ENVY, POISON, AN

At the heart of this volume are three trials held in Athens in the fourth century BCE. The defendants were all women and in each case the charges involved a combination of ritual activities. Two were condemned to death. Because of the brevity of the ancient sources, and their lack of agreement, the precise charges are unclear, and the reasons for taking these women to court remain mysterious.

Envy, Poison, and Death takes the complexity and confusion of the evidence not as a riddle to be solved, but as revealing multiple social dynamics. It explores the changing factors—material, ideological, and psychological—that may have provoked these events. It focuses in particular on the dual role of envy (*phthonos*) and gossip as processes by which communities identified people and activities that were dangerous, and examines how and why those local, even individual, dynamics may have come to shape official civic decisions during a time of perceived hardship.

At first sight so puzzling, these trials reveal a vivid picture of the socio-political environment of Athens during the early-mid fourth century BCE, including responses to changes in women's status and behaviour, and attitudes to ritual activities within the city. The volume reveals some of the characters, events, and even emotions that would help to shape an emergent concept of magic: it suggests that the boundary of acceptable behaviour was shifting, not only within the legal arena but also through the active involvement of society beyond the courts.

Esther Eidinow is Professor of Ancient History at the University of Bristol.

Envy, Poison, and Death

Women on Trial in Classical Athens

ESTHER EIDINOW

OXFORD
UNIVERSITY PRESS

Great Clarendon Street, Oxford, OX2 6DP,
United Kingdom

Oxford University Press is a department of the University of Oxford.
It furthers the University's objective of excellence in research, scholarship,
and education by publishing worldwide. Oxford is a registered trade mark of
Oxford University Press in the UK and in certain other countries

© Esther Eidinow 2016

The moral rights of the author have been asserted

First published 2016
First published in paperback 2018

All rights reserved. No part of this publication may be reproduced, stored in
a retrieval system, or transmitted, in any form or by any means, without the
prior permission in writing of Oxford University Press, or as expressly permitted
by law, by licence or under terms agreed with the appropriate reprographics
rights organization. Enquiries concerning reproduction outside the scope of the
above should be sent to the Rights Department, Oxford University Press, at the
address above

You must not circulate this work in any other form
and you must impose this same condition on any acquirer

Published in the United States of America by Oxford University Press
198 Madison Avenue, New York, NY 10016, United States of America

British Library Cataloguing in Publication Data
Data available

Library of Congress Cataloging in Publication Data
Data available

ISBN 978-0-19-956260-2 (Hbk.)
ISBN 978-0-19-882258-5 (Pbk.)

Links to third party websites are provided by Oxford in good faith and
for information only. Oxford disclaims any responsibility for the materials
contained in any third party website referenced in this work.

Acknowledgements

The seed of this book was planted in 2007, in a seminar paper given at the University of Manchester during a Leverhulme Early Career Research Fellowship: I thank both the Leverhulme Trust and the University of Manchester, especially Stephen Todd, for giving me that opportunity. The paper became an article in *Past & Present*, and I am very grateful to the anonymous referees for that journal, who offered so many useful and interesting comments. After it developed into a book proposal, Hilary O'Shea and the two anonymous reviewers at Oxford University Press (one of whom also read the book when it was nearing completion) gave invaluable encouragement and advice; and in its progress towards publication, Annie Rose and Charlotte Loveridge continued to give it patient support. In between, a Solmsen Fellowship at the Institute for Research in the Humanities at the University of Wisconsin, Madison provided some crucial time, for which I am very grateful. The editorial and production teams at OUP have been marvellous, and I also wish to thank Simon Hornblower, Robin Osborne, Charles Stewart, and the anonymous reviewer for the press, who gave so much of their time, encouragement, and counsel. This book is dedicated to Simon.

Contents

Figures ix
Abbreviations xi

PART 1: THE WOMEN

1.1 Introduction: Overview and Approach 3
1.2 The Evidence 11
1.3 What Charges? 38
1.4 Conclusion: 'If Anyone Has Cursed Me...' 65

PART 2: ENVY

2.1 Introduction: 'As Rust Eats Iron' 71
2.2 Defining Emotions 80
2.3 Narratives of *Phthonos* 102
2.4 *Phthonos* and Misfortune 140
2.5 Conclusion: 'Careless Talk...' 162

PART 3: POISON

3.1 Introduction: 'A Relish for the Envious' 167
3.2 Identifying Gossip 171
3.3 Genres of Gossip 180
3.4 Gossip... In Public 191
3.5 Gossip... In Private 212
3.6 Public, Private,... and Secret 224
3.7 From Gossip to Action 254
3.8 Conclusion: 'A Covert Form of Witchcraft' 261

PART 4: DEATH

4.1 Introduction: 'Killed by Idle Gossip'   265

4.2 After the War...   267

4.3 Dependence and Vulnerability   292

4.4 'Dangerous Women'   312

4.5 Conclusion: Envy, Poison, and Death   326

Epilogue: Social Trauma?   328

Bibliography   337
General Index   381
Index Locorum   403

Figures

1. Conceptual Blend of 'Death, the Grim Reaper' 245
2. Conceptual Blend of a Generic Binding Spell 248

Abbreviations

For ancient authors and works, and modern collections of ancient evidence, I have used the abbreviations in S. Hornblower, A. Spawforth, and E. Eidinow, eds, *Oxford Classical Dictionary* (4th edn, Oxford, 2012) where available. Additional abbreviations are listed below:

Arist. *Virt. Vit.*	Aristotle *de Virtutibus et Vitiis* (*On Virtues and Vices*)
Clairmont	C. W. Clairmont, *Classical Attic Tombstones*, 9 vols (Kilchberg, 1993–5)
Dion. Hal. *Din.*	Dionysius of Halicarnassus *De Dinarcho* (*Concerning Dinarchus*)
DT	A. Audollent, ed., *Defixionum Tabellae* (Paris, 1904). Numbers refer to items not pages.
DTA	*Inscriptiones Graecae*, iii *Inscriptiones Atticae aetatis Romanae*, Pars 3: *Appendix. Defixionum Tabellae*, ed. R. Wunsch (Berlin, 1897). Numbers refer to items not pages.
Joh. Chrys. *In 1 Cor. Hom.*	John Chrysostom *Homily On Corinthians 1*
Joh. Chrys. *In 2 Cor. Hom.*	John Chrysostom *Homily On Corinthians 2*
Max. Tyr.	Maximus of Tyre
Men. *Kith.*	Menander *Kitharistes* (*The Lyre-player*)
Men. *Sik.*	Menander *Sikyonioi* (*The Sicyonians*)
NGCT	D. Jordan, 'New Greek Curse Tablets (1985–2000)', *Greek, Roman, and Byzantine Studies* 41 (2000) 5–46. Numbers refer to items not pages.
Pl. *Ly.*	Plato *Lysis*
Plut. *De am. prol.*	Plutarch *De Amore Prolis* (*On Affection for Offspring*)
Plut. *De cohib. ira*	Plutarch *De Cohibenda Ira* (*On the Control of Anger*)
Plut. *De inim. util.*	Plutarch *De Capienda ex Inimicis Utilitate* (*How to Profit By One's Enemies*)
Plut. *De invid.*	Plutarch *De Invidia et Odio* (*On Envy and Hate*)
Plut. *De rect. rat. aud.*	Plutarch *De recta ratione audiendi* (*On Listening to Lectures*)

Plut. *Para.*	Plutarch *Parallela Minora* (*Greek and Roman Parallel Stories*)
SGD	D. Jordan, 'A Survey of Greek Defixiones not included in the Special Corpora', *Greek, Roman, and Byzantine Studies* 26 (1985) 151–97. Numbers refer to items not pages.
TM	Trismegistos Texts Database, coordinated by M. Depauw, www.trismegistos.org.

Note: I have usually adopted familiar Latinized spelling for personal names; in most cases, other Greek words are transliterated directly from Greek. I have used transliteration for single words and short phrases in order to help make the text as accessible as possible, but have included Greek for longer quotations and/or where it seemed useful.

Part 1

The Women

1.1

Introduction: Overview and Approach

Politics 'happens' where one may be led to least expect it—in the nooks and crannies of everyday life, outside of institutionalized contexts that one ordinarily associates with politics.[1]

The events that form the kernel of this book took place in Athens, in the middle years of the fourth century BCE. They comprise a number of intriguing trials in which the defendants were all women—puzzling targets for a society like Athens, where the law courts are largely regarded as the domain of the male political elite. These cases are *graphai*, or public cases, but just what kind of charges they included is debated: the evidence for each trial is multiple, various, and sketchy. It seems likely that at least two of them were *graphai asebeias* or trials for 'impiety'; the implication that these women were involved in magical activities is a consistent theme throughout the ancient sources and the modern scholarship. It is hard to say more than this: the sources are either too brief, or too late, or simply too contradictory to provide clarity. Little is known about the three women in question, the sparse historical evidence throwing only the faintest of silhouettes down through time.

These are obviously not novel problems: in general, the evidence for the lives of ancient women is usually voiced by others, and inextricably entangled in the conventions of different genres. There is now a burgeoning field of scholarship grappling with the problems of identifying and exploring the roles played by women in ancient communities. Marilyn Katz's analysis of over twenty years ago offers a useful framing of the ways in which these explorations have moved from consideration of 'women' to a more comprehensive exploration

[1] Besnier 2009: 11.

of gender, and from writing a history of women to writing 'a history of women in society'.[2] In line with these approaches, most scholarly studies of these trials have focused on the question of the nature of the charges, in the process of which these women fall into familiar, static social categories—be those sexual, magical, religious, or legal. The danger of such analyses is that we cease to see these women as anything more than cyphers for a kind of male violence understood to be endemic in Athenian society, the inadvertent victims of political struggles, their appearance in court the by-product of an attack by one elite male on another, a spin-off of episodes of religious intolerance, a side effect of the struggles of an elite patriarchy.[3]

And yet, the little evidence we have alludes to both the agency and power of these women; indeed, it was this that brought two of them to their deaths. Moreover, the extent of their influence may be inferred by the role they appear to have played in the cultural imaginary[4]: we can glimpse it in a number of stories or anecdotes that relate crimes and legal cases that seem remarkably similar to these trials.[5] A fable from Aesop's collection, a model speech for the law courts, a philosophical exemplum: each of them relates how a woman's ritual

---

[2] Katz 1992 (quotation, p. 96). The field of scholarship on ancient women is too great to cite here. However, the question of how and why women's lives may have changed has not been much explored. Exceptions include Osborne (1997), who raises the question of how changes in Athenian legislation prompted shifts in the social attitudes to, and representations of, women, with repercussions for lived experience of both genders; also van Bremen (1996), who considers the role of women as benefactors in Greek cities of (predominantly) Asia Minor, over a period of four centuries.

[3] Filonik (2013: 83) argues that there was no systematic religious repression at Athens and that 'the historical record cites a handful of individual trials for impiety out of nearly two centuries of Athenian democracy, more often than not placed in a very particular political context. Those individual trials or sometimes groups of trials reflect important turning points in the life of the community, more often than not being linked to various periods of instability, crisis, anxiety, sometimes even coups d'état, war, and, last but not least, either a threat of falling under foreign domination or frustration at the defeat.' However, he does not attempt a closer analysis than this, nor does this seem to account for the list of trials and potential trials he provides (82); he also does not explain those trials that do not fall into such an obvious category, such as the trials of these women.

[4] By this term I am referring not to the imagination of the individual, but to the set of shared ideas and images, narrative structures, and symbologies that members of a culture or society draw upon to organize their world view, and which gives shape and boundaries to their imaginations. For a useful discussion, see Dawson 1994: 48.

[5] Other scholars have suggested that one or other of these fictional characters be directly identified with the historical women, but have not raised the possibility that these characters indicate the development of a common cultural narrative.

Introduction: Overview and Approach

actions led to her death. For us, looking back over time, fact and fiction seem to be converging in a larger cultural narrative of a particular kind of risk. When we approach these women from this perspective—asking what risks they represented, how they developed, and why these women played such a key role in their expression—these trials start to assume greater significance, raising questions about the social and political environment of fourth-century BCE Athens. In this light, the complexity and confusion of the evidence is not so much a riddle to be resolved, but may rather be seen as articulating multiple dynamics. This study suggests that it forms the starting point for a historical investigation, one that places these women and their trials at its heart, and explores the changing factors—material and ideological—that may have provoked these events.

Rather than writing a history of these women in society, this study sets out to build on previous approaches to recover a history of society through the experiences of these women. The most obvious dimension of this is the larger changing political and economic situation of Athens—and this will be the focus of part 4 of this book. But the approach of this study is based on a sense that 'large-scale processes such as state formation, subsistence change and population movements need to be understood in locally meaningful contexts of feeling and understanding'.[6] Thus, before exploring events at the macro-level, this study will pursue some more everyday expressions of feelings, focusing on the emotion of *phthonos*, or envy. It will examine first the role of *phthonos* in local social dynamics, and then how these dynamics may have interacted with the larger civic processes of the law courts. It is a truism that the detailed information needed to assemble an account of local circumstances rarely survives; nevertheless, by bringing together a wide variety of different kinds of evidence from across the ancient world, as well as by drawing on resources from other periods and disciplines, it may be possible to assemble an alternative account that allows us to suggest, if not fully describe, more local or individualized events.

---

[6] Tarlow 2000: 719. Recent scholarly approaches offer helpful tools. In particular, research into the role and power of the emotions and connected work on cognition raise key questions about, and offer insights into, the nature and development of social relations. See Chaniotis (2012: 14–16), who provides a seminal overview of the role of 'emotions history', as well making a similar point about the connection between emotion and cognition.

Underpinning this analysis is an assumption that there are cross-cultural, and diachronic similarities between emotions. This book does not attempt to explain how this occurs, or in what ways vernacular emotion concepts connect across cultures, which categories they belong to, or the ways in which they have evolved.[7] However, it also does not assume that those similarities are absolute and that the modern concept can simply be mapped onto its ancient counterpart. Quite the contrary: the argument made here is that whatever element of emotions can be held to be universal, crucial aspects are culturally specific. We must take careful account of these aspects in any description of a culture and/or events affecting or affected by members of that culture. This means that rather than arguing for either a universal or a cultural-relativist point of view of emotions, this study embraces both approaches, treating emotion as inseparable from cultural context, and emphasizing its role as a social phenomenon, that is, the ways in which our knowledge and expression of an emotion are crucially affected by social relations, and how in turn social interactions are shaped by emotions.[8] This is not to deny the intrapsychic or physiognomic experience of emotion, but the focus of this study is on the ways in which social interactions give those experiences significance and meaning, and lead, in turn, to action. It is attempting to delineate not so much what an ancient emotion comprises, so much as what it might do.

This approach can perhaps be summed up by regarding emotions as cultural models or schemas: this incorporates not only their responsive mode, but also their expressive and creative roles,

---

[7] For an examination of these questions, a useful start is Griffiths 1997.
[8] In general, the focus of existing studies in this area has been on trying to distil the individual's experience of an emotion from our evidence. See, for example, Braund and Most 2003; Cairns 1993, 2003a and 2003b, 2008, 2009, and 2011; Harris 2001; Konstan 2001; Konstan and Rutter 2003; Kaster 2005; and Sanders 2014. Chaniotis (2012: 16) emphasizes how perceptions of, and responses to, emotions are to a great extent socially and culturally determined.

The approach used here is based on research on the emotions in both cultural anthropology and psychology that highlights the social and psychological construction of emotions. Although emotions may feel like private personal experiences—and certainly involve multiple, complex, probably iterative mental processes—they are also profoundly shaped by an individual's interactions with the world at interpersonal, group, and broader cultural levels (see especially Parkinson 1996). The question of the extent to which personal and social factors interact in this context is a source of much debate, especially in the field of psychology: see further part 2, section 2.

Introduction: Overview and Approach

encompassing the ways in which emotions appear to help us organize and evaluate our experiences. It offers a way to contemplate how emotions participate in both individual and group experience; and it grounds a method for their examination, through the analysis of the varieties of cultural discourse or 'emotion talk'. Part 2 uses this approach as the basis for examining some of the different cultural schemas of *phthonos*, revealing how narratives of *phthonos* differ across contexts and genres. It examines the power of '*phthonos* talk' for creating explanations for events and experiences, and how it was used to elicit meaning from otherwise inexplicable events or experiences.[9] In particular, it highlights the ways in which attributions of *phthonos* relate to the reciprocal relationships that structured many aspects of ancient Greek society, specifically the darker emotions arising from the process of giving gifts and all the responsibilities and attendant risks that come from being socially interdependent. This approach can, I suggest, help to explain not only the dynamics of mortal *phthonos*, but also the puzzling ancient phenomenon of the *phthonos* of the gods.

As this analysis will illustrate, *phthonos* talk includes both formal and informal discourses, and part 3 examines one of the more informal genres, namely gossip. Its informality increases its social potency: not just a vehicle for narrative, gossip is rather a 'reconstructive genre' from which an account of events will emerge.[10] This study explores how this aspect of gossip creates, supports, and develops the power of *phthonos* across different contexts, public, private, and secret.[11] Gossip as a discourse may offer us an insight into those

---

[9] See Eidinow (2011a) for use of cultural models to analyse ancient Greek discourse about fate, luck, and fortune.

[10] See Eidinow (2011b) for the ways in which narratives are crucial creative forces in social networks: the stories that we tell are shaped by, but also help shape, the context—the relationships and institutions—in which we tell them.

[11] Riess (2012) has indicated envy as a link between courtroom and binding spells (citing Eidinow 2007: 204 and 231, but rather misstating her approach, which turns on risk management). He asserts (169) that 'many forensic speeches must have been motivated by envy' and that 'although envy could not be openly expressed in court and was literally driven underground through the use of curse tablets, it still lingered in the background of many lawsuits'. It is not clear why he argues that binding spells had this effect. He does not examine the use of *phthonos* in forensic speeches; nor does he provide analysis of the ways in which envy may be connected to magical action, beyond mention of the evil eye (29, 165, 169, 177) and as a ritual to frame negative emotions (177). The argument that 'one could at least wish in malign magic what one could not openly say in court' (230) does not seem to take into account the substance

whose voices are rarely heard; but even when those voices are familiar, the presence of gossip deepens our understanding of the dynamics that lurk beneath the surface of our usual historical documents. Gossip provides a lead into 'the interstices of respectability' by following 'exactly the contours of local and regional concerns'.[12] This approach goes beyond arguing that gossip reveals values and the formation of values—the context for social action—to assert that gossip *is* social action. Thus, in our attempt to understand the historical past, it is important to see how, why, where, and when particular nuggets of gossip became credible, powerful—and, finally, acted upon.[13]

In doing so we gain insights into the ways in which people were actively making sense of their surrounding environment. As demonstrated by anthropological and historical work concerning other times and places, gossip (with envy) is a 'sense-making technique', and it frequently encompasses cosmological elements. Thus, local explanations of otherwise inexplicable events within communities, particularly misfortunes and suffering, though rooted in social tensions, may include accusations of supernatural violence.[14] Sometimes such accusations, like gossip, identify people—not fate, or luck, or accident—as the agency behind unfortunate experiences; sometimes they seek out the role of the divine; often, the two are inextricable.[15] This study similarly argues that the relationship between *phthonos*, gossip, and the menace of supernatural power is inextricable. The book's fourth part, 'Death', examines the larger political and

---

and intent of forensic speeches, and is contradicted by his own argument that (228) 'the new discourse on moderation and self-control had a profound impact on the language inscribed on the early tablets by making them sound temperate and restrained'.

[12] White 1994: 78.
[13] See Tonkin 1992: 89, as White 1994: 79. See Stewart and Strathern (2004: ix–x) for the relationship between gossip and witchcraft in terms of a processual model of social action.
[14] Favret-Saada (1980: 6): 'An onslaught by witchcraft, on the other hand, gives a pattern to misfortunes which are repeated and range over the persons and belongings of a bewitched couple.' See also and perhaps most famously, Evans-Pritchard (1937: 63): 'the concept of witchcraft provides a natural philosophy by which the relations between men and unfortunate events are explained and a ready and stereotyped means of reacting to such events. Witchcraft beliefs also embrace a system of values which regulate human conduct.'
[15] This is a topic of much ethnographic research: for example, see Evans-Pritchard 1937: 63–83 and 99–106. There is discussion in Stewart and Strathern 2004: *passim*, but see especially 1–28, and Ashforth 2005: *passim* and especially 20–5.

Introduction: Overview and Approach

economic situation of Athens in which such micro-social forces might gain deadly traction. Finally, in the Epilogue the book explores an additional psychoanalytical interpretation, introducing the idea of social trauma to explain how individual concerns might be transformed into group and/or civic action.

In making these connections, I am building on the insights of other ancient scholars, who have noted the role of gossip in accusations of magic;[16] and, in a broader historical context, this is drawing on studies of other times and places that have linked envy, gossip, and supernatural power. In particular, one of the influences on this study has been the approaches used in cross-cultural studies of the phenomenon of witchcraft. This is, of course, not an argument for the precise replication of historical or cultural circumstances across time and place, and this book is certainly not claiming that these trials are simply identifiable as the pursuit of 'witches' for 'witch-craft'.[17] Nevertheless, this book does explore the idea that these trials reveal some familiar societal response, of a sort that has occurred within other cultures within a certain pattern of circumstances: in some ways the evocation of what has been called a synthetic image.[18] It might also be argued that witch-hunts offer one example, and the trials of

---

[16] See, for example, Gordon 1999, Versnel 1999, and more recently Graf 2010. In the same volume Edmonds III (2010) uses similar material to emphasize the uncertainty of such accusations, also noted by Versnel (1999: 133). See also Salvo (2012: 260), whose analysis follows Versnel (2002: 73 and 37–40) in arguing that one manifestation of these accusations (prayers for justice) was a form of social control, and was intended to calm tensions (further discussed on pp. 221–3); and Sanders (2014: 30) who mentions the link between gossip and *phthonos* and the evil eye, and (45) briefly examines the link between envy and gossip.

[17] Nor is this the approach of the work done in different disciplines on the phenomenon of witchcraft across the world, which has stressed the crucial importance of exploring this phenomenon against its cultural background, and helped to clarify the wide variety and differences that emerge in the spaces between particular cultural manifestations of a concept that may, at first, look very similar. Scholars in this area have argued that a detailed reading of the social, political, legal, and religious forces at work in the trial of any particular individual or coven is necessary. See, for example, Roper 1994, Purkiss 1996, and Rowlands 2003. Stewart (2014 [2008]: 9) notes the context of beliefs about the devil in Greece, which 'never experienced a phase of witchcraft persecutions during the late middle ages and renaissance'.

[18] See Needham (1978: 41), who describes the make-up of synthetic images (they comprise 'primary factors' such as certain numbers and colours) which capture the imagination and persist across time, place, and culture, but importantly with specific modifications. Galt (1982: 669) uses this to describe the cultural ubiquity of the concept of the evil eye; Ostling (2011: 6) uses it to think about 'the imagined witch'.

these ancient women another, of a moral panic, 'a scare about a threat or supposed threat from deviants or "folk devils", a category of people who, presumably engage in evil practices and are blamed for menacing a society's culture, way of life, and central values. The word "scare" implies that the concern over, fear of, or hostility toward the folk devil is *out of proportion* to the actual threat that is claimed.'[19] The important aspect here is not the specific activities or social categories that are represented (although these play their part), but the perceived threat that they present.

In reflecting on the nature of a society's objects of fear, this book picks up on some of the themes of a previous publication, *Oracles, Curses, and Risk*, including the social construction of risk, explanations of misfortune, the overlap between those social dynamics and the search for responsibility and blame, and, finally, the point where the fear of risk prompts action. In that earlier book, I examined the selection of, and response to, risk at the level of the individual; in this book I am interested in group selections and responses. Of course, the two are inextricable, but it is precisely the nature of the interface, and subsequent interaction, between individual and group that is of interest here: why do individual emotions become so powerful? What are the wider circumstances in which that occurs? And how and why does a private feeling become a public action?

---

[19] Goode and Ben-Yehuda 2009: 2, their italics. This is a debated topic in sociology, but as the authors emphasize, this is not about panic in the sense of a headlong stampede, but moral panic, although they regard both as (3) 'emotionally charged social phenomena entailing fright and anxiety.'

1.2

The Evidence

To begin this inquiry we will first lay out the evidence for the historical trials of Theoris, Ninon, and Phryne, and then examine the concomitant (fictional) stories about similar trials.

THEORIS OF LEMNOS

Of the three women, we have most information about the trial of a woman called Theoris, who appears briefly in three sources, reproduced below. These are a law-court speech by the fourth-century BCE orator Demosthenes against a certain Aristogiton; a biography of Demosthenes, written four hundred or so years later by the essayist Plutarch; and a brief reference by a second-century CE lexicographer, Harpocration, to the work of a Hellenistic historian, Philochorus.

οὑτοσί—τὰ μὲν ἄλλα σιωπῶ, ἀλλ' ἐφ' οἷς ὑμεῖς τὴν μιαρὰν Θεωρίδα, τὴν Λημνίαν, τὴν φαρμακίδα, καὶ αὐτὴν καὶ τὸ γένος ἅπαν ἀπεκτείνατε, ταῦτα λαβὼν τὰ φάρμακα καὶ τὰς ἐπῳδὰς παρὰ τῆς θεραπαίνης αὐτῆς, ἣ κατ' ἐκείνης τότ' ἐμήνυσεν, ἐξ ἧσπερ ὁ βάσκανος οὗτος πεπαιδοποίηται, μαγγανεύει καὶ φενακίζει καὶ τοὺς ἐπιλήπτους φησὶν ἰᾶσθαι, αὐτὸς ὢν ἐπίληπτος πάσῃ πονηρίᾳ.

Demosthenes 25.79–80

It was this man [Eunomus]—the other matters I will not mention—who took the potions and incantations from the maidservant of Theoris of Lemnos, the filthy sorceress whom you executed for those things, both her and all her family.[1] The maidservant informed against her mistress, and

---

[1] See n. 13 for discussion of *miaros*, here translated as 'filthy'.

this evildoer has had children by her, and with her help performs his tricks and acts of deceit, and says he treats those who are seized by fits, when he himself is caught in acts of wickedness of every kind.[2]

This first passage mentions Theoris in passing, during the trial of one Aristogiton, a politician in Athens on trial as a state debtor.[3] It is has been argued that the speech was given sometime in 325/4 BCE, on the basis of a reference made by the orator Dinarchus to the trial's initial speech for the prosecution (made by Lycurgus), in which his use of the term 'lastly' is taken to indicate that the speech was fresh in his audience's minds.[4] Dinarchus was speaking against Aristogiton after the Harpalus affair in 323, and thus, it is argued, it is likely that this speech dates to just before that time. This, of course, only gives us a *terminus ante quem* for the events relating to Theoris that it describes. Throughout this speech, Demosthenes is painting, in broad and colourful strokes, a picture of Aristogiton's family background as shameful and chaotic. This description of Aristogiton's twin brother Eunomus, the man being discussed here, is intended to add to this impression. Eunomus, we have been told earlier, has prosecuted his brother for selling his sister (whose father, it is implied, was a slave, 25.55); his connection with Theoris, through her maidservant and her magical paraphernalia, is clearly meant to imply the worst.

Theoris' appearance is brief but vivid. Demosthenes describes her as a *pharmakis* from Lemnos, which, since this trial takes place after 390, could still indicate that Theoris was an Athenian citizen rather than marking her as foreign.[5] The term *pharmakis* can be translated as 'witch', but with a particular emphasis on the use of drugs.[6] But the meaning is more complex than this suggests, involving a significant double ambiguity, also present in the related noun *pharmaka*, which can be used to mean 'drugs' or 'spells' that may be either harmful or healing (or both), and which may be either natural or supernatural (or both).[7] In this passage, *pharmaka* appear as one of the reasons for

---

[2] Tr. Vince 1935.   [3] Following MacDowell 2009: 300–1.   [4] Ibid.: 298.
[5] Since this is the date when it is thought that the Athenians regained control over the island after losing it in the Peloponnesian War; see Salomon 1997: 76ff. and Cargill 1995: 13–14. Albeit, she could have been one of the 'dispossessed' of the island (see Zelnick-Abramowitz 2004 and for further discussion on this aspect, pp. 14 and 64).
[6] See, for example, Ogden 2002a: 98.
[7] Scarborough (1991: 139) notes the use of *pharmakon* in Homer to mean magic, charm, or enchantment, with appropriate adjectives to indicate what kind of effect it is meant to elicit in each case. He argues that drugs were understood to comprise both

Theoris' execution: it seems that when Demosthenes says to the jurors 'whom you executed *for those things*', he is referring back to *ta pharmaka kai tas epoidas*, 'drugs/spells and incantations'. This is the first appearance of this hendiadys; it will stay in use for some time, coming to express a complex idea of secret knowledge and supernatural power.[8]

Was Theoris practising harmful spells, and was that why she was taken to court? She may have been engaged in such activities, but it is difficult to establish that they were illegal in ancient Athens. Drawing on evidence for such legislation from later periods risks overlooking the very different context in which it emerged, and the changing profile of 'magic' as a category of ritual activity separate from 'religion'.[9] The details that Demosthenes supplies about Eunomus' activities may help to position Theoris in a professional context: he notes that Eunomus claims to be able to cure the falling sickness, or epilepsy.[10] This sets him, and perhaps therefore also her, in the realm of the self-proclaimed experts in healing whom we find criticized by, for example, the author of the Hippocratic treatise *On the Sacred Disease*.[11] The author of that text uses a list of abusive terms—*magoi, kathartai, agurtai, alazones*—to describe those who, in his opinion, wrongly attribute the disease (among others) to divine intervention, and thus prescribe *katharmous... kai epaoidas* [sic] ('purifications and incantations'), alongside other—as he sees it—pointless prescriptions.[12]

---

supernatural and agricultural elements, and that the power of drugs was a result of both their divine properties and the knowledge brought to bear by those who grew or used them (162). Derrida (1981) analyses the rich semantic ambiguity of the term *pharmakon* in the writings of Plato.

[8] A 'hendiadys' is a figure of speech in which a single complex idea is expressed by means of two words joined by a conjunction. For the long-term influence of this hendiadys in the fourth century BCE 'through the trial of cases involving harm caused by magical means', and its continued use, see Gordon 1999: 251. It seems still to be potent in contemporary popular ideas about witchcraft (a Google search [02/05/2015] for 'witchcraft "spells and incantations"' produced 18,400 results). See pp. 167–8 for further discussion of this phrase in the context of Xenophon's recollections of Socrates.

[9] As Hopfner 1928: 384. Ogden (1999: 83–4) argues 'that harmful magical practice was generally illegal throughout Graeco-Roman antiquity', but struggles to find evidence for Athens and has to admit that there was no 'comprehensive outlawing of magic'; for a more cautious consideration, see Phillips 1991.

[10] Dem. 25.80.   [11] This point made by Scarborough (2006: 23).

[12] Hippoc. *Morb. sacr.* 2.3–4; he points out that they do this on the basis of claims to being pious (θεοσεβέες, literally 'god-honouring') and of having superior knowledge.

To return to Theoris, if the kinds of 'magical' activities she practised were illegal, it would surely have been enough for Demosthenes simply to point out that Eunomus practised this trade himself, without further qualifying his remarks by reference to Theoris. The fact that Demosthenes does not do this, and instead specifically calls this woman to mind, suggests there was something further about her practice that the audience was expected to find objectionable. This is reinforced by Demosthenes' use of the adjective *miaros*, which can be translated as 'filthy', but can have the much stronger sense, 'polluted', indicating a metaphysical stain.[13] But the reasons for its use remain unclear: it seems problematic to explain this as caused simply by her use of *pharmaka*, which Eunomos has inherited and is using.

It may be, as Kai Trampedach has suggested, that this term is associated with her description as 'Lemnian', and together these are intended metaphorically to associate Theoris with the mythical 'women of Lemnos' who murdered their husbands.[14] Trampedach links this to the fact that, as Demosthenes observes, Theoris' crime led to the execution both of her and of her *genos* or clan. However, this is not really equivalent to the killing of husbands that takes place in that myth, and there is nothing, at least at first sight, in the passage that suggests any similar crime. The term *miara* may be simply a term of opprobrium, one that condemns and isolates Theoris.[15]

---

[13] LSJ s.v. *miaros*. Some further examples of its use in this speech will help define its area of meaning, and also help to illuminate the associations that the audience will have with this term before it is used of Theoris. Demosthenes is building the prosecution's case by depicting Aristogiton as a thoroughly bad character. He uses the adjective repeatedly to describe Aristogiton in terms of crimes, such as being a state debtor, but still participating in civic activity (25.28); displaying unfit political conduct (25.32); sycophancy (25.41); abandoning his father (exiled in Eretria) and refusing to bury him (25.54); biting off a fellow prisoner's nose, and swallowing it (25.62); as well as in reflection on the collective activities comprising non-burial of his father, sale of his sister, and the denunciation of Zobia (the metic woman who had looked after him) for not paying the metic tax (25.58—the adjective is repeated). The sense of *miaros* that emerges is of wrongdoing that (i) powerfully undermines the city, (ii) is repulsive to right-thinking fellow-citizens, and (iii) cannot be forgotten or forgiven. In Christian exorcisms and spells, the term is used as an adjective to describe the devil and demons (my thanks to Charles Stewart for this latter point).

[14] Trampedach 2001: 147.

[15] Similarly, it is worth noting here that any possible 'contamination' which might be thought to be the reason for Theoris being called *miara* does not seem to have attached in any way to her magical paraphernalia. It seems to have been quite acceptable for Eunomus to have inherited her tools and techniques and to go on to use them, even if Demosthenes treats him and his activities with contempt.

The Evidence 15

However, there may be a further reason that explains the introduction of Theoris' name here: she was, according to Plutarch's *Life of Demosthenes*, prosecuted by Demosthenes himself. If Demosthenes wanted to remind his audience of his devotion to ridding the city of evils, then introducing her name was a powerful interjection. The description that Plutarch gives is brief, but introduces some new material. The source of Plutarch's information is unknown: as he notes in the introduction to this 'Life', he used a variety of sources:[16]

κατηγόρησε δὲ καὶ τῆς ἱερείας Θεωρίδος ὡς ἄλλα τε ῥᾳδιουργούσης πολλὰ καὶ τοὺς δούλους ἐξαπατᾶν διδασκούσης· καὶ θανάτου τιμησάμενος ἀπέκτεινε.

Plutarch *Demosthenes* 14.4

He also accused the priestess Theoris of many other evil deeds, and in particular of teaching slaves to deceive and he had her killed by fixing the penalty as death.

There are a number of differences of detail with the preceding Demosthenic passage: first, use of the term *hiereia* or 'priestess' carries far more implicit respect than the description there. Moreover, as Plutarch's use of this word in other parts of his voluminous writings suggests, it indicates some role of leadership in a regular ritual activity: an externally granted office, rather than a claim to authority, with specific responsibilities towards a particular sanctuary and the rites carried out there.[17] Plutarch usually employs the word with some indication of the goddess to which the priestess was attached; this reference to Theoris stands out because it lacks such an affiliation.[18] New terms are also used to describe the

---

[16] He cites over twenty names throughout the text, many of whom were writing between the late fourth and late third centuries, most of whom are lost, as well as alluding to oral sources at the end of the piece (*Dem.* 31.7); see Holden 1893: xi and MacDowell 2009: 11. Theopompus' name appears most closely to the detail about Theoris, in connection with a story about Demosthenes' refusal to conduct a certain impeachment (he would not act as a sycophant). He was prosecutor in both the examples that follow (a case against Antiphon, and the prosecution of Theoris); however, this does not mean they have the same origin.

[17] See Flower 2008: 189. The term *hiereia* is not found in dedicatory inscriptions for portrait statues until the first half of the fourth century (see Connelly 2007: 135).

[18] A selection: *Tim.* 8.1.2, a priestess of Persephone; *Rom.* 3.3.4, a priestess of Hestia (that is a vestal virgin); *Nic.* 13.6.3, a priestess of Athena. These are examples from other *Lives*, but there are further examples from across his other writings,

16   Envy, Poison, and Death

charges: 'criminal deeds' and 'teaching slaves how to deceive'. The former is simply too vague to evaluate, while the latter is difficult to relate to Greek legal practice, and does not, at first sight, seem to be relevant to our questions here about Theoris' ritual activities.[19] Rather, this seems to be concerned with social control, a theme that is explored in a later section, and which may suggest a connection between slaves and particular kinds of religious practice, although none is mentioned explicitly here.

Finally, we turn to Harpocration, who cites the passage given above from Demosthenes' *Against Aristogiton*, but introduces a further set of terms to describe both Theoris and her crime.

ΘΕΩΡΙΣ Δημοσθένης ἐν τῷ κατ' Ἀριστογείτονος, εἰ γνήσιος. μάντις ἦν ἡ Θεωρίς, καὶ ἀσεβείας κριθεῖσα ἀπέθανεν, ὡς καὶ Φιλόχορος ἐν ς' γράφει.

Philochorus *ap.* Harpocration, s.v. *Theoris*
(Dindorf = *FGrH* 382 F 60)

THEORIS: Demosthenes in his speech *Against Aristogiton*, if legitimate. Theoris was a *mantis* and was put to death on a charge of impiety, as Philochorus writes in his sixth book.

First, the charge is here described as one of impiety (*asebeia*). Yet, although this was, at least officially, an offence tried in the Athenian courts, nevertheless, it is very difficult to define (and, probably for that reason, it has been argued, was often used in legal battles between political rivals).[20] This source also introduces a further term to describe Theoris: *mantis* is usually translated as 'seer', and customarily indicates the practice of foretelling the future. However, it has been argued that the appearance of a variety of terms for those who practised supernatural arts is typical of ancient Greek evidence.[21] Although each term may once have been used to denote a specific skill, in general the ancient Greek market for such services does not seem to have demanded so much precision. A *mantis* might be involved in supernatural activities other than fortune-telling,

including *De mul. virt.* 257f1, a priestess of Artemis, and 262d2, a priestess of Demeter; *Para.* 314f5, a priestess of Hera; and *Quaest Rom.* 292a6, a priestess of Athena.

[19] Ziehen (1934: 2238) urges caution in our use of this passage of Plutarch and suggests (2237) that this text indicates that Theoris taught her slaves how to poison.
[20] See Cohen 1991, ch. 8; Todd 1996: 115, with n. 23.
[21] See Bowden 2003: 61; also Eidinow 2007: 26–30; cf. Dillery 2005: 169–70.

The Evidence 17

including the creation of *pharmaka*.²² Whether we agree or not, across these three sources the specific nature of Theoris' activities remains vague, perhaps reflecting the imprecise reality of her actual practice. However, it is the use of *hiereia*—indicating a more official role—alongside the more loosely used terms *mantis* and *pharmakis* that is most puzzling.²³ We may gain some insight from a comparison with our second case, that of Ninon.²⁴

NINON

Ninon's trial and execution is mentioned in passing by Demosthenes in three speeches, their very brevity suggesting that the case in which she was involved was well known to his audience. In the first passage, Demosthenes is discussing the behaviour of Glaucothea, the mother of his political opponent Aeschines. He says that she brought together *thiasoi* in which Aeschines played an active, and somewhat embarrassing, role.²⁵ Demosthenes then goes on to mention that there was another *hiereia* or priestess who was executed for this kind of activity.

τὸν δ' Ἀτρομήτου τοῦ γραμματιστοῦ καὶ Γλαυκοθέας τῆς τοὺς θιάσους συναγούσης, ἐφ' οἷς ἑτέρα τέθνηκεν ἱέρεια, τοῦτον ὑμεῖς λαβόντες, τὸν τῶν τοιούτων, τὸν οὐδὲ καθ' ἓν χρήσιμον τῇ πόλει, οὐκ αὐτόν, οὐ πατέρα, οὐκ ἄλλον οὐδένα τῶν τούτου, ἀφήσετε;

Demosthenes 19.281

And then, when you have in your power a son of Atrometus the dominie, and of Glaucothea, the fuglewoman of those bacchanalian routs for which another priestess suffered death, will you release the son of such parents, a man who has never been of the slightest use to the commonwealth, neither he, nor his father, nor any member of his precious family?²⁶

---

²² Pl. *Resp.* 364c.
²³ See the discussion in Henrichs (2008: 5–6) on the terms for *mantis* and *hiereus* in particular.
²⁴ Most scholars give her name as Ninos, except for Collins (2001), who gives Nino. In the sources her name appears in the accusative case: Ninon, so the nominative is unknown. In calling her Ninon, I have followed the appropriate entry in *LGPN*, ii, Attica.
²⁵ Dem.18.259-60. ²⁶ Tr. Vince and Vince 1926.

18 Envy, Poison, and Death

We learn the name of this priestess from one of the two ancient scholia on this passage: it was 'Ninon'. It seems that Ninon, like Glaucothea, was organizing some form of cultic group.[27] But the scholion that gives Ninon's name goes on to provide a very different explanation of her activities, and this, in turn, diverges from those given by a second scholion.[28] The first comment, which names not only Ninon, but also her prosecutor, goes on to link Demosthenes' phrase, 'what Glaucothea did', to a non-existent antecedent '*pharmaka*'. It then explains that Ninon was actually accused of making love potions (*philtra*) for young people.[29] In contrast, the second scholion, although it does not give a name for the priestess, reads the Greek correctly, and elaborates that it was her rituals (which mocked the Mysteries) which led to her prosecution. It also offers an explanation as to why her activities led to a court case, while Glaucothea was allowed to practise unharmed; some scholars have argued that this is a creation of the scholiast.[30]

495a <ἐφ' οἷς ἑτέρα τέθνηκεν ἱέρεια>] ἐφ' οἷς φαρμάκοις καὶ ἄλλη ἱέρεια τέθνηκεν. λέγει δὲ τὴν Νῖνον λεγομένην. κατηγόρησε δὲ ταύτης Μενεκλῆς ὡς φίλτρα ποιούσης τοῖς νέοις.

495b ἐφ'... ἱέρεια] ἐξ ἀρχῆς γέλωτα εἶναι καὶ ὕβριν κατὰ τῶν ὄντως μυστηρίων [ὅτι] τὰ τελούμενα ταῦτα (νομίζοντες) τὴν ἱέρειαν ἀπέκτειναν·

---

[27] From the later fourth century onwards, the term *thiasos* appears to have been used more regularly and specifically of subgroups within a *phratry*, and of organized cultic groups. Earlier, there is evidence of its being used of gatherings or groups of revellers or cult worshippers, some, perhaps, spontaneous; it might also be used more generally to indicate a group or association. See discussions in Poland 1909: 16-22, and on *phratries* esp. Lambert 1993: 81-93 and Andrewes 1961: 9-12. Arnaoutoglou (2003: esp. 63-70) offers an overview of scholarship, and examines later use of terminology; he also argues that originally *thiasoi* were not necessarily Dionysiac, but simply convivial. Harp. and Suda s.v. *Thiasos* (theta 379 and 380, Adler) indicate it has a religious purpose; Hesych., s.v. *thiasos* (theta 573), discusses *choreutai*, but no specific religious setting. See *IG* II² 2343-61 for organized cult *thiasoi* dating mostly to the end of the fourth century BCE. Revellers: Ar. *Ran* 156 and Eur. *Bacch.* 680. Group or association: see Ar. *Thesm.* 41, Eur *IA*. 1059, Eur. *Phoen.* 796.

[28] Scholia to Dem. 19.281: 495A and B (Dilts); see MacDowell 2000, esp. 327.

[29] Dickie (2001: 52) discards this charge on the basis that although it may still have been a part of Menecles' case, it is a quite unexpected spin on the story that does not emerge from the Demosthenic account. Hansen (1995: 26), albeit in a very brief account, appears to accept it (she 'was charged with having administered a potion, probably an aphrodisiac, to her devotees of young people').

[30] Parker (1996: 194-5 n. 152) describes the oracle giving Glaucothea permission as 'a transparent scholiast's invention to explain a supposed contradiction in the text'.

The Evidence

μετὰ τοῦτο τοῦ θεοῦ χρήσαντος ἐᾶσαι γενέσθαι τὴν Αἰσχίνου μητέρα μυεῖν ἐπέτρεψαν.

Scholia to Demosthenes 19.281: 495A and B (Dilts)

495a <for which another priestess was executed> for which spells/ potions another priestess was executed. He says it is Ninon that is spoken of. Menecles accused her of making potions for young men.[31]

495b for which another priestess was executed] First of all, believing that her initiations/services brought ridicule and insult to the real mysteries, they executed the priestess; then, once the god had given permission through an oracle, they allowed the mother of Aeschines to conduct initiations.

Two further passages of Demosthenes, from two speeches made *Against Boeotus*, reveal a little more about Ninon's accuser, Menecles. In both he is given the epithet 'the man who secured the conviction of Ninon' and described as one of the leaders of a gang of young sycophants. In the first speech Demosthenes associates him with the defendant of that case. But little further information is given about Ninon in either of the speeches; rather, the case is referred to as if everyone knew about it.[32]

νῦν δὲ λαχὼν δίκην τῷ πατρὶ τὠμῷ καὶ μεθ' ἑαυτοῦ κατασκευάσας ἐργαστήριον συκοφαντῶν, Μνησικλέα θ', ὃν ἴσως γιγνώσκετε πάντες, καὶ Μενεκλέα τὸν τὴν Νῖνον ἑλόντ' ἐκεῖνον, καὶ τοιούτους τινάς, ἐδικάζεθ' υἱὸς εἶναι φάσκων ἐκ τῆς Παμφίλου θυγατρὸς καὶ δεινὰ πάσχειν καὶ τῆς πατρίδος ἀποστερεῖσθαι.

Demosthenes 39.2

But, as it is, he brought suit against my father, and having got up a gang of blackmailers to support him—Mnesicles, whom you all probably know, and that Menecles who secured the conviction of Ninon, and others of the same sort—he went into court, alleging that he was my father's son by the daughter of Pamphilus, and that he was being outrageously treated, and robbed of his civic rights.[33]

ἐπειδὴ δ' οὗτος αὐξηθεὶς καὶ μεθ' αὑτοῦ παρασκευασάμενος ἐργαστήριον συκοφαντῶν, ὧν ἡγεμὼν ἦν Μνησικλῆς καὶ Μενεκλῆς ἐκεῖνος ὁ τὴν Νῖνον ἑλών, μεθ' ὧν οὗτος ἐδικάζετό μου τῷ πατρὶ φάσκων υἱὸς εἶναι ἐκείνου.

Demosthenes 40.9

---

[31] See Dickie 2001: 51.
[32] Dem. 39.2 and 40.9.
[33] Tr. Murray 1936.

But after Boeotus had grown up and had associated with himself a gang of blackmailers, whose leaders were Mnesicles and that Menecles who secured the conviction of Ninon, in connexion with these men he brought suit against my father, claiming that he was his son.[34]

These speeches, while giving us little information about the trial itself, do allow us to speculate about the date of the trial: Demosthenes 19 was delivered in 343 BCE, three years after the negotiations that it discusses, but the speeches against Boeotus were made in 348 and 347 respectively, giving a slightly earlier *terminus ante quem*.[35] The details of the latter speech may allow a possible further refinement: they tell us that Boeotus had brought together his gang of sycophants, including Menecles, before he prosecuted his father Mantias (39.2 and 40.9), and we know that Mantias died before 358 BCE (when Mantitheus initiated a prosecution against Boeotus and his mother Plangon).[36] Demosthenes' phrasing does not make it certain that Menecles had already charged Ninon by the time that Boeotus met him, but it is certainly possible from what he says, since the implication is that Boeotus was establishing connections with some disreputable characters. If this is the case, then the trial of Ninon could well have taken place before 358 BCE. If we want to narrow it down still further, we can work with the approximate age of the protagonist of these speeches: MacDowell argues that Mantitheus was born around 380 BCE.[37] If Boeotus demanded to be registered in the deme Thorikos after his brother had been registered, then that must have been soon after 362 BCE. This may mean, therefore, that the trial of Ninon can be located as occurring between 362 and 358 BCE.[38] This brings her a little closer in time to the case of Glaucothea, who, if Aeschines was born around 390 BCE, would presumably have required (oracular) permission sometime between

---

[34] Tr. Murray 1936.
[35] MacDowell (2009: 74) notes that trials were not held in the latter part of 349/8 BCE because there were insufficient funds to pay juries (citing Dem. 39.17).
[36] See Dem. 40.3 and 18.
[37] On the grounds that Mantitheus was a taxiarch in 349/8 (39.16–17) and that to hold that office it was necessary to be around 30 years old.
[38] Trampedach (2001: 138) states that the trial took place in 350 BCE, but most scholars do not try to identify a specific date: Dickie (2001: 52): in 'the 350s or 340s'; Parker (2005a: 163): the fourth century; Versnel (1999: 115): 'Somewhere in the fourth century, at any rate before 343 BCE'.

The Evidence

380 and 370 BCE—before her son reached manhood and began to assist her, as Demosthenes describes.[39] Further, but clearly unreliable information about what happened next is added by Dionysius of Halicarnassus writing about the orator Dinarchus, and the speech *Against Menecles* that was attributed to him: 'For the defendant is the Menecles who successfully accused the priestess Ninon, and who was prosecuted by her son.'[40] However, he goes on to observe that this is a spurious attribution since Dinarchus would have been too young to deliver the speech:

Κατὰ Μενεκλέους ἀπαγωγῆς· 'ὦ ἄνδρες δικασταί, καὶ τῶν νόμων καθ' οὕς.' καὶ οὗτος εἴρηται παιδὸς ὄντος ἔτι Δεινάρχου. ὁ μὲν γὰρ κρινόμενός ἐστι Μενεκλῆς ὁ τὴν ἱέρειαν Νῖνον ἑλών, ὁ δὲ κατηγορῶν υἱὸς τῆς Νίνου. ἔστι δὲ ταῦτα πρεσβύτερα τῆς Δεινάρχου ἀκμῆς. ὁ μὲν γὰρ Δημοσθένους περὶ τοῦ ὀνόματος [δεδηλώκαμεν] λόγος, ἐν ᾧ τούτων μέμνηται, κατὰ Θέελλον ἢ Ἀπολλόδωρον ἄρχοντα τετέλεσται, ὡς ἐν τοῖς περὶ Δημοσθένους δεδηλώκαμεν. εἰ δ' ὡς τεθνηκότος ἤδη τοῦ Μενεκλέους ὁ Δημοσθένης ἐκεῖ μέμνηται λέγων· 'ἑωρᾶτε γὰρ πάντες αὐτὸν χρώμενον, ἕως ἔζη, Μενεκλεῖ', παλαιὸς λόγος τίς ἐστιν. ὅτι δὲ οὗτος ὁ Μενεκλῆς, ἐν αὐτῷ τῷ λόγῳ δεδήλωκεν ὁ κατηγορῶν.

Dionysius of Halicarnassus *Dinarchus* 11

Against Menecles, on his arrest: 'Gentlemen of the jury, even of the laws by which...' This too was delivered when Dinarchus was still a minor: for the defendant is the Menecles who secured the conviction of the priestess Ninon, and the prosecutor is the son of Ninon. These events are earlier than the prime of Dinarchus: for the speech of Demosthenes *On the Name*, in which he recalls these events, was completed during the archonship either of Theëllus or of Apollodorus, as we have shown in our work on Demosthenes. And if Demosthenes is referring to Menecles as already dead when he says 'For you all observed his association with Menecles while Menecles lived', the speech is an old one; and that this Menecles is the one in question the prosecutor has shown in the speech itself.[41]

Finally, the first-century Jewish historian and priest Josephus supplies us with a very specific charge: he gives a list of those put to death by the Athenians because they 'uttered a word about the gods contrary to their laws'. Mostly consisting of men, the list includes

---

[39] Dem. 18.258; Harris 1988 and Trampedach 2001: 138.
[40] Dion. Hal. *Din.* 11; see Dickie 2001: 52.
[41] Tr. Usher 1974; slightly adapted.

such famous characters as Socrates, Anaxagoras, Diagoras, and Protagoras. However, if we accept the emendation of *nun*, then the name of the woman may be 'Ninon'—otherwise it could be a reference to Theoris, or another unlucky priestess.[42]

τί δὲ δεῖ θαυμάζειν, εἰ πρὸς ἄνδρας οὕτως ἀξιοπίστους διετέθησαν, οἵ γε μηδὲ γυναικῶν ἐφείσαντο; Νῖνον γὰρ τὴν ἱέρειαν ἀπέκτειναν, ἐπεί τις αὐτῆς κατηγόρησεν, ὅτι ξένους ἐμύει θεούς· νόμῳ δ' ἦν τοῦτο παρ' αὐτοῖς κεκωλυμένον καὶ τιμωρία κατὰ τῶν ξένον εἰσαγόντων θεὸν ὥριστο θάνατος.

Josephus *Against Apion* 2.267-8

Can one wonder at their attitude towards men of such authority when they did not spare even women? They put Ninon the priestess to death, because someone accused her of initiating people into the mysteries of foreign gods; this was forbidden by their law, and the penalty decreed for any who introduced a foreign god was death.[43]

Along with the second scholion to Demosthenes' 19.281 cited above, Josephus' account suggests that there was a profound intolerance in Athens of religious innovations. However, this statement has been received by scholars with different degrees of scepticism. Some have dismissed it out of hand, arguing that it originates in Josephus' experience of his own Jewish culture and that there is no contemporary evidence that supports this, and only a very little from a later period.[44] Others have argued that although there may have been a law against the introduction of foreign gods, it is difficult to identify just what it comprised and/or how it developed;[45] moreover, for those

---

[42] Dover (1975) argues that this is based on a tract written by Demetrius of Phaleron intended to describe how there has always been tension between Athenian people and intellectuals, and illustrating this with a description of the fifth-century trials for impiety.
The emendation that results in the identification of Ninon is adopted by St. J. Thackeray (1926), who attributes it to Weil; the emendation appears in Blum 1902.
[43] Tr. Thackeray 1926.
[44] See Trampedach 2001: 140; later supporting evidence for Josephus is found in Serv. *Aen.* 8.187: 'Among the Athenians, it was stipulated that no one be allowed to introduce religious cults [or 'objects']: for which reason Socrates was condemned to death' ('cautum fuerat apud Athenienses ne quis introduceret religiones: unde et Socrates damnatus est'). However, Krauter (2004: 237) argues that Servius worked from the same sources that we have and used these to come to his conclusion about the existence of a law (rather than the other way around).
[45] See Derenne 1930: 223-36; Rudhardt 1960; Versnel 1990: 123-30; Parker 1996: 214-17.

taking this position, the consensus seems to be that even if such a law was available, it was seldom used.[46] In the context of this discussion it is also important to note that the various sources draw attention to two different kinds of innovation. The scholion appears to condemn the introduction of new activities in light of existing practices, while Josephus' comments emphasize the crime of religious practice that introduced foreign gods. These two sources do not mention other ritual activities—for example spells of some description designed for young people—that the scholia interject; and none of our sources for Ninon's case uses the term *asebeia*. The question of Athenian intolerance will be considered in the next section, but, as we shall see, these charges against Ninon are echoed, to a certain extent, in those that were brought against the *hetaira*, Phryne.

PHRYNE

Represented in court by the renowned fourth-century orator Hyperides, Phryne was the only one of these three women to be acquitted. The date of her trial is uncertain, but it probably occurred between 350 and 340 BCE.[47] The case has received a great deal of attention, both ancient and modern, and it provides, at least in comparison with those of the other women discussed here, a wealth of evidence. The reasons for this are manifold, and touch on some of the themes discussed already in the introduction. In particular, the celebrity of the characters involved and especially their occupations, seem to have captured the imagination of commentators.

---

[46] e.g. Parker (1996: 216): 'In practice therefore individuals seem to have "introduced new gods" with some freedom... They were called to account only if they or their religious associations proved objectionable on other grounds.' And, despite a later description of the suspicions generated by foreign cults (1990: 102), Versnel also notes that (128) 'Many private cults of foreign gods must have passed unnoticed or were condoned.'

[47] Raubitschek (1941: 904) gives this date on the basis of the report that Anaximenes wrote Euthias' speech, and must have done this before Anaximenes' arrival in Macedonia, the date of which is uncertain. The *Suda*, s.v. *Anaximenes* (alpha 1989, Adler) describes Anaximenes tutoring Alexander (late 340s); on the basis of his dedication to Alexander of the *Rhetorica ad Alexandrum*, Berve (1926, ii: 35–6) suggests that Anaximenes knew Alexander before 342 BCE; Flower (1997: 21–3) suggests Anaximenes may have been at the court by 343/2 BCE.

24 Envy, Poison, and Death

The story of the trial that survives offers a beguiling blend of fact and fiction. Hyperides' speech, hugely admired in antiquity, became a victim of its own success.[48] Although only fragments survive, the speech is perhaps best known for what it was said to have achieved without words: a peroration in which Hyperides opened Phryne's clothing to reveal her breasts. But this startling scene in fact almost certainly never occurred. Plutarch and Athenaeus both provide a description of this moment, their respective versions each giving a slightly different emphasis:

ὡμιληκὼς δέ, ὡς εἰκός δή, καὶ Φρύνῃ τῇ ἑταίρᾳ ἀσεβεῖν κρινομένῃ συνεστάθη· αὐτὸς γὰρ τοῦτο ἐν ἀρχῇ τοῦ λόγου δηλοῖ· μελλούσης δ' αὐτῆς ἁλίσκεσθαι, παραγαγὼν εἰς μέσον καὶ περιρρήξας τὴν ἐσθῆτα ἐπέδειξε τὰ στέρνα τῆς γυναικός· καὶ τῶν δικαστῶν εἰς τὸ κάλλος ἀπιδόντων, ἀφείθη.

Plutarch Lives of the Ten Orators 849e

And, as it is indeed reasonable to suppose, it was because he had been intimate also with Phryne the courtesan that when she was on trial for impiety he became her advocate; for he makes this plain himself at the beginning of his speech. And when she was likely to be found guilty, he led the woman out into the middle of the court and, tearing off her clothes, displayed her breasts. When the judges saw her beauty, she was acquitted.[49]

ἦν δ' ἡ Φρύνη ἐκ Θεσπιῶν, κρινομένη δὲ ὑπὸ Εὐθίου τὴν ἐπὶ θανάτῳ ἀπέφυγεν· διόπερ ὀργισθεὶς ὁ Εὐθίας οὐκ ἔτι εἶπεν ἄλλην δίκην, ὥς φησιν Ἕρμιππος. ὁ δὲ Ὑπερείδης συναγορεύων τῇ Φρύνῃ, ὡς οὐδὲν ἤνυε λέγων ἐπίδοξοί τε ἦσαν οἱ δικασταὶ καταψηφιούμενοι, παραγαγὼν αὐτὴν εἰς τοὐμφανὲς καὶ περιρρήξας τοὺς χιτωνίσκους γυμνά τε τὰ στέρνα ποιήσας τοὺς ἐπιλογικοὺς οἴκτους ἐκ τῆς ὄψεως αὐτῆς ἐπερρητόρευσεν δεισιδαιμονῆσαί τε ἐποίησεν τοὺς δικαστὰς τὴν ὑποφῆτιν καὶ ζάκορον Ἀφροδίτης ἐλέῳ χαρισαμένους μὴ ἀποκτεῖναι.

Athenaeus Deipnosophistae 590d–e

Phryne was from Thespiai, and when Euthias successfully indicted her, she escaped the death penalty; Euthias was so angry about this that he never argued another case, according to Hermippus.[50] Hyperides spoke in support of Phryne, and when his speech accomplished nothing, and

---

[48] For the fragments, see Jensen 1917, who provides ten (frr. 171–180); cf. Marzi 1977, who supplies only eight, but retains Jensen's numbering. O'Connell (2013) proposes a further fragment in Poll. 8.123-4 (see discussion on p. 30, n. 74). Ancient praise: Quint. *Inst.* 10.5.2; Dion. Hal. *De imit.* 5.6; [Longinus] *Subl.* 34.2-4.
[49] Tr. Fowler 1936. [50] Hermippos *FGrH* 1026 F 46 (= 68a I Wehrli).

the jurors seemed likely to convict her, he brought her out in public, ripped her dress to shreds, exposed her chest, and at the conclusion of his speech produced cries of lament as he gazed at her, causing the jurors to feel a superstitious fear of this priestess and temple-attendant of Aphrodite, and to give in to pity rather than put her to death.[51]

Plutarch stresses the impact of her beauty, but Athenaeus gives the scene a distinctly religious tinge. His account describes her as the 'servant and devotee of Aphrodite' (which, it has been suggested, may be Hyperides' own formulation); moreover, we learn that the display of Phryne's body prompted in the jurors a profound sense of religious awe (*deisidaimonesai*).[52] This story hints at others that make a similar divine association: for example, Athenaeus relates how Phryne removed her clothes and let down her hair in front of everyone at the Eleusinian festival, inspiring the artist Apelles to create his Aphrodite Anadyomene.[53] In relating this detail, Athenaeus does not condemn Phryne's behaviour; rather the implication is that this woman, in her body and behaviour, and above all in her beauty, teetered on the divine. And finally, according to Athenaeus, the plaintiff Euthias was apparently so upset by the outcome of the trial that he never prosecuted again. Across these two accounts there is surely some irony, and no little humour.

Although numerous modern scholars have accepted the account of the trial at more or less face value, it seems likely that its infamous culmination was an invention.[54] Athenaeus' patchwork of anecdotes enables us to pinpoint the timing of its creation when he quotes another version of the scene preserved in verses from the *Ephesian Woman* of Posidippus, a writer of comedies active from around 290 BCE. The extract describes how Phryne stood before the *Heliaia* on a capital charge, 'said to have corrupted all the citizens', but pleaded in tears with the judges, and so saved herself. Despite its comic potential, no mention is made of Hyperides or the infamous peroration.[55] It suggests that this memorable incident, far from providing a historical report, was developed sometime after 290 BCE. Scholars have

---

[51] Tr. Olson 2010.   [52] See Naiden 2006: 102.   [53] Ath. 13.591f.
[54] As Cooper (1995: 305–6) notes: see Cantarelli 1885: 465–82; Semenov 1935: 271–9; Foucart 1902: 216–18; Raubitschek 1941: 893–907; Kowalski 1947: 50–62; to which we can add Versnel (1990: 118), who refers to the 'unconventional methods of her counsel' and does not question it.
[55] Ath. 13.591e–f.

identified its originator as either Idomeneus of Lampsacus, who wrote a work on the Athenian demagogues, or Hermippus of Smyrna, or perhaps a combination of the two.[56] Moreover, this was not the only embellishment. These two accounts, prefaced as they are by descriptions of Hyperides' multiple relationships with a variety of prostitutes kept at a number of locations, draw on a biographical fiction that depicts Euthias and Hyperides going to court to fight over the famous *hetaira*.[57]

These elaborations do not mean we should throw out the whole briefing with the biography. There is some historical evidence to support the idea that Hyperides and Phryne were known to be connected, since other enemies of Hyperides also brought cases against Phryne.[58] And a political motivation seems the most obvious explanation, especially since Hyperides apparently accused Euthias of being a sycophant.[59] In the end, whichever viewpoint we take, it is clear that we need to approach this material with some awareness of the ways in which the layers of storytelling have been assembled, and the strong appeal of such narratives to both ancient and modern imaginations.

Let us start with the original charges made against Phryne, which are summarized in an anonymous treatise on rhetoric (*techne tou*

---

[56] Bollansée (1999: 386 n. 22) gives a succinct overview of the different attributions; as noted there, Cooper (1995: 304 and 312–16) has suggested a combination of the two ancient authors.

[57] Cooper 1995: 303–18. Described in Ath. 13.590d and Plut. *X orat* 849e, who claim to be drawing on Hyperides' own speech, probably Hyp. fr. 172 (Jensen = Syrianus *Ad Hermogenem* 4.120 Walz). See Cooper 1995: 309–10: Idomeneus was probably the first to interpret the passage in this way, but it becomes part of the biographical tradition about the orator (e.g. see Alciphron 4.4.4 and 5).

[58] Other accusations made against Phryne by enemies of Hyperides: Aristogiton, described in Ath. 13.591e.

[59] Sycophant: Harpocration, s.v. *Euthias* (= *Suda* s.v. *Euthias*, epsilon 3497, Adler) reports that Hyperides accused Euthias of this (Hyp. fr. 176 Jensen); it was supported in antiquity by the tradition that Anaximenes of Lampsacus had been hired by Euthias to write his speech (see Hermippus *FGrH* 1026 F 67). Other motivations put forward by modern scholars include Raubitschek (1941: 904), who suggests that Euthias was trying to avoid paying Phryne her fee. This is based on Alciphron 4.3.1 (= Hyp. fr. 179) in which a *hetaira* called Bacchis complains to Hyperides that Euthias' prosecution of Phryne threatens any *hetaira* chasing a fee—and may mean a charge of *asebeia*; and Alciphron 4.5.3 (= Hyp. fr. 179), which depicts Bacchis scolding another *hetaira* called Myrrhine for turning to Euthias to revenge herself on Hyperides (see O'Connell 2013: 113–14).

The Evidence 27

politikou logou), and are followed by what is usually taken to be the actual epilogue of the prosecutor of the case, Euthias.[60]

οἷον, ἀσεβείας κρινομένη Φρύνη· καὶ γὰρ ἐκώμασεν ἐν Λυκείῳ, καινὸν εἰσήγαγε θεόν, καὶ θιάσους ἀνδρῶν καὶ γυναικῶν συνήγαγεν. Ἐπέδειξα τοίνυν ὑμῖν ἀσεβῆ Φρύνην, κωμάσασαν ἀναιδῶς, καινοῦ θεοῦ εἰσηγήτριαν, θιάσους ἀνδρῶν ἐκθέσμους καὶ γυναικῶν συναγαγοῦσαν.

Phryne charged with *asebeia*. For she held a *komos* in the Lyceum. She introduced a new god and she held *thiasoi* for men and women. (Euthias) 'So I have shown that Phryne is impious because she joined in a shameless *komos*, because she has organized the introduction of a new god, and unlawful *thiasoi* for both men and women.'

Phryne's impiety is linked here with what appear to be a list of three separate charges: the joining in of a 'shameless' *komos*, the introduction of a new god, and the assembly of mixed-sex *thiasoi*. The first and the third accusations are perhaps the most puzzling. Why should Phryne's *komos*—which is something like a religious festival or celebration—have been described as shameless?

One reason may be the reference in the summary to the public space where these gatherings took place. The Lyceum lay outside the walls of the city, to the south-east. Although it eventually became famous as a philosophical school, it was originally a sanctuary dedicated to Apollo Lyceus and it retained this association.[61] This god was, as Michael Jameson has clarified, very much concerned with the hoplite citizens of the community, and the use of this space reflected this ideology.[62] During the Archaic and Classical periods it was used for mustering troops, military drills, and exercise, with perhaps an Archaic gymnasium, and then under Pericles a more elaborate set of buildings; it may be that the gymnasium was part of a larger sanctuary space.[63] The Assembly also seems to have met there before the Pnyx

---

[60] Anonymous Seguerianus 215 = Euthias fr. 2 Baiter–Sauppe = Spengel 1.390.
[61] According to Paus. 1.9.3, and see *SEG* 19.227.
[62] See discussion in Trampedach 2001: 143, and Hintzen-Bohlen 1997.
[63] Kyle 1993: 78, and see Jameson 1980, Travlos 1980, and Lynch 1972. Harpocration (s.v. *Lykaion*) notes the disagreement among the sources about the dates of the gymnasia (Theopompus *FGrH* 115 F136 attributes it to Pisistratus, while Philochorus *FGrH* 328 F 37 associates it with Pericles; Hesychius, s.v. *Lykaion kai Thumbraion* (lambda 1368), agrees with the latter). Xen. *Eq. mag.* 3.1.6-7 describes cavalry displays; Ar. *Pax* 353-7 marshalling troops; Xen. *Hell.* 1.1.33 military drills; a gymnasium structure and trainers are found in Pl. *Euthphr.* 272d–273b and Socratic Aeschines fr. 15 Krauss (see Lynch 1972: 15).

was established as a permanent location.[64] As well as gathering to exercise or for military and civic purposes, the Platonic dialogues also suggest that individuals would meet there to talk, perform, and debate.[65] Since this would mean the presence of a number of young men, it may be that the charge had connotations of the corruption of youth (recalling the charges made against Socrates). With the emendation of a word, this charge may also be traceable in the extract from Posidippus, quoted in Athenaeus: what reads now as corruption of 'all the citizens' (*tous bious*), may in fact be corruption of the youth (*tous neous*).[66]

Another reason for the disapproval of the *komos* may lie in the nature of the groups assembled there; indeed, the *thiasoi* are described as 'unlawful'. However, the grounds for use of this term are not made clear. It seems unlikely that legal approval was needed to hold such a gathering, and a law attributed to Solon (from the far later *Digest*), suggests that a *thiasos* was recognized as legal so long as it did not infringe 'public law'; however, the date and thus the specific contextual concerns of this passage are much debated.[67] The presence of individuals of both genders may have been the problem. Women were certainly involved in *thiasoi* (think of Lysistrata's gripe at the beginning of Aristophanes' play of that name that her sisters are always ready to trot off to random religious festivals)—but were these usually single-sex events?[68] In general, the epigraphic evidence that could illuminate this question is available only for later periods. However, a few inscriptions survive that appear to be lists of *thiasotai* and these include both male and female names.[69] Other sources also

---

[64] *IG* I³ 105.
[65] End of fifth century: Socrates and his companions in *Euthyd.* 271a, *Euthphr.* 2a, *Symp.* 223d; Prodicus of Keos in [Plato] *Eryxias* 397c–d; and Protagoras in Diog. Laert. 9.54. Isocrates taught rhetoric in the Lyceum during the first half of the fourth century BCE, as did other sophists and philosophers. Performances of poetry are mentioned in Alexis fr. 25 K-A, Antiphanes fr. 120 K-A, and Isoc. 12.18–20 and 33.
[66] See Cooper 1995: 314 n. 28.
[67] *Dig.* 47.22.4 (= Solon fr. 76a Ruschenbusch); see Versnel (1990: 119 n. 92), who appears to interpret it as evidence that all gatherings had to be ratified by public law, but it seems more likely that it renders any association a legal person for the purpose of enacting agreements, provided those agreements are themselves legal in their terms (with thanks to Robin Osborne, priv. comm.).
[68] Ar. *Lys.* 1–5.
[69] See Jones 1999: 307–10 (App. 1). *IG* II² 2346, first half of the fourth century: *Aristola*, l.100 and *Agathokleia*, l.105, although the end of the word here is supplemented; *IG* II² 2347 (Salamis, second half of the fourth century, but see Threatte

offer some insight. For example, from Demosthenes' attacks on Aeschines it becomes apparent that the revels of Glaucothea—initiations into the mysteries of the god Sabazius—involved both men and women, while imagery from vases may indicate that both men and women could be present at ecstatic religious revels.[70] In another source, Harpocration, a different kind of disapproval of these gatherings is evinced. They are now described as single-sex, but comprise women of much lower status and, Harpocration suggests rather coyly, of doubtful virtue:

Ὑπερείδης ἐν τῷ ὑπὲρ Φρύνης. ξενικός τις δαίμων, ᾧ τὰ δημώδη γύναια καὶ μὴ πάνυ σπουδαῖα ἐτέλει.

Harpocration, s.v. *Isodaites* (Dindorf)

Mentioned by Hyperides in his oration for Phryne. Some foreign *daimon* in whose honour women of the lower classes and particularly the ones that did not excel in virtue used to hold *teletai*.[71]

This brings us to the question of the god, according to Harpocration one called *Isodaites*. Described as 'foreign' in this definition, and as 'new' in the other extract, the name is nevertheless a Greek word, and was recognized as an epithet of Dionysus in later sources, although there is also evidence, from Hesychius, that the name was associated with Pluto, either as a name of that god, or as the name of his son.[72] The name, meaning something like 'equal shares', may, at least at first, carry insinuations to modern ears of some kind of social programme, but as an epithet or name of Dionysus it more probably alludes to the joys (and pains?) of drinking wine.[73] The possible risks

---

1980: 661), face B right col. 2 includes (l.30-3) *Parthenion, Hesychia, Erotis, Aitherion*; see discussion in Ascough (2003: 55), who notes that these women were not identified with reference to fathers or husbands.

[70] Dem. 18.259ff. and see also 19.199 for Glaucothea; for the image of women and men celebrating what appears to be worship in honour of Cybele on the Ferrara krater (dated 440-430 BCE), see Dillon 2002: 160-1. Parker (2005a: 326 n. 126) doubts the arguments from iconography put forward by Moraw (1998: 199-200, 259) that mixed private *thiasoi* developed in the fifth century; however, these show Dionysiac revels involving satyrs and maenads.

[71] Tr. Versnel 1990: 119.

[72] Harp. s.v. *Isodaites*; Hyp. fr. 177; Plut. De E 398a; or Pluto (Hesych. s.v. *Isodaites* [iota 952]).

[73] As Versnel (1990: 119 n. 93) notes: Eur. *Bacch.* 421-3: 'In equal measure to rich and humble he gives the griefless joy of wine.'

of introducing worship of a new divinity into Athens will be discussed in more detail in the next section, but it should be noted here first that 'Isodaites' does not sound like a new god or even a foreign god; moreover, Harpocration's phrasing also suggests that such assemblies in honour of such a god were not, in fact, such a rare event.

Perhaps it was instead the way in which these meetings were being organized that contravened acceptable religious practice? Some indication of this may survive in fragments of the speech by Hyperides that include some terminology from the Eleusinian Mysteries referring to the revelatory aspect of the Mysteries' ritual: *anepopteutos* 'someone who has not experienced the *epopteia*' and *epopteukoton* 'the people who have experienced the *epopteia*'.[74] It has been suggested that these were references to the participants of Phryne's rites, but Peter O'Connell has argued that it seems more likely that these references to aspects of the Eleusinian Mysteries were part of Hyperides' rhetorical strategy, offering a way of ridiculing Euthias' attack on Phryne.[75] Instead, the *teletai* may bring with it associations with independent ritual practitioners, like those *agurtai* ('beggar-priests') and *manteis* described by Plato as knocking on rich men's doors and trying to sell a range of supernatural services.[76]

We end this discussion of the evidence for Phryne's trial, as we did for those of the other women, trying to configure a scattering of vivid splinters of evidence. Anecdotes and arguments, assumptions and archetypes: the pieces can be assembled now one way, now another. In Phryne's case, perhaps, we can see the creative process most clearly at work, as the figure of the 'celebrity *hetaira*'—already a fabrication—is gradually muffled in further layers of fiction.

---

[74] Hyperides frr. 174 and 175 (Jensen) = Harp. *anepopteutos* and *epopteukoton*, respectively.

[75] Foucart 1902: 216-18 and Marzi 1977: 306-7; Raubitschek (1941: 905) argues that the terms refer specifically to the ritual bathing of the participants, but see O'Connell 2013: 111. O'Connell argues that Hyperides provided an extensive description of legal procedures for cases involving the Eleusinian Mysteries; he suggests that Poll. 8.123-4, which also includes these rare terms for participants, comprises a missing fragment from that speech. For ridicule as one of Hyperides' rhetorical weapons, see O'Connell 2013: 114-15, Cooper 1995: 301-12, Bartolini 1977: 118. O'Connell also suggests that Hyp. fr. 198 (Jensen) may indicate that another line of attack was to imply that Euthias was guilty of some misdemeanour with regard to the Mysteries.

[76] Pl. *Resp.* 365a.

FICTIONAL WOMEN

In addition to these historical cases, a number of fictional accounts of women being taken to court convey some more murderous stereotypes. These narratives bear a striking similarity to the historical cases: they each feature a woman who has been taken to court because she has used either *pharmaka* or incantations. They suggest that the figure of a woman standing trial for supernatural activities may have become a stock figure of the cultural imaginary of ancient Greek society.

The first is an Aesop's fable. From among the many manuscript variants, two versions of the story have been gathered: one, listed first below, is probably from the oldest rescension of the fables, the *Augustana*; the other from more recent rescensions.[77]

a) **Γυνὴ μάγος.** Γυνὴ μάγος ἐπῳδὰς καὶ καταθέσεις θείων μηνιμάτων ἐπαγγελλομένη διετέλει πολλὰ τελοῦσα καὶ ἐκ τούτων οὐ μικρὰ βιοποριστοῦσα. ἐπὶ τούτοις γραψάμενοί τινες αὐτὴν ὡς καινοτομοῦσαν περὶ τὰ θεῖα, εἰς δίκην ἀπήγαγον καὶ κατηγορήσαντες κατεδίκασαν αὐτὴν ἐπὶ θανάτῳ. θεασάμενος δέ τις αὐτὴν ἀπαγομένην ἐκ τῶν δικαστηρίων ἔφη· ὦ αὕτη, σὺ τὰς τῶν δαιμόνων ὀργὰς ἀποτρέπειν ἐπαγγελλομένη, πῶς οὐδὲ ἀνθρώπους πεῖσαι ἠδυνήθης; Τούτῳ τῷ λόγῳ χρήσαιτο ἄν τις πρὸς γυναῖκα πλάνον, ἥτις τὰ μείζονα κατεπαγγελλομένη τοῖς μετρίοις ἀδύνατος ἐλέγχεται.

Aesop *Fables* no. 56 (Perry 1952)

A female *magos* who promised to make incantations that calmed the anger of the gods did a good trade and from these activities made a handsome living. On these grounds, certain people charged her with innovating in divine matters and they accused her and condemned her to death. A certain person, seeing her leaving the court, said to her: 'You claim to be able to calm the anger of the gods, how come you could not persuade ordinary mortals?' Someone might use this tale against a

---

[77] I have used the variants given by Chambry 1925/6: no. 91 (but using Perry 1952: no. 56 for the older version). See Perry 1936 and Kurke 2011: 43–5 for an overview of the complexity of the prose fable tradition. Perry (1952: 156) argues that although we cannot know the history of the *Augustana* before the tenth century, it is likely that it reflects 'an ancient recension or combination of recensions, dating from sometime between the death of Alexander and the third century after Christ'. It has been argued that Demetrius of Phaleron was the first to collect Aesop's fables, in the fourth century BCE, and that the *Augustana* has aspects that reveal an Athenian influence (see Diog. Laert. 5.80 with Perry 1936; also Keller 1862: 361; Perry 1959: 32–5.) Perry (1962: 340) suggests that we may have the text 'of Demetrius himself' in PRyl.

wandering woman, who although she promises greater things, proves incapable of ordinary achievements.

b) **Γυνὴ μάγος.** Γυνὴ μάγος καὶ θείων μηνιμάτων ἀποτροπιασμοὺς ἐπαγγελλομένη πολλὰ διετέλει ποιοῦσα καὶ κέρδος ἐντεῦθεν ἔχουσα. Γραψάμενοι δέ τινες αὐτὴν ἀσεβείας εἷλον καὶ καταδικασθεῖσαν ἀπῆγον εἰς θάνατον. Ἰδὼν δέ τις ἀπαγομένην αὐτήν, ἔφη· Ἡ τὰς τῶν θεῶν ὀργὰς ἀποτρέπειν ἐπαγγελλομένη, πῶς οὐδὲ ἀνθρώπων βουλὴν μεταπεῖσαι ἠδυνήθης; Ὁ μῦθος δηλοῖ ὅτι πολλοὶ μεγάλα ἐπαγγέλλονται, μηδὲ μικρὰ ποιῆσαι δυνάμενοι.

Aesop *Fables* no. 91 (Chambry 1925–6).

A female *magos* who promised to be able to turn away the anger of the gods by sacrifice did a roaring trade and from this made a good income. Certain people accused her and charged her with impiety. They found her guilty and led her to her execution. Seeing her being led away, one person said, 'You claimed to be able to turn away the anger of the gods; how come you were unable to change the decision of a group of men?' The story shows that many may boast of great things, and are not able to achieve even small things.

In the older version, the *gune magos* has an expertise in *epoidai* (incantations); in the more recent versions she makes a profit dispensing *epoidai* to quell the anger of the gods. In the older version, she is taken to court on a charge of 'innovating in divine matters'; in the more recent version, this has become a charge of *asebeia*. In both versions, as she leaves the courtroom the *gune magos* is asked why, if she can control the gods, she was unable to persuade the jury. The content of the morals of these alternative versions is of some interest: neither mentions the legal machinery involved, or the role of justice (as a virtue or a judicial process);[78] rather, they both focus on more general conclusions. The newer version is banal, a general insight into the likely reality behind claims of greatness. The older version, however, gives slightly more social detail, and with it brings a heightened sense of personal interactions.[79] The story is positioned as being relevant to those women who wander and, presumably, offer similar supernatural services.

---

[78] As Zafiropoulos (2001: 117) observes of this tale and of the fables in the *Augustana* in general.
[79] Zafiropoulos (2001: 118) argues that 'the presentation of interpersonal relationships in the *Augustana* usually supports the stronger protagonist's demand for self-interest and his need for victory and survival'.

The accusations in each version, and the questions they raise, are, by now, familiar. The charge of innovation in the first version is one that we have already met in the cases of Ninon and Phryne. It has been argued that it is the procedure used by the woman that opens her to this charge.[80] However, the acts in question (using incantations to placate the gods) are scarcely innovative.[81] In the second version, incantations have become sacrifice—again, hardly novel—and the case is referred to as one of *asebeia*. From the point of view of legal process, the use of different terms in these two accounts is unproblematic: *asebeia* can be seen as simply providing the general category of offence, while innovating could have been the content of the specific indictment. The two versions of the story could be said to be focusing on different aspects of the charge.[82] This is not surprising. Philochorus the fourth-century historian apparently noted the charge against Theoris as being one of *asebeia* for practising similar activities. The parallel may extend beyond this. Although in referring to Theoris Demosthenes gives no indication that she was suspected of innovative religious ritual activities, nevertheless, he does mention that her servant was able to take on her 'drugs/spells and incantations', and in later evidence the term *hiereia* is used to describe her.

Both versions also lead us to reflect on the apparent difference between general opinion and legal charge. It is implicit in both accounts that while some people found the activities of the *gune magos* indictable, others were quite happy to employ her for the same reasons. Similarly, Theoris must have been doing business when she was arrested for her activities—and it has been suggested that this Aesopian woman may be Theoris. But the parallel does not quite work, since, as we have seen, Theoris is the only one of the women in the cases examined who does not seem to have been accused of religious innovation.[83]

---

[80] Dickie (2001: 52): 'The offence committed by the woman was not then sorcery, but attempting to placate the wrath of the gods by means that were felt to be at odds with Athenian tradition, presumably because they involved sorcery.'

[81] Neither Versnel (1990: 117) nor Iles Johnston (1999: 113) suggests that this character was trying to invoke the dead (*contra* Dickie 2001: 330 n. 20).

[82] Compare the indictment against Socrates (quoted in Diog. Laert. 2.40), which does not mention the general charge of *asebeia*, only 'wrongdoing' (*adikein*), and then lists the individual charges (see Gagarin 2012: 296).

[83] Gordon 1999: 274 n. 56.

We move to the final three examples in this section, which are perhaps the most straightforward of these accounts in the sense that they continue the themes of *pharmaka*, but make no mention of impiety. The first is a model forensic speech, the second a philosophical exemplum, the third, a biographical narrative. In each case, a woman stands accused of murder or attempted murder and defends herself by arguing that she thought she was restoring her victim's love, not taking his life; in the last example, we learn a little more about the social pressures that could be involved in such a situation.[84]

The first example is found in a model speech by Antiphon: the infamous *Against the Stepmother for Poisoning*.[85] The case concerns the poisoning of one Philoneus and his friend during dinner at Philoneus' house in the Piraeus. The speech lays out the events leading up to their deaths (14–20) and fills in at least some of the background. Initially, the murderer was assumed to be a slave woman, the mistress of Philoneus, who had served the two men poisoned wine after dinner. She was arrested, tortured for information, and executed. But the case was reopened when an illegitimate son of Philoneus' friend, at the behest of his dying father, charged his father's wife, his stepmother, with the murders. He argues that the slave woman was merely an accessory to his stepmother's plot to kill her husband, and supplies the intriguing information that this was, in fact, her second attempt to kill her husband in this fashion. The first time, her husband had caught her slipping something into his drink, but she had denied that it was poison, pleading that it was, in fact, a love philtre. According to the stepson, this was also the line of argument she had used to persuade Philoneus' mistress to carry out her plan. Philoneus was threatening to discard this woman and place her in a brothel. The stepmother promised her that she had the means

---

[84] This story pattern is familiar from myth, but again shows interesting nuances: the story of Deianeira poisoning Hercules 'in ignorance' appears to be told in Hes. fr. 25.18–25 M/W; in Soph. *Trach.* the figure of Deianeira is a more domesticated character than her mythic heritage might suggest (see Dickerson and Williams 2009: 100–1). This might be thought to bear some connection to the story patterns and stereotypes apparent in Antiphon 1, but the date of the play is uncertain (see Easterling 1982: 19–23).

[85] Gagarin (2002: 139) suggests that this court speech was probably written around 419/18 (a secure date for Antiphon 6); he observes that this is 'likely to be later, or at most just a few years earlier'.

The Evidence 35

to ensure that this would not happen: the love philtre would restore his feelings for her.[86] It is likely that this case would have gone to the Areopagus. As Aristotle tells us, this court judged 'Trials for homicide and wounding, if the killing or wounding is committed deliberately... so are those for *pharmaka*, if one causes death by giving it, and arson'.[87] Arguments have been made for the Palladium, on the basis that the jury is addressed in the speech as *dikastai*; but the term appears to have been used across the different Athenian courts.[88] Moreover, the prosecution does not seem to respond to the speaker's argument that even if his stepmother only meant to seduce his father, she still deserved to die, which would suggest the context of the Palladium.[89] Quite the contrary, in fact: the plaintiff seems at pains to emphasize how his stepmother had *planned* the death of her husband, stating that 'she killed him intentionally, planning the death... by sending the drug and ordering [the slave] to give it to him to drink, she killed our father'.[90] The emphasis on intent here is surely intended to

[86] This case also brings to mind the story of Medea as portrayed by Euripides; this would have been performed around fifteen years before, as Gagarin (2002: 147) points out.
[87] [Arist.] *Ath. Pol.* 57.3, tr. MacDowell 1963: 44.
[88] *Dikastai* at Antiph. 6.1: This argument is made by Wallace (1989: 103–4), but see MacDowell (1963: 56), who suggests that it was possible that this term could be used of jurors across all the courts, including, he notes, the Twelve Gods themselves (e.g. Dem. 23.66).
[89] Parker 2005a: 133.
[90] Antiph. 1.26: ἡ μὲν γὰρ ἑκουσίως καὶ βουλεύσασα τὸν θάνατον <ἀπέκτεινεν>... ἡ δὲ πέμψασα τὸ φάρμακον καὶ κελεύσασα ἐκείνῳ δοῦναι πιεῖν ἀπέκτεινεν ἡμῶν τὸν πατέρα (*contra* Gagarin 2002: 149–50), who quotes this sentence while at the same time arguing that the plaintiff 'is clearly not interested in her intent or state of mind when she provided the drug' and that the plaintiff 'is not concerned to show that she knew the drug was a poison, rather than a love potion' (150). Granted that the plaintiff only asserts that she is a murderer, it still does not seem to be the case that 'the speaker seems to have no interest in the question of whether his stepmother deliberately intended to kill or not' (149). The prosecutor repeatedly draws attention to the intention of the defendant not just to deliver the drug (as Gagarin argues), but to commit murder (Antiph. 1.26: ἑκουσίως καὶ βουλεύσασα τὸν θάνατον; see also 1.22, stressing the forethought of the defendant: ὑμεῖς δ' οὐ τῶν ἀποκτεινάντων ἐστὲ βοηθοί, ἀλλὰ τῶν ἐκ προνοίας ἀποθνῃσκόντων, 'you are not here to champion the murderers, but those who were wilfully murdered' (tr. Maidment 1941), and for a similar contrast between those unwillingly murdered and those planning to commit murder, see 1.6). He contrasts this with the position of the defence (that she killed him ἀβούλως τε καὶ ἀθέως, 'without thought and without scruple', 1.23; similarly, see also 1.27, where he contrasts involuntary crimes with those committed ἐκ προνοίας, 'with forethought'). It is hard to see how this can be interpreted as indicating that (Gagarin 2002:

counteract the impression of the letter of the law, which mentions the 'giving' of poison. In this case, the stepmother is the will behind the act; the slave woman who gave it was purely instrumental.[91] We do not know the imagined or intended outcome of this prosecution, but it is possible that a second example offers some insight.

This is found in the *Magna Moralia*, a treatise on ethics traditionally attributed to Aristotle, in which the writer explores the role of *to hekousion*, 'the voluntary', in actions. In this example, he describes how an anonymous woman was brought before the Areopagus, charged with administering a fatal potion. She claims she had only meant her target to fall in love, not to die, and so had acted without understanding of the consequences of her actions; as a result she is acquitted.

οἷόν φασί ποτέ τινα γυναῖκα φίλτρον τινὶ δοῦναι πιεῖν, εἶτα τὸν ἄνθρωπον ἀποθανεῖν ὑπὸ τοῦ φίλτρου, τὴν δ' ἄνθρωπον ἐν Ἀρείῳ πάγῳ ἀποφυγεῖν· οὗ παροῦσαν δι' οὐθὲν ἄλλο ἀπέλυσαν ἢ διότι οὐκ ἐκ προνοίας. ἔδωκε μὲν γὰρ φιλίᾳ, διήμαρτεν δὲ τούτου· διὸ οὐχ ἑκούσιον ἐδόκει εἶναι, ὅτι τὴν δόσιν τοῦ φίλτρου οὐ μετὰ διανοίας τοῦ ἀπολέσθαι αὐτὸν ἐδίδου. ἐνταῦθα ἄρα τὸ ἑκούσιον πίπτει εἰς τὸ μετὰ διανοίας.

[Aristotle] *Magna Moralia* 1188b35–8 (= 1.16.2)

We are told that a woman once gave a man a love-potion that proved fatal to him. She was put on her trial before the court of Areopagus; and was acquitted expressly on the ground that she acted without understanding the consequence. Affection prompted the deed; and she failed of her loving purpose. Because, then, the cup was given with no thought of the man's death, it was regarded as an involuntary homicide. In this case, then, the Voluntary falls under the head of Understanding.[92]

As the narrative explains, the reasons for the woman's release were quite straightforward: the Areopagus was for deliberate, wilful planned acts of murder, so someone who did not intend to kill her victim could not be convicted there.[93] Some scholars regard this

---

150) 'Antiphon's strategy, in other words, is to portray the stepmother as the primary agent in a plot to give her husband a drug.' Rather, the text seems to draw particular attention to the stepmother as the primary agent in a plot to commit murder.

[91] See the discussion in MacDowell 1963: 44–5, 62–4.
[92] Tr. Tredennick and Armstrong 1935.
[93] Parker (2005a: 133) expresses surprise on the grounds that 'one might expect any unsolicited use of *pharmaka* against another for whatever motive to be highly objectionable', but this overlooks the role of intention in the remit of the Areopagus. Parker seems to accept Plato's legislation against *pharmakeia* as an Athenian

The Evidence 37

anecdote as offering further elucidation of the case described in Antiphon 1, explaining what would have happened to the woman on trial; others have argued that it may also connect directly with aspects of some of the historical cases discussed above, helping to cut through the confusion surrounding at least one of these cases.[94]

But just before we turn to examine those charges, there is a final tale to set among this collection. In his treatise on the *Virtues of Women*, Plutarch gives an account of Aretaphila's attempt to kill the tyrant of Cyrene, Nicocrates. Aretaphila is caught red-handed and, in her defence, she claims she had created her own potions to make her husband love her more deeply. At first sight, this seems very similar to the stories we have already explored here, in which a woman fears the loss of her partner. However, Aretaphila offers a little more detail about the social context that prompted her actions, when she provides a further justification. She states that she created her potions because she herself feared the potions and devices of 'bad women' for whom she knew she was *epiphthonos*, that is, they felt *phthonos* towards her.[95] We will return to some of these details, especially the question of the associations between *phthonos* and accusations or actions relating to *pharmakeia*, later.

---

legislative reality (on this see further pp. 43-4), but does observe (133 n. 72) that since the stepmother's alibi (used twice) was that it was only a potion, there was little likelihood of such a charge.

[94] Parker (2005a: 133 n. 72) links the example in the *Magna Moralia* with the case discussed in Antiphon's speech. However, although he discusses these examples alongside the historical cases, he makes no mention of any association between them.

[95] Plut. *De mul. virt.* 256b-c: καρποῦμαι πολλαῖς ἐπίφθονος οὖσα κακαῖς γυναιξὶν ὧν φάρμακα δεδοικυῖα καὶ μηχανὰς ἐπείσθην ἀντιμηχανήσασθαι, μωρὰ μὲν ἴσως καὶ γυναικεῖα, θανάτου δ' οὐκ ἄξια· πλὴν εἰ κριτῇ σοι δόξειε φίλτρων ἕνεκα καὶ γοητείας κτεῖναι γυναῖκα, πλεῖον ἢ σὺ βούλει φιλεῖσθαι δεομένην.

1.3

What Charges?

The Athenian law courts were an arena for displaying and disputing political, and so male, power: in such a context, why bother to put these women on trial? One answer may be that they were closely associated with (male) political figures, and their indictments were part of the ongoing feuding of the Athenian political class. We will look at further cases that illustrate this aspect as we proceed.[1] However, although this is possible (especially in the case of the well-connected Phryne), too little, if anything, is known of these women's families or friends, let alone the substance or context of the trials, to substantiate this claim. Besides, even if we prefer such an explanation, then the choice of charges against these women (taken individually and in combination) remains puzzling. From supernatural activities of various kinds, including introducing new gods, making religious innovations, casting spells, and brewing potions; to various social offences, such as illicit gatherings, teaching slaves how to deceive; to involuntary murder using drugs or potions, we are left wondering about the plausibility and significance of these accusations.

MURDER?

That the main charge was one of murder is possible in at least some of the cases discussed here. Mirroring the charges brought against the

---

[1] For example, see the case against Archias, described in [Dem.] 59.116; discussed on pp. 319–20 and 51, n. 51. We can draw a slightly indirect parallel with those women we find cursed in the texts of binding spells that target important political figures; see Eidinow 2013a: 177.

What Charges? 39

stepmother in Antiphon's speech, or the anonymous woman in the *Magna Moralia*, it could be argued that this is the implication of the references to love philtres or *pharmaka* in the cases of Theoris and Ninon. This is the conclusion that Derek Collins draws about the case of Theoris: focusing on the discrepancy between what we know of Athenian law and the charges described in the fullest account (the passage from *Against Aristogiton*), Collins argues that Theoris was brought to trial (and executed) simply for applying *pharmaka*, specifically with an intention to kill.

Collins's argument draws in part on an inscription from the island of Teos on the coast of Asia Minor which dates to the early fifth century (*c*.470 BCE).[2] The inscription recorded the public curses that the Teans required their magistrates to pronounce against those who would harm their community. The original stone is now lost, but the discovery of another similar inscription has helped to clarify the text.[3] One of the clauses concerns 'whoever makes *pharmaka* against the Teans as a community or against an individual', and threatens death for them and their family.[4] This parallel, Collins argues, not only provides an explanation why Theoris was executed for *pharmaka*, but could also illuminate the reasons for the execution of her family as well.[5]

However, this parallel needs to be treated with caution. The Tean curses may not indicate a straightforward legal penalty, but rather an invocation for divine punishment, which would work whether or not the malefactor was detected; although presumably it is possible that there was accompanying legislation that ensured mortal penalties if he was caught.[6] More significantly, perhaps, is that fact that no

---

[2] Collins 2001: 486-7.
[3] The second document, *SEG* 31.985, dates to *c*.480–450 BCE. It also demonstrates the close relationship between Teos and its colony Abdera; see Graham 1992: 54-6.
[4] ML 30.
[5] Collins (2001: 489, drawing on Harris 2001) argues that the family could possibly have been found guilty of being accomplices in the crime, perhaps charged with *bouleusis* of intentional homicide for a victim who had died.
[6] Collins (2001: 486-7) discusses the Tean curses as part of his argument that Theoris was indicted for murder; he understands it literally as threatening public execution. But see the discussion in Parker (1983: 193-4 and again, 2005b: 77), who suggests that these were not legal provisions. Latte (1920: 76) argues that by 300 CE, if not earlier, the role of the curse in offering effective legal protection had played out in the Hellenistic world, although the formulae could still be seen in inscriptions. This decline is marked by the appearance of secular penalties alongside those of the supernatural at the beginning of the third century BCE.

similar example is known from ancient Athenian law. The closest parallel may appear in the curse uttered at the beginning of meetings of the Council and Assembly, as far as we can tell from our sources.[7] These covered plotting against the people of Athens, negotiating with the Persians against the people of Athens, and attempts to become or restore a tyrant. The threatened penalty does appear to have been the destruction of the wrongdoer, along with his family, but there does not appear to have been a clause covering use of *pharmaka*.

Further support for a lack of legislation in this area may come from Plato's *Laws*, in which the philosopher himself advocates the need for legislation that distinguishes between harm caused by *pharmakeia* through, on the one hand, natural and, on the other, supernatural means. It may be that his suggestions arose from actual cases conducted in the fourth-century BCE courts, cases of harm or *dike blabes*, caused by objects that had no actual physical contact with their victim.[8] Indeed, Richard Gordon has insightfully suggested that, in a context in which there was no charge for harm caused by supernatural means, Demosthenes' hendyadic phrase, 'drugs/spells and incantations', could have been understood as verbal shorthand for 'poisoning of an unnatural kind' by the jurors, perhaps because such a charge was not yet officially recognized in Athenian courtrooms.[9] This is ingenious; nevertheless, it suggests that the reason for Theoris' execution, along with that of her family, requires a different explanation.

A further possibility may emerge from another of Demosthenes' speeches, a blatantly political confection, written for Diodorus in his legal feud with Androtion. At the very beginning of that speech Diodorus describes the judicial machinations of his opponent: they have included not only indicting Diodorus for parricide, but also accusing his uncle of *asebeia* ('impiety') on the grounds that he associated with his nephew.[10] He does not give us details of the charges made against him, but he does note that his opponent failed to get a fifth of the votes, implying that this was a *graphe* procedure.

---

[7] The primary source for this is Ar. *Thesm.* 332–67 (with Sommerstein 1994, and Austin and Olson 2004, *ad loc.*); see also Isoc. 4.157, Dem. 18.30, 19.70 (with MacDowell *ad loc.*), and 23.97, Din. 2.16.
[8] Plato *Leg.* 932e–933e.
[9] Gordon 1999: 250.   [10] Dem. 22.2–3.

He also uses the term '*asebeia*' to refer to his crime when he proclaims to the jury that if he and his uncle had been found guilty, then 'who, whether friend or stranger, would have consented to have any dealings with me? What state would have admitted within its borders a man deemed guilty of such impiety?'[11] Diodorus tells us that his uncle escaped the charge, but the reason was that Diodorus himself was not convicted of parricide. This suggests that the two cases were being pursued, if not together, then at least in close temporal proximity.[12]

Could it be that, similarly, Theoris' family was indicted on a charge of impiety, on the grounds that they had associated with a woman accused of impiety, and that, therefore, when she was found guilty, so were they? Could we take this parallel even further to suggest that Theoris' original crime, whatever it was, had been *against* a member of her own family?[13] This could then return us to the earlier comparison with the

---

[11] The case *Against the Stepmother for Poisoning* may provide another apposite example. Although the plaintiff does not accuse his stepbrother of impiety explicitly, he repeatedly brings up the idea, using terms such as *atheos* ('godlessly') and *anosios* ('profanely') to describe both the killing (21, 23, and 26), and the impropriety of his stepbrother's position (5). In turn, he emphasizes his own piety in bringing the case, and the piety of the jurors if they convict the defendant using terms that indicate piety (25), including the term *eusebeia* (25). Finally, he mentions the underworld gods (31), which Gagarin also takes as a hint of the 'idea of pollution'. He argues that the speaker's final remark here 'seems almost perfunctory' (1997, *ad loc.*), but this may be because Gagarin does not seem to place much emphasis on the other references to holy/unholy behaviour throughout the rest of the speech. If we take Gagarin's point that references to homicidal pollution are to be understood as rhetorical, this speech is interesting for the careful course that the speaker steers between an accusation of impiety and more general statements of unacceptable behaviour.

[12] MacDowell (1963: xx) argues that the charge was for associating with Diodorus and for not taking the legally required action in the law courts against his own brother's killer; the 'association' between Diodorus and his uncle refers to the time that has passed with the uncle taking no legal action. However, in *Demosthenes the Orator* (2009: 169 n. 54) he accepts Parker's correction (1983: 123 n. 72) that there was no legal requirement for a relative to prosecute, only a 'moral duty'. Parker argues that '"association" with the killer' is the key issue here, on the grounds of the pollution that thus arose; he points out that this would not normally be a problem in cases where the killing had occurred between families. He does not mention the case of Theoris and her family.

[13] Murder cases were expected to be conducted by members of the victim's family (see Dem. 43.57 and Poll. 8.118, and *IG* I³ 104, with discussion in MacDowell 1963: 16-22 [where it is cited as *IG* I² 115]), so the plaintiff would not have been a family member employing the usual procedure. If this did not happen (as would be the case here, if the family is still associating with the murderer), then a non-family member would have to select an appropriate legal process. Examples of non-family members taking action occur in cases where slaves have been murdered, e.g. Pl. *Euthphr.* 3e-4b and [Dem.] 47.68-73. In both cases, religious guidance is sought from the *exegetai* or expounders of religious/unwritten law (see MacDowell 1963: 11-16).

women of Lemnos; it would also provide an implicit explanation of Demosthenes' use of the word *miaros* (discussed above, p. 14, n. 13), to describe Theoris, as well as his apparent reluctance to state the charge explicitly: both aspects suggest that Theoris was strongly polluted. In turn, memory of such a train of events could explain the disapproval that Demosthenes appears to be trying to draw down onto Eunomus. Thus, finally, it is not the tools as magical devices, or the activities related to those tools, which are meant to prompt condemnation, but an association, however indirect, with this woman.

But what then of the mention of *pharmaka kai epoidai*? Collins argues that the fact that the speaker mentions *epoidai*, the casting of incantations, would have been irrelevant to the original charge against Theoris. It was included by the speaker simply in order to sully those involved in the case by associating them with a woman who cast spells and uttered incantations. In particular, he hopes it would attach to Eunomus, who, it becomes clear, has a relationship with Theoris' maidservant and inherited Theoris' drugs and incantations, which he also uses. The 'magical features' of the case 'are rhetorical embellishments marshalled for the purpose of discrediting a witness' and the speaker may even have 'misremembered or deliberately embellished the facts of the case, while relying upon sensationalism and the lack of expertise of the jurors to make the point that Theoris had been executed for magic'.[14]

It is an ingenious argument, but in the end it begs—and raises—a number of questions. First of all, would the jurors fall for the kind of rhetorical embellishment that Collins describes? If the charge was intentional murder, then the case would have been held in the Areopagus, as the model from the *Magna Moralia* describes.[15] The jurors there were experienced ex-magistrates: would they have been befuddled by slippery forensic rhetoric confusing magic or murder?[16]

---

[14] Collins 2001: 477. Gordon (1999: 251) similarly ends his argument with the suggestion that society simply found Theoris unimpressive and tiresome (and the suggestion is not unrelated to her gender). He notes that the speaker knew how to 'smear her convincingly: by representing her as nothing more than a female sorcerer, of the sort that anyone would thankfully be rid of'.

[15] MacDowell (1963: 60) suggests that the rule may have been that 'homicide was intentional whenever death resulted from an act which was intended to cause harm'. If Theoris' case were about an unpremeditated murder, then it would have been tried in the Palladium, in which case the penalty would have been exile (see Harrison 1968: 198).

[16] On the process of presenting an *enklema* or *graphe* to the magistrate, and its likely content, see Gagarin 2012: 295–6 and Harris 2013: 115–16.

Collins's argument suggests that it was feasible—or that the jurors would have thought it so—to be executed on a charge of 'practising magic'. Presumably this is not intended to mean that this was the overall procedure, but is meant to be a reference to one of the charges recorded in the *enklema* against Theoris as part of a larger charge. But this still raises the question of the nature of the wrongdoing: it would not be enough to charge someone with using drugs/spells and incantations.[17] If the answer is that these drugs/spells and incantations had been used to kill someone—and this was a charge of murder—then it raises the question of why Demosthenes does not simply refer to that crime. After all, in other similar cases, where *pharmaka* result in death, the crime is referred to as *phonos* or homicide, not a poisoning or bewitching.[18] The explanation of murder can be applied most obviously to two of the fictional trials, but it is significantly more difficult to relate it to those historical cases that involve the creation of *pharmaka* but make no mention of harm caused or an intent to murder; nor does it help to resolve the role of the ritual aspects of those cases.

MAGIC?

As described above, there is little if any evidence that one could be taken to court simply for creating *pharmaka* or using incantations per se.[19] The Tean curses do not provide evidence for Athens, and besides they focus on evidence for doing harm rather than simply the questionable activities themselves; similarly, Plato's discussion of legislation against those practising these arts is directed towards punishing the likely physical harm that these might effect, rather than the acts themselves.[20]

---

[17] As Gagarin (2012: 312) has argued in an analysis of relevance in Athenian forensic argument: 'For them, law was not just a matter of written statutes, but could include the broad set of customs or traditional rules that the Athenians generally accepted whether or not they were enshrined in statute.'
[18] MacDowell (1963: 64) observes that in Antiphon 1 and 6, the crime is referred to by those involved as a *phonos*, although *pharmaka* are involved.
[19] The difficulties of establishing the illegality of magical practice in ancient Athens are well illustrated by Ogden (1999: 83–4).
[20] Pl. *Leg.* 933b–e. Dickie (2001: 60) also makes this observation. He provides a succinct and compelling analysis of Plato's concerns: on the one hand, regarding the

Indeed, this also seems to be the point of the often-quoted observation in Plato's *Meno* that elsewhere Socrates would be arrested as a *goes* ('sorcerer') for the effect that he has on his audience (he is able to numb the soul and mouth of the speaker, so that he is unable to speak well on a subject [virtue] as he claims to have done many times before).[21] This episode also appears to contrast Athens' tolerance for such activities with that of other cities, although that alone does not indicate that there was no specific legislation against magic-working in Athens.[22]

Again, as above, it seems more likely that this charge would have accompanied other accusations, as part of a larger legal process. Scholars have argued that it was particularly likely to have accompanied the charge of introducing 'a new religion'.[23] That it was, as it were, an inseparable further dimension of a discourse of distrust that surrounded religious innovation, especially novel ideas introduced from abroad.[24] This might align with the periodic attempts by the Athenians to control the religious ritual activities taking place within their city, and the evidence for suspicion regarding the practitioners of supernatural services, especially those who lived off the proceeds or used them to garner political support.[25]

However, the association of these two charges is not inevitable. Although there is ample evidence for it from later periods, especially under the Roman Empire, this does not mean that it was also the case in Classical Athens. To help us better understand not only the events

---

harm potentially caused by sorcery, and, on the other, the threat posed by the impious; as Dickie observes, the two should not be conflated.

[21] Pl. *Meno* 80a.

[22] As Dickie points out (2001: 329 n. 6, criticizing Iles Johnston 1999: 122 for making this assumption).

[23] Derenne 1930: 232–3, Reverdin 1945: 215–16, Dodds 1951: 204–5; see Versnel 1990: 115–18.

[24] The ideas of new religion and foreign religion are somewhat elided by Versnel. In his initial analysis (1990: 16) he argues that: 'the present two charges are not contradictory at all as they represent the two sides of one very current coin. The universal tendency to associate prophets of a new religion with sorcery or magic, so typical of various periods in classical antiquity and especially of the Roman imperial period, was not lacking in classical Athens either.' In a more recent work, the argument is made again in discussion of what he calls 'the three priestesses'. Here Versnel (2013: 139) narrows down 'new religion' to the idea of foreignness: 'Introducing foreign cults and the suspicion of practicing magic are, throughout antiquity, two sides of one medal and at Athens might provoke an *asebeia* process of which there were several in the 4th c.'

[25] Ar. *Pax* 1052–119 and 1061–86, *Av.* 987–8, *Eq.* 1085, *Vesp.* 380, for examples.

themselves, but also the processes of historical change over time, it is important to try to distinguish, where possible, between, say, association with foreign gods vs new rituals, and new rituals vs new performances of old rituals. As we have seen, the accusations against these women are far from simple. In Ninon's case, the scholia make the link between her and, in this case, *philtra*, but this is based on a misunderstanding of the text that could well be born of associations frequently made at a later time. The most contemporary source, Demosthenes, mentions simply the bringing together of *thiasoi*, as part of the discussion of the activities of the mother of his enemy Aeschines. The brevity of this reference is puzzling: if Demosthenes wanted to raise suspicions against Glaucothea and Aeschines, then why did he not provide more details about Ninon's case? Although we are given to understand that her activities were like Glaucothea's initiations into the mysteries of the god Sabazius, no mention of the identity of Ninon's god is made here. If Demosthenes wanted to emphasize the alien nature of Glaucothea's activities and the dangers this posed to the city of Athens, why not reinforce this point with mention of the foreignness of Ninon's divinity? If this was because it was simply Sabazius again, then there would have been no harm in repeating the idea (although, we also have to observe that with at least twenty years separating the two events, this was hardly a new or foreign entity).[26] Although a later source, Josephus, argues that this case concerned the introduction of new gods, this demands cautious treatment, since he also tells us that such introductions were forbidden (which, as we shall see, is highly questionable).

One possibility for some resolution may lie in the scholion to this speech, which, rather than referring directly to new gods, mentions mockery of the Mysteries. This could mean new rituals, or existing rituals wrongly performed, perhaps in the wrong place (a problem that seems to have been at the heart of one of the most well-known impiety trials of the Classical period, the 'mocking of the Mysteries' in 415 BCE).[27] We will examine this possibility in more detail shortly. For

---

[26] Compare, in the case of Phryne, the description of Isodaites as 'foreign' by Harpocration, but only as 'new' in the quotation of the charge itself; the god has a Greek name, as Parker (1996: 163) observes and is 'not so new after all', as Versnel has noted (1990: 119).

[27] Similarly, the Aesopian parallel includes the accusation of introducing new things *peri ta theia*, 'regarding things divine', which need not necessarily mean a new god. 'In the wrong place' recalls the profanation of the Mysteries: see Murray 1990: 156.

now we can observe that, with regard to the associations that some scholars have made between magic and new ritual practice, this does not seem to be the case here. The argument that there is simply a 'universal tendency to associate prophets of a new religion with sorcery or magic' may be assuming a context that did not exist in fourth-century BCE Athens.[28]

Similarly, we must be cautious with our assumptions about the identity of these women simply as magic-workers. To stay with the case of Ninon, one scholar has argued (with reference to the famous description by Plato in the *Republic* of itinerant *manteis*) that she 'must have belonged to that elusive lot of *agurtai kai manteis*' offering 'prophetism, charlatanism, bigotry and hocus pocus': a description that certainly recaptures the dismissive tone of the philosopher's original phrasing.[29] Indeed, Plato's own approach to these activities is rather more cautious. Although he clearly dislikes the profit motive of these characters, he is more cautious in his handling of what we might call their prophet motives, and careful not to dismiss the power (both actual and social) of the rituals that they offer: 'it is not easy to know the truth about these and similar practices, and even if one were to find out, it would be difficult to convince others'. Moreover, he appears to struggle to find the words to make a clear distinction: 'promising to persuade the gods by bewitching them, as it were, with sacrifices, prayers, and incantations'.[30] This may be because the clear distinction between 'magic' and 'religion', which an unqualified use of these two modern terms suggests, is not at play in the Classical

---

[28] Vernsel 1990: 116. We can note in passing here that they do not appear in the charges brought against Socrates in 399 BCE—although the highly reminiscent phrase *philtra kai epoidai* does occur in descriptions (by his friends) of Socrates' powerful use of persuasion (see pp. 167–8).

[29] Versnel is here bringing together the description of the itinerant *manteis* in Pl. *Resp.* 364b–c and the description of the more harmful type of atheist in *Leg.* 908d and 909b. His precis introduces aspects that are hard to find in the original Greek. Moreover, Versnel's example of the suspicious attitude towards *manteis* (117; Soph. *OT* 386f., in which Oedipus berates Tiresias for being a *magos* and a *dolios agurtes* 'tricky beggar-priest'), is undermined by the fact that Tiresias, as the audience knows and Oedipus will come to know, is proved right in the end.

[30] Pl. *Leg.* 933b (tr. Saunders 1970). In his account in the *Republic* (364e), Plato quotes the wrongdoers themselves as they, in turn, quote Homer as support for their services.

material.³¹ Rather, those who were offering ritual services to the gods were not necessarily stepping so far outside a familiar ritual context. This is borne out when we turn to Plato's proposed legislation against magic-working, where we find he also does not equate these activities directly with impiety. Rather, he is concerned about the impious nature of such practitioners, and the attitude they show towards the gods when they promise to be able to bend them to their will through these activities (as we will see, this focus on a mindset, rather than specific actions, also appears in other evidence). Plato's proposed punishment for these wrongdoers is physical isolation in order that their ideas cannot be transmitted.³² Indeed, it is for activities that are more recognizably 'religious' (the setting up of shrines on private or public ground, sacrificing to any god whatsoever, sacrificing in a state of impurity) that Plato reserves the penalty of death 'for their impiety'.³³

But what is also clear from his discussion of such activities is that Plato's view of impious action included activities that were common within the city of Athens. Plato himself tells us that,

ἔθος τε γυναιξί τε δὴ διαφερόντως πάσαις καὶ τοῖς ἀσθενοῦσι πάντῃ καὶ κινδυνεύουσι καὶ ἀποροῦσιν, ὅπῃ τις ἂν ἀπορῇ, καὶ τοὐναντίον ὅταν εὐπορίας τινὸς λάβωνται, καθιεροῦν τε τὸ παρὸν ἀεὶ καὶ θυσίας εὔχεσθαι καὶ ἱδρύσεις ὑπισχνεῖσθαι θεοῖς καὶ δαίμοσιν καὶ παισὶν θεῶν, ἔν τε φάσμασιν ἐγρηγορότας διὰ φόβους καὶ ἐν ὀνείροις, ὡς δ' αὔτως ὄψεις πολλὰς ἀπομνημονεύοντας ἑκάσταισί τε αὐτῶν ἄκη ποιουμένους, βωμοὺς καὶ ἱερὰ πάσας μὲν οἰκίας, πάσας δὲ κώμας ἔν τε καθαροῖς ἱδρυομένους ἐμπιμπλάναι καὶ ὅπῃ τις ἔτυχε τῶν τοιούτων.

---

³¹ The cases of these women bring into sharp relief the difficulties of understanding the ancient perception of the relationship between (the modern categories) of magic and religion. Parker's approach over time illustrates these issues: in an earlier discussion of these women (1996: 163 with n. 34) he draws an implicit line between magic and religion. His discussion of the introduction of new gods brings up the 'prosecution of three "priestesses"', but only the case against Phryne is discussed in the text; the evidence for Theoris and Ninon is given in a footnote. His argument is that the case of Phryne along with that of Socrates reveals 'the Athenians... affirming their right of ultimate control over all the religious practices of Attica' (1996: 217). In contrast, in later work (Parker 2005a: 133), Ninon and Theoris are discussed without mention of Phryne, religious practice, or the introduction of new gods. They are described as 'two women cunning in spells', although other associations are also alluded to: 'in both cases, the expertise in spells or philtres may have been a symptom of a broader impiety rather than the core of the case'.
³² Pl. *Leg.* 907d4–909d2.   ³³ Pl. *Leg.* 910d.

> It is customary for all women especially, and for sick folk everywhere, and those in peril or in distress (whatever the nature of the distress), and conversely for those who have had a slice of good fortune, to dedicate whatever happens to be at hand at the moment, and to vow sacrifices [910a] and promise the founding of shrines to gods and demi-gods and children of gods; and through terrors caused by waking visions or by dreams, and in like manner as they recall many visions and try to provide remedies for each of them, they are wont to found altars and shrines, and to fill with them every house and every village, and open places too, and every spot which was the scene of such experiences.[34]

This brings us to the question of the range, nature, and relative wrongdoing of independent, let alone innovative, religious activities. If 'magical activities' might be one of the constitutive charges of a larger general charge, then it was likely that the larger charge was one of impiety, or *asebeia*.

ASEBEIA

Before sifting through the details of the charges related to ritual activities, and the various ways in which they have been approached by different scholars, it is useful to examine one particular significant legal process: the *graphe asebeias*, which, in Athens, was one of a number of legal charges that concerned some kind of offence against the gods.[35] *Asebeia* can be translated variously as 'impiety' or more

---

[34] Pl. *Leg.* 909e–910a (tr. Bury); cf. Men. *Dys.* 260–3.

[35] We know most about those cases that were conducted in Athens—although, even here this information is relatively sparse—where, alongside the charge of impiety, such cases included 'wrongdoing concerning a festival' (usually conducted by means of a *probole*), temple robbery (*hierosulia*), 'theft of sacred money' (Dem. 19.293 and Antiph. 2.1.6), and offences against olive trees (Lysias 7, although it does not mention *asebeia* at all). Not all such charges were equivalent: the *graphe asebeias* with some exceptions (see Harrison 1968: 82) appears to have been an *agon timetos*, that is, the penalty would be set by the prosecutor, with an alternative offered by the defendant if he was found guilty. In contrast, those found guilty of *hierosulia* were automatically punished with death or exile, along with property confiscation and loss of burial rights; there was no room for debate (see Xen. *Hell.* 1.7.22, and *SEG* 12.100 for the case of Theosebes of Xypete). On the impossibility of working out the attitude in the rest of Greece, and how this does or does not contrast with Athenian attitudes, see Krauter 2004: 235.

What Charges?

broadly as 'religious offence',[36] and a *graphe* was a 'public' charge, so any willing person could bring a *graphe asebeias* against an individual.[37] Indeed, in the Platonic dialogue the *Euthyphro*, which is set just before Socrates' trial, Socrates mentions that he has never met the man who has brought the *graphe* against him.[38] This, of course, laid the charge open to abuse: the use of the *graphe asebeias* against political rivals has been well documented.[39] And if not attacked directly by their enemies, individuals might still be prosecuted by proxy, that is, by sycophants. Indeed, in the case of the women under consideration here, Ninon and Phryne were accused by individuals who had reputations for being sycophants. Of course, this does not negate the possibility that there may also have been genuine concern about religious matters among those who were involved in bringing these prosecutions.[40]

In the process that followed, a preliminary hearing or *anakrisis* took place in front of a magistrate, the *archon basileus*, before the case went to a court with a jury of 500 or more.[41] Beyond a straightforward decision between guilt and innocence, a *graphe* charge had potential

---

[36] Religionsvergehen, as Krauter (2004: 231) translates the Greek term.
[37] Procedures may have varied, as I have noted elsewhere (see Eidinow 2015: 66 n. 49).
[38] Pl. *Euthphr.* 2b7–9.
[39] They include the fifth-century BCE 'attacks on intellectuals' associated with Pericles (although by now, it is well established that the historicity of a number of these cases is doubtful); the late-fourth-century proceedings against pro-Macedonian sympathizers (Demades in 324/3 and Aristotle in the following year; then in the period of democratic revival 318/17 BCE, Theophrastus, Demetrius of Phaleron, Theodorus the atheist, and Stilpo the Megarian). See a compelling discussion in O'Sullivan 1997; as she notes (145), there is evidence to suggest that the prosecution of Theodorus was, as Bauman (1990: 125) puts it, an 'unequivocal case of "pure" asebeia'.
[40] Filonik (2013: 80) gives a stark statement of this approach ('the use of religion in those trials appears as a purely instrumental measure, serving various forms of political agenda, even if feeding on existing superstition and fear'). A more nuanced view is found in Todd (1996: 115 n. 23): 'It is a striking fact, and one which has never been adequately explained, that charges of impiety at Athens often seem to have been highly politicised.' Todd gives as examples the trials of Socrates, Andocides, and the case of the sacred olive stump (Lysias 7, where the speaker appears to have retained his property under the regime of the oligarchs). Indeed, we see this demonstrated in the way that charges of impiety were themselves part of the great game of litigation: so in Lysias 21.20 it appears that the charge of taking bribes has been levelled by a group already on a charge of impiety. Janko (2001: 14) gives an overview of the mixed motives of those who prosecuted Socrates and points out that the fear of the intellectual was crucially mixed with fear of 'atheism'; Connor (1991) argues that Socrates was killed on religious grounds, and see also Parker 1996: 202.
[41] [Arist.] *Ath. Pol.* 57.2–3, Dem. 35.48. See MacDowell 1963: 33 ff., Harrison 1971: 9 and 48.

implications for both sides. For if the person bringing the charge failed to capture one-fifth of the votes at trial or abandoned his case, he would be fined 1000 drachmae and suffer at least partial *atimia*.[42] Since the *graphe* was an *agon timetos*, it meant that the penalty was not fixed by law. Once the defendant was found guilty, the jurors had to choose between penalties proposed first by the prosecutor and then by the defendant—a process that Socrates, for one, did not appear to take seriously.[43]

This leaves the question of what actions might come under the charge of *asebeia*—and here we meet with some greater uncertainty. At one level, we might argue that the general charge of *asebeia* might be held to include any smaller charge that could be made to sound relevant;[44] on the other hand, it is worth looking at which particular activities the Athenians themselves were likely to include. In terms of what the Athenians understood *asebeia* to mean, as Cohen has pointed out, the 'unreflective ordinary language conception of the Athenian citizen' is probably captured by Euthyphro's response to Socrates in Plato's dialogue of that name: he states that 'impiety is that which is not pleasing to the gods'.[45] Aristotle offers us a more detailed definition that turns on the meaning of the term *plemmeleia*, which means 'error', but may also convey an element of impious offence. It can, as Aristotle explains, be committed against gods, *daimones*, the dead, parents, or the fatherland.[46] The cases brought or crimes referred to in the forensic corpus give some idea of the variety of misdemeanours that might be included under this heading. For example, as noted above, the speaker of Demosthenes' speech *Against Androtion*, Diodorus, tells us that it was possible to bring an impiety charge for murder. The example in that speech is the murder of a kinsman (his father); but a puzzling fragment of a speech

---

[42] On prosecutions with the potential for partial *atimia*, see Hansen 1975: 29 (and for exceptions MacDowell 1978: 64). The extent of the *atimia* is discussed by Harris (1992: 79–80), reviewing MacDowell (1990); Rubinstein (2000: 92 n. 43) offers an overview of the debate.

[43] See Todd 1993: 134.

[44] As one anonymous reader of this text has observed (pers. corresp.). For systematic listings of the evidence for trials in Athens and beyond, see Krauter 2004 and Filonik 2013.

[45] Pl. *Euthphr.* 7a. See Cohen (1991: 204–5), who notes (205) that 'it is reasonable to suppose that the legal scope of the term is narrower'.

[46] Arist. *Virt. Vit.* 1251a30. The additional nuance is apparent also in the noun's cognates; see entries in LSJ s.v. *plemmeles* (2).

by Hyperides suggests that the murder, or the mistreatment of the dead, need not be that of a kinsman.[47] Returning to Diodorus, we learn that it was also possible to prosecute under this charge if someone had not brought a homicide charge against the murderer of a kinsman.[48] These cases raise questions about the perceived sanctity of family ties, and may be explained by the pollution caused by murder.[49]

However, the majority of crimes prosecuted through a *graphe asebeias* were what Hyperides elsewhere calls *peri ta hiereia* (and he distinguishes these crimes from, for example, mistreating parents or making illegal proposals).[50] Again, law-court speeches offer some idea of the many different kinds of 'errors' the category might encompass: for example, offences against priests or private individuals 'with a religious mission', and the actions of officials who represented the people in religious activities but failed to fulfil the customary criteria.[51] Two famous trials from 399 BCE supply examples that are particularly salient for this study. First, the trial of Andocides is itself a case of *asebeia*. Andocides was part of the prosecution against those who profaned the Mysteries, and this case was brought against him for breaking a law that banned those convicted of impiety from entering temples (Isotimides' decree, passed shortly after the events of 415).[52]

---

[47] Hyperides (fr. 70) suggests that after a number of wealthy Aeolians had been found dead at Rheneia, the Delians accused the Rheneians of impiety, followed by the Rheneians bringing the same charge, in turn, against the Delians, but we lack important contextual and detailed evidence to understand why this event seems to have resulted in these particular charges.

[48] Dem. 22.2; see discussion on pp. 40–1.

[49] *Tetralogies* I and III make these points at some length. It seems likely that there was a conception of *asebeia* by association for the kinsman—and perhaps for the city—but see Parker 1983: 130.

[50] Hyp. 4.5.

[51] Examples of offence: *IG* II^2 1635 (B, frg. a111).135–6 (= *IDélos* 98 [B, frg. a1] ll. 26–7; see RO 28) (against Delians who had chased the Athenian representatives of the Amphictyony from the temple and beaten them). Cf. Versnel (1990: 123), who gives an overview of offences against religion, drawing on Derenne (1930: 9–12). Versnel (1990: 123–4) includes Dem. 21.1, 12, 20, 34, 51, 55 (but although Meidias' offences were described as *asebeia* during the trial, this was not prosecuted as such; see the discussion in Eidinow 2015); and the case of Archias ([Dem.] 59.116), which he argues demonstrates that a priest who sacrificed at the wrong time and place would have 'offended both state and gods' (see further discussion on pp. 319–20).

[52] For the original events: Thuc. 6.53.1 and Andoc. 1.10, 29–32, 58, and 71. On his return to Athens in 403 BCE, Andocides tried to bring a prosecution against one Archippus for mutilating his family's herm (Lys. 6.11–12).

But his case also introduces three other types of *asebeia* relating to those events and the famous desecration of the herms in 415 BCE: the defacing of sacred objects, the revelation of the secrets of the Mysteries, and the mocking of the Mysteries.[53] The other example is the most well documented and thoroughly discussed of all impiety cases, that of the philosopher Socrates. The charges against Socrates famously included that he 'has broken the law by not duly acknowledging (*nomizein*) the gods whom the [Athenian] polis acknowledges [and] introducing other new divinities (*daimonia*). He has also broken the law by subverting/corrupting the young.'[54] These two cases together introduce some useful comparative material for reflection on the charges that we find in the cases made against these women: the question of the legality of introducing new gods, treatment of particular ritual activities, and, perhaps somewhat more surprisingly, the teaching of those of lower status. We turn to these next.

RELIGIOUS MISDEMEANOURS

The passage from Josephus relating to Ninon which was cited earlier indicates a society with no tolerance for the introduction of new gods; but from the same period, but in contrast, we find Strabo praising the Athenians for their tolerance, 'for they welcomed so many of the foreign rites that they were ridiculed by comic writers'.[55] These two

---

[53] Other examples of the defacing of sacred objects: *I Ephesos* 2; of revelations: (Aeschylus) Arist. *Eth. Nic.* 1111a10, Ael. *VH* 5.19; (Diagoras of Melos) Diod. Sic. 13.6.7, Schol. Ar. *Av.* 1071, Lys. 6.17; of mockery: the charge against Alcibiades is preserved in Plut. *Per.* 22 (it does not mention *asebeia* explicitly, but we are told he was charged with impiety in *Per.* 19; and see also Thuc. 6.27, 53, and 60, and Xen. *Hell.* 1.4.13, 14, and 20).

[54] Favorinus *ap.* Diog. Laert. 2.40; Xen. *Mem.* 1.1–2 and *Ap.* 10; Pl. *Ap.* 24b–c (tr. Parker 1996: 201). The verb, *nomizo*, translated here as 'acknowledge', straddles both the idea of 'customary practice' and 'belief' (see Derenne 1930, Fahr 1969, Versnel 1990: 125, Parker 1996: 201). Dover (1975) has argued that only Socrates can be taken to have been prosecuted for his attitudes towards the gods; in his edition of Aristophanes' *Clouds*, he translates *nomizo* as 'accept (*or* treat, practise) as normal', which captures both physical and mental attitudes. Yunis (1988: 62–6) provides a neat and effective analysis of the way in which *theous nomizein* (65) 'must be something distinct from worshipping gods, but must be a necessary concomitant of worshipping gods'.

[55] Strabo 10.3.18. He mentions specifically 'the Bendideian rites mentioned by Plato, and the Phrygian by Demosthenes when he casts the reproach upon Aeschines'

statements appear to illustrate two clear and contrasting positions—and, indeed, some scholars have adopted one or other, for example arguing that certain kinds of cults which smacked of 'being foreign' were more likely to be regarded with suspicion and intolerance by the Athenians.[56] However, the difference between them may not be as clear as first appears. In particular, the question of how to apply the terms 'new' or 'foreign' to either divinities or ritual practices poses significant problems.

In terms of gods, 'new' or 'foreign' could mean divinities known from other Greek communities, but not yet enjoying cult in Athens, as well as deities from further afield. If a god required civic space and funds, and all the trappings of institutionalization, there were regular procedures by which Council and Assembly would grant official sanction.[57] However, some gods designated as 'new' to the civic pantheon were already being worshipped in Athens by groups or individuals before they received this official recognition: the cults of Pan and Bendis are good examples. It was also possible to rent land on which to conduct worship, and to remain privately funded. Some cults did not even go this far: the cult of Adonis, for example, was famously celebrated by groups of women on their domestic rooftops, and its devotees do not seem to have arranged for or been designated a location of civic cult.

It has been described as 'standard practice' for Athenians to introduce new gods, but the details of this practice varied. Gods might be introduced by individuals or groups. They might stay the same or be transformed; remain the concern of subgroups or be absorbed into the pantheon of the city.[58] As this suggests, in terms of 'new' or 'foreign' ritual practice, evidence for myriad smaller cult activities indicates that individuals and groups could, and did, perform

---

mother and Aeschines himself that he was with her when she conducted initiations' (tr. Jones 1928).

[56] e.g. Burkert (1985: 316), who states: 'From the helplessness of those who wish to hold on to tradition there springs an irritation which can be dangerous, especially if political or personal motives are involved as catalysts.'

[57] Large cults needed a number of different resources: Garland 1992: 19–21, Parker 1996: 124–31 and 2005b: 61–2. Foreigners needed two permits to found a temple for their gods in Athens. These covered both the right to acquire a piece of land (*enktesis*) and permission to build a temple on it: for Bendis *IG* II^2 1283; Egyptian devotees of Isis and the Cyprian ones of Aphrodite Ourania *IG* II^2 337 = *LSCG* 34 333/332 BCE; see Pecírka 1966, Versnel 1990: 122, with Parker 1996: 216 and Purvis 2003: 9.

[58] See Parker 1996: 199 for the quotation and ch. 9 of that volume for evidence.

unregulated ritual acts of worship around the city—just as Plato portrays, with some anxiety, in the *Laws*.[59] Sometimes this took place in unoccupied land, sometimes on sacred land that had been rented, sometimes celebrants gathered unofficially.[60]

However, little of this suggests that there was a wide diversity in the activities brought to bear in worship. Much has been made of the strangeness of ecstatic cult to Athenian sensibilities, but as Robert Parker has succinctly noted: 'One can scarcely insist enough on the paradox that ecstatic dancing... was, in all seeming, indigenous in Greece.'[61] We should bear in mind the nature of the sources from which any such impression arises. For example, Demosthenes is scarcely a neutral witness in his description of Aeschines' participation in the cult of Sabazius under the direction of his mother, but even so, his partisan report does not, in fact, suggest that Aeschines should be regarded with suspicion.[62] Rather, Demosthenes places emphasis on Aeschines' shameful poverty and his lack of opportunity and experience. He ends the account with an ironic comment on Aeschines' undoubted pride in his good fortune. This is not about Aeschines' religious activities being dubious, but their role in marking him as a young man of no account.[63] With all this in mind, the next two sections set out some further aspects to consider as we explore the possible religious misdemeanours committed by these women, and the ways in which scholars have tried to understand them.

---

[59] Pl. *Leg.* 909d–910a.

[60] Archaeological evidence for individual shrines in Wycherley (1970), and Purvis (2003: 8) observes the random distribution of shrines to gods and heroes among private dwellings in Athens and (11) examines how use of the terms *demosia* and *idia* and *hiera* and *hosia* suggest that the category of 'sacred' encompassed both public and private. See Hdt. 5.66 and Ar. *Aves* 1534; also shrines built by nympholepts offer further examples (see Connor 1988). These unregulated examples may have been the focus of worship by individuals and/or small groups, if only families. A larger group example is the cult of Adonis, celebrated at the Adonia, which suggests that ecstatic cult activity did not per se receive regulation, nor, more specifically did it require a space of its own for celebration (see Ar. *Lys.* 3; and *IG* II² 1177, dating to the mid-fourth century, which forbids anyone from bringing together regular spontaneous revels in the Thesmophorium in the deme Piraeus; see Parker 1996: 162).

[61] Parker 1996: 160.   [62] Dem. 18.259–60.

[63] Krauter makes this point more generally about the evidence from law-court speeches for cases of *asebeia* (2004: 234): 'Diese aber sind nicht in erster Linie Zeugnisse für das antike Recht, sondern für die antike Rhetorik.'

TRADITIONAL GODS: NEW APPROACHES

A number of scholars have argued that these women were prosecuted on charges of impiety because they had dared to play the part of priests in private religious ceremonies.[64] However, their likely offences are often left somewhat vague, in part, because, as we have seen, there are difficulties in giving a clear account of the nature of what was considered new or foreign, and, in part, because we are somewhat hampered by perceptions of what counted as innovatory activities.

Matthew Dickie argues that Ninon was probably condemned on a charge of impiety for the way she was conducting mysteries, and he sees the same offence as the basis for the accusation and execution of the *gune magos* in the first version of Aesop's fable for innovating in divine matters (*kainotomousan peri ta theia*). This he takes as implying that this woman's crime was 'attempting to placate the wrath of the gods by means that were felt to be at odds with Athenian tradition, presumably because they involved sorcery'.[65] This suggests it was the innovatory nature of what this woman was *doing*, apparently here the use of incantations, which was judged to be problematic. However, it is hard to find corroborating evidence that shows that the use of incantations was regarded with particular suspicion.[66] More generally,

---

[64] See discussion by Parker (1996: 158–63). Dickie (2001: 51) on Theoris, argues that Philochorus was likely to have got these kinds of details correct because he is a historian who was interested in cult. Parker (1996: 163 n. 34) by implication regards these women as 'priestesses' but does not try to distinguish between their likely offences (except for Ninon, where he indicates a slight preference for the charge of 'initiating in rites of foreign gods'). Garland (1992: 150) argues that Ninon was a priestess for a civic cult, and that was what prevented her from taking part in these rituals, but cf. Krauter 2004: 238 n. 36. Krauter (2004: 233 and 237–8) is reluctant to consider the trials of Theoris and Ninon as historical cases since the evidence is obscure.

[65] Dickie (2001: 51–2, quotation, p. 52), taking the older version of the fable as being closer to a fourth-century rendering; see also Gordon 1999: 249.

[66] Versnel (1990: 117) appears to suggest this, although the thrust of his argument is not wholly clear to me here. He notes the claims of the sorceress and her '*epoidas*', and observes that 'these practices were generally associated with professionals of foreign cults', but the further example that he gives (Max. Tyr. 19.3) concerns priests of Cybele who will *apothespizousin* ('give oracles') for 2 obols. He states that Pentheus in Euripides' *Bacchae* 'does not hesitate to expose the foreign prophet as a *goes epoidos*', but cites l. 234, where the phrase is one of a number of descriptions of Dionysus that Pentheus is reporting; the emphasis of his criticism seems to be on the stranger's seductive activities and allure. The additional citations, Pl. *Meno* 80a–b and

the glimpse of everyday religious creativity provided by Plato (described above, pp. 53–4) does not seem to portray a context of intolerance; similarly, his description of itinerant salesmen also suggests that there was, in actuality, something of a 'market in magic'. And when we remember the sanctioned activities of Glaucothea, this appears even more puzzling. Innovation alone seems insufficient to condemn Ninon to death.

Two possible, and not necessarily mutually exclusive, routes to resolution are apparent. The first is to attempt to narrow down the nature of the activities that Ninon and her group may have been pursuing. With regard to the problems outlined above concerning the difficulties of identifying new gods and new activities, there is a notable exception—and we return to the possibility that Ninon was accused of profaning the Eleusinian Mysteries. The Athenians in the Classical period appear to have perceived a strong link between the preservation of the Eleusinian Mysteries and the well-being of the democracy; and it has already been noted how often the profanation of the Mysteries appears in trials for impiety.[67] Details of the fifth-century prosecutions for 'the mocking of the Mysteries' survive in the charges against Alcibiades preserved by Plutarch.[68] These offer an account of all the ways in which his activities were understood to be 'mimicking the Mysteries'. These included where they happened, how he was dressed, what he called himself, and the way he distributed other official titles, including his 'initiates'.

Is it possible then that Ninon's misconduct—or that of any of the women here discussed—was somehow connected to a misrepresentation of Eleusis? In the case of Phryne, we know the name of the god in question, and this does not resonate with an Eleusinian context; nor is such a charge made explicitly in the summary of the case or the record of Euthias' words that survive. However, as noted above, some of the language found in the fragments of Hyperides' speech suggest that references to Eleusis may have been introduced into the case, either by Euthias as part of his argument, or, indeed, by Hyperides to

---

Hippoc. *Morb. sacr.* 1.9 (6.358 ff.), are similarly given with little contextual discussion, e.g. the apparent comparative tolerance of Athens revealed by the Platonic comment, or the element of competition motivating the remarks of the Hippocratic author.

[67] Mylonas (1961: 224): 'divulging the secrets of the cult was considered comparable to the destruction of the democracy'; see also Graf 2002 and Gagné 2009. Contemporary views of the significance of the Mysteries: e.g. Isoc. 16.6, Lys. 6.54.

[68] Plut. *Alc.* 22.

ridicule the charges. In the case of Theoris, despite some scholars' attempts to link her to such innovations, there is no mention of rituals of this kind.[69] Perhaps Demosthenes does not mention this aspect because it would undermine his arguments against Aeschines, since Glaucothea's activities were therefore fundamentally different; at the same time, however, the brevity with which he mentions Ninon suggests that her crimes were well known anyway. Returning to the scholiast's elaboration of this material, we have to ask whether or not the writer was drawing on specific knowledge of events or, alternatively, on general ideas of what was a possible charge.

'NEW' GODS?

An alternative possibility is that these women were, at least in part, taken to court because they had introduced the rites of gods that were, as yet, unknown in the city of Athens. In favour of this argument, the case against Socrates may confirm that there was a law against introducing new gods. It has been argued that the specific charge originates in a fifth-century decree by the diviner Diopeithes. This, according to Plutarch, provided for 'the public impeachment of such as did not believe in gods, or who taught doctrines regarding the heavens', and enabled the prosecution of the philosopher Anaxagoras as an indirect attack on Pericles himself.[70]

The existence of this original decree—and trial—has been challenged on the grounds that the only evidence for Diopeithes is late and the account of the trial muddled.[71] The nature of its relation to Socrates' trial is unclear. There are similarities of language between the two accounts, but, it has been objected, (i) it would be impossible for Socrates to be prosecuted by means of a decree of the mid-fifth century, and (ii) Socrates was prosecuted with a *graphe*

---

[69] Gordon (1999: 250) argues that she was taken to court on the grounds that she had perpetrated an 'undesirable religious innovation', but just what this was, and whose target this made her, remain opaque (see further below).

[70] Plut. *Per.* 32 (tr. Perrin 1916); supporting this we find Derenne 1930: 168ff. and Dodds 1952: 189. See also Burkert 1985: 467 and Versnel 1990: 124. Dover (1975: esp. 39–40) raises questions about the accuracy of this account.

[71] Cohen (1991: 212–13) dismisses law and trial as inventions; cf. Parker (1996: 208–9), who comes to no 'confident conclusion'.

asebeias, whereas Diopeithes' decree introduced an *eisangelia*.[72] In response it has been suggested that either a law was developed as part of the reforms of 403/2, or that the prosecution of Socrates was an interim 'improvisation of sorts' before a law was developed later in the fourth century BCE.[73] Presumably, it is also possible that the late account of the trial actually draws on the account of the trial of Socrates. In the end, however we analyse this material, the evidence of Socrates' own trial brings us to the undeniable conclusion that, although it seems to have been a rare occurrence, it was possible to be condemned on such a charge.[74]

We can perhaps get some further help from Socrates' own attempt at analysing the charges made against him in the version of his defence given by Plato. He offers a range of possible implications of the different accusations and the ways in which they relate to each other.[75] This examination offers echoes of the accusations concerning innovation that were levelled at Ninon, Theoris, and Phryne: for example, Socrates was 'teaching them not to believe in the gods the state believes in, but in other new spiritual beings', while Ninon and

---

[72] Dover 1975: 40; see Versnel 1990: 128–9. But a charge of impiety using *eisangelia* was brought by Lycurgus against Menesaechmus, probably after 324 BCE (Lycurg. fr. 14.1 [Berlin Papyrus 11748]). The case concerned the annual pilgrimage to Delos; the papyrus seems to suggest it was illegal to offer certain sacrifices unsupervised. The dating of the case assumes that Lycurgus had probably ceased to be responsible for Athens' finances (see Plut. *X orat.* 841b, 852b; Diod. Sic. 16.88.1 with Faraguna 1992: 197–205 and Harris 2001b: 156) after which Menesaechmus attacked him at his last *euthynai* (Harris 2001b: 216).

[73] See Versnel 1990: 128–9 (quotation, p. 129); the idea that a law—either the law that sanctioned the trials of Phryne, Ninon, etc., or a precursor of it—was developed during the archonship of Euclides draws on Derenne 1930 and Reverdin 1945: 213, 217.

[74] Cohen (1991: 213–15) examines the characterization of charges made against Socrates in the beginning of Plato's *Euthyphro* (3b–c) and *Apology* (23) and Xenophon's *Memorabilia* (1.1.9–16). The first depicts the charges as concerning religious innovation and not conforming to traditional beliefs and myths—and Cohen observes that this is never challenged as an inappropriate charge; the last two raise the question of speculation about the universe and natural phenomena—and it is denied that Socrates was interested in these topics. Krauter (2004: 239, citing also Garland 1992: 145–50) argues that it is not clear that *kaina daimonia* meant the introduction of a foreign god.

[75] Pl. *Ap.* 26a–c (tr. H. N. Fowler); Xen. *Mem.*1.1.5 explains of Socrates, πιστεύων δὲ θεοῖς πῶς οὐκ εἶναι θεοὺς ἐνόμιζεν ('And since he had confidence in the gods, how can he have disbelieved in the existence of the gods?'), where he seems to be drawing a distinction between a sense of trust or confidence and one of customary practice illustrating belief (see also the discussion in note 72 above).

Phryne were introducing new or foreign gods.[76] It also places emphasis on the significance of the spread of these ideas. In the case of Socrates, the charge of corrupting youth was underpinned, as later writers recalled and most scholars now argue, by Socrates' role as the teacher of Critias, a leader of the vicious revolution of the Thirty in 404 BCE.[77] Because of the Amnesty of 403/2, this material could not be introduced in the official charge. But it could apparently be brought up in the courtroom, even fifty years after the original trial.[78] In this regard, there are no direct parallels with any of the cases of the women who have been discussed. But some concern about the extent of these women's influence may still be apparent; for example, in the charge against Ninon that she was making *philtra* for young men and against Theoris that she was teaching slaves; while Phryne's pejorative social influence is surely shown by her assemblies of either men and women or women of a lower class and doubtful virtue. We can even, perhaps, link these three concerns to each other via the context of cult activity. There is no evidence that slaves were prohibited from being initiated into mysteries, and indeed some evidence that they were able to participate in the cult of Sabazius. Since initiations for Sabazius involved the gathering of men and women in *thiasoi*, and since Sabazius was worshipped with ecstatic rights, as was Isodaites, these different accusations may therefore be connected by ritual.[79] However, in none of these cases is this aspect highlighted, as it is in the case of Socrates. It seems less likely that these women were feared for the extent of their social or political influence. That said, perhaps it is most likely that these details appear in the sources as projections of the concerns of writers of later periods.

---

[76] Pl. *Ap.* 26b: διδάσκοντα μὴ νομίζειν οὓς ἡ πόλις νομίζει, ἕτερα δὲ δαιμόνια καινά.

[77] Aeschin. 1.173 for Critias, and see Xen. *Mem.* 1. 2. 9 and 12–46 (Alcibiades is included alongside Critias as someone who did the city great harm). The complexity of the motives behind the trial of Socrates is manifest in the range of emphases brought to bear in modern analyses: see, as a small selection, Taylor 1932: 104, Finley 1977, Rankin 1987, Connor 1991, Garland 1992: 136–51, Parker 1996: 201, Krauter 2004: 240–1, Waterfield 2009.

[78] Hansen (1995) has argued for a similar situation in the case made by Lys. 30, but see Todd 1996: 116 and 2000a: 297–8.

[79] Slaves: *SEG* 24.223, dated to the second half of the fourth century, shows *thiasoi* including slaves honouring gods at Eleusis; *IG* II² 2934 and *IG* II² 4650, from Attica, are both dedications to the nymphs, which appear to include slave names. For later evidence for *thiasoi* of Bendis on Salamis in five mid-third-century texts (Osborne 2004–9), see the discussion in Parker 2011: 237. For slaves in the cult of Sabazius, see Ar. *Vesp.* 9.

Nevertheless, we may be able to follow this trail a little further. It has long been claimed that the crime of *asebeia* was one that concerned the threat posed by what one thought alongside what one did.[80] Teaching implies a claim to knowledge, and its involvement in a charge of *asebeia* indicates a concern with the wrong kind of knowledge and its transmission.[81] This is explicit in the accusations against Socrates, and we also see it realized in the physical isolation that Plato imposes on his impious practitioners of magic in the *Laws*; indeed, for Plato, the level of punishment is calibrated according to the psychological state of his wrongdoer. The knowledge that these women may have been thought to claim is not made explicit in the evidence for the historical cases, although we might see the potential to innovate tacitly attributed in the employment of particular paraphernalia. However, there is one fictional story that offers a different perspective. The Aesopian fable, although at first sight appearing to focus on innovation in terms of activities, makes a quite different point with its moral. This concerns not the woman's use of incantations or any other specific activity, but rather her claim to the power to placate the gods. This moves us away from the usual poles of religious debate to a different concern altogether: that of a claim to a particular private power, namely, a specific and personal relationship with the gods. As we will see, this could be viewed as posing a particular threat to the city and its inhabitants.

ASEBEIA REVISITED

What is profoundly clear here is the fluidity of the charge of *asebeia* and its apparently capacious nature.[82] This impression lies partly in

---

[80] Cohen (1991: 210) gives an overview of this debate and some of the ancient evidence that suggests impious thought was as important as behaviour; cf. Krauter 2004: 236–40.

[81] As Saunders (1996: 97) says: Plato 'calculates penalties on the assumption that the degree of the technical knowledge misused by the offender is a measure of his psychic vice'.

[82] Scholars' opinions have varied: some have considered a fairly circumscribed set of charges; others have emphasized the greater fluidity of the charge. Rudhardt (1960: 91–3) argued that the law strictly defined impiety (even in the fifth century), but, as Cohen (1991: 207) points out, this has not been influential (and is not well supported by the evidence). Cf. Thalheim (1896: 1529), who described it as

the nature of Athenian law itself, which, it has been argued, offered litigants flexibility in both interpretation of law and procedure adopted.[83] In the case of *asebeia*, this would be supported by (and support) the perceived nature of the offence. Much of what we have already discussed is concerned with the protection and conservation of traditional ritual activity within the polis: this is the yardstick against which the charge of *asebeia* is measured out. The gods were 'sometimes benevolent and sometimes malign, with an unstable devotion to moral virtue', so, as observed earlier, the law of impiety dealt with 'a wide variety of acts supposed to be likely to attract the gods' hostility'.[84] However, as other scholars have argued, and, as we have seen, it is possible to gain some idea of the kinds of concerns that provoked prosecution.

The nature of *asebeia* meant that the potential danger of disrupting the relationship with the gods was one that the entire city had to confront.[85] Plato suggests that the judgement of what counts as impiety should turn on the opinion of the citizens about each other.[86] Something like this seems to have happened to Theoris, although it was her servant who denounced her. But some have argued that this makes it more likely that she was charged with *asebeia*; because *asebeia* was viewed as an offence that could draw down the wrath of the gods on the whole state, slaves would be encouraged to denounce their masters or mistresses.[87] Moreover, the term *asebeia* does seem to have been used in forensic oratory in a way that suggests the audience was expected to react to its appearance. There are plentiful examples of

---

exhibiting 'Unbestimmtheit und Dehnbarkeit' ('indeterminacy and extensibility'; repeated by Lipsius 1984: 359–60) but with clear central cases; cf. also Cohen 1991: 205. Ostwald (1986: 528–36) argues that the use of the *eisangelia* procedure in the fifth century intimates that the definition of the offence was left to the prosecutor; although there was a change of procedure in the fourth century, he doubts that this marks a stricter definition of the crime.

[83] See Osborne 1985 (and see the 2010 reprint for responses to critics of this view); this point is also made by Cohen (1991: 207–10).
[84] Saunders 1996: 91.
[85] On the question of whether or not impiety was connected to fear of wrath of gods, see Pl. *Leg.* 910b1–6, cited by Dickie (2001: 329 n. 13) as ordinary Athenian attitudes, but cf. Parker 2005b: 68. It is seldom found in other sources, but this could simply mean that it is taken for granted.
[86] Pl. *Leg.* 910d.
[87] See Dickie 2001: 51. Lys. 5.3–5 is a charge of sacrilege that prompts reflection by the speaker on the temptation for slaves to lay such charges in order to acquire their freedom (see also Lys. 7.16).

the term *asebeia* being introduced into a speech, and attached to a particular legal decision, even in a case that was not a *graphe asebeias* (and with no reference to an obvious religious misdemeanour) in order, it seems, to increase the sense of shared danger provoked by a particular offence.[88] Importantly, this need not mean that the ideas that were raised in these arguments reflected actual cult practice.[89] But these apparent attempts by speakers to infuse a situation or decision with a sense of danger appear to be intended to leverage an implicit understanding that confronting the risk of *asebeia* was a shared responsibility.[90] In at least some cases, then, the law of *asebeia* can be understood to have reflected understanding of a profound cosmological connection between the well-being of the city and the relationships of its citizens (both as individuals and as a group) with the gods.

SOCIAL CONTROL?

Attention to the incidental details of the charges has led some scholars to suggest that it was not simply the introduction of new gods or rituals that may have been perceived as problematic: there may have been other factors at play. Most generally, scholars have drawn attention to the need of the Athenian state simply to exercise control. Thus, Robert Parker has argued that the cases of Socrates and Phryne reveal 'the Athenians... affirming their right of ultimate control over all the religious practices of Attica'. He suggests the problem was not that Isodaites was a new, foreign god, but that he was not approved by the Athenian state.[91] With regard to these trials, Richard Gordon has suggested that there were individuals within the state dispensing discipline. In the case of Theoris, these were 'the legitimate specialists', who would consider her as 'as aiming at untoward religious or "salvific" capital'. But the identity of these specialists is unclear; nor is it plain what or why this capital was perceived as

---

[88] See Eidinow 2015.   [89] As Krauter 2004: 234.
[90] See Eidinow 2015; cf. Cohen (1991: 205), who, in looking for the bases for actual legal prosecutions, sets these examples aside as simply 'exaggerated usages' of the term.
[91] Parker 1996: 217.

dangerous.[92] Moreover, there does not seem to be further evidence for this kind of concern, although we can trace the occasional attempt at local regulations.[93] Similarly, in this context of exerting order, Plutarch's comment on Theoris that she was 'teaching slaves how to deceive' may be taken as significant. However, there is little evidence to indicate concern with slave unrest at this time (and few, if any, stories of slave revolts from the time of this trial). The charge seems more likely to express fears appropriate to Plutarch's own time.[94]

The gender of these three defendants has also been raised as a possible exacerbating factor in their trials. Frequently these explanations draw attention to the sexuality of these women: for example, some have assumed that all three women, not just Phryne, must have been *hetairai*. The argument is made solely on the basis that their names were mentioned in court, and this was not usual for respectable women.[95] But there are indications that their social status may have been higher than this implies: for example, the suggestion that Ninon's son may have hired a speech-writer so as to attack the man who took his mother to court. Even if the story is judged to be spurious, it suggests that Ninon was thought to have come from a family of some standing.[96] Moreover, it seems likely that women who had been condemned to death and executed were probably no longer considered 'respectable', whatever their status beforehand. But even were we to accept that these women were *hetairai*, the argument that follows is unconvincing, that is, that they were therefore considered dangerous because of their

---

[92] Gordon: 1999: 250.   [93] See note 60 above on *IG* II² 1177.

[94] Versnel (1990: 118 n. 87) draws a parallel between this and a judicial prayer from Amorgos that features a slave who has run off with other slaves (*SGD* 60), but he does not elaborate on the implications. It suggests that the writer was unable to have recourse to a civic judicial process (he does not threaten this in his prayer). However, the text has been dated to between the second century BCE and second century CE (Gager 1992: 165; it is discussed further in this volume on pp. 226–9). The hero Drimacus, a leader of runaway slaves, seems specific to Chios; but even he occupied a middle ground, both in myth (he would send back runaway slaves) and in cult (both slaves and masters offered him dedications); see Nymphodorus of Syracuse *FGrH* 572 F 4 *ap*. Ath. 6.265c–266e (cf. Graf 1985: 121–5).

Arnaoutoglou (2007) analyses literary and epigraphic legal texts for evidence of the areas of life in which communities demonstrate a fear of slaves. His findings reveal concern with the behaviour of individuals, not groups. The areas of life that he notes receive legislation include non-performance of duties, betrayal of the family to which they belonged, conduct that might disrupt the hygiene of sacred and secular public places or disturb civic relations with the divine, uncontrolled sexual behaviour, and economic offences.

[95] e.g. Trampedach 2001: 148.   [96] See Dickie 2001: 53.

essential social ambiguity (neither prostitute, nor wife). Apart from imposing a distinctly modern analysis on lived ancient experience, it fails to account for how and why these three women/*hetairai* in particular became so dangerous that they had to be put on trial for their lives.

An alternative, but not unrelated approach posits links between these women and the various more dissipated aspects of ecstatic worship of 'foreign' cult and/or erotic magic; but as we have seen, such aspects alone cannot offer an adequate explanation for these events.[97] The foreignness of the women themselves is another aspect on which commentators have focused, but it is difficult to establish the identity of these women closely enough to understand what role it could have played in their trial.[98] It is true that Theoris is specifically described as a Lemnian: but at this point Lemnos was a possession of the Athenians, one that they had regained after the Peloponnesian War. The use of the term may indicate that Theoris was one of the 'dispossessed' of Lemnos (i.e. not from an Athenian settlement), but it could also be a rhetorical device by which Demosthenes distanced her from his Athenian audience—or, in the end, simply a way to identify her. For the other women, this aspect seems to have been irrelevant: although we know that Phryne was from Thespiai in Boiotia, little seems to have been made of that in the trial, while we have no evidence of origin for Ninon.

---

[97] See e.g. the discussions of Hansen 1995: 26 and Parker 1996: 214–15.

[98] Not only as a characteristic that leads to suspicion, but also one that enabled innovation, at least in the case of Theoris (Gordon 1999: 250).

1.4

Conclusion: 'If Anyone Has Cursed Me...'

Across the different cases examined here, certain charges, and the reasons for bringing them, appear more significant than others. But this does not mean that the details of the other, possible charges (including, for example, the creation of *pharmaka*) should be elided or dismissed as simply irrelevant.[1] The attempt to distinguish a single accusation may be an understandable legacy of our own court system (and, before that, of the Roman legal system). However, it does not necessarily help us to understand what went on in an Athenian courtroom, where a variety of accusations against the plaintiff may have been introduced into a case to elaborate the main charge.[2]

So, why bring those particular accusations to bear? We can gain some foothold on this question by turning again to the procedure of *graphe asebeias*: scholars have rightly noted that this seems often to have been employed with political as much as religious intent—and that this was appropriate to a culture characterized by the inextricable association of these two dimensions.[3] The variegated nature of such cases is well illustrated by the trial of Socrates, where the minor or even unofficial indictments reveal the sociopolitical context of this event, and the nature and content of local popular feeling that

---

[1] The section title is from a *pharmakon* or binding spell discussed later in this section.

[2] Todd (1996: 108) goes so far as to argue that 'in order to be found guilty in an Athenian court, you did not actually need to have done (or not done) anything in particular'.

[3] Parker 1996: 207; Krauter 2004: 241 (cf. Garland 1992: 151). Connor (1991) provides a thought-provoking account of the ways in which religion and politics were integrated.

was working against the philosopher. More apposite to this study, perhaps, is the account given by Plutarch of the trial of Aspasia, wife of Pericles, who was accused of *asebeia*. The basis for the charge is unknown, but an additional accusation is also reported: the procurement of freeborn women for Pericles.[4] After mentioning the decree of Diopeithes, and the case against Anaxagoras, the narrative observes the delight with which the people accepted these divisive stories (*tas diabolas*); the mention of *diabole* in this context is something to which we will return later in this book. Meanwhile, although the source is late and must be treated with caution as evidence for what actually happened, it does indicate, in parallel to the events of the trial of Socrates, the malicious dynamics that could surround and support a public charge of impiety.

These examples in turn suggest that the charges brought against Theoris, Ninon, and Phryne would somehow have resonated with a jury of Athenian citizens, and therefore reflect current social dynamics. To explore these more deeply, in particular those that might lead to accusations linking women and *pharmaka* being brought into the courtroom, I want to return now to the story of Aretaphila (mentioned in section 2).[5] When she was discovered trying to kill the tyrant of Cyrene, Nicocrates, she argued that she had created her potions in part because she was aware of the *phthonos* of others. Although we know this was a fabrication (in the sense that Aretaphila intended to commit a murder), it was put forward as a credible excuse.

This association between *phthonos* and magic-making is one that we also find attested in epigraphic evidence. A binding spell dating to the fourth century BCE is one of very few that gives us explicit information about the motivations behind aggressive magical action:

Εἴ τις ἐμὲ κατέδεσεν | ἒ γυνὴ ἢ <ἀ>νὴρ ἒ δ<ο>ῦλος ἒ ἐ- | λεύθερος ἒ ξένος ἒ ἀσ- | 'σ'τος ἒ οἰκεῖος ἒ ἀλλώτ- | ρτος[sic] ἒ ἐπὶ φθόνον τὸν | ἐμὲι ἐργασίαι ἒ ἔργοις, | εἴ τις ἐμὲ κατέδεσ- | εν πρὸς τὸν Ἑρμεν τὸ- | ν ἐριόνιον ἒ πρὸ's' τὸν | κάτοχον ἒ πρὸς τὸν δό- | λιον ἒ ἄλλοθί πο, ἀντι- | καταδεὸ'σ'μενύω τὸς ἐχ'ρ'θ- | ὸς ἅπαντας.

If anyone has cursed me, whether woman or man or slave or free or stranger or citizen or household member or outsider, from envy (*phthonos*) of me, my work and deeds. If anyone has cursed me in the presence

---

[4] Plut. *Per.* 32.2.   [5] Plut. *De mul. virt.* 256b–c.

of Hermes the Erionios or in the presence of [Hermes] the Binder or in the presence of [Hermes] the Trickster or elsewhere, I curse, in turn all my enemies.

This is one side of a curse tablet dating approximately to the time of these trials, the early fourth century BCE, and known now by its catalogue entry as *NGCT* 24.[6] Although its writer clearly suspected he had been the victim of supernatural attack, he did not know the identity of the perpetrator and in writing his own spell he took an all-encompassing approach. But just like Aretaphila centuries later, the motivation he identifies in his unknown aggressor is *phthonos*. We turn to an examination of this emotion next, in order better to understand its role in ancient Greek culture more generally, and, in particular, its links to accusations of *pharmaka*.

[6] For text and dating, see Jordan 1999.

Part 2

Envy

2.1

Introduction: 'As Rust Eats Iron'

Phthonos is a virulent, powerful, toxic force. The quotation that heads this section is from one of the entries on this word in the *Suda*. This offers a number of definitions of *phthonos*, sourcing them from across different Classical literary genres.[1]

Φθόνος, νόσημα ψυχῆς ἀνθρωπικὸν καὶ ἐσθίον ψυχήν, ἣν ἂν καταλάβῃ, ὥσπερ ἰὸς τὸν σίδηρον. καὶ ὁ ἔρως ταὐτόν ἐστιν. οἷς ἐκεῖνος ἔχθιστον καλῶς τὸ θεῖον, περιτρέπων τὸ συμφυὲς ἀρρώστημα εἰς αὐτοὺς τοὺς ἐκφύσαντας αὐτά. καὶ ἴαμβοι: τὸ δευτερεῦον τοῦ φθόνου γράμμα ξέσας εὕροις ἐν αὐτῷ τὸν φόνον γεγραμμένον. καὶ Σοφοκλῆς: ὁ φθόνος ἕρπει πρὸς τὸν εὖ ἔχοντα. καὶ αὖθις: πιστὰ τοῖς ἀκούουσι τὰ κατὰ τῶν μεγάλων διὰ τὸν φθόνον. καὶ Πίνδαρος: ὄψον δὲ λόγοι φθονεροῖς. καὶ αὖθις: σφόδρα δὲ λαμπρὸς ὢν παρὰ τοῖς Ἀθηναίοις ὅμως ἐσκοτίσθη καὶ αὐτὸς ὑπὸ τοῦ τὰ πάντα διεσθίοντος φθόνου: δίκην γὰρ θανάτου ὦφλε.

Phthonos, [Meaning a] human sickness of the soul and [one] eating whatever soul it seizes, just as rust [eats] iron. And erotic desire is the same thing. For them[?], *phthonos* calls the divine a most hateful thing, turning the congenital ailment towards those who engendered it.

And iambic verses [sc. are attested as follows]: 'having scraped away the second letter of *phthonos*, you could find written in it *phonos* ["homicide"]'.

And Sophocles [writes]: '*phthonos* creeps towards the one who is well-placed.' And elsewhere]: 'listeners place credence in what is said against the great, because of *phthonos*.' And Pindar [writes]: 'speeches [are] a relish for the envious.'

---

[1] *Phthonos*: phi 510 Adler, *Suda On Line*, tr. Boeri, 23 July 2008 (accessed 3 Feb. 2015), http://www.stoa.org/sol-entries/phi/510.

72 *Envy, Poison, and Death*

And elsewhere [it is written]: 'despite being a great celebrity among the Athenians, he too was eclipsed by all-consuming *phthonos*; for [...] he was condemned to a sentence of death.'

The several quotations cover a wide span of time. The first is probably the latest, a fragment attributed to Aelian, writing in the second century CE: 'A human sickness of the soul and [one] eating whatever soul it seizes, just as rust [eats] iron'.[2] We might dismiss this as a colourful expression of the Second Sophistic, a period characterized by a focus on rhetoric as a significant and prestigious art form. However, the entry goes on to list a number of quotations that date from much earlier and express related sentiments. Examining these is a useful way to start building our understanding of the perceived effects of this emotion, the situations in which *phthonos* was understood to be manifest, and something of how it was regarded.

The second definition in this entry, from the *Greek Anthology*, reports that having scraped away the second letter of *phthonos*, you could find written in it *phonos*, that is, 'homicide'.[3] A similar thought, not listed here, is found in Sophocles' *Oedipus at Colonus*, where the chorus provide a list of the unavoidable travails of mortal existence. These consist of the suffering that man imposes on man—and they are, to a certain extent, the evils that we might expect: *phonoi, staseis, eris, machai* ('murders, revolutions, strife, warfare') and, finally, *phthonos*.[4] To modern ears, perhaps, the final item seems somewhat anticlimactic, but it echoes the implied relationship of the quotation from the *Greek Anthology*, drawing attention to the violence with which *phthonos* was imbued.[5]

The following passages in the *Suda* entry describe some of the kinds of relationships in which *phthonos* was understood to be

---

[2] Ael. fr. 335 Domingo-Forasté (338 Hercher). The online entry notes: 'here mangled ("locus desperatus": Adler). Read καλεῖ (manuscript G) for καλῶς, and Hercher's αὐτό for the final αὐτά'. Compare the similar imagery of Men. fr. 761 K-A in which *phthonos* consumes an individual, 'as rust in iron tools, moths cloaks, and wormwood wood.' Cf. also Joh. Chrys. *In 1 Cor. Hom.* 31.4 (*PG* 61.264).

[3] cf. *Anthologiae Graecae*, App. VII (*Problemata, aenigmata*) 47, 42.6-7 (Basilii Megalomytis) (Cougny) (Καὶ πρῶτον ἕν μου, δεύτερον, γράμμα ξέσας, | πανευφυῶς εὕρῃς με χεῖρα θανάτου· [sic]).

[4] Soph. *OC* 1234-5.

[5] Most (2003: 132) notes the anticlimactic aspect, citing Jebb 1907: 195 *ad* 1233, Kamerbeek 1984: 174 *ad* 1234, 5, and Fähse, who suggested transposing *phthonos* and *phonoi* (opposed by Lloyd-Jones and Wilson [1990: 252 *ad* 1234-5]; but cf. Silk 2000: 149 n. 110).

manifest. The first passage is a quotation from Sophocles—this time from the *Ajax*—which describes how *phthonos* operates within society: '*phthonos* creeps towards the one who is well-placed'.[6] What may be a scholiast's comment on the line follows: 'listeners place credence in what is said against the great, because of *phthonos*'. This introduces some aspects of the mechanics of the operation of *phthonos*.[7] There is more detail in the final two, brief quotations in this entry. The first dates to the fifth century, and is from the poetry of Pindar. It gives some insight into the experience of the one who speaks: ὄψον δὲ λόγοι φθονεροῖσιν, that is, 'words [are] a relish for those who are *phthoneroi*'.[8] And just how deadly this combination of *phthonos*, speech, and willing audience may be is evinced by the last definition, dating to the third century CE, in which Diogenes Laertius describes how the politician Demetrius of Phaleron fell victim to *phthonos*: 'despite being a great celebrity among the Athenians, he too was eclipsed by all-consuming *phthonos*; for [. . .] he was condemned to a sentence of death.'[9]

Having worked our way through this entry, we might be more tempted to understand that last phrase as '*because* of being a great celebrity'; and certainly the definition found in another of the *Suda* entries for *Phthonos* (phi 509, Adler), can be taken to support that:[10]

Φθόνος: πάθος λύπης ἐπὶ τῇ τῶν πέλας εὐπραγίᾳ. τῶν ἐπιεικῶν τινος. ἐκ τούτου δῆλον, ὡς καὶ φθονερὸς ἂν εἴη ὁ λυπούμενος ἐπὶ ταῖς τῶν ἐπιεικῶν εὐπραγίαις. οὗ κειμένου, ἐπεὶ προδήλως ἀλλότριον τοῦ σπουδαίου τὸ λυπεῖσθαι ἐπὶ ταῖς τῶν ἀγαθῶν εὐπραγίαις [οἱ γὰρ ἐπιεικεῖς ἀγαθοί], οὐκ ἂν εἴη ὁ ἐπιεικὴς φθονερός.

This states first that the term means '[an] emotion of distress at the prosperity of those nearby'. It then reinforces this idea, while also giving an explicit condemnation of the characters of those who feel such an emotion:

[But if *phthonos* is distress at the evident prosperity] of one of the decent [people], from this it is clear that he who is grieved at the prosperity of decent people would be [sc. called] *phthoneros*. This being given, since

---

[6] Soph. *Aj.* 157.
[7] Schol. Soph. *Aj.* 154. Boeri notes that the quotation is unidentifiable.
[8] Pind. *Nem.* 8.21, further discussed on p. 112.
[9] Diog. Laert. 5.76 (abridged).
[10] *Phthonos*: phi 509 Adler, *Suda On Line*, tr. Roth, 7 Oct. 2011 (accessed 3 Feb. 2015), http://www.stoa.org/sol-entries/phi/509.

obviously being grieved at the prosperity of the good is alien to the virtuous man (for decent people [are] good), the decent man would not be envious.[11]

The final *Suda* entry on *Phthonos*, phi 508 Adler, introduces some further phthonetic vocabulary: Φθόνος· ἡ ἐπὶ τοῖς καλοῖς τοῦ πλησίον βασκανία παρὰ τῷ Ἀποστόλῳ ('Phthonos: a malignant attitude to the fine things of someone close by, in the Apostle').[12] Although it gives its source as a later period—and which gospel writer it means is unclear—the sentiment it offers aligns with some aspects of the other entries, for example the notion that this emotion is exercised towards those close to you and is provoked by their 'fine things', their prosperity, or good fortune.[13] The term *baskania* is one that we will explore further in a later section of this book. Suffice to say here that over time it develops connections with the uncontrollable and potentially extremely harmful form of malignant attitude, the 'evil eye', which is, in turn, also associated with *phthonos*. Explicit discussions of these forces, as well as examples of amulets to protect against them, are found in greatest profusion after the first century CE, but there are earlier allusions to various aspects of them in the corpora of tragedy and oratory.[14]

---

[11] As notes to the online entry detail (tr. Roth, ed. Whitehead and Roth): similar entries are found in other lexica, see Photius s.v. *Phthonos* (phi 154) (Theodoridis); the second quotation is from Alexander of Aphrodisias, *Commentary on Aristotle's Topica* 141.31–142.2, but omitting the beginning of the sentence. The final *Suda* entry on *Phthonos*, phi 508 Adler, raises the question of *baskania* and is discussed in section 2.3, on pp. 135–6.

[12] 'Phthonos': phi 508 Adler, *Suda On Line*, tr. Whitehead, 21 Oct. 2010 (accessed 3 Feb. 2015), http://www.stoa.org/sol-entries/phi/508.

[13] See a list of references to apostolic writings on *phthonos* in Walcot 1978: 86–7. This entry is from Gennadius of Constantinople's fragmentary commentary on Romans (Theodoridis 1998: LXIX–LXXIII); for this and further notes, see the online entry (tr. Whitehead, ed. Roth and Whitehead).

[14] The most explicit discussion can be found in Plut. *Quaest. conv.* 5.7.680–3, which draws on Democritean explanations of how the eyes work to depict the eye as giving off a stream of particles harmful to the person being observed. See Bryen and Wypustek (2009: 546 n. 21) on how, among the documentary papyri, many of the personal letters include the wish that the recipient and their family (especially their children) should remain *abaskanta*, i.e. 'untouched by the evil eye'.

Earlier examples include the role of the eye of an envious mortal in causing damage to the observed: Aesch. *Ag.* 947; but it may also be the eye of a god, Aesch. *Ag.* 468–70; see Walcot 1978: 34. In fourth-century forensic sources *baskanos* and *baskainein* already convey a sense of malignancy; see further discussion on pp. 135–6.

Introduction: 'As Rust Eats Iron' 75

We will return to a number of the different themes raised above, but first, we will take a closer look at *phthonos*. The definitions above offer an initial idea of the modern emotions concept that *phthonos* evokes: the closest English translation for it is probably 'envy'. According to Aristotle, *phthonos* is one of the emotions provoked by the prosperity of others and manifesting as 'a pain that arises at the sight of the good fortune of another... like themselves', for example in birth, family, age, reputation, that is, someone who has what we could have:

ἐστὶν ὁ φθόνος λύπη τις ἐπὶ εὐπραγίᾳ φαινομένῃ τῶν εἰρημένων ἀγαθῶν περὶ τοὺς ὁμοίους, μὴ ἵνα τι αὐτῷ, ἀλλὰ δι᾽ ἐκείνους· φθονήσουσι μὲν γὰρ οἱ τοιοῦτοι οἷς εἰσί τινες ὅμοιοι ἢ φαίνονται. ὁμοίους δὲ λέγω κατὰ γένος, κατὰ συγγένειαν, καθ᾽ ἡλικίαν, καθ᾽ ἕξιν, κατὰ δόξαν, κατὰ τὰ ὑπάρχοντα.

Phthonos is a kind of pain at the sight of good fortune in regard to the goods mentioned; in the case of those like themselves; and not for the sake of a man getting anything, but because of others possessing it. For those men will be envious who have, or seem to have, others 'like' them. I mean like in birth, relationship, age, moral habit, reputation, and possessions.[15]

This sounds a little like what may, in contemporary English-speaking cultures, colloquially be called jealousy. Modern usage suggests that they share a similar context, in which an object of desire sets up tension between two individuals. Those competing in such a zero-sum paradigm must be of roughly equal status for this to occur, because otherwise there can be no sense of rivalry.[16] But the ancient concept draws out some key nuances between the two: whereas *zelos* ('jealousy') is concerned with wanting for oneself something that someone else has, the key element of *phthonos*, at least as Aristotle understood it, was not necessarily the desire to get something for oneself, but essentially the desire that someone else not have it.[17]

---

[15] Arist. *Rhet.* 1387b (tr. Freese 1926).
[16] Walcot 1978: 28–9. Elsewhere Aristotle (*Eth. Nic.* 1108a35) distinguishes three emotions that occur in response to the fortunes of one's neighbours: *phthonos*, *nemesis* 'indignation at undeserved good fortune', and *epichairekakia*, 'spitefulness'. Aristotle organizes them in terms of his tripartite system made up of excess, deficiency, and mean, so that *nemesis* is the mean between *phthonos* and spitefulness.
[17] Definition of *zelos*: Arist. *Rhet.* 1388a30-3, where it is described as a characteristic of virtuous men, in contrast to those who feel *phthonos*. The pain caused by the achievements of others is mentioned in Pind. *Pyth.* 1.83-4 and *Parth.* 1.8-10. For a

76 Envy, Poison, and Death

A similar definition is given by Socrates in Xenophon's *Memorabilia*. He carefully delineates the nature of *phthonos*: not pain at a friend's misfortune, nor at an enemy's good fortune, but irritation at a friend's success, even a friend whom one has been willing to help when they were in trouble:

φθόνον δὲ σκοπῶν, ὅ τι εἴη, λύπην μέν τινα ἐξηύρισκεν αὐτὸν ὄντα, οὔτε μέντοι τὴν ἐπὶ φίλων ἀτυχίαις οὔτε τὴν ἐπ' ἐχθρῶν εὐτυχίαις γιγνομένην, ἀλλὰ μόνους ἔφη φθονεῖν τοὺς ἐπὶ ταῖς τῶν φίλων εὐπραξίαις ἀνιωμένους. θαυμαζόντων δέ τινων εἴ τις φιλῶν τινα ἐπὶ τῇ εὐπραξίᾳ αὐτοῦ λυποῖτο, ὑπεμίμνῃσκεν ὅτι πολλοὶ οὕτω πρός τινας ἔχουσιν, ὥστε κακῶς μὲν πράττοντας μὴ δύνασθαι περιορᾶν, ἀλλὰ βοηθεῖν ἀτυχοῦσιν, εὐτυχούντων δὲ λυπεῖσθαι.

Considering the nature of *phthonos*, he found it to be a kind of pain, not, however, at a friend's misfortune, nor at an enemy's good fortune, but he said those who feel *phthonos* are only those who are annoyed at their friends' successes. Some expressed surprise that anyone who loves another should be pained at his success, but he reminded them that many stand in this relation towards others, that they cannot disregard them in time of trouble, but aid them in their misfortune, and yet they are pained to see them prospering.[18]

---

thorough overview of *phthonos* in the ancient world, see Walcot 1978, with Sanders 2014.

Toohey 2014, Ben Ze'ev 2000, and Parrott and Smith 1993 are among the most useful discussions of the differences between the modern emotions; Konstan 2003b explores the evidence for ancient equivalents of jealousy focusing on *zelotupia*; Sanders 2014 discusses envy and jealousy, comparing modern as well as ancient meanings, and finding overlaps between the two. Although the approach of establishing modern colloquial uses of the terms 'envy' and 'jealousy' is useful, it can become confusing. Thus, emulation is given as part of the table of envy scripts by Sanders (2014: 31), but elsewhere in ancient (and modern discussion) is identified as an element of *zelos* or *zelotupia*, 'jealousy' (see Konstan 2003b: 13–14).

[18] Xen. *Mem.* 3.9.8, cf. Isoc. 1.26. Sanders (2014: 39) suggests a script of 'covetous envy', in which there is 'also a desire to obtain the goods ourselves'. However, the examples he provides do not necessarily illustrate this. For example: Eur. *Supp.* 241, which provides evidence of resentment against the rich, but not of desire for the acquisition of wealth; Ar. *Eq.* 580, which concerns the care given by the chorus members to their hair and toilet (why would this be coveted?); Thuc. 6.16.3, which concerns the wealth of the liturgist—but presumably no one would wish to be in the position of paying liturgies; Philemon fr. 92.2 K-A, which describes wealth stirring up envy, hate, and abuse, but without mention of desire for the wealth; Xen. *An.* 1.9.19, where the individual in question is Cyrus, who is unlikely to desire his subjects' wealth (although he might not want them to have it); and Xen. *Cyr.* 7.5.77, which again makes no mention of the desire for the rich person's wealth but rather seems to

This definition is closer in time to the events that form the focus of this study than some of the previous descriptions given above, but as we have seen from the references given in the *Suda*, *phthonos* is an emotion term that seems to remain both remarkably consistent and strikingly prevalent. The definitions we have examined here are largely about interpersonal relations, but they also encompass the dynamics between groups and individuals, and groups and groups. Picking up on this aspect, some scholars have suggested that the tension arises from a public/private dichotomy, that is, as 'a preference for private satisfaction to the detriment of public aims and goals'.[19] But this definition adds an emphasis that is not there in Aristotle's, at least. Aristotle is not concerned primarily with the impact of private desire on public policy—although that is surely part of the fallout of *phthonos*, and his later, brief mention of *phthonos*' role in exacerbating injustice reinforces this aspect.[20] Rather, his initial definition is actually a focus solely on the private realm, or—bearing in mind the difficulties of giving a definition of 'private' in the ancient world—the personal pitched against the personal.

Indeed, cautious though we must be about such generalizations, the evidence from these sources, and more widely across Greek literature, suggests that this emotion seems to have been regarded as an inevitable dimension of social relations. As analysed by Otanes in the constitutional debate of book three of Herodotus' *Histories*, *phthonos* was understood to be an unavoidable aspect of the human condition, rooted in most of mankind from birth—however virtuous one's character:[21]

---

indicate the potential for resentment at the way the wealth has been obtained, encouraging the wealthy to be virtuous, 'for we may be sure that the more a man has, the more people will feel *phthonos* towards him and plot against him and become his enemies, particularly if, as in our case, he draws his wealth and service from unwilling hands' (tr. Miller 1914, adapted). The analysis offered by Cairns (2003a: 239 n. 12) offers a subtle description of this kind of *phthonos* as focusing on the possessor of the privilege, rather than the privilege (object or person) they possess.

[19] Bulman 1992: 11; cited also by Guettel Cole 2001: 203.

[20] In the *Eudemian Ethics* (1234a30), Aristotle draws attention to the way in which *phthonos*, as an emotion, contributes to the not-virtue of injustice, just as the emotion of righteous indignation (*nemesis*) contributes to the virtue of justice (*dikaiosune*); so this does not appear to be concerned with a justified if malicious redistribution of goods.

[21] Hdt. 3.80.3–5. The innate nature of *phthonos* also receives implicit comment in other passages: see, for example, Hdt. 4.104 (on the Agathursi, who demonstrate lack of *phthonos* in their household arrangements).

καὶ γὰρ ἂν τὸν ἄριστον ἀνδρῶν πάντων στάντα ἐς ταύτην ἐκτὸς τῶν ἐωθότων νοημάτων στήσειε. ἐγγίνεται μὲν γάρ οἱ ὕβρις ὑπὸ τῶν παρεόντων ἀγαθῶν, φθόνος δὲ ἀρχῆθεν ἐμφύεται ἀνθρώπῳ. δύο δ' ἔχων ταῦτα ἔχει πᾶσαν κακότητα· τὰ μὲν γὰρ ὕβρι κεκορημένος ἔρδει πολλὰ καὶ ἀτάσθαλα, τὰ δὲ φθόνῳ. καίτοι ἄνδρα γε τύραννον ἄφθονον ἔδει εἶναι, ἔχοντά γε πάντα τὰ ἀγαθά. τὸ δὲ ὑπεναντίον τούτου ἐς τοὺς πολιήτας πέφυκε· φθονέει γὰρ τοῖσι ἀρίστοισι περιεοῦσί τε καὶ ζώουσι, χαίρει δὲ τοῖσι κακίστοισι τῶν ἀστῶν, διαβολὰς δὲ ἄριστος ἐνδέκεσθαι.

Give this power to the best man on earth, and it would stir him to unaccustomed thoughts. Insolence is created in him by the good things to hand, while from birth *phthonos* is rooted in man. Acquiring the two he possesses complete evil; for being satiated he does many reckless things, some from insolence, some from *phthonos*. And yet an absolute ruler ought to be free of *phthonos*, having all good things; but he becomes the opposite of this towards his citizens; he feels *phthonos* towards the best who thrive and live, and is pleased by the worst of his fellows; and he is the best confidant of slander.[22]

This final ancient idea about *phthonos*, alongside the disturbing familiarity of this emotion to modern eyes, leads to a series of questions about our access to the emotional experience of the historical individual subject, and the kind of phenomenon we are trying to analyse: how do we go about such an investigation? If we can accept that 'emotions are materially constituted and material culture is emotionally constituted',[23] then when we look at historical objects, or historical documents, are we managing to access something of the individual subjective experience or 'reactions to emotions rather than emotion itself'?[24] Since subjective experiences by their very nature vary so widely (not only from person to person, but also within a single individual), the risk is that historians import their own values into evaluation of historical contexts, ignoring radically different conceptions of self and agency, for example.[25] Yet, at the same time,

---

[22] Tr. Godley 1920 (slightly adapted).
[23] See Gosden (2004: 39), whose theoretical approach emphasizes the importance of trying to understand the relationship between emotions and objects.
[24] Quotation from Stearns and Stearns (1985: 826) on what they think is to be found in historical documents.
[25] On this problem, see Weinstein 1995: 302 and Tarlow 2010: 184 (on Harris and Sørensen 2010a, and their response, Harris and Sørensen 2010b: 189). Voutsaki (2010: 75) argues that before we discuss individual agency in any particular society, we should aim to understand 'the notions of the person held in that society' and identify

Introduction: 'As Rust Eats Iron' 79

it is hard to imagine how historians can attempt to tell the stories of past cultures without approximating the historical 'experiencing self'.[26] Historians and archaeologists have argued that although full empathetic understanding of historical individuals may not be possible, it is important that we not 'suspend... our personal expectations of emotions in our analysis', lest our analyses become 'even more abstract or even pale reflections of past worlds'.[27] In the next section I lay out a necessarily brief overview of some trends in the wide range of research into the emotions, which I hope will help to clarify the approach taken in this study. It sets out a relational view of emotions, and emphasizes the analysis of 'emotion talk' as a way of accessing the cultural narratives of a 'social emotion'.

specific cultural and moral traditions in order to do this. Questioning conceptions of the self raises further questions about perceptions of agency and personhood in a premodern, relational world, which may involve non-human entities. Bill Sillar (2004: 183) addresses this problem in detail using an anthropological approach in the context of Andean peoples, comparing and contrasting their (modern) ritual activities with what is recorded of those of their forbears, the Inkas. He interrogates the idea of agency, and perceptions of agency as cultural/historical constructs, but underlines the importance of continuing to consider, and seek, individual motivation, without which we can only see 'people as unmotivated automatons who unconsciously maintain tradition... or people who merely react to changes in their environment'. Gardner (2004b and c) addresses questions of understanding agency in archaeological approaches; he also raises the question of group/institutional agency.

[26] The idea that study of the emotions can make a significant contribution to scholarship is now firmly established across the study of different periods of history.

[27] Harris and Sørensen 2010b: 189. A new set of terms may be needed to provide a language for such analyses: Harris and Sørensen 2010a and b, with Smith 2010: 174. Tarlow (2000: 728) draws on the idea of 'ethos' to sketch a link between emotional standards and subjective emotional experiences (see Jenkins 1991: 389). A common theme across many of these analyses is the importance of the physical body as the basis for analysis; as Tarlow (2000: 718) puts it 'bodies... can be considered as part of the way in which emotion is culturally enacted, experienced and represented'; see also Meskell 1998a and b.

2.2

Defining Emotions

'HE NEVER DISSECTED A MONKEY'

We start in the nineteenth century, as a crucial debate—one that is still not resolved—begins to spark. In 1806, the anatomist and physician Sir Charles Bell publishes *Essays on the Anatomy of Expression in Painting*. His book is something like a handbook for artists, and yet it offers much more. Drawing on an analysis of ancient art, it sets out a concept of beauty, focusing on the importance of emotional expression. But his approach is based on his extensive knowledge of human anatomy, and he urges the artist to become a scientist, and study dissection. As well as practical advice, he imparts a philosophical viewpoint, careful to distinguish the more elevated beauty of humans from that of animals, who are only capable of a lower form of expressiveness. In humans, 'in the muscles of the face there is a provision for a superiority of expression', he states.[1] In the expanded version of the book (its third edition, titled *The Anatomy and Philosophy of Expression as Connected with the Fine Arts*, first published in 1844) these observations about physiognomy and emotional expression are linked to the will and design of God.[2] The book proves extremely popular, going through seven editions in that century alone.[3]

Much is at stake here. In the copy of his old tutor's book (the expanded edition), Charles Darwin scribbles his responses. Where Bell notes 'the most remarkable muscle in the human face is the *corrugator supercilii* which knits the eyebrows with an energetic effect which unaccountably, but irresistibly conveys the idea of

---

[1] Bell 1824 (1806): 56.   [2] On links to God, see Bell 1865: 105.
[3] After the expanded version (or third edition) was published in 1844, there were editions in 1847, 1865, 1872, 1873 (NY), 1877, 1890 (see Cummings 1964: 191, n. 2).

Defining Emotions 81

mind,'[4] Darwin comments in the margin: 'monkey here?...I have seen well developed in monkeys...I suspect he never dissected monkey.'[5] His notebooks for 1838-9 are full of similar and related material, making observations on both non-human primates, and humans in other cultures and other countries.[6] Alongside his other work, he continues to explore and develop what would become his 'Three Principles of Expression'.[7] He makes inquiries, through journals, of the emotional expressions in other countries; he sends out 'Queries about Expression'; he even makes notes about his own newborn son, William.[8] Darwin does not seek to explain what emotions are or how they evolved; he even denies that they are useful. He argues, simply, that the muscle actions of humans, praised as unique by Charles Bell, are also found across mammal and primate species, which use them to express similar emotions.[9] They may no longer serve that same purpose in humans now, but as a vestige of those earlier responses, they still offer a powerful mode of communication.[10] Actions that were once intentionally undertaken, or instinctively occurred, could become habitual, and, in turn, hereditary. Darwin intends to write another chapter for his *Descent of Man*, but it proves too long. Two days after he finishes correcting the page proofs of that volume, and before he begins work on the sixth and final edition of *On the Origin of Species*, he starts to write *The Expression of the Emotions in Man and Animals*: it is finished in four months, and first published in Great Britain in 1872.[11]

But the debate was far from over. In 1884, the psychologist William James published a paper entitled 'What is an Emotion?' In it he outlined a theory that took the opposite point of view from Darwin.

---

[4] Bell 1865: 137. See Ekman 1999: xxv (who, however, misquotes Bell: 'knits the eyebrows with an enigmatic effect').
[5] Ekman 1999: xxv. This is the source of the quotation used above as a subtitle. Elsewhere (e.g. Matsumoto *et al.* 2008: 227 n. 1) this is quoted as 'He never looked at a monkey.'
[6] Ekman 1998: xxvii, and see Ekman 2009.
[7] Richards (1989: 232-3): the three principles are (i) the principle of 'serviceable associated habits', (ii) the 'principle of antithesis', and, finally, (iii) 'The principle of actions due to the constitution of the Nervous System, independently from the first of the Will, and independently to a certain extent of Habit'.
[8] Burkhardt and Smith 1988 and Burkhardt *et al.* 2010. Darwin 1867; Darwin 1892: 131-2.
[9] Matsumoto *et al.* 2008: 226, with 227 n.
[10] See Griffiths 1997: 44-5, who calls this a 'pattern of "adaptive-historical" explanation'.
[11] Criticized by James 1884, 1890, and 1894.

Whereas Darwin argued for fundamental feelings that were innate, not learned, and which were expressed through the body, in James's view the emotions were perceptions of one's own physical reactions. There may be a contextual trigger, but this simply stimulates the body, and 'our feeling of the same changes as they occur is the emotion'.[12] The symptoms of the emotion may vary from person to person (so a single category of emotion may be indicated by different sets of physical symptoms), but this occurs within limits.[13] Conscious emotional experience was, as he put it, 'not a primary feeling, directly aroused by the exciting object or thought, but a secondary feeling indirectly aroused'.[14] In responses to criticism, it has been suggested, he seemed to enlarge on this to argue that the context of perception is important to what is perceived.[15] But in essence, as one scholar has argued, his presentation of the division of body and mind can be described as 'export quality Cartesianism machined to a high standard by means of nineteenth century positivism'.[16] In this brief snapshot, we see the way in which emotions have been wielded as part of the armoury of beliefs about the nature of humanity, and in particular, human rationality. Both Darwin and James emphasized the difference between body and mind. For Darwin, our emotions were shared with our animal ancestors, a product of instinct and inheritance. For James, there was a clear division between body and mind: we perceive, we respond physically, and we feel.[17] These two approaches are still influencing modern theories of emotions.

WHAT IS AN EMOTION?

In modern, western cultures, the popular view of emotions sees them as 'private, unlearned and physiological': phenomena that can perhaps be tamed or repressed, but are an integral part of our precious, personal,

---

[12] Although he also argued in his articles that emotions are multiply determined, so not all emotions are caused by physiological reactions. See James 1884b: 189 (cited by Larsen *et al.* 2008: 182): how the body feels those changes is raised in a footnote on p. 193, where, he argues, 'The question is too minute for discussion here', and directs the reader to 'The Feeling of Effort' (in the *Anniversary Memoirs of the Boston Natural History Society*, 1880, and a summary in *Mind* 20: 582).
[13] See Gendron and Barrett 2009: 9 and Black 2002.   [14] James 1884a: 516.
[15] See James 1884a; Gendron and Barrett 2009 324–5.   [16] Lyons 1999: 31.
[17] Richards 1989: 437–40.

Defining Emotions

sometimes secret, selves.[18] However, the study of emotion across a number of different academic disciplines—philosophy, psychology, anthropology, and history—suggests a different perspective. The ways in which emotions have been understood to operate or function, the very meaning of 'emotion' itself, have been interrogated, with each part of that initial triad challenged, fragmented and, in some cases, more or less discarded. The idea that emotions in different times and places can be considered with a 'common-sense' approach in which we simply assume an understanding of the nature of the emotional expression—that *they* felt the same as *us*—has now largely been laid to rest.

Nevertheless, the answer to James's question—just what is an 'emotion'?—and how emotions work, is far from settled. The arguments are cross-disciplinary and complex; emotions theorists differ as to the variety of experiential components that may comprise the experience of 'an emotion' (e.g. cognitive, feeling, motivational, somatic, or motor components), even as to how they define those components.[19] These arguments are stimulating, but not necessarily appropriate, for the analysis of the emotions of historical subjects. In what follows, I will try, necessarily briefly, to outline what I understand to be the main strands of this debate, concentrating on those that seem to be most relevant to this project.

The 'Basic Emotions'

Acknowledging that this is a profound simplification, I start with two contrasting fundamental approaches. The first, sometimes called affect programme theory, posits that certain emotions—surprise, anger, fear, sadness, joy, and disgust—should be regarded as a distinct category of 'natural kinds'. These are basic or fixed emotions that are biologically given (with a unique neural circuit, or other neural signature), as a result of evolution. These emotions exist independent from our perception of them.[20] As such, the theory suggests, it is possible to draw reliable conclusions about the category from one member of it, and thus conduct a scientific research programme.[21]

---

[18] Lutz 1986: 284.   [19] See Moors 2010, esp. 1-3.
[20] See Moors 2010: 20-1. Barrett (2006b: 21) argues (22) that the psychological study of emotion is dominated by the paradigm of natural kinds.
[21] See, challenging this, Barrett 2006a and 2006b. See also Griffiths 2004 (where he qualifies his understanding and use of the term). On developments in the meaning of the term 'natural kinds' across disciplines, see e.g. Griffiths 1997: 4-5.

This initial approach, in which Darwin's work played a seminal role, heralded an ongoing interest in and debate about the nature of emotion (in particular, the question of whether bodily activity causes emotions or vice versa).[22] But this lapsed during 1940–60 as other theories gained dominance.[23] In the 1960s, however, the pioneering research of Magda Arnold, Stanley Schachter and Jerome Singer, and Sylvan Tomkins began to reopen the subject, and since the 1980s study of the emotions has grown rapidly.[24] More recent work now emphasizes how these fundamental emotional expressions play a key role in individual human interactions, and are crucial communicative processes. Perhaps most famously, Paul Ekman, drawing in part on the work of Sylvan Tomkins, has argued that there are six universal 'basic emotions'. These are happiness, surprise, fear, sadness, anger, and disgust combined with contempt, with each of these emotion words indicating a 'family of related states', whose members share nine characteristics (distinctive universal signals, presence in other primates, distinctive physiology, distinctive universals in antecedent events, coherence among emotional response, quick onset, brief durations, automatic appraisal, and unbidden occurrence).[25] Another way of thinking about this idea of a family is in terms of a theme and variations, where the variations are the result of individual, cultural, and contextual differences.[26]

---

[22] Darwin 1872.

[23] Some say behaviourism (see Gendron and Barrett 2009: 317), others anthropological relativism (see Ekman 1998: xxiii) diminished this approach. Rosenberg (2005: 10) notes that, in addition, (i) early work indicated that the study of facial expressions did not supply useful data and (ii) even if it had, there was no way to measure it. Gendron and Barrett (2009: 316–17) argue that, in fact, a number of key works in the field of what has now been labeled psychological constructionism were published during this period.

[24] Magda Arnold's work offered an initial 'appraisal model' of the emotions (see Arnold 1960). Appraisal models place emphasis on the 'meaningful interpretation of an object by an individual' (see Gendron and Barrett 2009: 317 and Clore and Ortony 2008: 628–9).

[25] Tomkins 1962 and Ekman 1992a. Carol Izard was also a pioneer in this area, influenced by Tomkins's initial work (see Izard 1971). As Ekman (1992a: 550) notes, Tomkins and McCarter (1964) and Izard (1971) also found evidence for the recognition of interest and shame, but Ekman has reservations about these findings (first, on the grounds that interest may not be an emotion, and second, on the evidence for shame). Ekman (1992c: 191–2) also raises the possibility that embarrassment, awe, and excitement may be candidates for this status. For 'family of related states', see Ekman 1992c: 172 and Ekman and Friesen 1975.

[26] Ekman 1992c: 173.

As Ekman explains, the 'basic' in the phrase 'basic emotions' refers primarily to two key ideas: first, that there are 'a number of separate, discrete, emotional states' that can be identified and differ in their expression through the face; and, second, that the function of these tasks and their universal attributes were shaped by evolution. In response to anthropological findings that, across cultures, different facial expressions may signify differently, he has formulated the notion of 'display rules' to explain how universal facial expressions might be modified according to cultural strictures.[27] This approach has provided the basis for much of the research into emotions that has followed. As Ekman himself has stated, its value lies 'in the questions it directs attention to and the research findings that are generated by those who work from this stance'.[28]

Ekman's use of 'basic' also suggests how other non-basic emotions may be formed, that is, as combinations of the basic emotions, in blends or mixed emotional states.[29] However, before this analytical step is taken, he suggests considering whether non-basic emotions are indeed to be classified as such: are they simply part of the family of a basic emotion? If not, then there are a number of other possible distinct categories, including moods (e.g. apprehension, irritation), emotional attitudes (e.g. love or hatred), traits (timorous, hostile), or disorders (depression, mania), and finally 'emotional plots', which involve specific information, such as settings and stories (examples include grief, infatuation, and jealousy).[30]

Ekman himself has dealt robustly with challenges to his methods, and to conflicting anthropological research.[31] It is important to realize that his theory of the basic emotions involves room for

---

[27] Ekman and Friesen 1969.
[28] Ekman 1992a: 552. For example, his work on the links between facial expression and emotion is also supported by work on autonomic nervous system (ANS) physiology, and he has proposed that each emotion produces distinctive 'patterned changes in both expression and physiology' which are not linked to the cause of the emotion (see Ekman *et al.* 1983 and 1990, and Ekman 1984 and 1992b).
[29] Ekman 1992c: 170 and see Ekman and Friesen: 1975.
[30] Ekman 1992c: 194. Other scholars have suggested that experiences of more complex emotions can be explained in two ways: either because some of these basic emotions are triggered simultaneously—the imagery used is of particular circuits of emotions firing simultaneously—or because of the way we communicate our personal experience: see Lindquist and Barrett 2008: 513-14.
[31] Ekman 1992b: 34 and 1999a.

individual and cultural variation. He recognizes, indeed emphasizes, the important role played by the language of emotion, not only in terms of the nuances of expression and understanding that a particular term can introduce, but also the possible effects on a culture of not having a word for a particular emotion.[32] Work in this field remains vibrant and constructive. There is ongoing research into the ways in which recognition of particular emotional expressions may be related to brain activation.[33] These new findings support the conclusions that humans have evolved physiological systems for recognizing certain emotions—and that this has an obvious social function.[34] In addition, research that involves measuring facial behaviour itself, rather than using inferential judgements, may also prove useful to students of emotions.[35]

However, as approaches become increasingly influenced by constructionist theories of emotion, the argument that there are emotions that are 'natural kinds' and can be identified objectively has been criticized as conveying key assumptions that are not demonstrated by scientific research, and as presenting an obstruction to the development of productive scientific research into the nature and process of emotions.[36] In an overview of work in the field in 2003, James A. Russell et al. concluded that 'Emotion expressions may not be expressions and may not be related to emotions in any simple way.'[37] Others have posed different criticisms. Paul Griffiths, for example, has argued that a scientific research programme on 'emotion' as a category is impossible, since, in fact, too many different types of phenomena exist under this heading. He compares the category 'emotions' to that of 'vitamins'—on closer inspection this comprises a variety of different chemicals that are best described individually.[38]

[32] Ekman 1999a: 317. He gives the example of the German *Schadenfreude*, which of course does not exist in English, although the emotion it describes is recognized (see further on this emotion pp. 225 and 250).
[33] Roesch et al. 2011 provides a useful overview of the different approaches that such research has taken.
[34] Russell et al. 2003: 342; cf. Matsumoto et al. 2008.
[35] e.g. using the Facial Action Coding System (FACS); see Rosenberg 2005.
[36] Barrett 2006a and b; constructionist theories are discussed further on pp. 87–95.
[37] Russell et al. 2003: 342.   [38] Griffiths 1997 and 2004.

Evaluating Emotions

One alternative route to research in this area is to tackle emotions as processes of cognitive evaluation. Based on an approach developed by Magda Arnold, appraisal theories emphasize the experience of emotions as intentional, that is, concerned with an individual's particular experience of an object or situation rather than simply being caused by that object or situation.[39] Different theories suggest that different aspects of a situation may be appraised, which leads to the experience of different emotions. Some theorists use a structural approach, looking at the dimensions of the individual's relationship with the object or situation; others focus on the qualitative nature of the relationship.[40] Many of these appraisal models introduce a second cognitive stage or stages, which follow an initial stimulus, and which (either simultaneously or cumulatively) shape the initial data. Criticisms of the idea of cognitive appraisal often depict it as involving the articulation of an explicit proposition. In fact, most cognitive approaches suggest that the appraisal process is, like many of our cognitive processes, rapid and inaccessible, and that there may be a number of different cognitive routes to emotional appraisal.[41] Thus, some theorists have argued that emotions are more like instinctual reactions to different situational structures, so we are like chameleons, responding to our changing environment by simply reflecting appropriate emotions.[42]

With some similarities of approach, theorists who argue for a distinct 'psychological constructionist' approach lay particular emphasis on the role of the social context in our cognitive processing.[43] They tend to

---

[39] Arnold 1960.

[40] e.g. for the structural approach, see De Rivera 1977; Kemper (1978) focuses on concerns with power and status. For overviews of the different dimensions of appraisal that various theorists have proposed for different emotions, see Frijda 1986: 201–4 and Ellsworth and Scherer 2003.

[41] The sequence of the appraisal may also vary and there are a number of 'dual-process' models of appraisal (see Scherer 1984, 2001). See discussion in Gendron and Barrett 2009 and Clore and Ortony 2008.

[42] Chameleons: Clore and Ortony 2008: 633; they cite Parkinson 2007, who argues (22) for emotions 'as direct adjustments to relational dynamics'; Roseman (1991) argues for a theory that categorizes how combinations of five appraisals will lead, in any given situation, to thirteen qualitatively different emotions.

[43] As Gendron and Barrett 2009. Brosch 2013 provides a compelling comparison of appraisal and psychological constructionist theories of emotions.

argue that emotions comprise basic psychological components that are involved in other mental states, either a mental feeling ('affect') or physical stimulation, a low-level affective reaction. Emotional states occur through a process of categorization, using conceptual knowledge.[44] This approach suggests that emotions are grounded in core affect—'continuous and fluctuating affective states'—so-called because they occur in changes of body state (face, voice, nervous system) or the 'core' of the body.[45] But the two are not equivalent: what people know and how they process what they know about an emotion and how it works inform them of what they are feeling. Importantly, the context of the event (both in the here and now, and in memory) is crucial to this mental process.[46] Lisa Feldman Barrett compares this process to the way we see colour: the wavelengths of particular colours remain the same, but whether we see blue and green as two separate colours will depend on whether our culture has separate concepts for blue and green.[47]

Neuroscientific research supports this emergent variable approach, offering insights into the ways in which mental and social events interact. Research demonstrates how fundamental domain-general neural processes underpin diverse emotional experiences—rather than being directly related to a limited number of emotions—with implications for the ways in which we understand and explain the

---

[44] Toobey and Cosmides (1990) argue that some of this knowledge arises from mankind's evolutionary history (419): 'emotions...constitute a treasure-house of information about the nature of ancestral conditions and about the power of various evolutionary processes'.

[45] Wilson-Mendenhall *et al.* 2013.

[46] Barrett (2006b), who points out that other psychological phenomena have been studied as emergent properties rather than (21) 'entities to be found'. She notes (2006a: 48) that core affect may be supported by a kind of 'hard-wiring' in the human physiognomy; see also Lindquist and Barrett 2008: 514. Damasio (1994: 131-9) argues for a split between primary emotions that are 'preorganised' and secondary emotions 'which occur once we begin experiencing feelings and forming systematic connections between categories of objects and situation, on the one hand, and primary emotions, on the other'. He recognizes 'a large biological component' to what he calls primary emotions, noting the experiments that have demonstrated links between affect and particular parts of the brain. Primary emotions are emotions that we experience early in life, and these become the basic scaffolding of our emotions, while secondary emotions are shaped by an individual's experience when they are older, and 'are relative to particular cultures' (285 n. 16).

[47] Barrett 2006b; other models of this process have been put forward, e.g. Russell (2003) has suggested a process of attribution, in which a person is prompted by a change in his mood (core affect) to attribute that change to a particular object, and this process is followed by a fuller appraisal.

variability of emotions.[48] Moreover, it appears that the less typical an emotion is (e.g. pleasant sadness, unpleasant happiness), the harder the neural system has to work to process it, and the more difficult it is for the person experiencing the affect to identify it within social emotions categories. In turn, it appears that emotional language also contributes to how we perceive representations of emotion.[49] This process may be iterative, leading us to reinterpret and refine our interpretations, resulting in increasingly reflective evaluations.[50]

Whereas psychological constructionist theories attempt to tackle the variability of emotion by looking at the experiences and neurophysiology of the individual, social constructionist theories focus on the way that emotions vary between cultures. Some cultures seem to have emotions that do not occur elsewhere. An often-quoted example is the Japanese *amae*, which is described as a sense of childlike dependency on someone or something, which gives a sense of great comfort. However, the extent to which such emotions are constructed is debated, and a spectrum of approaches has developed. Across the social sciences, what has been called 'the affective turn' has prompted provocative and profound reflection both on the role and process of the emotions in individual and community life—and on how we study these phenomena.[51]

Socially Constructing Emotions

We might start, along with Paul Griffiths, by identifying two models of the social construction of emotion, which he calls, respectively, the 'social concept' model and the 'social role' model.[52] The social concept model describes an emotion as fundamentally conceptual, the act of classifying situations; moreover, it is the concept of a particular culture or group, rooted in cultural beliefs and understandings. Griffiths is highly critical of this propositional attitude account of emotions on a number of grounds, including the idea that emotions may be felt without beliefs (for example, because the object of the emotion

---

[48] See Coan 2010.
[49] Gendron *et al.* 2012, Wilson-Mendenhall *et al.* 2013 and 2015, and Russell and Fehr 1994.
[50] See Cunningham and Zelazo 2007. (As Clore and Ortney 2008: 15 argue, this has implications for how we think about the relation between apparently unconscious attitudes and explicit attitudes, e.g. with regard to race).
[51] Greco and Stenner 2008.   [52] Griffiths 1997.

is either imagined or does not exist), and, in turn, that beliefs may be held without emotions—or that we deny those emotions; he has also argued that this approach takes no account of the connections between emotions and physiological changes.[53]

Leaving the 'social concept' model, we turn to what Griffiths calls the 'social role' model, which also involves cognitive elements with a similar focus on engagement with the world.[54] A number of scholars emphasize the key part played by the psychologist J. R. Averill in opening this avenue of research, in particular in an article titled 'A Constructivist View of Emotion', published in 1980.[55] This approach sets an individual firmly and integrally in his or her social context, applies social constructionist theories, and focuses on the relational nature of the emotions. In other words, it concentrates on 'the unfolding of social practices', which, in turn, opens up the possibility that 'many emotions can exist only in the reciprocal exchanges of a social encounter'.[56] Although we may not go so far with this argument, it inevitably prompts consideration of the nuances inherent in

---

[53] Griffiths (1997: 27) finds this approach among philosophers such as Robert Solomon (1976). As he puts it (2008: 10): 'We should identify the *experience* of having an emotion (as opposed to just a simple "feeling") as embodying thoughts, judgments, and other cognitive elements', and (11) 'the emotion is first of all a mode of engagement'. Solomon himself continued to argue that 'emotions are judgments'; and—a further crucial point—that we are responsible for our emotions (see 2003a, esp. the preface). He expresses concern that psychological approaches, which tend to see emotions as preceding cognition, pay little attention to this aspect (see Solomon 2003b: viii). His research programme has proved highly influential. Examples of philosophical analyses that examine the role of cognition in the emotions (exploring different aspects), include, Michael Stocker (2003) who has explored cognitive theories and 'affectivity'; Cheshire Calhoun (2003), who has offered 'cognitive sets' as a way of thinking about the discontinuities between beliefs and emotions; and Martha Nussbaum (2003) who draws on and develops the ancient Greek Stoic view that (22) 'emotions are forms of evaluative judgments that ascribe great importance to things and persons outside one's control'.

[54] As Harré describes it (1986b: 5): 'It turns out that the dominant contribution to the way that aspect of our lives unfolds comes from the local social world, by way of its linguistic practices and the moral judgements in the course of which the emotional quality of encounters is defined.'

[55] Averill 1980.

[56] Harré 1986b: 5. Constructionist approaches have also received criticism. As part of the thoughtful siege Ian Hacking (1999) lays to the notion of social constructionism in general, he observes (18–19) with regard to the social construction of emotion in particular, that such an approach dilutes the meaning of construction to a code rather than a description—and the code stands for (19): 'not universal, not part of pan-cultural human nature, and don't tread on me with those heavy hegemonic (racist, patriarchal) boots of yours'. Nevertheless, he credits the approach with raising our

the interpretation of some emotion terms. A particular social context may lead to distinct emotional expectations and reactions, even if, at first sight, they resemble each other. And differences in the representation of emotions may indicate more than simply diverse ways of talking about the same thing, raising questions about differences in the construction or composition of emotion experiences.[57]

For example, take the emotion acedia or accidie (in Greek, ἀκηδία) described by St Evagrius of Pontus, a monastic theologian of the fourth century CE, who spent much of his later life in Egypt transcribing the wisdom of the Desert Fathers. Acedia appears in the *Praktikos*, a volume providing guidance for purifying the soul (a process called *praktike*). It is one of eight generic *logismoi* '(tempting) thoughts' (forerunners of the seven deadly sins, instituted by Gregory the Great, in which acedia does not appear), and it feels like this:

> The demon of acedia—also called the noonday demon [*Ps* 90:6 LXX]—is the one that causes the most serious trouble of all. He presses his attack upon the monk about the fourth hour and besieges the soul until the eighth hour. First of all he makes it seem that the sun barely moves, if at all, and that the day is fifty hours long. Then he constrains the monk to look constantly out the windows, to walk outside the cell, to gaze carefully at the sun to determine how far it stands from the ninth hour, to look now this way and now that to see if perhaps [one of the brethren appears from his cell]. Then too he instils in the heart of the monk a hatred for the place, a hatred for his very life itself, a hatred for manual labour. He leads him to reflect that charity has departed from among the brethren, that there is no one to give encouragement. Should there be someone at this period who happens to offend him in some way or other, this too the demon uses to contribute further to his hatred. This demon drives him along to desire other sites where he can more easily procure life's necessities, more readily find work and make a real success of himself. He goes on to suggest that, after all, it is not the place that is the basis of pleasing the Lord. God is to be adored everywhere. He joins to these reflections the memory of his dear ones and of his former way of life. He depicts life stretching out for a long period of

---

consciousness about ideas that are otherwise simply taken to be inevitable. He suggests instead that we unpack the meaning of social construction, distinguishing its relevance to, respectively, objects and ideas, and exploring how the latter exist within a 'matrix' (34), that is 'the individuals falling under the idea, the interaction between the idea and the people, and the manifold social practices and institutions that these interactions involve'.

[57] Harré 1986b: 5 and Heelas 1986: 258.

time, and brings before the mind's eye the toil of the ascetic struggle and, as the saying has it, leaves no leaf unturned to induce the monk to forsake his cell and drop out of the fight. No other demon follows close upon the heels of this one (when he is defeated) but only a state of deep peace and inexpressible joy arise out of this struggle.[58]

The experiences and feelings that Evagrius describes here are probably all too familiar to some of us—we might describe them in terms of *ennui*, boredom, or even depression—and yet the emotion of acedia itself, by that name, is no longer current.[59] Crucial to our understanding of this emotion are the particular contexts in which it originated and then developed. So, for example, acedia was associated with the challenges of monastic life, but as that lifestyle became less popular, and as the Church began public teaching on the vices in the early thirteenth century, its meaning shifted.[60] Where once it had described a state of mind, over time it became associated more with the behaviour that state of mind evoked. Moreover, the term acquired a different nuance for those more preoccupied with seeking worldly rewards, rather than the spiritual insights of contemplation. It began to be associated with the concept of *amaritudo* or bitterness: for example, the parson in the *Canterbury Tales* describes how the mother of 'Accidie', which makes a man 'hevy, thoghtful and wraw', is 'bitternesse' (which is, itself, made from 'Envye' and 'Ire').[61] Although elements of the description of the emotion may seem familiar to many of us, for Evagrius, the experience was integrally bound up with a specific context.

The implications for the historian are manifold. In our attempts to describe emotions in a historical or cultural context other than our

[58] Description from Driscoll 2003: 9; translation from Evagrius Ponticus *Praktikos* 12 in Bamberger 1971: 18–19. W. V. Harris (2001: 21) translates it as '"listlessness" or something similar', and observes that it was known to Cicero (*Att.* 12.45.1). Wenzel (1967) translates the Greek as 'lack of care, *incuria*' and notes its appearance in a Hippocratic text, *Glands* (the date of which is disputed). Luciani-Zidane (2009: 29) notes that it is also found in Empedocles and Lucian but does not give references. 'Accidia' is the normal form in the later middle ages (and is found at least as early as the ninth century CE; see Wenzel 1967: 206 n. 1).

[59] For a history of *acedia* see Luciani-Zidane 2009 and Wenzel 1967, cited in Harré and Finlay-Jones 1986. Solomon (2001) uses the phrase 'the noonday demon' as the title for his examination of depression (both his own experience and an examination of the history of this disease across cultures).

[60] Wenzel 1967: 68–9.

[61] Ziolkowski 2003: 105. The parson: Chaucer's *Canterbury Tales* X (I) 676–7 in Benson 2008: 310.

own, the ways in which they are embedded in and emerge from social interaction is an essential aspect—and this may deftly change the nature of our focus. We are no longer talking (just) about the private meaning of emotion or the experience of the individual, but focusing on emotions as sociocultural constructions, linked to specific contexts. This leads, in turn, to consideration of the crucial role played by the emotions in the formation of a moral order and the establishment of what is considered normative.[62] In this view, emotions are not only socioculturally determined, but prescribe 'a function of shared expectations regarding appropriate behaviour'.[63] They not only inform ideas about the nature of the self, but also about relations between self and other, and concern questions of moral order.[64] Thus, if the Dinka of Sudan understand envy in terms of witches and witchcraft, not only does this suggest that their 'envy' is not the same emotion as that experienced by those who do not, but also that their understanding of envy links to and has implications for a realm of cultural knowledge about, at least, the nature of social interactions and supernatural power.[65] And, of course, these implications are relevant not only to our subjects of study: the historian

[62] Harré 1986b: 6. For example, in this context, Stearns and Stearns (1985: 813) distinguish between what they call 'emotionology' and emotions. The latter refers to the familiar although 'complex set of interactions among subjective and objective factors, mediated through neural and/or hormonal systems, which give rise to feelings', while the former is 'the attitudes or standards that a society, or a definable group within a society, maintains toward basic emotions and their appropriate expression; ways that institutions reflect and encourage these attitudes in human conduct'. This view has been criticized on the grounds that it suggests that emotions can form a subject of research (Weinstein 1990: 301; although some might take issue with this characterization). Emotionology is (833) a 'powerful force...shaping the behavior of individuals and groups', but the way in which it will shape them, and why, and how those changes link to the wider social context and other historical forces, is far from predictable. Emotionology provides an overall framework; its creators raise but leave unexplored the possibility that there may exist subgroups within a specific emotionology (828).
[63] Averill 1980: 308.
[64] Lutz and White 1986: 417. Something of this aspect is found in the analyses of ancient anger that have been presented by Douglas Cairns (2003b: 13–16), who links this prescriptive aspect to an argument for the evolutionary origin of emotions and their role in the development of human sociality and in ensuring cooperation.
[65] Heelas 1986: 258.

must also retain a reflexive awareness about his or her own assumptions about the emotions. These too are shaped by the experiences, institutions, and social structures where they occur.[66]

In terms of the transmission of sociocultural concepts, it is clearly not accurate to stop at what Claudia Strauss calls a '"fax" model of socialization'—that is, the idea that we simply receive and follow, largely unconsciously, a set of norms imposed by the hegemonic cultural structure within which we live.[67] Instead, she emphasizes how the communication and expression of culture is made complex by the ways in which the information that individuals receive about their culture is ambiguous and diverse, received and understood differently by different individuals, and, of course, experienced with diverse emotions. How we perceive, describe, and respond to situations in turn creates the emotional culture in which we live. As Michelle Rosaldo succinctly put it: 'Feelings are not substances to be discovered in our blood but social practices organized by stories that we both enact and tell.'[68] Averill argued that emotions were transitory social roles, and others have developed this idea to consider the ways in which emotions provide us with narratives or plot structures, in some cases, regarding these almost as scripts where we play out dramatic roles that are recognizable to others as particular emotions.[69]

---

[66] Averill (1992: 16) notes how researchers tend to find most natural or fundamental those emotions that have that status in their own culture. Sanders (2014) analyses current feelings about envy and jealousy as part of his examination of similar ancient emotions.

[67] Strauss 1992a: 10.

[68] Rosaldo 1984: 143.

[69] Sarbin (1995; see also 1986a and 1986b) uses metaphors drawn from drama and rhetoric to examine the ways in which narratives inform our emotional comprehension and interactions. He argues that we use rhetorical actions of two sorts in our emotional interaction: dramaturgical actions occur in the moment, and the actor is the author of a 'concurrent script'; dramatistic rhetoric comprises the cultural 'plots' or narratives that we absorb from plays, films, stories, songs, folktales, fables, myths, legends, etc. (these become guides to actions). For the usefulness of examining ancient emotions in terms of narrative processes or scripts, which can be used to elicit an emotion term's 'emotional terrain', see Kaster 2005: 7–9 and Sanders 2014: 36ff.

Scheer 2012 offers an insightful development of the idea of 'emotional practices', exploring the concept of emotion in light of practice theory, that is '*as* a kind of practice' (194, italics in original).

The 'Nervous System'

The analysis so far suggests that in thinking about the social construction of emotion—or rather the social practice of emotion—we need to set the individual into a larger circuit of creativity. This is to borrow imagery from Kathleen Stewart's moving account of 'ordinary affects', which she describes as 'an animate circuit that conducts force and maps connections, routes and disjunctures. They are a kind of contact zone where the overdeterminations of circulations, events, conditions, technologies and flows of power literally take place.'[70] It is a reminder to us of the emergent nature of emotion, of the matrix of information that comprises lived experience: emotions 'are public feelings that begin and end in broad circulation, but they're also the stuff that seemingly intimate lives are made of'.[71]

This is, in some ways, reminiscent of Michael Taussig's conception of the 'nervous system', as a way of examining the manipulation of biological and social bodies (meaning both the individual and institutional, and the relations between them).[72] It draws our attention to emotions, not as discrete, individualized phenomena, but as dynamics developed within networks of relationships, socially conceptualized and enacted within familiar schemas, comprising rhetoric and narratives that are both verbal and physical. As Parkinson argues, some of these will be influences that work as it were 'top-down', cultural influences that work through processes of socialization, while others will be dynamic, situational processes that generate emotional meaning in real time.[73] Rather than thinking of any of these processes as monolithic, the scale and timing of interactions need consideration.[74] Recent work in psychology also supports these

---

[70] Stewart 2007: 3. As she points out, this draws inspiration from Raymond Williams's 'structures of feeling', which he describes (2009: 132) as 'meanings and values as they are actively lived and felt'. These, he stresses are 'a social experience which is still *in process*, often indeed not yet recognized as social but taken to be private, idiosyncratic, and even isolating, but which in analysis (though rarely otherwise) has its emergent, connecting and dominant characteristics, indeed its specific hierarchies'.
[71] Stewart 2007: 2.
[72] As Charles Stewart notes (pers. corresp.); Taussig 1992.
[73] Parkinson 1996, 2007, 2012.
[74] See Parkinson 2012, with esp. Scherke 2012. Rosenwein (2002: esp. 36 and 43; and 2006) has highlighted the possibility of identifying 'emotional communities', which are similar to social communities, but defined by their own system of feeling. Within a single community or culture, there may also be subgroups holding different

ideas that emotions are not simply intrapsychic events, but rather processes that emerge through both cultural and social (group and interpersonal) interactions.[75] And, recently, in sociocultural anthropology, Henrietta Moore has argued for the role of 'sociality' (defined as 'a dynamic relational matrix within which subjects are constantly interacting in ways that are co-productive, and continually plastic and malleable') as a crucial part of understanding how human beings work with affect and emotion.[76]

The notion of the cultural model or schema may provide a lens with a wide enough angle to encompass these various aspects—social and individual, structured and fluid, defined and ambiguous, identified and emergent.[77] These are powerful ideas about how the world works that are learned and shared by individuals within a culture, often without their being aware of this process. Usually taken for granted, these flexible sets of mental associations of objects and relations are used to represent, organize, and evaluate experiences. They enable us to interact swiftly with the world around us and it is possible to hold alternative models simultaneously.[78] As well as reflecting the regularities of a culture, these models or schemas are also understood to be flexible and to evolve. This approach describes knowledge or action as emerging from interaction between these mental phenomena—be they statements or non-verbal experiences, sensations, or symbols—as they stimulate or inhibit each other. Certain neural pathways may become repeatedly activated, but novel pathways

---

values, working with diverse models of emotions, and expressing themselves in contrasting ways to each other or to the dominant configuration.

[75] Averill (2012: 216, quoting Kroeber and Parsons 1958: 583) draws our attention to the distinction between social and cultural systems in such an overview. These two separate spheres of influence are interrelated, but indicate different processes: whereas culture operates by transmitting and creating 'patterns of values, ideas and other symbolic-meaningful systems as factors in the shaping of human behaviour and the artifacts produced through behaviour', society comprises a 'specifically relational system of interaction among individuals and collectives'.

[76] Quotation from Long and Moore 2013: 4, and see Moore 2013: 30–1. Moore (see esp. 2013: 26–30) argues that this interrelational aspect is what is missing from the view of affect suggested by, for example, Massumi 2002, who views it as autonomous.

[77] See Eidinow 2011a, who uses the concept of cultural models to analyse representations of luck, fate, and fortune in ancient discourses.

[78] D'Andrade 1995: 122–3.

can also be forged.[79] As a result, two people may be aware of the same schema, but have very different responses to it; moreover, the emotions that a person associates with a particular schema will develop over time, shaped by that person's life experiences.[80]

This links schemas at one level to appraisal processes;[81] but they also align with network theories of emotions, which can explain their development as a gradually increasing set of links between biologically relevant stimuli. The idea of a network of associations that underpins these theories was initially developed when 'a computational metaphor of the mind ruled'; more recent approaches are influenced by the connectionist or dynamic systems metaphor.[82] This involves a model of parallel, rather than sequential processing of information, and mirrors some of the observations of iterative neural processing that occurs during and as part of emotional experience, already described in this section, as well as psychological and neuroscientific research into the variability of emotional experience, and the possibilities for new directions of research into emotion as a social phenomenon. For the purposes of this study, the primary emphasis must be on finding ways of exploring that phenomenon in historical subjects, and the model of networked schemas offers a way to do this, through the analysis of cultural discourses, or emotion talk.[83]

EMOTION TALK

The 'emotion talk' of a society offers crucial insights into the nature of both the cultural schemas and the individual experiences of an emotion.[84] As Paul Heelas puts it, 'emotion talk functions as a kind

---

[79] This is a very brief summary of Strauss and Quinn 1997: 50-5. For a useful overview of the history of the development of schema theory and connectionist models (in artificial intelligence), see D'Andrade 1995: 122-49 and Moors 2010: 18-20. Interaction emerges from within social life, so neural pathways are shaped not just by shared information, but by associations with particular emotions, unconscious knowledge and desires, the influence of other people, indeed, by the interaction of different schemas (see Strauss 1992a: 13-15; D'Andrade 1995: 148-9).
[80] See Holland 1992; summarized by Strauss (1992a: 15).
[81] D'Andrade (1995: 222) has suggested that 'an appraisal is the activation of a schema'. He suggests that in fact there are two appraisals, a primary appraisal that is 'innate' and a secondary one in which cultural knowledge plays a major formative role.
[82] Moors 2010: 20.   [83] Strauss 2005.   [84] Edwards 1999.

of spotlight'.[85] If an emotion remains vague and ill-defined ('hypocognized'), then it may receive little attention in a society; if, in contrast, it receives much cultural elaboration ('hypercognized'), then that emotion is likely to hold particular significance for that culture, which is likely to enhance an individual's experience of it.[86] The nature of that elaboration matters: for example, what kinds of metaphors are used to describe it, which body parts do these metaphors refer to, and what sensations do they evoke?

A brief example can be made using the emotion of anger. George Lakoff and Zoltán Kövecses have explored the imagery used in relation to the concept of anger in US English, showing its 'elaborate cognitive structure', one which is interestingly motivated by bodily experience. They draw attention to the ways in which the cultural model of anger and its physiological effects emphasizes heat and highlights the ways in which it is dangerous, both to the person with the emotion and to those around him or her.[87] In contrast, as Michelle Rosaldo has clarified, although 'anger' among the Philipino Ilongots (a tribe of headhunters) is superficially similar to modern Western models, it appears to differ from them in important ways, and is associated with different metaphors and images. She notes how we may be able to deny our true feelings (and be tormented internally), but, unlike the Philippine Ilongots, 'We cannot be "paid" for "anger" which, so satisfied, then dissolves, and we cannot "forget" an "anger" whose expression would prove undesirable.'[88] Rosaldo also found that, although the Ilongots could hide their feelings, they did not, like us, think of them as toxically bubbling away beneath the surface. As this suggests, the metaphors of an emotion can provide insights into the underlying schema of an emotion from a variety of

---

[85] Heelas 1986: 259; Kaster (2005: 8) claims that emotion talk 'is just the lexicalized residue of what happens when the data of life are processed in a particular way—through a sequence of perception (sensing, imagining), evaluation (believing, judging, desiring) and response (bodily, affective, pragmatic, expressive)—to produce a particular kind of emotionalized consciousness, a particular set of thoughts and feelings'.

[86] See also D'Andrade 1995: 224. In particular, the extent to which an emotion is culturally elaborated—that is, whether it is tightly defined and seems significant—will influence the way in which it is consciously experienced. As Tarlow (2000: 727-8) discusses, the question of the authenticity of emotion—public or private, personal or collective, spontaneous or pre-coded—thus becomes somewhat more difficult to identify, but this may not matter 'to a delineation of social emotional *values*'.

[87] Lakoff and Kövecses 1987.

[88] Rosaldo 1984: 144, but cf. Spiro 1984. See also D'Andrade 1995: 227.

perspectives, which encompass both its individual experience and its social role: for example, the origin of an emotion, the extent to which it is understood to be controlled by or in control of the person feeling it, the ways in which it may be brought to an end or changed, are just some of the perceptions that will influence how it plays out in social interactions.[89] As Rom Harré points out, 'emotions are strategic. They play roles in forms of action. And actions occur in situations . . . Emotions do not just happen. They are part of the unfolding of quite standard dramatic scenarios.'[90]

This raises the rhetorical role of emotion talk, and the ways in which the expression of emotional schemas relates to individual and group motivations. In examining these aspects of emotion talk, Holly F. Mathews analysed the 'directive force of morality tales', exploring the telling of the tale of La Llorona or the 'Weeping Woman', a folktale that recounts the story of a troubled marriage. Her account of her fieldwork in Mexico describes how the story's telling differed according to the gender of the teller, conveying diverse emotional cultural schemas that motivated the behaviour of the characters in different ways, and drawing out different lessons for the story's audience, according to the goals of the teller.[91] Thus, in a version of the folktale told by a father to chastise his errant daughter, when the wife goes crazy and begins to walk the streets, the husband experiences anger or rage that prompts him to seek revenge—and he kills her or her lover. But in another version of the story told by the daughter's mother, when the wife finds out that her husband has another woman, she feels sadness—and she kills herself. As these examples suggest, these tales tend to reflect on the suffering caused by 'bad' behaviour, but also on attitudes to male dominance; different versions communicate various models of marriage and gender.

The morality tale is a cultural form that offers a representative series of events, a slow burn, as it were, of cultural values. A contrasting form of emotion talk is evoked by Michael Taussig's description of the 'cultural elaboration of fear' in the nineteenth century rubber plantations of the Congo. There, narratives of savagery, cannibalism, and potential rebellion shared by white workers in the Congo were crucially combined with the experiences of torture, by both victim and victimizer. Talk and reality became horribly and violently intertwined: 'Far from being trivial daydreams indulged in after work was over, these stories and the imagination they sustained were a potent political

---

[89] A point made by Heelas 1986: 258. [90] Harré 1986b: 12.
[91] Mathews 1992: 127–62.

force without which the work of conquest and of supervising rubber gathering could not have been accomplished... they functioned to create, through magical realism, a culture of terror dominating both whites and Indians.'[92]

How do these tales acquire their power? D'Andrade, for example, argues that the motivational force of a particular schema for an individual comes from the emotional content the schema conveys when it is learned. This may happen through socializing agents within our culture, and he posits a hierarchy of internalization levels with corresponding levels of motivation for the individual. Strauss takes a similar approach, but stresses the ways in which the process of internalizing a cultural model—and its motivational force—will vary from individual to individual, shaped by their emotionally salient personal experiences and conscious self-understanding ('personal semantic network'[93]). For example, her research into the goals of a group of blue-collar workers in America reveals that they may have shared similar models of success, but held these models with diverse levels of awareness. The result was what she calls 'different *ways of believing*' which, in turn, resulted in different goals.[94]

These different examples illustrate how emotion talk and emotion actions take place within specific social structures—which encompass both individual experiences and actions as well as institutions—both drawing from and giving meaning to the occasions in which they are used. They conform to certain schemas, but these are, importantly, more than just a system of rules. They are explanatory narrative structures, closely related to a society's moral order, and an individual's personal experience: 'People thus define how and what they should feel in terms of externalized forms of emotion talk.'[95] An expression of personal emotion is also a statement about oneself, or others, as social beings.

Emotions are cognitive, linguistic, embodied, and social manifestations—all of which relate to, and shape, each other. Without denying the role of individual and individual processes, examining this aspect directs us 'away from the "private" and instead concentrate[s] on what it means to be emotional as that is socially defined'.[96]

---

[92] Taussig (1984: 492 and 494): 'The systems of torture they devised to secure rubber mirrored the horror of the savagery they so feared, condemned—and fictionalised.' See further the development of these ideas into the 'nervous system' described in Taussig 1992.
[93] Strauss 1992b: 211.   [94] Strauss 1992b.   [95] Heelas 1986: 260.
[96] Ibid.

This brings us back to the text with which we started this exploration: a binding spell from ancient Athens that offers *phthonos* as its core motivation. The larger context of emotion studies provokes a host of questions about the significance of this emotion term, and the schemas it may comprise: What events provoked its use here? What kinds of relationships might it signal? What social meanings could it hold? To start to answer these questions, we need to explore this emotion concept and the variety of narratives in which it occurs, setting this text in the nexus of cultural meanings that *phthonos* evoked.

2.3

Narratives of *Phthonos*

A proverb found in Theopompus suggests that from the Greek point of view you were only really safe from the *phthonos* of your fellow men once you had died:

Ἐπίσταμαι γάρ, ὅτι τοὺς μὲν ζῶντας πολλοὶ μετὰ δυσμενείας ἐξετάζουσι, τοῖς δὲ τετελευτηκόσι διὰ τὸ πλῆθος τῶν ἔτων ἐπανιᾶσι τοὺς φθόνους.

For I know that many people scrutinize the living invidiously, but on the dead, because of the number of intervening years, they are sparing with their *phthonos*.[1]

Although care is needed over the extent to which we judge such individual statements to represent broadly held views, nevertheless, it is notable how widespread this thought is across other literature of the Classical period, particularly rhetorical texts.[2] The emotion talk around *phthonos* in ancient Greek literature has a startling prevalence. This is in part because of the kinds of sources that have survived, but it is surely not the only reason.[3] It has been suggested that it is an important element of *phthonos* that it is limited to those

---

[1] Theopompus FGrH 115 F 395 = Theon. *Prog.* 1 (II 63, 18 Sp.), translated in Shrimpton 1991: 114, who urges caution in its interpretation: see 112 and 115.

[2] Dem. 18.315: τίς γὰρ οὐκ οἶδε τῶν πάντων, ὅτι τοῖς μὲν ζῶσι πᾶσιν ὕπεστί τις ἢ πλείων ἢ ἐλάττων φθόνος, τοὺς τεθνεῶτας δ' οὐδὲ τῶν ἐχθρῶν οὐδεὶς ἔτι μισεῖ ('Everybody knows that against the living there is always an undercurrent of more or less *phthonos*, but no one hates the dead, not even their enemies'); and 19.313. Thuc. 2.45.1–2: Φθόνος γὰρ τοῖς ζῶσι πρὸς τὸ ἀντίπαλον, τὸ δὲ μὴ ἐμποδὼν ἀνανταγωνίστῳ εὐνοίᾳ τετίμηται ('*Phthonos* confronts the living, but those who are no longer in our path are honoured with a good will that holds no rivalry'). Also Cic. *Balb.* 16, Hor. *Carm.* 3.24.31, and Quint. 3.1.21.

[3] As Sabini and Silver (1986: 167) observe, 'Traditionally, envy has an important place in the account of human misbehaviour.'

of similar social standing.[4] But as has been noted, the description of the bad behaviour of kings towards their subjects given by Herodotus' character Otanes (in the constitutional debate of book three of the *Histories*) demonstrates that things are not so simple. And this is reinforced when Herodotus makes Achaemenes say to his brother, King Xerxes of Persia, as he contemplates invading Greece: 'For these are the ways that gladden the hearts of the Greeks: they feel *phthonos* towards success and hate those who are more powerful.'[5]

It is impossible to pursue the evidence for the development of *phthonos* in detail here, but I will explore some examples of the differences in nuance—the manipulation and formation of its cultural models—between and among genres and authors over time. In what follows, I want to draw attention to the ways in which *phthonos* and its cognates were used rhetorically, first in praise poetry of the sixth/fifth centuries BCE, and then in forensic oratory of the fourth century BCE. I have chosen these examples because their juxtaposition creates some illuminating contrasts, including form, genre, and context of composition. In both studies, it can be seen how, '*phthonos* talk' offered a potent force for the negotiation of significant social dynamics; and how, as these dynamics changed over time, they prompted different narratives about *phthonos*. The final sections of this part of the book will be on the nature of the cultural institutions from which these diverse narratives emerged, and the supernatural context in which they operated.

ENVY AND PRAISE

Perhaps we should not be surprised to find that Pindar, a writer of praise poetry, also offers some useful insights into the nature of *phthonos* and its role in community relationships. Carey has pointed out how the possibility of *phthonos* is a rhetorical topos of the praise

---

[4] Lanzillotta (2010: 81) appears to be asserting this in his description of the sociological aspects of *phthonos*: 'a sort of existential proximity is necessary'; he draws on Hes. *Op.* 25–6.

[5] Any Greek: Hdt. 7.236.1; cf. also Hdt. 3.80.3, with further discussion on p. 77. Envy of friends: Aesch. *Ag.* 832–7.

poetry of Pindar and Bacchylides.[6] There is a startling plethora of forms of the term across the extant and fragmentary praise poems, from *phthonos* to *phthoneros* ('envious'), to *aphthonos* ('lack of envy'), and *aphthonetos* ('being without envy'). Whether these terms convey negative or positive reflections on human nature, they were selected with a 'conscious controlled artistry' and were intended to speak to an audience's concerns.[7] However, in exploring the ways that *phthonos* appears and is manipulated across Pindaric poetry we are not piecing together an intricate philosophical thesis. The range of its uses in these poems reveals a shared culture of ideas and feelings, and the ways in which diverse contexts and audiences might shape the careful creative choices being made.[8] Pindar presents a *phthonos* that is a crucial part of a distinctive cultural value system: at first sight it may seem a long way from everyday experiences of envy. But his insights quickly convey his audiences into the heart of the communities he describes, offering a complex and nuanced perspective on attitudes to *phthonos* and the network of relations within which it could develop; it provides modern readers with an almost programmatic view of this ancient emotion.

In general, *phthonos* is the unavoidable response of others to great achievements.[9] For example, in *Pythian* 1, addressed to Hiero of Syracuse, the poet explains how 'townsmen are grieved in their secret hearts | especially when they hear of others' successes'; in *Pythian* 7 we hear how the noble deeds of Megacles of Athens are met with *phthonos*; in *Olympian* 6 (for Hagesias of Syracuse) the poet makes a general statement about the *phthonos* accruing to those who 'drive first around the twelve-lap course' and are blessed with divine favour (*charis*).[10]

---

[6] Carey 2007: 203.
[7] Carey 1981: 4. For example, 'more generous', *Ol.* 2.94; 'ungrudging' *Ol.* 6.7; 'without stint', *Ol.* 11.7; or even 'an abundance', *Nem.* 3.9: these are all translations of forms of *aphthonetos*, and see also *Isth.* 5.24; cf. *Ol.* 13.5, where *aphthonetos* seems to translate as asking the god to be, literally, 'without *phthonos*'.
[8] As opposed to Bulman's (1992) systematic world view and complex association of concepts.
[9] Instead, when the event prompts an aspiration for things that are possible, other terms are used: for example, in *Ol.* 7.7 Pindar evokes in a few swift lines a prosperous man's flourishing home life that makes his friends 'jealous' (that is, *zalotos*) for his harmonious and well-chosen marriage.
[10] All translations in this section are from Race 1997a and b. Hiero: *Pyth.* 1.83–4; Megacles: *Pyth.* 7.18–19: this is possibly a reference to his ostracism; *Ol.* 6.74–7.

In contrast, but to the same point, he tells us that there are men whose achievements deserve praise that is given *me phthoneraisi*, that is, 'without begrudging it'.[11] In epinikian poetry, *phthonos* is the unavoidable fellow traveller of victory, but this is not to say that *phthonos* is simply 'the antithesis of victory' as one scholar has suggested.[12] Rather, it presents a closer, almost symbiotic phenomenon, which could be said to play a natural and even necessary role.[13] It appears at both the mortal and the divine levels, and Pindar presents himself, the poet, as standing in the front line in an ongoing and pervasive battle against it.[14]

To understand its significance we need to understand the cultural attitudes towards a successful individual, his place in a community—and the risks attendant on holding such a position. On the one hand, for the city, the success of a local athlete was a glorious thing. On the other, the enhanced status of the athlete separated him from his community, not only in terms of his physical location, but also in terms of his sense of himself and his limits.[15] Some approaches have focused on the more supernatural aspects of the risks involved: success in the games could be viewed as superhuman, and indeed the heroization of historical athletes was not unknown.[16] But as other sources remind us, there was marked ambivalence around such a phenomenon: the relevant myths tend to be accounts of complicated and painful relations between community and individual, in which the athlete in life or death punishes his fellow citizens for their behaviour towards him, and is then appeased with cult.[17] And to

---

[11] Pind. *Isth.* 1.41–5.

[12] Crotty (1982: 7) in discussion of Pind. *Pyth.* 2 argues that 'it sets on its head everything which makes victory good and desirable'.

[13] Scholiast on *Ol.* 6.6–7 agrees: τοῦτο δὲ προστίθησιν ἐπειδὴ οἵ πολῖται κατὰ φύσιν ἀλλήλοις φθονοῦσιν (see Boeke 2007: 88 n. 157, citing Bulman 1992: 87 n. 51).

[14] It is rather surprising to read (Kurke 2013: 175), 'Generally though, if such tensions exist in the community, the poet does not reveal them. Instead, his is a picture of complete harmony, between the individual and his family and between the family and the polis.'

[15] Crotty (1982: 107) describes how the journey to the games was a journey out of the community, 'not only in a spatial but a moral sense as well'.

[16] Fontenrose 1968, Currie 2005, Hornblower and Morgan 2007: 25. Redfield (2003: 95) has observed how particular individuals—oikists, lawgivers, and athletes—are separated from their community by a particular status, and not reintegrated. Hornblower discusses these categories in the context of heroization, and adds the element of healing, in the sense that, as heroes, all three may acquire healing powers.

[17] Crotty (1982: 122–4) gives stories of returned athletes who are rejected by their communities. These include Oebatas of Dyme (Paus. 6.3.8; 7.17.6–7), Cleomedes of Astypalaia (Paus. 6.9.6–8), and Euthycles of Lokri (Callim. frr. 84–85 Pfeiffer). Crotty

seek any kind of heroization for oneself was, of course, to claim more than one's mortal status; Pindar himself warns against this: 'Do not seek to become Zeus; you have all there is, if a share of these blessings should come to you. Mortal things befit mortals.'[18]

More mundane ambitions also presented risks. Leslie Kurke has drawn attention to the ways in which Pindar carefully manipulates the victories of individuals and the associated *megaloprepeia* ('lavish public expenditure'), a quality that if taken too far, could indicate a tyrannous intent. She argues that Pindar represents it not only as a personal, aristocratic achievement but also a civic benefaction, drawing it into the rhetoric of civic and personal gift exchange.[19] In Pindar's poems, the fear that a returning athlete might overreach his political status is not stated explicitly (and, in a number of cases, where the poem's honorand is already in such a position of power, this sentiment would be irrelevant). Nevertheless, the topos remains, traceable in the encouragement the poet offers to his subjects that their displays of wealth and power should be tempered with virtue, wisdom, and self-control.[20] In response, as Pindar himself repeatedly observes, this kind of behaviour will garner the kind of praise that the victory deserves—praise that he, the poet, is instrumental in shaping, praise that encompasses both individual and community.[21]

This brings us to the risks attendant on a victory from the point of view of the athlete. Not only is there the possibility of failure, but

---

(*ibid.* 129) notes the ambivalence of rejection—how what is judged to be 'bestial' (and therefore rejected) may be later lauded for its superhuman nature.

[18] *Isth.* 5.14-15: μὴ μάτευε Ζεὺς γενέσθαι· πάντ' ἔχεις, | εἴ σε τούτων μοῖρ' ἐφίκοιτο καλῶν. θνατὰ θνατοῖσι πρέπει; see also *Isth.* 4.12, *Pyth.* 10.29-30, *Ol.* 3.44-5, 9.27-39, *Nem.* 3.19-22.

[19] As Kurke (2013: 149) notes: 'Pindar can represent athletic victory within the closed circuit of aristocratic gift exchange. On the other hand, victory at the games can be located within the public sphere of *megaloprepeia*, as a common benefaction bestowed on the city by the victor.' She compares (2013: 159ff.) the ideology of *megaloprepeia* expressed across the poems of Pindar with that in evidence for Athens (e.g. Thucydides' depiction of Alcibiades' presentation of his achievements to the Athenians, where he describes his athletic successes both in terms of their meaning to himself and his family, and as bringing glory to the city and its inhabitants: Thuc. 6.12 and 16.3-6). See also Plut. *Nic.* 3.1-3; Lys. 21.1-5 and 25.12-13; and cf. discussion in Pl. *Resp.* 560d8-561a8. As Kurke observes, modern scholarship on *megaloprepeia* is plentiful (see for example, Ober 1989: 199-247, Whitehead 1983, with further references in Kurke 2013: 149 n. 20), but little applied to Pindar.

[20] *Pyth.* 5.1-4, 11.50-8; *Ol.* 2.53-6; *Nem.* 3.70-5. See the hint to Hiero at *Ol.* 1.99-100, and Thero, *Ol.* 2.5-7.

[21] *Isth.* 3.6-7: the debtors who must respond with hymns.

there is the potential for a success not to be recognized, for there to be no *kleos* ('good report') for the victor and, as importantly, for his family.[22] Kurke has explored the larger economy of *kleos*, and what she calls its 'inevitable entropy', which she sees arising from the impact of a largely oral culture on the collective memory. As a result, 'even while the integrity of the house requires spatial and temporal continuity, it also necessitates the continual renewal of the family's achievements by each new generation'.[23] The essential need for achievements to be recognized is apparent throughout Pindar's poems. Men are known and judged by the reputation that follows them, and if glory is silenced then 'a noble deed dies'[24]: praise for deeds that deserve them is just, something that Zeus himself might take care of.[25]

Thus, the praise expressed with and within epinikian poetry can be seen to be part of a larger social, even cosmological, system of exchange between individual and community: each party has its office.[26] It not only ensures that both parties receive the recognition they deserve, thus achieving harmony, but it reaches into the very personhood of the individuals involved and the structure of the community in which they live and will die.[27] As the poems themselves indicate, *epinikia* of the kind Pindar writes may themselves provide *kleos*. But they are also intended to help elicit recognition and praise from within the community, smoothing the successful athlete's return.[28] The journey home, the welcome back, were far more significant than a simple celebration: they were part of an individual's restoration, setting him back into a political and mortal community he had briefly left behind. The poet and his work play a key role in easing that transition, in highlighting the roles and activities to be performed that would keep both the system of reciprocal exchange and community dynamics well oiled with praise and favours. In a

---

[22] Pind. fr. 94a (Maehler).   [23] Kurke 2013: 18, with n. 10.
[24] *Pyth.* 1.98–101; fr. 121 (Maehler).   [25] *Nem.* 3.29, *Ol.* 7.89–90.
[26] Crotty (1982: 61–2) shows how Pindar's argument about the need for praise (and the need for people to give that praise) draws on Homeric sentiments (e.g. Hom. *Il.* 9.318–20: that the individual who achieves fine things must be praised, or else he suffers the same as the man who does nothing). In turn, 'without just praise, the community cannot fulfil its office of assuring individual *kleos*. It then ceases to be of any use... it offers nothing to distinguish itself from the state of nature.'
[27] Report goes even to the dead: see *Ol.* 8.74–84 and Kurke 2013: 58.
[28] e.g. *Ol.* 11.7.

number of places Pindar explicitly notes his role as a 'shepherd' of the words of renown that follow hymns of praise, and he sets his own praise beside that of the community.[29]

But praise poetry also reveals to us the weak points in this system. On the one hand, the returning victor may have ambitions; on the other, the members of the community, far from being passive recipients, could also exhibit disruptive behaviours and emotions. And chief among them, as described by Pindar, was *phthonos*. The term and its cognates are used, on the one hand, to evoke their opposite, referring to the giving of 'ungrudging' praise: the townsmen of Hagesias are asked to be unreserved in such a context (*aphthonon aston*); praise of Hagesidamus opens with a description of 'praise without stint' (*apthonetos d'ainos*) for Olympic victors; in the hymn for Herodotus of Thebes, the poet announces, 'it is necessary to give praise to those who deserve it with no begrudging thoughts' (*me phthoneraisi . . . gnomais*); and, while praising Phylacidas of Aegina, he instructs his audience, 'if someone has entered into the clear road of divinely granted deeds, do not grudge (*me phthonei*) to blend into your song a fitting vaunt in return for toils'; finally, for Aristoclidas of Aegina, he asks from the muse herself that he be granted 'an abundance (*aphthonian*) [of song]'.[30] This pattern of recognition of and reciprocity for victory, which underpins Pindar's poetry, includes only one example in which encouragement to be ungrudgingly generous is directed at a victor—the tyrant Thero.[31] In all other cases Pindar uses these concepts to discuss the attitudes and behaviours of the townsfolk, those receiving the victor and giving praise, including, of course, himself. In turn, for *phthonos* in, as it were, its positive sense, we learn of its prevalence: for those who are successful it is impossible to escape;[32] for those who are not successful, it is almost inevitable that they will feel it towards those who are.[33] Those on the

---

[29] *Ol.* 11.8–9, *Pyth.* 5.108–15.

[30] Hagesias, *Ol.* 6.6; Hagesidamus, *Ol.* 11.7; Herodotus, *Isth.* 1.43–5; Phylacidas of Aegina, *Isth.* 5.22–5; Aristoclidas of Aegina, *Nem.* 3.9.

[31] *Ol.* 2.94: a man more generous—Thero.

[32] *Parth.* 1.8: 'upon every man lies *phthonos* for his achievement'; *Pyth.* 7.18–19: 'but this grieves me, | that *phthonos* requites your noble deeds'; *Isth.* 2.43 '*phthonetic* hopes hang about the minds of mortals'; fr. 94a (Maehler) '*phthonos* attaches to every excellent quality a man possesses'. (And see p. 115, n. 73 for discussion of *Pyth.* 11.54–8.)

[33] *Pyth.* 1.81–3: 'and townsmen (*aston*) are grieved in their secret hearts | especially when they hear of others' successes.'

receiving end of this emotion include, in particular, the athletes for whom Pindar is writing, men like Hagesias of Syracuse, who drive 'first around the twelve-lap course', and, on whom '*Charis* sheds a glorious appearance'.[34] *Phthonos* is perceived to be a part of the nexus of dynamics between an individual and his fellows: after all, *politai* are the last people to recognize a glorious achievement.[35]

But alongside this vision of *phthonos* produced by athletic victory, Pindar also gives us a glimpse into the broader life of this emotion. It is not just male victors who risk exposure to this most virulent of emotions; *phthonos* reaches into all parts of the adult community. In his poem for Thrasydaeus, Pindar vividly evokes the gossip that follows young wives, his questions about the reasons for Clytemnestra's behaviour mimicking its spiteful speculations.[36] Moreover, not only does *phthonos* for individuals arise from the wider community, but it also lurks at the heart of the family itself. In a *Paean* written for the Abderites, Pindar notes how 'hate-mongering *phthonos* | has now disappeared | for those who died long ago', but the next line suggests that the *phthonos* arises from within the family rather than the community: 'a man must give his forefathers | their due portion of ample glory'.[37] The juxtaposition of these lines suggests that those who might have felt *phthonos* do not, but this is only because of the passage of time, and the fact of death.[38] Similarly, the dangers threatened by a lack of recognition between father and son is suggested by Pindar's urging at the end of *Isthmian* 2 that 'the son never keep silent his father's excellence'.[39] And *Isthmian* 7 may offer another example of the potential for this danger by celebrating its opposite. Written to

---

[34] *Ol.* 6.73-7.
[35] *Ol.* 5.15-16: those who strive are recognized 'even by their fellow citizens'. Kurke (2013: 175) notes that Stoddart (1990: 24) takes this to be a Pindaric 'joke' on the topos of envy. Whether it is or not, it alludes to a common understanding of civic relations.
[36] *Pyth.* 11.22-9. On the meaning of l. 30, see Hubbard 1990.
[37] *Paean* 2.50-8.
[38] Rutherford (2001: 270) interprets these lines in a similar way but reads this reflection on envy as serving 'a double function: (i) it refers to the bad political situation in the past (in which case the envy is that felt by different groups of ancestors for each other); and (ii) it serves as a foil for the following exhortation to praise (in which case it is the envy of present and future generations for their ancestors). He observes (n. 36) that Pindar may intend both meanings at once.
[39] *Isth.* 2.43.

honour Strepsiades of Thebes for his victory in the Pancration, the poem focuses on his uncle, also called Strepsiades, who died in battle. In this poem we see, perhaps, reciprocity of the gift of recognition, and the confirmation of its importance within the family, as well as the community. As Pindar says: 'But the ancient | splendour sleeps; and mortals forget | what does not attain poetic wisdom's choice pinnacle, | yoked to glorious streams of verses.'[40] Finally, a fragment raises interesting questions of interpretation in this context: ὁ γὰρ ἐξ οἴκου ποτὶ μῶμον ἔπαινος κίρναται.[41] It has been argued that this must mean 'self-praise or partisan praise is no praise at all or worse'. But there is another possibility, supported by the material above, that this is neither an observation about the general relationship of praise and blame, nor a comment on the interaction between an individual family and the surrounding community. Instead, it refers to emotional reactions to success from within a family.[42]

But why and how is *phthonos* so powerful? When Pindar evokes the sensation of being the recipient of *phthonos*, he describes it in physical terms, as like being struck with a rough stone. The imagery suggests the punishment of stoning and ideas of retribution that arise from within the community without judicial intervention.[43] *Phthonos* is thus not only associated with ideas of impulsive grassroots justice, but also implicated as a cause of death.[44] Indeed, as we will see, it becomes apparent from the poems that *phthonos* can cause just such

---

[40] *Isth.* 7.16–19: ἀλλὰ παλαιὰ γὰρ | εὕδει χάρις, ἀμνάμονες δὲ βροτοί, | ὅ τι μὴ σοφίας ἄωτον ἄκρον | κλυταῖς ἐπέων ῥοαῖσιν ἐξίκηται ζυγέν·. See Kurke (2013: 66), who sees this as referring back to Thebes, but also ahead to the family of the two Strepsiadai, and notes 'the reciprocal exchange of good offices between ancestors and descendants' also in *Ol.* 8 and *Pyth.* 5. In *Ol.* 10.86–94 the imagery of familial descent is used to describe the role of song and its relationship to achievement and *kleos* (Kurke 2013: 77).

[41] Pind. fr. 181 (Maehler).

[42] Kirkwood argues for the first interpretation (1984: 21–2) against Nagy (1979), who gives 'for praise is by nature mixed with blame'. Kurke summarizes (2013: 76): since praise is part of an exchange system, the house that produces the achievement cannot then produce its own praise, which must come from outside. The fragment is included in the scholia to *Nem.* 7.61–3, which describes how a 'guest-friend' creates praise and holds back blame. Kurke sees this as the poet drawing on networks of *xenia* among the dark households; this is surely part of the image, but it is also a statement made by the poet, emphasizing his key role in creating *kleos*.

[43] On stoning as a form of popular justice, see Rosivach 1987 and Forsdyke 2008.

[44] *Ol.* 8.54–61: 'But if I have recounted in my hymn Melesias' glory gained from beardless youths, | let no ill will cast a rough stone at me, | because I will likewise declare | a glory of this sort at Nemea too, | and the one gained thereafter in the men's bouts | of the pancratium. Truly teaching is easier for one | who knows, and it is

Narratives of Phthonos

damage to one's presence and person in the community, although not necessarily through physical means.

Talking and Not Talking

Pindar reveals not just the sensations associated with *phthonos*, but some of the ways in which it was perceived to operate within a community. It is described as working in two ways, which are often found together. As we might expect, bearing in mind our source, these play out through the game of words and the world of talk. On the one hand, *phthonos* may lead to the repression of the achievements of an individual, and therefore prevent the correct allocation of glory; on the other, it may provoke attributions of blame against the victim, and the spreading of lies about him or her. One of the most poignant examples of *phthonos* operating in both directions is depicted in *Nemean* 8. This refers to the story of how Ajax was driven to his death, in effect by the lies of the Greeks, who favoured Odysseus and awarded the armour of Achilles to him rather than Ajax. Pindar compares the physical wounds that the Greeks were able to inflict on their enemies to the wounds they caused Ajax with their 'hateful deception that existed long ago'. Ajax, dead, cannot speak for himself: the great warrior's glory is silenced, his reputation destroyed by gossip.[45] Another mythical scene provides a further example. Clytemnestra's murder of Agamemnon becomes a scenario in which the dynamics of *phthonos* play out, in both the envy of young brides (as we have seen already) and the *phthonos* that attaches to men of more than 'low ambition', like Agamemnon.[46] A final example comes with a twist, since this time Pindar deliberately rewrites the myth to make his point. Rather than the usual story—that Tantalus tried to trick the gods by serving them his own son—Pindar recounts how the disappearance of Pelops, stolen by Poseidon who had fallen in love with him, provides fodder for gossip of the neighbours. It was they who spread the rumour that Pelops' mother had cut him up, boiled him,

---

foolish not to have learned in advance, | for less weighty are the minds of men without experience.'

[45] *Nem.* 8.33; see further Crotty 1980.
[46] *Pyth.* 11.29–30: ἴσχει τε γὰρ ὄλβος οὐ μείονα φθόνον· | ὁ δὲ χαμηλὰ πνέων ἄφαντον βρέμει. (I interpret l. 30, following Hubbard (1990), as referring to the poor and envious man.)

and served him for dinner.[47] By presenting the generally accepted myth as a result of malicious talk, Pindar demonstrates how powerful such slander is, and how those who are blessed by the gods are always at the mercy of those who spread it. But these events are not limited to myth, as Pindar notes incidentally in a famous phrase, *kakologoi de politai* ('For townsmen are scandalmongers').[48] And so he illustrates, with vivid evocations of real-world situations, how even mythical individuals react to their neighbours' fortune or misfortune with *phthonos* and evil talk. And the same is true for his clients: for example, the kind of success that Hagesias of Syracuse has enjoyed is likely to meet with *momos* ('blame') coming from those who feel *phthonos*.[49] An elaborate, circumspect warning for Hiero creates a link between talking too much (about one's own successes) and stirring up *phthonos*, which links to slander.[50] Finally, we see the rarity of a neighbour who minds his own business, when Pindar announces how, 'If man has any enjoyment | of his fellow man, I would say that a neighbour who loved | his neighbour with fixed purpose is a joy to him worth | everything.'[51]

The slanderer's stories are described as ὄψον δὲ λόγοι φθονεροῖσιν: that is, for those who feel *phthonos*, they are a treat to be savoured, to be rolled around the tongue.[52] Nevertheless, the image of the *phthonetic* man that Pindar evokes is one of isolation, perfectly capturing the sterile, obsessive, and ineffectual thoughts associated with this emotion: 'Another man, *with phthonos* in his eye, rolls an empty thought in the dark that falls to the ground'.[53] The obsessive, unremitting nature of this kind of thinking means that even the unpredictability of fortune is not a comfort for those who feel this emotion.[54] In contrast to the praise poetry that Pindar himself creates, *phthonos* and the slander associated with it are conducted in secret, whispered, a benefit neither to those who spread the slander nor to those who receive it, dependent on the company of men who are bad by nature.[55] Slanderers cannot flourish among good men;

---

[47] *Ol.* 1.47–51.   [48] *Pyth.* 11.29.   [49] *Ol.* 6.74–7.   [50] *Pyth.* 1.81–3.
[51] *Nem.* 7.86–9. Crotty (1982: 134–5) on *geuetai* (translated here as 'having enjoyment of'), as 'coming to know someone through particular social institutions, closely associated with the trial of others' character of strength'; as he notes, it can be used to mean trial in battle (Hom. *Il.* 21.60–3), but in the *Odyssey* it is also used in contexts of literal 'tasting'; see Hom. *Od.* 17.411–13, 20.178ff., 21.98, 22.8–14.
[52] *Nem.* 8.21.   [53] *Nem.* 4.39–40.   [54] *Pyth.* 2.89–91.
[55] *Pyth.* 2.75–7, and 81–2. Most (1985: 111 and 112 n. 79) notes how 'the general moral tenor of this passage suggests the inadvisability of confining the reference of *oi*

indeed, they often end up impoverished.[56] An example of this thinking occurs at the end of *Pythian* 4, in Pindar's final plea for the ruler Arcesilaus to take back Damophilus, a young Cyrenean who had been exiled. One of the virtues that Pindar highlights is Damophilus' capacity to oppose violent acts and nasty talk: he 'deprives a malicious tongue of its shining voice | and has learned to hate the person who is violent'.[57] In *Pythian* 2, Pindar portrays the slanderer as a fox, and himself, in turn, as a wolf, chasing the fox, who 'fawns on all and weaves his utter ruin', one of a series of images that sets up the poet and his work as being on the offensive against this kind of language.[58] Elsewhere, he keeps away dark blame, and brings praise like streams of water;[59] he is water against smoke;[60] the visible and bobbing cork of the nets, rather than the weights, labouring in the depths of the sea;[61] or he is like an athlete himself, making great efforts, taking on these many risks.[62]

Poetic Strategies, Poet's Strategy

Thus, as Leslie Kurke has persuasively argued, these poems map the dynamics of a system of reciprocity that may both comprise and help to negotiate the challenges presented by the return of a victor. She sets it in the turbulence of a society moving from a pre-monetary to a monetary economy, and makes the compelling suggestion that this enables the use of 'many different, even competing, symbolic systems and ideologies', a number of them drawing on different models of exchange.[63] Kurke argues that the 'poet's strategy to allay the envy of

---

agathoi too strictly to the nobility, cf. *kakagorian* 53, *ariston* 56, *kalos* 72–3, *kakon* 76, *agathois* 96'. See also *Ol.* 1.47, *Nem.* 8.26.

[56] *Ol.* 1.53.   [57] *Pyth.* 4.283–4.

[58] Fox and wolf: see *Pyth.* 2.81–2. Goldhill 1991: 141, where he cites Lefkowitz (1980: 42): 'the poet in speaking the truth portrays himself as a combatant'.

[59] *Nem.* 7.61–2.

[60] *Nem.* 1.24: as Carey (1981: 113) notes, smoke has a number of associations with undesirable emotions, such as anger (Hom. *Il.* 18.110), *phthonos* (Plut. *An seni* 787c, *Prae. ger. reip.* 804d), or bad governance (e.g. incipient tyranny, Alc. 74).

[61] *Pyth.* 2.78–80: see Most 1985: 108–9.

[62] See Crotty (1982: 137) on *Nem.* 7.64–74, who also makes the point about risk; Pindar compares songs to the pentathlon. He defines himself in contrast to those poets who have been deceptive in *Nem.* 7. His insistence on his good will here and the comparison to athletes is not unusual, but receives unusual emphasis.

[63] Kurke 2013: 226.

the victor's fellow citizens is to include them emphatically, both in the poem as paradigm of *megaloprepeia* and in the victory itself'.[64] As Kurke has shown, these processes of inclusion consist of integrating myths of landscape, cities, and peoples into the poems; associating the origin of a victor with more general praise of his city of origin and its inhabitants; and encouraging and developing a shared celebration of the victory and its victor, as we have seen above.[65] But the nature and extent of inclusion in the victory itself or the glory arising from it is far from straightforward; nor is it clear-cut just how such an approach might relate to the presence of *phthonos*, especially when praise itself may feed this dread emotion.[66]

It is essential for Pindar's purposes that the two parties—the victor and the city (and its inhabitants) to which he returns—while related, remain distinct, each fulfilling the particular roles that maintain their relationship. On the one hand, he highlights the choice that a successful individual makes to share his glory with his city.[67] On the other, any glory that the individual will enjoy turns on the choices that the city and its inhabitants make to offer praise and celebration of the victor and his success.[68] Thus, in *Olympian* 5.1-7 (in honour of Psaumis), the reciprocal relationship between city and victor is described—both the gift of the victor to his city and the request for a celebratory reception of the victor by the city:

Ὑψηλᾶν ἀρετᾶν καὶ στεφάνων ἄωτον γλυκύν
τῶν Οὐλυμπίᾳ, Ὠκεανοῦ θύγατερ, καρδίᾳ γελανεῖ
ἀκαμαντόποδός τ' ἀπήνας δέκευ Ψαυμιός τε δῶρα·
ὅς τὰν σὰν πόλιν αὔξων, Καμάρινα, λαοτρόφον,
βωμοὺς ἓξ διδύμους ἐγέραρεν ἑορταῖς θεῶν μεγίσταις
ὑπὸ βουθυσίαις ἀέθλων τε πεμπαμέροις ἁμίλλαις,
ἵπποις ἡμιόνοις τε μοναμπυκίᾳ τε.

---

[64] Kurke 2013: 170 and 173: Pindar's poetry aims at 'merging' the *oikos* of the victor and polis, although elsewhere this image is less strong, e.g. the statement that Pindar 'skilfully assimilated the interests of these two spheres' (6).

[65] Kurke 2013: 170: e.g. *Ol.* 13, 19.97-9, *Nem.* 10 (examples are myriad).

[66] e.g. *Ol.* 2.95-8, *Pyth.* 1.42-5, *Nem.* 8.20-2.

[67] e.g. in *Nem.* 5.4-5 and 7-8 Pindar notes how 'Pytheas | has won the crown for the pancratium in Nemea's games... and he has glorified the Aiakidai, heroic warriors... and his mother city'; in *Ol.*4.8-12 we find Psaumis, 'crowned with Pisan olive, is eager to arouse glory for Kamarina'; while in *Isth.* 1.64-7, Herodotus brings honour to seven-gated Thebes. See also *Nem.* 4.12-13, where Timasarchos of Aegina brings 'a wreath of crowns'.

[68] In *Nem.* 4.11, the poet asks that the victory be received by the city; in *Pyth.* 12.4-6 the city of Akragas is asked explicitly by the poet to receive the crowns of the victor.

Daughter of Ocean [Kamarina], with a glad heart receive this finest | sweet reward for lofty deeds and crowns won at Olympia, | gifts of the tirelessly running mule car and of Psaumis, | who, exalting your people-nourishing city, Kamarina, | honoured the six double altars at the gods' greatest festival | with sacrifices of oxen and the five days of athletic contests | with chariots, mules and single-horse racing.

Victor and city are separate, and each receives instruction about appropriate behaviour towards the other. The care with which such relationships are presented suggests some of the difficulties that were perceived as likely to be involved.[69] Similarly, when at the end of *Olympian* 7, we see that 'at the celebrations of the Eratidai | the city too holds festivals' the 'too' (*kai*) is important because of its acknowledgement of difference and of the potential for that difference to become tension.[70] Pindar's following and final line, 'But in a single portion of time | the winds shift rapidly now here, now there,' is an image that implicitly evokes such potential.[71]

The reassurance Pindar gives that the glory accruing to an individual will also have significance for his city may ameliorate certain bad feelings, in particular, concern about the political ambitions of an individual.[72] However, as a strategy for defusing *phthonos*, this approach can only ever be partly successful.[73] As noted earlier in this

---

[69] See also *Isth.*1: both the community and the victor must make sure they play their part. Similarly, *Ol.* 7 opens with an address to Rhodes and describes the victor and his father as 'members of Herakles' mighty race', bathing the reader/audience in the warm glow of mythical digression. But as the poem moves towards its close, it reminds the audience that the victories that this poem celebrates are Diagoras' alone, and they are listed at some length (80–5); the poem ends with a plea to Zeus that the victor be granted 'respectful favour | from both townsmen and foreigners' on the grounds that he 'abhors insolence'; while the very last lines mention the separate celebrations held by the victor's clan and the city. Kurke (2013: 173) uses this example in her argument that Pindar 'succeeds in merging the oikos and polis through the narration of foundation myths'; she does not discuss the end of the poem.

[70] *Ol.* 7.93–4: Ἐρατιδᾶν τοι σὺν χαρίτεσσιν | ἔχει θαλίας καὶ πόλις

[71] Cf. Kurke (2013: 170), who sees the *kai* as an acknowledgement of the tensions or hostilities 'likely to exist'.

[72] Kurke (2013: 181–9) discusses *hubris*, *koros*, and fear of tyranny.

[73] *Pyth.* 11.54–8 appears to suggest that simply avoiding dire *hubris* can keep away the envious, but these lines are extremely corrupt. Kurke (2013: 188) argues, with Young (1968: 21), that the phrase 'the envious are warded off' (l. 54) should be taken as an apodosis to the following lines, which continue 'But if a man has won the peak | and dwelling there has avoided dire | insolence . . .', going on to talk about his noble death and provision of good name to his descendants. Her supporting examples (*Isth.* 3.1–3 and 5.21–5; *Nem.* 11.13–17) each describe how victors should avoid arrogance,

section, achievements generate *phthonos*.⁷⁴ Instead, in some of his *phthonos* narratives he offers some more direct advice, making it plain both how the emotion works and why it is to be despised.⁷⁵ In this context, his comments might be taken as directed towards those who might feel *phthonos*, suggesting that it is a desirable characteristic to be able to avoid it. He points out that this is not hard if one is *sophos*, 'wise', or that a 'good man' might have the means to praise a young victor; whereas *phthonos* is 'the companion of empty-minded men' (κενεοφρόνων ἑταῖρον ἀνδρῶν).⁷⁶ Similarly, he implicitly compares the behaviour of the *phthoneroi* with that of the tyrant, in so far as *phthonos* is explained as a result of not understanding mortal limits. In a difficult metaphor that appears to use the imagery of a measuring line or a plumb line, he argues that the man who feels *phthonos* hurts himself, because he does not understand either his own limits, or the fact that it is the gods that hand out favours, and that they do so unpredictably:

ἀλλ' οὐδὲ ταῦτα νόον
ἰαίνει φθονερῶν· στάθμας δέ τινος ἑλκόμενοι
περισσᾶς ἐνέπαξαν ἕλκος
ὀδυναρὸν ἐᾷ πρόσθε καρδίᾳ,
πρὶν ὅσα φροντίδι μητίονται τυχεῖν.

But not even that soothes the mind of those men who feel *phthonos*; by pulling, as it were, a measuring line too far, they fix a painful wound in their own hearts, before they gain all that they contrive in their thoughts.⁷⁷

and the first two link this to deserving (ungrudging) praise, which support the interpretation of ll. 55–8; while the last offers reflection on how those who achieve are still mortal, but should be praised. With this reading, these lines provide the only explicit instruction about how to avoid *phthonos*, which otherwise, the poems tend to imply, is inevitable for deeds that are admirable (e.g. *Pyth.* 7.18–19, *Parth.* 1.8). In contrast, others have read them as offering a more dire vision of the persistence of *phthonos* (see Race 1997a: 375): 'Those who feel *phthonos* fight back in their delusion. Who, having won the peak and dwelling there in peace avoids (their) dread insolence?' With this reading the apodosis is no longer reversed, and the death and good name of the next lines offer the achieving man some solace. However, even if the first reading is correct, this is not the same as saying that *phthonos* is destroyed through sharing an achievement: it is merely kept at a distance.

⁷⁴ See p. 104.
⁷⁵ *Contra* Kurke (2013: 193), who argues that he adopts a pose of pained resignation, giving as examples *Ol.* 6.74, *Pyth.* 7.19, and *Nem.* 8.21.
⁷⁶ As reported by Plutarch to be Pindar's comment on *phthonos* fr. 212 (Maehler), in Plut. *De inim. util.* 10.91f, and compare *Isth.* 1.41–6, *Nem.* 4.39–40.
⁷⁷ *Pyth.* 2.90–1. The metaphor is vivid but difficult. Gildersleeve (1885: *ad loc.*) offers the image of a measuring line with two sharp pegs; Most (1985: 119 and 1987)

In contrast, the poet sees clearly, and explains the way of the world: that the gods glorify some at one moment, and others the next.[78] To guide them through the baffling and obstacle-filled context that he depicts, Pindar offers his patrons and audience his own extraordinary talents. All this poisonous talk provides a setting for him to draw attention to the value of his poetry and an opportunity to advertise his own skills as both a creator of *kleos* and a warrior against rumour.[79] In the creation of reputation, he is anxious to emphasize, poetry can achieve what other forms of commemoration cannot.[80] But praise cannot be indiscriminate; it must be handled with care.[81] Words are powerful, and a successful individual must avoid too many of them—even at times be silent.[82] After all, as he admonishes himself, in his hymn to Epharmostus of Opous, 'boasting inappropriately sounds a note of madness'.[83]

Demonstrating excess or *koros* is linked by Pindar to *hubris* and, among many other hazards, it may lead in turn to *phthonos*—in the sense of both a hostile response from the audience and/or divine hostility.[84] Instead, as the opening of *Isthmian* 3 states, the right kind of behaviour for victors is very clear: 'If a man is successful, | either in glorious games | or with mighty wealth, and keeps down nagging

---

understands it as referring to a plumb line; Carey (1981: 61) offers a switch in metaphor, from measuring line to a wound from a spear or sword.

[78] *Pyth.* 2.89–90.

[79] As Mackie (2003: 20 n. 38) has observed, between epinikian and rumour, there is a 'complex and endlessly interactive relationship'; see her illuminating discussion (pp. 19–20) on the intersection between poetry, rumour, and reputation.

[80] He competes not only with other professionals, but also with other forms of commemoration, in particular statuary, as an anecdote by the scholiast to *Nem.* 5.1a illustrates: the Aeginetans choose a bronze statue rather than an ode as giving better value, and then change their minds; see Smith 2007: 92 and Thomas 2007: 149; also *Nem.* 6.28–30 and *Isth.* 2.44–6.

[81] *Ol.* 2.94.   [82] The need for silence: *Isth.* 1.63 and *Isth.* 5.51.

[83] *Ol.* 9.38–9.

[84] Dangers of overdoing it: for tyrants, *Pyth.* 1.82–4, *Ol.* 2.92–7; for others, *Ol.* 5.23–4, *Nem.* 8.19–21, *Pyth.* 3.59–60, 8.15 and 32, *Nem.* 10.20, and somewhat indirectly, *Isth.*1.62–3. Linked explicitly to *hubris*: *Ol.* 13.10. *Hubris* is here the mother of *koros*, which reverses the usual relationship. These concepts linked to *phthonos*: *Nem.* 8.19–21; or to a painful response: *Nem.* 10.20. See Mackie (2003: 16–19) for discussion of this theme as a 'break-off' in Pindar's poetry and Mackie (2003: 33–5) and Dickie (1984) on the ways in which Pindar urges the victor not to overreach himself. See also the story of Tantalus (*Ol.* 1.55–64), in which greed for more *olbos* ('happiness') becomes greed for the nectar and ambrosia of the gods, which he steals, and which leads to punishment from the gods; and compare the story of Ixion, *Pyth.* 2.24–9.

excess in his mind, | he deserves to be included in his townsmen's praises.'[85] In turn, for those who witness success, as *Pythian* 9 describes, it is essential 'to praise even one's enemy | wholeheartedly and justly when he performs noble deeds'.[86]

The poet steps in to offer his song as a mode of praise that ameliorates these complex issues of reception, while satisfying the needs of the victor, and making clear why and how this praise is necessary in the first place.[87] Across the odes, he underlines the need for a good reputation, now and into the future, as well as advising, guiding, and demonstrating just how he can help to build that reputation. In addition to offering praise himself, he leads citizens into celebration, and works to shape their everyday attitudes. He also demonstrates an understanding of, and works with, the 'things that are said', the everyday rumours that shape common understanding.[88]

In an environment filled with verbal risks, Pindar shows himself doing battle with two groups of slanderers who are named explicitly. These include not only the multitudes of envious fellow citizens, who bad-mouth and blame their victims, but also the professionals, specifically Archilochus, the seventh-century 'blame poet' or writer of *iambos* (what we might call 'epimomic' poetry).[89] Where the former

---

[85] *Isth.* 3.1–3.

[86] *Pyth.* 9.93–6: the quotation describes the behaviour of the old man of the sea, who commands that others do the same.

[87] Encouraging praise: *Isth.* 2.44–5; spreading the news: *Nem.* 5.2–6, 6.57b; the power of verse: *Pyth.* 3.114–15, *Nem.* 7.20–3; the need to hymn success: *Pyth.* 1.91–3, *Nem.* 7.11–13 and 9.6–7; fr. 121 'but a noble deed dies when left in silence', a plea to the gods not to keep the line of Diagoras of Rhodes in obscurity; *Ol.* 7.93–4.

[88] The poet's task: *Pyth.*10.57–60, *Nem.* 1.24, 8.21, 9.53–5; encouraging both victor's and citizens' righteous behaviour: *Ol.* 5.23–4, 6.72–4, 7.89–92, *Nem.* 11.13–16; *Isth.* 1.42–6, 2.37–42, 6.69–72; and encouraging citizen's celebration *Isth.* 7.20–3; *Nem.* 2.23–35, 5.40, 9.6–7, 11.17–21, *Ol.* 11.8–11, *Pyth.* 10.55–9. Now and into the future: *Ol.* 11.5–6, *Isth.* 4.37–45. Working with citizen gossip: *Pyth.* 5.108–15. Things 'that are said': *Isth.* 4.7–12, 6.24–5; *Ol.* 1.28–29 'I think, in men's talk | stories are embellished beyond the true account | and deceive by means of elaborate lies'; *Ol.* 7.11 'fortunate is the man who is held in good repute'. On Pindar's own refusal to lie, see p. 119, n. 91.

[89] I use the modern colloquial term 'bad-mouth' here and elsewhere in this study because it not only draws attention to the power of abusive and critical speech, but also the range of types of relevant speech acts, including and especially gossip or slander, which is a theme of this study; as such it seems to offer a helpful reflection of such ancient Greek terms as *kakologia* and cognates. For 'blame poet', see Kurke 2013: 88, with further discussion of the imagery of poetic resources, p. 101. *Pyth.* 2.82 may be a further reference to the genre of Archilochian 'blame' poetry. Pindar brings himself into the poem almost immediately afterwards: 'May I never have such a

group is criticized as empty-headed and deceitful, concealing their maliciousness, Archilochus is quite blatant in his hostile craft, offering a stark contrast with Pindar and his own work.[90] His presence in the poem illuminates Pindar's particular skills as a verbal warrior. His comments on Archilochus add to the emphasis he has already given to his own careful management of words, his measured use of affect, his refusal to lie.[91] Indeed, he scolds himself when his speculations about the gods appear to be going too far: 'But cast that story | away from me, my mouth! | For reviling the gods | is a hateful skill.'[92] *Phthoneroi* and Archilochus are connected through the imagery used to describe nasty talk, and it is worth examining this in some more detail, since here we find these activities embodied, through metaphors for the experience of giving and receiving gossip and abuse, and the evocation of the bodily sensations involved.

Bite, Feast, Gnash, and Fatten

Across the Pindaric corpus, there are a great many images concerned with links between perverse appetites, modes of eating, blame, and *phthonos*, which bring to mind the visual depictions of *phthonos* from later periods. For example, Archilochus is described as fattening himself on his hatred, which recalls the tasty morsel of hatred enjoyed by the *phthoneroi* in *Nemean* 8;[93] while the way in which this indiscriminate feeding leaves the malicious poet *en amachaniai* or 'resourceless' brings to mind the isolation of the man 'who rolls his empty thought in the dark that falls to the ground'.[94] The kind of censure that Archilochus employs has a bite *(dakos)* to it, which

---

disposition'—that is, to write such poetry. This poem also contains other Archilochian elements, such as animal imagery. For Archilochian blame poetry and Pindar, see Most 1985: 125–6.

[90] *Pyth.* 2.76–7.
[91] Careful measure: e.g. *Ol.* 13.43–50. Refusal to lie: *Ol.* 4.17, *Ol.* 13.52, *Nem.* 1.17–21; see discussion in Brown 2006.
[92] *Ol.* 9.35–9; the dangers here are linked with those of 'boasting' about oneself. The verb for reviling (*loidoresai*) appears only here in the *Odes*. The activity it describes, and the way it links to *phthonos* will be a point of discussion in section 2.4.
[93] *Pyth.* 2.55–6 and *Nem.* 8.21.
[94] *Pyth.* 2.55 and *Nem.* 4.39–40. For the idea that the feeding itself leaves the poet resourceless, see Steiner 2002: 305; others have argued that it represents his poetic sterility.

Pindar seeks to avoid, but it brings to mind the behaviour of *phthonos*, personified in the story of Ajax told by Pindar in *Nemean* 8, as it feasts on the body of the dead warrior, once it has 'rolled him onto his sword', and then consigns his real achievements to oblivion.[95] Failure behaves the same way. Those who were beaten by Aristomenes of Aegina in the wrestling match at the Pythian games of 446 BCE are described as 'shrinking home down alleyways... bitten by failure' (κατὰ λαύρας... | πτώσσοντι, συμφορᾷ δεδαγμένοι).[96] While at the end of *Olympian* 2, Pindar warns against those greedy men who, out of envy, praise a man's achievements to excess—and eclipse them.[97]

The poet is drawing on a set of associations between nasty eating habits—animalistic or even cannibalistic—and those who use invective, as depicted in lyric or epic poetry.[98] With this in mind, we can see that those who are described as gossiping about the fate of Pelops in *Olympian* 1, blaming Pelops' mother for his disappearance and accusing the gods of cannibalism, are invoking the very activities of which they would typically, as spreaders of malicious rumour, be understood to be guilty.[99] In fact, we could go a step further and argue that, through indulging in *phthonos*, they are themselves actually engaging in the cannibalistic activities that they describe, by, as it were, consuming their targets. This idea of *phthonos* as 'consuming' is found in later literature and iconography, vividly evoking the violence of the power of envy. For example, we have seen the description of the fall from grace suffered by Demetrius of Phaleron, who 'suffered eclipse through all-devouring *phthonos*'.[100] But importantly, it should be understood not just as consuming the victim of *phthonos*, but also the *phthoneros* himself.[101] One of the physical features of some of the later representations of the *phthoneros* is emaciation.[102] The earliest

---

[95] *Nem.* 8.23: κεῖνος καὶ Τελαμῶνος δάψεν υἱόν, | φασγάνῳ ἀμφικυλίσαις; *Pyth.* 2.53: δάκος... κακαγοριᾶν, 'bite of censure'.

[96] *Pyth.* 8.86–7.   [97] *Ol.* 2.95–8.

[98] See Nagy (1979: 226–7) and discussion by Steiner (2002: 300–1). The idea of biting and feasting may bring to mind, in turn, the 'gnashing jaws' of Euryale, the fearsome gorgon (younger sister of Medusa), whose killing is described in *Pyth.* 12.21—although in this instance she is wailing, not feeding.

[99] See Steiner 2002: 303–4.   [100] Diog. Laert. 5.76–7 (tr. Hicks 1925).

[101] Plut. *De rect. rat. aud.* 39e. Dunbabin and Dickie (1983) give a thorough analysis of the later evidence for the pain of the individual afflicted by *phthonos*.

[102] e.g. as a characteristic of a group of Hellenistic-Roman terracottas (perhaps particularly those from Smyrna); see *LIMC* 8.1 *Phthonos* 1–9 (993). Dunbabin and Dickie (1983: 20–1) explain that previous work on these figurines identified them as 'a

literary description of *Phthonos* with this feature appears in Menander, but it was also, apparently, one of the characteristics of the figure's earliest known depiction by the fourth-century painter Apelles, who, according to Lucian, painted *Phthonos* leading *Diabole* (an image to which we will return).[103]

Viewed like this, *phthonos* and the associated activity of blaming can be seen as a very violent set of behaviours. Were there specific situations in which such behaviour was particularly feared? Glenn Most has suggested that these references to *phthonos* were written for individuals who were, because of their context, exposed to 'a situation of exceptional political instability and unrest'—and he gives as examples of the former, the Athenian tyrants;[104] and of the latter, Aegina[105] and Thebes.[106] References to *phthonos* also occur in the odes written for the Sicilian tyrants where it shows some distinctive characteristics. For example, in contrast to its usual functions of repressing or eclipsing achievements with lies, *phthonos* against the tyrant Thero plays out in people talking too much—and thus obscuring his reputation.[107]

Nevertheless, this explanation of *phthonos* as a symptom of political instability is not wholly satisfactory. Although there seem to be many references to *phthonos* in odes for Aeginetan victors, this may be because there are a number of these odes (Pindar wrote eleven poems for Aeginetan victors, some of them concerning the same families as those poems mentioning *phthonos*). With that in mind, it is perhaps more striking that only half of these have references to *phthonos*. Moreover, the political explanation risks eliding a number of distinctive aspects of the Aeginetan odes themselves, as well as the historical context, which might lead to different explanations. In

---

rendering of a tubercular subject suffering from a respiratory spasm'; see also the bronze statuette, *LIMC* 8.1 *Phthonos* 10 (993); and in literary descriptions, e.g. Joh. Chrys. *In 2 Cor. Hom.* 27.3 (*PG* 61.587). Other physical characteristics include exaggerated body parts, and hands grasping the throat along with other features suggesting choking. However, it is important to note that these characteristics are not consistently applied: there are a number of representations of *Phthonos* as a handsome young man (see, for example, *LIMC* 8.1. *Phthonos* 11, 16, 21 and 22, and 26).

[103] Men. fr. 761 K-A; Luc. *Cal.* 5.
[104] *Ol.* 1.47, 2.94, 6.7, and 74, *Pyth.* 1.85, 2.90, 3.71, and *Isth.* 2.43.
[105] *Ol.* 8.55, *Pyth.* 8.72, *Nem.* 3.9, 4.39, 8.21, and *Isth.* 5.24.
[106] *Pyth.* 11.29 and 54; *Isth.* 1.44 and 7.39; see Most 2003: 135.
[107] *Ol.* 2.96–100.

particular, the careful acknowledgement of the achievements of family members other than the victors themselves reminds us that *phthonos* was also possible between family members. Of the appearances of *phthonos* listed by Most, the majority seem to have little reference to the political atmosphere. Among them, we find a plea that the poet himself not be a victim, which has been read as referring to the poet's embarrassment, disgust, or defiance at mentioning an Athenian trainer; others see it as a rhetorical marker, the 'artfully negated form' of in effect announcing a shift in topic—'Watch me now!'[108] This leaves two very striking descriptions of *phthonos*: the consumption of Ajax, discussed in *Nemean* 8, and the vivid image of the envious man and his empty thoughts in *Nemean* 4. The latter image seems most likely to be a way for Pindar to highlight the power of his own poetic offering, in contrast to the ineffectual words of the envious man (ll. 39–40).[109] In contrast, the poignant tale of Ajax reverses this dynamic: lies becomes powerful, and the good man is swallowed by silence. This could be a powerful commentary on the kinds of trouble that a community split by political differences might suffer.[110] However, its setting in the poem suggests a different emphasis: it follows discussion of the achievements of the victor's father, Megas. It illustrates how praise excites *phthonos*, and offers reflection on the responsibility of the living towards the dead; the role of right speech and the dangers of silence; and the poet's own choice of poetic form and style.[111]

Similarly, the argument that the three poems for Theban victors in which *phthonos* is mentioned all concern situations of instability and unrest is hard to maintain when we look more closely at the examples adduced in support. These include, first, a reference to Herodotus of Thebes' father, which may refer to his exile or that he had fought for the Persians at Plataea;[112] second, mention of the uncle of Strepsiades, also called Strepsiades, who fell in battle—and to whom the victor has

---

[108] *Ol.* 8.55, as Burnett 2005: 216.
[109] The plots lurking in the water (l. 36) mentioned just before the *phthonetic* man have been taken as referring to specific enemies; but more recent scholarship suggests it refers to any poet who cannot brave these dangers as Pindar does (see Burnett 2005: 125).
[110] The date of the poem is unknown, which makes it more difficult to speculate about what these events might be.
[111] See *Nem.* 7.64–9; use of silence, see this section, n. 87.
[112] *Isth.* 1.32–8.

dedicated part of his crown, while Pindar praises him for defending his 'dear country', all of which scarcely suggest current political instability;[113] and, finally, *Pythian* 11 for Thrasydaeus of Thebes, in which Pindar praises a city where 'I find the middle estate flourishing'.[114] This latter sentiment has been read in a number of different ways over the years (e.g. as a personal apology for Pindar's own involvement with the Sicilian tyrants, as a rejection of tyrannical behaviour, or of Athens), but most recently it has been seen as part of a tradition of admonition against the arrogance of athletes, which could be seen as 'quasi-tyrannical'.[115] It might, as we have seen, carry the potential to be politically dangerous, but, as Chris Carey indicates, we should not exaggerate this connection—and, besides, it is hardly in evidence here.[116] These latter references do not seem to indicate a situation of political instability and unrest; rather, they offer comment on or describe the kinds of social dynamics that might beset those who are politically involved or prominent, or both.

Of the individual poems, the ode written for Athenian Megacles, who was exiled by ostracism before his victory, does refer to a political event. But this raises questions about what we mean by 'political unrest', since this was, after all, a process intended to pre-empt such troubles.[117] That political instability might provide the context for the ode to Hippocleas of Thessaly is possible, since the poem was commissioned by one of the ruling families of Thessaly, and it seems true that there was increasing rivalry between elite families during the fifth century.[118] However, the reference to *phthonos* in this poem is not to mortal *phthonos*, but part of a wish that the boy athlete, so successful up to now, not encounter divine *phthonos*. As Most points out, there are also three other poems that reference *phthonos*, with no such politically unstable context: these were written for, respectively, a Rhodian, a victor from Epizephyrian Lokri, and Xenophon of Corinth.[119] In turn, there are poems that concern *stasis* but do not mention *phthonos*: for example, *Olympian* 12, which hymns

---

[113] *Isth.* 7.23–5.   [114] *Pyth.* 11.50–4.
[115] See Hornblower 2006: 59, citing in particular Young 1968: 1–26.
[116] Carey 2007: 203.   [117] *Pyth.* 7.19.
[118] *Pyth.* 10.20; see Stamatopoulou's (2007) overview of the Thessalian. See also fr. 109, which was intended for a Theban audience. Polybius (4.31.6) reports of the Thebans medizing that 'we do not praise Pindar for encouraging them to remain active with these verses'.
[119] *Ol.* 7.6, 11.7, 13.25.

Ergoteles, now of Himera, Sicily, but originally from Knossos, Crete, and deprived of his homeland by an unnaturing or hostile faction (*stasis antianeira*); or Paeans 9 and 14, the latter too fragmentary to provide a sense of context, but the former including *stasis* among a list of possible catastrophes facing Thebes.[120]

Phthonos may be seen as an element of political instability, but it is far from an indication of such. In general, Pindar's odes reveal some of the common ideas and cultural models concerning mortal behaviour and expectations of behaviour with regard to victory and its celebration—along with the darker emotions and activities that trailed in their wake. We can see that *phthonos* could develop a particular political potency, as it is depicted in Pindar's poetry. It may be that the developing polis ideology, which turned on a carefully balanced choreography of benefaction between elite and citizen, threw into high relief the role of *phthonos*, and its potential for political catastrophe.[121] But the presentation of *phthonos* varies in response to the tensions and concerns of each particular context.[122] Thus, it may also have a positive value;[123] sometimes silence is better; sometimes boasting is encouraged.[124] The concept of *phthonos* was already familiar across Archaic communities: *phthonos* was part of the expected and accepted emotional reaction to a victorious or prosperous individual who vaunted his success.[125] It was an acknowledged risk for communities in which there were powerful individuals whose authority might generate resentment. But there were certainly other settings in which it might emerge. And Pindar shows us how it works at the mortal level: people talk.

---

[120] See Hornblower 2006: 77, with Silk (2007: *ad loc.*), translating *antianeira* as 'unnaturing'.

[121] Goldhill (1991:128): 'there is a *rewriting* of the terms of praise in the context of the developing ideology of the collectivity of the polis'.

[122] See Carey (1981: 51 ff.).

[123] *Pyth.* 1.85: it is better to be a victim of *phthonos* than to be an object of pity.

[124] Boasting: *Isth.* 2, in which Thrasybulus of Akragas, nephew of the tyrant Thero, is urged not to keep quiet about his dead father Xenocrates' achievements; cf. the discussion in Kurke (2013: 190). Silence, or caution: in the case of the non-tyrannical victor, encouragement to praise oneself, if it occurs at all, is treated with some circumspection, for example, *Isth.* 1.62-8.

[125] Rather than seeing the final three examples as simply 'statistical outriders that confirm an evident trend', as Most (2003: 135). With Most, we can compare Bacchylides' presentation of envy, which presents the emotion as an obstacle for all to overcome (though we might emphasize its persistence a little more than Most allows).

ENVY AND BLAME

Evidence from fourth-century Athens, largely from the forensic corpus, provides another perspective on *phthonos*. Across these speeches, we find envy of others' fortunes—that is, often their material wealth—used to explain the (bad) behaviour of individuals. At its simplest, and commonest, *phthonos* is used to explain individual action, most often by calling into question the motivation behind the accusations and associated behaviours of one's rival.[126] This may be achieved in a variety of ways: for example, by attributing it to one's opponent, perhaps through a description of an action, or listing it among possible motivations; or by asserting that in contrast to one's opponent, you will not sink to being motivated by *phthonos*.[127] Once this is established, it then becomes possible to weave this into a larger argument about the case. For example, the speaker of Lysias 24 (*On the Refusal of a Pension to the Invalid*, written in around 403 BCE) cites *phthonos* as the ultimate cause for the court case against him—and, in the process, scores a number of other rhetorical points. Against an opponent who seems to be making an argument that concerns material possessions, the speaker states that he himself is poor, not a beneficiary of good fortune. Thus, he cannot explain the *phthonos* of his adversary as a response to his wealth, only his own virtuous character: 'It is clear that he feels *phthonos* towards me because, although I have to bear this sore misfortune, I am a better citizen than he is.'[128]

As with the poetry of Pindar, the discourse of *phthonos* in the forensic corpus shows how this emotion was inseparable from the networks of relationships in which it occurred. Take for example, the accusation of *phthonos* made against Theramenes in Lysias 12

---

[126] Sanders (2014: 82) provides a useful analysis: he finds ninety-eight accusations, prohibitions, and denials of *phthonos* (breaking down into twenty-eight direct accusations, fifty-two indirect, nine prohibitions, and nine denials). He points out (35) that such accusations of *phthonos* are also made against cities, but it should be borne in mind that these uses of *phthonos* describe the motivations of groups in narrative accounts (e.g. Lys. 2.48, 2.67, Dem. 15.15), explain the actions of groups in political calls for action (Isoc. 14.20), or are observations about human characteristics (Isoc. 4.47) and function rather differently from how the litigious accusations do.

[127] Opponent's actions are *phthonos* and unjust: Is. 2.23, Dem. 39.34; among a list of possible motivations: Dem. 9.54; denying that one will have the same *phthonos* as one's enemy: Isoc. 15.259.

[128] Lys. 24.3, tr. Lamb 1930.

(*Against Eratosthenes*). The speaker uses *phthonos* to describe the motivations of Theramenes (who had led the more moderate section of the Thirty before Critias had done for him): 'So long as he found favour, he showed himself loyal; but when he saw Pisander, Callaeschrus and others getting in advance of him, and your people no longer disposed to hearken to them, immediately his *phthonos* towards them, combined with his fear of you, threw him into cooperation with Aristocrates.'[129] The generation of *phthonos* is not only about the relationship between those who succeed and those who do not, but also turns importantly on the social context and the evaluations that take place within it. Success prompts recognition and attention from some, and it is losing this that concerns Theramenes and provokes his *phthonos*; and his *phthonos*, in turn, motivates his desire for the public reputation of others to be destroyed.[130] In these ways, the attribution of *phthonos* in law-court speeches in Classical Athens suggests a clear line of descent from the concerns of Pindar's poetry. It is an emotion stirred up by those who see others succeed, which makes a person not only unwilling to offer acknowledgement of that success, but also desirous to see it destroyed, along with the ruination of any broader public recognition of that success.

However, shaped by the relational structures of the democratic context and the contentious arena of the law court, it also acquires some further dimensions. It becomes almost a technical term to describe the kinds of emotions that one *should* experience in certain circumstances, in particular when confronted by either those who have goods they do not deserve, or those who have fortune that they do not use to benefit the city.[131] The result is a righteous emotion that can be wielded against one's opponent, as Demosthenes demonstrates in *Against Meidias*:

μεγάλην μέντἂν ἀρχήν, μᾶλλον δὲ τέχνην εἴης εὑρηκώς, εἰ δύο τἀναντιώταθ' ἑαυτοῖς ἐν οὕτω βραχεῖ χρόνῳ περὶ σεαυτὸν δύναιο

---

[129] Lys. 12.66 (tr. Lamb 1930). Fear of the loss of public reputation because of *phthonos* is also demonstrated by the defendant in Lysias 3.9, who reports how he is at risk of ridicule from those who feel *phthonos* towards him, and for this reason does not seek redress for the assaults on him and his family by the prosecutor, Simon.

[130] Guettel Cole (2001) argues that, over the period of the fourth century, the Athenians had found a new political maturity that enabled them to develop rituals for the recognition and commemoration of successful individuals, which also protected them from the dangers of *phthonos*; see further, this section, p. 134.

[131] See the discussion in Konstan 2007: 80; Cairns 2003a: esp. 246–7.

ποιεῖσθαι, φθόνον ἐξ ὧν ζῇς, καὶ ἐφ' οἷς ἐξαπατᾷς ἔλεον. οὐκ ἔστιν οὐδαμόθεν σοι προσήκων ἔλεος οὐδὲ καθ' ἕν, ἀλλὰ τοὐναντίον μῖσος καὶ φθόνος καὶ ὀργή· τούτων γὰρ ἄξια ποιεῖς.

It would be indeed a great method that you have devised, or, rather, a great trick, if you could in so short a time make yourself the object of two contradictory sentiments, rousing *phthonos* by your way of life and compassion by your deceptions. You have no conceivable claim to compassion; no, not for an instant. On the contrary, hatred, *phthonos* and wrath—those are what your conduct calls for.[132]

This is a righteous *phthonos*, one that can be used against rivals in the courtroom. It can become, in turn, linked with an oppositional merit, as shown in Isaeus 6, *On the Estate of Philoctemon*: 'No *phthonos* ought, therefore, to be felt against them, but rather, by Zeus and Apollo, against our opponents, if they obtain what does not belong to them.'[133]

As a result, as Hippias of Elis described, there developed 'two types of *phthonos*: one type is just, when a person feels *phthonos* towards bad men who are honoured; the other is unjust, when one feels it in regard to good men'.[134] But, as the forensic corpus reveals, any such clear conceptual demarcation brought with it considerable rhetorical complexity, in which adroit manipulation of *phthonos* talk was a requirement of effective persuasion. As others have noted, there are no explicit attempts by speakers to incite what we may call 'bad' *phthonos* in the jury—as we have seen already in the example from Isaeus 6.[135] But this does not mean that speakers did not try to instil 'bad *phthonos*' in more subtle ways. Indeed, the *Rhetorica ad Alexandrum* draws our attention to the skills involved in depicting the

---

[132] Dem. 21.196 (tr. Vince 1935, adapted).
[133] Isae. 6.61 (tr. Forster 1927). Comparative appeals include: Isoc. 8.51, Dem. 28.18, Dem. 37.52. Konstan (2007) argues that *phthonos* acquired a negative reputation in the Classical period (from a neutral or positive status in the Archaic period) on account of its role in the ideological struggles of the democracy.
[134] D-K 86 B16 (Stob 3.38.2, from Plutarch's lost *On Slander*; see Konstan 2007: 195 and Walcot 1978: 12). Some modern scholars have also adopted this categorization: see Sanders 2014: esp. 10 and 78.
[135] See Cairns 2003a: 245–6.; cf. Sanders (2014: 83), who argues that 'orators openly call on their audience to feel *phthonos*'—but he means 'good *phthonos*'. The invitation is offered to the group as a whole, rather than an individual. Sanders (2014: 35–6 and 87) suggests that this is one way of not accusing an individual of feeling *phthonos*, but it is hard to see how this ameliorates the social power of this invitation.

circumstances of one's rival in order to incite *phthonos* in the jurors.[136] In turn, 'good' *phthonos* also posed risks, which must be confronted rhetorically. Sometimes this could be dealt with directly: speakers simply ask that their audience look on their previous actions or current status with understanding, and not *phthonos*.[137] But a speaker may inadvertently arouse *phthonos*, for example, by relating what he sees as the truth, but which others judge differently. And so we find speakers asking their audience to treat their words with care, and expressing the hope that they will not provoke undeserved *phthonos*.[138]

Thus, the handling of *phthonos* in fourth-century forensic rhetoric was no simple matter. In the adversarial environment of the law court—enhanced by the underlying tensions implicit in the social structures of the democracy—there were certain situations in which speakers described *phthonos* as justified. Moreover, references to *phthonos* in the forensic corpus reveal a further ambiguity: although it is treated as a hateful emotion, destructive and 'un-Athenian', it is also clearly understood to be an emotion that everyone can relate to, or has felt themselves, and, most importantly, may be expected to feel in a democracy. The ways in which the speakers play across these different cultural models of *phthonos* allow us to appreciate its powerful presence in Athenian social relationships. A couple of more detailed examples will show the subtlety with which these 'blame games' were played.

Righteous and Destructive

In *On the Crown*, written in 330 BCE, Demosthenes is not only defending his political ally Ctesiphon, but also, and perhaps more importantly, his own reputation. In arguing that Ctesiphon's proposal to award him a crown was not illegal, he sets himself an intriguing political challenge: he must discuss his achievements, but he must also avoid explicit and unapologetic self-praise. That this was the

---

[136] [Arist.] *Rh. Al.* 1440a35–1440b4 and 1445a13–29; see also discussion in Cairns 2003a: 247.
[137] Past actions: Andoc. 2.6; current status: Lys. 21.15.
[138] See, for example, Isoc. 9.39, Dem. 20.74.

challenge he faced was recognized by ancient commentators, who praised the rhetorical techniques he used.[139]

In this speech, perhaps unsurprisingly, Demosthenes is extremely concerned with the emotion of *phthonos*—and for a number of different reasons. First, he must avoid evoking in his audience the emotion of *phthonos*. One of his key ploys is to redirect this emotion so that it is associated quite clearly with his opponent.[140] As a number of scholars have observed, Demosthenes appears to argue that the case is brought because of *phthonos*.[141] In this speech, the term itself occurs six times, spaced across the text so that it creates a 'red thread' of vicious emotion around which the case expands, and to which Demosthenes repeatedly returns. But the meanings it conveys do not remain static; rather, Demosthenes gradually builds a set of associations, emphasizing particular dimensions of the concept that align with, and reinforce, the different aspects of his argument.

From the beginning Demosthenes clearly associates the emotion of *phthonos* with his opponent. The term is used first (18.13) as part of a description of Aeschines' position or stance in bringing Demosthenes to court. The metaphor is militaristic—ἐν ἐπηρείας τάξει καὶ φθόνου τοῦτο ποιεῖν—bringing to mind a line of troops. The way in which Demosthenes arranges his speech, the repetition of *epereia* from the preceding section (18.12), means that we also associate *phthonos* with a whole host of nasty verbal activities. He lists *loidoria* ('abuse'), *propelakismos* ('insulting treatment'), as well as referring to vicious concepts of personal enmity: *hubris* ('outrage') and *echthrou men epereia* ('malice of hostility').[142] The theme of private hostility and uncivic behaviour is firmly established, and then gradually expanded. As Demosthenes

---

[139] For example, Quintilian (*Inst.* 11.1.22) on how his approach redirects the blame towards his opponent.

[140] In this respect, he may be recalling the argument of Aeschines made against him thirteen years before in *On the Embassy* (Sanders 2014: 85 implies that the two speeches are related in this way). However, this seems like a long period over which to seek such revenge; and, to be rhetorically effective, it would depend on the jurors being similarly aware of the previous speech. Besides, it would be rather self-defeating for Demosthenes to remind his audience of those charges. It seems more likely that these kinds of charges were part of the armoury of an orator, as ps-Aristotle's comments (*Rh. Al.* 1445a12–26) on uses of *phthonos* indicate.

[141] See Cohen 1995: 77–81 (envy and enmity) and also Sanders 2014: 87, with n. 43.

[142] Dem. 18.12: ἐχθροῦ μὲν ἐπήρειαν ἔχει καὶ ὕβριν καὶ λοιδορίαν καὶ προπηλακισμὸν ὁμοῦ καὶ πάντα τὰ τοιαῦτα· '[the prosecution] includes private malice and violence, railing and vituperation, and the like'. Tr., here and throughout, Vince and Vince 1926.

depicts it, Aeschines' nasty language of accusation reaches out to threaten not just the orator, but also the city and citizens, because Aeschines is misusing the law courts and, to an extent, shaping the law to his own advantage (15–16).[143]

The next mention of *phthonos* (121) repeats the argument of the first—that Aeschines is motivated by this emotion—but then expands on it: 'Then why this miserable pettifogging? Why these insincere arguments? Why do you not try hellebore for your complaint? Are you not ashamed to prosecute for *phthonos*, not for crime; misquoting this statute, curtailing that statute, when they ought to be read in their entirety to a jury sworn to vote according to their direction?' The fact that Aeschines confuses his own *phthonos* with the crucial concept of injustice shows how far he has gone. Demosthenes compares this activity with the uncivic behaviour of sycophancy; but he also associates it with madness, referring to the use of hellebore (a traditional treatment for that ailment).[144]

The next occurrence of *phthonos* (279) moves the concept of *phthonos* from an external emotion that motivates Aeschines to act, to a personal characteristic of Aeschines, alongside private enmity and mean-spiritedness: 'But for a man who never once sought to bring me to justice for any public, nor, I will add, for any private offence, whether for the city's sake or for his own, to come into court armed with a denunciation of a crown and of a vote of thanks, and to lavish such a wealth of eloquence on that plea, is a symptom of private hostility, *phthonos*, and small-mindedness.'[145] As noted above, Demosthenes associates *phthonos* with nasty verbal activities, and this emphasizes again that it is a private enmity that brings Aeschines to court, rather than concern for public welfare. At the beginning of the speech, he notes how Aeschines 'as prosecutor... enjoys an advantage' because 'people listen with delight to insults and accusations'.[146]

---

[143] Sanders (2014: 87) suggests that Demosthenes may be marking *phthonos* as a characteristic not of political rivalry but of a vicious character. See Sanders (2008) on Aristotle's associations of *phthonos* and bad character.
[144] Dem. 18.121–2. For hellebore, see Ar. *Vesp.* 1489.
[145] Dem. 18.279.
[146] Dem. 18.3–4.

Narratives of Phthonos

The final three occasions of *phthonos* talk broaden the meaning of the word to include the emotions and motivations of the jurors themselves. Here we find *phthonos* portrayed in a subtly different light, as one that every citizen naturally may feel towards those who are more fortunate, in particular, if they are wealthier. This could present a dilemma: how can Demosthenes discuss this aspect when he has already made it clear that Aeschines' *phthonos* is so very un-Athenian? He resorts to referring to *phthonos* as an increasingly anonymous and anodyne quantity. So (303), the jurors are asked to listen to a list of Demosthenes' achievements and judge them *aneu phthonou*, that is, 'without *phthonos*', as dispassionate witnesses and judges of this case. The phrasing of such a request underlines just how natural it is that one citizen, in the presence of another's success, should feel this emotion—but is achieved without making a direct accusation. Moreover, it could be argued that the jurors have in effect been told that they have the capacity to be better men than Aeschines. Nevertheless, the risk is still there, both for Demosthenes and for the jurors. He proceeds (305) to explain that he wishes to guard against *phthonos*; whose *phthonos* is not spelled out—but after the previous mention the implication is obvious. However, he makes it clear that he too is implicated if they feel this emotion: he must himself ensure that their *phthonos* is not aroused.

Finally, in 315, he quotes a proverb (that we have noted earlier) concerning the unavoidable nature of *phthonos* among the living, and this is directly followed by a plea not to judge him unfairly in comparison with previous generations: 'Everybody knows that against the living there is always an undercurrent of more or less *phthonos*, while the dead are no longer disliked even by their enemies. Such is human nature; am I then to be criticized and canvassed by comparison with my predecessors?'[147] The proverb normalizes *phthonos*, clarifies that it is a common reaction to good fortune. Without identifying the jurors, it lets them slip gently off the hook, while emphasizing how they also must reciprocate in their treatment of him.

In *Against the Crown* Demosthenes moves from the *phthonos* of his accuser, which he argues is a private emotion, and which is, moreover, un-Athenian, uncivic, and disrespectful of citizen ideals,

---

[147] Dem. 18.315; see the beginning of this section, and cf. Thuc. 2.45.

to the potential *phthonos* of his audience, which becomes, in contrast, increasingly acceptable. The contradiction this entails is made less of a reproach to his fellow citizens by his first not attributing it (305), and then normalizing it as a part of everyday human nature (315), which the speaker emphasizes by himself taking some responsibility for keeping it under control. In turn, Demosthenes' attitude to his own achievements—this careful *phthonos* talk—recalls aspects of *phthonos* in Pindaric poetry, in which the poet warns his subjects away from boastfulness.

Ungrateful and Inevitable

At one level, Demosthenes' speech (20) *Against Leptines* concerns a law to abolish the privilege of *ateleia*, that is, exemption from all taxes and liturgies.[148] At another level, it investigates, and constructs, the qualities of the ideal Athenian citizen's character—and one of its chief concerns is the nature and role of *phthonos*.[149] The background to the speech is as follows. The privilege of *ateleia* extended not only to those who had been granted it directly, but also to their descendants, which meant that the burden fell more heavily on those who still had to pay. As has been extensively documented elsewhere, the fourth century had seen increasing resentment among those who were liable for liturgies and capital levies; the system of collection seems to have been breaking down by the late 360s.[150] It was particularly resented in a time of increasing military costs, especially in the aftermath of the Social War.[151] Leptines proposed not only removing existing grants of *ateleia* (except for the descendants of the tyrannicides, Harmodius and Aristogiton), but also making it illegal to confer it on anyone in future.[152] This speech comes from what was actually a second attack on the law: a man called Bathippus had initiated a *graphe nomon me epitedeion theinai* ('a case against an unsuitable law') against Leptines,

---

[148] In some cases it meant just liturgies, but see MacDowell 2004.

[149] As Hesk 2000: 40–51.

[150] Dem. 51: trierarchic obligations hired out; [Dem. 50]: deme-based collection rather than *proeisphora*; [Dem.] 47.20 and 44: no equipment in the dockyards; Dem. 50.7: trierarch must provide own crew. See Hornblower 2011: 273–4.

[151] As Isoc. 8 and Xen. *Vect.* attest; see Kremmydas 2012: 33 for the dating of the speech and likely chronology regarding the Social War.

[152] MacDowell 2000: 231.

but died before he could see it into court.[153] This second attack, by Bathippus' son Apsephion, used the same procedure, but because it took place two years after the original law was enacted, Leptines was no longer personally liable.

Demosthenes (along with another man, one Phormio) was a *synegoros* (a 'co-speaker'); this would have been the second speech from the prosecution. At the beginning of the speech, Demosthenes gives his reasons for supporting the case: that he thinks its abolition will benefit Athens in general, and more particularly, he wants to support the son of Chabrias, a famous Athenian general killed at the battle of Chios in 357/6, who had been awarded *ateleia*.

Demosthenes develops a discourse of risk that highlights the dangers of *phthonos*. This speech famously demonstrates how acceptance of Leptines' law will lay the city open to this emotion, since it prevents the citizens from showing appropriate gratitude to their benefactors. *Phthonos* is positioned as a key danger to the ideal image of Athenian civic behaviour, a threat to the individual, to the citizen, and to the city itself. He sums up its risks for a person's character thus: 'For to give no reward in the first instance is an exercise of judgement; to take it away when given shows *phthonos*, and you must not seem to have been prompted by that.'[154]

Repeatedly, Demosthenes sets *phthonos* amongst other undesirable characteristics, in opposition to the ideal values of a well-ordered and harmonious city, lining up triads of adjectives against each other as if they were doing battle.[155] In this argument he stresses again and again that the city itself is not naturally given to *phthonos*—and yet, there are incidental comments that suggest otherwise. An example of this occurs when Demosthenes asks the jurors to rethink their valorization of Themistocles, and their admiration of his deceit and trickery. Far better to venerate Conon, he argues, and his open approach to military action.[156] In the process, he apologizes to the jurors, and asks them not to feel *phthonos*. The implication here, in contrast to the

---

[153] On the translation of this term, see Kremmydas 2012: 48.

[154] The danger of *phthonos* summarized in Dem. 20.56–7 (tr. here and what follows by Vince 1930, with some adaptations).

[155] Adjectives arrayed in 10 and 157 (the ethos the law will engender); 13 and 142 (current national character); while 164 comprises examples of both the latter, and 165 offers the bad characteristics against which the jurors of Athens are arrayed.

[156] Dem. 20.74: 'Therefore it is not right that so great a man should be wronged by you, or should gain less than those orators who will try to prove that you ought to

rhetoric of the rest of his speech, is that it is a default setting for his audience.[157]

Across the two speeches examined in this section, the role and nature of abuse merits some attention. In the first speech, *On the Crown*, Demosthenes frequently returns to the role of *loidoria* ('abuse'), remarking, for example, on how people like to listen to the abuse of others, and discussing the accusations made against him in these terms.[158] Obviously, Demosthenes is anxious to draw a line between Aeschines' accusations and those that the jurors should take seriously.[159] Soon after the second mention of *phthonos*, Demosthenes spells out the difference between accusation and abuse: 'Accusation, I would say differs from abuse in that accusation presupposes an offense punishable by law, but abuse entails insults of the kind that enemies naturally direct at each other.'[160]

But other examples show that it was also useful to be able to blur this distinction: on a number of occasions Demosthenes refers to the charges brought against him and the abuse of his enemies in the same phrase, the one devaluing the other by association.[161] There may also be some further implications relevant to our investigation in this discourse about abuse, since, as Demosthenes himself makes clear, *loidoria* describes the kind of ritualized abuse encouraged during the Dionysian procession.[162] Susan Guettel Cole argues that the Dionysian procession with its *phallephoria* complete with abuse, which occurred just before the public proclamation of honours, was intended to 'decontaminate a space and make it unsafe for *phthonos*'.[163] She does not return to Demosthenes' accusations against

---

deduct something from what was bestowed on him.' From the account, the Athenians appear to have admired Themistocles' behaviour; see Hesk 2000: 48.

[157] Kremmydas (2012: 317) explains that this is a 'variation of a standard rhetorical formula to pre-empt potential hostile reactions on the part of the audience, since what Dem. is about to say undervalues the Athenian hero'; other examples include Dem. 18.321 and Isoc. 15.8.

[158] Abuse of others: 18.3; accusation against him: 18.11, 12, 15, 123, and 138.

[159] In 10.75, Demosthenes points out the strategy (of the Athenians themselves) of turning the subject 'into laughter and ridicule' (εἰς γέλωτα καὶ λοιδορίαν) in order to avoid doing their duty.

[160] Second mention of *phthonos*: 18.121; accusation and abuse: 18.123.

[161] e.g. Dem. 18.3, 22.21, 22, and 23, 57.17.

[162] He refers to the unrestrained talk of the ritual procession: τῆς δὲ πομπείας ταύτης τῆς ἀνέδην γεγενημένης.

[163] Guettel Cole 2001: 212. The phallus is a well-known ancient apotropaic symbol. Charles Stewart notes (pers. corresp.) that a phallus in public could be *geloion*

Aeschines, but the implication is that Aeschines' use of abusive language in the wrong setting transgresses this ritual arrangement, and so lays the way open for *phthonos*, endangering those receiving honours and, by association, the city and its citizens.[164] These observations by Demosthenes about Aeschines' language also reinforce Demosthenes' argument about Aeschines' private motivation: his personal enmity has brought him to the point of using language that is only publicly acceptable when used in a ritualized setting.

Turning to the second speech, we find an additional term, which can be translated as 'to abuse', *baskainein*. Demosthenes instructs the jurors that if a man has great wealth but has not done them wrong, then (he pleads) you need not *baskainein*.[165] The precise meaning here is unclear: it could refer to the attitude of the citizens or to the temptation to bad-mouth a person. Whichever it is, it seems to follow a similar pattern to the operation of *phthonos* and/or *loidoria*, which we have already seen. Here and elsewhere, the term is sometimes linked indirectly to *phthonos*.[166] In *On the Crown*, Demosthenes uses *baskanos* as an adjective six times. All except the first and last citations refer to Aeschines, whose *phthonos* Demosthenes has repeatedly mentioned,[167] while in *Against Meidias*, Demosthenes uses it as an example of perhaps excessive abuse that might be employed against a member of the jury if he offended Meidias or one of his retinue.[168] In later use, *baskania* and related vocabulary will come to describe the phenomenon of the evil eye, and there may be some indications of these developments in *On the Crown*, when Demosthenes observes that Aeschines' use of the term *goes* (sorcerer) against him is better applied to Aeschines himself;[169] while in *Against Aristogiton*, the term appears to be used in association with the activities

---

('laughable') or *atopon* ('absurd'), both of which were techniques for defusing the evil eye in Byzantium; he suggests that this was probably taken over from antiquity.

[164] Elsewhere, the relationship depicted between the two phenomena is less elaborate: e.g. Dem. 9.54, where he lists the motivations driving the Athenians: 'λοιδορίας, φθόνου, σκώμματος' ('abuse, envy, jesting'); Demosthenes speculates that these may be divinely inspired (see further p. 154). That abuse is expected in court seems to be the case in Pl. *Tht.* 174c.

[165] Dem. 20.24: οὐχὶ δεῖ δήπου τούτῳ βασκαίνειν.

[166] cf. Dem. 8.19 and 22, 16.19, 18.189 and 307, and Isoc. 5.11, 12.155, 15.62 (the latter used in association with *phthoneo*).

[167] Dem. 18.108, 119, 132, 139, 242, 317.

[168] Dem. 21.209.

[169] Dem. 18.276 and cf. 19.109.

of a ritual practitioner.[170] None of these examples directly associate this term or its cognates with supernatural aggression, nor do they necessarily manifest a direct association with *phthonos*. However, they do refer to the kind of malicious gossip employed to disparage others' achievements, or to terms of abuse, and the idea that *baskania* may be connected with a disruptive reaction to the acquisition of good fortune by others is still apparent in these earlier sources.[171]

A Discourse of Attribution

These examples demonstrate the power of what I have been calling *phthonos* talk. The attribution of *phthonos* creates an explanation, and makes meaning out of the inexplicable. It identifies a perpetrator and his action, gives the context of that action, offers an explanatory agency or means by which the action is achieved, and intimates the perpetrator's purpose.[172] These heuristic categories are the five 'basic forms of thought' that Kenneth Burke used to break down the notion of motives: Act, Scene, Agent, Agency, and Purpose. And this framework, called 'dramatism', has been successfully used by Adam Ashforth to think about the presumption of malice underpinning life in a world of witches in Soweto, South Africa. In that culture, the assumption is that 'everyone is jealous of everyone else, regardless of appearances... especially despite appearances of comity'.[173] This has some parallels in ancient Greek culture, in particular the concern with the potential for occult attack from among one's friends and neighbours, and I will return to this later. However, it is a different aspect of Burke's approach to motive that I want to draw attention to here, that is, his emphasis on the role of discourse in its social context.[174]

---

[170] Dem. 25.80. Cf. also Ar. *Eq.* 103 and *Plut.* 571. In Pl. *Phd* 95b5–6, Socrates famously observes to Cebes that *baskania* may disrupt their discussion if the claims they make about it are too great. It is not clear from where this danger emanates, but the idea that claims to achievement are under threat would suggest an association with *phthonos*.
[171] See Hesk 2000: 213 n. 33.   [172] See Lanzillotta 2010: 75.
[173] Ashforth 2003: 217.
[174] In interpreting Burke's dramatism (1945) I am guided here by Benoit (1996), who is in turn guided by Mills (1940), but notes other interpretations of Burke's meaning.

Burke focuses on 'discourse intended to explain, interpret, rationalize, characterize, justify, or account for our actions'.[175] Rather than it being an examination of the cognitive functions and/or internal motivating states that underpin a person's actions, we can consider an attribution of *phthonos* as a discursive entity that creates a narrative of causality linked inextricably to social norms and values. In thinking of *phthonos* claims in this way, I am working with a conception of the Greek self as comprising an objective–participant model (as described by Christopher Gill), which emphasizes how, in ancient Greek culture, communal values and norms shaped and were shaped by participation in shared dialogue.[176]

Phthonos talk is another example of a participant discourse in which we can see the bases of an ethical life being established, but it demonstrates the darker, more disruptive aspects of this conception. When *phthonos* is attributed to another, we see that those who are involved (the agents) are known to each other and to the others before whom this discourse is played out (the scene); the act is some kind of attack. As with an attribution of *phthonos*, this emotion also acquires its agency by means of a discourse of some kind. This may be explicit, for example, a speech in the law courts, perhaps the slander or *diabole* that precedes or accompanies it; it may be hidden, which means that, in the case of a spell, the attribution of agency is more difficult (we will return to this aspect of occult agency in the next section of the book); or it may be a missing discourse, for example, a lack of acclamation where an achievement suggests it.

Burke's analysis of the elements of motive reveals the construction of the storyline in such a discourse. In making an attribution of *phthonos*, the speaker is not of course giving his audience the 'true' motivation of the perpetrator; rather, he is presenting a rhetorical action that directs an audience's attention to a particular configuration of events—a familiar narrative of blame. But that narrative will also confer a couple of significant rhetorical benefits on the speaker himself. First, it will draw attention to his state of good fortune (otherwise why would he attract *phthonos* in the first place?). Second, it will draw attention away from his own role in the creation of any

---

[175] Benoit 1996: 77.
[176] Gill 1996: 175; Eidinow 2013b uses this notion to discuss the process of oracular consultation.

problematic situation, be it the overweening pride of an Olympic victor, or the less than civic behaviour of an Athenian politician.

This analysis leads us to the content of *phthonos* talk, and a realization about the fundamental set of values that underpin it. This is a discourse that concerns the shared, normative understanding of the allocation and recognition of good fortune in Greek society. In all the cases above, *phthonos* is understood to be a response to someone else's experience of good fortune, and the cause of disruption of the usual cycles of reciprocity that otherwise develop from such an experience. Thus, Pindar's poetry urges ordinary mortals to engage in the rituals of recognition of great men who have been blessed with good fortune by the gods; *phthonos* prompts the breakdown of these relationships. In turn, in Demosthenes' speeches, we see *phthonos* called out explicitly as the emotion that obstructs the cycles of mutual benefaction (among mortals) that follow divinely granted episodes of good fortune. The speech *Against Leptines* offers a forceful disquisition on the cycle of civic benefaction—good fortune leads to benefits granted, which leads to (gifts of) gratitude—and a full and clear explanation of how *phthonos* impedes or prevents its fruition. And this makes sense of Demosthenes' almost incidental request to the jurors not to feel *phthonos*, rather than, say, simply anger, regarding his comments on Themistocles and Conon.[177] If we understand *phthonos* to be concerned with the emotions related to benefactions, its use here is appropriate: Demosthenes is suggesting that the reputation and recognition of one individual be given to another. It is not the undervaluing of Themistocles that poses the risk—Demosthenes does not suggest that he be stripped of honour—but the gift of additional respect to Conon.

The implications are that *phthonos* is an inevitable human response. Yet both authors also give us some further insight into the relational, emergent nature of *phthonos* in different civic contexts. In Pindar's poetry, the plea to ordinary mortals not to show *phthonos* towards those who have achieved is, in turn, also a subtle instruction to the successful individual not to ignore their responsibilities. Compare the caution with which Demosthenes presents his own good fortune in *On the Crown*: he must defend his right to this award, but he also recognizes that his own presentation of the good fortune that

---

[177] Dem. 20.74.

led to this situation is a key part of the generation of *phthonos*. As both Pindar's poetry and the rhetoric from the courts demonstrate, the occurrence of *phthonos* marks a particular breakdown of the reciprocal relationships that run like nerves through the ancient social body. A culturally specific emotion term, *phthonos* highlights the profound social tensions that accompanied perceptions, and performances, of good fortune—the gifts of the gods.

2.4

Phthonos and Misfortune

PHTHONOS AND 'THE GIFT'

The dynamic of reciprocity—a sense and system of mutual obligation—oiled the wheels of ancient Greek life, but its accompanying negative aspects also played a crucial role in shaping social action.[1] Marcel Mauss, in his work on the gift, commends the gift-exchange system as a way of creating social harmony, but he also consistently refers to the potential dangers of 'the gift'.[2] This negative aspect is multifaceted, and most obviously includes declining to be drawn into the process of giving gifts. As we might expect with the 'total' social phenomenon of the 'the gift', the dangers of stepping

---

[1] e.g. Dewald (2008) discusses gift exchange as a key dynamic in Archaic society, while Van Wees (2002) argues for changing patterns of acquisitiveness in the *xenia* relationships of the Archaic period. On reciprocity in Homer and Hesiod, see Ulf 2006, esp. p. 87; on the complexities of reciprocity in the *Iliad*, Gould 2001b; and on the role of benefaction, including negative examples, as a system of explanation in Herodotus, Gould 2001a. Van Wees (1998: 32–3) discusses examples from anthropology of competitive reciprocity, noting (33) that 'the antagonistic nature of reciprocity as a force for status differentiation seems to sit uneasily with its conciliatory nature as a force for social integration'. He goes on to stress that such competitive reciprocity is 'most of the time . . . an effective, and on the whole preferable, alternative to violent competition for status'.

[2] e.g. Mauss (1990: 22) on the mistrust with which the gift is regarded among the Trobrianders (mentioned again with more emphasis in discussion of the Germanic 'pledge' (62; see further below); (27), he also notes the potential threat of death from not reciprocating among the Maori; (59) in his description of classical Hindu law, he notes that 'the gift is therefore at one and the same time what should be done, what should be received, and yet what is dangerous to take'; and (62) in his description of the pledge in Germanic law, he notes how 'the pledge, the "gage", like the thing that is given, holds danger for both parties', giver and recipient. It is important to stress that 'the gift' is not just an object that is representative of social relations: it is a process that creates them; see Mauss 1990: 72–3.

outside the rituals of giving are potentially catastrophic.[3] But gifts themselves involve risk: for example, the danger that I, the giver, will lose out, that the recipient of my giving will not recognize my gesture, or not repay it in full.[4] And, of course, it is possible to reciprocate actively, but still involve negative emotions. In his spectrum of reciprocity, organized according to emotional and physical distance from the familial group, Sahlins reminds us that even giving itself can be aggressive.[5] First, 'generalised reciprocity' describes transactions that

[3] Mauss (1990: 3) describes a 'total' social phenomenon as one in which 'all kinds of institutions are given expression at one and the same time'. The point is made most explicitly in his description of the potlatch among the Native American societies of the American Northwest (39–43): the obligation both to give and to receive—and the extreme social and spiritual consequences if one refuses to play one's role. Mauss (12) put it in terms of spirits. He argued that in Maori law, 'to make a gift of something to someone is to make a present of some part of oneself'. He goes on to explain just how dangerous it is for the recipient to retain that thing, because it exerts a magical or religious hold over them. Mauss famously attributed this power to the *hau*, that is, the soul of the thing itself. However, his account of Maori beliefs has been extensively criticized: see Firth 1959 and Sahlins, 1972: 149–83. Although scholars have largely rejected the idea of the *hau*, Mauss's notion that 'by giving one is giving *oneself*, and if one gives *oneself* it is because one "owes" *oneself*—one's person and one's goods—to others' is sustained (46). Lévi-Strauss (1987: 46–9) argued that Mauss had mistaken an indigenous belief for the objective reason for gift exchange—he set the circulation of exchange in the unconscious mind; Godelier (1999: 52) in turn re-roots it in the social, arguing that the *hau* means the original donor has an inalienable ownership of an object, which is socially acknowledged. Osteen (2002: 3) gives alternative analyses of the meaning and role of the spirit of the gift. For example, in exploring examples of apparently irrational giving, Sykes (2005: 74–5) comes to the conclusion that the *hau* of a gift is relational in its nature (166–7): 'the gift you take into your hands begs you to think of yet another person, maybe the one who gave it to you, or maybe another person you have not met. That is how the gift works. This is the hau of it, not bush spirits or spirits of the dead, but the spirits of living others that insist themselves upon you, the additional, unexpected share of the transaction that remains with you.' In this context, gifts then can be described as being both relational and as representative, signifying a particular social relation (see Osteen 2002: 3, who cites also Berking 1999: 5).

[4] Mauss (1990: 3) reminds us of these tensions at the very beginning of his essay, when he refers to 'the present generously given even when, in the gesture accompanying the transaction, there is only a polite fiction, formalism, and social deceit, and when really there is obligation and economic self-interest', but he does not offer any detail about these emotions, who holds them, at what point in the ritual, and why. Osteen (2002: 26) observes that in the moment, the obligation conveyed by a gift may be far from the thoughts of the giver (and, we can add, perhaps from the mind of the recipient). Caillé (2001: 34) discusses the 'Dale Carnegie paradox', in which one must behave as if one is spontaneously sincere, in order to further one's goals.

[5] Sahlins 1972: 193–9. This model has been challenged and modified to fit the ancient Roman relationship of the client (which was expressed in terms of kinship, although this kinship was fictional); see Crook 2005, and cf. Kirk 2007.

are 'putatively altruistic', most usually found among family members, friends, or neighbours, where obligations are seldom made explicit and there is little sense of any time limit on their repayment. 'Balanced reciprocity' occurs between individuals who are not so close— perhaps between those in a market context. This is 'direct exchange', in which transactions are expected to be timely and equivalent. Finally, 'negative reciprocity', usually between strangers, involves aggressive behaviour, which is intended to maximize one's own interests, and which may result in exploitation.

As these examples and models indicate, gift-giving both creates and is given meaning through a process of transactions between people.[6] We have only to think of gift-giving and the desire for social approval to realize the importance of the relations surrounding a gift.[7] The gift only comes to be realized as a gift by the response of the recipient: 'the donor knows that she gives, she does not know what she gives, since only the recipient actualizes the value of the gift'.[8] The relationship gives meaning to the gift—and the gift to the relationship.

James Laidlaw (2002) provides an intriguing example of these dynamics, in his examination of the giving and receiving of *dan*, particular types of charitable gifts given in India, which are not only unreciprocated, but can convey misfortune from giver to recipient. Those who receive *dan* in different relationships are affected by it in different ways. Thus, the priests of Banaras, who willingly receive *dan*, but do not reciprocate, also receive the misfortunes of their donors. In contrast, the Jain renouncers avoid this disaster by means of a ritual of giving in which those who give such a gift mark it as their gift, but never refer to it as such, while those who receive it do not acknowledge it as a gift—and so there is no reciprocity, rather, the *dan* becomes a 'free gift'.[9]

---

[6] Godelier 1999: 104. In modern societies processes of giving may appear to be less personal: Godelier (14) gives the example of charitable giving, in which the beneficiaries of the charity are shown on television. However, in tracing the history of the modern form of production in the USA and UK, James Carrier (1995a, esp. pp. 6–8) has focused on the relationships between people and objects (how they are (7) 'really made, bought, given or even used' rather than seeing them in terms of (10) 'mass structures of meaning and identity') and how this then shapes the relationships between people who share or transact objects, and vice versa. See further Carrier (1995b: 91): 'commodity logic is... a social value that binds and obligates potential transactors to each other'.

[7] See Van de Ven 2002. [8] Caillé 2001: 34.

[9] Laidlaw (2002) is building on the work of Parry (esp. 1986) on 'pure-gift' ideology. As Laidlaw points out, Malinowski identified the existence of the free gift

The meaning of a gift reaches well beyond the momentary response of giver and recipient. The giving of a gift is an assertion of identities, while rejecting it may be to reject a definition of oneself.[10] This can also be extended to gift-acquiring for others. Thus, if a person buys a gift for a close friend which does not align with the giver's sense of identity, it may come to form an identity threat to them. Some research suggests that the giver may then try to correct this feeling by buying 'identity-expressive products'.[11] These kinds of implicit dynamics indicate how and why gift-giving may be used as an instrument for acquiring or maintaining status and control.[12] And, of course, underpinning these dynamics, these private meanings are shaped by public structures of meaning, which are 'regenerated, modified and subverted in part by what people do in their private lives'.[13] It is much more than the thought that counts.

In this context, my suggestion is that *phthonos* expressed a spectrum of negative responses to the expectations and obligations involved in the social networks of reciprocity that pervaded ancient Greek society: these comprised specifically, resentment at giving (that is, at the expectation that one has to give); resentment at receiving (which is, in the end, a resentment at the expectation that one has to

---

among the Trobrianders, an analysis that Mauss was quick to correct; see Douglas 1990: viii.

[10] Bergadaà 2006: research on charitable giving illustrates how the self-identity of givers motivates their giving of donations; Schwartz (1967) describes an office game called the 'Office Pollyanna', which vividly evokes gift-giving as an expression of the views of others. It involved choosing the recipient of a gift (at random) and presenting them with an inexpensive item which made (1) 'comical or witty reference to that part of their personal makeup which in the eyes of the giver, is most worthy of exaggeration'. These examples help to demonstrate the way in which a gift is a confirmation of self-identity by the giver, and an imposition of identity upon the recipient.

[11] Ward and Broniarczyk (2011) point out that research suggests that we tend to give presents that conflate our own tastes with those of the recipient, which leads to unwanted or disliked gifts. They argue (165, citing Mintel 2008) that this may be why gift registries are increasingly popular (annually in the United States gifts worth $19 billion are registered for and more than $5 billion purchased).

[12] Ward and Broniarczyk 2011: 177. This dynamic can be seen in studies of charitable giving in villages of northern Thailand, which show it to be 'a complex language expressing both domination and resistance' that 'should not be located in the margins of volition and religion. Rather it is central to the political dynamics of the relations between elites and subalterns in class-stratified societies' (see Bowie 1998, quotation from p. 478). Lévi-Strauss (1965: 76) argued that the exchange of goods is a way of creating and shaping personal relationships, as a strategy for ensuring security.

[13] Carrier 1995a: 7.

give in return); resentment at others giving (that they have the gifts to give in the first place); and resentment at others' receiving (even if you already have what they have). The last appears to take us close to what is nowadays (in modern Britain at least) colloquially known as jealousy—especially if you are the one charged with making this gift.

Indeed, Aristotle appears to support this argument when he describes how those who are already great and have good fortune are *phthoneroi*. But the emphasis here is not (as has been translated) on the fear of having their own fortune carried away, but rather on a sense of resentment that others also take or have what they regard as an appropriate possession for themselves.[14] Indeed, Aristotle himself gives us a variety of 'scripts', emphasizing how *phthonos* may be made worse if the individual in question also wants the possession in question, or thinks they should have it.[15] The hand that feeds us may not only be bitten; it may bite back.[16]

Mortal *Phthonos*: Reciprocity and Resentment

In diverse literary and sociopolitical contexts, the cultural model of *phthonos* emphasized different aspects of the gift-giving relationship.

---

[14] Sanders (2014: 39) identifies a 'possessive jealousy' script of envy that he conflates with Arist. *Rhet.* 1387b28–31. The crucial aspect of this emotion is the desire to retain one's own possessions, and it describes the *phthonos* of the great man. However, some caution is necessary: when Aristotle explains the *phthonos* of the great man as πάντας γὰρ οἴονται τὰ αὑτῶν φέρειν, we can translate this as 'because they think that everyone is trying to deprive them of their own' (tr. Freese 1926, and see also Sanders 2014: 54), but translating *pherein* as 'deprive' imports an extra nuance. Compare another translation: 'for they think everyone else is taking what is theirs' (Ross); here *phthonos* arises not from losing something of one's own, but from others gaining something that one regards as one's own—while one has actually lost nothing oneself. This is borne out by the examples Sanders gives that can be read (in accordance with Aristotle) as concerned with not seeing another possess something that by rights is theirs: e.g. in Xen. *Cyr.* 3.1.39, the king of Armenia may feel *phthonos* that his son may admire the man he goes hunting with more than him, but it does not say that the son stops admiring the King; in Ar. *Thesm.* 249 Agathon is told that he has begrudged helping Euripides (which does not prevent him helping others), and in 252 he does not grudge a material gift, which he can spare; finally, in Ar. *Lys.* 1192, the speakers deny *phthonos*—that is, they do not mind seeing another acquire something they have—but it is also apparent that they can spare it. Although there is an element of not relinquishing something of one's own, the aspect of denying another is just as strong here—it is the root of Aristotle's set of 'scripts'.

[15] Arist. *Rhet.* 1387b.

[16] The original quotation is from Emerson 1929: 286.

Phthonos *and Misfortune*

The examples that have been discussed are from specific genres of praise and blame. But the connections they have enabled us to trace between *phthonos*, or cognates of *phthonos*, and responses to benefactions and good fortune can also be seen in other genres of writing. I have written elsewhere about the ways in which uses of *phthonos* and its cognates in the Homeric epics illuminate the crucial role of the gift in the communities described in those poems, and the complex customs, implicit assumptions, expectations, and resulting behaviours that accompanied it.[17] In epic, when individuals talk about *phthonos* and themselves, they tend to deny the emotion; in contrast, statements made about others and *phthonos* tend to be statements of attribution. These are usually challenging—either reprimands or insults (or the one understood as the other)—and can lead to conflict. As these examples show, when individuals deny that they have *phthonos*, they are stating their capacity, and willingness, to be involved in basic reciprocal relationships; in contrast, an attribution of *phthonos* makes an accusation that a person is unwilling to do so. In the Homeric poems, *phthonos* talk is a way of signalling information about the nature of one's participation in the crucial social system of reciprocity. In particular, it flags the darker emotions: feelings of resentment and anger at being involved in a system that required one to give or to receive, or to observe others giving or receiving.

In later work, as we have seen, the emphasis of *phthonos* falls more on the instinctive response to an individual's actual or even potential good fortune, and draws attention to actions, potential actions—or,

---

[17] See Eidinow forthcoming a. The observation of Walcot (1976: 26) that *phthonein* 'can be used in Homer when it means not much more than "to be unwilling"' supports the idea that the notion of resentment regarding processes of benefaction was a part of the meaning of *phthonos* and the social tensions it described already in these works. Of the ten examples of its use in the Homeric poems, eight occur in the *Odyssey*, a work that comments particularly on the importance of gift exchange. Von Reden (2003: 59–66) argues for a difference in the meaning of gifts between the two epics. The gifts of the *Odyssey* are still often made in contexts of gift exchange. In the *Iliad*, the context of battle serves to underline the characters' views that there are more important values than survival, and gifts tie into a system of exchange that emphasizes individual heroic values (e.g. Hom. *Il.* 12.310–21, where Sarpedon's explanation to Glaucus that the land they receive from their people means they must fight well in order to earn *kleos* in battle).

indeed, lack of action—that disrupt the cycle of reciprocity.[18] Herodotus' *Histories* repeatedly offers examples of this *phthonos* talk: for example, Aristodemos' valiant death in battle is not granted recognition, because it is said to have occurred because he wished to die, a story that Herodotus attributes to the *phthonos* of those spreading the story. Presumably they did not wish actually to die themselves, but are unwilling to recognize his sacrifice.[19] Similarly, after the battle of Salamis, the Greek generals are constrained by their *phthonos*: although the benefits it has brought are obvious, they cannot bring themselves to honour Themistocles' successful leadership. Able to vote twice, they each put themselves in first place, their *phthonos* exacerbated by the sense that they should have this recognition.[20] In contrast, when Themistocles returns from Sparta, one Timodemus of Aphidna, who is otherwise unknown—and in fact his insignificance and lack of political weight are stressed—repeatedly claims the victory of Salamis for the whole Athenian people; 'crazed' with *phthonos*, he cannot bear to see the gift of recognition granted only to Themistocles.[21]

These examples concern extraordinary battle honours, but the same pattern emerges at a domestic level, according to Xerxes, King of Persia. Defending his friend Demaratus, he provides a programmatic statement of *phthonos*: 'if one citizen prospers, another citizen has *phthonos* towards him and shows his enmity by silence, and no one (except if he has attained the height of excellence; and such are seldom seen), if his own townsman asks for counsel, will give him what he thinks to be the best advice'. Xerxes opposes a stranger's attitude to that of a citizen: the stranger will give good advice, and is 'beyond all men his well-wisher'; he offers a tidy opposition between

---

[18] Examples from Herodotus: potential good fortune: Hdt. 3.146.1, Maeandrius does not want (*phthonesas*) Syloson to recover Samos. Actual good fortune: Hdt. 3.30.1, Cambyses' response of *phthonos* (*phthonoi*) to his brother's facility with the bow; Hdt. 3.52.5, Periander invokes the *phthonos* his son will gain (*phthoneesthai*) by returning home; Hdt. 7.139.1, Herodotus' own allocation of honour to the Athenians may provoke *phthonos* (*epiphthonon*); Hdt. 8.69.1, those who feel *phthonos* (*phthoneontes*) at Artemisia's good fortune.

[19] Aristodemus: Hdt. 9.71.4–9.72 (*phthonoi*). Another example: Demaratus slanders Cleomenes (*phthonoi*) in Hdt. 6.61.1.

[20] Hdt. 8.124.1 (*phthonoi*).

[21] Hdt. 8.125.1: *katamargeon* ('crazed') is rare, poetic, and strong. In Pl. *Resp.* (329e6–330a), the man comes from Seriphos, 'an island noted for its insignificance' (see Bowie 2007).

an ideology of aristocratic gift exchange (the gift being that of trust) and rivalry between citizens.[22] With acknowledgment that Xerxes is making a case for his friend—and that what he presents is surely a simplification of social relations—we may still see some reflection here of the concerns about the disruptive nature of *phthonos* in a civic context.[23]

Across all these examples, whether they are voiced by a character or by Herodotus as narrator, the power of *phthonos* attributions is apparent. Most obviously, in the latter example, Demaratus slanders and is in turn slandered; when he is accused of *phthonos*, Xerxes asks that Achaemenes not subject him to *kakologia*, that is, not 'bad-mouth' him. But it is also true of Herodotus' own narrative: the Spartans are subtly demeaned by their inability to recognize a brave soldier; while Themistocles' eligibility for honour is only emphasized by the figure of the raving Timodemus—who offers a stark parallel to the Greek generals.

In contrast, Thucydides rarely uses the term in his own narrative, preferring to put it in the mouths of his characters. Nevertheless, we gain a strong sense of its role in the war: its appearance introduces a further layer of explanation, one that supports the sense of contingency that emerges from his experiential account of events. His earliest use of it sets the context most clearly: he is describing the destruction wrought by *stasis*; *phthonos* appears in a devastating final sentence about the possible reasons why citizens who would not join a political faction had to die.[24] It may have been because they were disliked for keeping apart, or, he suggests, they were killed because others felt *phthonos* that they might survive. It also occurs again after the siege of Amphipolis: the Spartans will not support Brasidas; they give some strategic reasons.[25] But Thucydides' emphasizes their emotional response to Brasidas' success: that they acted in this way 'partly through *phthonos* of their leading men, partly because they wanted to recover their men'. This almost incidental comment forms a powerful assessment of Spartan character.

---

[22] Hdt. 7.237.2 (*phthoneei*) and 3 (tr. Godley 1920).
[23] Opposition is a simplification in Kurke (2013: 80), who reminds us (91) that the polis is a complex institution, with many strands: 'aristocratic ideology may not always be coextensive with the aristocratic group'. The sharing of women prevents the Agathursi from feeling *phthonos* (4.104.1).
[24] Thuc. 3.82.8.   [25] Thuc. 4.108.7.

Other examples of the use of *phthonos* for characterization occur in speeches. These rhetorical uses of *phthonos* resonate with those in forensic oratory, not only in their content, but also in the ways that speakers manipulate the term. They also reveal a variety of contexts in which *phthonos* may emerge. Pericles crafts his employment of *phthonos* so as to discourage its expression—only a man who cannot achieve is unable to praise another or hear him praised because of *phthonos*.[26] But in fact, as he admits, *phthonos* is such a common emotion that, as noted before, only the dead are safe from it.[27] Meanwhile, Diodotus perhaps gives us the context for these remarks when he sets out his argument in the Mytilene debate (3.43.1). He observes that his fellow Athenians do not even need to feel certain that a man will gain success from the advice he gives in the Assembly before their *phthonos* towards him is aroused.

Thucydides also uses *phthonos* talk to reinforce individual characterization. Examples of some of the more belligerent comments about *phthonos* include Alcibiades confronting head-on the *phthonos* that he provokes;[28] and Hermocrates' address to the Camarineans, where he is unapologetic about the *phthonos* and fear that other states in Sicily feel towards Syracuse.[29] And, still in Sicily, one might compare Nicias' desperate reasoning about the *phthonos* of the gods: the Athenians may have been the object of *phthonos* when the fleet set out, but surely cannot deserve it any more.[30] We will address the topic of the *phthonos* of the gods next in this section; for now, it reminds us of the sense of *phthonos* mentioned earlier, in which a great man simply cannot bear to see another enjoy good fortune.

Across all these examples we see *phthonos* linked to episodes that describe responses to good fortune or its absence—the emotional difficulties of granting public praise, or accepting with equanimity the good fortune granted to others. They reinforce the wider social and cosmological associations of *phthonos*. Gifts and reciprocity are part of the social system by which the members of a community take care of each other, protecting groups and individuals from experiences of misfortune. But, as the example of Nicias demonstrates, this

---

[26] Thuc. 2.35.2 and 2.64.5.   [27] Thuc. 2.45.1.   [28] Thuc. 6.16.3.
[29] Thuc. 6.78.2.   [30] Thuc. 7.77.3 and 4.

idea also relates to divine behaviour. Before leaving this topic, I want to suggest that this mortal model can help us to understand divine *phthonos*—although it comprises fundamental differences from the mortal dynamic of reciprocity, in both the nature of the gifts and the perception of the giver.[31]

Divine *Phthonos*: A Different Currency

Ancient Greek narratives about divine *phthonos* repeatedly draw attention to the ways in which the gods undermine mortal notions of reciprocity, and how unexpected and often unpredictable provisions of fortune, both good and bad, destabilize the mortal system of reciprocity.[32] For example, Pindar's descriptions of the dynamics of *phthonos* reveal that it is not only individual and mortal communities that are involved. Crucially, this system of exchange is underpinned by the presence and role of the gods.[33] It is their granting, or not, of favour, their gifts, that can bring a man success or cause him to topple from victory to disaster.[34] Pindar's words remind both his subject and his audience of their mortal fragility, their dependence on unseen powers.

The role of the gods in this system has been described as a reflection and reinforcement of social dynamics among the elite, and it is true that Pindar introduces divine favour to reinforce mortal status.[35] But

---

[31] Cf. Siegel (2006: 9), where he argues that naming the source of fortune and misfortune (in his study, this is witchcraft) means that these experiences are 'possibly recovered for the social'.

[32] A detailed discussion of divine *phthonos* can be found in Eidinow forthcoming a.

[33] *Ol.* 7.89-91, 9.28-9 and 100-4, 10.21, 14.5-6; *Pyth.* 1.41-2 and 8.76-7; *Isth.* 5.11. See Kurke (2013: 129-131) for gift-exchange imagery reinforced by the victor's relationship with Apollo in *Pyth.* 5. 23-31, Dioscuri in *Nem.* 10.49-54, Hermes in *Ol.* 6.77-81; and (131-2) for invented relationships in *Pyth.* 5.30-1, *Isth.* 1.52-4, 2.13-19, 6.3-7, and 8.61-60. It is not clear whether or not Kurke sees these relationships only as metaphorical references to gift exchange or not (see esp. 134, 136).

[34] *Pyth.* 7.19-21. The sentiment is perhaps most succinctly and famously expressed in *Pyth.* 8.95: 'Creatures of a day! What is someone? What is no one? A dream of a shadow is man.' The unpredictability of life, except for families blessed by the gods, is also described in *Ol.* 8.12-14, 12.10-12a, 13.105-6; *Pyth.* 5.54-5 and 7.19-21; *Nem.* 6.1-7; *Isth.* 3.18b, 4.4-21. Tuche: *Isth.* 4.31-5, fr. 38 (Maehler). The fates: *Isth.* 6.16-18. Fate: *Ol.* 2.21 and 35, *Pyth.* 12.30; fr. 232 (Maehler), and Charis' vacillation: *Ol.* 7.11-12.

[35] Kurke (2013) recognizes the role of the gods in the system of gift exchange, but her concern is with how the model relationship between divinity and mortal ratifies aristocratic gift exchange (see, for example, pp. 110, 131, 136-9).

there is another side to Pindar's presentation of the role of the gods, in which the nature of divine favour introduces a note of uncertainty about mortal status. Pindar works hard to create a picture of the ideal chain of reciprocal relationships, in which benefit and thanks are, as it were, nested within each other, across the levels of god, elite, and citizen. But he also makes clear how the gods are not bound into this mortal system of reciprocity. Their presence and indeed their gifts introduce a crucial note of uncertainty, a strong sense of risk, into this structure.

Pindar provides a reminder of the unknowability of one's own fate—both to the individual athlete, so that he not seek higher status, and to the citizen audience, so it gives praise to those who deserve it. The gods may deny their favours just as easily as they give them. As he notes: 'One must not contend with a god, | who at one time raises up these men's fortunes, then at other times gives great glory to others... | It helps to bear lightly the yoke one has taken upon one's | neck, and kicking against the goad | you know, becomes a slippery path.'[36] At the root of this profound unpredictability is the risk of the envy of the gods. Thus, at *Olympian* 13.24, as he hymns Xenophon of Corinth, Pindar asks that Zeus may be *apthonetos* ('without *phthonos*')—for all time to come—concerning words of praise; at *Isthmian* 7.39, as he sets out to sing in honour of Strepsiades of Thebes, he asks that the *phthonos* of the gods cause no disruption (ὁ δ' ἀθανάτων μὴ θρασσέτω φθόνος). In *Pythian* 8.72–3, Pindar intervenes on behalf of Aristomenes of Aegina to ask the gods for their 'favour without *phthonos*' (*opin aphthonon*),[37] and assumes a similar role in *Pythian* 10.20 for Hippocleas of Thessaly, when he asks that his subject and his father not encounter 'phthonetic reversals from the gods' (φθονεραῖς ἐκ θεῶν | μετατροπίαις). When he then implores, 'May the god not be pained in heart' (ll. 21–2: θεὸς εἴη | ἀπήμων κέαρ), the physical suffering of the god brings to mind the pains that afflict mortals suffering *phthonos*.

At the root of both mortal and divine *phthonos* is the risk inherent in the gift of good fortune itself.[38] Pindar shows how this danger reverberates through three different levels. First, there is the divine

---

[36] *Pyth.* 2.89–90, 93–6.
[37] As translated by Race, but note that *opis* usually means 'vengeance', not 'care' or 'favour' (LSJ gives no other examples), and can mean 'regard'.
[38] Hornblower (2006: 30–3) discusses the role of the gift in Pindar.

Phthonos *and Misfortune*

gift of good fortune, which produces success or prosperity, but may just as easily be reversed, or produce such self-belief that the individual destroys himself.[39] Second, there is the gift of the glory of that success or prosperity (material or not) by the individual to the community. And finally, comes the gift of recognition and honour from the community back to the individual.[40] In each case, *phthonos*, both mortal and divine, may rear its head and bite.

Confronted with the possibility of this danger, any successful individual must manage his gift of the glory of that success or prosperity (material or not) to the community; in return, the community must achieve a fitting gift of recognition for the individual. Bridging the dangerous distance between individual and community is the poet, trying to keep *hubris*, *koros*, the inevitable mortal *phthonos* all in check by keeping the nexus of gifts in circulation.[41] And yet this may not be enough: as Pindar stresses again and again, divine *phthonos* is the inherent cosmological risk of good fortune— unavoidable, yet unpredictable, desired and feared.

Herodotus provides a similar sense of the pervasive nature of divine *phthonos*, reinforcing the sense of supernatural involvement that suffuses his work. This begins with Solon's almost programmatic instruction to Croesus, where the sage describes the divine as *phthoneron te kai tarachodes* ('prone to *phthonos* and troublesome').[42] This is not, as some scholars have suggested, criticism of the gods for being acquisitive or competitive.[43] Despite its context—the tour of the King's treasury—this is a lesson about the risks involved in the reception of divinely maintained fortune, not the dangers of excess. Similar vocabulary occurs with regard to the events that befall Xerxes.

---

[39] The latter is illustrated by the story of Ixion (*Pyth.* 2.21–41), which provides a powerful illustration of the dangers of the divine gift.

[40] Crotty (1982: 120) notes that success is 'neither wholly human nor wholly divine; it both violates and respects the injunction to be content with what one has'.

[41] Pindar works to ensure that the gods are on his side, and his patron's. With the gods on side: *Ol.* 6.101–2, 7.87–95, 8.10–11, 9.21–30; *Pyth.* 6.7–9; *Nem.* 7.31–2. *Ol.*11.10 has been read as meaning that the poet also needs a god's help to succeed. Dickie (1987: 122) observes that Pindar's poetry is apotropaic—intended to keep away the dangers of *phthonos*—but Dickie links this directly to the evil eye.

[42] Hdt. 1.32.1.

[43] *Contra* Lanzillotta (2010: 91), who suggests that in this episode (Hdt. 1.32.8–9) and that of Polycrates' ring (Hdt. 3.40) the gods are motivated by avarice (the gods 'simply keep for themselves, as divine privilege, the right to enjoy happiness without counterpoint').

For example, in the commentary by Xerxes' uncle Artabanus, who echoes Croesus' conclusion that the gods are simply *phthoneros* towards men.[44] And in Themistocles' account of Xerxes' defeat, although he describes Xerxes as impious and wicked, this is not an explanation about the Persian king's lack of success in conquering Europe and Asia.[45] Instead, Themistocles states that the gods and heroes simply 'begrudged' (*ephthonesan*) them. The impression that Xerxes is the victim of more elaborate divine machinations is also reinforced by the mysterious dream figure, who will not let Xerxes turn back from his plans to conquer the Greeks.[46]

And this latter episode highlights a further dimension of the *phthonos* of the gods: while these divine dynamics seem closely to follow the mortal model, simply disrupting the dynamic of reciprocity, they also diverge in important ways. First, divine gifts occur in a very different currency from that of mortal gift exchange. Again, Herodotus offers some instruction: Solon tells Croesus about the glorious death of Tellus, then the unexpected deaths of Cleobis and Biton. Perhaps, in part, these stories are about Croesus' shortcomings (although his pride in the wealth he has amassed is only human), but they also underline the very different currency of divine gift exchange.[47] This is highlighted by the detail that the mother of Cleobis and Biton, albeit indirectly, asks for the deaths of her sons. They are the deserving recipients of ultimate good fortune from the gods—who take their lives. These divine 'gifts' are delivered in a currency that subverts our mortal understanding of what is valuable.

Related to this is the divine gift that leads to destruction: Pheretime, queen of Cyrene, mother of Arcesilaus III, and her horrible death offer a good example.[48] In Pheretime's case the divine opportunity to avenge herself is a gift that destroys her. The explanation is that 'Revenge that is too extreme attracts the *phthonos* of the gods'.[49]

---

[44] Hdt. 7.46.1.
[45] Hdt. 8.109.3. See Macan (1908 *ad loc.*), who argues that the description of Xerxes' destruction of sacred places should be seen 'not as the justification of the ways of gods to man, but as a statement of pure matter of fact —a fact inevitable, since what mortal invested with such power could avoid pride, presumption, impiety, sin?'.
[46] Hdt. 7.16–18.   [47] See Pelling 2006.   [48] Hdt 4.205.
[49] αἱ λίην ἰσχυραὶ τιμωρίαι πρὸς θεῶν ἐπίφθονοι γίνονται. The term used here, *epiphthonos*, also occurs when Herodotus is explaining how the Athenians played the crucial role in the Persian defeat—and he admits that his opinion may be *epiphthonon*, that is, it may be looked on with *phthonos* (Hdt. 7.139.1); see also Hdt. 9.79.2, where the general Pausanias uses the verb *epiphthoneo* to indicate

At one level, the excesses of her actions are certainly significant—and yet this aspect was not enough to condemn the eunuch Hermotimus, whose revenge on Panionius for his castration fails to provoke divine *phthonos*, despite being, as Herodotus tells us, 'the greatest that we know of'.[50] Compare the story of Polycrates, whose fate is sealed by his constant, unremitting good fortune. Polycrates considers himself to be *eutuches* ('fortunate'), but, as Amasis explains, this can only be temporary. The gods are envious ('the divine is *phthoneron*'), and their 'gifts' set up an impossible dynamic: the obligation they establish cannot be repaid, but nor can the gift be returned.[51]

With these latter examples in particular, we hear something of the bewilderment that Nicias expresses to his men in the passage, mentioned earlier in this section, from Thucydides. Whereas for Pindar, and in fact much of Herodotus, references to divine *phthonos* can seem to provide a systematic explanation of events, Nicias' observations underline the gulf between divine and mortal status and perception. Although Nicias offers it as encouragement to his men, it seems rather to communicate a sense of their helplessness, in particular, his inability to understand divine reasoning.

Coming finally to evidence from the fourth century, and the forensic speeches examined earlier, we find the role of *phthonos* as a mortal phenomenon is by far the greatest focus of this *phthonos* talk. At first sight there is little that obviously links to the behaviour of the gods. This is perhaps its own explanation: the complexity of mortal *phthonos*, in particular its link to a vicious character (as in *Against Leptines*), may have made it conceptually difficult to associate it with the gods. Certainly, when it does occur—for example, in Aristophanes' *Wealth* in the mouth of Wealth himself as he explains his blindness—it appears (in this context, comically) as venomous.[52]

---

condemnation of the act of insulting the dead. (See Nilsson 1967: 761 for the argument that this difference in treatment turns on gender: because Pheretime is a woman, revenge is less acceptable than it would be for a male.)

[50] Hdt. 8.105–6.

[51] Hdt. 3.40.2, linking it to Solon's earlier explanation by this phthonetic vocabulary. Kurke (1999: 109) notes that Polycrates must give something back to the gods, and sees the anthropological parallels (making the Maussian reference), but does not link this to *phthonos*.

[52] Ar. *Plut.* 87–92. Wealth explains Zeus was motivated by *phthonos* to blind him, so as to prevent him from rewarding those who deserve it.

Yet similar patterns of explanation can still be found. Even as Demosthenes is criticizing Aeschines in *On the Crown*, he refers to the cycle of fortune that Solon describes: 'Seeing that a man who thinks he is doing very well and regards himself as highly fortunate is never certain that his good fortune will last till the evening, how can it be right to boast about it, or use it to insult other people?'[53] Similarly, as already noted, reference to *ti daimonion* ('some divine power'), which may drive a state or a person to ruin, also echoes preceding patterns of divine causation.[54] In general, however, it seems that although divine *phthonos* still occurs as an explanation in certain writers, its role in the cultural imaginary is slowly being taken over by a personification of the phenomenon that divine *phthonos* once directed: *Tuche* ('chance' or 'fortune').[55]

In the material examined above, divine benefactions mirror, but pervert, a mortal system of benefaction, destabilizing expectations and assumptions, and drawing attention to the power of the gods and their unfathomable motivations. Solon emphasizes to Croesus the difference between being *olbios* (prosperous) and *eutuches* ('fortunate'): *olbios* may look better at first glance, but it cannot be relied upon. Divine gifts are unpredictable in terms of both their nature (are they in fact good fortune?) and steadfastness (they may appear or disappear without warning). Where *phthonos* talk provided Homeric characters with a potent force for their negotiations of status, the *phthonos* talk we find in later narratives of divine *phthonos* offers another kind of negotiation, as mortals attempt to explain their experiences of fortune and misfortune.

---

[53] Dem. 18.252 (tr. Vince and Vince 1926): ἦν γὰρ ὁ βέλτιστα πράττειν νομίζων καὶ ἀρίστην ἔχειν οἰόμενος οὐκ οἶδεν εἰ μενεῖ τοιαύτη μέχρι τῆς ἑσπέρας, πῶς χρὴ περὶ ταύτης λέγειν ἢ πῶς ὀνειδίζειν ἑτέρῳ; This follows a reference to Aeschines' *baskania*, but the implications do not seem to be supernatural.

[54] See Dem. 9.54, where Demosthenes seems to link it to mortal *phthonos*, referring to the madness of the men of Athens whom he addresses, which may be motivated by 'love of *loidoria*, *phthonos*, and jesting', as he notes his fear that 'some divine power' is driving Athens to its doom (see also Aeschin. 3.117). Cf. Whitehead (2009: 331), who does not note the reference to mortal *phthonos*.

[55] See Eidinow 2011a. Dover (1974: 78) argued that belief in divine *phthonos* still prevailed in the fourth century; Dickie (1987) makes this argument, drawing attention (120) to links between *tuche* and *phthonos* in the poetry of Pindar and in tragedy (although he offers no examples). Whitehead (2009) agrees, but emphasizes the lack of evidence to support this position and argues for the burgeoning role of *tuche* in Polybius, Pausanias, and Plutarch (he does not adduce the orators).

Stories of divine *phthonos* have a particular sense structure of their own, revealing the gap between mortal expectations of reciprocity and divine unknowability. In these narratives, different authors emphasize different aspects of events, some stressing links with excess, others with pride, still others with cosmological order, or a blend of all three. But what all of these stories direct our attention to is man's unbearably uncertain relationship with his gods, and the sense of insecurity and ignorance that accompanies experiences of fortune and misfortune, one's own and those of others. Attributions of *phthonos* between mortals are a crucial element in this matrix of uncertainty, offering a mortal cause, but one that is inextricably linked to the manipulation of occult powers.

PHTHONOS AND OCCULT AGGRESSION

We have seen how narratives about divine *phthonos* could be used to explain random and inexplicable events of fortune and misfortune by offering justifications, validations, consolations, and explanations. Here I want to draw attention to the ways in which mortal *phthonos* also played its part in structuring experiences of otherwise inexplicable misfortune, and in reinforcing a sense of insecurity. In making this argument, I am drawing on research into other societies in other times and places, to highlight a recurring cross-cultural pattern. From the villages of Germany in the sixteenth century, to the forests of Colombia, from the bocage in northern France, to the townships of Soweto, South Africa in more modern times, we find similar interpersonal behaviours and narratives of explanation in which the envy of another's success is pinpointed as the root cause of that person's misfortune.[56] Across these cases, in the terms of Kenneth Burke's 'dramatism', the attribution of motive involves the identification of an agent—usually a person within the community, and often known, if not related, to the victim—whose agency is supernatural

---

[56] e.g. Ashforth 2005 (Soweto, South Africa), Campbell 1964 (Greece), Favret-Saada 1980 (northern France), Galt 1982 (Italy), Roper 1994 and 1996 (early modern Germany), Taussig 1991 (Colombia). There are of course myriad more examples that could be mentioned here; some of these will be introduced as part of the discussion that follows.

power.[57] As has been noted, Adam Ashforth has used this approach to explore the experiences of witchcraft in modern Soweto. He uses it to highlight the problems of epistemology that this mode of explanation presents: one can never know who is a witch and who is not, whose jealousy has been activated.[58]

Ashforth emphasizes the ways in which friends and neighbours are the likely source of such attacks—and this is a pattern that other scholars of witchcraft in other African countries have observed.[59] I want to suggest that a similar pattern of occult insecurity pertained in ancient societies. The two examples I will put forward are both from later than the period under study here. I use them because they offer, in each case, unusual access to the behaviour and concomitant thoughts of individuals going through these experiences. My suggestion is that these patterns of behaviour, at least, can also be traced in earlier evidence.

The first case dates to 197 CE, and concerns one Gemellus Horion, a landholder in Karanis in the Egyptian Fayyum, whose neighbours were stealing his harvests. We know about this case because Horion filed a number of petitions, first with the prefect Quintus Aemilius Saturninus, who authorized him to approach the *epistrategos*, then, before that latter hearing occurred, with the *strategos*, Hierax.[60] This case is distinctive because of the use of particular rituals by the thieves. To begin with, Horion's neighbours, Sotas and Julius, along with Julius' wife and a friend called Zenas, had marched into Horion's field and demanded to repossess his land; next, they arrived with a *brephos* or 'fetus', and stole his harvested crops. When Horion and two village officers visited Julius to complain, he threw the fetus at Horion in the presence of the village elders. He then proceeded to gather in the remaining crops in the field, taking them and the fetus home with him.

---

[57] In interpreting Burke's dramatism I am guided here by Benoit (1996), who is in turn guided by Mills (1940), but notes other interpretations of Burke's meaning.
[58] Ashforth 2003; see this volume, p. 136.
[59] See especially Geschiere 2013.
[60] *P. Mich.* VI 422 (copy *SB* XXII 15774; TM 12261) and *P. Mich.* VI 423 (copy 424; TM 12262); text published by Youtie and Pearl 1944. See Bryen and Wypustek 2009 for details of the case and (ibid.: 536 n. 2) for discussion; and the Leuven Homepage of Papyrus Collections (http://lhpc.arts.kuleuven.ac.be/archives/texts/90.pdf, accessed 1 December 2014) for details about the collection of papyri concerned with Gemellus Horion and his family.

Gemellus associates the use of the fetus with the emotion of *phthonos*—and here that emotion seems to have taken on almost physical dimensions.[61] The fetus, he reports, is intended to encircle his tenant farmer with *phthonos* (l. 13 *phthonoi periklisai*), and later, when Julius throws it at him in turn, to do the same to him (ll. 17–18). This imagery brings to mind the operation of a binding spell, which is intended to prevent its victim from acting; and we could say that it is remarkably successful in this respect—it even prevents the village officials and elders from doing anything to stop Julius.

We have one narrative here, which depicts Horion as the victim of magical activity and of *phthonos*. But, as Ari Bryen and Andrzej Wypustek observe, there are other perspectives that can be extracted from the evidence.[62] Gemellus Horion's family, it seems, had moved to Karanis relatively recently: his grandfather had bought a house there in 154 CE.[63] The family had grown quite wealthy quite rapidly, and at the time of these events owned a lot of land (by 189 CE, at least four houses, seven courtyards, and shares in other dwellings and courtyards).[64] Horion himself occupied a privileged position in the community: he was a citizen of Antinoopolis, with access to provincial Roman magistrates.[65] However, it is possible he did not spend a great deal of time in Karanis itself. Moreover, it appears that he was not prepared to support a liturgy (he petitioned to be excused on the basis that he was blind in one eye and had a cataract developing in the other), and there seems to have been some trouble with the collection of taxes.[66] It may be that

---

[61] See Frankfurter 2006 for the argument that the fetus was likely to be real, Bryen and Wypustek 2009 for the analysis of its relation to *phthonos*.

[62] Bryen and Wypustek 2009: 539–42.

[63] *P. Mich.* VI 428 (sale of a house; TM 12266).

[64] *P. Mich.* VI 370 (census declaration; TM 12174).

[65] On Gemellus Horion's family see especially Biezunska-Malowist 1957, cited by Bryen and Wypustek (2009: 540), along with the archive of Gemellus Horion (Smolders 2013). Alston (1995: 129–32) argues that Gemellus Horion did not inherit Roman citizenship from his grandfather, but see Smolders 2013 and Bryen and Wypustek 2009: 540 n. 10. For evidence that he was an Antinoite citizen (his right to wear the *chlamys*), see *P. Mich.* VI 426.18 (TM 12264). He appears as a representative of landowners and public cultivators of the village of Kerkesoucha: *SB* XIV 11478 (Youtie 1974: 149–52; TM 14456).

[66] That he may not have spent a lot of time in Karanis, see Smolders 2013: 3–4 n. 12; the property in *P. Mich.* VI 370 is listed through the estate manager. In *P. Mich.* VI 425 (TM 12263) Horion complains that a tax collector's assistant has demolished the

in such a context, it was in fact Gemellus who was seen as the source of *phthonos*, since he disrupted the cycle of benefaction in the community by taking from its resources, and then refusing to contribute.[67] This may be reinforced by the possibility that his eye diseases were also perceived as being related to the evil eye, which, as we have seen, is a phenomenon closely linked to *phthonos*.[68] It may be that a fetus was thought to offer protection, and the neighbours had brought it with them to shield themselves from Gemellus, rather than to attack him, while they asserted what they perceived to be their rights to property that he refused to share.[69]

A second example takes us forward two centuries to Antioch and the precarious, intensely competitive world of the professional orator. Libanius had trained in Athens, and taught rhetoric in Athens, Constantinople, and Nicomedia before becoming municipal sophist of Antioch, in ancient Syria, in 354 CE; within and beyond the city he was connected to an impressive network of scholarly and government notables, which both supported and endangered him, in turn. He also ran a school of education, and had to attract students by competing in public-speaking competitions, an experience that he himself describes in terms of extreme aggression.[70]

---

doors of the house there (198 CE). Petition to be released from liturgy: *P.Mich.* 426.1–24, 199/200 CE.

[67] Bryen and Wypustek (2009) introduce the parallel of C. Furius Chresimus.

[68] Plutarch's essay *On Envy and Hate* makes parallels between *phthonos* and sore eyes (Plut. *De invid.* 537e), and see also Philodemus, περὶ κακιῶν *Liber Decimus*, col. xii.15 (ed. Jensen). Discussions of the physical operation of the evil eye in Plut. *Quaest. conv.* 680c–683b and Heliod. *Aeth.* 3.7–9. Capelle (1953) argued that both were likely to be derived from the same source (Phylarchus), but cf. Dickie 1991. See Alvar Nuño 2012 for ancient associations between ocular pathologies and the evil eye. The only ancient description of the casting of the evil eye is in Ap. Rhod. *Argon.* 4.1669 ff. Later iconography certainly associates the evil eye with *phthonos*: see most famously the Kephallenia mosaic, where text and image establish the connection unequivocally: *LIMC* 8.1. *Phthonos* 16 (p. 994); for other examples, see Dunbabin and Dickie 1983. The *phallos* (an apotropaic symbol against the evil eye) is also found in images relating to *phthonos*: see examples in Dunbabin and Dickie 1983: 36–7. See also this volume, p. 120.

[69] Youtie and Pearl (1944: 125) note that a premature infant or animal would count as an *aoros* (that is, one that has died untimely); they also mention that it is *biaiothanatos* ('dead by violence' (?)) and *ataphos* ('unburied') and this 'might produce considerable agitation, to put it mildly, in those against whom its malignant force was directed'. *PGM* IV.2578 uses an *embruon gunaikos* as an ingredient in a sacrifice intended to subject a woman to the spell-maker's will.

[70] See Lib. *Or.* 1.91, 2.14 (tr. throughout this section are from Norman 1992); Cribiore 2007: 91–2.

But by the 380s, this life of feuding competition seems to have reached something of a peak: Libanius appears to have been facing increasing criticism and disapproval, which his own conduct did little to ameliorate. This is the context for a number of incidents that he describes, which provide first-person insight into the supernatural violence that pervaded interaction between professional rivals. The most famous example occurs in 386 CE, and is the culmination of a notable period of difficulties. These included a plague and famine in the previous year, marked disciplinary problems with students at his school, and a charge of magic made against his (dead) secretary, which culminated in a number of arrests, exiles, and floggings for the practice of various forms of divination.[71]

In this episode, Libanius is the victim: he describes how he finds himself unable to speak, read, or write; he suffers from gout; he becomes unsociable, not visiting the baths or going to dinner, and he cannot study.[72] He has a dream that seems to him to 'portend spells, incantations and the hostility of sorcerers'; he starts to wish to die.[73] He has his suspicions of who has done this to him, although nothing is said explicitly. When he falls ill, he reports, there were people 'prophesying that I would be dead before morning, and, in fact, in other cities it was said that I was dead already'. More to the point, throughout the earlier stages of his suffering, when the cause was still unknown, his 'friends kept urging me, and each other too, to prosecute certain individuals who were rumoured to be responsible for this'. Libanius restrains them, 'telling them to offer up prayers rather than to have folk arrested for secret machinations'.[74]

The cause of all his distress becomes clear to him when a mutilated chameleon 'turned up from somewhere or other' in his classroom. He observes how its head was tucked between its hind legs, a front leg was missing, while the other was covering its mouth to silence it.[75] This is

---

[71] Lib. Or. 1.241–2 (in this passage, note the double meaning of *cheimoni* to mean winter, and a charge of magic, as noted by Norman 1992, *ad loc.*). The ill-discipline included students leaving the teacher they were registered with and applying to work with another, thus cheating the original teacher out of payment. Petit (1979, *ad loc.*) suggests that Libanius resorted to some kind of magical action to diminish this mobility, noting that he is unwilling to give details about it; see Norman 2000: 112–14.

[72] Lib. Or. 1.243–4. See, for discussion of this incident, Bonner 1962 and Graf 1997: 164–5.

[73] Lib. Or. 1.245 φάρμακα δὲ καὶ μαγγανεύματα καὶ πόλεμον ἀπὸ γοήτων ἀνδρῶν ταῦτα ἐδόκει δηλοῦν; see Brown 1970: 127–9.

[74] Or. 1.247 and 248. [75] Lib. Or. 1.249.

no joke.[76] But although, according to his *Autobiography*, this discovery appears to allay his symptoms, a speech he wrote at about the same time suggests that it does not soothe his concerns. Instead, it confirms his sense that there are people plotting against him. In the speech, he works his way through the different constituents of the city with whom he is in contact. He explains how and why, if any of them is responsible for the spell, they cannot claim they are acting in revenge; rather, they have wronged him.[77]

What kind of injury they have done him, and the motivations behind it, become apparent from other anecdotes, in which we find Libanius has been allocated the role of magic-maker, accused of provoking other people's suffering. First, in Constantinople, one Bemarchius goes around spreading the story that Libanius beat him by using sorcery, specifically by hiring a 'man who controlled the stars'.[78] We are told that the accuser is supported by a group of accomplices: 'Chagrin, fear, and *phthonos* made them his accomplices—all these emotions in the case of the professors, *phthonos* in the case of the rest.'[79] Similar events occur when he moves to Nicomedia: a rival speaker asserts that he has been bewitched by Libanius (this is why Libanius has consistently beaten him in rhetorical competitions). The man accuses Libanius of afflicting mental illness on his wife by magical means, and then of having killed her.[80] The case goes to court—in the end, on Libanius' insistence—but is dismissed. The implications of this case ripple out through wider society: the man is reduced to buying students, and we are told therefore 'he became a laughing-stock throughout the city'. He is defended by only one citizen, who is upset that his own wife's name has become entangled in the gossip about the case.[81]

---

[76] Although some make this interpretation: Festugière 1959: 113, as observed by Norman 2000: 125.

[77] Lib. *Or.* 36, written soon after (he refers to the chameleon, in §3).

[78] Lib. *Or.* 1.43 (early 340s): ἀνδρὶ τυραννοῦντι τῶν ἄστρων.

[79] Lib. *Or.* 1.44: ἐποίει δὲ αὐτῷ τοὺς συνεργοὺς λύπη τε καὶ φόβος καὶ φθόνος· τοὺς μὲν σοφιστὰς πάντα, τοὺς ἄλλους δὲ τὸ φθονεῖν.

[80] Lib. *Or.* 1.49 and 62ff.

[81] Lib. *Or.* 1.64–6. There are yet more examples of accusations against Libanius: twice it is alleged that he has used body parts in magical activity. In one claim, a rival bribes a boy to accuse Libanius of decapitating two girls so as to use their heads in the creation of binding spells. In another, one Sabinus links Libanius to the head of a corpse and a forged letter (see Lib. *Or.* 1.98 and *Or.* 1.194).

The idea that it is *phthonos* that lies behind these interactions is reinforced by its appearance in further similar cases.[82] Thus, Libanius himself defends his secretary Thalassius by claiming that his accuser was envious of his brother, and sought his death through sorcery.[83] In another example, even as he casts himself as supporting his ex-pupil, he passes on the rumours that Severus' extraordinary successes at court are the result of sorcery.[84] And it is important to bear in mind that, under anti-pagan legislation, making this connection could have extremely serious consequences for the accused. In the case of the charge brought by Bemarchius, Libanius himself tells us that the (newly appointed) governor Limenius tried to indict him on an accusation of magic;[85] while the trials at Scythopolis in Palestine during the late 350s may have put Libanius directly in danger—as it was, some of his friends were put on trial.[86]

The destructive power of *phthonos* is emphasized again and again. It need not necessarily lead to overt accusations of sorcery, but the association appears to have been so common that it did not need to be made explicit.[87]

---

[82] That the focus on *phthonos* in Libanius' writing is not idiosyncratic is suggested by Basil of Caesarea's homily *On Envy*, which dates to around 364 CE. As Vasiliki Limberis' (1991) analysis makes clear, this work suggests that *phthonos* and the evil eye were 'pervasive problems' (184) in Basil's parish; Basil similarly links *phthonos* with gossip (see *De invid.* 10 Migne). The homily also uses the imagery of rust consuming iron that we saw in the *Suda* (see p. 72; *De invid.* 1a Migne), and provides vivid descriptions of the physical appearance of those suffering from *phthonos* (see *De invid.* 5 Migne).

[83] *Or.* 42.12.

[84] Bear in mind that Severus' father had pulled him out of class during his second year. See Cribiore (2007: 147), who suggests (211) that in his later works (*Or.* 58.30-1 and 38.6) accusations of pederasty and homosexuality take the place of magic in explaining the success of youths whom Libanius believes have not been properly trained.

[85] Lib. *Or.* 1.45-7.

[86] Sandwell 2005: 115-16; Cribiore 2013: 155-6; Libanius pleads for his friends *Ep.* 37 (= Norman 49) to Modestus (cf. Amm. Marc. 14.12.6ff.).

[87] In *Or.* 30.15, Libanius notes how spite and *phthonos* would be enough for neighbours to start proceedings against anyone they wanted to accuse of making sacrifices (forbidden: C. Th. 16.10.7, in 381 CE, and reinforced in 385 CE: C. Th. 16.10.9).

2.5

Conclusion: 'Careless Talk...'

Among the charges that our sources tell us were made against Theoris, Ninon, and Phryne are accusations that they were involved in magical activities.[1] Theoris is described as a *pharmakis* by the man who prosecuted her; Ninon is accused in a later source of creating *philtra* for young men; Phryne is implicitly associated with this charge by virtue of the effects of her beauty (a story type that recurs), and perhaps also her profession. This charge has been hard to make sense of in a strict legal sense, but, as has been argued in the first part of this study, it may provide us with a thread to follow as we try to understand the social dynamics and related emotions that motivated members of the Athenian community to bring these women to court and condemn them. To help examine those dynamics, at the end of part 1 this study introduced one of the few pieces of evidence that suggests the kinds of emotions associated with the casting of magic, a binding spell that is unusually eloquent about the suspicions of its writer. And now, if we return to that spell—written by a man who feared that he was himself the victim of occult aggression—we may have some greater sense of the resonances set up by its mention of *phthonos*.

Phthonos is the dark companion of good fortune: its appearance signals the breakdown of the reciprocal relationships that ran like nerves through the ancient social body. Our sources describe the experience of this emotion, for the person suffering it, for the afflicted victim, and, finally, for the wider community. But what gives

---

[1] The full quotation is 'Careless Talk Costs Lives': this was a British government propaganda campaign of the Second World War intended to discourage gossip and rumour that might aid the enemy. Taylor (2010) gives further details about the campaign and its chief designer, Cyril Kenneth Bird.

phthonos this capacity to spread its poison so effectively? At one level it is the idea, found across cultures, that this phenomenon was connected with supernatural interventions, sometimes explicit, sometimes assumed. However, our sources also suggest a more mundane aspect, one that underpins even the supernatural explanations: talk. From praise poetry to the law courts, from personal writings to magical spells, and in the accounts given by the historians, *phthonos* comes alive in the mouths of those afflicted by it.

Some of our sources are more detailed than others. This aspect receives perhaps the most sustained attention in Libanius' accounts of accusations and counter-accusations. Those attacking him do so by spreading rumours; those supporting him use those rumours to diagnose his illness. Similarly, the evidence relating to Gemellus Horion can be teased apart to suggest the kinds of local stories that formed the basis for the accusations of *phthonos* being made. But the role of talk in the power of *phthonos* has been manifest across the different case studies, from Pindar's 'relish for those feeling *phthonos*' to Demosthenes' concern with *baskania*. *Phthonos* acquires its power through what is said—or indeed, in what is carefully not said—about another person. *Phthonos* talk categorizes the victim and identifies the guilty party, and then builds a network of support for those judgements. Another term for this is 'gossip'.

Part 3

Poison

3.1

Introduction: 'A Relish for the Envious'

We are looking at the ways in which *phthonos* or envy acquired its social force. Let us start this section by returning to the *Suda* entry with which the discussion of *phthonos* began. The quotation from Pindar reveals something about the social mechanisms involved in the operation of *phthonos*: 'words [are] a relish for those who are *phthoneroi*'.[1] It is words, of various different kinds and genres, which will form the backbone of this section on 'poison'. To illustrate why, we turn again to the trial of Socrates. This may seem like an odd choice, since, as we have seen, unlike the women's trials, there is no mention of *pharmaka* or *philtra kai epoidai* in the accusations against him. Nevertheless, this phrase does occur throughout Xenophon's defence of Socrates in the *Memorabilia*—usually in the context of his making friends, but also of his gaining followers.[2]

The phrase *philtra* first occurs in this discussion as Socrates answers Chaerecrates' concerns about how he should win the friendship of his brother Chaerophon. In response, Socrates demonstrates to Chaerecrates his understanding of how to manage social relationships successfully. For example, how to get an invitation to dine with an acquaintance on the occasion of a sacrifice, by inviting him first. The *philtra* in question involve manipulating the dynamic of reciprocity—giving so that you will in turn receive—but importantly, they also comprise the clever use of words.[3] This is also true of the second example, where Socrates is discussing with Critobulus the

---

[1] Pind. *Nem.* 8.21.
[2] If these items could lead to a prosecution for *asebeia*, it seems unlikely that Xenophon would repeatedly describe Socrates as discussing, recommending, and claiming their use for himself.
[3] Xen. *Mem.* 2.3.11 and 14.

nature of making friends. He refers first to the singing of incantations, then to *philtra*—the two terms appear to belong together: 'There are spells (*epoidas*), they say, wherewith those who know charm (*epaidontes*) whom they will and make friends of them, and drugs (*philtra*) which those who know give to whom they choose and win their love.'[4] The Sirens are given as a first illustration, but more current examples soon follow. These include Pericles, who made the city love him using spells, that is, through his speeches. In contrast, the account continues, Themistocles made the city amulets (a metaphor for the ships and fortifications he constructed for Athens).[5]

Finally, in his meeting with the intriguing Theodote, Socrates describes again the techniques in which he is an expert, and how he (like her) uses *philtra* and *epoidai* to attract and retain his clients, who study these things with him, φίλτρα τε μανθάνουσαι παρ' ἐμοῦ καὶ ἐπῳδάς.[6] The parallels he draws between them highlight the similarities and differences of their fields of expertise. His potions and spells comprise his mastery of rhetoric, but are used with a similar intent to hers, that is to attract clients. In turn, although her potions and spells are for love, her sparring with him suggests that she is also expert in rhetoric. In the end, they tussle charmingly over who gets to use the 'wheel'—an erotic magical device—on whom first.

These examples illustrate the various dimensions and associations of drugs, spells, charms, and words that this part of the book, 'Poison', will examine—so, 'poisons' in both their literal and metaphorical senses. The multivalence of the Greek idea of spells or charms is well known. Socrates uses the term *philtra* here—since the emphasis is particularly on spells of attraction—but another commonly used term is *pharmaka*. This can allude to drugs that do harm and those that bring benefits; it can refer to natural forms of drug, but also supernatural forms; it may also indicate potions, amulets, and binding spells or curse tablets.[7] The link between drugs and spells is perhaps less obvious to a modern mind, but makes sense in a culture in which words were understood to be able to work some kind of change in the world, including on a person's

---

[4] Xen. *Mem.* 2.6.10 (tr. Marchant and Todd, rev. Henderson 2013): εἶναι μέν τινάς φασιν ἐπῳδάς, ἃς οἱ ἐπιστάμενοι ἐπᾴδοντες οἷς ἂν βούλωνται φίλους αὑτοὺς ποιοῦνται· εἶναι δὲ καὶ φίλτρα, οἷς οἱ ἐπιστάμενοι πρὸς οὓς ἂν βούλωνται χρώμενοι φιλοῦνται ὑπ' αὐτῶν.
[5] Xen. *Mem.* 2.6.13.   [6] Xen. *Mem.* 3.11.16–18.
[7] Scarborough 1991: 139, as discussed on p. 12 above.

Introduction: 'A Relish for the Envious'

physical or mental state. Thus, incantations could be used, for example, as part of a healing treatment; while, in turn, potions, amulets, and curse tablets were a physical instantiation of the verbal power that helped to create them, and might, in the last two cases, be inscribed upon them.

Pindar in his third *Pythian* ode offers a glimpse of the different ways in which *pharmaka* can be used when he describes Asclepius healing the sick: 'some he tended with calming incantations (*epaoidais* [sic]), while others drank soothing potions, or he applied remedies (*pharmaka*) to all parts of their bodies; still others he raised up with surgery'.[8] In contrast, we find Plato using *pharmaka* to describe binding spells;[9] and the Tean community calling down a curse on anyone who uses *pharmaka deleteria* (harmful *pharmaka*) against the Tean state or individual citizens.[10] The ambiguity of these terms is neatly on show in Plato's discussion in the *Laws* of the proposed penalties for *pharmakeia* (the creation and use of *pharmaka*). *Pharmaka* is used to describe the activities of practitioners of both medicine and magic, while *epoidai* are included (alongside curse tablets) as some of the supernatural 'weaponry' (intended to do harm) in the armoury of those who sell magical services.[11]

Turning back to Xenophon's *Memorabilia*, we see the speaker using this complex set of associations to describe the words that Socrates employs to persuade his audience. This power was not unique to Socrates: across a range of writers we see rhetoric and the associated skills of sophistry linked with supernatural power.[12] The idea that words could have supernatural power did not apply only to the polished formulations of professional speakers, but also to less formal forms of speech. We have seen that the term *baskainein* and its cognates, usually employed to describe someone bad-mouthing another, gradually developed to acquire associations of malevolent

---

[8] Pind. *Pyth.* 3.51–3 (tr. Race 1997a): τοὺς μὲν μαλακαῖς ἐπαοιδαῖς ἀμφέπων, | τοὺς δὲ προσανέα πίνοντας, ἢ γυίοις περάπτων πάντοθεν | φάρμακα, τοὺς δὲ τομαῖς ἔστασεν ὀρθούς.

[9] Pl. *Resp.* 364b–c.   [10] ML 30.   [11] Pl. *Leg.* 933a.

[12] See for example, Dem. 29.32, where Demosthenes links rhetoric, sophistry, and sorcery via skill in speaking; Din. 1.66 and 92, where Demosthenes is described as a *goes* ('sorcerer'). De Romilly (1975) discusses magic and rhetoric, and magic and sophistry in the writings of Gorgias, Plato, and Isocrates. Burkert (1962: 50–1) discusses the links made by Plato between rhetoric, sophistry, and deceit, and *goeteia* (e.g. Plato *Symp.* 203d); see further discussion in Hesk 2000: 213.

supernatural activity.[13] It is to these casual, everyday forms of verbal 'poison' that we turn our attention in this section of the book; in particular, to the gossip that itself concerned the creation, possession, and employment of *pharmaka*, natural and supernatural. Gossip will be the key to this code of social tensions and unofficial accusations. It will offer a way into the unspoken, the implicit, the untold stories of dread and harm in ancient Greek society; and it will also help to clarify how a community moves, as it were, from unsociable whispers to civic action.

In part 3 we start by examining how gossip has been analysed as a phenomenon, before looking at the ways in which scholars of ancient Greek culture have approached it, and how we may problematize and complicate their methodologies. Scholars of gossip have suggested a three-stage process as a model to describe how gossip operates, comprising circulation, formation of meaning (not necessarily consensus), and action.[14] In what follows, we will use this paradigm to trace different pathways of gossip through ancient society.

---

[13] See pp. 74 and 135. Aeschines calls Demosthenes a *goes* at Aeschin. 2.124, and 153, 3.137 (and a *magos*) and 207.
[14] Merry 1997: 54.

3.2

Identifying Gossip

The word 'gossip' originates from the Old English 'god-sibb' or 'gods-sibling' meaning godparent. The term was used of those (of both genders) who acted as 'sponsors' at a baptism, but it also seems to have developed a more specific meaning, describing those women who attended a mother 'before, during and after a birth'.[1] These god-sibbs were invited to witness the birth for the purpose of the child's baptism, and evidence suggests that the presence of a certain number of women was considered necessary.[2] Over time, 'gossip' has come to be associated with a particular activity, that of 'idle' talk, usually about a person, and evaluative in nature, and in some way 'superfluous (in the sense of being unnecessary or excessive)'.[3] We tend to be quite loose in our use of the term (unlike some other cultures);[4] in particular,

---

[1] Christening attendees: see Rosnow 2001; quotation, Sugg 2007: 112.

[2] Wilson (1990: 70–1, citing MacFarlane 1976: 50, 118 and 415) notes that there is evidence to indicate anxiety about the number of women present at a birth as god-sibbs, citing the diary entry for 14 January 1658 of Ralph Josselin, which describes how his wife gave birth to their eighth child 'so strongly and speedily that... only 2 or 3 women more gott in to her, but god supplied all'. Josselin seems to have gathered the local women to attend his wife, but other evidence suggests it was the woman's own choice whom she invited to attend her. Not being invited was considered a slight, but it was also sometimes linked to much more serious subsequent suspicions, such as accusations of witchcraft. Historical records suggest that women who were not invited to a birth ran a risk of being accused of witchcraft if anything happened to the baby, presumably because they were thought to be resentful (see Purkiss 1996: 101–5). (This is possibly the source of those fairy tales where lack of an invitation to an event involving a child is seen as a slight that must be supernaturally avenged.) The god-sibbs shared responsibility with the midwife for preparing the birthing room and protecting it from both natural and supernatural threats (see Wilson 1990: 73 and 74, and Purkiss 1996: 101).

[3] Rosnow 2001: 201–11.

[4] Compare the eleven different words for different types of gossip identified in a small Spanish community in Gilmore 1978.

there is an overlap with 'rumour'. But definitions suggest that whereas rumour may or not involve people and is always speculative, 'gossip' is always about people, and may include fact or supposition; moreover, in general, its use still bears a sense of contempt.[5]

And yet, recent research in evolutionary psychology suggests we should treat this activity with far more respect, since it seems it is 'what makes human society as we know it possible'.[6] Far from being a tool for more effective hunting, or for abstract discussion, 'language evolved to allow us to gossip'—and gossip facilitated social bonds.[7] Seeking gossip's origins, Robin Dunbar describes it as a 'kind of vocal grooming' for large social groups, comparable to the physical grooming that can be observed among primates.[8] This one-to-one activity allows them to build social bonds, developing trust with and knowledge of individuals. Gossip, he argues, allows us to do the same thing, but at a much larger scale, passing information through a broad network of individuals, to find out about mutual acquaintances, to assess personal contacts, and thus to oversee our social networks.

The basic motivation behind gossip in his account is that it helps to identify and deal with 'free riders', that is, individuals who do not cooperate with others. Research shows how free riders are less likely to be successful in a community that both cooperates and gossips, since their activities are more likely to be revealed.[9] Moreover, some simple experiments suggest that free riders themselves are less willing to step out of line if they think that others are commenting on them.[10] In agreement with these hypotheses, the neuroscientists Uta Frith and Chris Frith have observed that information about other people which is received through gossip plays a key role in how we behave towards them. If we

---

[5] The distinction between rumour and gossip follows Rosnow (2001: 211). Rosnow (207-8) argues that this must now be updated to include the ways in which rumours are spread other than by word of mouth, e.g. the Internet and newspapers, and that interest in rumours is not necessarily short-lived (he notes that some themes of rumours 'may endure virtually forever'). Allport and Postman (1947: ix) define rumour as 'a specific (or topical) proposition for belief, passed along from person to person, usually by word of mouth, without secure standards of evidence being present'. Stewart and Strathern (2004: 39) argue that scandal is always damaging, while rumour and gossip need not be; rumour circulates more widely than gossip. Besnier (1996: 544) states that scandal is 'gossip that has become public knowledge' and rumour is 'the unconstrained propagation of information about an event of importance to the group.'

[6] Dunbar 2004: 100-10. [7] Dunbar 1996: 79. [8] Ibid.: 78-9.
[9] Ibid.: 172, citing Enquist and Leimar 1993. [10] Dunbar 2004: 108.

hear good things about a person, then we are more likely to trust them, even more so than if we see those good things for ourselves.[11] In turn, as other scholars have observed, if you do not have gossip about a person, or know their precedents in behaviour, then that person can seem much more dangerous.[12]

Most popular understandings of gossip align, at least in part, with the analyses above: gossip does usually concern people's reputations, especially the difference between them and their actual behaviour, aiding the social processes involved in allocating responsibility, liability, and trust.[13] Overall, these approaches draw particular attention to the role of gossip as a powerful way of spreading information.[14] But as further examination suggests, this is only a small part of what it can do.

'ALL STRANGERS SHOULD BE SHOT!'

The idea that gossip helped to forge social bonds was the basis of the analysis of anthropologist Max Gluckman—but with a much less roseate glow. The quotation that heads this section comes from an example he provides of gossip being used to establish and then protect the identity of a small community.[15] Gluckman describes how in a Welsh village 'back tattle, gossip and scandal' were used to prevent differences of opinion among the villagers from exploding into direct confrontation. When the crisis point was reached and could no longer be avoided, a stranger was manoeuvred into taking

---

[11] Frith and Frith (2012, especially p. 302) describe the results of experiments concerned with the effects of reputation, conveyed through word of mouth. This is part of a larger argument about the ways in which we keep track of our own and others' reputations for cooperative and trustworthy behaviour.

[12] See Merry 1997: 67 for references.

[13] I say 'in part', because the analyses above stress positive evaluations (even if negative ones must be implicitly a part of the story they tell) and the positive role that this can play within an organization or small group (see Rosnow 2001 and Baumeister et al. 2004). Popular definitions of gossip tend to highlight its role in spreading negative evaluations (see, for example, Michelson et al. 2010, esp. 376).

[14] Some scholars use this basic definition to identify gossip, perhaps emphasizing a specific purpose: for example, to be able to make comparisons quickly and easily. See e.g. Hannerz 1967, Besnier 1989, Tannen 1990, Bergmann 1993, and Suls 1977 (who emphasizes comparisons).

[15] See Gluckman 1963: 312 (the story is from Frankenberg 1957).

the necessary crucial and controversial decision at a village meeting. Once this had been achieved, gossip then stepped in again, flooding over the apparent rift like a soothing balm. It blamed the stranger ('all strangers' according to the phrase that heads this section) for 'destroying village unity', and subsequently (consequently?) a sense of harmony among the villagers was restored.

As this anecdote suggests, Gluckman understood the social function of gossip to be largely focused on its role within a group, and he emphasized how it works 'to unite a group within a larger society, or against another group, in several ways.' He stated that 'The more exclusive the social group, the greater will be the amount of gossip in it.'[16] His explanation, inspired by the approach of the British structural-functionalist school, was based on the assumption that institutions promoted social cohesion and stability. Thus, Gluckman developed a notion of gossip as 'social glue', holding group members firmly within the boundaries of a homogenous, shared set of values, binding them together in harmony, preventing disagreements from emerging into the open, and ensuring that competition for leadership cannot get out of hand. Gluckman did mention (this is rarely observed in summaries of his work) that gossip of this kind depends on a pre-existing sense of community; and that, when a group begins to lose such a sense, then gossip will 'accelerate the process of disintegration'.[17] But, as one of Gluckman's early critics, Robert Paine, observed, this still means that gossip is made explicable only in terms of the social structure—be it integrative or disintegrative to that structure.[18] Moreover Gluckman's only nuancing of this picture was a brief discussion of the gossip about royalty, between social classes (lower about upper and vice versa), and about celebrities, which 'produces a basis on which people transitorily associated can find something personal to talk about'.[19]

Paine offered an alternative: 'It is the individual and not the community that gossips. What he gossips about are his own and others' aspirations, and only indirectly the values of the community.'[20] Writing a few years after Gluckman, Paine also understood gossip as playing a variety of social roles, but did not agree that it was primarily about advancing the values, and thus the 'overall unity' of the

---

[16] Gluckman 1963: 308–9, and 313 and 309 for quotations.
[17] Ibid.: 313–14.   [18] Paine 1967: 282.
[19] Gluckman 1963: 315.   [20] Paine 1967: 281.

Identifying Gossip 175

group. Instead, he saw it as instrumental, a conduit of communication used by individuals as a way of forwarding their particular interests. In this 'transactionalist stance', gossip may support social values, bringing people a sense of cohesion or belonging, but it may also be deeply disruptive to the community as a unit, pushing its members into opposing factions—even destroying a community.[21]

The distinctive dimensions of Paine's approach have been developed by others. On the one hand, in terms of its (destructive) individual power, scholars have explored how gossip can work as a weapon, often wielded without accountability.[22] Niko Besnier's work on the Pacific Ocean island of Nukulaelae has shown the power and reach of gossip within a small community. He notes that in gossiping conversations, 'reputations are made and undermined, actions are evaluated and condemned, motives are speculated upon and criticized, virtues are scrutinized and found wanting, and rumours are started and circulated'.[23] On the other hand, anthropologists have drawn attention to Paine's argument that gossip plays a significant part in managing information. For example, it may be described as performing a key role in the storage and retrieval of a group's information resources or in shaping legal precedents and disputes. Indeed, some cultures draw a distinction between this kind of gossip and gossip that is judgemental.[24]

Both Paine and Gluckman developed approaches that revolve around the interaction of the individual and institution, and emphasize gossip's role in establishing trust.[25] Returning to the insights on gossip offered by researchers in evolutionary psychology and neuroscience discussed earlier, these also draw attention to gossip as a vehicle for spreading information about people, since the individual, and his or her motivations for gossiping, are firmly situated within the group. Questions of trust and cooperation are about individual interactions within the compacts formed by social

---

[21] Paine 1967: 283; called 'transactionalist' by Handelman (1973: 210).
[22] Bailey 1977 and Goodwin 1982.   [23] Besnier 2009: 36.
[24] Storage and retrieval, as argued by Roberts (1964); legal precedent and dispute, as argued by Cox (1970); distinction between information and judgement in Hannerz (1967); and see Merry 1997: 50–1. Other distinctions between types of gossip include positive and negative gossip (Leaper and Holliday 1995), blame and praise gossip (Soeter and van Iterson 2002), and critical and uncritical gossip (Taylor 1994).
[25] Gluckman 1968: 31.

institutions. They lead us back to the fundamental need for group solidarity and harmony. And, in turn, these individual interactions both inform and are clearly informed by group experiences.

'HOW'S THAT? HER? HOW DID SHE GET TO DO THAT??'

However, recognizing gossip as a dynamic process of information 'management' between individuals peels back the lid of the functionalist approach. It prompts the recognition that society and information about society may interact at many different levels. And this leads to a more detailed interrogation of the nexus of interactions that underpin processes of gossip and their implications. As noted already, a three-stage process has been suggested to describe how gossip operates. This comprises circulation, formation of meaning (not necessarily leading to consensus), and action, and this will provide a basis for the approach of the rest of this part of the book.[26] The first two stages of this model will be explored across sections 3.2–6, and we will return to the final stage, action, in section 3.7.

First of all, in terms of circulation, there is the nature of the information exchange itself. The easiest model is one in which one party knows and another does not. Thus, gossip may be thought of in terms of patterns of economic exchange. As the market expands, so does the gossip in circulation. There are benefits for those involved (although probably not the subject of the gossip), including entertainment, information, the intimacy of the relationship involved, perhaps money, and surely status, and power.[27] However, the process of gossip is rarely so simple. To begin with, there is the nature of the 'currency' itself: the information that gossip transmits is far from certain, and this has a number of implications.[28]

As already mentioned, gossip does not produce an account that resembles the normative structure of a 'story', but is rather 'a

---

[26] Merry 1997: 54.
[27] Bergmann 1993: 67. Economic exchange: Rosnow 2001: 219; social status: see Baumeister et al. 2004.
[28] Merry (1997: 51–2): '[gossip] thrives when the facts are... neither publicly known nor easily discovered'.

reconstructive genre', a process that enables the creation of a narrative. This has a number of consequences. First, it may bear on how those who do the gossiping are regarded. Being a gossip, especially a judgemental gossip, is to risk the censure of the community.[29] This may be rooted in the impression that the gossiper has gossiped at all, let alone because he or she has gossiped too much, or the gossip itself is revealed to be inaccurate.[30] This can be illustrated by the dialogue that has supplied the quotation used above as a subtitle.[31] Two women are starting to gossip. The woman who has initiated the gossip begins by mentioning an absent mutual acquaintance; the response her friend makes establishes that she both knows the person and is prepared to enter into a relationship of gossip.[32] As this demonstrates, gossip can be a way of creating friendship and influence, but those who gossip need to play their hand carefully: the process may backfire on the person spreading the gossip in the first place.[33] Some studies have noted how, in some groups, particular phrases tend to be used around episodes of gossip, apparently to indicate that the speaker is not finally responsible for the content of the information that they are relaying.[34] But although we have focused here on the person providing the gossip, this reminds us that information management is more than information delivery: the audience of gossip also plays a crucial role. Far from being simply passive recipients, he, she, or they may also, at any moment, help to generate information.[35]

---

[29] See Merry (1997: 52) for a range of evidence, including her own research among urban African Americans (1981) and Campbell's work on Greek pastoral nomads (1964: 291), as well as research on Austrian mountain villagers (Heppenstall 1971), and Chinese peasants (Wolf 1972); see also Foster 2004.

[30] On the dangers of gossiping too much, see e.g. Bergmann 1993: 99.

[31] Bergmann 1993: 93; discussed further below.

[32] As Bergmann 1993: 93.

[33] Friendship and influence: Foster 2004: 83–4. Rosnow (2001: 219–22) offers the three functions of information or news-bearing, influence, and intimacy—although he does mention the incentive of 'fun' elsewhere (219). Emler (1994: 136–7) suggests that gossip is unscheduled, informal, face-to-face (one-to-one), and between acquaintances. The idea that gossip may backfire is based on examinations of different cultures (see Kurland and Pelled 2000 and Brison 1992, which are both concerned with small, close-knit, and relatively egalitarian communities; see Harrison 1993: 618).

[34] See Haviland (1977) on 'or so I hear' and Bernstein (1983) for 'It's just talk...'.

[35] See Roberts 1964. There are some cultures or contexts where the role of an audience is more visible than in others: for example, studies of gossip among Fiji islanders reveal how those listening join in the conversation (at different levels) and, in some examples, become co-authors of the story being told. Brenneis (1987) examines the aesthetic aspects of the gossip produced. Goodwin (1990: 229–57,

Gossip turns on the sharing of particular meanings: this is not just about understanding the content of the information being spread, but also its import in terms of values and principles—and, crucially, the ways in which these may have been transgressed.[36] This notion of ideals and gossip offers a useful basic model for the interaction between the values of a society and the way it prompts gossip. But it is also important to recognize that gossip will reflect the dynamic and diverse nature of society, drawing attention to the ways in which a particular ideal may be differently regarded by diverse parts of society, at different times. For example, the nature of a woman's background—slave or free, foreigner or citizen—may become a matter of gossip only when the identity of her son and his claims to citizenship are in dispute.[37] Gossip is, in this sense, co-created, as becomes clear when we think about these moments of telling, hearing, and judgement.[38]

This takes us from the circulation of gossip to the formation of meaning, demonstrating how these two stages overlap: although gossip is itself a creation (with noted aesthetic qualities), it is also a creative force. First of all, there is the process of cultural learning that occurs in the spread of gossip. Part and parcel of the maintenance of norms, gossip not only provides a system of policing, but also a process of teaching members of a group about what is acceptable.[39] The information in question involves shared cultural models, social meanings, references to commonly known events and people.[40] Without those shared references, gossip is unlikely to make sense—but at the same time, it is gossip that helps to create their sense.[41] It is

---

esp. 256–7) examines the ways in which stories offer participation structures: these provide situations for social organization as individuals choose which version or teller of a story they choose to support. The nature of participation may then result in changes to the structure of the recounting of the story itself (e.g. elaboration, topic shift, etc.). Abrahams (1970) describes how gossip is judged by the community (of the Caribbean island of St. Vincent) as to whether it has been used appropriately.

[36] See Almirol 1981.   [37] e.g. Dem. 57.18–19.

[38] Handelman (1973: 212), drawing on Goffman (1961), stresses the importance of the encounter, and its transformational nature.

[39] Baumeister et al. 2004.

[40] Merry (1997: 54) calls them 'cognitive maps of social identities and reputations'.

[41] But it can come together, as Donald Roy (1959: 161) describing his own experience of working in a factory: 'the disconnected became connected, the nonsense made sense, the obscure became clear, and the silly actually funny...the interaction began to reveal structure'. For the ways in which shared cultural meanings are necessary for gossip's subtleties to make sense, see Noon and Delbridge 1993,

illustrated literally by the topographical gossip of the Haiǁom Bushmen of southern Africa, which 'comprises the cognitive processes by which they orientate themselves'. As they travel, each bushman gathers information 'about plant use, the topographical transitions between countries, the travels and travel accounts of fellow Haiǁom, the exchanges between social groups and other relevant information'.[42] In the process of gossiping, these individuals are literally constructing a map of their world. In turn, this example highlights the dynamic, emergent nature of gossip.

Thus, in terms of the first two stages of gossip identified above—circulation and the formation of meaning—as well as 'a way of drawing a social map of reputations and as a means of political competition and conflict', gossip also sets an individual in their larger social context. It provides a system that allows personal identity to be constantly shaped and reshaped, as relationships are negotiated.[43] The idea that the narrative of gossip may play this role has received some support from more recent cognitive analysis of the role of narrative as the link between individual cognition and the surrounding culture. Cultural narratives of all sorts help to determine our sense of our own identity, setting ourselves not just in our current social position, but also in historical time—and, beyond that, establishing our cosmological location. As Armin W. Geertz puts it: 'our texts and narratives are not just hermetic containers of semantic worlds, but also and more significantly, producers of neural mappings, minds, selves, memories, histories and worlds'. And, alongside 'religious narratives, autobiographies, hagiographies, myths and legends, dreams and vision narratives', he explicitly includes 'even gossip'.[44]

Abrahams 1970, and, often quoted, the comments of Gluckman (1963: 313–14) on the frustration of not being able to access a group's gossip.

[42] Widlok 1997: 328.
[43] As Merry 1997: 69, and compare Bailey 1971: 281 and Dunbar 1996: 66.
[44] See Geertz 2004: 376.

3.3

Genres of Gossip

The previous material, starting with social harmony and ending with cosmological insights, gives us some idea of how scholars have analysed gossip as a social process.[1] This section and the following three sections of the book will use these approaches to examine the role and pathways of gossip in and through the ancient society of Athens. This one will examine the language and locations of gossip; the following three comprise case studies demonstrating the ways in which the presence of gossip can be traced in different kinds of ancient discourse. The first looks at 'public' gossip in the law-court speeches, and the question of the border between gossip and slander. The second examines gossip in epitaphs, and curse and confession inscriptions. I have called this kind of gossip 'private' to indicate its more personal nature. The third case study explores the relationship between gossip and binding spells, and the significance and meaning of secrecy in this context. Each case study explores its material not only for the presence of gossip, but also for the ways in which these different discourses may themselves have fostered gossip.[2]

---

[1] The idea that gossip is a key aspect of the Mediterranean social environment is far from new, and much work has been done on this in both ancient and modern Greek society, e.g. Du Boulay 1976, Cohen 1991, Hunter 1994: 108. See Cohen (1991: 38–41) for a compelling defence of comparing and relating social practices in the ancient and modern Mediterranean.

[2] Does the size of the community matter? It has been debated whether or not Athens was a face-to-face community (see Hunter 1994: 117, but cf. 97 and 150–1), but recent debates about the size of the Athenian population and how that affects interpersonal relations are not at issue here. Even in a modern city, 'the essential conditions for the existence of personal reputations still obtain for more people' (Emler 1990: 178). In Athens this consideration is supported by the fact that demesmen were considered synonymous with neighbours, and that both were called into court as witnesses (as Hunter 1994: 117).

The ancient vocabulary of gossip tells us a little about perceptions of gossip. As well as those words that associate gossip with babble and chatter or idle talk, such as the verbs *laleo* or *perilaleo* and *huthleo* (and related nouns, e.g. *lalia* or *huthlos*), other terms draw attention to diverse aspects of the creation of gossip.[3] Thus, the literal 'making of stories' is highlighted by the noun *logopoiema*, meaning an 'idle tale', 'piece of gossip', and the verb *logopoieo*, meaning 'to write or compose'.[4] This aspect of manufacturing a story is underlined (with horrible consequences) in Plutarch's account of the barber who spreads the story of the Sicilian disaster of 415 BCE. The man is punished because he is a *logopoios*, that is, a story-*maker*, who is unable to provide details of the event: 'But, on being asked from whom he had learned the matter, he was unable to give any clear answer, and so it was decided that he was a story-maker, and was trying to throw the city into an uproar. He was therefore fastened to the wheel and racked a long time, until messengers came with the actual facts of the whole disaster.'[5]

Where it is used to indicate gossiping, *logopoieo* is often in association with the idea of, literally, 'going around' (*perieimi*), alluding to the physical process of spreading the stories in person.[6] The activity of story circulation is also emphasized in another noun, *spermologos*, which is used to describe 'one who picks up and retails scraps of knowledge, an idle babbler', and originates in the imagery of a bird

---

[3] See LSJ, s.v. *perilaleo* 'chatter exceedingly, gossip', Ar. *Eccl.* 230, M. Aur. *Med.* 1.7, Ar. *Ran.* 376; *huthlos*: Pl. *Ly.* 221d, Dem. 35.25; old wives' gossip: Pl. *Tht.* 176b, Porph. *Abst.* 4.16; plural: Pl. *Resp.* 336d.

[4] Antiphanes 166.2 K-A; see also Andoc. 1.54, where he claims that the story that he informed against his associates to save his own skin is one that his enemies invented; and Andoc. 3.35, where he uses the term to criticize the ways in which the ambassadors negotiating peace between Athens and Sparta lay claim to resources that they do not in fact have.

[5] See Plut. *Nic.* 30.1 (tr. Perrin 1916): ὡς δ' ἐρωτώμενος παρ' οὗ πύθοιτο σαφὲς οὐδὲν εἶχε φράζειν, δόξας λογοποιὸς εἶναι καὶ ταράττειν τὴν πόλιν, εἰς τὸν τροχὸν καταδεθεὶς ἐστρεβλοῦτο πολὺν χρόνον, ἕως ἐπῆλθον οἱ τὸ πᾶν κακόν, ὡς εἶχεν, ἀπαγγέλλοντες.
As Danielle Allen (2003: 100) points out, the barber is a slave, and those who punish him are citizens. Thus, the story also clarifies gossip and social relations, and the nature of the city's control over both.

[6] Din. 1.32: It is used to describe Demosthenes' behaviour when he was attempting to associate himself in public with Charidemus' embassy to the Persian king by 'going around the agora telling stories'. In Dem. 21.198, Demosthenes himself uses it to describe Meidias' behaviour, and how he is 'going about' telling the story that Demosthenes has cancelled the prosecution. See also Dem. 4.48–9 and 6.14.

picking up seeds.[7] Demosthenes accuses Aeschines of being a *spermologos peritrimm' agoras*—that is, literally, a 'storyteller worn smooth by (his activities in) the marketplace'.[8]

This brings to mind the places where gossip would circulate, also highlighted by certain terms: thus, *lesche* indicates gossip of the sort that went on in the *leschai* or places where men would spend their time. (The word later came to be used of public buildings where meetings were held.)[9] Theognis uses the verb *leschazo* with *kaka* ('bad things') to indicate malicious gossip.[10]

But not all gossip is straightforwardly mortal. *Pheme* is perhaps more closely related to the concept of rumour than gossip, but the two are difficult to distinguish.[11] It indicates a report in general circulation, often about a person's reputation (and when it offers the information they want, litigants in the courts can become suspiciously anxious to deny that such stories are the same as mere malicious gossip).[12] The source of a *pheme* is often unknown and mysterious, and this can be seen to have several implications.[13] First, it allowed those who spread a story to distance themselves from it.[14] Second, and perhaps more importantly, this sense of an obscure origin may also have led the term to develop a distinctive 'other-worldliness'.[15]

---

[7] See LSJ, s.v. *spermologos*, 'picking up scraps, gossiping': D.H. 19.5, Plut. *De cohib. ira* 2.456c; one who picks up and retails scraps of knowledge, an idle babbler, gossip: Dem. 18.127, *Act. Ap.* 17.18, Ath. 8.344. See also *spermologia*, 'babbling, gossip': Plut. *Alc.* 36, 65b; and *spermologeo*, 'to pick up seeds' Plut. *De tranq. anim.* 2.473a, and 'to be a gossip' Philostr. *VA* 5.20.

[8] Dem. 18.127; cf. Ar. *Nub.* 447, where the same term *'peritrimma'* is used to describe someone practised in the law courts. Strepsiades uses this term alongside a number of others that are concerned with the glib, deceptive, and abusive use of speech by such characters.

[9] LSJ, s.v. *lesche*: as a place to hang about: Hom. *Od.* 18.329, Hes. *Op.* 493. Public building: Paus. 3.14.2 and Plut. *Lyc.* 16.24. Gossip: Eur. *Hipp.* 384; and in a less malicious sense, discussion: Hdt. 9.71.3 and 2.32.1, Soph. *OC* 167, Call. *Aet.* 1.1.16, *Epigr.* 2.3.

[10] *Leschazo*: Thgn. 613. Herodotus has *perilescheneutos* (2.135.5), and *prolescheneuomai* (6.4.1).

[11] LSJ, s.v. *pheme*: common report (not gossip): Aeschin. 2.145, Hdt. 9.100, Hom. *Od.* 20.100, Aesch. *Ag.* 938, Ar. *Eq.* 1320, Pl. *Leg.* 672b. Reputation: Hes. *Op.* 760, Thuc. 1.11, Aeschin. 1.127. Good report or fame: Hdt. 1.31, Isoc. 5.134.

[12] Aeschin. 2.145.

[13] e.g. report or rumour of mysterious origin: Hes. *Op.* 763; cf. Aeschin. 1.128 (see LSJ s.v. *pheme*).

[14] As Lewis 1996: 13.

[15] Prophetic utterance: *Od.* 2.35, 5.72; Soph. *OT* 43, 86, 475, 723, *El.* 1109, *Trach.* 1150; Eur. *Hipp.* 1056, *Ion* 180, *Hel.* 820; Pl. *Phd.* 111b; Isoc. 9.21; Xen. *Symp.* 4.48; cf. *Cyr.* 8.7.3 (see LSJ, s.v.).

Genres of Gossip 183

Herodotus uses it of a prophetic utterance about the fall of Babylon, and the appearance of the portent (*teras*) it foretold—a mule giving birth; more specifically, after Adrastus kills Croesus' son, *pheme* is used to describe the message of Croesus' dream that had foretold this death (the events had 'fulfilled the *pheme* of [Croesus'] dream').[16] And in his account of the banishing of Cleomenes, Herodotus uses the term *pheme* and the more explicitly prophetic *kledon* (an omen in a chance utterance) interchangeably to describe the words of the priestess of the Acropolis who had banned his entrance to the sanctuary.[17]

These are specific utterances or messages, but more general rumours can also acquire a portentous and even prophetic significance. For example, as the Greeks line up at Mykale, the story (*pheme*) goes around that there has been a victory for them in Boiotia, which does wonders for their morale—and Herodotus comments on how the timing of this message seems to be evidence of 'the divine order of events'.[18] And of course, it is this kind of message that gets talked about, as Isocrates suggests when he describes how he prefers not to join in the speculation about the birth of Evagoras of Salamis:

περὶ οὗ τὰς μὲν φήμας καὶ τὰς μαντείας καὶ τὰς ὄψεις τὰς ἐν τοῖς ὕπνοις γενομένας, ἐξ ὧν μειζόνως ἂν φανείη γεγονὼς ἢ κατ' ἄνθρωπον, αἱροῦμαι παραλιπεῖν, οὐκ ἀπιστῶν τοῖς λεγομένοις, ἀλλ' ἵνα πᾶσι ποιήσω φανερὸν ὅτι τοσούτου δέω πλασάμενος εἰπεῖν τι περὶ τῶν ἐκείνῳ πεπραγμένων, ὥστε καὶ τῶν ὑπαρχόντων ἀφίημι τὰ τοιαῦτα περὶ ὧν ὀλίγοι τινὲς ἐπίστανται καὶ μὴ πάντες οἱ πολῖται συνίσασιν.

> I prefer to say nothing of the portents, the oracles, the visions appearing in dreams, from which the impression might be gained that he was of superhuman birth, not because I disbelieve what is said, but that I may make it clear to all that I am so far from resorting to invention in speaking of his deeds that even of those matters which are in fact true I dismiss such as are known only to the few and of which not all the citizens are cognizant.[19]

As these examples suggest, it is not only the origins of the rumour, but also the way in which it spreads that suggest a supernatural power. Indeed, after 465 BCE, *Pheme* acquired a cult in Athens, in recognition of the role of rumour in announcing the victory won by the Greeks over the Persian forces at the battle of Eurymedon.[20]

---

[16] Hdt. 3.153.1–2; dream: Hdt. 1.43.2–3. See LSJ, s.v.
[17] Hdt. 5.72.2 and 4.   [18] Hdt. 9.100.2.
[19] Isoc. 9.21 (tr. Van Hook 1945).   [20] Aeschin. 1.128 and 2.145.

The meaning of *pheme* therefore ranges across a spectrum of registers, natural and supernatural, and contexts, personal and impersonal. These possibilities can, with no great fanfare, introduce greater significance to what may seem to be at first sight only idle chatter. With a little less subtlety, the more obviously prophetic term *kledon* also appears in contexts where the relation to gossip is unavoidable. First, an example from tragedy: in Euripides' *Alcestis*, Alcestis, facing her own death, laments for her daughter, fearing that a stepmother 'will cast some disgraceful slur (*kledona*) on your reputation and in the prime of your youth destroy your chances of marriage'.[21] But this idea of a reputation-in-the making is also found in the law courts. For example, when Andocides is describing the gossip about the 'evil spirit' which lives in the house of Hipponicus, the father of his rival Callias—and which, he argues, is in fact Callias himself—he describes it as a *kledon*, 'on the lips of little children and silly women throughout the city'.[22] In this context, this more poetic term with its supernatural resonance fits the content of the gossip that it describes; it highlights how Callias' monstrous deeds are more appropriate to a tragedy than to real life.

I start by drawing attention to this supernatural dimension of gossip because it is rarely discussed: instead, modern scholarly analyses have highlighted the role of gossip in maintaining shared sociocultural values. For example, Virginia Hunter has drawn attention to the role of gossip in 'sanctioning individual conduct and thereby ensuring appropriate standards of community behaviour'. She evokes Athens' reputation for being a shame culture, whose inhabitants were profoundly anxious about breaking implicit standards of behaviour and exposing themselves to public mockery.[23] Gossip was the overseer of this system: even as it elicited ridicule for deviant behaviour, it set the ideal standards to which individuals should conform. It bridged family and community values, dragging details of private life into the public spotlight, while penetrating deep into the privacy of the *oikos*, as Aeschines describes in *Against Timarchus*: 'But in the case of the life and conduct of men, a common report which is

---

[21] Eur. *Alc.* 315–16: μή σοί τιν' αἰσχρὰν προσβαλοῦσα κληδόνα | ἥβης ἐν ἀκμῇ σοὺς διαφθείρῃ γάμους (tr. Kovacs 1994); other examples where *kledon* means 'reputation' include Aesch. *Ag.* 927 and *Choeph.* 505; Soph. *OC* 258.

[22] Andoc. 1.130 (tr. Maidment 1968): παρὰ τοῖς παιδαρίοις τοῖς μικροτάτοις καὶ τοῖς γυναίοις κληδὼν ἐν ἁπάσῃ τῇ πόλει.

[23] Hunter 1994; see Dodds 1951: 28 ff.

unerring does of itself spread abroad throughout the city; it causes the private deed to become matter of public knowledge, and many a time it even prophesies what is about to be.'[24]

Hunter argues that gossip helped to maintain an Athenian sense of identity 'by the images it evoked, by the standards it proclaimed, and by the morality it enforced. For, in criticizing one another, Athenians declared what it was to be an Athenian. Gossip thus helped to sustain the position of Athenian citizens as an elite surrounded by slaves and aliens.'[25] Indeed, she suggests that such gossip, used in the courts, may have played a levelling role, weeding out those who did not conform to common values and behaviours, and she focuses, in particular, on gossip as a form of surveillance over women.[26]

David Cohen also emphasizes how gossip and its purveyors play a key part in containing social behaviour. He describes how the constant flow of information that occurs in densely packed neighbourhoods, whether it comprises fact or inference, enables the formation of 'moral taxonomies of public evaluation'. When these evaluations enter channels of gossip, they can make or break people's reputations.[27] He sees gossip, especially women's gossip, as providing an answer to the question of how Athenian women's lives, neighbourhood lives, overlapped and interacted with larger structures of social and civic control, arguing that they were 'themselves agents in processes of social control that governed both their lives and the lives of men as well'.[28] In both these analyses, we see how gossip does not simply reflect social realities, but is part of their creation. Gossip is a tool for encouraging social conformity, and thus social equilibrium. By generating reputation, it helps to maintain the social fabric,

---

[24] Aeschines 1.127–8 (tr. Adams 1919): περὶ δὲ τὸν τῶν ἀνθρώπων βίον καὶ τὰς πράξεις ἀψευδής τις ἀπὸ ταὐτομάτου πλανᾶται φήμη κατὰ τὴν πόλιν, καὶ διαγγέλλει τοῖς πολλοῖς τὰς ἰδίας πράξεις, πολλὰ δὲ καὶ μαντεύεται περὶ τῶν μελλόντων ἔσεσθαι. See Hunter 1994: 116.

[25] Hunter 1994: 118.

[26] Hunter 1994: 117: she mentions that Ober (1989: 150) suggests that gossip in the law courts could have been a topos encouraged by orators who composed for wealthy clients, but observes there is no way to confirm this. On gossip about women, see McLure 1999: 57.

[27] Cohen 1991: 50. Fact or inference: ibid.: 65; e.g. Isae. 3.13–14, in which the neighbours offer testimony that a woman must be a *hetaira* because of what went on in the house of the local man she visited.

[28] Cohen 1991: 161.

repressing open conflict and upholding normative categories of behaviour, without the imposition of rigid rules.

But as Paine challenged Gluckman, gossip has more divisive aspects. Laura McClure has observed in her analysis of ancient Athenian society that gossip may have a 'dual function', both reinforcing and subverting a dominant culture. It can thus become 'a vehicle of resistance for the socially marginal'.[29] This dimension of gossip, she argues, may have been what shaped its depiction in Classical drama, as potentially threatening male citizens and their polis.[30] As she notes, there were both male and female domains of gossip:[31] on the one hand, there is plenty of literary evidence indicating how ancient Athenian men gathered and chatted; and more, as we shall see later on in this section, emerges from the forensic speeches, where gossip could be transformed into slander, and acquire civic power.[32] But ancient Greek literature portrays women as particularly susceptible to talking, and women's gossip as less public—and therefore less controllable.[33]

A brief overview of the latter begins with Semonides of Amorgos, writing in the seventh century BCE, who offers us descriptions of at least two types of women—literally, 'a fox woman' and 'a dog woman'—whose behaviours include some of the worst aspects of gossip:

| τὴν δ' ἐξ ἀλιτρῆς θεὸς ἔθηκ' ἀλώπεκος γυναῖκα πάντων ἴδριν· οὐδέ μιν κακῶν λέληθεν οὐδὲν οὐδὲ τῶν ἀμεινόνων· τὸ μὲν γὰρ αὐτῶν εἶπε πολλάκις κακόν, τὸ δ' ἐσθλόν· ὀργὴν δ' ἄλλοτ' ἀλλοίην ἔχει. | Another the god made from a wicked vixen, a woman who has expertise in everything. Nothing of what is bad escapes her notice, nor even of what is good, since she often calls the latter bad and the former good. Her mood is different at different times. |

---

[29] McClure 1999: 56, drawing on Spacks 1982: 19–38.
[30] McClure 1999: 58.   [31] Ibid.: 57 (cf. Sanders 2014: 45).
[32] e.g. male places for gossip included workshops and shops, often in or near the Agora: Dem. 21.104, 24.15, 25.52 and 82; Hyp. 4.21; Isoc. 18.9; Lys. 23.3, 24.20; Ar. *Nub.* 1003; and Men. *Kith.* 64–5; cf. Ar. *Eq.* 1375–6, *Av.* 1441, *Plut.* 338; Antiphanes fr. 247 K–A; Men. *Sam.* 510. See Ober 1989: 148–9 and Hunter 1994: 98–100.
[33] See discussion by Hunter 1994: 99 and 220 n. 8, who also cites Ober's observation (1989: 149) that prostitutes and entertainers at parties 'may have been conduits of gossip between classes'; and Lewis 1996: esp. 10–11.

τὴν δ' ἐκ κυνός, λιτοργόν, αὐτομήτορα,
ἣ πάντ' ἀκοῦσαι, πάντα δ' εἰδέναι θέλει,
πάντῃ δὲ παπταίνουσα καὶ πλανωμένη
λέληκεν, ἢν καὶ μηδέν' ἀνθρώπων ὁρᾷ.
παύσειε δ' ἄν μιν οὔτ' ἀπειλήσας ἀνήρ,
οὐδ' εἰ χολωθεὶς ἐξαράξειεν λίθῳ
ὀδόντας, οὐδ' ἂν μειλίχως μυθεόμενος,
οὐδ' εἰ παρὰ ξείνοισιν ἡμένη τύχῃ,
ἀλλ' ἐμπέδως ἄπρηκτον αὐονὴν ἔχει.

Another is from a bitch, ill-tempered, her mother all over again. She wants to hear everything and to know everything and peering and prowling everywhere she yaps even if she sees no one. A man can't stop her with threats, nor even if in anger he should knock out her teeth with a stone, nor can he by speaking to her soothingly, not even if she happens to be sitting among guests, but she constantly keeps up her yapping which nothing can be done about.[34]

These vivid, repulsive images find more mundane counterparts in fifth-century drama and fourth-century rhetoric. In Aeschylus' *Agamemnon*, the chorus mutters about woman's tendency to be taken in too quickly by good news—and the difficulty of quashing a story that is spread by women. Phaedra in Euripides' *Hippolytus* gives us a 'woman's' point of view when she lists 'lengthy and idle chats' among the pleasures of life. In comedy, we find the women of Aristophanes' *Ecclesiazousae* proclaiming themselves to be familiar with 'talking'. In comparison, the women of the *Thesmophoriazousae* argue that being 'talkative' is one of the characterizations of women by Euripides that they find unfair.[35]

Turning to the law-court speeches, we find multiple examples of women's gossip described (with some contempt). For example, Demosthenes, describing the activities of one Zobia who has been ill-treated by the defendant (Aristogiton), says she behaved 'just like a woman' (using *gunaios*, a scornful term for 'woman'), when she 'went about among her acquaintance with complaints of his conduct'.[36] Compare the passage from Andocides' description of the evil spirit resident in Hipponicus' house, cited earlier, where he blames

---

[34] Sem. fr. 7.7–20 (Stob. 4.22.193, ed. and tr. Gerber 1999).
[35] Aesch. *Ag.* 483–7; Eur. *Hipp.* 384; Ar. *Eccl.* 120 and *Thesm.* 393.
[36] Dem. 25.57: ἀλλὰ γυναίου πρᾶγμ' ἐποίει καὶ πρὸς τοὺς γνωρίμους προσιοῦσ' ἐνεκάλει.

'little children and silly women' for spreading the story throughout Athens. We also find more subtle allusions to women's gossip. A memorable example occurs in Lysias 1, when the old slave woman brings Euphiletus news of his wife's lover. She carefully explains her particular role as a messenger, and anxiously denies that she is simply meddlesome (*polupragmosunei*, literally 'with interfering curiosity'). It may be that Lysias was alluding to a familiar neighbourhood character, and perhaps raising a sympathetic chuckle in an otherwise tragic tale.[37]

But as well as evoking an amusing stereotype, these literary examples also suggest the power of women's gossip. For individuals, its effects could be devastating, as incidental moments from tragedy suggest. We have already mentioned how Alcestis fears for her daughter's reputation, at the mercy of her future stepmother. Medea offers another example as she emerges from her house, fearing to leave the women of Corinth to gossip and find fault with her.[38] Such gossip may be feared because it brings with it threats of further repercussions. Aristotle's account of the Syracusan *potagogides* (translated as 'provocatrices') and the tyrant Hiero's so-called *otakoustai* ('eavesdroppers') builds on this very stereotype. He relates how Hiero would send these out 'wherever there was any gathering or conference'. Not only were these women intended to listen, but they also had other eristic purposes, that is, 'to set men at variance with one another and cause quarrels between friend and friend and between the people and the notables and among the rich'.[39]

Although these references may indicate contempt for a female stereotype, men were also perceived to be culpable: we have seen that local gossip in Pindar is spread by and about both men and

---

[37] Lys. 1.15–16. The comedy of Lysias' old slave woman may have been reinforced by the fact that slaves too were represented as having a role in spreading information—and, more importantly, of spreading information about their masters. Explicit comic scenes portray slaves as revelling in gossip: in Aristophanes's *Frogs* (750–3), Aeacus confesses to Xanthias how much he loves to eavesdrop on his masters when they gossip (the verb used here is *laleo*)—and then blab it all to outsiders. In Menander's plots, the gossiping slave often becomes the linchpin of events (see Hunter 1994: 84–5, 89). Such slave gossip also has significance beyond the domestic sphere: in [Dem.] 50.48, it is the slaves who have discovered that the ship they are on will bring home an Athenian exile. To what extent such literary references represent real-life events is uncertain, but it seems likely that the audiences of all these narratives would need to find the behaviour described plausible, if not familiar.

[38] Eur. *Alc.* 315–16 and *Med.* 214–15.

[39] Arist. *Pol.* 1313b11–15 (tr. Rackham 1932): καὶ τὸ διαβάλλειν ἀλλήλοις καὶ συγκρούειν καὶ φίλους φίλοις καὶ τὸν δῆμον τοῖς γνωρίμοις καὶ τοὺς πλουσίους ἑαυτοῖς.

women. Of the examples just mentioned, after Medea's initial protests to the chorus of Corinthian women, she goes on to blame neighbours in general. She laments how 'before they get sure knowledge of a man's true character [people] hate him on sight, although he has done them no harm'.[40] And we have plenty of evidence in the courts for the generally accepted idea that men's private gossip could be both malign and damaging. A few examples from Demothenes' speeches include abuse of Meidias for gossip; observation of jurors' gossip (in the process of abusing Aristogiton); a description of the kinds of gossip the Athenians spread about Nicobulus; and a claim that he will be accused in court by Boeotus, 'as he is wont to do also in private life'. Similarly, we see Isaeus accusing his opponent Diocles of continually spreading malign gossip about the speaker's father; mentioning the stigma arising from having rights disputed; and protesting that he will not 'give those who wish to do so, a good occasion to speak evil of me'.[41]

Rather, the difference between the sexes appears to be more about a division of subject matter: women were concerned with events concerning family members and neighbours, in particular other women.[42] In turn, it has been observed that, in the masculine realm, 'gossip had a special power in classical Athens' because of the particular procedures of the democratic system.[43] This encouraged the examination of one's fellow men for qualification to participate in everything from being a citizen to holding office, and has been described as a system that 'allowed people, strangers even, to interact *as if* they trusted each other'.[44] However, I want to argue that while that may be true of such objective systems of evaluation as weights and measures for marketplace transactions, the arena of social and political relationships was somewhat more ambiguous and complex. It may be the case that the administrative structures that were

---

[40] Eur. *Med.* 219–21 (tr. Kovacs 1994): ὅστις πρὶν ἀνδρὸς σπλάγχνον ἐκμαθεῖν σαφῶς στυγεῖ δεδορκώς, οὐδὲν ἠδικημένος. Aristotle (*Pol.* 1277b) acknowledges the different expectations of male and female behaviours: 'for a man would be thought a coward if he were only as brave as a brave woman, and a woman a chatterer if she were only as modest as a good man' (tr. Rackham 1932).

[41] Dem. 21.148, 25.67–71, 37.52, 40.22; Isae. 8.36–7 and 44, 2.43.

[42] Aristotle (*Pol.* 1313b) notes that it is in his final form of democracy that women acquire dominance in the home and 'carry abroad reports against the men' (tr. Rackham 1932).

[43] Hunter 1994: 116.   [44] Johnstone 2011: 3.

instituted were intended to provide an objective framework. However, the processes of evaluation—the interactions by which decisions were obtained—were highly subjective, dependent on personal feelings, and often achieved through presentation, performance, and persuasion. In this rhetorical game, gossip played a key role.

The law courts will offer material for my first case study, but I will not be presenting arguments to show how important honour and reputation were to an Athenian male. That 'men judged others, and expected to be judged by reputation' has been thoroughly argued by other scholars, and there is no need to revisit it here.[45] Instead, I will focus in this case study on one of the ways in which that reputation might be undone: though the power of gossip, and, in particular, the ways in which that gossip was made present in court.

---

[45] Cohen 1991: 97.

3.4

Gossip ... In Public

GOSSIP VS. SLANDER

ἔπειτα οἱ μὲν ἐπειδὰν πρότερον λόγον λάβωσιν, οὐ μόνον ἃ ἔχουσιν αὐτοὶ δίκαια περὶ τοῦ πράγματος λέγουσιν, ἀλλὰ συσκευάσαντες λοιδορίας ψευδεῖς κατὰ τῶν κρινομένων ἐξιστᾶσιν τῆς ἀπολογίας· ὥστε συμβαίνειν αὐτοῖς δυοῖν τὸ ἕτερον, ἢ περὶ τῶν ἔξωθεν διαβολῶν ἀπο[λογου]μένοις τῆς [περὶ το]ῦ πράγματος [ἀπολογία]ς ἀπολελ[εῖφθαι, ἢ] μὴ μεμνη[μένοις] τῶν προκ[ατηγορηθ]έντων, ο[ἴησι]ν καταλείπ[ειν παρ]ὰ τοῖς δικαστ[αῖς ὅτι] ἀληθῆ ἐστιν [τὰ εἰρ]ημένα.

Hyperides, 1 fr. IVb.9.

Also, accusers, speaking first, do not confine themselves to putting the just arguments which support their case, but trump up baseless slanders about the accused and so deprive them of the means of defence. The latter are thus affected in one of two ways. Either they defend themselves against the extraneous charges and fall short in the relevant parts of their defence, or else they forget the accusations which have just been made, and so leave the jury with the impression that these are true.[1]

In this carefully crafted passage from his *Defence of Lycophron*, Hyperides 'comes clean' about the tactics used by speakers in court. For modern readers, he succinctly sums up the evidence of the forensic speeches. It was clearly a common gambit to accuse one's opponent of a variety of types of wrongdoing. Here again, we see the language of *loidoria*, or 'slander', used to try to create a distinction between legal

---

[1] Tr. Burtt 1954. The heading for this section is a quotation from this passage.

charges and plain abuse.[2] But a further useful term occurs here, one that both reinforces this distinction and ratchets up the power of this accusation: *diabole*. Translated in this passage, rather neutrally, as 'charges', this term, by the fifth century, had acquired a strong negative sense of 'slander' or 'abuse'.[3] And we have seen it used (albeit by a later source) to describe the divisive courtroom environment in which Aspasia was charged with *asebeia*.[4] In this section, we see Hyperides manipulate the idea. His next move is to explain how his opponent Ariston has (unfairly) employed various rhetorical strategies against him. He leaves the charge of *diabole* percolating in the jurors' minds, while, explicitly, he accuses Ariston of 'robbing him of his defence' by (it seems) slandering his witnesses, and instructing them on his likely line of argument. Only after that does he deny the accusations made against him.[5] And, of course, what he does not explain to the jurors is that his defence, that one has been the victim of *diabole*, was just as common as the activity of slandering.[6]

But if it was possible to introduce such slanders in the courtroom, how far could one go? It has been argued that in a society in which there was no forensic evidence, there would have been a need for a broader conception of relevance, with more and different kinds of background information allowed as evidence than are in a modern courtroom.[7] However, careful analyses of forensic speeches suggest that, although irrelevant prejudicial material can certainly be found across the corpus of forensic oratory, most of the arguments presented by speakers can be assessed as having a direct or indirect bearing on the case in question.[8]

---

[2] See also Hyp. 4.10, Lycurg. 1.11–13, and Lys. 19.5–6, cited by Hunter (1994: 102). Such attacks also went on in the Assembly: see Thuc. 6.15.2.

[3] As Carey observes (2004: 2), although the word essentially means 'divide' and examples of its neutral use are found even in the fourth century (Pl. *Symp.* 222d), by the late fifth century, noun and verb forms have come to possess a negative sense, associated with false allegations and abuse.

[4] See p. 66 of this volume (discussing Plut. *Per.* 32.2).   [5] Hyp. 1 fr. IVb.10–11.

[6] Hunter 1994: 222: Antiph. 5.79, 6.7; Dem. 48.55, 57.30, 36, and 52; Din. 1.54; Hyp. 1 fr. IVb.14; Lycurg. 1.11 and 149; Lys. 9.1, 3, and 18–19.

[7] On what counts as relevant, see the analyses by Gagarin 2012 and Lanni (2006: chs. 3–4), who argues that there was a stricter emphasis on relevant material in the homicide courts, but even that was difficult to enforce; see Lys. 3.44–6. By the late fourth century there were rules in place intended to try to control speakers (see [Arist.] *Ath. Pol.* 67.1, and Carey 2004: 4).

[8] As Carey (2004), who also cites Rhodes 2004, observing (2) that Rhodes misses some examples (e.g. the irrelevant character attack on Agoratus and his brothers in

This is not to suggest that relevance was always wholly clear: the careful play of ambiguity was itself part of the rhetoric of the court, as the Hyperides passage makes clear. But when we turn to the question of *diabole*, we find that speakers are, at least superficially, careful to present this material as relevant. Thus, in making his case against Nicomachus, the speaker of Lysias 30 attacks his opponent for *diabole* (for the accusation that the speaker was one of the Four Hundred), and then brings up similar charges (his subversion of the democracy) in criticizing him.[9] He introduces the information first almost incidentally as part of his outraged rhetoric of self-defence (a kind of 'how could he do this to me, when in fact it's true of him!'). But then it becomes part of his rhetoric of a larger service that he is doing the jurors, and beyond that the city: 'I should have made no reference to these events had I not learnt that he was going to attempt, by posing as a democrat, to save himself in despite of justice, and that he would produce his exile as a proof of his attachment to the people.'[10] Moreover, he goes on to suggest that the city (represented by the jurors) also has a right to seek revenge in light of what he alleges has occurred:

ἐγὼ δὲ καὶ ἑτέρους ἂν ἔχοιμι ἐπιδεῖξαι τῶν συγκαταλυσάντων τὸν δῆμον τοὺς μὲν ἀποθανόντας, τοὺς δὲ φυγόντας τε καὶ οὐ μετασχόντας τῆς πολιτείας, ὥστε οὐδένα εἰκὸς αὐτῷ τούτου ὑπόλογον γενέσθαι. τοῦ μὲν γὰρ ὑμᾶς φυγεῖν μέρος τι καὶ οὗτος συνεβάλετο, τοῦ δὲ τοῦτον κατελθεῖν τὸ πλῆθος τὸ ὑμέτερον αἴτιον ἐγένετο. ἔτι δὲ καὶ δεινόν, εἰ ὧν μὲν ἄκων ἔπαθε χάριν αὐτῷ εἴσεσθε, ὧν δ᾽ ἑκὼν ἐξήμαρτε μηδεμίαν τιμωρίαν ποιήσεσθε.

But I on my part could point out others among those who combined to subvert the democracy who were either put to death or exiled and debarred from the citizenship, so that he cannot expect to get any credit on that account. For while this man did contribute his share to your exile, he owed his return to you, the people. And besides, it would be monstrous if you should feel grateful to him for what he underwent against his will, but should exact no requital for his voluntary offence.[11]

Lys. 13.65–9), but in general supporting his view that litigants tend to stick to subjects that are relevant to the facts of the case.

[9] Lys. 30.7–9 (Lysias' speeches, here and below, tr. Lamb 1930).
[10] Lys. 30.15. See Carey 2004: 7.
[11] Lys. 30.15–16.

However, more frequently, it is establishing the truth of these allegations, rather than their relevance, that is of concern to the speakers. Thus, for example, in *Against Leocrates*, we find Lycurgus arguing about the details of business done with and by Amyntas (the husband of his elder sister). Amyntas is dead (as he tells us) so cannot be produced as a witness. However, Lycurgus is anxious to reassure his audience that what he is saying is not simply 'talk' (*logos*, which he contrasts with *aletheia* or 'truth'), and so he has found others who are willing to testify.[12] As he and the jurors would have been well aware, it was perfectly possible for a speaker to make up information, even when it was fairly certain he would not be able to get away with his version of events.[13]

The basis for this concern with 'truth' is at one level obvious: it was more persuasive. The idea behind introducing this material into the courtroom was to persuade your audience that here was a character that deserved their punishment.[14] But it was surely more complicated even than this: the underlying aim of *diabole* was not simply to damage your opponent in court; its cold hand also reached beyond this arena, into daily life—as some of the speakers profess to fear. For example, in Lysias 3, the speaker repeatedly explains that he had been unwilling to come to court because they were, not want the events under discussion widely known. He was sure that if they were, he was then likely to become *periboetos*, that is, 'much talked of'.[15] A second example offers further illumination: the speaker of the first speech against Boeotus has the same name as the man he is prosecuting. His concern is that the reputation of his rival will tarnish his own. He refers to the ways in which someone may acquire a bad reputation, describing how this may happen either through the filing of a suit or 'a wholly disagreeable scandal'. As he introduces his rival's patchy military service, he mentions that this is something that 'all of you who were at home saw'.[16]

As we will see, when such allegations are made, there is often an appeal to 'what everyone knows' (sometimes, but not always,

---

[12] Amyntas dead: Lycurg. 1.123. He uses the phrase ἵνα δὲ μὴ λόγον οἴησθε εἶναι ἀλλ' εἰδῆτε τὴν ἀλήθειαν, 'so that you may not think this is just talk, but know it to be the truth' (tr. Burtt 1954).

[13] Harris 1988: esp. the discussion, p. 213.   [14] Carey 2000: 206.

[15] Lys. 3.3-4 and 30.

[16] Dem. 39.15-17 (tr. Murray 1936). Hunter (1994) includes this episode in her Appendix of Gossip under the theme 'Military Service' (118).

supported by witnesses or depositions). This gives another reason why such background material may have been considered relevant in the courtroom. If this is what everyone knows, and what everyone is talking about anyway with regard to the litigants, then it becomes relevant through association. For both sides it becomes important to shape that information to one's own advantage, perhaps as an attack, perhaps as a defence against allegations not yet made. Moreover, if people are not talking about this beforehand (and the appeal to general knowledge is simply rhetorical), then it is likely they soon will be.

The process of turning ordinary gossip into an accusation is a process of creating the means for action.[17] But we can add to this: the process of creating an accusation can, in turn, also create ordinary gossip. This social process is not a simple linear structure, but rather a self-sustaining cycle. In the law courts, it was certainly a case of 'I appeal to common report; you spread slander.' But, drawing on our evidence, and on the theoretical approaches to gossip outlined in the previous sections, we can develop this formulation so that it includes the audience of that gossip: 'I make genuine accusations, you spread slander, and we both draw on and foster common report.'[18]

Once we return to the courts themselves, these can become fine distinctions, but keeping them in view allows us to maintain sight of the different verbal genres at play—and the rhetorical feints that connected them.[19] Many of the juicy allegations or accusations produced by one speaker against another look ripe to be labelled as gossip, but the passages in question offer little evidence for this: the speakers give little or no indication that these accusations were being discussed elsewhere or were already regarded as common knowledge. A first example of this is from Isaeus 3 (*On the Estate of Pyrrhus*), in which Nicodemus is being prosecuted for giving false testimony when

---

[17] See White 1994: 1. She observes how earlier scholars of gossip linked gossip and 'scandal' (although see Besnier 1996, mentioned on p. 172 n. 5), and makes the same link, but replaces 'scandal' with 'accusation'. However, Gluckman's definition of slander appears to be gossip that has gone beyond 'general interest in the doings, and the virtues and vices, of others, which characterizes any group' (1963: 312).

[18] The original formulation ('I appeal to common report; you spread slander') is in Lewis (1996: 13).

[19] For example, there is some elision of gossip and slander in Virginia Hunter's argument (1994: 101–2): 'what they say about an opponent amounts to statements "making moral judgments" or what we have defined as gossip', and the habit of slander is summed up as a strategy that 'has left the forensic orations full of gossip'.

he swore he had betrothed his sister to Pyrrhus without a dowry.[20] Although the argument focuses on the dowry, a further dimension is briefly introduced: Nicodemus' own status as a citizen. Apparently, it had been challenged by a member of his own *phratry*, and Nicodemus won the case by only four votes. The plaintiff argues that his uncle, Pyrrhus, would not have married a woman whose brother was not a citizen. The case is neatly made, complete with a call for testimony, but it is not clear that this is a case of gossip. There is no report of general suspicions or common knowledge, and it is not clear what the testimony is about—the dowry or the citizenship.

Another example occurs in Isaeus' speech (7) *On the Estate of Apollodorus*, in which Thrasyllus is attempting to maintain his legal position as the adopted son of Apollodorus; he has been attacked by one of Apollodorus' female cousins and now attempts to strike back. His approach is to point out that she and her sister are not to be trusted with an inheritance; they have form. They have already inherited an estate from one brother, but not given up a son for adoption into his house. Again, although this account introduces past omissions or offences by the target, even describing the state of the inherited property in strong terms as 'shamefully and deplorably desolate', this is still not clearly gossip.[21] For the same reasons given earlier, the lack of any allusion to third-party discussion suggests that this is more likely to be an aggressive slanderous attack by the speaker. Such allegations are simply the accusations and denials, claim and counterclaim that make up much of the basic discourse of an Athenian law-court speech. If they are categorized too quickly as 'gossip', we risk losing sight of the distinctive nature of this reconstructive genre and its particular employment in the law court.

Gossip vs Truth

At first sight, the discourses of gossip and of forensic oratory might be thought to be fundamentally different; as Besnier has described: 'gossip is blurred, incomplete, and unframed, while oratory is clear, complete and framed. Oratory's form is predictable, its delivery poised, its voices seemingly monologic, while the gossip text is messy, full of pitch variations and heteroglossic.'[22] Both may be artful and aim to persuade,

---

[20] Isae. 3.37.
[21] Cf. Hunter 1994: 103. Speeches by Isaeus, here and below, tr. Forster 1927.
[22] Besnier 2009: 124.

but they take place in different settings (public vs private). Moreover, each has distinctive implications for the way they are prepared (one is polished, the other spontaneous), and for the likely effects they may produce. Although those who gossip in other settings may work hard to establish the truth of what they say, there is no requirement to do so.[23] But in the Athenian law courts, the two genres coincide and overlap, and this produces certain distinctive markers. When speakers introduce gossip, that is, unsubstantiated reports about people, into their speeches, they do so by means of a number of specific techniques. Moreover, they also play with the very framework of gossip, signalling that they are, as it were, performing gossip through the use of particular speech acts characteristic of that genre. Rather than giving the impression that they are untrustworthy, this allows them to imply a different kind of truth claim in their speeches.

The most obvious way in which gossip is introduced into the speeches is through explicit references to the things that 'people, in general, are saying' or things that 'everyone knows'. The speakers not only introduce nuggets of current gossip, but they also frame it in a way that is itself suggestive of the common discourse of gossip. An example occurs in Isaeus' speech *On the Estate of Dicaeogenes*, where the speaker describes how 'Everyone saw [Dicaeogenes'] mother seated in the shrine of Eileithyia and charging him with acts which I am ashamed to mention but which he was not ashamed to commit.' A second example occurs in Demosthenes' speech *Against Eubulides*, when the story of Eubulides' and his group's corrupt approach to creating citizens is followed by the account of his father's dishonest approach to the deme register. As verification, the speaker claims, 'These facts all the older ones know.'[24]

This kind of appeal means that one's own role in spreading this information can be played down: as Demosthenes observes as he lists vivid little nuggets of information about Aeschines' family in *On the Crown*, 'Everybody knows that without being told by me.'[25] It appears to have been a good ploy to seem to rely on the information that

---

[23] Ayim (1994) examines the acquisition of knowledge through gossip. She describes gossipers anxious to establish the truth of the information they gather, comparing gossip to scientific inquiry (87).

[24] Isae. 5.39. Dem. 57.59–60, and quotation, 61 (tr. Murray 1939b). For further examples where general knowledge is called upon, see Dem. 39.16, 54.34, and [Dem.] 45.63–5 and 70, and 58.28; Din. 1.30, 2.8 and 11; Lys. 6.32; Isoc. 17.33–4.

[25] Dem. 18.129 (tr., here and below, Vince and Vince 1926).

already existed among the jurors. For example, speakers might ask them to consult what they have heard, as, for example, does Demosthenes regarding Meidias: 'Who of you does not know the mysterious story of his birth—quite like a melodrama!'[26] Or they may instruct the jurors to think about what they know or remember about the defendant, and then consider what that means about their own behaviour towards him, as does Andocides of his opponent Cephisius, 'whom every one of you sitting in this court knows too well to trust with anything belonging to him'.[27] This approach may even include explicit appeals to what the jurors know that they do not know, for example, in *Against Stephanus* (1) (of Stephanus): 'Although he has so large an estate that he gave his daughter a marriage portion of one hundred minae, he has never been seen by you to perform any public service whatever, even the very slightest.'[28]

Such an allusion to ostensibly shared knowledge may be very brief: for example, where a speaker simply acknowledges an acquaintance in common: 'Cinesias, with the character we know';[29] or makes a reference to a shared experience, such as 'even those who have no dealings with you are exasperated'.[30] So long as it achieves a note of collusion with right-minded citizens (which, of course, includes the jurors), such an appeal is powerful. These moments of complicity with the jurors work not only to spread information, but also to draw them onto the speaker's side, helping to create the impression that they share the same perspective, and so what the speaker says cannot be called slander.[31] Less specific claims of knowledge may be phrased as reports by other people: 'he was seen by a number of people' or 'it is clear that he... [did such and such]'.[32] Although these appeals to more general knowledge may achieve less intimacy with their audience, they may still work as truth claims for the speaker, reinforcing the value of their particular allegations.

The speaker can also use descriptions of gossip of a more personal and explicit nature to bolster a claim. Thus, he may describe how he himself has discussed some aspect of the case with some group of people. For example, in *On the Estate of Ciron*, the speaker implies that

---

[26] Dem. 21.149–50 (tr., here and below, Vince 1935).
[27] Andoc. 1.139 (tr., here and below, Maidment 1941) and compare Dem. 2.22, Din. 1.30, and Isae. 3.37.
[28] [Dem.] 45.66 (tr., here and below, Murray 1939a).   [29] Lys. 21.20.
[30] Dem. 21.195.
[31] Compare also the suggestion in Hyp. 4.22 that even children know.
[32] e.g. Lys. 14.25 and Din. 1.15, respectively.

he has discussed the situation with his friends: 'And when my opponent claimed this house and everything else that Ciron left behind him, although he said that he had left nothing, I did not think (and my friends agreed with me) that in these painful circumstances I ought to use violence and carry off my grandfather's body.'[33] In other cases, it is clear that the speaker has been participating in gossip about the case, but the other parties remain anonymous: for example, in *Against Agoratus*, we are informed of Agoratus: 'I am told that he is concocting for his defence the plea that he went off to Phyle, and was in the party that returned from Phyle, and that this is the mainstay of his case.'[34] Sometimes this information is dropped inadvertently into the account: for example, Aeschines tells us about Timarchus: 'his mother begged and besought him, as I have heard...'—an almost incidental truth claim, inserted as the story develops.[35] It may be that the speaker makes a very strong point of his own role in passing on gossip. One example comes from Demosthenes' *Against Conon*, in which the plaintiff, Ariston, regales the audience with the appalling activites of the Triballi:

ἀκούω γάρ, ὦ ἄνδρες δικασταί, Βάκχιόν τέ τινα, ὃς παρ' ὑμῖν ἀπέθανε, καὶ Ἀριστοκράτην τὸν τοὺς ὀφθαλμοὺς διεφθαρμένον καὶ τοιούτους ἑτέρους καὶ Κόνωνα τουτονί, ἑταίρους εἶναι μειράκι' ὄντας καὶ Τριβαλλοὺς ἐπωνυμίαν ἔχειν· τούτους τά θ' Ἑκαταῖα κατεσθίειν, καὶ τοὺς ὄρχεις τοὺς ἐκ τῶν χοίρων, οἷς καθαίρουσ' ὅταν εἰσιέναι μέλλωσι, συλλέγοντας ἑκάστοτε συνδειπνεῖν ἀλλήλοις, καὶ ῥᾷον ὀμνύναι κἀπιορκεῖν ἢ ὁτιοῦν.

For I hear, then, men of the jury, that a certain Bacchius, who was condemned to death in your court, and Aristocrates, the man with the bad eyes, and certain others of the same stamp, and with them this man Conon, were intimates when they were youths, and bore the nickname Triballi; and that these men used to devour the food set out for Hecate and to gather up on each occasion for their dinner with one another the testicles of the pigs which are offered for purification when the assembly convenes, and that they thought less of swearing and perjuring themselves than of anything else in the world.[36]

---

[33] Isae. 8.38.
[34] Lys. 13.77 (such details could also be heard at the pre-trial procedure, Lys. 13.86–88) and cf. Lys. 31.27–9.
[35] Aeschin. 1.99 (all speeches by Aeschines, here and below, tr. Adams 1919).
[36] Dem. 54.39 (tr. here and below, Murray 1939b). Hunter (1994: 119) lists this passage under 'resort to false oaths'; this is one of the crimes committed by this group as listed by Demosthenes, but the gossip itself is clearly much broader than that, and deliberately includes other impious behaviour.

In this instance, the role of the speaker in finding out this information (for which he offers no further proof but his own inquiries) is heavily emphasized: 'The contempt, however, which this fellow feels for all sacred things I must tell you about; for I have been forced to make inquiry.'[37] In light of the nature of the crime, and the seriousness of the allegations being made, this act of gossip suddenly becomes a much-needed investigation on behalf of the city and its citizens.

Similarly, in his speech *On the Mysteries*, Andocides provides a detailed account of Callias' domestic chaos. Callias had married a woman (a daughter of Ischomachus); then made her mother, Chrysilla, his mistress (the daughter tried to hang herself); then grew tired of Chrysilla and (in various different contexts) denied that the child she had was his. He finally fell for her again and then tried to present the boy to his *phratry*, the Kerykes, which involved him swearing that the boy was his son. Andocides calls witnesses to this statement, but it is certainly possible that these are only testifying to the final allegation (Callias' appearance among the Kerykes and the oath that he was the father of Chrysilla's son). However, if that is the case, then the rest of the story stands as unsupported allegation—with only Andocides' own claim at the beginning of his account: 'You must let me tell you... it is quite worth hearing, gentlemen'.[38]

As noted in the previous section, Aeschines' vivid description of how *pheme* or reputation is created is phrased in a way that denies any suggestion that talk is created by individuals: 'But in the case of the life and conduct of men, a common report which is unerring does of itself spread abroad throughout the city; it causes the private deed to become matter of public knowledge, and many a time it even prophesies what is about to be.' It leaves instead the impression that gossip functions simply as an impersonal and objective witness, with a certain supernatural animation of its own. In contrast, the insinuations that we see here, that everyone is talking, and everyone must know the details of an individual's private life, are just as specious. The 'gossip' they allude to may not, in fact, be as widespread as they are suggesting or, in fact, exist at all.[39]

---

[37] Dem. 54.39.   [38] Andoc. 1.124–9.
[39] On *pheme*, see Aeschin. 2.145; see p. 182 of this volume for discussion. Unsurprisingly, Aeschin. 1 is full of such insinuations; see e.g. 44–5, 53, 55–6, 69, 116, 130, 158. Hunter (1994: 220) also gives the following references: Dem. 19.199–200 and 226, 21.149, 54.34, and [Dem.] 59.30; Din. 2.8; Isae. 3.40, 6.19 (and cites Ober 1989: 149). Hunter (1994: 102) suggests that speakers may assume 'or pretend to assume'

In the inheritance case on the estate of Astyphilus (Isaeus 9), this possibility is explored: the speaker describes what 'is said', but then notes how difficult it is to find people to testify in its support. In the end, the witness whom he finds swears an 'Oath of ignorance'. The effort to provide a witness neatly suggests that the speaker is anxious to tell the truth, painting a thin veneer of veracity over what may be, in fact, only allegations.[40] As noted, this kind of information, even if it does not in fact exist, may, through its airing in the court, *become* gossip—as some of the speakers profess to fear. Those who promulgate this kind of information may also fear the consequences. For example, in Demosthenes' *Against Olympiodorus*, the speaker, Callistratus, provides a vivid description of the mistress of his brother-in-law and rival Olympiodorus flaunting her luxury. The picture he creates appeals to widespread knowledge; he then follows this account with a deposition, intended, explicitly, to avoid the charge of *diabole*.[41]

This brings us to the framing of gossip, and its manipulation. As Niko Besnier has argued, for some genres, such as forensic speeches, a more complete and verbally attractive performance can increase a truth claim. In contrast, gossip is perceived as 'unsaid, understated or waiting to be filled in by the audience'.[42] When the two are brought together, we can see some examples of the ways in which 'performing gossip' (rather than reporting on gossip) also gives speakers further support for its introduction into speeches, by helping them to construct an impression of the truth of their claims. In the law-court speeches we find this artfully created through a repeated affect—*praeteritio* or *paraleipsis*—that of the apparent spontaneous second thought, in which the speaker suddenly decides to leave the worst accusation unsaid. This enables him to damage his opponent, while acquiring credit for his own care with language—and without requiring the provision of any actual evidence.[43]

Bringing up the military record of his accuser, the speaker of *Against Simon* offers a very clear example of the use of this technique

---

widespread knowledge of this gossip, but does not pursue the point of the truth claims of such references to gossip here; later in the same discussion she briefly raises the question of whether or not we can ever know if we are dealing with the truth.

[40] Isae. 9.16–18.
[41] Dem. 48.55. Similar use of vivid imagery that may or may not be connected to current gossip is found in Dem. 42.24.
[42] Besnier 2009: 124.   [43] As Fisher 2001 *ad* §39.

(and I have highlighted the relevant parts of the translation with italics):

ἐβουλόμην δ' ἂν ἐξεῖναί μοι παρ' ὑμῖν καὶ ἐκ τῶν ἄλλων ἐπιδεῖξαι τὴν τούτου πονηρίαν, ἵνα ἠπίστασθε ὅτι πολὺ ἂν δικαιότερον αὐτὸς περὶ θανάτου ἠγωνίζετο ἢ ἑτέρους ὑπὲρ τῆς πατρίδος εἰς κίνδυνον καθίστη. τὰ μὲν οὖν ἄλλα ἐάσω· ὃ δ' ἡγοῦμαι ὑμῖν προσήκειν ἀκοῦσαι καὶ τεκμήριον ἔσεσθαι τῆς τούτου θρασύτητος καὶ τόλμης, περὶ τούτου μνησθήσομαι. ἐν Κορίνθῳ γάρ, ἐπειδὴ ὕστερον ἦλθε τῆς πρὸς τοὺς πολεμίους μάχης καὶ τῆς εἰς Κορώνειαν στρατείας, ἐμάχετο τῷ ταξιάρχῳ Λάχητι καὶ ἔτυπτεν αὐτόν, καὶ πανστρατιᾷ τῶν πολιτῶν ἐξελθόντων, δόξας ἀκοσμότατος εἶναι καὶ πονηρότατος, μόνος Ἀθηναίων ὑπὸ τῶν στρατηγῶν ἐξεκηρύχθη. Ἔχοιμι δ' ἂν καὶ ἄλλα πολλὰ εἰπεῖν περὶ τούτου, ἀλλ' ἐπειδὴ παρ' ὑμῖν οὐ νόμιμόν ἐστιν ἔξω τοῦ πράγματος λέγειν, ἐκεῖνο ἐνθυμεῖσθε· οὗτοί εἰσιν οἱ βίᾳ εἰς τὴν ἡμετέραν οἰκίαν εἰσιόντες, οὗτοι οἱ διώκοντες, οὗτοι οἱ βίᾳ ἐκ τῆς ὁδοῦ συναρπάζοντες ἡμᾶς.

I could wish that I were allowed to expose this man's wickedness before you in all its other effects, so that you might understand how in justice he ought far rather to be on trial for his life than bringing others into peril of losing their native land. *I will, however, pass over all those things, and will mention only one which I consider you ought to hear, as being a sure proof of his brazen-faced audacity.* In Corinth, where he arrived after our battle with the enemy and the expedition to Coronea, he fought with the taxiarch Laches and gave him a beating; and when the citizens had set forth in full military strength, he was specially noted for insubordination and knavery, and was the only Athenian ordered by the generals to be banned by herald. *I could go on to relate many other things regarding this man; but, since it is not lawful to speak in your court beyond the limits of the case,* I ask you to reflect on this: it was these men who forced their way into our house, they who pursued us, and they who forcibly seized and dragged us out of our path.'[44]

A single example is made to generate infinite possible crimes, but with not a piece of evidence in sight; indeed, there is not even reference to evidence of gossip to support his accusation.[45]

---

[44] Lys. 3.44–6.
[45] For a similar approach to evidence, see Dem 21.130; he reads out his memoranda of Aeschines' crimes and finishes with the tantalizing observation: 'I have omitted other instances, for no one could compress into a single narrative the violent acts that he has spent a lifetime in committing.' See also Dem. 39.26, where the omission appears to have the advantage that he does not have to describe in detail his father's lack of business acumen; and Dem. 54.44, where the water clock prevents a detailed exposition of Conon and his son's lack of service to the state. Further

Lysias appeals to the limits apparently set by the nature of the proceedings to shape his narrative and justify his missing details. In *Against Ctesiphon*, Aeschines uses his fear of enmity as the reason why he omits information: 'Here he married a woman who was rich, I grant you, and brought him a big dowry, but a Scythian by blood. This wife bore him two daughters, whom he sent hither with plenty of money. *One he married to a man whom I will not name—for I do not care to incur the enmity of many persons*—the other, in contempt of the laws of the city, Demosthenes of Paeania took to wife.'[46] In Demosthenes 24, an attack on Timocrates, it is modesty that apparently restrains the speaker, Diodorus: 'Ah, but he was a good manager for his sister. Why, if he had committed no other crime, he deserves destruction on that account alone. He has not given her in marriage, he has sold her. An enemy of yours from Corcyra, one of the faction now in power there, used to lodge at his house whenever he came here on embassy, and wanted to have his sister—I will not say on what terms. He took the man's money, and he has given him the girl; and she is in Corcyra to this day.'[47] As this last passage demonstrates, the material becomes almost more persuasive if the information omitted is trivial: it sounds far more realistic if it is a detail that has been forgotten.[48]

The technique of leaving information unsaid and implicit is a powerful device in the context of the law courts in several different respects. First, it tantalizes: the implication is that the situation is as bad as it could be. Consider this example from Lysias' *Against Philon*, where the speaker is criticizing the defendant, Philon: 'the strange things of which his mother accused him while she was alive I will pass over'.[49] Second, it engages: creating 'gaps' in the narrative that draw an audience

---

examples include: Isae. 8.40–3: 'If you understood the impudence of Diocles and his behaviour on all other occasions, you would have no difficulty in believing anything in my story;' Lys. 13.67: 'Now, to tell of all the other injuries and infamies, gentlemen, which have been the practice of this man and his brothers would be a lengthy task;' Lys. 14.28: 'Well, to relate all the offences that he has committed, gentlemen, either against the citizens, or against foreigners, or in his dealings with his own relations or with ordinary people, would be a lengthy affair.'

[46] Aeschin. 3.172.   [47] Dem. 24.202 (tr., here and below, Vince 1935).

[48] Another example at Dem. 21.139, where the omitted detail is the precise sum of money used for bribery.

[49] Lys. 31.20.

in, involving them in the creative process of building the very story they are meant to judge. When combined with an explicit appeal to the jurors' existing knowledge, this approach not only heightens this sense that the speaker knows what he is talking about, but also builds a strong sense of collusion between speaker and jurors. An example occurs in a speech made by Apollodorus against Timotheus, where Apollodorus states: 'The specific instances of the perjuries which he has committed without scruple would make a long story; but I will call to your minds the most flagrant instances *and those of which you are all well aware*.'[50] In Aeschines' speech against Timarchus, the collusive aspect of such an approach is made more explicit with an invitation to the jurors to investigate the matter for themselves: 'But, you say, although he was worthless when he held office alone, yet when he was associated with others he was all right! How so?' Aeschines then recounts myriad stories of wrongdoing.[51] Finally, the language of 'I could tell you, but . . .' offers a rhetorical structure for supplying all the necessary information, with the implication that any omitted material would be simply superfluous anyway. Thus, for example, Diodorus declaims against Timocrates: 'Well, about his father I will say nothing disrespectful; though I could tell you a long story about thieving—however, so far as I am concerned, let his father be worthy of all the compliments that Timocrates may lavish upon him.'[52]

The interaction between the genres of gossip and forensic rhetoric is complex, dynamic, and interactive—and reaches beyond the law courts. As we have seen, gossip could move seamlessly into forensic rhetorical structures as part of the case being made. This occurs, for example, in a case already mentioned, concerning the estate of Pyrrhus, in which the legal status of Nicodemus, his sister, and her daughter is being questioned. Apparently, the neighbours 'have given evidence of quarrels, serenades, and frequent scenes of disorder which the defendant's sister occasioned whenever she was at Pyrrhus's house'.[53] A further example occurs when Lycurgus is attacking

---

[50] [Dem.] 49.66 (tr. Murray 1939a), with italics added for emphasis. See also [Dem.] 45.27, where the name of the speaker's mother is left unspoken, 'but whom you know of yourselves, even if I do not name her'. Further examples of the combination of these two approaches (the appeal to existing or widespread knowledge, and the 'I could tell you, but . . .'): Lys. 30.2 and [Dem.] 49.66–7. A variation on this theme is the combination of the 'I could tell you, but . . .' technique with a deposition by the neighbours in Isae. 3.10–14.
[51] Aeschin. 1.107–15.
[52] Dem. 24.127 and compare Dem. 23.213.
[53] Isae. 3.13.

Leocrates, and supports his allegations with the testimony of neighbours, family, and friends: 'first the testimony of the neighbors and the men living in this district who know that the defendant ran away during the war and sailed from Athens, next that of the people present at Rhodes when Leocrates was delivering this news, and finally the evidence of Phyrcinus, whom most of you know as the accuser of Leocrates in the Assembly for having seriously harmed the two per cent tax in which he had an interest.'[54] We must bear in mind that the speaker would have written the witness statements himself, for the witnesses to swear to their validity; nevertheless, the presentation of this information is certainly suggestive of the dynamics of gossip. This kind of rhetoric could also be 'reversed': the speaker of Lysias 7, *On the Olive Stump*, adduces the lack of knowledge of his neighbours in order to prove that an action did not occur. He cannot have chopped down the sacred olive stump because his neighbours, among others, including passers-by, previous owners of the plot of land, and his slaves, would have known.[55] He also cleverly points out that his opponent should have persuaded the hostile neighbours to give evidence against him.[56] As these and the other examples indicate, the insinuation of damaging information was a powerful form of attack that had the potential to reach beyond the confines of the court, and the litigants themselves, to involve the rest of the city. But even this could become a rhetorical feint: an example occurs in a curious speech written to attack Alcibiades. The speaker explains that he is unwilling to describe Alcibiades' many misdeeds—adultery, stealing wives, acts of lawless violence— because he would make public the injuries suffered by many of his fellow citizens.[57]

These techniques make play not only with gossip itself, but also with the distinctive aspects of it as a genre. They allude to what everyone knows; they introduce what no one knows but will come to find out; they play with implicit knowledge and manipulate the explicit. The difficulties this raises of distinguishing gossip from slander can be seen by comparing two passages from a speech written by Demosthenes in support of Phormio against Apollodorus. When the speaker

---

[54] Lycurg. 1.19. On witness testimony in the fourth century BCE see Carey 1995.
[55] Lys. 7.14–18, 28, and 39. See esp. 18–19 for evidence of hostile neighbours.
[56] See discussion of the role of neighbours in Cohen 1991: 87–90.
[57] Andoc. 4.10; see also Lys. 3.3–4 and 30.

first attacks Apollodorus for not spending what he should on liturgies, it is simply an accusation of wrongdoing. Demosthenes goes through the figures systematically—this is, if you like, one way of giving authority to these claims. He does not appeal to third-party discussion, and there is no indication that this is gossip.[58] However, as he turns to Apollodorus' private life, indications appear that show that we are dealing with this very different genre. He describes to Apollodorus how his brother has not complained about his licentious lifestyle: 'Archestratus, to whom your father formerly belonged, has a son here, Antimachus, who fares not at all as he deserves, and who does not go to law with you and say that he is outrageously treated, because you wear a soft mantle, and have redeemed one mistress, and have given another in marriage (all this, while you have a wife of your own), and take three attendant slaves about with you, and live so licentiously that even those who meet you on the street perceive it, while he himself is in great destitution.' What marks this as gossip is not the lascivious detail of these claims, but the phrase 'even those who meet you on the street', which signals to the audience that Demosthenes is aware of and indicating the kind of third-party discussion about Apollodorus' behaviour and its implications that lives and breathes in gossip.[59]

GOSSIP AND ANXIETY

What made these claims so powerful? It has been argued, by Virginia Hunter, that the gossip in these lawsuits 'often reached an ideological level in the demands it placed on the elite to conform publicly to the image of the good citizen deserving of *charis*'.[60] She assembles a list of themes of gossip, and suggests that gossip helped to preserve the descent group itself against outsiders by enforcing certain images, ideas, and standards of behaviour, such that 'in criticizing one another, Athenians declared what it was to be an Athenian'.[61] It is

---

[58] [Dem.] 36.36–9.   [59] [Dem.] 36.44–5 (tr. Murray 1939).
[60] Hunter 1994: 117.
[61] Hunter (1994: 115–17): 'to preserve the descent group itself against outsiders by the images it evoked, by the standards it proclaimed, and by the morality it enforced...in criticizing one another, Athenians declared what it was to be an Athenian'. Her themes of gossip (118–19) include: public service, military service,

certainly the case that these assertions, allegations, and reports concerning 'what everyone knows' or not, together generate an index of ideal behaviours. In a society in which a legal case was a political weapon, they reflect the concerns of a particular constituency of the population. (As Hunter herself points out, we do not know what kinds of uses of gossip other social classes may have made.)[62] However, they also reveal some further, darker dimensions of what it meant 'to be an Athenian'.

Among these, the most obvious to emerge from this material is the need to become adept in manipulating gossip: this analysis suggests a striking transparency to Athenian daily life. By instituting what was, in effect, a system of self-policing (and beyond that, of self-litigation), each citizen was perforce (by laws and decrees) an 'agent of law enforcement', not standing on the margins of dispassionate procedure, but employing and directing individual emotions and social processes of evaluation.[63] In the law courts, the idea that prosecutions were made on this basis is made quite plain by the emotional explanations of the speakers themselves, who sometimes explain that the public case they are bringing (*graphe*) is occasioned or accompanied by feelings of personal grievance (although this might well be coupled with statements about also benefitting the city).[64] Moreover, the system was structured in such a way that there were plenty of opportunities for individuals to play out their personal feelings, even in political settings. For example, the examinations of public officers allowed anyone to raise an objection at the *dokimasia* before a

---

treatment of kin, treatment of parents, care of patrimony, associates, private life and conduct, sexual mores, character, status, criminal record; less frequently, maltreatment of friends, resort to false oaths, dishonesty or other unacceptable conduct in public office.

[62] Hunter 1994: 117. [63] Ibid.: 124.
[64] See for example: Dem. 54.33, and [Dem.] 53.1–3 and 15, 58.49 and 52, 59.1 and 14–15; Lys. 7.20, 13.1, 15.12; Hunter (1994: 127) provides evidence of feuds. Kucharski (2012: 171–2) argues for the prominent role of personal enmity in public prosecutions, and lists five of thirty-one speeches where the speaker explicitly or implicitly denies personal enmity, eleven where he explicitly admits it, and eight where he presents himself as 'a disinterested agent of the state'. Making such personal statements would also indicate that the case was not being brought by a sycophant, which was another risk that this legislative structure posed; see Hunter 1994: 126–7; cf. Osborne 1990. But Kucharski (2012: 192) adds that even enmity could be coupled with charges of sycophancy, if it was the wrong sort of enmity. Lys. 24.2 lists envy, money, and vengeance as personal motives for court cases that are not acceptable.

citizen was appointed, or, after he had served his term, to bring forward a prosecution at the *euthyna*.[65]

But as well as thinking about the ways in which this structure was set up to encourage what Hunter has called institutionalized 'private initiative', we need also to think about how it felt to live within such a system, and balance it with the idea of 'institutionalised vigilance'.[66] Indeed, it becomes a regular plea at the end of law-court cases that the jurors exercise vigilance for their city and its future, in one way or another: for example, to protect her foreign policy,[67] her identity,[68] or her laws;[69] to safeguard the loyal service of her citizens[70] and the security of their families and women;[71] or to take care of the Athenians' relationship with their gods—and it becomes their liability if they do not.[72]

The need for such judicial vigilance can be set in a broader emotional context of anxiety. At the individual level, as Joseph Roisman has argued, the rhetorical material is replete with indications of a conspiratorial outlook (and this is reinforced by evidence from non-forensic sources).[73] As he notes, although, in part, these accusations of personal and political plotting are recurrent themes of law-court speeches, their use suggests that they were taken seriously by their audience.[74] Plotting was envisioned around, for example, cases concerning inheritance,[75] murder,[76] commercial transactions,[77] and citizen status.[78] Moreover, overlapping with these personal claims are accusations made on behalf of the state: political conspiracies—both national and international—appear across a number of cases.[79] Together these suggest that the imagination of the Athenian citizenry not only kept alive the memory of past conspiracies and their horrors, but that this also helped to prompt concern about the future of the democracy. The context this created was one within

---

[65] [Arist.] *Ath. Pol.* 55.2–4. Lys. 26 is a wonderful example of a case brought concerning a *dokimasia*.

[66] For institutionalized 'private initiative' (as opposed to 'self-help'), see Hunter 1994: 124.

[67] Dem. 23.188–9.   [68] Dem. 24.94.   [69] Lys. 1.48–50.
[70] Lys. 18.23, 20.32.   [71] [Dem.] 59.112.   [72] See Eidinow 2015.
[73] Roisman 2006.   [74] Ibid.: 152.   [75] Dem. 43.1–10.
[76] Antiph. 1.3, 5, 9, 21, and 25–7 (see Roisman 2006: 11–18).

[77] Specifically maritime fraud in Dem. 32 (see Roisman 2006: 35–7); and internationally, the grain trade Dem. 56 (see Roisman 2006: 145–9).

[78] Dem. 57 (see Roisman 2006: 88–94).

[79] National: Lys. 12, 13, 30; Isoc. 20.10–13 (see Roisman 2006: 66–94); and international: e.g. [Dem.] 7 (see Roisman 2006: 130).

which gossip could become a remarkably potent weapon, and one that must be handled with skill. After all, as Aeschines points out, it was possible to earn the hatred of one's neighbours by describing their outrageous behaviour in too much detail.[80]

Gossip and *Phthonos*

In these speeches we see the impacts of a hypervigilant environment, in which talk about others helped to shape and direct legal cases. Such a background makes sense of the need for the expert management of gossip, as it made its way from street corner to courtroom, and back again. More specifically for this study, it provides a context in which to draw connections between gossip and *phthonos*.

We have seen above how *phthonos* and abusive talk are closely related. Here we see how much of that abusive talk comprised gossip—and we begin to understand why the fourth-century painter Apelles is said to have painted *Phthonos* leading *Diabole*.[81] This relationship is also apparent in the accounts of the trial of Socrates. Both Xenophon and Plato put forward *phthonos* as part of the explanation for why the jury convicted Socrates. Xenophon, in the *Apologia*, explains that there were a number of individuals among the jurors who felt *phthonos*, specifically in response to Socrates' claimed relationship with the divine.[82] Just as we might expect from the previous discussion, they feel it in response to Socrates' assertion of his divine blessing. And Socrates' own behaviour makes it worse: Xenophon gives *phthonos* as the reason why Socrates' conviction by the jury was made more certain, describing how Socrates brought it upon himself (*phthonon epagomenos*) by his arrogant behaviour.[83]

---

[80] Aeschin. 3.174: 'I have seen people hated who recount too exactly the sins of their neighbours'.

[81] Luc. *Cal.* 5 (see discussion p. 121).   [82] Xen. *Ap.* 14.3.

[83] Xen. *Ap.* 32. 2. In the *Memorabilia*, Xenophon offers a broader view of the role of *phthonos* in Athenian society, as Socrates discusses with Critobulus what qualities make a man's friendship worth winning. Critobulus (2.6.20.6) reflects on how men who vie with each other for primacy in cities feel *phthonos* as well as hatred for each other. And Socrates agrees that there are 'hostile elements' in men, who hold the same things to be honourable and pleasant and then fight for them ('strife and anger lead to hostility, covetousness to enmity, *phthonos* to hatred', 2.6.22.1). His message is, in the end, one of optimism, but even this is cast in terms of *phthonos*: there are true friends who are able to share their wealth and supply one another's wants and '*phthonos* they take away entirely, regarding their own good things as belonging to their friends and

In Plato's account, there are similarly multiple references to *phthonos*, but here it is depicted as the cause of both the indictment and the verdict, linking the gossip of daily life to the courtroom. He depicts Socrates describing the prevailing atmosphere against him, in which people had been accusing him of activities that were linked with not believing in the gods.[84] They have apparently been doing this 'for a long time', when the jurors were children or youths. And of course, to this kind of rumour and gossip, there is no defence: 'But the most unreasonable thing of all is this, that it is not even possible to know and speak their names, except when one of them happens to be a writer of comedies.' He goes on to discuss the persuasive forces behind this spreading gossip, which includes *phthonos* and slander: 'And all those who persuaded you by means of *phthonos* and slander . . .'. He notes the way it spreads: 'and some also persuaded others because they had been themselves persuaded'.[85]

It becomes unclear whose *phthonos* is being referred to here—those persuading or those being persuaded. And this ambiguity continues as Socrates, first, indicates the *phthonos* and *diabole* of his accusers, Meletus and Anytus, noting how they have condemned many in the past, and then also describes to the jury how they, his fellow citizens, have found his words have moved them to *phthonos*.[86] The case seems, in some key respects, to be an illustration of the situation that Aristotle describes in the *Rhetoric*, as he discusses those who do wrong and those who are likely to be attacked by them. Among the latter he lists, 'those who have been slandered, or are easy to slander; for such men neither care to go to law, for fear of the judges, nor, if they do, can they convince them; to this class belong those who are exposed to hatred or *phthonos*'.[87] In conclusion, the evidence suggests that in a context of hypervigilance, making gossip public (or

---

thinking their friend's good things to be their own' (2.6.23.5). Finally, the conversation becomes more specifically focused on Athens and the Athenians, as Socrates and Pericles explore the reasons why the city has become so degenerate. They explore the lack of harmony in the city, arising from the attitudes of Athenians: 'they feel more *phthonos* and are more bitter against one another than against the rest of the world' (3.5.16.5; all tr. Marchant and Todd, rev. Henderson 2013).

[84] Pl. *Ap.* 18c: the accusations include being a thinker about 'things in the air and things below the earth, and who makes the weaker argument the stronger'.
[85] Pl. *Ap.* 18d (tr. Fowler 1914).
[86] Pl. *Ap.* 37d.
[87] Arist. *Rhet.* 1372b (tr. Freese 1926): καὶ τοὺς διαβεβλημένους ἢ εὐδιαβόλους· οἱ τοιοῦτοι γὰρ οὔτε προαιροῦνται, φοβούμενοι τοὺς κριτάς, οὔτε δύνανται πείθειν, ὡς μισούμενοι καὶ φθονούμενοι.

creating public gossip) harnessed popular feelings and social emotions, including *phthonos*, to create allegations, which then, in turn, created popular feeling, in an ongoing cycle.[88] In the next section, this kind of vicious cycle—between accusation and emotion—will provide the model for analysis of some more ambiguous accusations.

[88] Szwed (1966: 435): gossip 'is not only a means for an individual to assemble basic information on his peers, but it is also a technique for summarizing public opinion'.

3.5

Gossip ... In Private

'ACCUSATIONS AGAINST ME'

We have seen how gossip itself could be seen as a metaphorical poison. We come now to the question of how gossip coincides with more literal senses of poison—in accusations of deaths brought about by poison, spells, and/or dirty tricks. Trying to locate and pin down this kind of informal narrative is hard enough in our own society, let alone for the ancient world. Nevertheless, there is evidence that can help us to piece together something of how this social dynamic may have surfaced in ancient society. As is often the case when examining ancient sources for evidence of magical practices, much of the material is not from the place or time under discussion. Moreover, it is partial: although a few inscriptions will offer us a longer and more detailed narrative, the evidence in question usually gives only a very brief snapshot of events. Indeed, sometimes it is only iconography that leads the viewer to suspect that this is a text that includes an accusation of some kind of foul play.[1] However, these fragments can still offer some insight into a common pattern of responses to a particular experience of misfortune—usually the death of an individual—and the ways in which its effects may have rippled out through wider society.

Raising Suspicions

One of the primary sources for such information is ancient funerary inscriptions in which the gods are implored to punish those who are

[1] On *Fluchhände*, for example, see further p. 213.

responsible for the death of the deceased.[2] A number of these epitaphs also contain allegations of foul play, and they often include an image of two raised arms with open hands (so-called *Fluchhände*). This is not only a gesture of prayer or cursing, but seems to be specifically marked as an invocation of divine vengeance in cases of premature and unnatural death.[3] A famous example comes in the form of two very similar grave markers from Rheneia (an island near Delos), which date to the end of the second/beginning of the first century CE. The details of the text indicate that the provenance is a Hellenistic Jewish community, one which, not unusually, employed Greek language and practice.[4] Both epitaphs rail 'against those who have murdered with trickery or poisoned/bewitched the wretched, untimely dead'; the victims are a Heraclea and Marthine, respectively. They ask that 'thus the same fate may happen to those who murdered or poisoned/bewitched her, and to their children'.[5]

---

[2] There are collections made by Cumont 1923, 1926, and 1933, Björck 1938. See also Pippidi 1976/7 and Jordan 1979. This material has been the focus of increasing interest in recent scholarship: see Versnel 1991: 97 nn. 44 and 45. For more detailed discussion, see Versnel 1999, 130–1, and 2002a (in the former, he seeks to identify emotions that may have motivated certain curse texts, focusing on the intention to cause victims to lose face; in the latter, he discusses the role of these texts in processes of social control; Salvo 2012 comes to similar conclusions). Although my conclusions are different, this discussion owes much to his analyses. See also Graf 2007 and 2010; Edmonds 2010.

[3] As (Graf 2007: 145) notes, the ubiquity of this gesture as a symbol of prayer was already noted in antiquity ([Arist.] *Mund.* 400a16); see further Jakov and Voutiras 2005. Graf (2007: 146 and 150) refines the arguments of Cumont (1933, esp. 31) and Robert (*BÉ* 1968: no. 338) that this symbol in epitaphs indicated 'only and alone an invocation for divine vengeance of a death that was felt to be premature and to result from the action of a malevolent human'. Some only include this image with the name of the dead person, and no further information (see Graf 2007: 145–9).

[4] See further Gager 1992: 185–7 and van der Horst and Newman 2008: 137–43.

[5] The full text for Heraclea runs (*IG* XI 2532 I A): ἐπικαλοῦμαι καὶ ἀξιῶ τὸν | ὕφιστον, τὸν κύριον τῶν πνευμάτων | καὶ πάσης σαρκός, ἐπὶ τοὺς δόλωι φονεύ- | σαντας ἢ φαρμακεύσαντας τὴν τα- | λαίπωρον ἄωρον Ἡράκλεαν, ἐχχέαν- | τας αὐτῆς τὸ ἀναίτιον αἷμα ἀδί- | κως, ἵνα οὕτως γένηται τοῖς φονεῦ | σασιν αὐτὴν ἢ φαρμακεύσασιν καὶ | τοῖς τέκνοις αὐτῶν, Κύριε, ὁ πάντα ἐ- | φορῶν καὶ οἱ ἄγγελοι θεοῦ, ᾧ πᾶσα ψυ- | χὴ ἐν τῇ σήμερον ἡμέραι ταπεινοῦτα μεθ'ἱκετείας ἵνα ἐγδικήσῃς τὸ αἷμα τὸ ἀ- | ναίτιον ζητήσεις καὶ τὴν ταχίστην.
See for Heraclea: *IDélos* 2532 I A–B; *SIG* 1181; *CIJ*, no. 725; Björck 1938: 29 no. 11; *SEG* 14.505; Couilloud 1974, no. 485; Guarducci 1978: 236–8; *SEG* 37.687; Gager 1992: 185, no. 87; *SEG* 46.966; Noy *et al.* 2004, no. Ach70. Wilhelm 1901 gives details of the stone, now in the Bucharest National Museum; see also discussions in Deissmann 1911 and Bergmann 1911. See for Marthine: *IDélos* 2532 II; Noy *et al.* 2004, no. Ach71, now in the Epigraphical Museum, Athens. Salvo (2012: 244) argues that

Some epitaphs are phrased rather less precisely over the manner of death.[6] For example, an epitaph from Phrygia from a husband for his dead wife and child reads: 'If, by my particular fate, it had to be; if by dastardly hands, o Helios see this!'.[7] Another from Amisos: 'If a dastardly trick killed me, let there be divine, justice-dealing light'.[8] Indeed, the sense of uncertainty across these texts is often striking—both about the nature of the offence and the identity of the culprit.[9] Nevertheless, the indication of foul play remains, and if we recall that these inscriptions were likely to have been read out loud, then this reinforces the idea that setting up such an inscription was a way of 'voicing' suspicions within a community. This is even more likely in those cases where the epitaph was written as if spoken by the victim. For example, an inscription dating to the second/third century CE lists the travels and achievements of a doctor called Antiochus. Although his grave is in Thasos—the monument was set up by his parents, son, and wife—the inscription relates how he was apparently *allei pharmachtheis*, ('poisoned/bewitched in a foreign land').[10]

Marthine's stone was influenced by that of Heraklea on the grounds that the former is only inscribed on one side, and is missing the term *zeteseis* in l. 13, which is found in the similar inscription on the latter stone (A, l. 13 and B, l. 18). Graf (2007: nos 5 and 7) lists thirteen other texts that are similarly explicit about the cause of death and the desire for revenge. See Pippidi 1976/7 and Jordan 1979 on *IDélos* 2533 for consideration of solar invocations.

[6] The following examples are collected by Robert (1936: 122).

[7] εἰ μὲν ἰδίᾳ μοίρῃ ὤφειλεν· εἰ δὲ χερσὶ δολοποιοῖς, Ἥλιε, βλέπε Hadrianoi, Pisidia, or Phrgyia, c.200 CE; Graf 2007: 17; Ramsay 1888: 265, no. 7; Cumont 1923: 75, no. 12; Robert 1936: 122; Björck 1938: 26, no. 3; Bean 1959: 109, no. 78 (see also *BÉ* 1961: no. 739).

[8] εἰ δὲ δόλος με . . . [δαμάσσε?] θεῖον φάος ἔκδικον ἔστω Amisos (Pontus), c.200 CE; Graf 2007: 18. Björck (1938: 25, no. 2) leaves the lacuna blank; Anderson *et al.* (1910: 17, no. 9) and Robert (1936: 122) read εἰ δὲ δόλος με [κτάνεν? . . . θ]εῖον φάος ἔκδικον ἔστω.

[9] Uncertainty emphasized by Graf (2010) and Edmonds (2010). But Graf (2007: 143) notes how epitaphs for visible violent deaths often identify the perpetrator. The text may not preclude a legal process, but may also occur because the culprit was known but somehow out of legal reach (whether through a lack of evidence, or insufficient resources on the accuser's side to take that person to court); e.g. a text from Syria (Hauran, *SEG* 7.1239), where the murderer was a senior adminstrator and presumably, therefore, it was difficult for the family to seek mortal justice.

[10] Graf 2007: 13 (date given: late); *IG* XII 8.450 and Pfohl 1966, no. 23. Graf (2007: 141) states that this was more likely to be a suspicion of foul play than actual poisoning—on the basis of the fact that the victim died far from home.

Protesting Innocence

Texts from the corpus of curse tablets may offer some further insights into the social dynamics surrounding such suspicions and/or accusations of poisoning—and from another perspective. Among the corpus of binding spells is a group of texts from the temple of Demeter at Knidos in Asia Minor, protestations against injustice done to those who wrote them.[11] But these are not all simple victims: among them are those who feel they have been unjustly accused of crimes themselves, and we focus here on those that concern accusations of poisoning. In the first, a woman calls down a curse on herself if she is guilty as accused:

ἀνιεροῖ Ἀντιγό- | νη Δάματρι Κού- | ραι Πλούτωνι θε- | οῖς τοῖς παρὰ Δά- | ματρι ἅπασι καὶ | πάσαις· εἰ μὲν ἐ- | γὼ φάρμακον Ἀ- | σκλαπιάδαι ἢ ἔ- | δω[κ]α, ἢ ἐνεθυ- | μήθην κατὰ ψ- | υχὴν κακόν τι | [α]ὐτῷ ποῖσαι, ἢ ἐ- | κάλεσα γυναῖκ- | α ἐπὶ τὸ ἱερόν, | τρία ἡμιμναῖ- | α διδοῦσα ἵνα | {ι}αὐτὸν ἐκ τῶν | ζώντων ἄρῃ, | ἀναβαῖ Ἀντιγό- | νη πὰ Δάμα- | τρα πεπρημέ- | να ἐξομολ<ογ>οῦμ[ένα], | καὶ μὴ γένοιτο | εὐειλάτ[ου] τυ- | χεῖν Δάματρος, | ἀλλὰ μεγάλα- | ς βασάνους βασ- | ανιζομένα· εἰ δ'ἐ<ἴ>- | [πέ] τις κατ'ἐμοῦ π- | ρὸς Ἀσκλαπίδα<ν> εἰ κ- | [α]τ'ἐμοῦ καὶ παριστ- | ἀνεταλ[ι] γυναῖκα | χαλκοῦς δο<ῦ>σα | ĮAN δ'ἐμοῦ TA-

Antigone dedicates (this tablet?) to Demeter, Kore, Pluto, and all the gods and goddesses beside Demeter. If I have given a potion to Asclapiadas or conceived in my soul of doing anything bad to him, or have summoned a woman to the sanctuary, giving her 3 half-*minae*,[12] so that she might take him from the living, let Antigone come to the sanctuary before Demeter, burning (*pepremenos*), and confess, and may Antigone not find Demeter merciful, but may she be tormented with great

---

[11] These come from a group of fourteen or so curse tablets and date approximately from the first/second century BCE. See Newton 1862-3: (ii): 719-45 (= Blümel 1992: 85-103, nos 147-59). They are included in the category of 'prayers for justice' identified by Versnel (1991, 1998, 2002a, 2010), a genre distinguished from binding spells by their intention to persuade the divinity addressed to punish the perpetrator of a wrong that they have suffered. The majority of prayers for justice date to the Hellenistic or later periods, but see Versnel (2010) for some reconsideration of earlier cases.

[12] A unit of ancient Greek currency, a mina or mna was roughly equivalent to 100 drachmae.

suffering. And if anyone says anything against me to Asclapiadas, if [anyone] brings forward [as a witness] against me a woman giving her coppers.[13]

The other text was obviously written in similar circumstances of accusation and denial. The writer appears to be a woman cursing a man who has accused her of giving *pharmaka* to her husband:

[ἀνα]τίθημι Δάματρι καὶ Κούραι τὸν κατ' ἐμο[ῦ]
[ε]ἰπ[α]ντα, ὅτι ἐγὼ τῶι ἐμῶι ἀνδ[ρὶ] φάρμακα ποιῶ· ἀνα[βαῖ]
παρὰ Δάματρα πεπρημένος μετὰ τῶν αὐτοῦ [ἰδίων]
πάντων ἐξαγορεύων, καὶ μὴ τύχῃ εὐειλάτου
[Δ]άματρος καὶ Κούρας μηδὲ τῶν θεῶν τῶν παρὰ Δά[μα]-
τρος, ἐμοὶ δὲ ἦ{η} ὅσια καὶ ἐλεύθερα ὁμοστεγησάσῃ ἢ ὧι πο[τε]
τρόπωι ἐπιπλεκομένηι· ἀνατίθημι δὲ καὶ τὸν κατ' ἐ[μοῦ]
γράψαντα ἢ καὶ ἐπιτάξαντα· μὴ τύχοι Δάματρος καὶ
[Κ]όρας μηδὲ θεῶν τῶν παρὰ Δάματρος εὐιλάτων, ἀλλ' ἀ[ν-]
αβαῖ μετὰ τῶν ἰδίων πάντων παρὰ [Δ]άματρα πεπρημένος.

I dedicate to Demeter and Kore the man who spoke against me that I made poisons for my husband. May he come to the sanctuary of Demeter, burning, along with all his people and publicly confess, and may he meet with mercy neither from Demeter and Kore nor from the other gods with Demeter. But let it be holy and free for me under the same roof, whatever dealing [I have with him] at any time. I dedicate also the man who has written [accusations] against me or directed another man to accuse me. Do not let him find Demeter or Kore or the gods with Demeter merciful, but let him burn and come before Demeter with all his people.[14]

The two tablets share similar formulae with a third tablet—more fragmentary, but with some indications that accusations of poisoning had also prompted it to be written. However, in this case, it appears that the writer was afraid of being poisoned. The text is extremely fragmented, but two lines of the text appear to include mention of an attempted poisoning, possibly with an exotic, overseas concoction: ll. 14–15, εἴ τι ἢ ἐμοὶ πεποίκει φάρμ[α]- | [κον] ἢ ποτὸν ἢ

---

[13] *DT* 1 (*IK* I 147); see also Eidinow 2013: 391.
[14] *DT* 4 (*IK* I 150A1); see also Eidinow 2013: 392.

κατάχριστον ἢ ἐπακτὸν [ἢ] [τινι] ἡμῶν (that is, literally 'if anyone has made (for use) against me or one of my family, a drug or spell, a potion or an ointment or a charm imported from another country'.[15]

The formulaic similarities suggest a common source: Angelos Chaniotis suggests that these were 'angry and frustrated women, interacting with each other', and that the similarity of formula indicates that they 'talked to each other about their concerns'.[16] It is an appealing idea, but needs to be treated with some caution. Their own words rather suggest that these women may have felt isolated from their communities and by the gossip about them. It may be relevant to observe that curses from shared localities and contexts which share formulae, for example *defixiones* for the Athenian law courts, which are likely to have been written by men, are not taken to indicate that men are either very emotional and/or talking to each other about their concerns. In fact, quite the opposite: the suggestion has been made that the process of commissioning these texts did not allow for an emotional discharge because they were likely to have been written by an intermediary.[17]

Perhaps it is more likely that the texts draw on a shared oral tradition, and/or the same spell-seller. Alternatively, it may be that these texts were phrased by the priests of the sanctuary as part of a conflict resolution process. For example, the term *pepremenos* may indicate a divine punishment ('burning with fever)' or the impact of the discovery and publication

---

[15] *DT* 8; *IK* I 154. (possibly early first or second centuries BCE): *epakton*, translated here as 'spell', according to LSJ, s.v., may indicate something imported.

[16] Chaniotis 2009: 64. Although Chaniotis (54) warns the reader that our ancient sources provide us with men's views on women, he provides (65) a passage of Polybius concerning Oenanthe (15.29.8–14) to support his argument about the emotional interaction of women in a temple. But Polybius' comments elsewhere suggest that he may not be wholly objective in his view of women's mental and emotional faculties (see, e.g., on Teuta 2.4.8 and 2.8.12). Moreover, it seems unlikely that he meant this episode to be taken as representative of female behaviour: Oenanthe's behaviour is outrageous, and the response of the women around her is part of the overheated tension that will lead up to Agathocles' overthrow. (The Thesmophorium appears to provide a focus of stories about outrageous acts by and against Oenanthe: in 15.33.8, Oenanthe is dragged from the Thesmophorium to the stadium naked on horseback. It seems that a temple provides a useful setting for describing acts by and against women, especially those that violate customary norms, e.g. Polyb. 15.27.2–3, in which Danaë is dragged from the temple of Demeter, and through the streets of the city, unveiled.)

[17] Graf (1997: 146–7) emphasizes the importance of spontaneity, although elsewhere (157) he suggests that these texts were thought to offer individuals a way 'to master emotionally an otherwise difficult crisis'.

of a crime ('burning with shame'), or it may be an allusion to a particular ordeal set up by the sanctuary officials as a test of innocence—a 'burning by fire or water'.[18] It is possible that these protestations of innocence were made as publicly as the epitaphs already described above, that is, that these curse tablets were pinned up and on display, available to be read by any visitor to the temple of Demeter.[19] This would not have been an isolated phenomenon; there is a curse from Delos that bears some remarkable similarities to these texts. It is inscribed on a stele in the Sanctuary of the Syrian Gods, with an introduction in which the writer, one Theagenes, 'raises his hands to Helios and the Holy Goddess' and asks for justice against a woman to whom he has lent money for her manumission, and who has not returned it.[20]

Confessing Guilt

Some of the expectations and assumptions about the process and result of dedicating a wrongdoer to the gods, in particular the divinely caused suffering that will afflict them until they come to the sanctuary, is shared with other texts: the so-called confession inscriptions from Asia Minor, specifically Lydia and Phrygia. These texts, which date from the first to third centuries CE, appear to have been set up near sanctuaries in small towns or rural temples, and record an offence (social or religious) that the individual has committed, and the divine intervention that followed.[21] They were written by individuals, or their families, and concerned a realization that a misfortune being experienced was related to some offence that had been

---

[18] Chaniotis 2004: 7. Burning with fever: Blümel 1992: 85 (and see Kantzia 1997 = SEG 47.1291 in support). Burning with shame: Versnel 1999: 154, and burning as an ordeal: Versnel 1994: 150–4.

[19] Newton 1862–3: ii.724.

[20] Björck 1938: 30 no. 14. The text ends with a request that ἀξιῶ καὶ δέομαι πάντας τοὺς θεραπευτὰς βλασφημεῖν αὐτὴν καθ'ὥραν. It has been suggested by Versnel (1999: 141, followed by Salvo 2012: 252–3) that this means 'all the worshippers (*therapeutas* includes those 'devoted to the goddess, including the sacred personnel of the temple') gossip about this woman'; the phrase *kath'horan* (according to Versnel) should be translated as 'at the right time'. However, other uses of the phrase indicate something that happens early (see Polyb. 1.45.4 and 3.93.6; IGUR 1277), so the phrase may rather be an encouragement to be prompt.

[21] See Petzl 1994, with additional texts noted in Gordon 2004: 1 n. 4, and a list of more general studies in Chaniotis 2004: 4 n. 10.

committed against the gods. According to the texts, a visit to the sanctuary followed, where instruction was received about how to make atonement. It is likely that the local priests played some role in the process of divine instruction, but the nature of their activity is unclear.[22]

Again, these confession inscriptions covered a wide range of offences, but we focus here on one that concerns an accusation of the use of *pharmaka*. This *histoire curieuse*, as Louis Robert described it, was set up in public by the relatives of a woman called Tatias. It adds some further detail to our developing picture of the dynamics of social suspicion that revolved around episodes of misfortune.[23] First, we see the role of gossip in spreading suspicion, leading to the victim of the gossip (the alleged perpetrator of the crime) creating curses, which she 'sets down' in the temple (ll. 4–13): Ἰουκοῦνδος ἐγένετο ἐν | διαθέσι μανικῇ καὶ ὑπὸ πάν- | των διεφημίσθη ὡς ὑπὸ | Τατιας τῆς πενθερᾶς αὐ- | τοῦ φάρμακον αὐτῷ δεδόσ- | θαι, ἡ δὲ Τατιας ἐπέστησεν | σκῆπτρον καὶ ἀρὰς ἔθηκεν | ἐν τῷ ναῷ ὡς ἱκανοποιοῦ- | σα περὶ τοῦ πεφημίσθαι αὐ- | τὴν ἐν συνειδήσι τοιαύτῃ ('Iucundus had gone mad, and everyone was saying his mother-in-law Tatias had given him a poison/bewitched him. But Tatias raised her sceptre and set down curses in the temple, to defend herself against what was being said about her, although she knew she was guilty of the crime.')

In several ways, this process appears similar to that described in the two curses from Knidos discussed above. Tatias is setting up public curses with a conditional self-punishing clause; the Knidos curses also seem to have included clauses that asked for punishment for the curser if what she was claiming was untrue. The erection of the sceptre, however, can be argued to take this a step further: it seems likely that it was, or signalled, a ritual indicating the beginning of a

---

[22] Zingerle (1926: esp. 45–6) suggested legal trials, including capital punishment, but this view has been widely criticized. Although some still argue for a more formal judicial process (Petzl 1988 and 1994), there is some consensus that priestly interventions were limited to receiving or witnessing the vows made by different parties (those offending or offended against), possibly negotiating between them, helping to identify acts of atonement, and setting up the final texts recording these events. See Chaniotis 2004, esp. 5–9 and 26–43, and Ricl 1995, and below note 25.

[23] Smyrna, second century CE; SEG 4.648; TAM 318. See Gordon 1999: 246–7 and Versnel 1991: 76, who also discuss TAM 318 and note the similarities with DT 1, and the dangers of gossip that these texts indicate; Versnel (1999: 134) refers to 'the idiom of suspicion'.

divine judicial process—a way of alerting the gods, and the surrounding community, that justice was being sought.[24]

The story continues (ll. 14–23): οἱ θεοὶ αὐτὴν ἐποίησαν ἐν | κολάσει ἣν οὐ διέφυγεν· ὁ- | μοίως καὶ Σωκράτης ὁ υἱὸς | αὐτῆς παράγων τὴν ἴσοδον | τὴν ἰς τὸ ἄλσος ἀπάγουσαν | δρέπανον κρατῶν ἀμπελοτό- | μον, ἐκ τῆς χειρὸς ἔπεσεν | αὐτῷ ἐπὶ τὸν πόδαν καὶ οὕ- | τως μονημέρῳ κολάσει ἀ- | πηλλάγη. ('But the gods inflicted punishment on her, which she did not escape. In like manner, her son Socrates, going by the entrance of the sacred grove and carrying a pruning knife with a hook, dropped it from his hand onto his foot, and after only a day came release from this divine punishment.')[25] Thus, as the account notes, Tatias' request in fact came to pass. This tragic course of events, the inscription reveals, led Tatias' relatives to the conclusion that Tatias had been punished by her own curse, and so must have been guilty.[26]

This story aligns with, but provides a more complete narrative than, the previous examples of the social dynamics involved in these kinds of accusations. We see how the formation of an accusation, a protestation of innocence, the affirmation of guilt, and appeasement of a god all developed from within the general community. As with the curses from the temple of Demeter at Knidos, which mention the people who have spoken against the writers of these texts, accusing them of malicious supernatural activities, the confession inscription highlights the gossip of the community as the motivation for Tatias' initial curse. In turn, any resulting public claims of guilt and innocence were surely not only caused by, but also themselves generated, more talk. The text shows that Tatias' descendants

---

[24] See Petzl 1994: 4, Ricl 1995: 73, Chaniotis 1997: 366, Versnel 2002a: 64–5, Gordon 2004. It has been argued (Eger 1939: 290) that the sceptre was set up in the case of unknown offenders and curses laid down if their victims were known, but Versnel (2002a: 64–5) argues against this.

[25] Gordon (1999: 247) has argued that the phrase 'the gods inflicted punishment on her, which she did not escape' describes the workings of a religious court; but, although the significance of the sequence of events, and the setting up of the inscription itself may have been brokered by the local priests, it seems unnecessary to envisage any active power other than that of the divine, or to see this as anything other than a story of supernatural justice. More recently, the assembly of a larger collection of evidence has allowed scholars to argue more specifically that although priests were involved in the process of resolving conflict, it is unlikely that trials took place (see Ricl 1995: 69, Chaniotis 2004: 6).

[26] Robert 1936: 122–3.

saw what had happened to her as a demonstration of her guilt. I would argue that it is likely that the setting down of curses did not stop the community's gossip, but exacerbated it, as people reported to each other what they saw happening and tried to make sense of it. For Tatias' relatives, their perception of what had occurred would be rooted in the shared knowledge and gossip of the community, which developed a narrative of explanation in response to the sequence of experiences and events.

Written by both the accused and the accusers, these texts—epitaphs and curses—seem to reveal the powerful and disruptive role of gossip within a community, and at a different level from that of the public arena of the law courts. It has been argued that creating such inscriptions helped to contain the negative emotions of a community. Two approaches have been taken. The first views these texts as offering a process for seeking some experience of justice in a situation in which civic legal redress is otherwise unachievable.[27] This certainly seems likely; nevertheless, at the same time, it is clear that the type of experience would differ across the diverse texts. The Lydian confession inscription, for example, suggests some kind of centralized, semi-formalized process, in which a third party (the priests of the sanctuary), invested with the authority and power of the divinity they represented, offered not only a conduit to the god in question, but also some concrete negotiation and resolution among those involved. In turn, the curses from Knidos (and the stone from Delos), submitted to, and perhaps put on display in, the local sanctuary, offered at least a shared space, which formalized both the presence of the divine, and the scrutiny of the community. It may also indicate a system, more or less formalized, which helped produce the texts of the tablets in the first place. Whether this process resulted in a sense of resolution is unknown.[28] And finally the epitaphs, viewed here as individual cries for justice, seem not to have been supported by any such system, however informal, by which the authority of the god—and of the community—could be brought to bear.

Moreover, in terms of an experience of justice, it is not only the presence of the god or of the community that is more or less formalized in these texts; the identity of the culprit him- or herself is also in play. For example, the stories related in the confession inscriptions

---

[27] Versnel 2002a: 73 and 37–40, followed by Salvo 2012: 260.
[28] See Versnel 2002a and Chaniotis 2004.

name the culprit, offence, and punishment; their neat narratives of cause and effect confirm expectations of divine justice. This contrasts with the levels of uncertainty evinced in both epitaphs and curses: some of these texts name a culprit, some do not. This does not necessarily indicate a lack of knowledge: consider the curse from Delos, written against a woman to whom Theagenes had lent money—he certainly knew who she was. And, in a small community, the activities alluded to in the other texts (gossip, accusations, etc.) may also have been intended to identify an individual who was widely suspected to have done these things.[29] This suggests that the explanation that these curse texts and their production would have offered a process for seeking some experience of justice may be further developed. These texts may have been expressions of suspicions relating to particular people, and therefore represent an attempt to get them punished. Alternatively, they may have been written by people distressed by the situation in which they found themselves—with no understanding of what caused it. The same is the case with the epitaphs: their writers may have had their suspicions and been in search of justice. Alternatively, they may simply have been seeking an explanation for the mysterious death of a loved one.[30]

This leads us to examine the second kind of 'social containment' that has been suggested, in particular for the curse tablets. This emphasizes a sense of emotional release, which seems to draw on implicit contemporary theories that expressing oneself is a way of seeking closure.[31] This requires some further consideration of the contemporary ideas being applied, which depend on a specific therapeutic setting in which what is said is explicitly heard and validated—a very different environment from that under discussion here. It is, of course, possible that a random event that brought suffering to the target might provide divine validation; but if not, then what kind of emotional release was likely? It is also worth bearing in mind that these inscriptions are not addressed only to the divine. Setting out an account of events so

---

[29] Jordan 1979: 523 n. 5.
[30] An aspect that both Graf (2007) and Edmonds (2010) emphasize.
[31] e.g. Salvo (2012: 257), who argues for a process in which women's feelings were amplified through sharing them with each other, and then focused in concrete action through the setting-up of the curse tablets; thus, the social function of the display of emotions in the Knidian prayers 'was to satisfy and cool strong retaliatory emotions and to "detoxify" the social interrelationships within the city'.

clearly and in public suggests an attempt to redirect an existing shared narrative—the gossip of the community. These inscriptions, publicly displaying unresolved suspicions and likely to be read aloud by members of a community, seem more likely to have become the stuff of further talk, threads to be spun into substance through whispers and hearsay. If we then turn our attention to those individuals who were alluded to in these curses, or perhaps, better put, who feared they were the targets, then how might they react? It seems likely, from the evidence already discussed, that the suspicion that one had been cursed would lead one, in turn, to curse... And was it likely then that if one set up a curse, one expected, in turn, to be cursed?

Daniel Ogden's marvellous summary of this cycle of experience as a 'magical arms race' also brings to mind the paranoia that accompanies the source of that imagery.[32] And, indeed, that kind of extreme emotion also seems to emerge from the sentiments of the epitaphs, whose writers appear to have imagined people living alongside them who were prepared to plot and poison them, but whose identity remained concealed. In the end, rather than containing anxieties, we can imagine these texts doing precisely than opposite: as well as expressing the anguished state of than individual who set the text up in the first place, it seems likely that these vivid, public expressions of desperation would also heighten the anxiety of other members of the community. If their fear that they also could become the targets of an occult attack was exacerbated, it makes it more likely that they, in turn, might resort to such activities.

---

[32] Ogden 1999: 51. See Pl. *Leg.* 933a–b for the power of suggestion in this context. Hendershot (1999) uses evidence from popular culture to illustrate the levels of social paranoia engendered by the nuclear arms race.

3.6

Public, Private, . . . and Secret

'IF ANYONE HAS BOUND ME . . .'

The texts discussed in the previous two sections offer insights into some of the more overt responses that people might make to the social threats they perceived. However, there were other, less explicit reactions, and these included the creation of binding spells that were similarly inscribed, but were not put on display.[1] One example, found near the banks of the Eridanos in the Kerameikos at Athens, appears to mention the threat of poison explicitly, with the phrase 'whoever gave a *pharmakon* to Hyacinthus'. We do not know if this Hyacinthus was the writer of the text or a third person, but this phrase may indicate that a suspected poisoning provoked the writing of this text.[2]

Other spells (as I have argued elsewhere) provide evidence for the risks that other people were perceived to present across a number of specific areas of life—including the law courts, political, performative, and commercial activities, as well as erotic relationships. However, although there have been attempts to assign these spells to particular categories, and argue that they were in general concerned with competition, a number of those spells that date to the pre-Imperial period are ambiguous. These include, for example: spells that have been categorized as concerned with commercial competition, but which address too many other types of profession, or other areas of life, for this to be their (only) motive; judicial spells that mysteriously target

---

[1] The quotation that heads this chapter comes from the first line of the binding spell *NGCT* 24; Attica, very early fourth century BCE (Jordan 1999), discussed on pp. 66–7.

[2] Listed under *SGD* 14; it is also possible that Hyacinthus was a corpse involved in the curse ritual. Compare also *DT* 8, a text from Knidos (possibly early first or second centuries BCE), discussed on p. 217.

women among their list of 'litigants'; and 'erotic' spells that also seem to be concerned with the professional aspects of their victim's life.[3]

The ambiguous nature of these spells may signal an environment in which hostilities were not confined to particular categories of life, but in which there had been a more general breakdown of social relations. This prompts a more detailed analysis of what these spells were intended to achieve. The writing of binding spells was a practice firmly set in the context of Athenian everyday experience, but it was not only expressive; it was also creative. As Bruce Kapferer has argued, we should not regard magical practices simply as representations of social realities, but foremost as 'exercises in the construction and destruction of the psychosocial realities that human beings live and share'.[4] This approach enables us to move away from focusing on the feelings of the spell-writer (and such questions as whether or not a spell text can express real feeling if it has been commissioned from a third party).[5] Instead, it turns our attention to the way in which the ritual of cursing was intended to address and reshape relations between victim and spell-writer.

The Language of Humiliation

One analysis that touches on the relationship created between victim and spell-writer has been developed by Henk Versnel, who argues that *Schadenfreude* or 'malicious laughter' underlies the creation of binding spells in ancient Greek culture. This posits that some binding spells can be construed as protests against the pain of ridicule, while others were clearly intended to ensure that their victims would become a laughing stock, by binding their targets so that they would be incapacitated and unable to perform their social roles effectively.[6]

---

[3] See Eidinow 2013a.   [4] Kapferer 2003: 302.
[5] Spell-writer, see Graf 1997: 146–7.
[6] Versnel (1999: 127) was inspired in particular by Campbell's work (1964), specifically on the uses of ridicule and mockery as forms of social control in a community dominated by social values of honour, shame, and competition. Much work has been done on the role and power of public mockery in ancient society and there is no question that fear of public mockery played a significant part in the Athenian value system and is one of the multiple emotions involved in the 'arms race' of binding spells (as described by Ogden 1999: 51).

Although use of the term *Schadenfreude* does need some more reflection, processes of mockery and laughter are certainly useful for this analysis, since, as Versnel demonstrates, they are often expressed through gossip.[7] His perhaps most vivid example is the Amorgos curse (now lost, but a text and translation is provided below), which he argues was written by a man who felt himself to be ultimately humilitated, made a fool of by the charming and aptly named Epaphroditus, who has encouraged his slaves to flee.[8] Versnel argues that this tablet is prompted by anticipation, or indeed, experience of, *Schadenfreude*, because, after all, 'we must realise that being deserted by one's slaves is—especially in the context of a face-to-face society— both a very *public* (in the sense of conspicuous) event and a grievous attack on the victim's dignity'.[9]

Side A
Κυρία Δημήτηρ, Βασίλισσα, ἱκέτης σου, προσπίπτω δὲ ὁ δοῦλός σου· τοὺ (ς) ἐμοὺς | δούλους ὑπεδέξατο, του(ς) κακοδιδασκάλησε, ἐγνωμοδότησε, συνεβούλευσε, | ὑπενόθευσε, κατέχαρε, ἀνεπτέρωσε ἀγοράσαι, ἐγνωμοδότησε φυγῖν | τις Ἐφαφρόδ[ει]τ[ος], συνεπέθελγε τὸ παιδίσκην αὐτός, ἵνα, ἐμοῦ μὴ θέ- | λοντος, ἔχειν αὐτὸν γυναῖκα αὐτήν. δι᾿ἐκήνην τὴν αἰτίαν δὲ αὐτὴν πεφευ- | γέναι σὺν καὶ τοῖς ἄλλοις. Κυρία Δημήτηρ, ἐγὼ ὦ ταῦτα παθὼν ἔρημος | ἐὼν ἐπί σε καταφεύγω σοῦ εὐγιλάτου τυχεῖν καὶ ποῖσαί με τοῦ δικαίου τυχεῖν, | ποιήσαις τὸν τοιαῦτά με διαθ[έ]μενον μὴ στάσιν μὴ βάσιν μηδ(αμ)οῦ ἐμπλησθῆναι | μὴ σώματος μήτε {ο}νοῦ, μὴ δούλων μὴ παιδισκῶν μὴ δουλεύθοιτο, μὴ ὑπὸ μυ[κρ]- | ὧν μὴ ὑπο

---

[7] Versnel 1999: 136–9. *Schadenfreude* may be a misleading term to use here, since recent research has suggested that it is 'not a public mocking intended to humiliate someone; it is typically a private enjoyment lacking any element of severe mocking or humiliation' (Ben Ze'ev 2014: 88). It does not seem an appropriate description of situations in which a person enjoys another's pain and suffering in a situation of extreme violence and even death (as, for example, Versnel 1999: 151, referring to *damnatio ad bestias*, a punishment in which people were thrown to wild animals). We can compare the story that Socrates tells of Leontius' son Aglaeon (*Resp.* 439e–40a), who does not want to look at the bodies of the executed, but is overcome by desire. Such an emotion is coherent, but is not *Schadenfreude*: see Ben Ze'ev (2014: 88), who argues that 'we should distinguish between schadenfreude and cruelty as expressed, for example, in sadism or when the other person experiences great suffering'. See further in n. 20, on the passive nature of *Schadenfreude*, which also does not fit Versnel's analysis.
[8] *SGD* 60; text Bömer 1963: 992 ff.; tr. Eidinow 2013: 423–4.
[9] Versnel 1999: 127–8 (italics in original).

μεγάλου μὴ ἐπιβαλόμενός τι ἐκτελέ{σε}σαιτο, καταδε{ε}σμὸ(s) αὐτοῦ | τὴν οἰκίαν λάβοιτο ἔχ[ο]ι, μὴ παιδὶν κλαύσετο. μὴ τράπεζαν ἱλαρὰν θῦτο. μὴ κύων | εἰλακτήσαιτο, μὴ ἀλέκτωρ κοκκύσαιτο, σπείρας μὴ θερίσαιτο, καταντίσας καρποὺς | μὴ ἐπί[στα]ιτο ετεραν(?), μὴ γῆ μὴ θάλασσα καρπὸν ἐνένκαιτο, μὴ χαρὰν μ[ακ]αρίαν | ἔχ[ο]ιτο, αὐτός τε κα[κ]ῶς ἀπόλοιτο καὶ τὰ παρ' αὐτοῦ πάντα.

Side B
Κυρία Δημήτηρ, λιτανεύω σε παθὼν ἄδικα, ἐπάκουσον, θεά, καὶ κρῖναι | τὸ δίκαιον, ἵνα τοὺς τοιαῦτα ἐνθυμουμένους καὶ καταχαίροντε(s) καὶ λύπας | ἐπιθε(ί)ναι κἀμοὶ καὶ τῇ ἐμῇ γυναικὶ Ἐπικτήσι, καὶ μισοῦσιν ἡμᾶς ποιῆσαι αὐ- | τοῖς τὰ δινότατα καὶ χαλεπώτερα δινά. Βασίλισσα, ἐπάκουσον ἡμῖν | παθοῦσι, κολάσαι τοὺς ἡμᾶς τοιούτους ἡδέως βλέποντες.

Side A
Mistress Demeter, O queen, I, your suppliant, throw myself before you, your servant. A certain Epaphroditus, has enveigled my slaves, he has taught them evil, he has counselled them, he has hatched conspiracies, he has corrupted them, he has rejoiced over them, he has incited them to run about, he has counselled them to run away. He has bewitched a slave girl, without my permission, so that he can have her as his. For that reason she fled with the other runaways. Mistress Demeter, I have suffered these things and, all alone, I run to you, may you be merciful and help me find justice. May you make this man who has perpetrated these acts against me find no fulfilment, neither at rest, nor in motion, neither of the body, nor of the soul, let him not be served either by slave boys or girls, let him not achieve anything, whether he takes on something small or great. May a binding spell seize his household, let no child cry for him and let him not prepare a gracious table. Let no dog howl, let no rooster crow. When he sows, let him not reap, if he produces a good harvest, let him not produce (another?), let neither land nor sea bring forth fruit. Let him have no delight or bliss. But let him be horribly destroyed and everything with him.

Side B
Mistress Demeter, I, who have suffered injustice, pray to you, hear me, goddess, and make a just judgement, so that on those who think such things and rejoice and bring grief on me and on my wife Epictesis, and hate us, on them you make the most terrible and and painful horrors. O Queen, listen to us, who suffer, punish those who look happily on us.

Before examining this text, it is worth briefly pausing to consider whether ancient evidence supports the claim that shame would have been a first reaction to such a situation. In Xenophon's *Memorabilia*, Diodorus says that he would ask friends and neighbours to help recover runaway slaves. He also mentions offering a reward—a very public strategy if this was a shameful event.[10] That fear might be a more appropriate emotion is suggested by the description of neighbours helping to guard neighbours against runaway slaves.[11]

When we turn to the text itself, we find similar nuancing is necessary. Side A is squarely aimed at Epaphroditus, but the idea that the primary motivation behind the writing of the curse was the *Schadenfreude* that Epaphroditus was relishing is hard to establish. Vernsel has translated the lines τοὺ(ς) κακοδιδασκάλησε, ἐγνωμοδότησε, συνεβούλευσε, | ὑπενόθευσε, κατέχαρε, ἀνεπτέρωσε ἀγοράσαι, ἐγνωμοδότησε φυγῖν as '[he] has led them into evil ways, indoctrinated them, advised them, misled them, he rejoiced (in my misery), he has them wandering round the market place, he persuaded them to run away'. It seems unlikely that *katechare*, 'he rejoiced', occurring in the midst of this long list of wrongdoing, should be the only verb that does not take the object *tous*, 'them'. The verb *katachairo*, 'I rejoice', certainly carries an idea of malicious joy, but the exultation described is perhaps more accurately translated as the rejoicing of the villain over his spoils.

The text on Side B may offer some more useful material: it continues the enraged howl of the spell-writer, and provides a list of types of people against whom the spell is targeted—the enemies of the spell-writer and his wife. This includes those who have thought about hurting them, and those who have found pleasure in plotting against them, and those who hate them. We are reminded of the paranoid statements of the epitaph writers described in the previous section, who felt themselves the victims of secret plots and dirty tricks. But the key phrase is the final request: κολάσαι τοὺς ἡμᾶς τοιούτους ἡδέως βλέποντες. Versnel translates this as 'punish those who rejoice in our misery'. In fact, the Greek is more restrained than this: it refers to those who look on what has happened and find it pleasurable. Taken out of context it might be interpreted as showing that the writer of the spell text was afraid of *Schadenfreude*, but if we bear in mind the list of offences that precedes it, again, it is difficult to identify it as the primary

---

[10] Xen. *Mem.* 2.10.1–2.
[11] Xen. *Hiero*, 4.3 and Pl. *Resp.* 578e–579a. See Fisher 1993: 81.

motivation behind the writing of the spell. In situ, it offers yet another circumlocution for 'our enemies', and depicts one more of a number of activities that the writer fears from those who are hostile to him. In sum, the text does not appear to be primarily motivated by fear of the mockery or *Schadenfreude* of others.

Evidence of the desire to engender ridicule does appear in a group of seven spell texts from a cache of twelve found together in the Agora at Athens in a well 'sunk into the courtyard of the Poros building'. The relevant targets across this cache comprise wrestlers (five, with three of them against a wrestler called Eutychian), a runner, and sets of lovers (three).[12] The repetition of formulae and the handwriting of this group of texts indicates that they were probably prepared by two or possibly three persons—perhaps a professional and an apprentice (as David Jordan has suggested)—and possibly in advance of their specific commission, as the configuration of one text suggests.[13]

The seven spells relevant to this inquiry include four of the five spells written against wrestlers (three against a wrestler called Eutychian), one against a runner, and two of the erotic type: these all include a formula asking that the victim *aschemonesei*, that is, 'disgrace himself' (or, in the case of the last type of spell, 'themselves'). The formula is both rare and late—the spells date to the mid-third century CE—and it seems to have been used without much thought, since it is applied inappropriately in the erotic texts.[14] Although the desire for the victim to fall over and make a fool of himself is certainly expressed, when it is viewed in context, it becomes apparent that this is far from the primary aim of these spells. Rather, the overriding intent of each spell is to prevent the target from functioning at all. To illustrate this analysis, below is the translation of the first spell

---

[12] *SGD* 24–35 (Agora inv. 948+949, 950, 952, 953, 955–60, 964, 1000), which describes the location (Well V; see Jordan 1985: 210–11). (There are further curses in this collection that share aspects of the relevant formulation, but are unclear, e.g. 33–4; 35 addresses a ghost.)

[13] Jordan 1985: 210–11. For the configuration that suggests the name of the target was added after the text, see *SGD* 38.

[14] Date from context, SGD 24; but cf. Jordan 1985: 212. There is one curse on a pair of lovers (Agora Inv. No. IL 1000) in which it is asked that the male partner 'must fall and disgrace himself'; Versnel (1999: 150) admits that it is not appropriate to this context. Agora Inv. No. IL 952 only involves the lovers disgracing themselves; there is no wish that they fall down. This formula does not appear at all in 948 + 949; among the spells against wrestlers, it occurs in all three spells against Eutychian (Agora Inv. Nos 950, 957, and 960) and the one against Petres (Agora Inv. No. 955), but not the spell targeting Attalos (Agora Inv. No. IL 956).

against Eutychian (the text begins with 'Borphor syllables', that is, a magical invocation, and continues):

> -babaie, mighty Betpyt, I hand over to you Eutychian, whom Eutychia bore, that you may chill him and his purposes, and in your dark air also those with him. Bind in the unilluminated *aion* of oblivion and chill and destroy also the wrestling that he is going to do in the ... this coming Friday. And if he does wrestle, in order that he may fall and disgrace himself, Mozoune Alcheine Perpertharona Iaia, I hand over to you Eutychian, whom Eutychia bore. Mighty Typhon, Kolchoi Tontonon Seth Sathaoch Ea, Lord Apomx Phriourinx over the blacking out and chilling of Eutychian, whom Eutychia bore, Kolchoicheilops, let Eutychian grow cold and not be strong this coming Friday, but let him be weak. As these names grow cold, so let Eutychian grow cold, whom Eutychia bore, whom Aithales promotes.[15]

The second spell against Eutychian again focuses on making sure he cannot function—and reinforces this message with some further phrases:

> -babaie, mighty Betpyt, I hand over to you Eutychian, who is going to wrestle with Secundus, that you may chill Eutychian and his purposes, and his power, his strength, his wrestling, and in your dark air also those with him. Bind in the unilluminated *aion* of oblivion and chill and destroy also the wrestling of Eutychian, wrestler. If with regard to Secundus you chill him and do not allow Eutychian to wrestle, in order than he may fall and disgrace himself, Morzoune Alcheine Perpertharona Iaia, I hand over to you Eutychian. Mighty Typhon, Kolchoicheilops, let Eutychian the wrestler grow cold. As these names grow cold, so let Eutychian's name and breath, impulse, charm, knowledge, reckoning, knowledge grow cold. Let him be deaf, dumb, mindless, harmless, and not fighting against anyone.[16]

The desire for the victim to 'fall and disgrace himself' is certainly one of the aims of the text, but it is far from the only or even the primary motivation. The spell appears to be intended to cover all aspects of the situation, just in case the target does manage to wrestle (or in the case of the runner, to 'get past the starting line'). Indeed, some of the other texts make no mention of this aspect at all.[17] If we are

---

[15] Agora Inv. No. IL 950 (tr. Jordan 1985: 215).
[16] Agora Inv. No. IL 960 (tr. Jordan 1985: 216).
[17] Inv. No. IL 956 (tr. Jordan 1985: 218) for the wrestler Attalus: this focuses on the desire for 'blacking out and chilling and powerlessness'. It also includes the *similia similibus* formula: 'just as these names grow cold, so too let Attalos' name and breath,

looking for a primary motive for these texts, it appears to be that the victim not be able to compete at all. That he also cut a sorry figure is sometimes made explicit—but almost only as a last resort—and that he become an object of mockery is not mentioned. Nor does such a desire, implicit or explicit, appear in any other binding spell text to my knowledge.[18] Even in those texts that seem to have been written in response to an injustice or harm already done, where an appetite for revenge including humiliation might be expected, there is no mention of such intent. As with the majority of binding spell texts, they restrict themselves to binding, that is, inhibiting the functioning of their enemies, and reducing specific, contextual risks, in the person of mortal enemies.[19] It appears that rather than the desire to humiliate the target being explicit or a primary goal of a binding spell, it was perhaps taken as one possible result of the inability to function that it might inflict.[20]

In conclusion, it is hard to locate in these texts the desire for malicious pleasure that has been claimed. It does not seem to be present either as a source of motivation in writing the spells, or in descriptions of their desired outcome. If we pause and consider the nature of *Schadenfreude*, this absence makes sense. If this emotion arises from observing the misfortunes of others—which have come about as a result of contingency or happenstance[21]—actually writing a binding spell to bring about a situation of misfortune (in order then to enjoy it) seems to be a different matter. The situation requires an initial emotion to motivate the writing of the spell in the first place, and this raises the question of the nature of that emotion.[22]

---

impulse, knowledge, reckoning grow cold'. There is no mention of what should happen if he does wrestle.

[18] As Versnel admits (1999: 129 and 156). He appears to suggest that this is because they display 'mere lists of names and simple instructions to bind the opponent', but there are a number of more elaborate formulas, and derision or humiliation does not appear among them.

[19] See Eidinow 2013a.

[20] But fear could work just as well: Eur. *Alcmene* F 88a (Collard and Cropp 2008). Among the few times that curses are explicitly mentioned in ancient literature, people are using them to explain or excuse a particular misfortune or failure; see Brown 1970: 25 and Dover 1974: 133–56. Magical explanations might coexist with more spiteful ones: Cic. *Brut.* 217 and Libanius *Or.* 1.43, 62, and 245–9, discussed in more detail on pp. 158–61.

[21] As Charles Stewart points out (pers. corresp.). Ben Ze'ev (2014: 83–4) observes that *Schadenfreude* is typically seen as a passive emotion. Van Dijk and Ouwerkerk (2014) note the ways in which scholars have sought to identify different kinds of *Schadenfreude* (6), 'ranging from the mildly to the seriously morally negative joy'.

[22] See van de Ven 2014 on the relationship between *phthonos* and *Schadenfreude*, discussed in more detail on pp. 250–3.

As even the few spells we have looked at above suggest, these texts are concerned with causing the immobility of the victim, at least, and sometimes their suffering as well, frequently using a metaphor of binding. Recalling the discussions earlier in this book about the imagery of emotion talk, I suggest here that an examination of the formulae of the texts of these binding spells may be helpful. Focusing on the figurative language relating to binding, which is particularly common in Attic binding spells, may help us understand how these activities were understood to address and reshape the relations of victim and spell-writer. They can offer some insight into not only what those who wrote or used these spells may have imagined that they were doing to their victims, but also the origins of the perceived power of this practice.

Deducing Intention

In later Greek and many Roman tablets, the apparent intention of binding spells appears to become markedly more violent, and spell-writers may even set their sights on murder—asking not just that their victims be bound, but that they be wholly destroyed.[23] This vicious approach is, most scholars have come to agree, in contrast to the desires generally expressed in earlier spells, which may be agonistic, but are not intended to be fatal or even cause suffering.[24] These deductions about the purpose of these earlier spells tend to draw on

---

[23] *DT* 93a (Brigantium, first century CE), *DT* 129 (Arezzo, mid-second century CE). Apparently rare early examples of the death wish may appear in *SGD* 89 (Sicily, second century BCE); *DTA* 75 (Athens, fourth century BCE); and *DT* 92 (Black Sea, third century BCE), although, as with most curse tablets, the texts are fragmentary and some of the readings speculative.

[24] e.g. Graf (1997: 157) argues that they were 'a means to master emotionally an otherwise difficult crisis'; Versnel (1998: 232) has recognized this aspect in some tablets, designating them as 'prayers for justice', whose writers explicitly express their intention to punish the target for a wrongdoing. In these texts, body parts may be listed in detail, or not mentioned at all, but the passion of the writer is manifest, and the victim is clearly intended to suffer: 'there is a strong and often explicit link between the wish that a person shall suffer, struck by an affliction or even by death, on the one hand, and the enumeration of body parts or the mention of the body as a whole, on the other'. This he contrasts with texts in which (Versnel 1998: 222) 'all these formulas can be qualified as functional and instrumental in that they can be understood as instruments to bind—that is to restrain—competitors without the explicit, and perhaps even implicit, aim of physically hurting or tormenting them'. There is some overlap between the two categories: Versnel has identified spells that occupy a middle

some later literary evidence that offers few details, for example, the report of Galen, who mocks the claims of ritual experts who targeted their opponents in court with binding spells.[25] Neveretheless, other anecdotes hint at different outcomes from the use of binding spells, including the affliction of severe pain and disablement, or even, albeit indirectly, the potential to cause death (as an example, consider the account of the suffering of Libanius, already described).[26]

Unfortunately, there is little equivalent literary material that can help us to clarify the motivations of those who wrote the earlier

---

ground (so-called 'border-area curses') which involve elements of both these formulae. These tend not only to ask the god for help, offering some kind of justification for the appeal, but also to dedicate the stolen item to the deity's charge in the case of stolen goods, or to deliver the wrongdoer to the gods. A full description of their characteristics can be found in Versnel 1991: 64-8, updated in Versnel 2010: 280. Nevertheless, he has recently drawn attention to the way in which (in accordance with his analysis) the listing of body parts in some of these 'border-area' curses suggests that they should be labelled as prayers for justice rather than binding spells, and this category should be enlarged (some prayers for justice may not be 'written out in full'; see ibid.: 337). (For elements of supplicatory prayer, see ibid.: 332-3; the importance of lists of body parts, ibid.: 339-40; and reducing the number of 'border-area' cases, ibid.: 340.) Erotic binding spells may also be considered as occupying some kind of middle ground, since they tend to list a victim's body in detail, and have the clear intention of invoking torment. In his earlier work, Versnel suggests that this is because lovers feel a '"legitimate" indignation' about their situation, similar to the emotions of those seeking revenge for harm done, although they are in fact seeking not a negative but a positive final result. Versnel (1998: 264): 'In both types of texts, judicial prayers and erotic magic, torture and punishment unequivocally presuppose that the practitioners are wrong, aggrieved, deprived of something they feel entitled to.' In a footnote (Versnel 1998: 264 n. 131), he qualifies this as not being concerned with 'offences not tolerated by society' but rather as a 'personal "affront", demonstrably assessed as an act of injustice by the lover' (see also Versnel 2010: 280 n. 21). I am not concerned here with the category of 'prayers for justice': there is no doubt that it has been a tremendous advance in the study of curses, and has been adopted productively by many prominent scholars (Versnel 2010: 276). Rather, my aim is to explore the language of binding spells, specifically the metaphor of binding itself.

[25] e.g. Gal. XII p. 251 Kühn; see Faraone 1991: 15 and related discussion.

[26] Libanius *Or.* 1.245-9, as discussed on pp. 158-61 Graf (1997: 164) offers another example from the *Account of the Miracles of Saints Cyrus and John*. Sophronius describes the binding of a man called Theophilus, who is afflicted with dreadful pains, until a dream of Saints Cyrus and John reveals to him how to undo the binding spell that has been cast upon him (Graf 1997: 165; also discussed in Gager 1992: 121). Although Graf provides a number of later examples that suggest that curses were intended to do more harm than disempower their victim, he does not accept this as part of the 'ideology of ritual binding' (Graf 1997: 142). This is on the grounds, it seems, that it does not fit the five categories of binding established by modern scholarship and that 'the mechanism [of binding] is not so direct.'

tablets. However, in the texts of the spells themselves there may be some clues. There, we find a number of formulae that indicate that the writers of binding spells intended slightly more than simply to neutralize their opponent. Different so-called *similia similibus* formulae are included, aimed at transferring to the victim of a spell the characteristics of some object or action mentioned in it (e.g. that the victim be like the corpse with which the victim is buried, or the lead on which the spell is written, or even resembling the way the curse tablet itself has been set apart).[27] Some spell texts are inscribed with scrambled letters, or written backwards, which is then mentioned in the spell as the desired effect that the spell will have on the target or on his or her thoughts, words, or deeds.[28] The figurines found with some spells seem to be included for a similar purpose: these little dolls are bound and sometimes twisted; some appear in miniature coffins.[29] These early spells do not mention pain or death for the target; nevertheless, it is hard not to connect these representations—the twisted body, the boxed figures—with such an outcome, and with the impression that the writers intended to cause their targets pain. So, is this what was meant by 'binding'?

Analysing Metaphor

Most scholars are now agreed that binding is a metaphor, and use of the verb 'to bind' indicates that we are entering a realm of analogical thinking.[30] But what is the analogy here? Fritz Graf argues that binding is a description of a larger sequence of actions that involved piercing or nailing a ritual object, and which aimed, more or less explicitly, to transfer to the victim the characteristics of these or some of these actions.[31] So, for example, on DT 49 we find the instruction 'I bind, I make disappear, I bury, I nail down', and on SGD 48, similarly, 'I bind, I bury, I make disappear among men', while other tablets

---

[27] Examples of each are found on *DT* 68 (Attica, fourth century BCE), *DTA* 105 (Attica, third century BCE), and *DT* 85 (Boiotia, third/second century BCE), respectively.
[28] *DTA* 65 (Attica, fourth/third century BCE).
[29] *SGD* 9 (Athens, early fourth century BCE).
[30] Kagarow (1929: 9) suggested that the verb 'to bind' must once have referred to a real act of binding, and had since become symbolic.
[31] Graf 1997: 135ff.

include mention of burying their victim.[32] It does not appear that these are included as a summary of ritual actions; they were more likely part of a common formula.

As to why this metaphorical language may have been perceived to work, Graf turns to Stanley Tambiah's theory of performative power: in civic oaths that include magical acts, the ritual act gives a different intensity that uses 'other codes than just the linguistic one'.[33] The participants themselves are caught by the strangeness of the metaphor, which, as he puts it, 'they must first decipher'. However, when he talks of curse tablets he gives this explanation a slightly different twist, arguing that the magical acts that gave rise to binding spells were performed alone, and this isolation crucially shaped the nature and content of the formulae. In this context, he states, the action of binding the tablet, or piercing a tablet or a doll, was done by the magician as a record of his action: 'a lasting condensation of his words'.[34] And rather than the metaphor working as a code, the spell made 'explicit what the sorcerer wishes'. He attributes the origins of this practice to similar practices in Mesopotamia—but makes no comment about how and why they may have transferred to Greece.[35]

Henk Versnel also stresses the performative power of analogical language in magical spells: under a larger category heading of analogy, he lists comparison, simile, metaphor, and *historiolae*.[36] He notes of all these techniques that 'for some reason or other' they are powerful in themselves, and 'if incorporated into the formula impart their power, in other words persuasive force'.[37] But quite how this power is created or how these analogies are selected, he admits is puzzling: 'In this process we often observe that the *logical relevance* of a particular comparison is *not* the decisive consideration.'[38] Elsewhere, he focuses on the listing of body parts, maintaining that anatomical curses draw on ideas of punishment. However, he observes that 'although we are well informed about the different procedures and instruments of ancient torture, such as whip, wheel, rack, and corporal punishment in general, lists of body parts being tortured in a judicial context are conspicuously lacking in our evidence'.[39] Instead, like Graf, he turns to

---

[32] For example, on curses, DT 49 (Athens, c.300 BCE), SGD 170.
[33] Graf 1997: 209, drawing on Tambiah 1985: 18–21.
[34] Graf 1997: 212. [35] Ibid.: 170. [36] Versnel 2002b: 122.
[37] Ibid. [38] Ibid.: 129 (italics in original).
[39] Versnel 1998: 245.

Near Eastern influences to explain the origin of this approach, and to explain its power argues that 'these forms of expressive intensification... are intended to exert an irresistible rhetorical pressure upon the addressee'.[40]

In an initial approach to this material, Derek Collins rejected the use of metaphor and the idea of 'sympathetic magic' in favour of a more literal approach to binding: 'the binding of a figurine is the binding of its agency, not a symbolic or persuasive act'.[41] However, in later work, he has tried again to explain the metaphor of binding and its links to the listing of body parts via the appearance of binding in ancient Greek myth. He argues that 'binding' is a 'metaphorical precedent in Greek religious thinking' that acquires its power because of its use by the gods in (chiefly) Homeric epic: they cannot kill each other, but they can constrain each other, and other creatures. On this basis, Collins asserts that binding is associated with divine power, and this precedent leads to mortals asking gods to bind their mortal enemies in binding spells.[42] However, this approach also raises numerous questions: for example, there is no reference to these precedents in the binding spells themselves; moreover, the binding of the gods in these stories includes descriptions of ropes and shackles, and the spells do not.[43] Finally, the obsessive focus on particular body parts found in binding spells does not seem to fit the cursory mention of hands and feet in the literary texts he cites. Although the idea of the body part representing the whole person

---

[40] Ibid.: 224–5. The list should be thought of as resembling a 'camera's "panning-shot"' and its effect on our attention, such that it enables 'the period of the practitioner's projective fixation upon the victim... [which] can be extended as long as possible'. This idea introduces intriguing questions about the cognitive experience of binding—although a culturally more appropriate metaphor, in terms of the gaze, might be the evil eye—but it remains unclear how and why the metaphor of binding relates to the use of body parts.

[41] Collins 2003: 43; see Riess 2012: 200. Riess himself sets binding spells in the context of 'curses' more generally, linking the *agos* of a broken conditional curse to the binding produced through a spell, through the fact that both could be undone by a ritual (205): 'Very clearly, *defixiones* and *loimos*, and, consequently, *arai*, belong together in the imagination of ancient believers.' Despite his own acknowledgement of the differences (203), this approach appears to conflate these two genres.

[42] Collins 2008: 67–9.

[43] Collins (ibid.: 67) notes mention of a rope in a later spell, but is cautious about attributing that explicit form of binding to earlier spells. Elsewhere in his argument (ibid.: 80), he observes that binding is 'a realization, through magic, of Greek notions of disability and impairment' and inverts 'cultural notions of health'.

makes this connection clearer, it leaves unanswered why these specific body parts should be singled out for inclusion.[44]

The Imagery of Punishment

From myth to Near Eastern influence to torture—these suggestions illustrate the difficulty of identifying the origins of this binding metaphor. But perhaps the answer lies closer to home: the realm of civic punishment. In Athens the most common verb for magically binding a victim seems, from current evidence, to have been built around verbs of binding (*-deo*), often the verb *katadeo*.[45] In turn, both *katadeo* and *deo* were used to describe being physically tied up, and can indicate being attached to something, being detained, and being sent to prison (*deo* is the commoner).[46] That the two ideas were related is illustrated very clearly in some binding spell formulae:

---

[44] Ibid.: 16.

[45] See Wunsch *DTA*, p. v (he finds it sixty times in his collection) and p. iii for discussion of the meaning of binding; and see Kagarow 1929: 25–8 for discussion of the two categories of types of verb—those to do with binding and those to do with registering the victim.

[46] Riess (2012: 214) also argues that binding spells had more violent implications than have previously been suggested by scholars and makes this connection between binding in the spells and physical binding, arguing that *katadeo* was used as a metaphor of Athenian origin for the binding of those awaiting execution. However, he does not examine the language of the spells beyond this verb form, nor does he offer examination of texts about civic punishment. Rather he argues that it indicates that 'the victim was to be bound metaphorically to face trial in front of the gods' and that 'the gods defined what καταδῶ meant in each individual case and mobilized the dead to impose all kinds of adverse conditions on the intended targets of spells' (see also p. 229, where he emphasizes the role of the gods in determining 'if and how καταδῶ was supposed to harm the victim in each individual situation'). This is a vivid image, but, unfortunately, it is not supported by the curse texts. The role that he allocates the dead (to do the killing) does not align with the explicitly acknowledged immobility of the dead in certain spells (see e.g. *DT* 43, and compare Eidinow 2013a: 152–4). It is difficult to see active dead in the spells he cites (*DTA* 99, 100, 102, 103) even indirectly; however, he argues (213 n. 243) that the Greeks did not have clear-cut ideas of the dead.

Examples of *deo* used to mean 'to bind': Hom. *Il.* 5.385–91, *Od.* 22.189–90; Hes. *Theog.* 652 and 718; Hdt. 6.75.2; Aesch. *Pers.* 744–5; Soph. *Aj.* 108, 240; Eur. *Cyc.* 234; and *Andromeda* frr. 122 and 128 (Collard and Cropp 2008); Xen. *Hell.* 3.3.11; Andoc. 1.45; Ar. *Eq.* 367 and 1048, *Ran.* 619, *Thesm.* 942, 1019, 1022, and 1031; Pl. *Leg.* 882b, 855c; Arist. *Pol.* 1306b; Herod. 5.10, 18 (with *desmos* in Lys. 6.21). See further Halm-Tisserant (1998: 72). Examples of *katadeo*: Hdt. 3.143.2 and 5.72.4, Thuc. 8.15, Pl. *Ti.* 70e.

DTA 45, for example, asserts: 'I bind Euandrus, in a lead binding' (Εὔανδρον [κ]ατα- | δῶ ἐν δεσμ[ῶι] μο- | λυβ[δίν]ωι).[47]

One striking aspect of binding spell formulae is the lists of parts of the body. Can this be explained by reference to ancient types of detention? The Greeks themselves do not seem to have been very precise in their terms or descriptions for different mechanisms of physical binding as a civic punishment. Indeed, it is often hard to tell which specific type of device or approach is being referred to in the sources. Among them are the *kuphon* ('pillory'), *kloios* ('collar'), *podokakke* ('stocks'), *tumpanon* (defined by LSJ as 'name of some instrument of torture of execution'; this term also means 'cudgel', and so may indicate that a form of beating was involved).[48] The most common, but perhaps most confusing, was the *xulon*. This term for 'an instrument of punishment', is translated literally as 'the wood', but could indicate a 'wooden collar', the 'stocks', or a *pentesuringon xulon*, which combined collar and stocks 'with holes for the neck, arms, and legs'; it might also refer to a 'gallows' or a 'stake on which criminals were impaled'.[49]

This ambiguity may be explained as part of the Athenian 'unwillingness verbally to go into too much detail in the face of death, and specifically perhaps the death of citizens'.[50] Nevertheless, both texts and images suggest that there was a wide range of punishments to draw on, with a variety of configurations of restraint. Victims could be seated or standing;[51] the hands, arms, legs, or feet, or throat of the prisoner might be bound. For example, if a prisoner was wearing a *kloios*

---

[47] But, I would argue, for the purposes of this argument an exact parallel of this sort is not necessary: in the curse texts there are other rarer verbs such as *katadesmeuo* or *katecho* for example, and they too emphasize the restraining of the victim.

[48] But this may be undermined by the lexical approach to *apotumpanismos*, also once thought to be related to *tumpanon*, meaning cudgel, and now shown to be more like crucifixion, although there were variations over time and place (see pp. 240–2, and Gernet 1968: 302–3 and 307).

[49] Definitions from LSJ. *kloios*: Xen. *Hell.* 3.3.11, Eur. *Cyc.* 235; *kuphon*: Ar. *Plut.* 476 and 606, Arist. *Pol.* 1306b; *xulon*: Ar. *Eq.* 367, 705, and 1048, *Nub.* 592, *Lys.* 680; Andoc. 1.45; Dem. 18.129 and 24.105; Hdt. 6.75.2 and 9.37.2 (Spartan examples: King Cleomenes and Hegesistratus, the seer, share a topos of self-mutilation while imprisoned in a *xulon*—Cleomenes dies and Hegesistratus escapes); *podokakke*: Lys. 10.16; Dem. 24.105; *tetremenon xulon*: Ar. *Lys.* 680; *pentesuringon xulon*: Ar. *Eq.* 1048; see discussion in Hunter (1994: 179–81). See also discussion by Allen (2003: 200), where *apotumpanismos* and other forms of being 'fastened' are discussed.

[50] Todd 2000b: 36–7.

[51] See in particular Pl. *Leg.* 855c, [Arist.] *Ath. Pol.* 45.1, where the man sent for *apotumpanismos* is already seated in preparation for his punishment, and, as Gernet (1968: 295) points out, depictions of punishment of Prometheus.

or bound to a *kuphon*, then perhaps his legs and hands would be left free, and must be bound separately; in turn, there were also specific devices for binding the feet, including the *podokakke*. This might well explain why, in binding spells, we find lists of the different parts of the body as separate targets, with, in particular, a repeated use of 'hands' and 'feet', especially in Attic binding spells; and why we find curse figurines with their hands and feet bound.[52]

In addition, it does not seem far-fetched to suggest that the binding of the tongue, which is also common in Attic binding spells, could be a reference to the desired effects of a collar or neckband: the writers of these spells wanted to prevent their victims from talking. The description of Hercules' suffering in Euripides' *Hercules Furens* (1092) suggests that one side effect of the collar was to lose one's breath—part of the process of asphyxiation that led to death; Hercules also mentions his limbs going numb (ll. 1395–8). And the idea is also supported by the scene in Aristophanes' *Thesmophoriazousae* (1002–6) where Mnesilochus complains about the excruciating pain in the throat that being 'fastened to the plank' causes—which the Scythian Archer set to watch over him 'inadvertently' tightens. It is something of a theme of this episode in the play that Mnesilochus just keeps talking: the Scythian makes this explicit when he asks (1110) how *apotanoumene lalais*, that is, literally, 'even though you are about to die, you are babbling'.[53] It seems plausible that part of the joke here is the contrast between the punishment Mnesilochus is undergoing (a binding of his neck that is meant to stop his tongue) and his constant flow of chatter.

This raises questions about the likely targets of such texts. The binding of a victim's tongue is often taken as a sign that a spell text is likely to have been written for a judicial context, and to relate specifically to making speeches or giving evidence in court.[54] But perhaps a broader

---

[52] More obscurely perhaps, are the occasional references to the binding of the genitals found, albeit rarely, in some tablets (*DTA* 77, *SGD* 57, and *SGD* 58). Some images from pottery may depict prisoners or slaves who have some kind of object or weight fastened to their penis (fragment of kantharos from Boiotia, now Leipzig, Antikenmuseum der Universität T 326, 575–550 BCE: see Seeberg 1967: pl. IIIb and Halm-Tisserant 1998: pl. 11, C70; and image on a skyphos from Boiotia, now Antikenmuseum, Basle 51, c.420 BCE: see Seeberg 1967: 28, pl. 5 and Halm-Tisserant 1998: pl. 11, C71). Could these refer to some judicial binding practices—or even popular punishments?

[53] On the Scythian's mangled Greek as a source of humour, see Friedrich 1918, Brixhe 1988, and Willi 2003: ch. 7.

[54] Ogden 1999: 27.

scope is applicable. Although the binding of the tongue does occur in a number of tablets with judicial terminology, of the sixty-seven binding spells identified as judicial by Faraone, only seventeen bind the tongue of a victim. In comparison, of twenty-five tablets categorized as 'commercial', eight include mention of a tongue.[55] Moreover, a number of the judicial binding spells that mention the tongues of their victims also include the names of women who were unlikely to be giving evidence in court.[56] It may be that these are examples of the loose use of repetitive formulae, usually applied to male targets—but there is a further possibility. We have seen above the potency of gossip, both male and female; perhaps these texts were aimed at preventing their targets from indulging in such nasty, idle talk.[57]

To turn to the intentions of the writers of binding spells: physically binding a victim would not normally have drawn blood. Moreover, some texts refer explicitly to a spell-binding being loosed, and these forms of punishment could, of course, be released. But some of those texts also refer to the spell *not* being loosed, some until they gain their purpose, another until their victim goes down into Hades.[58] How does the metaphor of civic punishment align with spells that have more explicitly darker ambitions, and do they help us to understand the intentions of those who leave this aspect implicit?

In the realm of civic punishment, it is clear that this type of physical binding could have far more deleterious effects than simply immobilizing a target, and, indeed, that some forms were used as a mode of bloodless execution.[59] And here I turn to a suggestion first made by A. Keramopoullos in 1923, that the idea of binding that we find in binding spells was linked to the punishment of *apotumpanismos*.[60]

---

[55] Of these, only the early Sicilian curse tablets (*SGD* 95, 99, 100, and 108) target the tongue specifically. Of the others, the tongue is mentioned in concert with other particular parts of the target—often the spirit, sometimes the hands, feet, perhaps the body: see *DTA* 65, 66, 68, 79, 88, 94, 95, 105, and 107; *DT* 49, 51, 87. Commercial: *DTA* 68, 74, 75, 84, 86, 87, and 97; *DT* 52; and *SGD* 75. See Eidinow 2013a: 195–209.

[56] *SGD* 46 and *DT* 50; see also *DTA* 68, 89; and *DT* 49, 50, and 87.

[57] *DT* 50: where the formula 'tongue and deeds' probably stands in for the more common 'words and deeds'.

[58] Not being loosed: *SGD* 18 and *SGD* 170; Hades: *DT* 50.

[59] It seems to have been important to the Athenians to select bloodless forms of peace-time execution: Allen 2003: 213; Todd 1997: 3.

[60] References for descriptions of *apotumpanismos*: Lys. 13.56, 67, and 68; Dem. 8.61, 9.61, 10.63, 19.137, and 21.104–5; [Arist.] *Ath. Pol.* 45.1, Arist. *Rhet.* 1382b and 1385a. An alternative term appears to have been *sanis*, 'the plank': Hdt. 7.33.1 and 9.120.4; Plut. *Per.* 28; and Ar. *Thesm.* 930–46, 1001–2, and 1012; see also Ar. *Eq.* 367 and 705, Pl. *Resp.* 362 and Dem. 21.105.

For a long time thought to be a punishment that involved being clubbed to death, *apotumpanismos* was reimagined by modern scholars as a kind of crucifixion, after the discovery at the site of ancient Phaleron of a common grave containing seventeen bodies, each wearing an iron collar and with clamps on their hands and feet.[61] Keramopoullos argued that this was evidence for a form of capital punishment, in which the victim was tied to a pole using five clamps, and left to die, but with his hands by his sides, and this must be, in fact, *apotumpanismos*.[62] He went on to provide a compelling case for this approach, using detailed philological and literary evidence.[63] In terms of the dates of this punishment, Keramopoullos noted that the graves in Phaleron were pre-Solonic in date, and argued for the introduction of *apotumpanismos* by Draco, and evidence for its continuing use to the end of the fourth century.[64]

In arguing its relationship to binding spells, he drew attention first to the similarities between *apotumpanismos* and the physical arrangement of certain of the magical figurines, but went on to argue for a connection to the larger idea of binding.[65] The later date of the evidence for binding spells (in comparison to that for physical binding) was not an issue, he suggested: earlier binding spells were written on perishable materials or simply sung as incantations.[66] The potentially powerful effect that this punishment might have had on the ancient Athenian imagination may be suggested by the many representations of it on the Athenian stage between 460 and 411, including Aeschylus' *Prometheus Vinctus*, Sophocles' lost *Andromeda*, Euripides' *Hercules Furens* and lost *Andromeda*, and Aristophanes' *Thesmophoriazusae*. It has also been

---

[61] See Kourouniotis 1911 and Pelekidis 1916, and discussion in Keramopoullos 1923: 19-20. Since then, other mass graves have been found; some of the individuals have fetters, others not (see Papadopoulos *et al.* 2007). Allen (2003: 234) suggests that the *podokakke* was an early form of *apotumpanismos*.

[62] Different versions or postures of *apotumpanismos* appear to have been possible; see below.

[63] Keramopoullos 1923, and see discussion in Gernet 1968: 291 and 305.

[64] Keramopoullos 1923: 84, with which Gernet concurs (1968: 306). In terms of evidence, Keramopoullos (1923, 60-1) argued that the depiction of Prometheus in Aeschylus differs from that in Hesiod, because of the influence of *apotumpanismos*, although others have argued that the punishment is recalled by Hesiod's description of Prometheus as chained around a pillar.

[65] Keramopoullos 1923: 67.

[66] See ibid.: 67-75 for the motivations underlying the creation of curse tablets, and 108 for discussion of dates. Faraone (1985) discusses the *humnos desmios* of the Erinyes, Aesch. *Eum.* 306.

argued that the frequently found imagery of a seated Prometheus may reflect a version of punishment for this crime, for which there is also literary evidence.[67]

If the realm of physical punishment, specifically *apotumpanismos*, is the source of this key metaphor of binding in these spells, then this gives a different perspective on their use, and may offer further insight into the mindset of the spell-makers, in particular, their implicit attitudes towards the victim. First, asking for someone to be bound in a binding spell could indicate wishing them something far nastier than, for example, temporary immobility for the sake of competition. It could actually be a request for that victim to be punished in such a way that he or she could end up suffocating to death. This would also explain the ways in which some of those texts make explicit their desire for the binding spell to be loosed—or not. Second, those who used these spells wanted their victims to suffer a devastating loss of status: Stephen Todd emphasizes the public aspect of the resulting penalty, and its implications, arguing that it involved 'a humiliating expulsion from the community'.[68] Third, and building on this last point, physical 'binding' may have been associated with a particular type of crime. Louis Gernet has argued that *apotumpanismos* was originally used to punish certain *kakourgoi*, a category that included highway robbers, slave traders, wall piercers, purse-snatchers, and thieves, the last in particular, a class of target very familiar from a number of binding spells.[69] He goes on to suggest that *apotumpanismos* was likely to be used on those discovered red-handed, who were then executed without trial (by means of *apagoge*). This was a sort of private, personally directed justice, but, importantly, still receiving the support and approval of the community—therefore, a sort of 'popular

---

[67] Visual evidence: Attic proto-Attic krater, Nettus Painter, 600 BCE, now National Museum, Athens, 16384; see Halm-Tisserant (1998: pl. 25, E6a); cup, Arcesilas Painter, 570–555 BCE, now Vatican Museum, 16592; see Halm-Tisserant (1998: pl. 26, E12). Literary evidence: Pl. *Laws* 855c, [Arist.] *Ath. Pol.* 45.1, and possibly Hes. *Theog.* 522; see also discussion in Gernet 1968: 292 and 295.

[68] Coleman 1990; Todd (2000b: 45–7) has emphasized the public aspect of *apotumpanismos* ('crucifixion'), and its implications, arguing that it involved 'a humiliating expulsion from the community'; and see the example of Mnesilochus in the *Thesmophoriazusae* (943–4), who is told that part of his punishment is the humiliation of being exposed to public view.

[69] Gernet 1968: esp. 314–25; [Arist.] *Ath. Pol.* 52.1; see also Isoc. 15.90, Antiph. 5.9, Lys. 10.10, 13.67 and 68.

justice'.[70] But can we explain the creation of such a metaphor in the ancient Athenian imagination?

Mapping to Blending

Initial ideas about how metaphor 'works' are clearly described by George Lakoff, who in collaboration with Mark Johnson, developed Conceptual Metaphor Theory. This posited that metaphor is at the heart of human thought processes, not just in particular settings, but rather 'our ordinary conceptual system, in terms of which we both think and act, is fundamentally metaphorical in nature'.[71] Metaphors allow us to understand one domain of experience in terms of another: so time is money; argument is war; love is a journey. On the whole, this theory posits, we understand a less ordered and more abstract conceptual domain by means of structures from a more ordered and more experientially concrete domain.[72]

Importantly, these metaphors are 'primarily a matter of thought and action and only derivatively a matter of language', that is, they develop from the way we interact with our physical and cultural environments.[73] So, for example, we understand an experience such as 'love' primarily in terms of concepts for other natural kinds of experience, which emerge from our interactions with each other and with the world. We might use metaphors of journeying to describe the experience of being in love ('Look how far we've come', 'It's been a long bumpy road', 'This relationship isn't going anywhere', 'We'll have to go our separate ways') or we might think of love in terms of an exchange ('What am I getting out of this?', 'She invested a lot in this relationship', 'I'm putting more into this than you are!', 'Giving and receiving love').[74] Working in conjunction with these conceptual metaphors are image schemata: these are what Beate Hampe has called 'the "embodied" anchors of the entire conceptual system'.[75]

---

[70] Gernet (1968; esp. 318–22; quotation from 321) discusses the development of *apagoge* originating from private vengeance, but which (320) 'se renforce de la collaboration ou de l'assistance d'une collectivité'.
[71] Lakoff and Johnson 1980: 5.
[72] For discussion of the term 'domain', see Langacker 1987: 147.
[73] Lakoff and Johnson 1980: 153.   [74] Kövecses 2010: 23.
[75] Hampe 2005: 2. Johnson (1987: xiv and xvi) describes an image schema as 'a recurring dynamic pattern of our perceptual interactions and motor programs that gives coherence and structure to our experience'.

These are rooted in, and develop from, our own experience of our bodies moving through space, interacting with, and manipulating objects. A basic list was developed by Lakoff and Johnson, but it has continued to evolve: it includes for example, CONTAINMENT/CONTAINER, PATH/SOURCE–PATH–GOAL, ENABLEMENT, BLOCKAGE, RESTRAINING, CONTACT, SCALE.[76] Further research has developed and refined these analytical tools: identifying, for example, different schematic systems, which draw on our sensory-motor experiences, such as force dynamics.[77] Metaphors can then extend the use of image schemata into abstract or imaginative thinking.

Conceptual metaphor theory well describes this common cognitive process of understanding one thing in terms of another. Nevertheless, it has its limits: it allows only for the mapping of associations in one direction, and fundamentally it seeks to describe a stable knowledge system that is stored in long-term memory, rather than being able to account for emergent concepts that are constructed during discourse.[78] In reality, as Mark Turner and Gilles Fauconnier have described, we often draw on more than one source when we create concepts. They offer a helpful example, involving the popular image of the hooded and skeletal Grim Reaper, which is created by the bringing together or 'blending' of a number of 'mental spaces': these are a space with an individual dying; one with a prototypical human killer; one relating to harvest; and, finally, one that describes the personification of Death itself (a so-called causal tautology, in which a particular kind of event is caused by an abstract causal element—Death causes dying).[79]

The blend allows the bringing together of metonymic elements from each of these four spaces to create a final concept. The skeleton is metonymically related to death, its outcome; this, in turn, is brought together with the scythe, which stands metonymically for a reaper and for the manner of killing.[80] Through these associations, the idea of the

---

[76] See Johnson 1987: 126, and Lakoff 1987: 267.
[77] See Talmy 2000: ch. 7 (409–70). [78] Evans and Green 2006: 437.
[79] The blend for Death, the Grim Reaper is described by Turner and Fauconnier (1995), as well as Fauconnier and Turner (1998) and (2002), to which this discussion is indebted. Fauconnier and Turner (1998: 138) describe mental spaces as 'small conceptual packets constructed as we think and talk for purposes of local understanding and action'.
[80] Some of the metonymic associations only appear in a single input space. This is true for example of the cowl that the Reaper wears, which is part of a priest's habit. Although priests themselves do not feature in an input space, they are metonymically associated with humans dying, since they are often present at deaths and burials, and concerned with the hereafter (see Fauconnier and Turner 1998: 161–2, 170 and 177).

Public, Private, ... and Secret 245

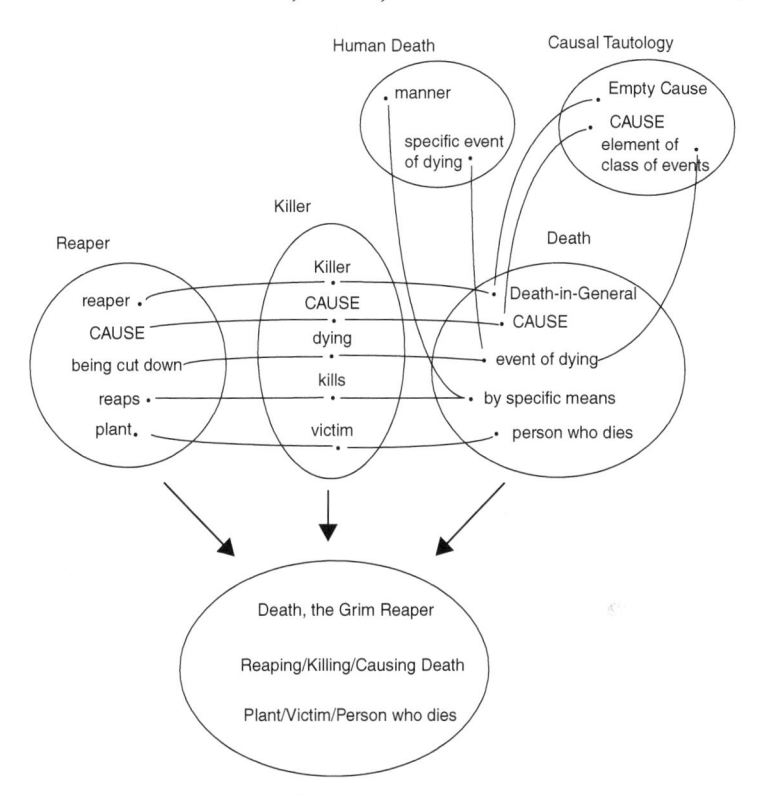

Fig. 1. Conceptual Blend of 'Death, the Grim Reaper' (Source: Fauconnier and Turner 2002: 292).

Copyright 2002 Gilles Fauconnier and Mark Turner, *The Way We Think: Conceptual Blending and the Mind's Hidden Complexities.* Reprinted by permission of Basic Books, a member of the Perseus Books Group.

cause of deaths, death-in-general, becomes 'Death the killer'; through association with the scythe, it becomes 'a reaper of men'. The Grim Reaper thus emerges from the blend itself, rather than simply mapping from one object to another, as with metaphor theory. Fauconnier and Turner describe this process in a diagram reproduced here (Figure 1).

The creation of the Grim Reaper describes how, instead of simply mapping concepts from one conceptual domain to another, we actually 'blend' selected elements from different conceptual domains. This is part of our everyday cognitive apparatus: the structure or elements from different domains are assembled in different configurations to create a new structure, and they produce new meaning. This assembly occurs by means of three constitutive processes. The first, composition, is the bringing together of elements from separate inputs: an example from the instance of the Grim Reaper involves the plants, the person who dies, and the victim being brought together to create the target of the metaphor. The second, completion, is the unconscious and effortless recruitment of background knowledge in the form of 'frames' or schematic knowledge that organizes meaning. The Grim Reaper blend invokes the schematic frame of death, that is, the unavoidability and authority of death and dying, and this has its counterpart in the agricultural frame of harvesting; these draw in part on image schemata, for example, COMPULSION, REMOVAL, COLLECTION, and CYCLE. Finally, the third process, elaboration is the online processing that produces the structure unique to the particular blend, introducing further ideas and emotions specific to the blend.[81]

Conceptual blending may offer new insight into the cognitive creation of a ritual space, as Jesper Sørensen has argued. In a powerful analysis of ritual, he argues that 'religious and magical rituals involve a blended space consisting of elements projected from input spaces themselves created by elements from two general domains—sacred and profane—and structured by a ritual frame'.[82] Within the ritual space that this creates, further instances of conceptual blending take place. In transformative or manipulative magic, the aim of these blends is to effect a change in the state of affairs in one domain, either through the transfer of qualities from one domain to another, or via the manipulation of elements in another domain.[83]

Blending and Binding

On the basis of this analysis, I suggest that ancient Greek binding spells are examples of manipulative magic, and that we may see some of them

---

[81] See Fauconnier and Turner 1998: 144 and 179–81 for discussion of these processes, and the role of image schemata.

[82] Sørensen 2007: 63. Sacred is carefully defined as involving (53) 'special beings violating ordinary ontological assumptions, special and privileged discursive repertoires, and special modes of interaction'; while 'profane' refers to the everyday world (65). In this model, religious concepts gain their potency through their connection with the profane. The efficacy of a ritual will emerge from a particular element with 'magical agency'. The agency emerges from the operation of the blend, the connections it creates between the sacred and profane domains, and the elements within them.

[83] Ibid.: 96–7.

as explicitly involving a process of conceptual blending that engages specific image schemata and schematic frames. The blending may have been expressed through language or action, or both (the relationship between action and language in the creation of many of these binding spells is uncertain); the emphasis may have varied not only across practitioners and practice, but even between individual spells.

In this blending process, the structure from one input space is imposed on the elements projected from the other input space, configuring the relation between the elements in the final blend.[84] The first input space is the configuration of elements that are involved in the creation of the ritual act: we can call it the Ritual space. It comprises one person who hates or fears another and seeks to acquire supernatural support to restrain the risk their enemy poses. The other input space is that of a civic Courtroom during the imposition of state-sanctioned penalties. The structure of this second domain is imposed on elements from the first domain, configuring their relationship and creating the blend of the target domain, the binding spell.

The composition process of the blend maps diverse elements from these two domains: the subject of the Ritual space is functionally related to the litigant of the Courtroom space, and this invests the spell-writer with power; the personal enemy maps onto the criminal of the Courtroom space, creating a legitimate victim in the blend; and, the jurors of the Courtroom space may find their counterpart in those gods and supernatural figures that a spell-writer frequently invoked as witnesses.[85] Finally, the (often repeated) appeal to 'bind' in the language of the spell finds its closer counterpart in the state-sanctioned penalties of the judicial process. This creates in the final blend an authoritative means of punishment. In some spells, the use of further similes, such as those that make comparisons between the target of the spell and lead, on which it is inscribed, will introduce further metaphoric associations that emphasize the effects of that punishment; use of materials such as lead tablets, even lead figurines, reinforce the connections already established by this conceptual blend, and strengthen the metaphoric connection with a metonymic connection.

This can be illustrated in a diagram that shows the two input spaces, a generic space (which shows the general instances, and the

---

[84] Ibid.: 125; this is a one-sided topology network; see Fauconnier and Turner 1998.
[85] Eidinow (2013a: 151–4) gives examples of different formulae, involving supernatural personnel in different roles.

Generic Space
a: agent (CONTAINER/SOURCE)
b: instrument (COMPULSION)
c: supporters (ENABLEMENT)
d: target (OBJECT)

Input Space 1: Ritual
a1: Petitioner
b1: Binding
c1: Divinity
d1: Personal enemy

Input Space 2: Courtroom
a2: Litigant
b2: Penalty
c1: Jurors
d2: Criminal

The Blend: A Generic Binding Spell
a3: Spell-writer/commissioner, allied with supernatural powers
b3 and c3: Legitimately and authoritatively imposing penalty
d3: Wrongdoer

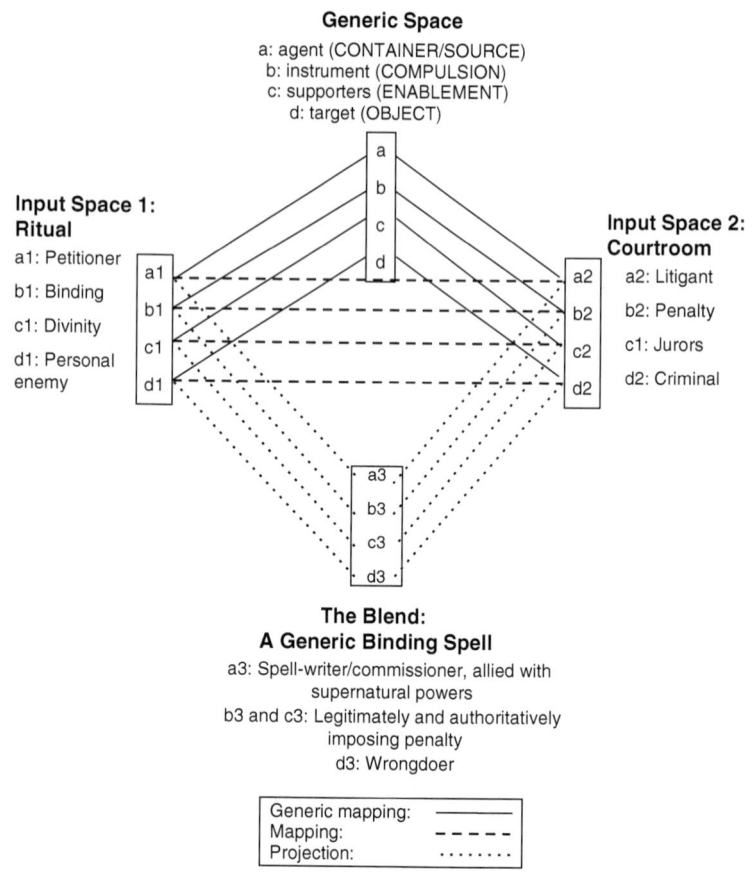

Generic mapping:	————
Mapping:	– – – –
Projection:	········

Fig. 2. Conceptual Blend of a Generic Binding Spell.

related image schemata that enable connections between the elements of the two input spaces) and the final blend (see Figure 2).[86] This shows how image schemata in this blend also facilitate connections between the different elements of the input spaces by setting up counterpart connections: litigant and spell-writer can be linked by their role as a CONTAINER—of the authority of the court, on the one hand, and of the knowledge of the ritual, on the other; they are also the SOURCE of the process. The image schema COMPULSION facilitates the connection between the language of binding and the penalty imposed in a judicial process: one offers a legal and social

---

[86] For description of generic space, see Fauconnier and Turner 1998: 143.

force, the other a metaphysical force. Divinity and jurors are both supporters, their authority providing ENABLEMENT to the two respective processes. Finally, the personal enemy and the criminal are connected as OBJECTS of these two processes.

As a result of the conceptual blend, the desired manipulation of the spell is more than simply the imposition of a metaphor of binding. Rather, it takes place within a new structure in which the spell-writer or commissioner becomes an agent of justice, allied with the power and authority of a supernatural agent, and instituting a process of legitimate punishment against a deserving target—a source of potential wrongdoing. This blend of civic and supernatural authorities lends the binding spell a strong sense of legitimacy. The use of the Courtroom as the input space for the spell draws our attention to the ways in which binding spells could be viewed, through a particular perspective, as instruments of civic order.

The blend brings together a supernatural power, appealed to by an individual, with the power of the state.[87] Within the blend, the authority of divinity becomes the individual's claim on divine help to bind his or her enemies. But state and divinity are also connected outside the blending space, since the power of the god supports the power of the state to punish. Meanwhile, the blend supports the spell-writer's case, by simultaneously hiding and highlighting aspects of his situation. On the one hand, it draws attention to a sense of having been wronged in some way, since it invokes a legitimate form of punishment; on the other hand, by evoking the moment of civic judgement, it conceals the idea that there could be any kind of plea in defence.

The idea that this was the mental space that supported the idiom of binding may be supported by the development of further judicial imagery in other contexts. The language of Attic binding spells encompasses verbs of dedicating or consigning victims, and more explicit use of judicial language is found in spells from outside Attica. For example, a curse from Alexandria in Egypt uses the language of orders for arrest and delivery (as recorded in the documentary papyri) to present its target to the chthonic powers.[88]

---

[87] Gernet's analysis of the penalty of *apotumpanismos* in a context of *apagoge* as allowing a free hand to personal acts of cruelty (1968: 329: 'les cruautés légitimes ont le champ libre') shows how this profane domain is particularly appropriate for this role in the conceptual blend of the binding spell.
[88] *Suppl. Mag.* 2, no. 54 (Alexandria, Egypt, third century CE): ll. 21–2, comm. 'similar wording is used in orders for arrest and delivery in the documentary papyri,

In the Attic binding spells, whether or not we accept the cognitive process described above, the use of this metaphor provides a powerful image of punishment that disables the victim, precludes the possibility that they will continue to pose a risk to the spell-writer, and conveys potent associations of a range of suffering, from physical pain to extreme humiliation. If this is the basis for the metaphor on which binding spells draw, then it supports the idea that these are a personal, direct mode of punitive action against one's enemies; it also introduces the additional notion that Athenians may have associated the binding spell with processes of punishment that were legitimized by their fellow citizens, and by the state.

The Emotions of Binding

If these are the connotations of the use of the metaphor of binding in these spell texts, then it is hard to see how this kind of occult attack can be seen as having been generated simply by the desire to generate, or from fear of, *Schadenfreude*. Rather, these spells, in general, seem to have been intended to remove the risk that their target posed, while the imagery invokes a legitimate and painful punishment or execution.[89] We have seen what kind of emotion an ancient Greek assumed might fit such a context. It is named explicitly in the binding spell *NGCT* 24 as *phthonos*. This does not mean that *Schadenfreude* is totally unrelated. It has been argued that '*phthonos* includes the idea of malice or *Schadenfreude*'. However, closer examination of the major passage used to support this statement—a discussion of comic laughter (both on and off stage) in Plato's *Philebus*—does not sustain this assertion.[90] The

e.g. *P. Hib.* I 54, 20–2, (TM 8204). See also *SGD* 150 (Cyrenaica, third century BCE), *DT* 69 (Attica, undated), NGCT 89. This analysis may help to explain something of the conceptual relationship between binding spells and prayers for justice. This is not an attempt to dissolve the boundaries between these categories, but to suggest how they may have been conceptually associated for those writing these spells (manifest in the border-area curses that Versnel has identified).

[89] In that case, they seem designed to neutralize situations that might generate such misfortunes, pre-empting the potential for our enemies to enjoy them by attacking them first.

[90] See Sanders 2014: 102, who also cites Frede 1993: 56, n. 2; Wood 2007: 78; Halliwell 2008: 301 and Munteanu 2011: 95–7 as describing this as *Schadenfreude*. Of these, Munteanu does unquestioningly assume that *phthonos* and *Schadenfreude* are the same. However, the other authors offer more nuanced readings: Frede (1993: 56 n. 2) is actually explaining the decision to translate *phthonos* as 'malice' rather than envy;

paidikos phthonos ('playful *phthonos*') that Socrates evokes is an idiosyncratic version of this emotion that, in fact, does not translate easily as 'envy', or 'malice', or '*Schadenfreude*'.[91]

In order to persuade us of his interpretation, Socrates elides a number of aspects of what are quite different contexts. By assuming that we must feel some resentment when we laugh at others—whatever the context—he persuades us that the experience of watching a comic performance is equivalent to that of participation in daily life. Our attitude to characters on stage is assumed to be the same as that towards, first, our neighbours, and then our friends.[92] The result is that the 'playful *phthonos*' we feel towards those on stage is gradually transmuted to the *phthonos* of the social sphere, which, as we have seen, is scarcely playful.

For this to work, however, Socrates achieves two further elisions. The first makes *phthonos* and the enjoyment of the ridicule of others appear to be virtually the same thing: Socrates says, 'But certainly we see the envious man rejoicing in the misfortunes of his neighbours', and similarly, later on he asks, 'Did we not say that pleasure in the misfortunes of friends was caused by envy?'[93] However, although in each case we can see that *phthonos* may lead to expressions of ridicule, in neither case is it necessary for them to be equivalent.[94] But it is easy to be misled by this into thinking that they

---

at lii, she also describes how such laughter 'presupposes at least some kind of inherent malice', which suggesting that she sees the two as separate emotions/states. Similarly, Wood (2007: 78 n. 3), although he raises the possibility of translating *phthonos* as *Schadenfreude*, distinguishes the difference between *Schadenfreude*, envy, and malice, and ends his observations with 'malice is a more appropriate translation'; Halliwell states that the connection between laughter and phthonos 'posits a kind of mild Schadenfreude', again, suggesting that the two emotions are distinct.

[91] I challenge the use of *Schadenfreude* here, as I have previously in this section (p. 226), on the grounds that the modern analyses of *Schadenfreude* argue that it does not comprise public mocking.

[92] Pl. *Phil.* 48a (comedies); 48b (neighbours); 49d (friends). Delcomminette (2006: 445) observes how this elision allows Socrates to discuss a kind of *phthonos* (and resulting ridicule) that offers no real risk to those who indulge in it.

[93] Pl. *Phil.* 48b and 50a, respectively (tr. Fowler 1925). As Cerasuolo (1980: 16) observes, Socrates appears to be dealing with *epichairekakia* (as defined by Aristotle; see discussion p. 75).

[94] Modern research into the emotions makes specific links between envy and *Schadenfreude*, arguing that envy can be an important antecedent of *Schadenfreude* (see, for example, Van Dijk *et al.* 2006 and van de Ven 2014).

must be the same emotion, and this is because of the second, and perhaps more important, elision: Socrates' curious description of the nature of *phthonos* itself.

Socrates creates a version of *phthonos* that is unlike any we have come across so far.[95] In the case of comic laughter, the ridicule and laughter that Socrates describes as evidence for *phthonos* is provoked, not by the target's possession of some aspect of fortune that we do not want them to have, but by the target's acknowledged *lack* of self-understanding of his own faults. The dialogue then turns from ridiculing the weak on stage to a discussion of the *phthonos* we feel towards our friends—and this also is rooted in the idea that our friends are deluding themselves. It is difficult to understand how this can be perceived to be the *phthonos* that we have seen operating across our other sources, which is a response to the good fortune of others, not to their mistaken belief that they are fortunate.[96] Socrates' discussion of comedic *phthonos* has transformed it into something quite pleasant, even therapeutic, in nature.[97] It bears little resemblance

---

[95] Sanders (2014: 102) cites three further passages, which he says 'show *phthonos* encompassing a malicious pleasure': Pl. *Lach.* 184c1–4, where those who claim excellence in fighting must really excel, because otherwise they will be mocked; Pl. *Phdr.* 240a5–6, where a lover is envious of his boys when they have property but rejoices when they lose it; and Dem. 9.54, where Demosthenes cannot safely identify *phthonos* as the emotion that prompts the Athenians to urge Philip's 'henchmen' to speak and then laugh at them.

However, although these episodes demonstrate that feeling *phthonos* may, in different ways, lead to an emotion that looks in some ways like *Schadenfreude*, none of them indicates that the two emotions are identical. The Demosthenes passage perhaps most clearly separates *phthonos* from ridicule, since the orator can only make a possible connection between the two (see Halliwell 2008: 301 n. 93). The emotional processes described in the other two passages, although more complex, lead to similar conclusions: in the *Laches*, *phthonos* is felt towards those we feel have something we want—and it is only when we discover that they do not have it that we feel we can ridicule them; while in the *Phaedrus* the lover feels *phthonos* that his beloved might have independence, and then rejoices when he does not—but this is an expression of relief, not ridicule. Halliwell (2008: 301) offers examples of situations where *phthonos* at someone's success leads to laughter at their undoing: these include Lys. 3.9, Arist. *Rhet.* 1387a1–3; examples where *phthonos* seems connected with ad hominem ridicule include Dem. 9.54, Alexis fr. 52 K-A, Ar. *Thesm.* 146.

[96] Pl. *Phil.* 49d–e; the conflation of misfortunes and self-deception is made clear in 50a: Socrates declares that 'when we laugh at the ridiculous qualities of our friends, we mix pleasure with pain, since we mix it with envy; for we have agreed all along that envy is a pain of the soul, and that laughter is a pleasure; yet these two are present at the same time on such occasions'.

[97] Socrates provides 'a prescriptive (and not descriptive) notion of the "laughable"', as Prauscello (2014: 199) has observed.

to the vicious emotion that we have seen elsewhere, in which the verbal expression of *phthonos* is far more extensive, far more poisonous, far more dangerous than Socrates allows.

To return full circle, then, to the discussion with which we began, it seems unlikely that *Schadenfreude* (either fear of it or the desire to generate it) is an adequate description of the kind of emotion that motivated the writing of binding spells. Instead, the emotion of *phthonos* seems a far more appropriate candidate. Not only is it named as playing this role in a spell text, but the analysis of the previous sections reveals how well it participates in the nexus of likely social dynamics in play. *Phthonos* was an emotion that was aimed at others within one's social network who had enjoyed or might enjoy good fortune. As we have seen, it generated, and was generated by, gossip and abuse. Similarly, binding spells were intricately bound into social networks of hostility and suspicion; they were created to restrain those whose success or potential achievements were perceived as threatening. Their creation was likely to have been one of the responses to, and provocations of, gossip, and the result was itself a form of abuse.

The roles of *phthonos* and gossip in binding spells draw our attention back to the metaphorical associations between binding spells and judicial activity. The analysis created by the conceptual blend above highlights a further important parallel. It suggests that, although binding spells may have been motivated by dark emotions, such as *phthonos*, they would not necessarily have been written or commissioned with a sense of shame, as we might expect. Drawing on ideas of civic punishment, the blend transforms the spell's victim into a deserving target; it illuminates the psychology of the aggressor, who sees himself as a victim. And this, in turn, aligns with a sentiment made explicit in fourth-century forensic rhetoric—that feeling *phthonos* is not only understandable, but also in some situations justified, and should even be encouraged.

3.7

From Gossip to Action

We have explored poisonous words and words about poisons, and evidence for the links between these two, across public, private, and secret arenas. We return to the mechanics underpinning these activities, and Merry's three-stage process of gossip: circulation, formation of meaning (not necessarily consensus), and action.[1] Our case studies have revealed some of the ways in which these first two stages occurred, albeit in diverse ways—and how they might lead to the third stage, action.

Curse tablets, vengeful epitaphs, and binding spells are all fodder for gossip, and these texts suggest how gossip played a key role in leading a community to interpret events, and allocate blame and responsibility. Reading this evidence, we enter a world of half-hidden hatreds and fears, whispered suspicions, and anonymized accusations, all generated by, and helping to generate, what Georg Simmel, in his analysis of the power of secrecy, called 'the possibility of a second world', one in which powerful mortal emotions interacted with supernatural powers to create desperate and terrible scenarios.[2]

Among scholars of ancient Greek magic, discussion about whether or not the practice of binding spells is secret has largely revolved around the question of whether or not it was illegal.[3] There is little evidence to suggest that it was, but the argument already presented concerning the final intention of these spells may offer some reasons why this form of occult attack appears to have been little mentioned. The desire to cause this kind of suffering, perhaps possible death, to

---

[1] Merry 1997: 54–69.
[2] Secrecy secures, as Simmel (1906: 462) puts it, 'the possibility of a second world alongside of the obvious world, and the latter is most strenuously affected by the former'.
[3] For details of the discussion, see Eidinow 2013a: 297 n. 69.

an opponent, was not something to publicize, even if one felt it was justified. But does this mean these activities were 'secret'? Even if they were never directly talked about, these texts and the emotions that prompted them would have been hard to conceal: plenty of people were involved. There were those caught up in the relationships of hatred and hurt that prompted the creation of these spells in the first place; perhaps a professional spell-writer or other experts; and finally friends and neighbours who would have spread information about the situation, the actions taken, and any resulting effects.

The result would have been not so much a situation of secrecy, but rather what we might call 'secretism', borrowing the term from Paul Johnson's analysis of the role of secrecy in Brazilian Candomblé.[4] This comprises 'the active milling, polishing and promotion of secrets', in which secrecy does not so much conceal as advertise: viewed in this way, secrecy becomes a kind of 'flirtation', revelling in the 'unspoken exchange between exhibition and voyeurism'.[5] We have seen this process at work in the techniques of the forensic orators as they hint at, are apparently shocked by, or refuse to disclose information about their opponents. We see evidence for it again in the social conflicts that can be glimpsed in the curse tablets, epitaphs, and binding spells. Secrets as secretism are intimately linked to social structures of gossip, each giving the other not only momentum, but also meaning.[6]

Thus, 'secretism' could be said to be an important part of the efficacy of these texts—although not necessarily in terms of individual validation or social containment (as others have argued).[7] Rather, such a social process could have helped to shape and reinforce existing community values. Simmel argued that a 'secret' acquires its greatest power, its meaning, in the moment of revelation.[8] That moment unveils a 'second world' of feelings and actions that was, to begin with, never suspected. Glimpsing it reshapes understanding of the world we see around us, both re-explaining past events and adjusting future expectations. This idea of secrecy and revelation may also help to explain how and why gossip, which plays a key role in 'secretism', is one of the processes by which communities at

---

[4] Simmel 1906: 486; see discussion in Johnson 2002: 3.
[5] Johnson 2002: 3.   [6] Ibid.: 4.
[7] See pp. 221-3.   [8] Simmel 1906: 465-6.

all levels of society establish how to interpret and then act on specific events.[9]

A social network analysis can help to clarify these processes further. The evidence considered in this study illustrates the dynamics of a dense social network, that is, where everyone is directly connected to everyone else.[10] This kind of network is understood to improve information flow, but it also allows for more efficient dissemination of social expectations, with closer monitoring and pressure to conform and cooperate with the normative expectations of the network.[11] Individuals will tend to share information that is consistent with the flow of conversation—and likely to gain them approval.[12] They will select from their available material to find a story that 'echoes' the tenor of the existing discussion or dispositions that have been displayed.[13] This process leads to the reinforcement of

---

[9] See discussion in section 3.2, p. 176. Marjorie Harness Goodwin's study of the interactions of children on a street (Maple Street) in Philadelphia in the 1970s provides a vivid example. She notes (1990: 286): 'the particular way in which talk is structured creates *participation frameworks*: an entire field of action including both interrelated occasion-specific identities and forms of talk; a speaker may transform the social order of the moment by invoking a different speech activity'. She offers an analysis of a particular phase of gossip among the girls she studied—the so-called 'he-said-she-said' argument strategy, in which accusations are framed as something said originally by someone else (thus allowing both sides to deny direct responsibility for their part in the confrontation). The resulting dispute is much more complex and long-running than the typically two-party strategies, used, for example, by the boys she studied, e.g. (p. 195) Annette: 'and Arthur said that you said that I was showin' off just because I had that blouse on'. Goodwin (1990: 190 ff.) examines how a particular type of gossip dispute can shape the social organization of a group, going through a series of recognizable stages, and paralleling Turner's formulation of 'social drama' (citing Turner 1980: 150–1). We can compare studies of community policing in the US that have established how local knowledge of individuals, their behaviours, and their reputation all play a part in enforcing laws, sentencing decisions, and disposition recommendations (see Merry 1997: 68–9).

[10] Merry (1997: 59–62) distinguishes between small-scale and complex societies, in order to examine how gossip leads to action at these different levels. On the significance of the density from a network analysis perspective, see Foster and Rosnow 2006: 170. The effect of third-parties on dyadic relationships within such networks is explored by Burt 2001 (see also Coleman 1988 and 1990: esp. 283–6, and Putnam et al. 1994: 174–5).

[11] Foster and Rosnow 2006: 170, citing also Pfeffer and Salancik (1978) for work on the dissemination of social expectations through denser gossip networks. Ellickson (1991: 57) reports that some individuals use gossip intentionally to enforce social control.

[12] Burt 2001: 40.

[13] See ibid., esp. 41–2; he argues that this occurs because of an individual's sense of etiquette; while Sobel (2001: 79) highlights the individual's self-interest.

predispositions; and, if the echo is repeated, as is probable in a closed, dense network, and gets 'louder', it is likely to push predispositions to their extremes.

In the context of this study, this analysis is useful for thinking about how and why local gossip might come to generate a legal charge; that is, how the first two stages of our three-stage process of gossip may lead to the third—action. But at the same time, of course, we have to bear in mind that this process was not automatic. A model of this type can illustrate a generic pattern of activity, but the contextual details are crucial. For that reason, it is useful to pause here and consider an example where gossip failed to find purchase in the Athenian law courts.

The 'case of Nicodemus' is mentioned again and again across a number of legal speeches over a period of roughly twenty years. However, despite apparent attempts to turn these accounts into something more serious, they remained at the level of gossip.[14] As far as we know, the basic facts are as follows: some time after 348 BCE, a man called Nicodemus, from the deme of Aphidna in Athens, was horribly murdered, his eyes gouged out, and his tongue cut off.[15] He had been a supporter of Meidias and Eubulus, enemies of Demosthenes, and been part of a group, formally led by Euctemon, who had tried to convict Demosthenes of deserting from the campaign by Athens against Euboea in 348 BCE.[16] The story was put about that Demosthenes had, apparently, bought Nicodemus off.[17] After his death, a young man called Aristarchus, a friend of Demosthenes, was found guilty of the crime and went into exile. But this was not the end of it.

---

[14] The story will resurface centuries later, in Athenaeus, in a convoluted form, relating how Demosthenes, once, when he was drunk, because of his feelings for Aristarchus, insulted Nicodemus and struck out both his eyes (according to Idomeneus *FGrH* 338 F 12 *ap*. Ath. 13.592-3). Fisher (2001 *ad* §170) suggests that this may indicate that the killing was thought to have taken place at a drunken party, and could at least suggest mixed motives (sexual as well as political). Worthington (1992: 180) argues for political motives only and discounts this evidence. It could be argued that this case offers a study of the relationship between rumour and gossip (as defined by Difonzo and Bordia 2007). In particular, it is noticeable that while his accusers tried to elevate the allegations against Demosthenes to rumours (unverified information, used to make sense of events), the story retained its character as gossip (that is, lacking urgency and largely concerned with details about Demosthenes' private life).

[15] Aeschin. 1.172.

[16] Dem. 21.103-4 and Aeschin. 2.148. Demosthenes argues (103) that Meidias was behind this prosecution, planning it after his attack on him in the theatre in 348/7; Demosthenes returned to serve as *choregos* (responsible for funding a dramatic or lyric chorus) at the Great Dionysia.

[17] Aeschin. 2.148.

It appears that Meidias regarded Demosthenes as responsible for the murder—and we hear this from Demosthenes himself.[18] In his case against Meidias, which must have occurred soon after these events (347/6), and which concerned quite different matters, Demosthenes relates how his opponent 'went round the Agora and ventured to spread impious and atrocious statements about me to the effect that I was the author of the deed'. When this failed, he goes on, Meidias tried to persuade the relatives of the dead man (who were prosecuting Aristarchus) to accuse Demosthenes of the crime.[19] Demosthenes emphasizes how Meidias continued to socialize with Aristarchus: he pictures Meidias in Aristarchus' house, putting his hand in his, treating him as a friend, just the day after denouncing him in the Council Chamber.[20] Of course, in relating such a vivid picture, Demosthenes was working hard to distance himself from the crime of which Aristarchus was being accused and for which he was eventually found guilty. But the case continued to haunt Demosthenes.

In 346 BCE, Aeschines was prosecuted by Timarchus and Demosthenes for his role in Athens' negotiations with Philip; in defence, some time between late summer 346 and spring 345, Aeschines prosecuted Timarchus... and the Aristarchus story resurfaced.[21] In that speech, Aeschines tells us that Aristarchus was one of a number of fatherless young men whose relationship with Demosthenes fitted a particular pattern; nowadays we might describe it as 'grooming'. Aristarchus, apparently, was vulnerable: his father was dead, his mother unable to manage, and he himself was mentally unstable.[22] The household was quite wealthy: Aristarchus is said to have given Demosthenes three talents. Aeschines relates how Demosthenes pretended to become the boy's lover—and fed his ambition.[23] Although Aeschines is quite vivid in his description of the growing friendship between the two, he is nonetheless quite careful in his insinuations that Demosthenes was involved in plotting murder. Nevertheless, it is hard to miss his meaning, particularly when he underlines the link

---

[18] Dem. 21.102–22; and see MacDowell 1990: 325–44.
[19] Dem. 21.104–5 (tr. Vince 1935).   [20] Dem. 21.116–19.
[21] Fisher 2001: 2–20: Aeschines 1, which was given some time between late summer 346 and spring 345, and Aeschines 2, in 343 BCE.
[22] Unstable: Aeschin. 1.171.   [23] Lover: Aeschin. 1.171.

between the cutting out of Nicodemus' tongue and his 'tendency to speak out freely, trusting in the laws and in you'.[24]

The introduction of this material into the case has been called irrelevant, but it illustrates the deployment of gossip in the law courts as discussed in this study.[25] By introducing what seems to have been current gossip about Demosthenes himself, Aeschines reinforces his arguments about Timarchus' corrupt lifestyle, transforming the accusations he is making against an individual into an indictment of both Timarchus and Demosthenes—and he is successful. Moreover, without turning this into an outright accusation, Aeschines' account of these events makes clear the threat he poses to Demosthenes. By the time Aeschines presents *On the Embassy* (343 BCE) his accusations against Demosthenes are stated more baldly: 'you saved yourself by buying off the man who indicted you, Nicodemus of Aphidna, whom afterward you helped Aristarchus to destroy'.[26] Although he is still careful not to deny that Aristarchus was the main protagonist, he nevertheless argues that Demosthenes should not enter the marketplace because he has been polluted—presumably through association with the murderer.

Finally, twenty years later, we see the same story return, in the case against Demosthenes brought by Dinarchus.[27] Demosthenes was one of a number of men being prosecuted for taking bribes from Harpalus—and a team of ten prosecutors spoke against him.[28] Rather than providing any evidence for the charge, the case turned on a thorough presentation of Demosthenes' character as corrupt, venal, and deceitful. The case and context were obviously more extensive and complex than this one particular charge—the Athenians were, for example, incensed by Demosthenes' handling of the city's relationship with Alexander and the Exiles' Decree, but it is worth noting that

---

[24] Aeschin. 1.172 (tr. Adams 1919). The punishment of cutting out the tongue of those whose speech somehow betrays their culture is found in other times and places, from heretics in medieval France (Pettegree 2005: 60) to traitors among the modern Mafia (Hess 1998: 114). Could the cutting out of Nicodemus' tongue be an example of a more violent version of binding the tongue of an enemy who was and who threatened to be talking against you?

[25] Carey (2000: 22): 'an irrelevant character assassination'.

[26] Aeschin. 2.148 (tr. Adams 1919). He does not bother to support this with any kind of testimony, or reference to general knowledge, but leaves it as a bald accusation.

[27] Dinarchus 1 (*Against Demosthenes*) was probably delivered in March 323 BCE (Worthington 2001: 8).

[28] Worthington 2001: 41.

the story of Nicodemus' murder resurfaces here again. First, it provides evidence of Demosthenes' corruption (because he had bought off Nicodemus). Then it blossoms into the tale of the murder, in which Demosthenes is described explicitly as a conspirator, and one who, moreover, betrayed Aristarchus—even, finally, being responsible for expelling him from the city.[29] The case brought by Dinarchus was successful; Demosthenes fled into self-imposed exile.

That Demosthenes had played a key part in the murder of Nicodemus was a powerful accusation; moreover, it seems to have drawn on stories about Demosthenes that were in widespread and long-running circulation. Across the speeches, the uses of this gossip vary in detail and success according to the prominence of the politicians in question, and the favour with which the city regarded them; for example, Aeschines' employment of the story becomes more explicit as his own political stature develops. But although his enemies persisted in airing this gossip in both the formal setting of the courtroom and the informal arena of the Agora, Demosthenes was never prosecuted on a charge of murder.

---

[29] Not only does Dinarchus invite the audience to bring their own knowledge to bear, he also gives us Aristarchus' point of view, describing Demosthenes as a *daimon* or 'supernatural force', responsible for all his misfortunes (a description that perhaps deliberately echoes the language used of Demosthenes by Aeschines in *Against Ctesiphon*); see Eidinow 2011a: 143–50.

3.8

Conclusion: 'A Covert Form of Witchcraft'

The cases made against Theoris, Phryne, and Ninon provide us with a complex of accusations concerned with magical practice for which we have little context, and which it is difficult to align with possible official charges. In trying to understand the social dynamics that might have given rise to such accusations—and brought them into the courtroom—we have followed a thread suggested by a binding spell, *NGCT* 24. This gives a possible motivation for writing such spells—that of *phthonos*—and we have examined the meaning of this emotion term across a variety of literary genres and social contexts.

In this part of the book, we have looked at some of the social processes that made *phthonos* so powerful, in particular, the crucial role played by certain types of 'talk': on the one hand, talk between mortals, from the gossip of the family and on the street corner to the exercise of *diabole* in the law courts; and, on the other hand, talk between mortals and between mortals and gods, in the toxic formulae of curses, spells, and epitaphs, and the fears and accusations that they encompassed. We have seen the close relationship between these kinds of poisonous talk and talk of poison: a vicious cycle of suspicions and allegations.[1]

The kinds of accusations that circulate in malignant gossip can result in real harm, but this may occur in different ways, through diverse processes. The case of Nicodemus demonstrates the failure of

---

[1] Charles Stewart (pers. comm.). Stewart and Strathern (2004: ix) call gossip 'a covert form of witchcraft against persons'; Stirling (1956) states that, in literate society, gossip as an outlet for aggression that is anonymous and so avoids conflict is a descendant of witchcraft and sorcery; see also Foster and Rosnow 2006: 161.

gossip to take root and develop into a legal case of its own. During his description of it, in the prosecution of Timarchus, Aeschines asks his fellow citizens about another victim of gossip, Socrates: 'Did you put to death Socrates the sophist, fellow citizens, because he was shown to have been the teacher of Critias, one of the Thirty who put down the democracy?'[2] Aeschines' question highlights again the crucial role of 'charges' that were not part of an official indictment, but which were clearly circulating in the community. It also underlines how particular individuals were more vulnerable to such accusations than others. And this leads to a final question, perhaps in fact the most basic for this study, that must be asked in the investigation of the charges brought against Theoris, Phryne, and Ninon: if there is gossip circulating about a person's activities, what is it that creates the right environment and what makes that person seem a suitable target, for that gossip to become transformed into legal action?

[2] Aeschin. 1.173 (tr. Adams 1919).

Part 4

Death

4.1

Introduction: 'Killed by Idle Gossip'

What is it that allows a seed of gossip to take root and flourish, which takes it from the street corner into the law court, and gives it such heft that it can be used to condemn a man, or woman, to death?[1] In the case of Socrates, the context is well known: the strength of the anger against Critias and his fellow oligarchs, the fear of sophistic world views, the concern about offending the gods. All of these factors would have come together to form a compelling case against Socrates. But in the trials of Theoris, Ninon, and Phryne such circumstances are difficult to identify. As we noted at the beginning, these are women, with little or no public, political role: what are the stories that transform them into figures that presented such risks that two of them were executed for their activities? To get a better understanding of the phenomena of these trials—and the deaths to which they led— we need not only to examine the charges involved, and the likely operations of gossip and envy, but also the context in which these dynamics grew powerful.

This final part of the book will examine the wider environment in which these trials occurred, setting them in the larger context of Athens and Attica in the early fourth century. It will argue that the

---

[1] The title of this section comes from the title of Rosnow and Georgoudi 1985; it refers to the jury's verdict recorded on the death of one Ida Bodman, who shot herself eighteen months after moving to Western Springs, Milwaukee. The cause was, apparently, poisonous telephone calls. *The Milwaukee Sentinel* (October 16, 1915) records that 'she knew others were receiving them by the lifting of eyebrows and breaking up of scattered groups of her new friends whenever she went near them'. More recently, cyberbullying ('deliberately using digital media to communicate false, embarrassing, or hostile information about another person'; see Schurgin O'Keeffe and Clarke-Pearson 2011: 800) can generate 'gossip' that can reach a wider audience extremely quickly, and can be extremely difficult to confront.

evidence for this period of Athens' history indicates that there was particular concern about the role of women in society, and the potential risks this could present. It will suggest that this was related to the context of the socio-economic impacts of the Peloponnesian War, and, importantly, contemporary perceptions of those impacts. These included not only physical dimensions, such as changes in the population, but also what we might describe as the metaphysical dimensions, by which I mean effects on the community's understanding of its relationship with unseen powers.

This approach will not comprise an argument for a radical breakdown of Athenian society, and nor is it intended as a definitive description of its state. It will be exploratory and speculative, an arrangement of some of the pieces to evoke a particular picture. And necessarily even more tentative will be the questions and possibilities it will raise about the situation of women in that environment. Nevertheless, it will be an attempt to set the trials of these women in a historical context, and one that encompasses the psychological and emotional dimensions of its subject.

4.2

After the War...

ἐπεὶ νῦν γε τίς οὐκ ἂν ἐπὶ τοῖς γιγνομένοις τῶν εὖ φρονούντων ἀλγήσειεν, ὅταν ἴδῃ πολλοὺς τῶν πολιτῶν αὐτοὺς μὲν περὶ τῶν ἀναγκαίων, εἴθ' ἕξουσιν εἴτε μή, πρὸ τῶν δικαστηρίων κληρουμένους, τῶν δ' Ἑλλήνων τοὺς ἐλαύνειν τὰς ναῦς βουλομένους τρέφειν ἀξιοῦντας, καὶ χορεύοντας μὲν ἐν χρυσοῖς ἱματίοις, χειμάζοντας δ' ἐν τοιούτοις ἐν οἷς οὐ βούλομαι λέγειν, καὶ τοιαύτας ἄλλας ἐναντιώσεις περὶ τὴν διοίκησιν γιγνομένας, αἳ μεγάλην αἰσχύνην τῇ πόλει ποιοῦσιν;

For as things now are, who among intelligent men can fail to be chagrined at what goes on, when we see many of our fellow-citizens drawing lots in front of the law-courts to determine whether they themselves shall have the necessaries of life, yet thinking it proper to support at their expense any of the Hellenes who will deign to row their ships; appearing in the public choruses in garments spangled with gold, yet living through the winter in clothing which I refuse to describe; and showing other contradictions of the same kind in their conduct of affairs, which bring great shame upon the city?[1]

In this section I want to take a closer look at what is known—and not known—about the socio-economic situation of Athenians in the early to mid-fourth century. The quotation that heads this chapter may give substance to some of the more immediate difficulties of this endeavour: it is from Isocrates' *Areopagiticus*, written in c.357 BCE. The passage describes the kinds of conditions in and contradictions with which some Athenians may have been living, brought about by economic deprivation. Among them are citizens happy to appear,

[1] Isoc. 7.54 (tr. Norlin 1929).

dressed in spangled garments, as 'dancers' in a public chorus, but who would then live through the winter in clothes that Isocrates finds so appalling he refuses to describe them.

But to what extent can we trust this image? Isocrates is one of our chief sources for this period, but his writings have an intellectual and moral agenda that makes it difficult to calibrate them as evidence. This image of the conflicted Athenian, for example, is presented as part of a systematic but emotional comparison of the city's idealized past with the moral and social problems of the present. It was intended to highlight the virtues of the city's ancestral constitution and institutions, above all those of the Areopagus, whose restoration as a guardian of the city's laws Isocrates is pleading for here.[2] We need to bear these underlying ideas in mind: Isocrates' political philosophy and his vision of civic education underpin and shape his arguments, and he presents his views with complex rhetorical audacity.[3] Moreover, we must also consider the context of this writing. It is possible that Isocrates' political speeches were written to be read, and so not actually delivered to their audience: they therefore cannot necessarily be interpreted as having to appeal to widespread popular values.[4] Nevertheless, the images they offer, while perhaps rendered in starker lines so as to support Isocrates' particular purpose, need not simply be discarded. They may emphasize some of the bleaker aspects of life in Athens, but they still spoke to an audience that lived in that city, and it is likely that they captured some sense, some perception, of what life was like for some of its inhabitants.

A NEW START?

The Athenians had been at war for twenty-seven years—and they had lost. The sequence of events at the end of the Peloponnesian War is well known: narrowly avoiding the destruction of the city and the enslavement or annihilation of its inhabitants, Athens lurched from

---

[2] Too 2000: 182–3.

[3] For an overview of Isocrates' life and work, see the introduction to Mirhady and Too 2000. Some speeches had a more rhetorical focus than others: compare Isoc. 8 (with Moysey 1982) with Isoc. 6 (Harding 1974). His self-characterization as a writer (not declaimer) of political speeches probably indicates a critique of contemporary political oratory (see Too 1995: 74–112).

[4] Hunt 2010: 21.

democratic to oligarchic to democratic regime. There is no doubt that this period was one of immense upheaval for the inhabitants of the city, both immediately and with longer-term consequences.[5] At the ideological level, it suggested not only that Athens could be beaten 'in every way at every point' on the battlefield, but also that the idea of democracy itself could be defeated.[6] More mundanely, a lot of men had been lost. Isocrates makes particular reference to the debilitating effects of Athenian military campaigns on the size of the population (although some of these comments are clearly connected to and coloured by his own views of the importance of autochthony).[7] This is not to suggest this was a radical phenomenon suddenly brought about by the Peloponnesian War.[8] Indeed, the events that followed the Persian Wars—the ongoing campaigns in the early part of the period and the slow build-up of momentum towards the First Peloponnesian War, coupled with events further afield—may have worsened this situation.[9]

The demographic evidence for fourth-century Attica has been closely debated on the basis of different models and interpretations

---

[5] For a marvellous and curiously neglected analysis of the trauma and its effects of the last years of the Peloponnesian War and its immediate aftermath, see Rubel 2000 (and now, in translation, 2014).

[6] The quotation is from Thuc. 7.87.6, describing the completeness of the Sicilian disaster; see Osborne 2003: 257. In 411, the Athenians themselves voted democracy out of existence; but in 404 the Spartans imposed its end.

[7] Isoc. 8.88; cf. 50. See the discussion in Davidson 1990: 35. The importance of autochthony is also found elsewhere in this speech (94) and in the *Areopagiticus* (7.74).

[8] So, for example, in Herodotus some Spartan speakers claim that the Athenians were suffering economically from the Persian Wars (8.142.3, but see Bowie 2007 *ad loc.* for the rhetorical exaggeration here).

[9] It is, of course, difficult to know what that would have meant in terms of actual casualties or fatalities in the Persian Wars. Raaflaub (1998: 31) observes that whereas hoplite warfare, which was intermittent, probably left enough survivors in a social group to provide support for extended families, naval warfare would have killed a lot more a lot more quickly, producing casualties in huge numbers and leaving many families in desperate conditions. He notes that these were also likely to be predominantly lower-class casualties, leaving families in more difficult conditions, and suggests that the problem was brought to public attention after a major naval disaster. For example, in 454 BCE Athenian troops had been involved in a campaign against the Persians on Cyprus, but they diverted these forces to aid Inarus, a Libyan who was leading an Egyptian revolt against the Persians. A casualty list (ML 33) from that campaign lists 177 men from one tribe alone. We also know that despite initial successes, the entire fleet of 200 plus a relieving squadron of fifty were wiped out. Thucydides (1.110.1) reports that few, out of many, escaped alive.

of the evidence. Mogen Herman Hansen's work has provided scholars with a clear and compelling line of argument, from which various different approaches have subsequently been developed; I will run through the key points here. If we start by comparing the size of the population in 431 BCE with its size by the end of the Peloponnesian War, we find that estimates of that first number have ranged fairly widely.[10] However, it is generally agreed that during the late fifth century Athens lost more than half of its adult male citizenry.[11] The most obvious cause of this was losses in battle itself, but there would also have been deaths off the battlefield, while men were on campaign.[12] This links to the second fundamental cause of the city's drop in population, disease—the most obvious and devastating example being that of the plague: 'Nothing did the Athenians so much harm as this or so reduced their strength for war.'[13] From what Thucydides tells us, the plague devastated the soldiers in their camps. And when we turn back to the city, the evacuation of the countryside would have created even better conditions for the spread of infection.[14] As well as through disease, Athens' population—and importantly the numbers of able, working bodies—would also have been reduced through emigration of non-Athenians and the loss of slaves.[15]

[10] Numbers in 431 BCE: Hansen (1988a: 14–28) suggests a minimum of 60,000 citizen males over eighteen, which implies a very large total population; Garnsey (1988: 90) suggests 250,000 for the total population; Rhodes (1992: 83; and 1994: 567) and Akrigg (2007: 31) estimate 300,000 (the total population of 300,000 comprising about 45,000 adult male citizens, slightly over 100,0000 wives or children of citizens, somewhat under 50,000 metics, free men, and women metics, or visitors, and somewhat over 100,000 slaves). Rhodes (1994: 567 n. 6) notes that the crucial question for the fourth century is whether the number of citizens before the poorest were disfranchised in 321 was 31,000 (Diod. Sic. 18.18.4–5) or 21,000 (Plut. *Phoc.* 28.7); he observes that Ruschenbusch (1979) argues for the lower figures, and Hansen (1985), more persuasively, for the higher (and see Hansen 1988b). For an overview of the literature, see Scheidel's addenda in Garnsey 1998: 195–200.
[11] See Scheidel 2007: 58, summarizing Hansen 1988a: 14–28. Following Ehrenberg 1969, Rhodes (1994: 567) posits a total population of 210,000 (29,000 citizens, 71,000 wives and children, 35,000 metics, and 75,000 slaves).
[12] See Akrigg 2007: 30–3.
[13] Thucydides 3.87.2. Akrigg 2007: 33 highlights the importance of this quotation. This section of this volume is indebted to his considerations of the impacts of the war on the Athenian population.
[14] See Hanson 1983 and Foxhall 1993.
[15] Thuc. 7.27.4–5. Emigration outweighed, as Akrigg (2007: 32–3) argues, the number of Athenians returning to Athens after the loss of overseas possessions.

The literary evidence for fighting forces suggests that there was a significant depletion of manpower: for example, from the 25,000 hoplites of the Peloponnesian War to 9,000, and then around 11,000 in the Corinthian War in the 390s.[16] Similarly, Xenophon suggests a shortage of recruitable men when he mentions a decree put out to support the battle of Arginusae (406 BCE) that ordered slaves and freemen, as well as all those of military age, to embark, and observes that many *hippeis* also joined the force.[17] It seems likely that the Athenians themselves were extremely aware of the loss of men, at least in the years directly after the war: Andocides, in pleading for his life, points out that the Athenians are 'ready to give Athenian citizenship to Thessalians and Andrians because of the shortage of men'.[18] Even when read in its rhetorical context, it seems plausible that Andocides is alluding to a common discourse of the time. It may also be reflected in the payments given to encourage attendance at the Assembly, which rapidly rise during the first decade of the fourth century (attendance is in fact better than in the fifth century).[19]

The drop in numbers did not necessarily mean more plentiful resources. During the war, Decelea had been occupied by the enemy since 413 BCE, and the evacuation of that area meant a higher concentration of people in the city, all struggling to find the wherewithal for survival.[20] The occupation meant that property had been destroyed, and for some Athenians, this may have meant financial ruin.[21] The forensic speeches may offer further insight into this situation. For example, in a speech by Isaeus which concerns the estate of Nicostratus, who died while serving abroad as a mercenary, one Chariades is making a claim on this estate, arguing that he was Nicostratus' business partner and had been adopted by him while they were both serving abroad. During his attack on Chariades, the speaker

---

[16] 25,000 hoplites, Thuc. 2.13; 9,000, Lys. 20.13 (confirmed by van Wees 2001); 11,000, Xen. *Hell.* 4.2.17 (but not a full turnout); see Hornblower 2011: 209.

[17] Xen. *Hell.* 1.6.24. Gabrielsen (1994: 107): conscription of oarsmen and *hyperesiai* was 'the exception rather than the rule' during the fifth and fourth centuries.

[18] Andoc. 1.149.

[19] Probably around 400 BCE: Loomis 1998: 20–2. [Arist.] *Ath. Pol.* 41.3; Ar. *Eccl.* 184–8, 293, 308, 380–90 (note that the payment was made to the first to arrive); and see [Arist.] *Ath. Pol.* 62.2 and Rhodes 1994: 568; attendance better in fourth than fifth century: see Hansen 1976.

[20] Thuc. 2.17.

[21] See Thuc. 7.27–8; Strauss (1986, esp. 50) notes that the results of the occupation are likely to have been highly diverse, depending on individual situations; this is supported by Ar. *Eccl.* 591–3.

notes that 'many others before now have claimed the property of men who have died abroad, sometimes without even knowing them'.[22] Athens had also lost her empire. This drastically diminished the prosperity of her citizens, both rich and poor, with no overseas possessions for the former, and no cleruchies for the latter. Xenophon recounts a meeting between Socrates and one Eutherus in which Eutherus explains how 'I came home when the war ended, Socrates, and am now living here... Since we have lost our foreign property, and my father left me nothing in Attica, I am forced to settle down here now and work for my living with my hands. I think it's better than begging, especially as I have no security to offer for a loan.'[23]

This is not to say that aspects of these kinds of experiences did not occur in Periclean Athens, but literary evidence from the early part of the fourth century seems to offer increasing numbers of stories about experiences of poverty. In Aristophanes' *Ecclesiazusae*, for example, which was presented in the first decade after the war, we hear about Athenians with no cloaks and nowhere to sleep, who are catching pneumonia.[24] The 'heroine' Praxagora is particularly aware of the need to feed the inhabitants of the city, and this becomes the basis for the reassignment of public space in the city under the new regime.[25] The problems of poverty, in particular not having enough to eat, were also the theme of *Ploutos* (*Wealth*), presented four years later, a play that offers a vivid overview of the gap between rich and poor. Wealth is blind, and cannot find honest men to help; instead he stops with the unjust and dishonest. Chremylus offers a vivid description of the life of the poor (ll. 535–47):

σὺ γὰρ ἂν πορίσαι τί δύναι' ἀγαθὸν πλὴν φῴδων ἐκ βαλανείου | καὶ παιδαρίων ὑποπεινώντων καὶ γραϊδίων κολοσυρτόν; | φθειρῶν τ' ἀριθμὸν καὶ κωνώπων καὶ ψυλλῶν οὐδὲ λέγω σοι | ὑπὸ τοῦ πλήθους, αἳ βομβοῦσαι περὶ τὴν κεφαλὴν ἀνιῶσιν, | ἐπεγείρουσαι καὶ φράζουσαι· 'πεινήσεις· ἀλλ'

---

[22] Isae. 4.21 (tr. Edwards 2009: 73).
[23] Xen. *Mem.* 2.8.1 (tr. Marchant and Todd, rev. Henderson 2013); see also Pl. *Euthphr.* 4.
[24] Ar. *Eccl.* 415–21; dated 392/1 BCE.
[25] Ar. *Eccl.* 676–90. The theme of food in these two plays is examined by David (1984: 5–8). Sommerstein (1984) draws out the change in Aristophanes' point of view in his last two surviving plays, and attributes it to the author's own perceptions and perhaps experience of poverty in Athens.

ἐπανίστω.' | πρὸς δέ γε τούτοις ἀνθ' ἱματίου μὲν ἔχειν ῥάκος· ἀντὶ δὲ κλίνης | στιβάδα σχοίνων κόρεων μεστήν, ᾗ τοὺς εὕδοντας ἐγείρει· | καὶ φορμὸν ἔχειν ἀντὶ τάπητος σαπρόν· ἀντὶ δὲ προσκεφαλαίου | λίθον εὐμεγέθη πρὸς τῇ κεφαλῇ· σιτεῖσθαι δ' ἀντὶ μὲν ἄρτων | μαλάχης πτόρθους, ἀντὶ δὲ μάζης φυλλεῖ' ἰσχνῶν ῥαφανίδων, | ἀντὶ δὲ θράνου στάμνου κεφαλὴν κατεαγότος, ἀντὶ δὲ μάκτρας | πιθάκνης πλευρὰν ἐρρωγυῖαν καὶ ταύτην· ἆρά γε πολλῶν | ἀγαθῶν πᾶσιν τοῖς ἀνθρώποις ἀποφαίνω σ' αἴτιον οὖσαν;

> What benefits can you provide, except blisters in the bathhouse and masses of hungry children and old ladies? Not to mention the lice, gnats, and fleas, too numerous to enumerate, that annoy us by buzzing around our heads and waking us up with the warning, 'get up or you'll go hungry!' And on top of that, you have us wearing rags, not coats, and sleeping not on a bed but a bug-infested twine mat that doesn't let you get any sleep, under threadbare burlap instead of a blanket, with our heads not on a pillow but a hefty stone. And to eat, not bread but mallow shoots, not cake but withered radish leaves. We sit not on chairs but on broken crocks, and instead of a kneading trough we get one side of a barrel, and that's broken too. Now haven't I revealed the many blessings you bring to all humanity?[26]

Supporting these comic presentations of Athens' problems is evidence from the law courts: Andocides in his speech 'On the Peace with Sparta' (dated to 391 BCE) notes that: 'There are those who are already complaining that they cannot see the meaning of the treaty, if it is walls and ships which Athens is to recover. They are not recovering their own private property from abroad: and walls cannot feed them. This objection also requires an answer.'[27]

Scholars once argued that such details indicated that fourth-century Athens was in serious decline; however, views have now shifted in the other direction.[28] As scholars have observed, Athens appears to have managed her recovery from the war on a number of fronts relatively quickly:[29] that she could, for example, introduce pay for the Assembly is an important point.[30] And, on the international

---

[26] Ar. *Plut.* 535–47 (tr. Henderson 2002); and see also 218f., 503f., 627ff., 750ff.; see further David 1984: 7.
[27] Andoc. 3.36 (tr. Maidment 1941).
[28] See Herman 2011 and its review by Forsdyke (2012).
[29] French 1991.
[30] See n. 19 above. On the other hand, she was probably no longer paying her magistrates (see Hansen 1991: 240–1; cf. Gabrielsen 1981: 57–87 and 97–9).

political stage, she continues to play a significant role. Indeed, it is largely accepted that behind much of Athens' foreign policy over the next half-century lies the desire to regain her empire (and it will take only around five years before this can be stated explicitly by Xenophon, albeit through the Thebans' speech, on the eve of the Corinthian War).[31] In practice, what this means is that after an initial period in which she acts as a subordinate ally of Sparta, she soon develops an independent foreign policy.[32] Trading interests carefully between Sparta and Thebes, while maintaining both links and conflict with Persia, Athens was almost continuously involved in warfare, on a number of different fronts. As the 360s close, she is recovering from the battle at Mantinea, while fighting in the North Aegean, first for Amphipolis, then the Chersonese and the Propontis, as well as in Asia Minor and the islands. The early years of the 350s will see her embroiled in the Social War, her allies apparently accusing her, as Demosthenes put it to his fellow Athenians, of 'plotting against them' and grudging them 'recovery of what was yours'.[33]

'EVEN THE POOR HAVE LEISURE, SINCE THEY HAVE *MISTHOS*'

All this military activity might suggest a secure and powerful state; and, indeed, Athens and the Piraeus do relatively rapidly recover both wealth and prestige—and over the course of the fourth century, the Athenians will increase their public revenue to a remarkable level.[34] But to begin with at least, it is clear that times were hard: the reliable fifth-century sources of revenue were gone. There was no empire, and the mines at Laurion were not yet back in production;[35] some

---

[31] Xen. *Hell.* 3.5.10. See Rhodes 2010: 262. The Demaenetus affair (*Hell. Oxy.* 9–11; 396 BCE) reveals the anxiety of the Athenians about openly confronting the Spartans. For the Theban call for Athenian help against the Spartans, see Xen. *Hell.* 3.5.8–15; and for attempts to ally with Persia, see Andoc. 3.15.

[32] Austin (1994: 547): 'Athens was at war almost continuously from 378'; but she is embroiled in the Corinthian War (395-387/6), supporting Evagoras of Cyprus against Persia (Xen. *Hell.* 4.24) fighting alongside Egyptians (Ar. *Plut.* 179; Isoc. 4.140). There is fighting in Asia Minor and the Hellespont (Xen. *Hell.* 4.8.30); see discussion in Hornblower 2004: 227–8.

[33] Dem. 15.3 and 15.

[34] Dem. 4.37–38, as French (1991: 38). See Pritchard 2010: 51–5 on the Athenian recovery, especially the reassertion of her prowess in 'war-making'.

[35] This will take until the middle of the fourth century: see Hopper 1953.

attempts were made to extract money from allied cities early on: we hear of the Athenian general Thrasybulus squeezing money from cities in Asia Minor and setting up taxes in cities in the Black Sea area.[36] The Second Athenian Confederacy started to collect funds in 373 BCE—called *syntaxeis* or contributions (there was to be no tribute)—and the contributions were far lower than the money raised under the empire.[37]

And it is expensive to run the democracy, especially one that is determined to (and perhaps must) engage its poorer members, which is the emphasis of this new regime.[38] Not everyone agrees with this approach, of course. The quotation that heads this subsection is from Aristotle's *Politics*, and expresses criticism of the kind of democracy that has sufficient revenue that it may pay the poor so that 'they are not hampered at all by the care of their private affairs', and can take part in the government and administration of the state.[39] The danger Aristotle identifies is that 'the poor become sovereign over the government, instead of the laws'. But Athens in the early fourth century had far more practical concerns: primarily, how to structure its administration so that there was sufficient revenue to support this approach to government.[40]

Resourcing the Navy

As a snapshot of the city's financial circumstances, we can consider the evidence that suggests the difficulties the city experienced in maintaining her navy. Even as her military activities demonstrate Athens' burgeoning political confidence, they also reveal her financial needs. Despite the ubiquity of Athens on the international stage, the naval lists of the 370s reveal that Athens was building almost no new ships;

---

[36] Lys. 28 and Xen. *Hell.* 4.8.30. Taxing traders in the Hellespont: RO 18, and Xen. *Hell.* 4.8.27. Thrasybulus is killed at Aspendus in 389 BCE after his troops plunder the town (even though he has collected money from it): Xen. *Mem.* 4.8.26–30; Diod. Sic. 14.94, 99.4–5.

[37] Second Athenian League: *IG* II² 43 = RO 22. References are made to a gross sums of 45 talents (Dem. 18.234) and of 60 talents (Aeschin. 2.71).

[38] Pritchard 2015. As he makes clear (31), this expense was relatively cheaper than the fifth century: 'Yet it still added up to a significant public expense.'

[39] See Arist. *Pol.* 1293a1–10 (tr., here and below, Rackham).

[40] Payment of magistrates is a contested issue: in this approach I follow Pritchard 2014; he takes issue with Hansen 1979 and 1980; cf. Gabrielsen 1981.

two-thirds of the fleet comprised old vessels, many in poor repair and badly equipped.[41] The problem seems to have come to something of a head in the years 358/7 and 357/6, when it became impossible to send out a fleet because the equipment for the ships had not been returned or was not available, and the markets in the Piraeus could not supply the requisite sailcloth. At about this time, the first legislation to deal with the lack of effective organization and naval defaulters is introduced.[42]

Support for the crew was also hard to find: it seems to have become quite usual for generals to raise their own funds.[43] For example, in 375 BCE, when Timotheus sent out sixty ships to the Peloponnese (at the request of the Thebans, to distract the Spartans), he received 30 talents—a not inconsiderable sum—but needed more and, despite victories, was forced to send repeated requests for funds to Athens.[44] By the late 360s, the situation was not much better: in *Against Polycles*, Apollodorus tells us that when he was trierarch he received full pay for his crew for only two out of seventeen months—and only ration money for the other fifteen.[45]

Perhaps it is not surprising that generals might consider going freelance. As Athens is embroiled in the Social War, a lack of resources leads the general Chares to hire himself out to the rebellious Persian satrap Artabazus. This in turn leads the king himself to order the Athenians to recall him—or face his support for their rebels.[46] In the second of the Olynthiac speeches (349/8 BCE), Demosthenes

---

[41] On the lack of equipment, see *IG* II² 1613.284–310, where the triremes number 349, but there are full sets of oars for only 291 and steering oars for fewer: *IG* II² 1611. Trierarchs seem to have held on to equipment and/or equipped their own ships (Dem. 51.5 and [Dem.] 47.23; see Cawkwell 1984: 341). Gabrielsen (1994: 146–57) stresses the problems of 'lengthy retention or misappropriation' of equipment 'on naval administration and organisation'.

[42] Gabrielsen (1994: 158–9) sees the laxity about this issue of equipment as arising from the prioritization of the recruitment of trierarchs. Requests for *epidoseis* ('voluntary gifts'), which start in 394, also become more frequent from about this time (see Rhodes 2010: 236.

[43] Pritchard 2012: 48–9. The money was considered public property: see Pritchard 2014: 8, citing Dem. 24.11–14; Lys. 28.1–4, 6, and 10, 29.2, 5, 8–11, and 14; Xen. *Hell.* 1.2.4–5.

[44] Isoc. 15.109 and Arist. *Oec.* 1350a3. In the same year, a law of 375 reveals concern for purity of silver coinage; Stroud (1974) suggests that the growth of the confederacy led to the need for reputable currency, but, coupled with the financial distress of those years, may have encouraged forgery.

[45] Cawkwell (1984: 338) notes that Demosthenes (4.22–3 and 28) observes that only 'ration money' will be available for the ten ships he advocates as a standing force.

[46] Diod. Sic. 16.21–2. In the late 360s, King Agesilaus of Sparta hired himself out to the Egyptians in similar fashion in order to raise money for Sparta for the war against Messenia (Plut. *Ages.* 40).

suggests that this was not a unique situation: 'Why is it, think you, men of Athens, that all the generals you dispatch—if I am to tell you something of the truth about them—leave this war to itself and pursue little wars of their own? It is because in this war the prizes for which you contend are your own—(if, for instance, Amphipolis is captured, the immediate gain will be yours)—while the officers have all the dangers to themselves and no remuneration; but in the other case the risks are smaller and the prizes fall to the officers and the soldiers—Lampsacus, for example, and Sigeum, and the plunder of the merchant-ships. So they turn aside each to what pays him best.'[47]

In response to these kinds of difficulties, the first half of the fourth century saw a new system of financial administration instituted. This had advantages—not so great a dependence on a central body for decisions—but also brought disadvantages, in particular, that more people could pocket the money that moved between different parts of the system, and it was harder to keep track of overall funds.[48] The reform of finance in 378/7 involved a reassessment of the taxable wealth of citizens and metics.[49] But the property tax (*eisphora*) was difficult to collect, and this led to various administrative attempts to facilitate the flow of money into the city's coffers. One way was to embed the administrative apparatus within a structure of social relationships:[50] first, the organization of symmories;[51] then the creation of an advance full payment, the *proeisphora*, paid by the richest three members of the symmory, who then must collect what they were owed from the others.[52] A similar system was gradually instituted to resolve the problems of financial support and organization for the navy: in the early part of the century, there appears to have been some trouble recruiting trierarchs, even though the size of the fleet was reduced.[53] Initially, the city allowed for a system of syntrierarchies (two men sharing a

---

[47] Dem. 2.28–9 (tr. Vince 1930). [48] Rhodes 1979/80: 310.

[49] Perhaps this is also when the army fund (*to stratiotikon*) was created to receive surplus revenue not otherwise allocated (see [Dem.] 49.12 and 16). Although, in fact, under Eubulus it appears that much of this money went to the theoric fund under the direction of a treasurer who was able to join the Council in supervision of the old financial committees. This changed once Demosthenes and associates gained political supremacy.

[50] See Christ 2007: 65–7. [51] 378/7: Philoch. *FGrH* 328 F 41.

[52] Rhodes 1979/80: 310.

[53] Gabrielsen 1994: 180–1 and 178–9, respectively.

trierarchy), before Periander's reforms were passed (358/7 BCE). These established a *symmoriai* system for sharing the costs of a trierarchy among a group of sixty men, turning the trierarchy, like the *eisphora*, into a compulsory obligation to the state.[54]

But these changes also introduced unforeseen consequences, in so far as they made no distinction between the wealthier and poorer members of the group. As with the other financial demands on the wealthy, this system was likely to have exacerbated social tensions.[55] We have seen some evidence for this already in the forensic speeches, in the phenomenon of *phthonos* directed at the wealthy, and the discourse that develops around it. Whereas *phthonos* is at root the resentment felt by those without fortune towards those who have it, in the context of fourth-century Athens, the cultural model becomes more complex. We see it nuanced to express, in particular, resentment against those who have good fortune but do not fulfil their civic obligations; while those who do provide for the city use this as a shield against the *phthonos* that their good fortune might otherwise provoke.[56]

Osborne estimates that only around 1,000 citizens would have faced major demands for cash, and that this may have been a lower number than those supporting these demands in the fifth century.[57] In the material we have already observed, the case of Timotheus is illustrative. On his return to face charges of treason, he found himself in dire financial straits (if Apollodorus is to be believed). The description of his monetary arrangements—a series of loans, the mortgaging of his land, the need to distribute money for pay among the trierarchs in charge of the ships, all exacerbated by his own inability to repay his private debts—illustrate the kinds of demands faced by the wealthy. These included liturgies of various kinds, *eisphorai*, and the general requirements of civic

---

[54] Ibid.: 84, 157–60, and 198–9, and see discussion in Christ 2006: 167.
[55] This inequity was tackled by Demosthenes in his naval reform (in the 340s); see Dem. 18.102–8 and Gabrielsen 1994: 207–13; see further Christ 2006: 168.
[56] See pp. 132–6.
[57] Osborne 1991: 140. See Kron 2011: 130–1 for further evidence for the wealthiest Athenians numbering 1,200. Osborne notes (1991: 144) that the 'Old Oligarch' (3.4) alleges that there were 400 trierarchs in the middle of the fifth century. Certainly it seems that a trierarch was appointed for every trireme in the shipsheds (Thuc. 2.24.2). In the fourth century, trierarchs were only appointed once it had been decided to send ships out (*IG* II² 1629.180–271; Dem. 4.36).

philanthropy.[58] That the wealthy feel overburdened emerges from the sense of persecution that is apparent in some political and forensic rhetoric.[59] In turn, as is clear from the rhetoric of the law courts, there is suspicion of those who have money in an invisible form. Other evidence suggests that this may have been well placed.[60]

The appearance of mortgage *horoi* in the early fourth century BCE may have been, in part, a result of the attempt to conceal wealth, as well as being evidence of the need among the wealthy for an additional source of income.[61] But we should look beyond the simple desire for financial gain: 'In Athens, where the local community is closely linked to political identity and to financial contributions (landed wealth is visible and hence "good"), the economics of the exploitation of that land could not but be bound up with local social and political factors.'[62] These activities have further implications for our understanding of the fourth-century context: as French observes, these transactions suggest that land was an 'acceptable object for commercial negotiation', although to take this as far as selling that land in its entirety could be represented as financial mismanagement—not only undermining one's family, but also betraying one's obligations to the city itself.[63] Osborne also stresses the ways in which many of these leases, especially of orphan estates, are remarkable for their short-term nature and the risk involved. He suggests that they indicate a fear of being reduced to dependency in a context of financial need, if not crisis.[64] Although it may be true that leases might draw attention to one's property wealth, it is also worth

---

[58] He was removed from the command because the Athenians thought he was wasting time, and charged with treason. See [Dem.] 49.9–15 and 22–7 and Plut. *X orat.* 836d.

[59] See Xen. *Vect.* 6.1; the argument was made in the law courts that rich defendants were condemned so that property could be confiscated: Lys. 30.22, 19.11, 27.1, and later, Dem. 10.43–5.

[60] Isae. 5.43, 7.39–41, 11.44–50; Lys. 20.23; Dem. 21.156 and 160–7, 48.12, 33, and 35, and [Dem.] 45.66. Cohen (1992: 199–207) argues that the wealthy concealed their money in banks, and this perhaps explains, in part, the rise of private banks (see Shipton 1997: 416–17, 422); see also Christ 2006: 191–4, Gabrielsen 1994: 53–60.

[61] On the *horoi*, see Osborne 1988 and 1991. Christ (2006: 192) suggests that 'posting stone markers (*horoi*) on his property recording debt' might be a way for a landholder to reduce the appearance of landed wealth.

[62] Osborne 1988: 138.

[63] Aeschin. 1.94–105; see French 1991: 29–30; Osborne 1991: 141–2. See also Isae. 7.31–3, in which the end of a family's estate is taken as threatening the end of a family line.

[64] Osborne 1991: 318–19.

considering how this relatively rapid turnover of short-term leases of land might work for both lessor and lessee as a way of blurring the appearance of their property assets.[65]

Feeding the City

An additional effect of this system was to direct those with funds and resources into other forms of raising money, which helped to drive Athens' role as a centre of commerce. This was encouraged not so much by the pressures of empire, as in the fifth century, as by the profits to be made from trade, and was reinforced by the advantages that the city obtained for traders. By the middle of the fourth century, the Piraeus was again a trade hub, helping to support the costs of warfare and running the democracy. And this was also crucial in the ongoing efforts to feed the population of Attica, which seem to have been a continuous anxiety during this period.[66]

Foreign and military policy shows continued concern with protecting the corn trade route. For example, conflict in the North Aegean during the 370s and 360s related directly to problems of the supply of grain, and vice versa.[67] Athens was no longer self-sufficient, and corn shortages were likely to have been created by crop failure (disease and drought), by piracy, and by the unsettled conditions of the period.[68] It is true that over a period of 185 years (between 507 BCE and 322 BCE) there are only fifteen possible—and probably ten—attested occurrences of food shortage in Athens.[69] However, it is also worth noting for the purposes of this study that these all occurred in the fourth century, and half of them in the period 387/6–357.

---

[65] Gabrielsen 1986: 105; cf. Christ 2006: 192–3.
[66] During the fifth and fourth centuries the Athenians always needed to import over half of their annual requirements from overseas, as argued by Moreno (2007: 323).
[67] See Dem. 50.6, 12, and 19 (and Heskel 1997: 142–8).
[68] For this not to be the case for a period of time was worth remarking on (see Xen. *Hell.* 6.2.6, of Corcyra in 373; Plut. *Ages.* 31.1–2, of Lakonia in 370; and Diod. Sic.16.42.8, of Cyprus in 344/3). See the discussion in Austin 1994: 559.
[69] Moreno (2007: 311), using Garnsey (1988: 145–6) states nine, but lists ten likely periods of food shortage, all in the fourth century. Garnsey (1988: 145–6) gives as likely: (145–6) 388/7, 362/1, and 361/0, (147) 376/5 or 374/3 and 357; he notes further shortages in the years 350s [also possibly others in the 390s]; then (157) a further five in the years 338/7, 335/4, 330/29, 328/7, and 323/2 (with further discussion 154–62).

After the War... 281

The Athenians did their best to get the situation under control. The cleruchies that were founded during the fourth century (Skyros, Lemnos, Imbros, Sestos, the Chersonese, and Potidaia) were not only intended to remove hungry mouths, and lessen the chance of hunger-driven discontent, but were also designed—on the basis of fifth-century models—to ensure a considerable quantity of grain made it to Athens.[70] In these settlements, after the existing population was expelled, the landscape was divided into a few large holdings owned by *pentakosiomedimnoi*.[71] These were intended to be 'surplus-producing' landscapes.[72]

Meanwhile, the administration and regulation of the Athenian grain trade and market was 'by far the most heavily regulated part of the Athenian economy'.[73] An elaborate, systematic structure was set in place to control the movement of grain, along with laws intended to control the behaviour of individuals in this area. For example, hoarding and excessive profits were regulated;[74] and no Athenian citizen or metic was to engage in or lend money on the transport of grain to any destination other than Athens.[75] As well as these sticks, there were also carrots, in the form of the extension of the honours system. To refer back to the discussion above of the economic difficulties created for the population by Athens' engagement in conflict, it is notable that the award of honorary decrees by the Athenians for trade-related services develops most dramatically in periods after defeats (Peloponnesian War, the Social War, and the Battle of Chaeronea).[76]

---

[70] Moreno 2007: 103–15.
[71] Scholiast Aeschin. 1.53; Philoch. *FGrH* 328 F 154.
[72] Moreno 2007: 112–13, 319—on Samos (see Heraclides *FHG* II.216). Moreno argues that this was for protection of the grain supply, but it is not clear that this excludes the rationale of reducing population numbers in Athens.
[73] Moreno 2007: 334; the details are given in App. 4. The personnel involved included *agoranomoi* (who oversaw the agora); *metronomoi* (responsible for weights and measures); *sitophylakes* (supervised the grain market and enforced laws against individuals); *epimeletai tou emporiou* (oversaw the import market, including the unloading of grain); and *epimeletai tou sitou* (in charge of transport, weighing, storage of public grain, and sale at a price set by the *demos*). See also Reed 2003: 48–9 for Athens' control of trade.
[74] Hoarding: Lys. 22.5–6; profits: Lys. 22.8 and 12.
[75] Dem. 34.37 and 35.51; Lycurg. 1.27. Austin (1994: 562): laws attested in the second half of fourth century but may be older.
[76] Engen 2010: 136. She notes in particular that the defeat in the Social War in 355 marks 'a major turning point in Athens' use of honorary language' (ibid.: 133–5, and

'LYDIANS AND PHRYGIANS AND SYRIANS AND EVERY OTHER SORT OF BARBAROI'

The corn trade was just one small part of the commercial activity that was steadily growing again in early fourth-century Athens. That life had been difficult for metics in Athens after the Peloponnesian War, or that the difficulties were greater than the rewards, is suggested by the fact that their numbers seem to have dropped, at least if our commentators are to be believed.[77] Certainly, for those who had stayed to fight for the democracy, there was little recognition—for them or their orphaned children.[78] Isocrates notes, admittedly rather melodramatically, how Athens is deserted by *emporoi* (traders), *xenoi* (temporary non-Athenian visitors), *metoikoi* (metics); instead, there is a floating population that passes through the city.[79] In the *Ways and Means*, Xenophon agrees, in so far as he also wants to attract more foreigners to Athens; while at the same time he refers to them in a distinctively insular fashion as 'Lydians and Phrygians and Syrians and every other sort of *barbaroi*'.[80] He recommends better access to the legal system—and, in fact, in the mid-fourth century, the reorganization of the *dikai emporikai* offered non-residents more rapid resolution of their cases.[81] This weakened the status difference between visiting merchants and resident metics, as did the fact that economic power could enhance status.

citing Whitehead 1983: 67–8), when Athens begins to honour native citizens for services performed as public officials (only), in the same way that they honoured foreign benefactors, using the language of *philotimia*, and the formula of the 'hortative intention' (that the decree shall be inscribed so all should know Athens honours those with *philotimia*). She attributes this change in part to the severe crisis of revenue and food caused by the conflict, and also notes the possible evidence for a prolonged drought (Engen 2010: 59; Camp 1982: 9–17).

[77] The title of this subsection is from Xen. *Vect.* 2.3; dated to 355/4 BCE (Tuplin 1993: 32).

[78] Those non-citizens who survived had to buy back the moveable property confiscated by the Thirty (Lys. fr. 1.34–47 Carey). Thrasybulus' proposal to enfranchise those who had fought for the democrats in 403 was blocked; instead they were carefully examined to see if they had done what they claimed, then given en masse 1,000 drachmae for sacrifices and dedications (less than 10 drachmae per man) along with a crown of olive (see Aeschin. 3.187); the dead were granted (along with the citizen dead) public burial and perpetual honours (Lys. 2.66, [Arist.] *Ath. Pol.* 40.2, schol. to Aeschin. 3.195, Plut. *X orat.* 835f–36a); for attitudes towards orphans, see further pp. 298–302.

[79] Isoc. 8.21.   [80] See n. 77 above.

[81] As Demetriou (2012: 205) also notes.

The ambivalent attitude that may at first appear in Xenophon's comments is mirrored in law-court speeches. Opponents are criticized for their ill-treatment of metics, but Aeschines, for example, suggests that pederasts turn to 'foreigners and metics' so as not to harm citizens.[82] However, when we look more closely at the ideological approach that underpins such statements, it suggests that Athenian attitudes to foreigners should be seen more in terms of the larger struggle to safeguard Athenian identity that plays out across this period, rather than being based in aggressive racial prejudice. It is significant that the suspicion that some who claimed to be Athenians might be non-citizens (and there is evidence for this charge recurring in inheritance or property disputes) does not seem to have resulted in any actual convictions.[83] It may be taken to indicate how successfully Athens managed to 'enforce simultaneously an open immigration policy, but an exclusive citizenship policy, and rigorously guard the dividing line'.[84] It was an environment ripe for gossip.

When, in 346/5 BCE Demophilus proposed the scrutiny of the deme registers to expel non-citizens, this may have been because Athens was again in the ascendant (as when the citizenship law of 451 was introduced).[85] The Peace of Philocrates led Athenians to believe that they were again attaining a position of superiority—so must reinforce the boundaries between them and everyone else. But the policing of this dividing line produced a strong sense of watchfulness: some of the pleas made by those defending themselves in court suggest just what suspicions it could arouse if one even talked like a foreigner.[86] In

---

[82] After the restoration of the democracy the administrative approach to non-citizens remains ambivalent. The citizenship law of 451/0 is re-enacted, retroactively at first, and then with 403/2 as the terminus. Theozotides appears to have put forward a decree that gave support to the orphans of those citizens (and only citizens) who had died in the struggle; while Phormisius proposed the restitution of political rights only to landowners—a move that Lysias (see Lys. 34) and others opposed and won. Finally, in 401/0 it may be that around 1,000 non-citizens were enfranchised for their part in the *kathodos* (but the epigraphic evidence of *IG* II² 10 is unclear: see e.g. Osborne 1981–2, D6, Whitehead 1984, and Harding 1987). Bakewell (1999: 20) discusses this, and more broadly, the ways in which Lysias 12 and 31 play with the ideological oppositions of the good metic and the bad citizen.

[83] See Isae. 3.3 and 37, 6.12 and 52; and [Dem.] 44 and Din fr. 55 and fr. 62; Hyperides frr. 13–26 appear to be from two speeches *Against Aristagoras* in a *graphe aprostasiou* case.

[84] Kapparis 2005: 112: e.g. Isae. 12 and Dem. 57.

[85] Kapparis 2005: 94–5, who provides the comparison.

[86] Wallace 2010: 150.

particular, time and again it is the indefinable status of women that seems to have created a key vulnerability for those seeking to prove their Athenian citizenship. Sometimes this might turn on the question of their civic status, but the charge could even be made that these women did not actually exist.[87]

The presentation of metics and foreigners in forensic oratory at Athens makes it clear that members of the mobile population—those who chose to live away from home—were to be regarded with suspicion.[88] But it also suggests that mobility was an increasing factor in many people's lives.

'PROCURING THEIR DAILY LIVELIHOOD AS BEST EACH ONE CAN'

At Athens, the Peloponnesian War would have meant, if only briefly, that there were fewer people scattered across more land, so that scarcer labour may have been one of the consequences: parallels with the situation in England following the Black Death raise these possibilities.[89] In that context, the result was higher wages for labourers, who were in a position to make demands. But, of course, the situation depends in part on the ways in which systems of landholding were structured.[90] For example, in Roman Egypt, as Duncan-Jones has observed, a similar situation led to changes in the character of Egyptian land leases—less land being leased for longer periods.[91]

---

[87] Isae. 6.10–16 (see Kennedy 2014: 98).
[88] See the analysis of McKechnie (1989: 16), giving as examples Lys. 31.9, Dem. 29.3, and Isae. 4.7 and 27 (which gives the other side of this argument, praising his clients for not going abroad, unless they were commanded to by the Athenians).
[89] The quotation that heads this subsection is from Isoc. 14.48 (tr. Van Hook), discussed further below. Akrigg (2007: 41) cites Scheidel's comparison between England after the Black Death and the Antonine plague (2002).
[90] It is important to examine, as Scheidel (2010, esp. 20–3), how different institutional constraints might influence the outcome of such a situation differently. As he points out, this observation was made by Brenner (1976), who emphasized the role of peasants; but he also cites the more recent comparative work of Borsch (2005), who compares the effects of the Black Death in England and Egypt, revealing how the economic outcomes of each of the epidemics were shaped by the structure of landholding in each location.
[91] Duncan-Jones 1996, esp. 120–34, as cited by Scheidel (2002). A number of other pieces of evidence are cited in this context, but the types of information are not available for fourth-century Athens.

For Athens, there is conflicting evidence: one monolithic account of triumphant revival or serious decline will not do. The story will have been different for diverse parts of the population; but nuancing the account appropriately is difficult. The evidence suggests a time of change, with hardship for some. On the one hand, as John Davies has observed, there are a number of political dynasties that dominate fifth-century sources and then disappear in the fourth century, and it is usually argued that these have died out; it may be that financial difficulties render them invisible in the historical record.[92] On the other hand, as Claire Taylor has argued, the evidence for the involvement in politics of a higher proportion of citizens from non-city demes may suggest a change in the distribution of wealth, along with a higher percentage of the surviving population taking on some land ownership, and moving around the territory of Attica in patterns of 'circular' migration'.[93]

The images that Isocrates paints—the quotation that heads this section is from one such description—indicate that there were at least some families facing extreme poverty.[94] This may indicate that, even if the population had dropped by the end of the war, it was possible that there were too many people in Athens to be comfortably fed and employed, even allowing for help from what we might call 'extended families'.[95] Perhaps this was a situation that did not last for very long; nevertheless, we can still construct some idea of that experience. For someone living in Athens, a city that was busy, thriving, crowded, with lots of opportunities for work, and lots of people to do it, it may have meant that there was little land available, low wages, and probably low standards of living and increasing inequalities.[96]

---

[92] Davies 1981: 84–5. As Taylor (2007: 81) suggests of the family of Alcibiades (Lys. 14.31 and Isoc. 16.46 indicate financial difficulties; cf. Lys. 14.7–8 for Alcibiades' son in the cavalry, c.395 BCE); and for Cimon's family, see Davies 1971: 309–11.

[93] Taylor (2007: 81; she cites Foxhall 1992: 156–9, Osborne 1992: 23–4, Morris 2000: 140–1, and Foxhall 2002: 211) indicates that land distribution in Attica was 'remarkably egalitarian'. Kron's analysis (2011) supports an impression that mid- to late fourth-century Athens had a remarkably equal distribution of wealth, especially when viewed in comparative perspective. Circular migration: Taylor 2011.

[94] Isoc. 14.48–9 (tr. Van Hook), discussed on p. 289.

[95] Thuc. 2.14ff. See Hornblower 2011: 190, and the suggestion that a larger, recently uprooted, and distressed civic population may be one explanation for why Athenian oratory and politics grew more aggressive during this period.

[96] Akrigg 2007: 38–9.

Greater Mobility

These kinds of experiences, multiplied across Greece, may be, in part, why the fourth century is understood to have developed an increasing mobile working-population. In addition, there were those forced to move because of War or political violence.[97] There had been exilings throughout the Peloponnesian war, and these continue as modes of military and political control.[98] The evidence suggests that one response was to take up a profession in which it was an advantage to be mobile.[99] The idea was sufficiently familiar for it to become part of an anecdote about the philosopher Diogenes the Cynic, in which he explains impatiently to someone who has criticized him for his exile, that that was why he had become a philosopher in the first place.[100]

Many craftsmen had long been itinerant, responding to demands for those with specialist skills.[101] But on the road now, alongside these craftsmen, there were increasing numbers of philosophers and

---

[97] During the early fourth century, Sparta, Thebes, and Athens all use the exile and resettlement of populations as methods of political/military assertions of power, and see the concern of Aeneas Tacticus (*Poliorc.* 5–10; written in the 360s) with the precautions to be taken by a city if there are exiles. Not for nothing did Alexander order the Greek states to restore their exiles (324; Diod. Sic.18.8.1–5)—as many as 20,000 men gathered to hear this proclamation. See McKechnie's analysis of this figure (1989: 25–7, quotation on p. 27) as a plausible indication of the likely number of exiles '"left over" from the middle of the century who still needed settlement in 324 BCE'; he also draws attention to the movement of populations in Sicily and Italy during the late fifth to mid-fourth centuries (McKechnie 1989: 34–48).

[98] Examples of exilings during the Peloponnesian War because of *stasis* (supported by Athens) include: Samos 412 (Thuc. 8.21), producing 400 exiles; at Chios 409 (Diod. Sic. 13.65.4), 600 exiles. After that war: at Theban Cadmea 382 (Xen. *Hell.* 5.2.31) 300 exiles; Tegea 370 (Diod. Sic. 15.59.2; Xen. *Hell.* 6.5.10) 1400 exiled and 800 take refuge with the Spartans. There are also examples of exiled populations being made citizens ([Dem.] 59.104, Isoc. 12.94, 14.51–2, Lys. 23; cf. Thuc. 3.55.3 and 3.63.2), or founding a new city (Hdt. 1.164–8), or even captives being returned: Diod. Sic. 13.114.1 (see discussion in Schaps 1982: 206). Exilings are discussed in Seibert 1979: during the war (54–92) and afterwards (92–147).

[99] McKechnie (1989: 5) notes that particular occupations developed more than others (mercenary services demonstrate tremendous growth for example, more so than long-distance trading) and for different reasons—so some develop in response to forms of recruitment or developments in techniques of warfare.

[100] Diog. Laert. 6.49; Diogenes the Cynic described himself as 'cityless, homeless, deprived of a fatherland—a beggar, a wanderer, living from day to day': Diog. Laert. 6.38.

[101] See Burford 1965: 21–34, 1969, and 1972. Note in particular the explanation of how the usual pattern of work (fairly local mobility) may have changed as the impact of the Peloponnesian War on finance meant that greater distances had to be covered. McKechnie (1989: 145) reinforces this argument by pointing out that it was likely that these skills were closely guarded by their possessors, and passed down within families.

orators (encompassing practitioners and teachers), cooks, actors, *manteis*, and *hetairai*, alongside freelance generals and other military specialists, such as professional drill sergeants.[102] The protreptic literature of the period demonstrates how professional training was being promulgated across a variety of professions.[103] Freelancers included skilled generals, and they drew on the increasing numbers of available mercenaries.[104] This phenomenon was partly a matter of demand, and partly a matter of supply—the one feeding the other.[105] In the mid-370s, when Timotheus set out to defend Corcyra, it proved impossible to man the sixty ships he had been voted within Athens, and instead he recruited men as he sailed through the Cyclades—men he then had to find the money to pay.[106] Meanwhile Iphicrates, sent out to replace Timotheus, faced similar financial problems: he had to hire out his sailors as farm labourers to the Corcyraeans, and in 371 BCE he sent Callistratus to Athens with a request for funds or peace. This may have been in part a matter of the drop in manpower caused by mortality, but it is also likely that men had left Athens in search of work.

Family Stories

As we have seen, those who left their communities might go because they were forced to do so, or because they were prompted by their own political beliefs, as a quick way of making some

---

[102] Pl. *Lach.* 183a–b, Xen. *An.* 2.1.7. See also Meritt 1940, no. 8, col. 1, ll. 33–6; cf. [Arist.] *Ath. Pol.* 42.3, with Rhodes's commentary (1981) *ad loc*. For a travelling chorus trainer: *SEG* 27.19, l. 5. For these references, see McKechnie 1989: 157 and 174 n. 195.

[103] Ibid.: 157–8. For medicine, see the Hippocratic treatises, *The Art*, *Ancient Medicine*, and *Decorum*; for rhetoric, Isoc. I; for cookery, Ath. 14.661e; for philosophy, Aristippus (Diog. Laert. 2.85), Aristotle (Diog. Laert. 5.22), Theophrastus (Diog. Laert. 5.50), and Demetrius of Phaleron (Diog. Laert. 5.81).

[104] McKechnie 1989, ch. 4, with Whitehead 1991. Mid-century: Aeneas Tacticus expects mercenaries to be used alongside citizen armies (*Poliorc.* 10.7, 10.18–19, 12–13, 22.29).

[105] As McKechnie (1989: 101) argues: 'as the tendency to use mercenary armies gained strength so the numbers of unemployed and wandering mercenaries increased'.

[106] Timotheus: Xen. *Hell.* 6.2.11–12. See Isoc. 8.48 and 79 for mercenaries as hoplites while Athenians man the ships; but compare 7.54 (357 BCE), where foreign oarsmen are hired (and see Gabrielsen 1994: 96). Callistratus was sent to Sparta as one of the envoys for peace (Xen. *Hell.* 6.3.3 ff.); see Tuplin 1977.

money, or as a way of life. In most of these accounts, the emphasis is on the fate of the male citizens, but occasionally we are also given glimpses of the effects on their families.

Sometimes, we learn, families were forced to move together: thus, Thucydides mentions the women and children who were part of the expulsions of population from Aegina by the Athenians in 431 BCE, and from Potidaia in 430/29 BCE.[107] Such families might then become separated: Lysias 12 comments on what happens after the Thirty limited citizen rights at Athens to 3,000 men and also details how those men had to leave their children in foreign, sometimes hostile lands.[108] In other circumstances, those who chose to go had to decide whether or not to take their families with them. As Xenophon tells us of the men who came, like him, to fight for Cyrus: 'For most of the soldiers had sailed away from Greece to undertake this service for pay, not because their means were scanty, but because they knew by report of the noble character of Cyrus; some brought other men with them, some had even spent money of their own on the enterprise, while still another class had abandoned fathers and mothers, or had left children behind with the idea of getting money to bring back to them, all because they heard that the other people who served with Cyrus enjoyed abundant good fortune.'[109] Other evidence may suggest that women and children accompanied such campaigns.[110] (And scholars have argued that this became more usual during the Hellenistic period.)[111]

[107] Thuc. 2.27.1 and 2.70.3-4.
[108] Lys. 12.97; see discussion in McKechnie 1989: 23.
[109] Xen. *An.* 6.4.8 (tr. Brownson, rev. Dillery); discussion in Austin 1994: 534.
[110] For children on military campaigns, see Xen. *An.* 5.3.1, and on the Sicilian expedition, see Thuc. 7.60.3.
[111] Later evidence from Miletos (*Milet.* I.3 33–93) shows the granting of citizenship to mercenaries (most of those whose origins are known come from Crete), and reveals a complex picture of family ties within the settlement. However, this must be treated with caution, since the presence of women in the records does not mean that families were brought on campaign (see Loman 2004: 50; see also Thonemann 2007: esp. 160, and Chaniotis 2002). As Pomeroy has noted (1983: 207–22), the fact that some of the men are listed twice indicates that they came alone to fight, and then brought their families over. The small size of families and few daughters, and the fact that the sex ratio is (216) 'more skewed among the children of parents whose ethnics are given and who do not come from Crete' she attributes to the difficulties of their lifestyle, and, as a result, a higher likelihood of infanticide of girl children. The inscriptions provide evidence of single mothers, but only as part of extended family groups. One is a mother of two sons accompanied by her own father and mother; the other migrated with her adult son and his wife. There are eight single fathers with children; only one single parent has a daughter (member of extended family group,

Isocrates's speeches of 357 (*Areopagiticus*) and 355 (*On the Peace*) are particularly concerned with the effects on families of the increase in itinerancy and provide a dark view, disenchanted and despairing.[112] In these speeches he focuses on the bands of men and the trouble that they could cause, emphasizing the fear of mercenary activity. There is more detailed evidence about some of the possible effects on families in Isocrates's *Plataicus*. This speech concerns the state of the Plataeans, expelled by the Thebans in 374 BCE, who found refuge and citizenship in Athens and had to start their livelihood all over again. He describes the fate of children reduced to slavery, parents unworthily cared for, wives separated from husbands, and daughters from mothers. He describes how people are being forced to work for hire, 'the rest procuring their daily livelihood as best each one can, in a manner that accords with neither the deeds of their ancestors, nor their own youth, nor our own self-respect'.[113]

As was said at the beginning of this section, how far we can trust Isocrates' words as evidence for widespread destitution remains a question. He was willing to adjust his material in order to make a rhetorical point more powerful.[114] Nevertheless, he does suggest something of the tensions and questions that were under debate and may help to provide some insight into these kinds of experiences.[115] Somewhat dryer, but no less compelling evidence for the difficulties created by such situations can be found in the forensic corpus: we have noted above, for example, the court case over the estate of Nicostratus, who died while serving abroad as a mercenary.[116] Other cases indicate the troubles caused within families by male relatives absent or killed while on military campaign.[117] Often and

---

Milet. I.3.62). There are thirty-six *orphanoi*: they may have had mothers (listed with patronymics), but they appear to have no fathers. There are eleven adult daughters in families, and another seventeen women travelling alone.

[112] See Isoc. 4.167–8 and 8.24; the damage these groups could wreak: 5.119–23 and 6.8–9.

[113] Isoc. 14.48–9 (tr. Van Hook).

[114] e.g. in 8.77, where he references Pericles' policy of keeping Attic citizens within the city walls as if they were afraid to go out to fight, whereas in fact Pericles was restraining them from fighting.

[115] Fuks 1984: 39 [132]: 'the "roving population" of the poor (especially the mercenaries) and the miserable condition of the poor in general'.

[116] Isae. 4.21(tr. Edwards 2009: 73) see p. 271.

[117] See, for example, Isae. 7 and Isae. 9.

unsurprisingly in these cases, the focus is squarely placed on the male protagonists: we have to look carefully to find information about the experiences of other family members.

The *Aegineticus* of Isocrates, also a case about the rights to an estate, may offer one example. The estate in question was created by one Thrasyllus, who inherited the mantic books of a man called Polemaenetus. After travelling from city to city selling his services as a seer, he finally settled back at home in Siphnos: he had two sons, Sopolis and Thrasylochus. In this speech, the claimant explains that Thrasyllus had married his father's sister, and that he himself was adopted by Thrasylochus; he is in dispute for his estate with a half-sister of Thrasylochus (the result of one of Thrasyllus' relationships on the road).[118] The story he tells aims to show his emotional devotion to the family (as well as his legal right to the inheritance) and illustrates many of the themes of enforced itinerancy discussed above.

In the speech, he relates how, when exiles from Paros and Siphnos drove out an oligarchic faction from the island, the family left Siphnos.[119] We know that Sopolis was absent at this juncture, perhaps already gone to Lycia, where he died.[120] Taking their movable property with them, Thrasylochus and his family settled first in Melos—the speaker helping Thrasylochus, who then persuaded him to go with him to Troezen. The speaker agreed, but it only becomes apparent that he also took his own family with him when he reports that his mother and younger sister died of disease there.[121] That these women were dependent on him is clear from his earlier description of the slaughter of his father, uncle, brother-in-law, and three cousins.[122] The next move took them all to Aegina, where they lived as metics, and where Thrasylochus adopted the speaker (or so he claims) and died.[123] It then emerges that in all his travels, Thrasylochus was also accompanied by a mother and sister, who had been travelling separately; we also learn of their illness.[124]

In this narrative, the speaker employs the figures of these women, at least in part, to provoke pity and compassion in his audience. For this to be effective, it had to be plausible: it is likely that something of

---

[118] Isoc. 19.5–9.
[119] This probably dates the speech to the end of 394/early 393 BCE.
[120] Isoc. 19.40.   [121] Isoc. 19.20–2.   [122] Isoc. 19.19.
[123] Isoc. 19.24. See discussion in McKechnie 1989: 18–19.
[124] Isoc. 19.11 and 25; when the speaker describes Thrasylochus' final illness, he mentions how they have not yet arrived.

these women's real-world experiences can be glimpsed in the incidental detail that the speech provides. It seems likely that those experiences were not uncommon, although they were rarely recorded. It prompts us to ask how many other such women lurk in the interstices of our evidence, caught in such situations of dependence and survival—and whether and how they are represented by our sources.

4.3

Dependence and Vulnerability

'SO MANY REFUGEE SISTERS AND NIECES AND FEMALE COUSINS'

It has been stated about ancient Roman society that it is likely that, 'as a result of mortality and divorce, we must envisage societies in which widows and orphans were pervasive and vulnerable'.[1] This quotation also seems applicable to Athenian society, in which men, probably around their late twenties or early thirties, typically married women in their late teens or early twenties; the men probably had an additional life expectancy of around 25–30 years (if they lived in fairly healthy environments).[2] If we add to this the effects of the warfare that stretched across the fifth and fourth centuries, and, in Athens, the impacts of the oligarchic revolution (404–403 BCE) and the plague, then, this study suggests, the prevalence of widows and orphans would have been markedly increased.[3]

Can we assign some numbers to such observations? One study estimates that 558 Athenian wives in every thousand lost their husbands at some time after their marriage and that there were 200

---

[1] The heading of this section is from Xen. *Mem.* 2.7.2 (discussed further on p. 296). On the composition of Roman society, see Saller 2007: 90–1, with quotation from p. 91. Saller points out that the representation of the family in ancient texts is husband, wife, children—that is, 'nuclear'. See also Scheidel 2009.

[2] Limits of marriageable age: Pl. *Leg.* 721b (30–5 years old for a man), 772d (25–35 years old for a man), 785b (30–5 for a man, and 16–20 for a girl). Aristotle suggests that a man was in his prime physically between 30 and 35 and mentally at about 49 (*Rhet.* 1390b). He advocates marriage at age 18 for women and 37 for men (*Pol.* 1335a29), and this has been put down to his own age at the time of his marriage (see Sallares 1991: 148). Sallares (1991: 149) discusses variations across poleis in the age of marriage for women.

[3] Cudjoe 2010: 17–22.

more widows than widowers.[4] Losses in war are likely to have exacerbated such demographic factors. The demographic effects of the defeats in the years 413–403 would not have been felt on the number of citizens coming of age until the decade 395–385 BCE.[5] Over this period, it seems likely that the age structure of the population changed; fewer young people meant fewer dependants, but it also presented problems for family support and/or the continuation of family lines. Of course, the economic situation would have fluctuated—and it would have been perceived differently by different social groups according to the diverse pressures affecting them, as outlined in the previous section. In general, however, it seems likely that there would have been a substantial number of women who were left without direct male support.[6]

Widows

In Athens, we are famously told, women's legal ownership of property was very restricted—to one *medimnos* of barley.[7] But, as Lin Foxhall has explained, 'the relationships that Athenians perceived between people and property' were somewhat more complicated: 'the concepts of management, disposal and use could join together in several different ways, depending on social context to form what we call "ownership"'.[8] There is evidence, for example, of women owning slaves: in law-court speeches we are told that, in Athens, Pasion the banker left his wife, Archippe, her maids in his will; and that Neaera could buy and sell slaves (albeit, this is in Corinth).[9] We also hear of women's ownership of *himatia kai chrusia*. This technical term, literally meaning 'clothing and jewellery', described the personal possessions of a new bride, which may, or not, have been part of her

---

[4] See Golden 1981: 329.   [5] See discussion in previous section.
[6] See discussion in Golden 1981: 316–29 and Cudjoe 2010: 58.
[7] Isae. 10.10.   [8] Foxhall 1989: 26.
[9] Pasion: [Dem.] 45.28; Neaera: [Dem.] 59.18. Perhaps the emphasis on *nomoi poleos*, as Schaps points out (1979: 115 n. 47), draws attention to the fact that such a sale would have been illegal in Athens; Neaera's ownership of the slaves she had purchased is confirmed by a group of Athenian arbiters (Schaps 1979: 46) As Schaps observes (ibid.: 155 n. 48), it is not clear whether or not Phrynio has claimed the maids or just his own movable property. What this evidence may reflect is that ownership was a separate matter from commerce—in which the legal limit for women was one *medimnos* of barley.

dowry.¹⁰ This latter point was important, since if these items were not part of the dowry, they need not be returned to the wife if her husband died or the couple divorced, since, legally they belonged to the husband (while the dowry belonged to the wife).¹¹ In general, apart from the dowry, it seems likely that married women would not amass personal possessions, in contrast to women of independent means, such as Theodote, whose lovely house is admired by Socrates.¹²

Although there were legal limits to the value of the transactions they could conduct, there is evidence for women handling much larger sums, although this was likely to depend on the attitude of the husband, if he was still living.¹³ After his death, a woman could choose to stay in her husband's house, and there is evidence for widows doing this in various circumstances—alone, with son(s), or with a son and daughter. There appears to have been some particular recognition and protection (by the archon) of pregnant women, who could stay in their deceased husband's house.¹⁴ We also see wives taking over the management of financial affairs and of the household when their husbands were away or had died. After her husband's death, it seems likely that the woman was in control (*kyria*) of any property that her husband had left her.¹⁵ Aeschines refers to those households with rich young orphans whose 'fathers had died and their mothers were managing their property'—but with little respect, and an indication that they were vulnerable to mistreatment.¹⁶

---

[10] See Dem. 25.56, [Dem.] 59.35 and 46; Lys. 12.19; Dem. 41.11, cited in Schaps 1979: 115, nn. 56–9. Schaps (ibid.: 10–11) observes that a woman probably kept these items herself (as the example of Dem. 41.27 suggests); that husbands may return such property out of goodwill (e.g. Isae. 2.9), and that there is no example of a husband keeping such items for himself, despite his legal title to it.

[11] See Foxhall 1989: 32–7 and Schaps 1979: 10.

[12] Xen. *Mem.* 3.11.4.

[13] See Foxhall 1989: 36; Dem. 27.53–5 and [Dem.] 36.14–16. Evidence ranges from women as household managers (Ar. *Lys.* 492–7 and *Eccl.* 210–13; Pl. *Leg.* 805e; [Dem.] 59.122; and of course the famous Xen. *Oec.* 3.12) to situations where household management is kept by the men (Ar. *Thesm.* 418–23) or put in the charge of a slave (Men. *Samia* 301–3).

[14] Dem. 43.75: but she did not need to be a pregnant woman, as the law quoted there might be taken to suggest, as Cudjoe (2010: 65ff.) argues. There do not seem to be examples of widows choosing to remain in the house with a daughter only.

[15] Dem. 41.8–11, 17, and 21. Schaps (1979: 56) notes that it is usually non-Athenian women or widows who tend to become most freely involved in business affairs. Cudjoe (2010: 159–61) argues that the loss of these rights when a woman remarried appears to have been theoretical.

[16] Aeschin. 1.170.

The freedom of widows went beyond their financial affairs: stories from the orators show some women making choices about their relationships.[17] It has been suggested that this potential for freedom may have been viewed as dangerous to the status quo. Thus, some scholars have cited Pericles' famous words at the end of the funeral oration, when he urges the widows of the war dead to do nothing to excite men's blame, or even praise; while others have argued that the portrayal of sexually voracious widows in later plays of Aristophanes may also be indicative.[18]

Widows are mentioned in a number of the funeral orations of this period, but with little evidence that they received any kind of organized support.[19] Pericles, for example, focuses primarily on consolation rather than suggesting the possibility of practical help.[20] And, although in his *Funeral Oration* Lysias does mention aid for wives of the kind that their husbands would have provided, this appears to be as insubstantial as the other emotional consolations that he suggests for parents and children.[21] (They should all receive *charis*—the parents 'high regard' and the children 'affection'.)[22] Ps-Plato's *Menexenus* includes parents and children being directed to take care of widows and children. As evidence, this must be treated with care—the text is, after all, a parody—but even here, although orphans and mothers are described as being in the care of the city, only orphans are mentioned as receiving specific support.[23]

In sum, it seems that during the fifth and early to mid-fourth century, widows did not receive any specific support, although there is evidence for civic protection of pregnant widows. The expectation appears to have been that they would either be able to cope on their

---

[17] Andersen (1987: 43) cites Dem. 27.13–15 and 29.26; Hyp. 1 fr. IVb.3 and 7; Isae. 9.27–9 and 6.51. He suggests that a woman with small children, or who was pregnant, may have had a rare moment of choice about whose *oikos* (that of her father's or of her dead husband) she must return to (citing Levy 1963).

[18] Pericles: Thuc. 2.45.2; the argument is made persuasively by Andersen (1987); Aristophanes: see McGinn 2008: 24–5, who cites Henderson 1987: 118–19, 128.

[19] Also observed by Cudjoe (2010: 70). Hyp. 6.27 does not mention widows.

[20] See den Boer 1979: 34. Pericles: Thuc. 2.45.2.

[21] Lys. 2.75.

[22] Similarly, Demosthenes (60.33) reports that both the orphans and the parents of the war-dead will receive assistance (not only distinction but also 'tender care'), but this does not seem to include any particular material support.

[23] [Pl.] *Menex.*: orphans and mothers (248e), care for orphans (248d). In the *Phaedo* (116a), Plato tells us that after Socrates' death, his disciples felt like orphans.

own, or with their sons,[24] be looked after by their adult children, or return to their natal families. Some evidence suggests that women might live together.[25]

However, that a woman's natal family might provide the support and protection needed was far from certain, nor was it a matter of law.[26] There is some evidence of the strain such support could put on a household: Xenophon reports how Aristarchus prevails on his single female relatives, who are living with him as his dependants, to support themselves by their weaving and bread-making.[27] He complains of being in great need, and explains to Socrates that since the revolution there has been a great exodus to the Piraeus. But only the men seem to have gone, so that 'a crowd of my women-folk left behind, are come to me—sisters, nieces, and cousins—so that we are fourteen in the house without counting the slaves'.[28] He explains that 'there is nothing from the land because our enemies have seized it, and nothing from our house property, now there are so few residents in the city. Portable property finds no buyers, and it's quite impossible to borrow money anywhere.' The next statement is particularly striking: 'It's hard Socrates to let one's people die, but impossible to keep so many in times like these.'

Some commentators have argued that this account of hardship would not have been a typical situation: but this is difficult to judge, especially in light of the subject matter.[29] The women of a household were not a common topic of discourse in ancient Greek texts. Presumably this

---

[24] The sons would look after their mother on their majority; see [Dem.] 46.20 for the case of a son's duty to his *epikleros* mother, and Lysias 24.6 for a son looking after his mother without any inherited resources.

[25] Lys. 3.6 and 29: although this may just be an example of an extended family.

[26] Uncertain: see for example, the apparent lack of support for the widow of Diodotus in Lysias 32: her father and brother in fact appear to have defrauded her sons, and she gave evidence against her father (12–13, 15–17) to the rest of the family; Isaeus 8 is a horror story concerning Diocles and his behaviour towards his half-sisters and their families. Matter of law: see discussion by Cudjoe 2010: 95–7, citing Isae. 8.8–9 and Dem. 41.25–6.

[27] Xen. *Mem.* 2.7.2.

[28] Tr. here and below Marchant and Todd, rev. Henderson 2013. Taylor (2011: 127) uses this as an example of 'women moving alone'; it seems rather better to fit her pattern of 'circular migration' of men—but the two are not exclusive.

[29] Sallares (1991: 433 n. 69) says that this 'is an exaggerated example of the unbalanced sex ratio'.

Dependence and Vulnerability 297

was because such a situation was likely to remain undiscussed until something brought it, usually dramatically, into the public eye. Examples of this happening include the speaker of *Against Simon* describing how he has taken in his sister and her daughters, in his account of Simon's outrageous invasion of his home; or the speaker of *On the Property of Aristophanes*, who has taken on his sister and her many children after the execution of her husband.[30]

If there was no natal family to return to, a woman's future marriage prospects were likely to be limited.[31] A woman might remarry as soon as her husband had died; and, indeed, this might take place against a woman's will.[32] Generally, remarriage was much easier for wealthy women, who appear to have been much in demand, but it would have been desirable, even a necessity, for poor women.[33] As the example of Demosthenes' own mother, Cleobule, demonstrates, the question of remarriage was also potentially fraught with dangers.[34] It suggests that even wealthy households—whose affairs, presumably, were in sufficient order that they could be left for the wife to manage on her own—were potentially extremely vulnerable.

The case *Against Diogiton* reinforces this aspect with disturbing details.[35] The background to the case is the death of Diodotus, who is killed while on military service, but has provided for his family in his will. His wife is also his niece, and it is her father, Diogiton, who is executor of the will. But Diogiton's primary concern is not for the welfare of his daughter and grandchildren. First, he conceals the death from the family; then he marries off the bereaved wife, and sends away her children. When the boys come of age, he explains to them that he has had to spend most of their inheritance—now they must support themselves. They are fortunate: when they seek help

---

[30] Lys. 3.6–7 and 29; Lys. 19.9 and 32–5.

[31] Cudjoe (2010: 98–9) argues this on the basis that fathers and brothers appear to have been under a moral obligation to marry and dower their sisters. He cites as examples of fathers: Isae. 8.7–8, 11.39; Lys. 19.14–15, 32.6; Dem. 27.5, 28.15–16, 29.43, 40.6–7, 20–2, and 56–7; of brothers: Isae. 2.3–6, 11.38–9; Lys 19.33, 13.45.

[32] A frequent occurrence: of forty-eight widows in the orators, eighteen out of twenty-five who were young and of child-bearing age got remarried at the death of their husbands (see Cudjoe 2010: 114 n. 250; Hunter 1989: 294).

[33] Wealthy woman: Dem. 30.33; compare [Dem.] 59.7–8. Poorer woman: [Dem.] 59.113. There were particular legal protections ensuring marriage for wealthy heiresses; see Dem. 43.54.

[34] Dem. 27; see also [Dem.] 45 (for the example of Archippe) and Isae. 7.

[35] Lys. 32.

from their mother, she turns to her daughter's husband and this court case ensues. This example also draws attention to the potential for considerable tensions around the breaking up and reformation of households, with particular hazards for children. This is a common aspect of the forensic speeches, where embezzling male relatives appear with disturbing frequency.[36] And this brings us to consideration of the situation of orphans.[37]

Orphans

Model life tables suggest that in the ancient world the death of the father of a family before the children reached the age of fifteen was very common indeed.[38] As we have seen, taking care of widows and orphans was not necessarily viewed as a public duty, but rather as a private obligation that the state would protect.[39] Guardianship was the usual response: a father would arrange for this in his will. If he did not, the responsibility fell to the closest male agnate (but this could introduce conflicts of interest), or the eponymous archon would appoint a guardian. The guardian was meant to manage an orphan's estate and business affairs, handing it over when they came of age: the corpus of forensic speeches shows how often this was perceived to have been mismanaged.[40] As Aristotle tells us, the eponymous archon had a number of responsibilities towards orphans and heiresses, including overseeing the institution of a guardianship (and any rival claims made in these instances) and ensuring guardians provided maintenance; fining or supervising lawsuits brought against those who did orphans or heiresses or their property any harm, and granting leases of houses (receiving rents if necessary) of orphans and heiresses until they

---

[36] It is balanced by the folk-tale theme of the wicked stepmother; see Golden 1990: 143–4 and Watson 1995.

[37] Wives and children evacuated in times of crisis, for example, during the Persian invasion and the Peloponnesian War: Hdt. 8.41.1, Thuc. 1.89.3, Lys. 2.34, ML 23.6–8; cf. Thuc. 2.6.4, 2.78.3, 4.123.4; Isoc. 6.73–4; Lys. 12.97 and 16.4; cf. Dem. 19.194, Men. *Sik.* 281–2.

[38] Hübner and Ratzan 2009b: 9, as many as a third of all children 'in every social and economic stratum over the entire Mediterranean' and 'another third before they reached the age of twenty-five'.

[39] Ibid.: 13.

[40] A good example is found in Isae. 5.9–11; but that the topos was powerful and misused is discussed in Dem. 38.19–20 and again in [Dem.] 53.29.

reached the age of fourteen.[41] We also know that their property was protected by laws that precluded a guardian from putting their property at risk, for example through a bottomry loan.[42]

However, even if we argue that the joint family type prevailed in Classical Greece, this would not necessarily mean that there were male relatives available to offer support; this was perhaps especially the case in times of war or *stasis*.[43] In periods of heavy military losses, it seems likely that there would be more bereaved women and children needing support, and fewer extended families able to absorb them. Indeed, Plato in designing his own city, including marriage laws, suggests that there may be times when it is not possible for young women left fatherless to find an eligible male relative, or indeed suitable men in the city itself.[44] And this literary evidence is supported by Walter Scheidel's analysis of ancient demographic realities, which concludes that it was likely that there would have been few agnatic relations to fill the role of guardian, especially for those children born to older men.[45] In their place, non-relatives could be and were appointed: Cudjoe suggests that this might happen because of a lack of available or trusted relatives, or to enhance connections.[46] Children could also be sent out to work in order to support themselves, and could be apprenticed by either parent (although evidence for this is sparse); it is possible that some exposed children would have been rescued for precisely this purpose.[47]

---

[41] We also hear of *orphanophylakes* in Xen. *Vect.* 2.7; elsewhere *orphanistai*: see *Suda* s.v. *Orphaniston* (omicron 652, Adler); Soph. *Aj.* 512. Cf. 'Old Oligarch' 3.4 (with discussion in den Boer 1979: 52).

[42] [Arist.] *Ath. Pol.* 56.6-7, and see also Dem. 37.45, 43.75, Aeschin. 1.58, and Isae. 11.6. Other protections for orphans included exemption from public services for a year after they came of age: Lys. 32.24-5.

[43] Gallant 1991: 27-30; Lys. 13.45-6: children left orphaned because of the persecution of the Thirty.

[44] Pl. *Leg.* 925a-b.   [45] Scheidel 2009: 31-40.

[46] Cudjoe 2010: 181-2. For examples of friends appointed, see Dem. 27.4-5; cf. also Diog. Laert. 5.12-13.

[47] There is little evidence for apprenticeship, but a letter survives from a boy called Lesis, apprenticed in a foundry, complaining about his treatment (Harris 2004; Eidinow and Taylor 2010). Lesis writes to his mother, and a man (Xenocles) who is not his father. Golden (2003: 18) discusses apprenticeships within families. Later evidence suggests a mother or father could make the arrangement (see Golden 2009: 48). As an example of a girl child who appears to have been sold into slavery, and was possibly a foundling, the story of Neaera and her upbringing is a reminder that child prostitution was also part of this picture ([Dem.] 59). See discussion by Saller 2007: 108; see also Lys. 20.11, Isoc. 4.68, Arist. *Pol.* 1323a; and on infant

An overview of the evidence for Athens suggests that there was little regulated and consistent provision for families in which the father had died, at least before the end of the fifth century. There is some evidence for the provision of food made by Solon for widows and orphans, but this is contested.[48] By the fourth century, there appears to be some support for some male children.[49] Some more certain intervention by the state does seem to have occurred with regard to the effects of war in some locations. Outside Athens, for example, there is evidence that some cities made provision for families of the war-dead: a text from Thasos of uncertain date includes provision for the parents of the dead, along with their children, both male and female. According to Diodorus Siculus, similar provisions were found in a decree from Rhodes.[50] But in the case of Athens, the evidence for the support of family members—even male children—of those who had died in battle is patchy and uncertain. This may be the result of our evidence, or, indeed, of the nature of the legislation itself. The appearance of such legislation may have been intermittent, perhaps a response to some crisis, rather than a long-term promise of welfare support. We do not know the circumstances of the Thasian decree, but the Rhodians passed their measures while besieged by Demetrius at the end of the fourth century, and the result was, apparently, increased morale and support.

Pericles' statement in the funeral speech as recorded by Thucydides is the first unequivocal indication of there being a law to support the children of those who die in battle.[51] It has been argued by some, drawing on the phrasing of the Greek, that this was a new law of its time, and it appears from other evidence only to have lasted into the mid-fourth century.[52] If we take ps-Plato's *Menexenus* as offering some reliable account of previous practice, it appears that these children

---

exposure and enslavement, see Ael. *VH* 2.7, Plut. *De am. prol* 497e; and de Ste Croix 1981: 169–70.

[48] This is attributed to Solon; the sources are late: Diog. Laert. 1.55) and lexicographers, Harp, *Suda*, s.v. *Sitos* (sigma 502 Adler) and Phot. 514.6, argue that a law was introduced by Solon providing food to women and orphans; see Stroud 1971: 288.

[49] State support: Arist. *Pol.* 1268a8–11, [Arist.] *Ath. Pol.* 24.3.

[50] For Thasos, see *Thasos* I 141.5, and Pomeroy 1982: 116–18. Rhodes: Diodorus Siculus (20.84.3).

[51] Thuc. 2.46.1. Den Boer (1979: 46) argues that this is a new piece of legislation; see also Cratinus fr. 183 K-A.

[52] Den Boer (1979: 51) argues that 'there were rules governing the care of war orphans, but there is no trace of any "laws" before the fourth century'. Aeschin. 3.154 and Isoc. 6.82 seem to talk about it in the past tense.

were paraded in the theatre of Dionysus, dressed in their new armour. A herald announced that their fathers had died as brave men and the state had brought the boys up and was now about to let them manage their own affairs, since they had become adults. Thus, the sources suggest, they were separated from the ephebes, by attaining maturity without a period of transition.[53]

The evidence of a later law, dating to around 403–402 BCE—the final part of which survives on stone—seeks to prevent the extension of the provision of support given to the sons of citizens to bastards (*nothoi*) and (oddly) adopted orphans (*poietoi*) whose fathers died fighting against the Thirty.[54] The decree was proposed by one Theozotides, whose political career, and perhaps its contentious nature, may be attested by the discovery of an elaborate curse tablet on which his name is inscribed.[55] There was opposition: a papyrus fragment of a speech by Lysias, disputing the decree, survives.[56] The editor of the inscribed text, Ronald Stroud, suggests that Lysias' attack on Theozotides failed, but others are not so sure, since the wording of the inscription is ambivalent: it refers to the beneficiaries of the decree as 'the children of these men' (sc. the Athenian dead).[57] The context for the decree is likely to have been the re-enactment of the Periclean citizenship law—so that the *nothoi* and *poietoi* would have been born in a period when the legislation was relaxed (Lysias' argument), but now was re-enacted (presumably Theozotides' case).[58] If we take this legislation as an illustration of contemporary concern with maintaining Athenian identity, then the focus on bastard sons at least makes sense—but this does not provide an explanation for the decree's attempt to exclude adopted sons. Instead, as Niall Slater has suggested, this may instead be regarded as evidence for the city's concerns about its available finances. It may suggest that posthumous adoption was widespread, with many families finding they had no legitimate sons; it may also have been a process that was being abused by families seeking to take advantage of this benefit.[59]

---

[53] Loraux 1986: 57; details of the ritual: [Pl.] *Menex.* 249a3–b2, Aeschin. 3.154.
[54] Ogden (1996: 79) suggests that Theozotides may have thought that adopted children would have support from their new fathers.
[55] See Stroud 1971: 285–7. On the curse tablet, see Eidinow 2013: 174.
[56] *P. Hib.* I 14 (TM 61454; Lysias 128–50 Carey).
[57] Ogden 1996: 79.   [58] See Stroud 1971: 285–7.
[59] Slater 1993. He considers (84) that the decree may have been an attack on the legislation of the Thirty, specifically the revision of Solon's law on adoption, which

Whatever the outcome of this particular debate, however, the evidence as a whole suggests that any provision made was only for certain male orphans. In turn, for girl children, even less support seems to have been organized, although there was protection in place for heiresses, as Aristotle describes.[60] We know of no state dowry supply at Athens, as mentioned in regulations from fourth-century Thasos and Rhodes, although there is reference to a law that required the nearest kin to supply the poor, fatherless daughters of relatives with dowries (or marry them themselves).[61] Girl children who had no form of active male support in this environment were extremely vulnerable. As an example of possible dangers, the new fragment of Hyperides' *Against Timandrus* appears to give us a brief glimpse of one girl whose legal guardian separated her from her brother at the age of seven, carrying her away to Lemnos; the brother was unable to recognize her when they met again.[62] In many ways, this young woman was lucky: her case was pursued by her brother. But if, for example, she had had no brother, or if it was the brother who had sold her into slavery (as occurred in another case),[63] then she would have had little recourse.

Unmarried Girls

Girls without a dowry would find it hard to find a husband, but staying at home in a poor household was likely to be expensive and difficult.[64] Poverty was relative, but a drop in standards could prove

---

had been the cause of much litigation. Rubinstein (1993: 23, cited by Slater 1993: 82) notes that we know of ten testamentary adoptions where the testator is identified: of these, five died in war and five while travelling.

[60] [Arist.] *Ath. Pol.* 56.6–7.

[61] The fabled dowering of the daughters of Aristeides (Dem. 20.115, Aeschin. 3.258, Plut. *Arist.* 27.1–3) appears to have been highly unusual. Thasos and Rhodes: see above, note 50. [Plat.] *Menex.* 248d–249b appears to be following this precedent: his own system of state support for war orphans mentions only boys. Kin to supply: in Isae. 1.39 these are only referred to in terms of daughters; in Dem. 43.54 the law is given in more detail and refers to heiresses.

[62] Tchernetska *et al.* 2007. The two sisters had lost both parents; the brother appears to have had a mother still living.

[63] As Aristogiton sold his sister (and mother): see Dem. 25.

[64] Apollodorus is unable to give his daughter in marriage because of poverty: [Dem.] 59.8 and see further [Dem.] 59.112. For fathers faced with girl children whom they cannot feed, see Ar. *Pax* 119–23 and Ar. *Ach.* 731–5, where Dicaeopolis sells his daughters in the marketplace.

disastrous.[65] However, the problems presented by the lack of a dowry may have paled at times in contrast to the lack of available husbands. There is ancient evidence that seems to allude to just such a predicament during the war years themselves: in Aristophanes' *Lysistrata*, in conversation with the magistrate, Lysistrata explains how girls have not been able to get married, but must 'lie single because of the army'; this may mean that husbands have gone away, or allude to deaths in battle. She refers to older women who are 'left sitting at home clutching at any straw of an omen', and just before this comment, Lysistrata has referred to bearing sons and seeing them sent off to war as hoplites (the magistrate asks her not to raise painful memories).[66] Although this is a comedy, and so cannot be taken as a straightforward report on events, nevertheless, it is likely to have been making some reference to the contemporary situation (some scholars have argued that this may be an allusion to the impacts of the disastrous Sicilian expedition).[67]

Not only the war itself, but Athens' concomitant internal conflicts may also have been perceived to be a cause of this problem: Lysias in *Against Eratosthenes* tops his list of the crimes of the Thirty with the point that their actions 'prevented many men's daughters from being given in marriage'.[68] The remarriage of widows would also have removed eligible men from the available pool. This may have been one of the factors in the development of a decree we find recorded in later sources that allowed an Athenian citizen to marry one citizen woman and get citizen children from another.[69] Although the authenticity of this decree has been debated, others see it as having been prompted by a lack of manpower following the Sicilian disaster.[70]

---

[65] Dem. 28.21: Demosthenes says that, unless his patrimony is returned to him, his sister will not find anything befitting her status because of the poverty of the household. See also Men. *Aspis*, where a brother's death results in poverty for a young woman.

[66] Ar. *Lys.* 591–7 (tr. Sommerstein 1990).

[67] ll. 587–90; see Sommerstein 1990, *ad loc*. The plight of unmarried girls is also a theme of tragedies: cf. Aesch. *Eum.* 959–60; Soph. *El.* 188, *Ant.* 810–13 (cf. 654); Eur. *IT* 369–71, *Med.* 985, *Or.* 1109, *Hec.* 416–18 and 612, and *IA* 461.

[68] Lys. 12.21; see also Lys. 13.45 and Hyp. 1 fr. IVb.12–13. See Schaps 1979: 41.

[69] Sources for the decree: Hieronymus (frr. 44–5 Wehrli) in Diog. Laert. 2.26, who associates this decree with Socrates, as does Ath. 13.555d–556b; Aul. Gell. *NA* 15.20.6 relates it to Euripides; see also *Suda*, s.v. *Leipandrein* (lambda 377, Adler).

[70] Sceptical discussions: Hignett 1952: 344–5, Woodbury 1973: 24–5; but in favour: Harrison 1968: 17 and MacDowell 1978: 90. Golden (1981: 330), who cites these discussions, argues that it does not seem improbable, although 'best to regard this as

Without it, a young woman would have lived as a *pallake* (concubine) with a man, and any resulting children would have suffered civic restrictions.[71]

Across all this material, we can glimpse only fragments of women's lives—and distorted fragments at that. But even these suggest a lived experience in which the neat categories of citizen and non-citizen were often blurred by the demands of poverty and the need to survive, while the risk of destitution prompted the crossing of social boundaries. For example, both Demosthenes and Isaeus mention how the poor could be bribed to take on non-citizens, in the sense of claiming them as relatives or adopting them; and it has been suggested that this is, in fact, what (in [Demosthenes] 59) Stephanus did in marrying off Neaera's daughter Phano to Phrastor and Theogenes.[72] Another situation that might give rise to such an arrangement was when unmarried girls became pregnant, a situation which would ruin a daughter's chance of a respectable marriage. Such a catastrophe is found at the centre of a number of plays by Menander—along with the important resolution that the girl will be able to marry her rapist.[73] In the *Adelphoi*, for example, the conversation between Geta and Sostrata that follows the rape of Sostrata's daughter reveals the range of options—and the likely reality. Geta urges that the rape be kept secret, since the wealthy young man will probably deny it happened, and the daughter's reputation will be ruined, while Sostrata contends that she will take the rapist to court and force him to marry her daughter.

---

our sources do, as an exceptional situation caused by heavy losses in the war'. Some scholars focus on only the concern to produce citizen children; so Strauss (1986: 74) suggests the point of the decree may have been that the second woman could be a non-citizen, and that it coincides with abrogation of citizenship law. This is accepted by Cudjoe (2010: 21 n. 50 and 133 n. 300), but cf. Kapparis (2012), who argues against the decree on the grounds that only one citizen parent was needed to produce citizen children, according to Dem. 57.3. Ogden (1996: 72–7) traces the legislation that relates to citizenship, arguing that the Periclean citizenship law was probably revoked before 403 BCE (he speculates 411 BCE) and then reinstated with the restoration of the democracy in 403 BCE in the archonship of Eucleides (see Harrison 1968: 26 n. 1). [Dem] 59.16 (so, sometime before 340 BCE) indicates it is again illegal to cohabit with a non-citizen, but since this clearly continued, it suggests that cohabitation with the intention of producing legitimate children was not possible (see Just 1989: 62–3).

[71] See Ogden 1996, esp. 152–65 for restrictions on citizenship. Children excluded from *anchisteia*: Ar. *Av.* 1649–68, Isae. 6.47, Dem. 43.51.

[72] See Isae. 12.2; Dem. 57.25: those who are forced by poverty to adopt foreigners. On Phano [Dem.] 59.50 and 72, see Ogden 1996: 124.

[73] Omitowoju 2002: 166–203.

However, as we are told by a lamenting slave in a fragment from Menander's play *Plokion* or 'Necklace', those parents who were too poor to make arrangements would have to find some other way to take care of the future of their daughter. An extreme solution (presumably intended to be comic) is threatened by Niceratus in the *Samia*, who, when he thinks his unmarried daughter is pregnant, threatens to burn the baby and then to kill the woman (Chrysis) protecting it.[74] More mundanely, away from the comic stage, it is also possible that some young women would simply have been left to fend for themselves.[75]

With no economic support from a relationship, a woman would have to find work. Some might follow the armies, perhaps involved in food preparation, although it was more likely that many went along as personal attendants, entertainers, and sexual partners.[76] If we return to the situation in European communities following the Black Death, one result may have been that changes in the social structure created more opportunities for women to enter the workforce at home.[77] For some women it was more essential that they take advantage of this situation because they had no other means of survival, as the speaker of Demosthenes' speech *Against Eubulides*, one Euxitheus of Halimous, explains. As described elsewhere, Euxitheus has been evicted from his deme, in response to the scrutiny of the demes instigated by the decree of

---

[74] Men. *Adelphoi* 337–41 and 350, respectively. Men. *Plokion* fr. 298 K–A (Aul. Gell. *NA* 2.23.15). Men. *Sam.* 553–4 and 560–1.

[75] Omitowoju (2002: 215) suggests that it is unclear 'whether these negative responses would result in fathers repudiating daughters so that they are forced to cross the boundary and lose all claims to respectability'.

[76] Dalby (1992) argues that, in relation to the campaign described in Xenophon's *Anabasis*, it was important for the men of the Ten Thousand to prepare and serve their own food, but Loman (2004: 49–50) argues more generally that women were 'probably' responsible for food production on foreign campaigns. Her argument is logical: the 'fewer men were tied to food production, the more men were available for fighting'. However, she offers no evidence for this (although it may be that there is no evidence). Note that at Thuc. 2.78.3, 110 women are left in Plataea to bake bread; while in the preparations for the Sicilian expedition (6.22), we find Nicias detailing the need to take bakers ('from the mills'; their gender is unclear); the implication is that this is unusual. For women as entertainers: Xen. *An.* 6.1.12; women accompanying the Greeks: Xen. *An.* 4.3.19 and 5.4.33; women smuggled in to the camp: Xen. *An.* 4.1.14; daughters given to mark an agreement: Xen. *Hell.* 4.1.14.

[77] French (2011: 9) gives a succinct overview of the situation, and of the ensuing debate by scholars over whether or not this is to be considered a 'golden age for women'. See, for example, Mate (1998: 11–20), who stresses that traditional gender roles did not change. She also emphasizes the fluctuating nature of this employment, such that women found themselves out of work as the male labour force met demand.

Demophilus of 346/5 BCE.[78] He must show that both his parents were citizens. First, he defends his father's foreign accent on the grounds that he was held prisoner during the second half of the Peloponnesian War (the Decelean War). Then he protests that his mother's status has also been questioned because she has been forced to take on a series of jobs that are not respectable: she sells ribbons in the market; she worked as a wet nurse.[79] However, he argues, this was because of the misfortune that Athens was suffering at the time, and he refers to her husband being absent on military service.[80] He points out that there were many Athenian women citizens who worked in such jobs, or at the loom, or in the vineyards.[81]

Similarly, recent analysis suggests that, although we may not have much palpable evidence, many women were employed in agricultural tasks.[82] The law limiting their transactions to one *medimnos* (if we accept it had influence) would still allow participation in petty commerce: women could take part in various crafts, especially woolworking.[83] We also find evidence among grave epigrams for women working: in fact, a profession is a separate theme *only* in grave epigrams from Attica—for both men and women, appearing in 75 per cent of the grave epigrams for men and 25 per cent of those for women.[84] The professions named for women are one priestess, two nurses, and one midwife, also called a physician;[85] but there are also a couple of epigrams in which the vocabulary appears to indicate some kind of labour, without designating a particular profession.[86] As Tsagalis has observed, this is an important indicator of shifts in the attitudes and expectations of this society: bridging public and private, it emphasizes with pride that work is essential for personal survival as

---

[78] See in this volume, pp. 197 and 320.
[79] Dem. 57.18–19, 35.   [80] Dem. 57.42–5.
[81] The plays of Aristophanes show women engaged in various occupations, as do images on vases, but with concomitant difficulties of knowing the status of these women, e.g. Ar. *Thesm.* 443–58 for a woman who is employed in garland-weaving after her husband dies in Cyprus.
[82] Scheidel 1995.
[83] Schaps 1979: 19, Brock 1994, but cf. Scheidel 1995. For the idea that this was not always observed in practice, see Cudjoe 2010: 120 n. 262, 157–8, and discussion, 293.
[84] Tsagalis 2008: 208, citing Breuer 1995: 48; further discussion, this volume, pp. 323–5.
[85] See also Stears 1995: 123–4. Priestess: *CEG* 566; nurse: *CEG* 534 and 571; midwife: *CEG* 569.
[86] Tsagalis 2008: 212; see *CEG* 491 and 537.

Dependence and Vulnerability 307

well as political well-being, and highlights the role of the individual.[87] This is a development typical of the fourth century more generally, but even more remarkable when we consider that this focuses, albeit rarely, on women.

However, there were professions that were not such sources of pride: how representative a type is the girl described by the fourth-century comic poet Antiphanes who has no relations to act as her guardians and so works as a *hetaira*?[88] The fear that this might be the fate of oneself or of that of the women in one's family may have been greater than the reality. Nevertheless, Apollodorus is certainly appealing to a strong image when he argues that the acquittal of Neaera would create a precedent by legitimizing Neaera's conduct: it could mean that poor women of citizen status would be unable to marry if they had to compete for husbands with prostitutes who could provide a substantial dowry, and so would themselves be forced to turn to prostitution.[89] Similar fears are referred to in a speech by Isaeus, which reports that Athenian men would keep marrying prostitutes. These passages suggest that there was concern that some prostitutes must therefore have managed to conceal themselves as citizen women.[90]

Prostitution could involve mobility: for example, we have considered those who moved with the armies. Even for a free woman, the nature of her economic dependency would dictate where she had to live. If the prostitute was also a slave, this mobility would be enforced by those who had bought her. Neaera, for example, moves according to the requirements of her owners, or to whom she owes money. The *hetaira* Lais seems to have had a similar career: born at Hykkara, Sicily in 422 BCE, she arrived in Corinth after Hykkara was plundered (415 BCE), as a prisoner of war. She clearly spent time in Athens, perhaps through her association with the philosopher and student of Socrates, Aristippus, who travelled widely, and seems to have written a piece about her ('To Lais'). Her death is said to have occurred in Thessaly, where she had gone as companion to a

---

[87] Tsagalis 2008: 213 (further discussion, this volume, p. 325).
[88] Antiphanes fr. 210 K-A. [89] [Dem.] 59: 111-14.
[90] Isae. 3.17-18, since [Dem.] 59.16 tells us that Athenian men could not marry foreign women. See also Dem. 22.61: both parents must have been citizens as well as prostitutes, since the children were Athenian citizens; Lys. fr. 299 (Carey) tells us that the *hetaira* Nais had a *kyrios*; see discussion in Cohen 2000 and 2008.

Thessalian returning home.[91] It was possible for some of these women to make considerable sums of money (Sinope from the Black Sea is one famous example).[92]

But, as the almost incidental stories of the orators reveal, to live such a life in Athens could be highly precarious. The story of Zobia, as recounted in *Against Aristogiton* (1) is a fine example: it describes what happens to a woman of metic status who requests the return of a loan from a man (Aristogiton) who is unwilling to pay it back. When she starts to complain to other people about him, he charges her with not paying her metic tax. Zobia manages to avoid being sold into slavery because she has the support of her *prostates*; but, as noted above, Aristogiton's mother and sister were not so lucky. And they also illustrate how a relationship to a citizen family member might not only not provide security, but could even present further danger.[93]

'AMONG THE PRISONERS BROUGHT TO APOLLO AT DELPHI WAS MANTO'

The story of Manto, daughter of Tiresias, albeit legendary, brings together a number of themes discussed so far. According to Pausanias, Manto was taken prisoner after the fall of Thebes to Thersander and the Argives. Her father had died during the journey to Delphi. She is told to go to Klaros, and is then captured by the Cretan leader Rhacius—her son will be the seer, Mopsus.[94] Although there is no direct evidence that she is a seer herself, Manto's story connects experiences of dependency on male relatives, enforced itinerancy, enforced sexual service—and introduces one last dimension: mantic powers.

---

[91] Birth: Steph. Byz., s.v. *krastos*; Ath. 13.589a, [1. 182]; arrival in Corinth: Plut. *Alc.* 39, Ath. 13.588c; associated with Aristippus: Diog. Laert. 2.75, Ath. 13.588e; and Diogenes ('the Cynic') of Sinope: Ath. 13.588e. She is said to have died in Thessaly, in a temple of Aphrodite, at the hands of a group of envious women: Plut. *Amat.* 767f and Ath. 13.589a–b; see Strothmann 2014.

[92] See Amphis fr. 22.12 K–A. [93] Dem. 25.57 and 25.55 and 65; see this volume, p. 302.

[94] See Paus. 7.3.1–2. We might also turn to another Manto, daughter of Polyidus (great-grandson of Melampus), whose grave could be seen by Pausanias at Megara (1.43.5); she and her sister Astycratea had journeyed there with their itinerant father, who had come to Megara to purify Alcathous for the murder of his son Callipolis.

In Greek texts, the word *agurtes* and related terms are used to refer to beggars.[95] But by the fifth century, this family of terms has acquired a more nuanced meaning: to describe itinerant sellers of ritual practices of various kinds, and it has become instantiated as a term of abuse.[96] An illustrative example—one of the most famous uses of the term—shows Oedipus insulting Tiresias in Sophocles's *Oedipus Tyrannus* as 'a crafty *agurtes* who has sight only when it comes to profit, but in his art is blind'.[97] But the earliest occurrence of the term, linking beggary and ritual practice, seems to be around 458 BCE, in Aeschylus' *Agamemnon*, where it is used by Cassandra, the sad, mad Trojan princess, cursed with a gift of prophecy that no one will believe, as she describes how she has been mocked by friends who have turned on her, and abused her.[98] A related term, *ageirousan*, appears in a fragment of a play by Aeschylus, the *Semele or Hydrophoroi*. We know very little about it, except that it features Hera transformed into a priestess, begging (*ageirousan*) on behalf of the Nymphs of the river Inachos in Argos.[99] In both these examples, one a first use of the term, the description is of a woman fallen on hard times, and she is associated with ritual practice. In the first instance, the woman is a *mantis* forced to take to the streets; in the other, a poor woman who begs in a ritual context. They are both remarkable women, and this draws attention to how far they have fallen. The idea of the bereft and begging woman is far from new (think of Andromache's heart-rending description in the *Iliad* of the miserable future her son will endure, without a father, forced to live as a beggar and an outcast).[100] However, perhaps these representations of begging

---

[95] See LSJ s.v. *agurtazo*, 'to collect by begging' (e.g. Hom. *Od.* 19.284).

[96] This process is charted in Eidinow Forthcoming b, on which this discussion draws. See also Flower (2008: 66) and Giammellaro (2013), who argues that it was simply a term intended to indicate a beggar, and that it was the marginal status of beggars that brings it inevitably to have associations with supernatural powers, comparing this to the modern idea of the gypsy.

[97] Soph. *OT* 388-9.   [98] Aesch. *Ag.* 1269-74.

[99] Aesch. fr. 220a-c (Sommerstein 2008) (= fr. 168 Radt) and see Pl. *Resp.* 381d4-7 (ὡς ἱέρειαν ἀγείρουσαν); two lines from the fragments (fr. 220a 16-17) are attributed by Asclepiades to the *Xantriai* (Schol. Ar. *Ran.* 1344), followed by Dillon (2002: 96) and Dickie (2001: 80), but Sommerstein (2008: 224-7) argues for the *Semele or Hydrophoroi*. The practice of women collecting gifts in honour of divinities that aid childbirth also seems to be alluded to in Herodotus' description (4.35.3) of the Delian women collecting gifts for Arge and Opis (two Hyperborean virgins).

[100] Hom. *Il.* 22.446ff.

women on the Athenian stage indicate that the prominence of this group in society had become more marked.

In literature of the fourth century, the term continues to present this associations between beggardom, travelling, and ritual. This is largely a tale of male seers: they are, by far, more prominent in our sources.[101] However, their situation also has relevance to the environment we have been describing: the increasing and increasingly bitter comments about (male) seers across literary genres turn on the perceived monetization of magic, reinforcing the impression that this activity was increasingly a resort of those forced to make a living.[102] Meanwhile, evidence for women *manteis* is much rarer and more partial, found in assorted literary and epigraphic sources from across places and centuries that comes together to allow a glimpse of a half-seen underlying reality. Sometimes these are allusions to groups of women. For example, we find in Hippocratic treatises the female *engastrimuthoi*, or 'belly-talkers', described with some contempt; and in an early third-century BCE decree, from Miletos, women who 'perform initiations for Dionysus in the city or in the country' are required to report to the priestess of Dionysus in the city and pay a regular fee.[103] Sometimes we learn of individuals: 'Asterie the seer' appears in a collection of epigrams; one 'Satyra the seer' is commemorated in an epitaph dating to the third century BCE; and a stele from Mantinea, dating to the fifth century BCE, depicts what must surely be a female seer.[104]

Such women may once have taken to the road, and then settled (bringing to mind the roaming pattern of the seer Thrasyllus, in Isocrates' *Aegineticus*).[105] For example, in Plato's *Symposium*, we famously meet Diotima, a priestess from Mantinea, who is described as having managed to delay the onset of a plague in Athens for ten years through her directions about sacrifices. This woman is teaching

---

[101] See Flower 2008: 212.

[102] The term is also used in Pl. *Resp.* 364b2–365a3 (cf. *Leg* 845e3); Cratinus in his *Drapetides* (Storey 2011a: fr. 62); and Lysippus (Storey 2011b: fr. 6b) in his *Bacchae*, where, according to Hesychius s.v. *Agursikubelis* (alpha 461), he used the term to mock the Athenian seer and politician Lampon.

[103] *Engastrimuthoi* in Hipp. *Epid.* 5.63 and 7.28 and in Philochorus (*FGrHist* 328 F 78); Initiations at Miletos: *LSAM* 48.19ff.; see Burkert 1987: 33.

[104] Satyra: *SEG* 35.626; see Flower 2008: 214. Asterie: the 'New Posidippus' (*P. Mil. Vogl.* VIII 309) AB 26 (IV 36–9).The stele from Mantinea depicts a woman with a liver in her hand: Flower 2008: 212; see discussion by Möbius 1967.

[105] See this volume, p. 290.

Socrates about love, and in the course of the conversation outlines the connections between skills in love and skills in such supernatural services as 'all divination and priestcraft concerning sacrifice and ritual and incantations, and all soothsaying and sorcery'.[106] As Michael Flower has argued, whether or not Diotima herself is a fictional creation, she represents a 'type of individual who was recognisable to Plato's contemporaries'.[107] She is discussed by modern scholars in terms of her presentation as a philosopher, but we must not forget her connections with the supernatural.[108] She is rare not only for her intellect but for the ease with which she is depicted discussing these techniques. As we will see, other such female practitioners of the fourth century seem to have engendered great anxiety.

---

[106] Pl. *Symp.* 201d.   [107] Flower 2008: 212.
[108] For example, Waithe 1987, Hawthorne 1994. Halperin (1990a: 113–52 and 1990b, a shorter version of the article) discusses the construction of Diotima as a '"woman"', representing (297) 'the erotics of (male) philosophical intercourse'.

4.4

'Dangerous Women'

In 'Women and Democracy in Fourth-Century Athens', Michael Jameson argued that the writings of certain fourth-century sources, specifically Plato and Aristotle, indicate a view that women enjoyed excessive freedom under the Athenian democracy.[1] Jameson posited that the true target of Plato's and Aristotle's 'fantasies of imminent or present *gunokratia*' was democracy and that their discourse not only brings to bear the rich resources of a misogynistic culture, but also the long-held anxiety of the upper classes that slaves, foreigners, and women will somehow undo the democracy. He notes that those women for whom we have evidence of their trials, Phryne, Ninon, and Theoris, along with other 'dangerous women' who are mentioned or brought to court in this period, tend to be foreigners, and in most cases are associated with slaves.[2] He sees these trials as illustrating the particular kinds of social weakness that the democracy engendered: although 'the public, political sphere remained impregnable so long as the democracy survived, in the area of social relations the discrepancy between ideal and the real had reached a point that it served to fuel anxiety over status relations in general'.[3] Jameson's focus embraces society more generally, and aristocratic dislike of democracy in particular; in what follows, I want to build on his initial arguments in a slightly different direction, by looking more closely at what this evidence reveals in terms of anxieties about 'dangerous women'.

---

[1] Jameson 1997: the title is from his reference (103 n. 11) to 'dangerous women'.
[2] Jameson 1997: 102, citing Plut. *Phoc.* 34, where Plutarch's source appears to blame the presence of slaves, foreigners, disenfranchised citizens, and women for the condemnation of the (anti-democratic) general Phocion and his associates.
[3] Jameson 1997: 103.

A number of such women appear in speeches written by Isaeus, playing a key role in the contestation about matters of inheritance that these present.[4] Alce, for example, appears in a speech probably written in 365/4 BCE, which concerns the estate of (originally) one Euctemon, who had three sons, Philoctemon, Ergamenes, and Hegemon, and two daughters.[5] The speech introduces a number of themes related to the context of warfare that we have explored earlier in this part of the book. All three sons predecease their father—the last to die is Philoctemon in a battle off Chios (6.27). On the death of Euctemon, Philoctemon's nephew Chaerestratus claimed the estate on the grounds that he had been adopted by Philoctemon, and was named in his will. This was opposed by one Androcles, a relative of Euctemon, who claimed the estate for himself, along with Euctemon's daughter in marriage (her husband had died) on the grounds that he was next of kin to this heiress. He then made two further claims: first, that Philoctemon had not made a will; and second that the estate was not liable for adjudication because Euctemon actually had two legitimate sons by a woman called Callippe (to whom he apparently called himself guardian). In response, Chaerestratus had no option but to prosecute Androcles on a *dike pseudomarturion* (case for false witness). This speech, delivered by a friend of Chaerestratus, sets out to prove that Callippe's sons were not legitimate heirs, but were in fact the children of a prostitute, the woman called Alce. And, according to the account given by the speaker, it is Alce who is at the heart of all the wrongdoing that has occurred.

The bulk of the speech is given over to narrating the ways in which Alce inveigled Euctemon, and then Androcles and his associate Antidorus, into committing crimes; in the process, we are given a full picture of Alce's life. It seems that Euctemon owned a building in Piraeus in which he kept a group of prostitutes, managed by one of his freedwomen. Alce was among the prostitutes, and the speaker implies

---

[4] All eleven of Isaeus' surviving speeches (there were perhaps fifty genuine speeches, according to ps.-Plut. *Life of Isaeus*, 839f) concern questions of succession, as do a number of the fragmentary speeches, although the individual charges vary (see Edwards 2007: 2). Harrison (1968: 123) argues: 'This predominance in its turn is probably partly due to the fact that the rules were in the fourth century both complicated and fluid, and this gave play to litigation and the skill of the logographer.'

[5] Isae. 6. Date: Edwards (2007: 100), based on §6.14: fifty years have passed since the departure of the Sicilian expedition in summer 415 BCE.

she had something of a reputation: 'I think many of you know her,' he says to the court, in a trope that we have seen used before.[6]

Alce had been in a relationship with a man called Dion, with whom she had had two sons whom Dion had brought up as his own. When Dion had been forced to flee because of a crime he had committed, Euctemon appears to have taken care of Alce, and she had become manager of an apartment block in the Kerameikos. Euctemon is described as becoming increasingly fond of her, spending 'much of his time in the apartment block; sometimes he even dined with her, abandoning his wife and children and the house he lived in. Despite the protests of his wife and sons, he not only did not stop going there but in the end, he lived there completely.'[7]

With this background filled in, the accusations become more focused—and start to include details that sound familiar. The speaker relates how Euctemon 'was reduced to such a condition by drugs or disease or some other cause', so that Alce was able to persuade him to introduce the elder of her two sons into his *phratry*, under his name.[8] Later, after the death of Philoctemon, the speaker describes how Androcles and Antidorus, in turn, 'fell under the influence of that woman' and together they plotted to acquire Euctemon's estate.[9] Alce is described as 'the woman who destroyed Euctemon's reason', and, more generally, as showing contempt 'not only for the members of Euctemon's family but for the whole city'.[10] She is portrayed as being at the heart of the plot to plunder Euctemon's estate—and, worse still, responsible for his not being properly attended to and buried.[11]

Then we turn from the personal to the religious: Alce, it seems, has disregarded a law concerning religious activity within the city, which the speaker asks to be read aloud for the benefit of the court. Although we do not know what the law was, it has been interpreted as one that regulated attendance at the Thesmophoria.[12] And the speaker follows it with a description of how Alce attended a festival, entering the temple, seeing the activities inside and seeing 'what she

---

[6] Isae. 6.19 (tr. Forster 1927, used throughout this section).
[7] Isae. 6.21.   [8] Isae. 6.21.
[9] Isae. 6.29; note the contemptuous use of *anthropos* to describe her, which may also signify her possible slave status.
[10] Isae. 6.48.   [11] Isae. 6.38–40.
[12] Isae. 6.48–50. Wyse (1904: *ad* 48): 'The law probably contained regulations concerning the Thesmophoria in which women of servile origin or of immoral life were not allowed to participate.'

was not entitled to see'.[13] He concludes with a reading of 'the decrees that the Council passed concerning her', making it sound as if regulation had been passed specifically in response to Alce's activities.[14] Although the speaker does not use explicit terms of impiety to describe her behaviour, the association of ideas is still clear: 'she has dared' to see what she should not have seen. Moreover, he frames this point by emphasizing how the people (and here he addresses the *dikastai* as 'you') framed the law in terms that were 'solemn and pious', and did this because they believed it important 'to honour these goddesses and the other gods'.[15] Alce comes across as a sinister figure, one who has scant respect for the values and structures of polis and *oikos*, who has tremendous influence over the men she meets—who may (possibly) use *pharmaka* to get her way—and who sets the city at risk with regard to the gods.

Alce is remarkably clearly drawn; she provides something of a set of characteristics that we also find used to portray other similar women. One example is the woman who is the focus of another speech by Isaeus (undated), *On the Estate of Pyrrhus*. She is the mother of a woman called Phile, and may or may not have been a slave, and/or a *hetaira*: the ambiguity and fluidity of her identity is the crucial problem in the case.[16] The estate in question was inherited from Pyrrhus by Endius, his nephew, whom he had adopted. When Endius died, because he had no children, a number of claimants appeared: on the one hand, Xenocles of Kopros, who claimed that his wife Phile was the legitimate daughter of Pyrrhus; and, on the other, Endius' younger brother (the speaker), on behalf of his mother. Much of the case depends on the outcome of a previous trial, in which Xenocles was prosecuted successfully for false witness after making a declaration that his wife's mother was married to Pyrrhus, and

---

[13] Isae. 6.50.
[14] It is possible that this could be an existing decree that he brings up here to reinforce his point, but, as Wyse (1904: *ad* 51.5) observes, the Council met in accordance with a law of Solon in the Eleusinion on the day after the Mysteries to receive a report from the Basileus Archon about the conduct of the festival. Although the Thesmophoria may not have received the same attention, perhaps the Council still received some kind of report and made some kind of judgment.
[15] Isae. 6.49–50.
[16] See discussion in Wyse 1904: 3.39. Date uncertain; Edwards (2007: 48) reports that it is possible that it was 389 BCE. Aspects of this case are also explored on pp. 196 and 204 of this volume.

therefore his wife, Phile, could legitimately claim his estate. He, in turn announced his intention to prosecute those who had witnessed Pyrrhus's will. In turn, and possibly to prevent this prosecution, our speaker took Nicodemus, the brother of Phile's mother, to court, with an indictment for false witness, since he had claimed at the previous trial to have given his sister in marriage to Pyrrhus, and that Phile was her child: this is the case for which this speech was composed.

According to the speaker, the woman-masquerading-as-wife seems to have remained unchallenged in her position, but quite what her position was is something of a mystery. It is far from clear that the woman was a *hetaira*—although the speaker stresses how she was available to any man who wanted her both before and after her marriage to Pyrrhus—or, even if she was a *hetaira*, she was not a citizen.[17] For our purposes, we can see how, in order to make his case against Phile and her mother, the speaker, Pyrrhus's nephew, seems to be appealing to familiar images of dangerous women. In the case of the mother, the speaker observes how other 'young men before now, having fallen in love with such women, and being unable to control their passion, have been induced by folly to ruin themselves in this way'.[18] Despite his claim that whenever she was at Pyrrhus' house there were fights, revelry, and frequent disorder, he is careful not to give the name of the woman in question, which suggests that her status was not so doubtful, nor her reputation so bad as he implies.[19] But the name of the daughter is bandied around quite openly; indeed, exactly what it was and who called her by it is part of the speaker's argument that she is not of the status that she claims. The character of the illegitimate daughter, poised to take away the property of an Athenian citizen woman, is scarcely realized, and yet she manages to personify all the dangers that arise from the absence of a genuine citizen identity that we have already seen above; the argument about her name may not be factually persuasive, but through it the speaker evokes 'the dangerous woman' of popular imagination.[20]

Similarly, in the speech *On the Estate of Nicostratus*, Hagnon and Hagnotheus, Nicostratus' brothers, assert that Chariades is

---

[17] Isae. 3.11.   [18] Isae. 3.17.
[19] Isae. 3.13; see Schaps 1977 on naming women in Athenian courts. It is also possible that she was in fact an Athenian citizen, albeit one who had lived as a *pallake*.
[20] Edwards 2007: 52.

attempting something of the same stratagem in his attempt to gain Nicostratus' estate. He has argued that he served with Nicostratus as a mercenary, was his business partner, and had been adopted by him; they argue that he is 'foisting in not only himself but also his child by the *hetaira*'.[21] We also find this character of the over-influential woman alluded to in other speeches: for example, in *On the Estate of Menecles* (c.354/3), the speaker denies the argument of the prosecution that he was adopted by Menecles when that man was 'under the influence' of his second wife (the speaker's younger sister).[22] The phrase calls to mind the Solonian law recorded by Demosthenes that discounted inheritance arrangements when they were made under the influence of *mania*, age, *pharmaka*, sickness, or a woman, or under constraint.[23] It has been suggested from the arguments put forward by the defence that the plaintiff will have tried to convince the court that the woman had no dowry, and that the couple were not properly married; and he may also have painted her as a *hetaira*.[24]

Finally, these characteristics also pervade the case made against another, more famous prostitute—and dangerous woman—Neaera. The law-court speech, delivered by Apollodorus and dating between 343–340 BCE, presents a particular view of Neaera's life story, as part of a prosecution against her for (illegally, as an alien) acting as the wife of a citizen.[25] The case is squarely aimed at Stephanus, her partner in crime and a long-time enemy of Apollodorus, so in some ways, Neaera is just a foil; but the speaker makes full use of the risks she presents as a dangerous woman. And not just her: before we turn to the details this speech provides about the life of Neaera herself, we can consider first its incidental introduction of two other such characters.[26]

The first is Neaera's daughter, Phano. The speaker has already established the doubtful status and character of this young women, explaining not only the ambiguity about her parentage (never satisfactorily resolved), but also just how like her mother she is in

---

[21] Isae. 4.10; date of speech uncertain—Edwards (2007: 68) reports a suggested c.350 BCE.

[22] Edwards 2007: 32.

[23] Isae. 2.19. Law: [Dem.] 46.14. The charge is also introduced at the end of Isae. 9.37, although no woman is identified in connection with this case.

[24] See Wyse 1904: 234–5 and Edwards 2007: 28–9.

[25] On date/authorship, Kapparis 1999: 28 and 48–52. Scholars have argued that this is a *graphe xenias*, e.g., Todd 1993: 176, but cf. Kapparis 2005: 78.

[26] [Dem.] 59: 116–17 (tr. throughout this section by Murray 1939b).

character, seeking 'to emulate her mother's habits and the dissolute manner of living in her house'.[27] There is a first marriage, to Phrastor, who indicts Stephanus on the grounds that he had represented Phano as his own daughter.[28] In this section of the speech we also find what may be an allusion to the working of magic: Phrastor falls ill after sending Phano away; he has no support from his relatives, and is in a helpless state. Neaera and her daughter then return, and, we are told, he is *psuchagogomenos* by their attentions.[29] The Greek word can mean something as simple as 'cajoled' or 'beguiled', but it has another meaning that alludes to supernatural persuasion, in particular that of summoning souls—of the living or the dead.[30] It may be intended to suggest that Neaera and her daughter have used wiles that are not wholly natural.

Phano is then married to Theogenes, who had been appointed as King Archon, and, as his wife, officiates at ceremonies in a role reserved for citizen women.[31] For some reason (in what may be another example of gossip at work) the problem of her identity is then raised before the Areopagus, but in this case, it appears to have been because she was accused of being an adulteress (this is the original reason why her husband Theogenes then cast her out, although his deposition states that he had found out she was not Stephanus' daughter).[32]

To the case that the speaker is making, the exact nature of Phano's offences is almost an irrelevant detail. The audience is allowed no doubt as to what kind of threat Phano's activities might pose to the city, as the speaker describes in some detail the ancient tradition that surrounded the election of the King Archon and the role of that officer's wife, one that was established even before the time of

---

[27] [Dem.] 59.38, 50–1 (quotation 50), 121–4; and see also the Epaenetus episode §§64–72 (in which Epaenetus is caught having sex with Phano, is discovered by Apollodorus, held to ransom, released on surety, fails to pay up, and then indicts him for unlawful imprisonment on the grounds [we are told] that Phano was not Stephanus' daughter). The two settled with, it is alleged, Stephanus putting Phano at Epaenetus' sexual disposal. See the discussion by Hamel (2003: 95–101) for the way in which the speaker draws out the implications for his case against Neaera—and the flaws in his arguments.

[28] [Dem.] 59.50–62; see also p. 304 of this volume. Phrastor brings a suit against Stephanus, but then tries to get his son with Phano entered into his own *phratry* and *genos*, the Brytidae; he takes them to court when they refuse.

[29] [Dem]. 59.55.

[30] The term is found with the more supernatural meaning in Pl. *Leg.* 909b, Xen. *Mem.* 3.10.6, Diod. Sic. 4.4.3.

[31] [Dem.] 59.72.

[32] [Dem.] 59.73–87. Kapparis (1999 ad loc.): argues that the document at 59.84 is a forgery.

Theseus.[33] We are left with the clear impression that in every dimension of both her birth and behaviour the figure of Phano is dangerous, to individual citizens, to the *oikos*, to the city and its venerable traditions and identity, and, finally, to the city's relationship with its gods.[34] In turn, these descriptions of Phano's behaviour exacerbate the dangers posed by Neaera's own status and actions. They allow the speaker to introduce the idea of impiety into the case, even though Neaera has not committed any straightforward offence. And Phano is not the only one to play this role. A further story makes this association even more directly and explicitly.

The speaker compares Neaera and a man called Archias, who had been a hierophant, or high priest, of the temple at Eleusis. It is likely that Archias was convicted of impiety. Among the charges brought against him is that he had sacrificed on the altar in the court at Eleusis when it was neither the right day for the sacrifice, nor his to perform; the sacrificial victim, we are told, had been supplied by the *hetaira*, Sinope. Archias, apparently, was punished; although we do not know what the punishment was, it was delivered so stringently that 'the pleading of his relatives and friends did not save him, nor the public services which he and his ancestors had rendered to the city; no, nor yet his office of hierophant'.[35] As we have noted earlier, it seems likely that there were also political motives underlying the case against Archias: if Plutarch is to be believed, Archias had tried to warn the ruler of Thebes (also Archias) that he and his men were to be ambushed by the anti-Spartan Theban faction led by Pelopidas, returning from exile in Athens.[36] Thus, even as this story explicitly described a dangerous woman who had led a man, a priest no less, into a perilous act of impiety, it also may have brought with it further resonances of treachery and deceit.

Sinope herself is not mentioned again, nor was she in fact necessarily guilty of anything. Nevertheless, the mention of her presence and her apparent influence in the moment of commission of an act of impiety reinforces the tenor of the speaker's argument against Neaera. The juxtaposition of these three women—Phano, Sinope,

---

[33] [Dem.] 59.74–7.
[34] These different levels of appeal are made explicit in the peroration, esp. §110–14.
[35] See earlier discussion of this case, p. 51, n. 51 of this volume. Krauter (2004: 233) regards this as a *graphe asebeias*.
[36] Plut. *Pelop.* 10.3–4.

320   *Envy, Poison, and Death*

Neaera herself—conflates and reinforces the threat of the dangerous woman who crosses civic and sacral boundaries, who leads individual citizens into impious actions, and who thus undermines the safety of the city. From Sinope's role in Archias' fate, the speaker slides neatly into a discussion of Neaera, and the idea that she might escape punishment, although 'she has committed acts of sacrilege against this same god, and has transgressed the laws'.[37] The jury is faced not only with the threat of letting women like Sinope and Neaera escape punishment for their crimes (while others who are of higher status and greater service to the city pay the penalty), but also the risk that, as jurors of the case, they will encourage others like them to do the same.[38]

There are still more dangerous women haunting the forensic corpus—although little beyond these salient characteristics is known about them. They include, for example, the sister of Lacedaemonius, mentioned by Demosthenes in his speech *Against Eubulides*. This trial probably took place on the occasion of the review of the deme register of 346/5: the speaker, one Euxitheus, was appealing against his ejection from the deme of Halimous, as discussed above. Eubulides had made the original demand for his disenfranchisement, and the other demesmen had voted to support him.[39] Euxitheus indicates that Eubulides had put forward various arguments to show that his parents were not Athenian. First of all, it was claimed that his father had a foreign accent. Euxitheus defends him on the grounds that he had been taken prisoner in the Decelean War and then sold as a slave; it was a long time before he had come home.[40] Second, it was argued that Euxitheus' mother sold ribbons in the Agora, and had worked as a wet nurse—apparently intimating that she was a poor foreigner. Euxitheus, as we have seen, argues that

---

[37] [Dem.] 59.119.

[38] Mentioned by Apollodorus in the context of the case of Neaera, is Metaneira, whose initiation Lysias arranged ([Dem.] 59.21). She seems to provide us with an exception to the image of the 'dangerous women': the story is presented as a contrast to the account of Neaera and her protector, the positive to their negative image of the perversion of citizenship. But we also have to bear in mind that the contrast runs deep. Lysias is, after all, a metic, and so already at some level, less than a citizen; it may be that this makes his consorting with a prostitute somehow more acceptable. See Goff 2004: 154.

[39] MacDowell 2009: 288; see discussion in this volume, p. 197.

[40] Dem. 57.

she was simply an Athenian who, like many who suffered during the Peloponnesian War, had to find a way to support herself.[41]

It has been suggested that the real issue of the matter (which the speaker has elided here) may have turned on this role as wet nurse: if Euxitheus's mother was pregnant while his father was away, then this casts doubt on his paternity.[42] However, Euxitheus focuses (unsurprisingly) on other motivations: not only long-held enmity between the two families, but more recently, another trial, in the course of which the speaker gave evidence against Eubulides. This was a prosecution against a woman—'the sister of Lacedaemonius'—for impiety. That she is not mentioned by name suggests her respectability.[43] That we have not heard more about her may be because Eubulides failed to gain a fifth part of the votes.

...AND AMBIGUOUS RELATIONSHIPS

The majority of these women emerge from the kaleidoscopic rhetoric of the forensic corpus drawn in hyperreal and unlikely colours. But their exaggerated characteristics also showcase the nightmares of the Athenian citizen imaginary. Marriage and adoption were strategies used in the fourth century to maintain family interests and property rights.[44] These women threatened those strategies: the potential ambiguity of their status became a weapon, wielded by acquisitive men and/or the women themselves. It confused and obscured kin and marital relationships, putting Athenian families and citizenship in jeopardy.

In a society in which the civic identity of women was hard to ascertain, a little gossip may have been enough to suggest that a wife was no straightforward citizen wife, but was, in fact a *pallake* or a *hetaira*—or vice versa.[45] We see this suggested in the forensic

---

[41] Dem. 57.30–45. [42] Dem. 57.42. [43] Dem. 57.8.
[44] Rubinstein 1993: 62–4 and 1999: 55–61.
[45] Underpinning this is the question of whether or not women who were citizens could be given as *pallakai* in the first place. In support, Sealey (1984) argues for the existence of dowries for *pallakai* on the basis of Isae. 3.39, and the idea that benefits other than a dowry are referred to there.. Ogden (1996: 151 and 158–63) argues that citizen *pallakai* were possible, but unlikely, and (159) that the Isaeus passage cannot be taken as evidence, since, he argues, there is no indication that the men in question

evidence: Demosthenes attempts to represent Plangon as a citizen and *pallake*; Isaeus represented Phile as a bastard, and her mother as a citizen–*hetaira/pallake*;[46] in turn, as we have seen, Apollodorus offers plenty of 'evidence' to support his allegations of Neaera's simulation of citizen–wife.[47] Although the facts that lie behind these accusations may be impossible to ascertain, we can see how, in the context of the law courts, speakers were able to use these common ideas, these shared fears, to manipulate perceptions of status.

Women who blurred these boundaries—the argument seems to be—could also cross others. The descriptions offered in these speeches show women luring men from their civic duty by inducing them to join in impious actions. And similar stories appear across ancient literature, ranging from allegations about Pericles and his relationship with the *hetaira* who became his wife, Aspasia (rumoured to have been brought

---

are Athenian citizens—but he does not engage with Sealey's argument. Indeed, in some ways he seems to agree with Sealey, since he argues with the support of New Comedy (citing Plautus *Stichus* 562 and *Trinummus* 612 and 685–91) that it was usual for a concubine to be given without a dowry—which is the conclusion that Sealey also comes to (1984: 117). Kamen (2013: 66) agrees with Ogden (in a passage on the status of *nothoi*), while Kennedy (2014: 114–15) states that, though citizen *pallakai* were possible, there is no evidence that the term was ever used about a citizen woman; later (117), she argues that the fact that Neaera was accused of pretending to be a citizen wife indicates that the difference between a *pallake* and a wife was citizenship. However, she argues that it was far from a servile status, and gave metic women legal protection (*contra* Patterson 1991: 284). Finally, Harrison (1968: 14) argues that the speaker is emphasizing the lack of a formal marriage agreement (by *engue*) between Nicodemus and Pyrrhus, and (15) supports the idea that *pallakai* would have included 'free women who formed these unions on their own initiative'.

[46] Dem. 39.26, 40.8 and 27. Cf. Ogden (1996: 158–9), who suggests that these examples are not convincing evidence, because in each case the woman was likely to have been a legitimate wife. But if this was the case, he does not explain what Demosthenes is trying to achieve, since presumably the jurors were aware of what was possible or not; perhaps these speeches may still reveal what was plausible. There is evidence for citizen *hetairai* in Plutarch's description of Alcibiades' happy home life (*Alc.* 8.3), but Ogden (1996: 160) stresses this is the only certain reference and dismisses descriptions of *hetairai* as coming from Attica (Thais 'need merely have hailed from the city'); he offers no comment on the evidence that Lamia was said to have a citizen father (Ath. 13.577c) and dismisses the famous Antiphanes fragment, which states that the *hetaira* 'is a citizen woman' with the assertion that this is about a 'pseudo-*hetaira*' (fr. 210 [*Hydria*] K-A; see Kurke 1997: 116 for the association of *hetairai* and gold).

[47] It is also represented in fictional situations: in Menander's *Perikeiromene*, we find gossip working precisely in support of such a situation, with characters referring to the relationship of Polemon and Glycera in terms of a proper marriage. See discussion in Konstan 1987: 127.

to court on a charge of *asebeia* and pandering), to the gossip that Athenaeus records concerning Demetrius of Phaleron (the Athenian statesman's grandson) and the way in which he seated his *hetaira* Aristagora at the Panathenaea and celebration of the Eleusinian Mysteries.[48]

This is the usual matted discourse of misogyny of ancient Greek literature. Nevertheless, the patterns repeated across these stories are striking: these women not only corrupt the individual, but they put the city itself in danger—in part, because they endanger the bloodlines of the *oikos*, but also because of the supernatural consequences of their actions or influence. And the forensic evidence itself indicates how closely these patterns interacted with reality.[49] When the orators refer to such women, they are generating and reinforcing, as much as drawing on, the cultural model of the dangerous woman.

It is striking that this discourse of risk was also reinforced from the opposite direction, as it were, through a discourse of public praise for a very different kind of woman. The commemoration of women in the form of inscribed epitaphs shows a marked increase during the fourth century BCE. There are 162 surviving epitaphs from fourth-century Attica, with family members attested in forty-five: eleven epitaphs for men, and thirty-four for women.[50] The grave stelai on which they are found also feature sculpted figure scenes—probably mass-produced, and likely to give some indication of what was considered to be an ideal family.[51]

Altogether, this evidence offer indications of the idealized characteristics of a woman: the standardized vocabulary notes how she was 'virtuous and moderate'.[52] It is also particularly striking how many of these appear to be concerned with family-oriented relations; in particular, the surviving epitaphs emphasize the role of the wife.[53] As well as the verbal emphases, there are a number of aspects of the

---

[48] Demetrius in Ath. 4.167; Pericles in Plut. *Per.* 32.

[49] As mentioned, there was a Solonian law (preserved in Dem. 46.14) that discounted inheritance arrangements when they were made under the influence of *mania*, age, *pharmaka*, sickness, or a woman—or under constraint.

[50] Tsagalis 2008: 184. [51] See Younger 2002: 172–3.

[52] *agathe kai sophron*; see Younger 2002: 181 (and tr.).

[53] Tsagalis (2008: 184–5) gives one epitaph to a woman for every three for men; this remains stable outside Attica during the fourth century, but within Attica, it changes to four epitaphs for men to every three epitaphs for women. Tsagalis (2008: 186–7): women are commemorated as wives in 41.02%, and as mothers in 25.64% of cases where family terms are employed. On women's control over the *oikos*, see

visual depictions that reinforce the idealized *oikos*-focused role of a woman: most generally the activities that occupy these women set them in a domestic sphere.[54] Typically, one woman is seated (usually regarded as the deceased) and another stands:[55] the relationship between these two figures (one seated, one standing) is often understood to be that of mother and daughter, but other figures are also depicted (for example, another woman, probably a maid, perhaps holding a baby) and sometimes the scenes appear almost crowded; one includes a small dog.[56]

In terms of further scene-setting, we also see *kalathoi* (or wool baskets) in various positions, and sometimes the women in the scene are working wool.[57] The seated figure may hold an object such as a *kithara* (lyre); she may be adjusting/holding a mantle or receiving or putting on (or taking off) jewellery.[58] The standing woman often has a box, and may be taking something from it;[59] often, the standing woman is holding a child.[60] In addition, we should also take note of the use of the *dexiosis* motif, in which individuals are shown clasping hands—and women are shown performing this action both with men

---

Tsagalis 2008: 187, and Breuer 1995: 65. Foxhall (1989: 22–44) explains how important a wife's dowry was to the well-being of her new home.

[54] Younger 2002: 178 (this description is indebted to his analysis); he emphasizes how the female viewer of these stelai would have been affected by them, causing her to (191) 'imagine the deceased individual's character and qualities, to feel for her the emotions that her loved ones once felt for her, and finally to remember that she will join her'.

[55] Younger (2002: 174) notes that in a survey of the images where figures are named, this tends to be a seated figure, and is often on the left of the image. He takes this to be what is conventionally termed the 'primary deceased'. Clear mother and daughter relationships: see Younger 2002: 174 with n. 32.

[56] Crowded: Clairmont no. 4.930 includes as well as the seated woman, two young women, one holding a baby, and a maid. Small dog: Clairmont no. 2.284.

[57] Kalathos: under or beside the chair: Clairmont nos 120, 247; 1.176, 1.184, 1.246, 1.691; 1.894, 1.986, 2.829, 2.948; 3.384b[?]) or in scenes of working wool: Clairmont nos 1.220, 1.309, and 2.650.

[58] Kithara: Clairmont no. 3.411. Bracelets: Clairmont no. 2.319a Mantle: Clairmont no. 2.464.

[59] Famously, the Archestrate stele, in which a young woman holds a box from which Archestrate (seated) takes a sash; Archestrate gazes at her daughter, who is leaning against her knees and holds a bird: Clairmont no. 2.820.

[60] Box: Clairmont nos 2.891, 3.404 and 423. Open box: Clairmont no. 2.306. Holding an infant: Clairmont no. 2.894, Clairmont no. 2.780, and Clairmont no. 2.806.

and with other women[61]—which seems to underline this role of responsibility and trust that women were expected to fulfil.[62]

After the initial and obvious contrasts, there are in fact some compelling similarities between our two discourses. First, both the stelai and the forensic speeches reveal a focus on the *oikos* and the important role played by individual women within that institution.[63] And although the women depicted in, on the one hand, the speeches, and on the other hand, the epitaphs, are playing quite different roles, both representations draw our attention to the importance of the family: first, the way in which a good woman or wife can support such a structure, and then, how her opposite can wholly undermine it, threatening family, city, state.

---

[61] Tsagalis 2008: 190. Younger (2002: 197 n. 31) notes that in Clairmont there are 224 two-figure stelai with a man and a woman, 75 where both figures are men, and 110 where both are women.

[62] On *dexiosis* as intimating relations between living and dead, especially in the context of the difficulties of burial during the Peloponnesian War, see Tsagalis 2008: 189, citing Pemberton 1989: 48, Davies 1985: 630, and Shapiro 1991: 654. Younger (2002: 178) suggests that it signifies the close relationship of deceased and survivor before and after death.

[63] Tsagalis (2008: 185) draws attention to the 'Entwicklung der Einzelpersonlichkeit' of this period (see discussion in this volume, p. 306). see Christes 1975: 32.

4.5

Conclusion: Envy, Poison, and Death

Pharmakeia was the starting point for our exploration: the poisons and curses with which these women's trials were imbued, but for which there was no certain evidence, or even clear statements. Trying to understand the reasoning behind these accusations, we followed the suggestion of a spell that *phthonos* might be the reason for their employment—and found that it might also be a motivation for the attribution of their use. This '*phthonos* talk', we saw, was engendered and expressed through gossip—a potent discourse of poison in itself, one that brings suspicion alive and makes it powerful—in the right circumstances. Those circumstances came under investigation in this part of the book, where we have examined the possible context for these events, setting out some ways in which the sociopolitical environment of fourth-century Athens might become fertile ground for gossip against three women, allowing it to develop into violent civic action.

To whatever extent the city of Athens did in fact suffer from depleted resources in the aftermath of the Peloponnesian War, there is some evidence that, for many, there were real and perceived economic difficulties. Moreover, even as the city recovered, these would have exacerbated existing social tensions. As the city of Athens fought to overcome the legacy of its defeat and to attain its previous dominance, what it meant to be an Athenian was a focus of concern. We see this issue raised indirectly across a variety of verbal and visual discourses, in legislation concerning civic recognition, and in the everyday vigilance over one's own and others' behaviours. Finally, in terms of family structures, it is likely that one result of the Peloponnesian War and its aftermath was that there were, and/or there were perceived to be, more single women and girl children—both Athenian citizens and those of more ambiguous status—living in the city without (adequate) economic support.

Conclusion: Envy, Poison, and Death

In the forensic speeches, charges of individual and political conspiracy offer evidence for a cultural mindset of suspicion—and at the centre of many of these discourses, in the context of fractured family relationships and fights over inheritance, we repeatedly find the figure of the 'dangerous woman'. Whether or not all these stories describe actual events, the cases of Theoris, Ninon, and Phryne suggest that these discourses of risk and real life could collide with devastating results.

Epilogue: Social Trauma?

'Cultural trauma is the most threatening because like all cultural phenomena it has the strongest inertia; it persists and lingers considerably longer than other kinds of trauma, sometimes over several generations, preserved in collective memory or hibernating in collective subconscious, and occasionally gaining salience when conducive circumstances arise.'[1]

In Demosthenes *Against Boeotus* (2), the speaker notes how dangerous his prosecutors are: he considers how they have conspired against him to bring the case, and how if they will do that, it becomes quite likely that they would also resort to other forms of wrongdoing—and he mentions explicitly *pharmakeia* or poison. I mention this final passage because it summarizes the kinds of social structures, interpersonal dynamics, and emotional behaviours that this book has been trying to examine as it explores the factors involved in shaping events that led to the trials of Theoris, Ninon, and Phryne. In this final section, I want to offer two further thoughts: the first adds one more dimension to the explanations we have been considering; the other reflects on the role of these trials themselves in historical change.

In examining the factors that gave rise to these trials, this study has attempted to combine macro- and micro-social dynamics, examining both the broader historical context and the individual emotions of those involved. However, in trying to bring these two elements together, there is always, inevitably, a gap, one which only the question of individual mental processes can bridge. Thus, this final addition to the causal

---

[1] Sztompka 2000: 458. Sztompka refers to 'cultural trauma', which is the focus of Alexander *et al.* (2004); Robben (2005) refers to 'social trauma' (346, citing Sztompka 2000). Argenti and Schramm (2010b: 14) describe the relationship between the two.

Epilogue: Social Trauma? 329

explanations put forward so far is a psychoanalytical interpretation of the phenomena of these trials. This brings us back to the role of context, and a desire to move beyond an explanation in which violence against women is simply taken as inevitable. Drawing on more recent studies of political violence and its impact on communities and society, I want to suggest the consideration of a crucial intermediary stage—trauma.[2]

By introducing this term, it is important to stress this study is not attempting to describe individuals within ancient Athenian society in terms of combat trauma or post-traumatic stress disorder, although individual and group experiences are integrally related.[3] Rather, the use of this term is intended to raise questions about the trauma experienced by a society, either as a whole or in groups, the damage 'inflicted by major social change' to 'the social body and its cultural frame', rather than the physical tissue of an individual.[4] This is to explore the ways in which traumatic experiences may exist in social

---

[2] Robben 2005, Siegel 2006. A version of this approach, phrased in terms of a religious crisis, has been put forward by some as an explanation for the apparent religious intolerance that the *asebeia* trials of the late fifth and early fourth centuries demonstrate (see Scholz 2000: 159–61 and Garnsey 1984: 3). Krauter (2004: 235) suggests that Parker (1996: 210) is sceptical about a religious crisis, but his position is more ambiguous: although he does not think that traditional religion was undermined, he does support the idea that 'in the sense that speculative thought was perceived by some as a threat, perhaps for the first time, a kind of crisis did arise'. He sees this lying specifically in the idea (found, for example, in the presentation of Socrates in Ar. *Nub.* and Pl. *Leg.* 886d–e, 889b–890a, 967a–d) that there was an 'alliance between a scientific determinism that was pushed to an atheistic extreme and sophistic determination'. Other scholars have explained this in terms of anxiety about the threat to tradition (Burkert 1985: 316); as a conflict between generations (Graf 2002: 126f.); or as political intolerance of intellectual developments (Dodds 1951: 189–93 and Versnel 1990: 127.

[3] The concept of combat trauma has been very successfully introduced into discussions of ancient military history: see Shay 2003: 199, Crowley 2012, Meineck and Konstan 2014. Nor should social trauma be understood as simply the sum total of individual traumas. Robben and Suárez-Orozco (2000: 346) give the following description 'it ruptures social bonds, destroys group identities, undermines people's sense of community, and entails cultural disorientation because taken for granted meanings become obsolete'.

[4] Robben 2005: 346 and Sztompka 2000: 450. Note that Sztompka argues that trauma is a collective phenomenon and is experienced by groups (communities or societies) and so 'cannot be treated as an individual psychological predicament' (458). Feuchtwang (2011: 12–13) is wary that the language of 'collective trauma' arises from 'a predominant political culture of being a victim', but this discussion seems to focus largely on individual trauma. Although he says at first (13) that he could not find evidence 'in any clinical sense' for 'collective trauma', later in his book (121,122, and 134) he does then use the term to refer to shared group experiences, the effects of which are transmitted through different social structures.

memory, bridging the gap between the individual and the collective, and transmitted between generations.[5] As recent work has stressed, such memories need not be expressed through straightforward modes of reference: they may emerge through non-discursive practices, embodied actions, ritual, and other performative practices.[6]

My suggestion is that the trials of these women are evidence for social trauma, and that they occurred within a society in which a sense of unity had been severely and catastrophically disrupted. Trust had broken down, not only between individuals, but also between individuals and 'the social institutions and cultural practices that structure experience and give meaning to social lives', including religious practices.[7] In short, the Athenians had experienced a severe social trauma, one which prompted a search for meaning and explanations of their experiences, and which was created by, and in turn itself led to, political, social, and supernatural violence.[8]

Piotr Sztompka, drawing on the work of Robert Merton, has suggested a sequence of responses to radical sociocultural changes, which can be summarized as resulting in a vicious cycle of cultural destruction and a virtuous cycle of cultural reconstruction.[9] In many ways, the steps taken to reconfigure the radical democracy of Athens in the early fourth century reveal a fierce commitment to responses of the latter kind. Similarly, if we pursue this kind of analysis, the evidence indicates activities that may be described as efforts at cultural reconstruction: the emergence of novel structures of employment, for example, and the instantiation of new cults, or ritual activities, can be seen in this light. Similarly, even crimes of certain kinds, although illegitimate, may also indicate a creative response to experiences of traumatic change.

Working in more detail with this typology, we might describe some of these activities simply as examples of 'adaptive innovation',

---

[5] See papers in Alexander *et al.* 2004.

[6] See papers in Argenti and Schramm 2010a; in particular Argenti and Schramm 2010b: 22–5.

[7] Robben and Suárez-Orozco 2000: 5.

[8] After the trauma there are attempts to make sense of this experience. Within society, different groups will find different kinds of meaning in their experiences of a particular event. See Weinstein (1995: 308), who suggests that we must be prepared for 'heterogeneity, discontinuity, and the capacity of people actively to construct versions of the world', rather than try to interpret historical events from a single perspective. The result may be a competition for meaning; see Robben and Suárez-Orozco 2000: 349.

[9] Sztompka 2000: 461, drawing on Merton 1938.

while others are more purposeful attempts to change the traumatic condition (either some aspect or the whole environment) with some form of cultural production (the latter is a strategy of 'rebellion' according to Merton's typology). However, if we take the trials of these women to be, in their turn, an extreme response to such creative activities, then this highlights a different, additional response to trauma. The nearest description in Merton's typology is what he calls 'ritualism': this involves coming back to established traditions and routines as a way of deflecting, or hiding from, trauma. But although this neatly captures the dynamic of turning to the established legal structures in order to find resolution, it does not help to explain the motivation of destruction that a capital charge appears to involve.

Some recent anthropological work may offer some further insights: I turn to the work of James Siegel in his examination of the witch-hunts of East Java which took place following the collapse of President Suharto's New Order in 1998.[10] In previous periods, jealousy and envy were at the root of witchcraft accusations in Indonesian culture; accusations of witchcraft tended not to surface explicitly, but remained at the level of gossip, related to specific events.[11] In contrast, these witchcraft accusations were a matter of collective action, and resulted in violence. Siegel argues that these events were responses to a long drawn-out experience of trauma that began for his subjects with the transfer of power between Sukarno and Suharto in 1965/6 and culminated in the fall of Suharto in 1998.[12] He evokes the primal uncertainty of the experience of loss that this trauma engendered;[13] in particular, the ways in which, under Suharto, the government's power was both a source of mortal danger and consuming fear, and the only basis of security against the dangers that, it is argued, were posed by society.[14]

---

[10] The witch-hunts and lynchings took place on the island of Java, especially the area of Banyuwangi: about 120 people were killed in a space of three months.

[11] Siegel 2006: 129–30, citing Geertz 1960: 109.

[12] Although Siegel emphasizes the novelty of these killings, Herriman (2007) and (2009) takes the opposite point of view (see discussion in Geschiere 2013: 196).

[13] Siegel emphasizes this primal uncertainty as a form of the sublime that we are unable to determine using our own cognitive powers; it is a form of the pure gift (see Siegel 2006, esp. 21–6).

[14] Siegel 2006: 72.

As well as being invasive and threatening, the government surveillance of the Suharto regime provided a source of identity and authority.[15] But when Suharto fell, any ability to appeal to authority was gone. In that context, in the popular imagination, the figure of the witch took a new shape, absorbing the sense of menace that previously the regime had embodied: 'Seen from the place of those possessed or obsessed by feelings of overwhelming catastrophe, those closest were the unrecognisable face of malevolence'.[16] The witch could be anywhere: in the absence of the structures of the regime, some of those accused of witchcraft were unable to verify even their own identity, and to be sure they were not themselves witches.[17]

I am not arguing that this provides a direct parallel with the situation in fourth-century Athens. This is not an attempt to find a single universalizing explanation (and recent work examining the transmission of social trauma in different contexts and cultures confirms the variability of this phenomenon).[18] Nevertheless, Siegel's marvellous study offers some guidance for thinking about the ways in which the trauma of past experience may integrate both with long-held fears and the lived emotions of current experience to create a novel sense of menace—one that demands action. In fourth-century Athens the trials of Theoris, Ninon, and Phryne can perhaps be seen as rooted in the traumatic experiences of the Peloponnesian War and its aftermath. Whereas once the behaviour of these women might result merely in gossip, perhaps the creation of further, defensive ritual practice, such local, specific responses were evidently no longer sufficient; instead another process was set in train—which led to violence, albeit through legal channels.

The differences between events in ancient Athens and those that Siegel describes are also instructive, in particular in thinking about how social trauma may become politicized, and the ways in which its meaning may be contested in various contexts by diverse groups. One example lies in the different roles played by state and civic processes in each example. In Indonesia, 'the appearance of the "witch" followed by the "witch hunt" offered a means for local control of

---

[15] Ibid.: 130–3.   [16] Ibid.: 160–1.
[17] Ibid.: 123–6. He describes how recognition by authority allows some of those accused of witchcraft to find their voice and deny the charges (146–53).
[18] Compare the diverse responses to trauma across the papers in Argenti and Schramm 2010a.

general—or national—malevolence when state control failed'.[19] In contrast, in Athens, where citizen and state were inseparable, the response was to turn to legal action. The trials of Theoris, Ninon, and Phryne, as part of the discourse that identified 'dangerous women', reinforced Athenian identity, individual and group, through the assertion of boundaries of behaviour, gender, and status. But they also reached beyond the mortal context, crucially encompassing—and attempting to control—claims on divine power. In bringing these aspects together, the Athenian court generated the image of a particular and unexpected enemy—not just a 'dangerous woman', but one more closely identifiable to modern eyes as the figure of the witch.[20]

As I have argued elsewhere, we might see these trials in terms of a resolution of conflict, one that reasserted the status quo. However, the repetition of the pattern—three trials at least—suggests that such a resolution was not achieved, and that the struggle for meaning continued.[21] And other evidence may also indicate that the issues these trials raised were under wider consideration. For example, Plato, in the *Laws*, seems to be tussling with questions that mirror some of the themes of these trials: how to punish the use of *pharmaka* (natural or supernatural) to inflict injury, and the appropriate penalties for professionals as opposed to private citizens.[22] As the fourth century advances, we might also consider the development of the *gunaikonomoi* as further evidence for concerns about the role and control of women in

---

[19] Siegel 2006: 161.
[20] Cf. Stewart 1991, who encourages the study of the witch (15) 'as a symbolic statement of what the society conceives witchcraft to be about'. See Stratton 2007 for discussion of the ways in which different historical contexts emphasize particular images of the witch; Edmonds (2010: 245) cites this work, but criticizes it as overly schematic, drawing attention to the role of genre and individual authorial preference in shaping these images. Roper (2012) provides a nuanced psychoanalytically informed cultural history of the witch, exploring both the vast range of representations of witches and the multiple ways that individuals made sense of witchcraft.
[21] Mendonsa (1982: 3-5) offers a model of conflict resolution that includes the perception of misfortune, the linking of that misfortune to deviance, the labelling of a deviant, and the resolution of conflict (see Eidinow 2010: 33).
[22] Pl. *Leg.* 932e–933e; Gordon (1999: 251–2) suggests that this 'reproduces a practical distinction which must have emerged in fourth-century Athens'; he emphasizes the role of cases involving harm by magical means, rather than 'death through direct magical action' such as the use of *philtra*.

Athenian society, especially with regard to their behaviour at gatherings related to religious events. What the *gunaikonomoi* comprised and when they were instituted in Athens is uncertain: that it may have been in the fourth century (perhaps by Demetrius of Phaleron) is suggested by Timocles. Timocles refers to an individual holding the position, while Athenaeus, Philochorus, and Lynceus seem to be talking about a group.[23] The responsibilities of the office in Athens included burial legislation, and, according to Pollux, the punishment of disorderly women.[24] Athenaeus connects it with a law about feasts, Menander refers to weddings, while Philochorus seems specifically to be concerned with private gatherings, especially marriage feasts and *thusiai* (sacrifices and associated feasting). Overall, the impression is that both at Athens and elsewhere, some care was being taken to control occasions in which group ritual activities took place, and that this was particularly focused on the behaviour of women.[25]

And this brings me back to my final point: this study began with the idea that 'large-scale processes such as state formation,

---

[23] See O'Sullivan 2009: 68 n. 52. Sources for the *gunaikonomoi*: Ath. 6.245a includes Timocles fr. 34 K–A, as well as the fragments of Men. fr. 208 (*Kekryphalos*) K–A and Philochorus *FGrH* 328 F 65 for the third century; see Nagle 2006: 257; perhaps supporting this is a fragment of Hyperides (Hyp. fr. 14 (Jensen) (= Harp. s.v. *hoti chilias*) which mentions that women who were *akosmousai* (without decorum) in the street were fined 1,000 drachmae; Hesychius s.v. *platanos* (pi 2475) tells us that the fines imposed by the officials at Athens were written on a white board and hung from a plane tree (see Ogden 1996: 366). Aristotle (*Pol.* 1300a4–8, and at 1322b37–1323a3) seems to relate such offices to aristocratic or elite women.

[24] Poll. 8.112; see O'Sullivan 2009: 66–71, esp. 66 n. 48 for earlier scholarship.

[25] The office is found, held by an individual or by a group, in other parts of Greece. For example, in all-female festival contexts, including Methymna, Lesbos, where the holder was responsible for preventing men from entering a shrine during a women's *pannychis* (*LSCG* 127.5-10, fourth century BCE, perhaps 340s); at Andania, where, as well as appointing those women with particular cultic roles, the holder oversaw other aspects, including the dress of participants (*Syll.*³ 736.26 and 32, 146 BCE; Gawlinski 2012: 133 dates the creation of the office to the fourth century BCE). At Thasos, with other civic officials, *gunaikonomoi* were responsible for overseeing the purity of those attending religious feasts (Pouilloux 1954, no. 141.5-7, dated 360–340 BCE). In Magnesia, *gunaikonomoi* selected nine girls to participate in a festival of Zeus Sosipolis (*LSAM* 32.20, 197–196 BCE). In Syracuse, it seems that there were very strict rules on what women were allowed to wear and when they were allowed to walk outside; during the day, the *gunaikonomoi* had to give permission (Phylarchus *FGrH* 81 F 45; third century BCE). In third-century BCE Gambreion, (*Syll.*³ 1219.17-25), where a *gunaikonomos* was elected by the people, he oversaw mourning behaviour. Ogden (2002b: 203) claims that the key role of *gunaikonomoi* was to select women for festivals and supervise their behaviour, but Osborne (2011: 174) argues that tasks related to cult activities were marginal aspects of their responsibilities.

subsistence change and population movements need to be understood in locally meaningful contexts of feeling and understanding'.[26] It ends here with the suggestion that one of those local contexts may have been an experience of trauma that, at the local level, shaped responses which, in turn themselves influenced larger processes of historical change. It seems likely that these trials played their part in helping to develop widespread attitudes to such activities. As we have seen, although supernatural activities were a source of gossip and accusation, they were not illegal, only condemned if their use resulted in death. And yet among these cases are charges of supernatural activity with no mention of murderous outcomes.

This suggests that the legal boundaries of acceptable behaviour were shifting, and that these cases indicate how attitudes to particular activities were developing not only within the legal arena, but also with the active involvement of society beyond the courts. By means of gossip of the kind that we have examined, the Athenian community was identifying the activities that it found threatening and deserving of social censure. In a legal setting in which character was evidence, gossip acquired official power and could be presented as an implicit social accusation alongside the explicit legal charge. Thus, the evaluation of events at the local level, shaped by emotions such as *phthonos*, became inextricably part of the judgements made in other, official civic spheres. The trials of these women, at first sight so puzzling, their myriad charges so hard to pin down let alone reconcile, may through their very confusion give us new insights into this period: not only into the conflicted nature of society in Athens during the early to mid-fourth century, but beyond this, to the characters, events, and local social processes that shaped an emergent, historical concept of 'magic'.

---

[26] Tarlow 2000: 719.

Bibliography

Abrahams, R. D. 1970. 'A Performance-Centred Approach to Gossip', *Man* NS 5: 290–301.
Adams, C. D., tr. 1919. *Aeschines: Speeches*. Loeb Classical Library. Cambridge, MA.
Akrigg, B. 2007. 'The Nature and Implications of Athens' Changed Social Structure and Economy', in Osborne 2007: 27–43.
Alexander, J., Eyerman, R., Giesen, B., Smelser, N. J., and Sztompka, P. 2004. *Cultural Trauma and Collective Identity*. Berkeley and London.
Allen, D. 2003. *The World of Prometheus: The Politics of Punishing in Democratic Athens*. Princeton, NJ.
Allport, G. W., and Postman, L. 1947. *The Psychology of Rumor*. New York.
Almirol, E. B. 1981. 'Chasing the Elusive Butterfly: Gossip and the Pursuit of Reputation', *Ethnicity* 8: 293–304.
Alston, R. 1995. *Soldier and Society in Roman Egypt*. London.
Alvar Nuño, A. 2006. 'Falsas consideraciones en los estudios sobre el mal de ojo en el mundo clásico', *Arys* 07 (2006–8), http://rabida.uhu.es/dspace/handle/10272/4910, accessed 8 May 2015.
Alvar Nuño, A. 2012. 'Ocular Pathologies and the Evil Eye in the Early Roman Principate', *Numen* 59: 295–321.
Andersen, Ø. 1987. 'The Widows, the City and Thucydides (2.45.2)', *Symbolae Osloenses* 62: 33–49.
Anderson, G. C., Cumont, F., and Grégoire, H. 1910. *Recueil des inscriptions grecques et latines du Pont et l'Arménie*. Studia Pontica 3.1. Brussels.
Andrewes, A. 1961. 'Philochoros on Phratries', *Journal of Hellenic Studies* 81: 1–15.
Ankarloo, B., and Clark, S., eds. 1999. *Witchcraft and Magic in Europe*, ii: *Ancient Greece and Rome*. London.
Argenti, N., and Schramm, K. 2010a. *Remembering Violence: Anthropological Perspectives on Intergenerational Transmission*. New York.
Argenti, N., and Schramm, K. 2010b. 'Introduction', in Argenti and Schramm, 2010a: 1–40. New York.
Arnaoutoglou, I. N. 2003. *Thusias heneka kai sunousias. Private Religious Associations in Hellenistic Athens*. Yearbook of the Research Centre for the History of Greek Law 37, Supplement 4. Athens.

Arnaoutoglou, I. N. 2007. 'The Fear of Slaves in Ancient Greek Legal Texts', in A. Serghidou, ed. *Fear of Slaves, Fear of Enslavement in the Ancient Mediterranean*, 133–44. Besançon.

Arnold, M. B. 1960. *Emotion and Personality: Psychological Aspects*. 2 vols. New York.

Ascough, R. S. 2003. *Paul's Macedonian Associations: The Social Context of Philippians and 1 Thessalonians*. Wissenschaftliche Untersuchungen zum Neuen Testament 161. Tübingen.

Ashforth, A. 2003. 'On Living in a World with Witches: Everyday Epistemology and Spiritual Insecurity in a Modern African City (Soweto)', in H. L. Moore and T. Sanders, eds. *Magical Interpretations, Material Realities: Modernity, Witchcraft and the Occult in Postcolonial Africa*, 206–25. New York.

Ashforth, A. 2005. *Witchcraft, Violence and Democracy in South Africa*. Chicago.

Austin, C., and Olson, D., eds. 2004. *Aristophanes: Thesmophoriazusae*. Oxford.

Austin, M. M. 1994. 'Society and Economy', in *The Cambridge Ancient History*, vi: *The Fourth Century*, 527–64. 2nd edn. Cambridge.

Averill, J. R. 1980. 'A Constructivist View of Emotion', in R. Plutchik and H. Kellerman, eds. *Emotion: Theory, Research and Experience*, i: *Theories of Emotion*, 305–39. New York.

Averill, J. R. 1992. 'The Structural Bases of Emotional Behaviour: A Metatheoretical Analysis', *Review of Personality and Social Psychology* 13: 1–24.

Averill, J. R. 2012. 'The Future of Social Constructionism: Introduction to a Special Section of *Emotion Review*', *Emotion Review* 4: 215–20.

Ayim, M. 1994. 'Knowledge Through the Grapevine: Gossip as Inquiry', in Goodman and Ben-Ze'ev 1994: 85–99.

Bailey, F. G. 1971. 'The Management of Reputations and the Process of Change', in F. G. Bailey, ed. *Gifts and Poison: The Politics of Reputation*, 281–301. Oxford.

Bailey, F. G. 1977. *Morality and Expediency: The Folklore of Academic Politics*. Oxford.

Baiter, J. G., and Sauppe, H. 1850. *Oratores Attici*, ii. Zurich.

Bakewell, G. 1999. 'Lysias 12 and Lysias 31: Metics and Athenian Citizenship in the Aftermath of the Thirty', *Greek, Roman, and Byzantine Studies* 40: 5–22.

Bamberger, J. E. 1970 [1972]. *Evagrius Ponticus: The Praktikos & Chapters on Prayer*. Cistercian Studies 4. Kalamazoo, MI.

Barrett, L. F. 2006a. 'Are Emotions Natural Kinds?', *Perspectives on Psychological Science* 1: 28–58.

Barrett, L. F. 2006b. 'Solving the Emotion Paradox: Categorization and the Experience of Emotion', *Perspectives on Psychological Science* 10: 20–46.

Bartolini, G. 1977. *Iperide: Rassegna di problemi e di studi*. Padua.

Bauman, R. 1990. *Political Trials in Ancient Greece*. London.
Baumeister, R. F., Zhang, L., and Vohs, K. D. 2004. 'Gossip as Cultural Learning', *Review of General Psychology* 8: 111–21.
Bean, G. E. 1959. 'Notes and Inscriptions from Pisidia I', *Anatolian Studies* 9: 67–117.
Bell, C. 1824. *The Anatomy and Philosophy of Expression: As Connected with the Fine Arts*. London. 1st edn 1824; originally published, 1806, as *The Anatomy and Philosophy of Expression in Painting*. London.
Ben Ze'ev, A. 2000. 'Why Do We Feel Bad When You Feel Good?', in *The Subtlety of Emotions*, 281–326. Cambridge, MA.
Ben Ze'ev, A. 2014. 'The Personal Comparative Concern in Schadenfreude', in W. van Dijk and J. W. Ouwerkerk, eds. *Schadenfreude: Understanding Pleasure at the Misfortune of Others*, 77–90. Cambridge.
Benoit, W. 1996. 'A Note on Burke on "Motive"', *Rhetoric Society Quarterly* 26: 67–79.
Benson, L. D. 2008. *The Riverside Chaucer*. Oxford.
Bergadaà, M. 2006. 'Le Don d'objets: dimensions centrales et profils de donneurs aux œuvres de bienfaisance', *Recherche et applications en marketing* 21: 19–39.
Bergmann, J. 1911. 'Die Rachgebete von Rheneia', *Philologus* 70: 503–7.
Bergmann, J. R. 1993. *Discreet Indiscretions: The Social Organisation of Gossip*. New York.
Berking, H. 1999. *The Sociology of Giving*. London.
Bernstein, L. M. 1983. *Ko e Lau Pē: (It's Just Talk): Ambiguity and Informal Social Control in a Tongan Village*. Ann Arbor, MI.
Berve, H. 1926. *Das Alexanderreich auf prosopographischer Grundlage*. 2 vols. Munich.
Besnier, N. 1989. 'Information Withholding as a Manipulative and Collusive Strategy in Nukulaelae Gossip', *Language in Society*, 18: 315–41.
Besnier, N. 1996. 'Gossip', in D. Levinson and M. Ember, eds. *Encyclopedia of Cultural Anthropology*, ii, 544–7. New York.
Besnier, N. 2009. *Gossip and the Everyday Production of Politics*. Honolulu, HI.
Biezunska-Malowist, I. 1957. 'La Famille du vétéran romain C. Iulius Niger de Karanis', *Eos*, 49: 155–64.
Björck, G. 1938. *Der Fluch des Christen Sabinus: Papyrus Upsaliensis 8*. Uppsala.
Black, J. 2002. 'Darwin in the World of Emotions', *Journal of the Royal Society of Medicine* 95: 311–13.
Blum, L. 1902. *Œuvres complètes de Flavius Josèphe traduites en français sous la direction de Théodore Reinach*, vii.1: *De l'ancienneté du peuple juif (contre Apion)*. Paris.
Blümel, W. 1992. *Die Inschriften von Knidos*, i. Bonn.
Boeke, H. 2007. *The Value of Victory in Pindar's Odes: Gnomai, Cosmology and the Role of the Poet*. Leiden.

Bollansée, J. 1999. *Felix Jacoby: Die Fragmente der griechischen Historiker, Continued. Part iv: Biography and Antiquarian Literature*, ed. G. Schepens, iva: *Biography*, Fasc. 3: *Hermippos of Smyrna*. Leiden.

Bömer, F. 1963. *Untersuchungen über die Religion der Sklaven in Griechenland und Rom*, iv, 992–4. Wiesbaden.

Bonner, C. 1932. 'Witchcraft in the Lecture Room of Libanius', *Transactions and Proceedings of the American Philological Association* 63: 34–44.

Borsch, S. J. 2005. *The Black Death in Egypt and England: A Comparative Study*. Austin, TX.

Bowden, H. 2003. 'Oracles for Sale', in P. Derow and R. Parker, eds. *Herodotus and his World: Essays from a Conference in Memory of George Forrest*, 256–74. Oxford.

Bowie, A. M. 2007. *Herodotus: Histories. Book VIII*. Cambridge Greek and Latin Classics. Cambridge.

Bowie, K. A. 1998. 'Charity and Class in Northern Thailand', *American Anthropologist* 100: 469–81.

Braund, S., and Most, G., eds. 2003. *Ancient Anger: Perspectives from Homer to Galen*. Cambridge.

Brenneis, D. L. 1987. 'Performing Passions: Aesthetics and Politics in an Occasionally Egalitarian Community', *American Ethnologist* 14: 236–50.

Brenner, R. 1976. 'Agrarian Class Structure and Economic Development in Pre-Industrial Europe,' *Past & Present* no. 70: 30–74.

Breuer, Ch. 1995. *Reliefs und Epigramme griechischer Privatgrabmäler*. Cologne, Weimar, and Vienna.

Brison, K. J. 1992. *Just Talk: Gossip, Meetings, and Power in a Papua New Guinea Village*. Berkeley, CA and London.

Brixhe, C. 1988. 'La Langue de l'étranger non grec chez Aristophane', in R. Lonis, ed. *L'Étranger dans le monde grec*, 113–38. Nancy.

Brock, R. 1994. 'The Labour of Women in Classical Athens', *Classical Quarterly* NS 44: 336–46.

Brosch, T. 2013. 'Comment: On the Role of Appraisal Processes in the Construction of Emotion', *Emotion Review* 5: 369–73.

Brown, C. G. 2006. 'Pindar on Archilochus and the Gluttony of Blame (Pyth. 2.52–6)', *Journal of Hellenic Studies* 126: 36–46.

Brown, P. 1970. 'Sorcery, Demons and the Rise of Christianity into the Middle Ages', in M. Douglas, ed. *Witchcraft Confessions and Accusations*, 17–45. London. Repr. 1972, in P. Brown, *Religion and Society in the Age of St. Augustine*, 119–146. London.

Brownson, C. L., tr. and rev. J. Dillery. 1998. *Xenophon: Anabasis*. Loeb Classical Library. Cambridge, MA.

Bryen, A., and Wypustek, A. 2009. 'Gemellus' Evil Eyes (*P. Mich.* VI 423–424)', *Greek, Roman, and Byzantine Studies* 49: 535–55.

Bulman, P. 1992. *Phthonos in Pindar*. Berkeley, CA.
Burford, A. 1965. 'The Economics of Greek Temple-Building', *Proceedings of the Cambridge Philological Society* NS 11: 21-34.
Burford, A. 1969. *The Greek Temple Builders at Epidaurus*. Liverpool.
Burford, A. 1972. *Craftsmen in Greek and Roman Society*. London.
Burke, K. 1945. *A Grammar of Motives*. Berkeley and Los Angeles.
Burkert, W. 1962. *Weisheit und Wissenschaft: Studien zu Pythagoras, Philolaos und Platon*. Nuremberg.
Burkert, W. 1985. *Greek Religion: Archaic and Classical*. Oxford and Cambridge, MA.
Burkert, W. 1987. *Ancient Mystery Cults*. Cambridge, MA.
Burkhardt, F., Secord, J. A., Dean, S. A., Evans, S., Innes, S., Pearn, A. M., and White, P. 2010. 'Appendix IV: Darwin's Queries about Expression', in *The Correspondence of Darwin*, xviii: *1870*, 451-2. Cambridge.
Burkhardt, F., and Smith, S., eds. 1988. 'Appendix III: Darwin's Observations on his Children', in *The Correspondence of Darwin*, iv: *1847-1850*, 410-33. Cambridge.
Burnett, A. P. 2005. *Pindar's Songs for Young Athletes of Aigina*. Oxford.
Burt, R. S. 2001. 'Bandwidth and Echo: Trust, Information and Gossip in Social Networks', in J. E. Rauch and A. Casella, eds. *Networks and Markets*, 30-74. New York.
Burtt, J. O., tr. 1954. *Minor Attic Orators*, ii: *Lycurgus, Dinarchus, Demades, Hyperides*. Loeb Classical Library. Cambridge, MA.
Caillé, A. 2001. 'The Double Inconceivability of the Pure Gift', *Angelaki: Journal of the Theoretical Humanities* 6: 23-38.
Cairns, D. L. 1993. *AIDOS: The Psychology and Ethics of Honour and Shame in Ancient Greek Literature*. Oxford.
Cairns, D. L. 2003a. 'The Politics of Envy: Envy and Equality in Ancient Greece', in Konstan and Rutter 2003: 235-52.
Cairns, D. L. 2003b. 'Ethics, Ethology, Terminology: Iliadic Anger and the Cross-Cultural Study of Emotion', in Braund and Most 2003: 11-49.
Cairns, D. L. 2008. 'Look Both Ways: Studying Emotion in Ancient Greek', *Critical Quarterly* NS 50: 43-63.
Cairns, D. L. 2009. 'Weeping and Veiling: Grief, Display, and Concealment in Ancient Greek Culture', in T. Fögen, ed. *Tears in the Graeco-Roman World*, 37-57. Berlin.
Cairns, D. L. 2011. 'Looks of Love and Loathing: Cultural Models of Vision and Emotion in Ancient Greek Culture', *Métis* NS 9: 37-50.
Calhoun, C. 2003. 'Cognitive Emotions?', in Solomon 2003b: 236-47. Chichester.
Camp, J. M. 1982. 'Drought and Famine in the 4th Century B.C.', in *Studies in Athenian Architecture, Sculpture, and Topography presented to Homer A. Thompson*, 9-17. Hesperia Suppl. 20. Princeton, NJ.

Campbell, J. 1964. *Honour, Family and Patronage: A Study of Institutions and Moral Values in a Greek Mountain Community*. Oxford.

Cantarelli, L. 1885. 'Osservazioni sul processo di Frine', *Rivista di filologia e d'istruzione classica* 13: 465–82.

Capelle, W. 1953. 'Zwei Quellen des Heliodor', *Rheinisches Museum* 96: 166–80.

Carey, C. 1981. *A Commentary on Five Odes of Pindar: Pythian 2, Pythian 9, Nemean 1, Nemean 7, Isthmian 8*. Salem, NH.

Carey, C. 1995. 'The Witness's Exomosia in the Athenian Courts', *Classical Quarterly* 45(i): 114–19.

Carey, C. 2000. 'Observers of Speech and Hearers of Action', in O. Taplin, ed. *Literature in the Greek and Roman Worlds*, 194–216. Oxford.

Carey, C. 2004. *The Rhetoric of Diabole*. http://discovery.ucl.ac.uk/3281/. Accessed 18 August 2015.

Carey, C. 2007. 'Pindar, Place and Performance', in Hornblower and Morgan 2007: 199–210.

Cargill, J. 1995. *Athenian Settlements of the Fourth Century B.C.* Leiden.

Carrier, J. G. 1995a. *Gifts and Commodities: Exchange and Western Capitalism since 1700*. London and New York.

Carrier, J. G. 1995b. 'Maussian Occidentalism: Gift and Commodity Systems', in J. G. Carrier, ed. *Occidentalism: Images of the West*, 85–108. Oxford.

Cawkwell, G. 1984. 'Athenian Naval Power in the Fourth Century', *Classical Quarterly* NS 34: 334–45.

Chambry, A. 1925-6. *Aesopi Fabulae*. 2 vols. Paris.

Chaniotis, A. 1997. '"Tempeljustiz" im kaiserzeitlichen Kleinasien: Rechtliche Aspekte der Sühneinschriften Lydiens und Phrygiens', in G. Thür and J. Vélissaropoulos-Karakostas, eds. *Symposion 1995: Vorträge zur griechischen und hellenistischen Rechtsgeschichte (Korfu, 1.–5. September 1995)*, 353–84. Cologne, Weimar, and Vienna.

Chaniotis, A. 2002. 'Foreign Soldier—Native Girls: Constructing and Crossing Boundaries in Hellenistic Cities and Garrisons', in A. C. and P. Ducrey, eds. *Army and Power in the Ancient World*, 99–113. Stuttgart.

Chaniotis, A. 2004. 'Under the Watchful Eyes of the Gods: Aspects of Divine Justice in Hellenistic and Roman Asia Minor', in S. Colvin, ed. *The Greco-Roman East: Politics, Culture, Society*, 1–43. Yale Classical Studies 31. Cambridge.

Chaniotis, A. 2009. 'From Woman to Woman: Female Voices and Emotions in Dedications to Goddesses', in C. Prêtre, ed. *Le Donateur, l'offrande et la déesse: Systèmes votifs dans les sanctuaires de déesses du monde grec*, 51–68. Kernos Suppl. 23. Liège.

Chaniotis, A. 2012. 'Introduction,' in A. Chaniotis, ed. *Unveiling Emotions: Sources and Methods for the Study of Emotions in the Greek World*, 11–36. Stuttgart.

Christ, M. 2006. *The Bad Citizen in Classical Athens*. Cambridge.
Christ, M. 2007. 'The Evolution of the Eisphora in Classical Athens', *Classical Quarterly* NS 57: 53–69.
Christes, J. 1975. *Bildung und Gesellschaft: Die Einschätzung der Bildung und ihrer Vermittler in der griechischen-römischen Antike*. Darmstadt.
Clairmont, C. W. 1970. *Gravestone and Epigram: Greek Memorials from the Archaic and Classical Period*. Mainz.
Clore, G. L., and Ortney, A. 2008. 'Appraisal Theories: How Cognition Shapes Affect into Emotion', in Lewis, Haviland-Jones, and Barrett 2008: 628–42.
Coan, J. 2010. 'Emergent Ghosts of the Emotion Machine', *Emotion Review* 2: 274–85.
Cohen, D. 1991. *Law, Sexuality and Society: The Enforcement of Morals in Classical Athens*. Cambridge.
Cohen, D. 1995. *Law, Violence, and Community in Classical Athens*. Cambridge.
Cohen, E. E. 1992. *Athenian Economy and Society: A Banking Perspective*. Princeton, NJ.
Cohen, E. E. 2000. 'Whoring under Contract: The Legal Context of Prostitution in Fourth-Century Athens', in Hunter and Edmondson 2000: 113–48.
Cohen, E. E. 2008. 'Athenian Citizens as Sex Workers', in P. Matthaiou and I. Polinskaya, eds. *ΜΙΚΡΟΣ ΙΕΡΟΜΝΗΜΩΝ: ΜΕΛΕΤΕΣ ΕΙΣ ΜΝΗΜΗΝ Michael H. Jameson*, 167–77. Athens.
Coleman, J. S. 1988. 'Social Capital in the Creation of Human Capital', *American Journal of Sociology* 94 Suppl. S95–S120.
Coleman, J. S. 1990. *Foundations of Social Theory*. Cambridge, MA.
Collard, C., and Cropp, M., eds. and trs. 2008. *Euripides: Fragments*. 2 vols. Loeb Classical Library. Cambridge, MA.
Collins, D. 2001. 'Theoris of Lemnos and the Criminalization of Magic in Fourth-Century Athens', *Classical Quarterly* NS 51: 477–93.
Collins, D. 2003. 'Nature, Cause and Agency in Greek Magic', *Transactions and Proceedings of the American Philological Association* 133: 17–49.
Collins, D. 2008. *Magic in the Ancient Greek World*. Malden, MA.
Connelly, J. 2007. *Portrait of a Priestess: Women and Ritual in Ancient Greece*. Princeton, NJ.
Connor, W. R. 1988. 'Seized by the Nymphs: Nympholepsy and Symbolic Expression in Classical Greece', *Classical Antiquity* 7: 155–89.
Connor, W. R. 1991. 'The Other 399: Religion and the Trial of Socrates', in M. A. Flower and M. Toher, eds. *Georgica: Greek Studies in Honour of George Cawkwell*. Institute of Classical Studies Bulletin Suppl. 58: 49–56.
Cooper, C. 1995. 'Hyperides and the Trial of Phryne', *Phoenix* 49: 303–18.
Cougny, E. 1890. *Epigrammatum Anthologia Palatina*, iii: *Appendix Nova*. Paris.

Couilloud, M.-T. 1974. *Les Monuments funéraires de Rhénée*. Exploration archéologique de Délos 30. Paris.
Cox, B. A. 1970. 'What is Hopi Gossip about? Information Management and Hopi Factions', *Man* NS 5: 88–98.
Cribiore, R. 2007. *The School of Libanius in Late Antique Antioch*. Princeton, NJ.
Cribiore, R. 2013. *Libanius the Sophist: Rhetoric, Reality, and Religion in the Fourth Century*. Ithaca, NY.
Crook, Z. A. 2005. 'Reflections on Cultural and Social-Scientific Models', *Journal of Biblical Literature* 124: 515–20.
Crotty, K. 1980. 'Pythian 2 and Conventional Language in the Epinicians', *Hermes* 108: 1–12.
Crotty, K. 1982. *Song and Action: The Victory Odes of Pindar*. Baltimore, MD.
Crowley, J. 2012. *The Psychology of the Athenian Hoplite: The Culture of Combat in Classical Athens*. Cambridge.
Cudjoe, R. 2010. *The Social and Legal Position of Widows and Orphans in Classical Athens*. Athens.
Cummings, F. 1964. 'Charles Bell and the Anatomy of Expression', *The Art Bulletin* 46: 191–203.
Cumont, F. 1923. 'Il sole vindice dei delitti ed il simbolo delle mani alzate', *Atti della Pontificia Accademia Romana di Archeologia, Memorie* 1, ser. 3, 1: 65–80.
Cumont, F. 1926–7. 'Nuovi epitaffi col simbolo della preghiera al dio vindice', *Rendiconti della Pontificia Accademia Romana di Archeologia*, ser. 3, 5: 67–78.
Cumont, F. 1933. 'Deux monuments du culte solaire', *Syria* 14: 385–95.
Cunningham, W. A., and Zelazo, P. D. 2007. 'Attitudes and Evaluations: A Social Cognitive Neuroscience Perspective', *Trends in Cognitive Sciences* 11: 97–104.
Currie, B. 2005. *Pindar and the Cult of Heroes*. Oxford.
Dalby, A. 1992. 'Social Organisation and Food among the Ten Thousand', *Journal of Hellenic Studies* 112: 16–30.
Damasio, A. 1994. *Descartes' Error: Emotion, Reason, and the Human Brain*. London.
D'Andrade, R. G. 1995. *The Development of Cognitive Anthropology*. Cambridge.
D'Andrade, R. and Strauss, C., eds. 1992. *Human Motives and Cultural Models*. Cambridge.
Darwin, C. R. 1867. 'Queries about Expression', in R. S[winhoe], 'Signs of Emotion Amongst the Chinese', *Notes and Queries on China and Japan* 1 (31 August): 105. In John van Wyhe, ed. 2002–. The Complete Work of Charles Darwin Online, http://darwin-online.org.uk. Accessed 18 August 2015.
Darwin, C. R. 1958 [1887]. *Autobiography of Charles Darwin (1809–1892)*. With the original omissions restored. Edited and with appendix and notes by his grand-daughter Nora Barlow. London.

Darwin, C. R. 1998 [1872]. *The Expression of the Emotions in Man and Animals*, 3rd edn (ed. P. Ekman). London and New York.
David, E. 1984. *Aristophanes and Athenian Society of the Early Fourth Century B.C.* Mnemosyne Suppl. 81. Leiden.
Davidson, J. 1990. 'Isocrates against Imperialism: an Analysis of the *De Pace*', *Historia: Zeitschrift für Alte Geschichte* 39: 20–36.
Davies, G. 1985. 'The Significance of the Handshake Motif in Classical Funerary Art', *American Journal of Archaeology* 89: 627–40.
Davies, J. K. 1971. *Athenian Propertied Families, 600–300 BCE*. Oxford.
Davies, J. K. 1981. *Wealth and the Power of Wealth in Classical Athens*. New York.
Dawson, G. 1994. *Soldier Heroes: British Adventure, Empire and the Imaging of Masculinity*. London.
Deissmann, A. 1911. *Light from the Ancient East*. London.
Demetriou, D. 2012. *Negotiating Identity in the Ancient Mediterranean: The Archaic and Classical Greek Multiethnic Emporia*. Cambridge.
den Boer, W. 1979. *Private Morality in Greece and Rome*. Leiden.
Derenne, E. 1930. *Les Procès d'impiété intentés aux philosophes à Athènes au Vme et au IVme siècles avant J.-C.* Liège.
de Rivera, J. 1977. *A Structural Theory of the Emotions*. Psychological Issues, Monograph no. 40. New York.
de Romilly, J. 1975. *Magic and Rhetoric in Ancient Greece*. Cambridge, MA.
Derrida, J. 1981. 'Plato's Pharmacy', in *Dissemination*, tr. B. Johnson, 173–276. Chicago.
de Ste. Croix, G. E. M. 1981. *The Class Struggle in the Ancient Greek World*. Ithaca, NY.
Dewald, C. 2008. 'Alternatives to the Golden Rule: Social Reciprocity and Altruism in Early Archaic Greece', in J. Neusner and B. Chilton, eds. *The Golden Rule: The Ethics of Reciprocity in World Religions*, 26–39. London.
Dickerson, G., and Williams, C. 2009. 'Introduction to Sophocles' *Women of Trachis*', in P. Burian and A. Shapiro, eds. *The Complete Sophocles, ii: Electra and Other Plays*, 97–108. Oxford.
Dickie, M. 1984. 'Hesychia and Hybris in Pindar', in D. E. Gerber, ed. *Greek Poetry and Philosophy: Studies in Honour of Leonard Woodbury*, 83–109. Chico, CA.
Dickie, M. 1987. 'Lo $\phi\theta\acute{o}\nu o\varsigma$ degli dei nella letteratura greca del quinto secolo avanti Cristo', *Atene e Roma* 32: 113–25.
Dickie, M. 1991. 'Heliodorus and Plutarch on the Evil Eye', *Classical Philology* 86: 17–29.
Dickie, M. 1995. 'The Fathers of the Church and the Evil Eye', in H. Maguire, ed. *Byzantine Magic*, 9–34. Cambridge, MA.
Dickie, M. 2001. *Magic and Magicians in the Greco-Roman World*. London.
Difonzo, N., and Bordia, P. 2007. 'Rumor, Gossip and Urban Legends', *Diogenes* 213: 19–35.

Dillery, J. 2005. 'Chresmologues and *Manteis*: Independent Diviners and the Problem of Authority', in S. Iles Johnston and P. T. Struck, eds. *Mantikê: Studies in Ancient Divination*, 167–231. Leiden.

Dillon, M. 2002. *Girls and Women in Classical Greek Religion*. Abingdon.

Dilts, M. R. 1986. *Scholia Demosthenica*, ii. Leipzig.

Dindorf, A. 1853. *Harpocrationis Lexicon in Decem Oratores Atticos*. Oxford.

Dodds, E. R. 1952. *The Greeks and the Irrational*. Berkeley, CA.

Douglas, M. 1990. 'Foreword' in M. Mauss, *The Gift: The Form and Reason for Exchange in Archaic Societies*, translated by W. D. Halls, vii–xviii. New York and London.

Dover, K. 1968. *Aristophanes: Clouds*. London.

Dover, K. 1974. *Greek Popular Morality in the Time of Plato and Aristotle*. Berkeley and Los Angeles.

Dover, K. 1975. 'The Freedom of the Intellectual in Greek Society', *Talanta* 7: 24–54.

Driscoll, J. 2003. *Evagrius Ponticus: Ad Monachos*. Ancient Christian Writers 59. New York and Mahwah, NJ.

du Boulay, J. 1974. *Portrait of a Greek Mountain Village*. Oxford.

du Boulay, J. 1976. 'Lies, Mockery and Family Integrity', in J. G. Peristiany, ed. *Mediterranean Family Structures*, 389–406. Cambridge.

Dunbabin, K., and Dickie, M. 1983. 'Invidia Rumpantur Pectora: The Iconography of Phthonos/Invidia in Graeco-Roman Art', *Jahrbuch für Antike und Christentum* 26: 7–37.

Dunbar, R. 1996. *Grooming, Gossip and the Evolution of Language*. London.

Dunbar, R. 2004. 'Gossip in Evolutionary Perspective,' *Review of General Psychology* 8: 100–10.

Duncan-Jones, R. P. 1996. 'The Impact of the Antonine Plague', *Journal of Roman Archaeology*, 9: 108–36.

Dundes, A., ed. 1981. *The Evil Eye: A Folklore Casebook*. New York.

Easterling, P. E., ed. 1982. *Sophocles: Trachiniai*. Cambridge.

Edmonds, III, R. G. 2010. 'Blaming the Witch: Some Reflections upon Unexpected Death', in S. P. Ahearne-Kroll and J. Kelhoffer, eds. *Women and Gender in Ancient Religions: Interdisciplinary Approaches*, 241–54. Tübingen.

Edwards, D. 1999. 'Emotion Discourse', *Culture and Psychology* 5: 271–91.

Edwards, M. 2007. *Isaeus*. Austin, TX.

Eger, O. 1939. 'Eid und Fluch in den maionischen und phrygischen Sühne-Inschriften', in *Festschrift für Paul Koschaker*, iii, 281–93. Weimar.

Ehrenberg, V. 1969. *The Greek State*. 2nd edn. London.

Eidinow, E. 2007. 'Why the Athenians Began to Curse', in Osborne 2007: 44–71.

Eidinow, E. 2011a. *Luck, Fate and Fortune: Antiquity and its Legacy*. London.

Eidinow, E. 2011b. 'Networks and Narratives: A Model for Ancient Greek Religion', *Kernos* 24: 9–38.

Eidinow, E. 2013a. [2007]. *Oracles, Curses, and Risk among the Ancient Greeks.* Oxford.

Eidinow, E. 2013b. 'Oracular Consultation, Fate, and the Concept of the Individual', in V. Roseberger, ed. *Divination in the Ancient World: Religious Options and the Individual.* Potsdamer Altertumswissenschaftliche Beiträge, Band 46. Stuttgart.

Eidinow, E. 2015. 'Ancient Greek Religion: "Embedded" . . . and Embodied', in C. Taylor and K. Vlassopoulos, eds. *Communities and Networks in the Ancient Greek World*, 54–79. Oxford.

Eidinow, E. Forthcoming a. 'Popular Theology? The "Embedding" of a Nasty Idea', in E. Eidinow, J. Kindt, and R. Osborne, eds. *Theologies of Ancient Greek Religion.* Cambridge.

Eidinow, E. Forthcoming b. 'In Search of the Beggar Priest', in R. Gordon, G. Petridou, and J. Rüpke, eds. *Beyond Priesthood: Religious Entrepreneurs and Innovators in the Imperial Era.* Berlin.

Eidinow, E., and Taylor, C. 2010. 'Lead-Letter Days: Writing, Communication and Crisis in the Ancient Greek World', *Classical Quarterly* NS 60: 30–62.

Ekman, P. 1984. 'Expression and the Nature of Emotion', in K. Scherer and P. Ekman, eds. *Approaches to Emotion*, 319–44. Hillsdale, MI.

Ekman, P. 1992a. 'Are There Basic Emotions?', *Psychological Review* 99: 550–3.

Ekman, P. 1992b. 'Facial Expressions of Emotion: New Findings, New Questions', *Psychological Science* 3: 34–8.

Ekman, P. 1992c. 'An Argument for Basic Emotions', *Cognition and Emotion* 6: 169–200.

Ekman, P. 1998. 'Introduction to the Third Edition,' in Darwin 1998: xxi–xxxvi.

Ekman, P. 1999. 'Facial Expressions', in T. Dalgliesh and M. J. Power, eds. *Handbook of Cognition and Emotion*, 301–20. Chichester.

Ekman, P. 2009. 'Darwin's Contributions to Our Understanding of Emotional Expressions', *Philosophical Transactions of the Royal Society of London*, Series B, 364: 3449–51.

Ekman, P., Davidson R. J., and Friesen, W. V. 1990. 'Emotional Expression and Brain Physiology II: The Duchenne Smile', *Journal of Personality and Social Psychology* 58: 342–53.

Ekman, P., and Friesen, W. V. 1969. 'The Repertoire of Nonverbal Behavior: Categories, Origins, Usage and Coding', *Semiotica* 1: 49–98.

Ekman, P., and Friesen, W. V. 1975. *Unmasking the Face: A Guide to Recognizing Emotions from Facial Clues.* Englewood Cliffs, NJ.

Ekman, P., Friesen, W. V., and Ellsworth P. 1972. *Emotion in the Human Face*. Elmsford, NY.

Ekman, P., Levenson, R. W., and Friesen, W. V. 1983. 'Autonomic Nervous System Activity Distinguishes between Emotions', *Science* 221: 1208–10.

Ellickson, R. 1991. *Order Without Law: How Neighbors Settle Disputes*. Cambridge, MA.

Ellsworth, P. C., and Scherer, K. R. 2003. 'Appraisal Processes in Emotion', in R. J. Davidson, K. R. Scherer, and H. H. Goldsmith, eds. *The Handbook of Affective Science*, 572–95. New York.

Emerson, R. W. 1929. 'Gifts', in *The Complete Writings of Ralph Waldo Emerson*, i. New York.

Emler, N. 1990. 'A Social Psychology of Reputation', *European Review of Social Psychology* 1: 171–93.

Emler, N. 1994. 'Gossip, Reputation, and Social Adaptation', in Goodman and Ben-Ze'ev 1994: 117–38.

Engen, D. T. 2010. *Honor and Profit: Athenian Trade Policy and the Economy and Society of Greece, 415–307 BCE*. Ann Arbor, MI.

Enquist, M., and Leimar, O. 1993. 'The Evolution of Cooperation in Mobile Organisms', *Animal Behaviour* 45: 747–57.

Evans, V., and Green, M. C. 2006. *Cognitive Linguistics: An Introduction*. London.

Evans-Pritchard, E. E. 1937. *Witchcraft, Oracles and Magic among the Azande*. Oxford.

Fahr, W. 1969. *ΘΕΟΥΣ ΝΟΜΙΖΕΙΝ*. Spudasmata 26. Hildesheim.

Fähse, G. 1804. *Sophokles. Trauerspiele*, vol. i. Leipzig.

Faraguna, M. 1992. *Atene nell'età di Alessandro: Problemi politici, economici, finanziari*. Rome.

Faraone, C. A. 1985. 'Aeschylus' *humnos desmios* (*Eum.* 306) and Attic Judicial Curse Tablets', *Journal of Hellenic Studies* 105: 150–4.

Faraone, C. A. 1991. 'Binding and Burying the Forces of Evil: The Defensive Use of "Voodoo Dolls" in Ancient Greece', *Classical Antiquity* 10: 165–220.

Faraone, C. A., and Obbink, D., eds. 1991. *Magika Hiera: Ancient Greek Magic and Religion*. Oxford.

Fauconnier, G., and Turner, M. 1998. 'Conceptual Integration Networks', *Cognitive Science* 22: 133–87.

Fauconnier, G., and Turner, M. 2002. *The Way We Think: Conceptual Blending and the Mind's Hidden Complexities*. New York.

Favret-Saada, J. 1980. *Deadly Words: Witchcraft in the Bocage*, tr. C. Cullen. Paris and Cambridge.

Festugière, A. J. 1959. *Antioche païenne et chrétienne: Libanius, Chrysostome et les moines de Syrie*. Paris.

Feuchtwang, S. 2011. *After the Event: The Transmission of Grievous Loss in Germany, China, and Taiwan*. Oxford and New York.

Filonik, J. 2013. 'Athenian Impiety Trials: A Reappraisal', *Dike* 16: 11–96.
Finley, M. I. 1977. 'Socrates and Athens', in M. I. Finley, ed. *Aspects of Antiquity: Discoveries and Controversies*, 58–72. 2nd edn. Harmondsworth.
Firth, R. 1959. *Economics of the New Zealand Maori*. 2nd edn. Wellington, NZ. Originally published 1929 as *Primitive Economics of the New Zealand Maori*. London.
Fisher, N. R. E. 1993. *Slavery in Classical Greece*. Bristol.
Fisher, N. R. E. 2001. *Aeschines: Against Timarchos*. Oxford.
Flower, M. A. 1997. *Theopompus of Chios: History and Rhetoric in the Fourth Century BCE*. Oxford.
Flower, M. A. 2008. *The Seer in Ancient Greece*. Berkeley, CA.
Fontenrose, J. 1968. 'The Hero as Athlete', *California Studies in Classical Antiquity* 1: 73–104.
Forsdyke, S. 2008. 'Street Theater and Popular Justice in Ancient Greece: Shaming, Stoning and Starving Offenders Inside and Outside the Courts', *Past & Present* no. 201: 3–50.
Forsdyke, S. 2012. Review of Herman, G., ed. *Stability and Crisis in the Athenian Democracy*. Historia Einzelschriften 220. Stuttgart, *Bryn Mawr Classical Review* (2012.10.37). doi: bmcr.brynmawr.edu/2012/2012-10-37.html.
Forster, E. S., tr. 1927. *Isaeus*. Loeb Classical Library. Cambridge, MA.
Foster, E. K. 2004. 'Research on Gossip: Taxonomy, Methods, and Future Directions', *Review of General Psychology* 8: 78–99.
Foster, E. K., and Rosnow, R. L. 2006. 'Gossip and Network Relationships: The Processes of Constructing and Managing Difficult Interaction', in D. C. Kirkpatrick, S. Duck, and M. K. Foley, eds. *Relating Difficulty: The Processes of Constructing and Managing Difficult Interaction*, 161–80. Mahwah, NJ.
Foucart, P. 1902. 'L'Accusation de Phryné', *Revue de philologie, de littérature et d'histoire anciennes* 26: 216–18.
Fowler, H. N., tr. 1914. *Plato: Euthyphro, Apology, Crito, Phaedo, Phaedrus*. Loeb Classical Library. Cambridge, MA.
Fowler, H. N., tr. 1936. *Plutarch: Moralia*, x. Loeb Classical Library. Cambridge, MA.
Foxhall, L. 1989. 'Household, Gender and Property in Classical Athens', *Classical Quarterly* NS 39: 22–44.
Foxhall, L. 1992. 'The Control of the Attic Landscape', in B. Wells, ed. *Agriculture in Ancient Greece: Proceedings of the Seventh International Symposium at the Swedish Institute at Athens, 16–17th May 1990*, 155–9. Stockholm.
Foxhall, L. 1993. 'Farming and Fighting in Ancient Greece', in J. Rich and G. Shipley, eds. *War and Society in the Greek World*, 134–45. London.
Foxhall, L. 2002. 'Access to Resources in Classical Greece: The Egalitarianism of the Polis in Practice', in P. Cartledge, E. Cohen, and L. Foxhall, eds.

Money, Labour and Land: Approaches to the Economies of Ancient Greece, 209–20. London.
Frankenberg, R. 1957. *Village on the Border*. London.
Frankfurter, D. 2006. 'Fetus Magic and Sorcery Fears in Roman Egypt', *Greek, Roman, and Byzantine Studies* 46: 37–62.
Frede, D. 1993. *Plato: Philebus*. Indianapolis and Cambridge.
Freese, J. H., tr. 1926. *Aristotle: Art of Rhetoric*. Loeb Classical Library. Cambridge, MA.
French, A. 1991. 'Economic Conditions in Fourth-Century Athens', *Greece and Rome* 38: 24–40.
French, K. L. 2011. *The Good Women of the Parish: Gender and Religion after the Black Death*. Philadelphia.
Friedrich, J. 1918. 'Das Attische im Munde von Ausländern bei Aristophanes', *Philologus* 75: 274–303.
Frijda, N. H. 1986. *The Emotions*. Cambridge.
Frith, C. D., and Frith, U. 2012. 'Mechanisms of Social Cognition', *Annual Review of Psychology* 63: 287–313.
Fuks, A. 1984. *Social Conflict in Ancient Greece*. Leiden.
Gabrielsen, V. 1981. *Remuneration of State Officials in Fourth Century BC Athens*. Odense.
Gabrielsen, V. 1986. 'ΦΑΝΕΡΑ and ΑΦΑΝΗΣ ΟΥΣΙΑ in Classical Athens', *Classica et Mediaevalia* 37: 99–114.
Gabrielsen, V. 1994. *Financing the Athenian Fleet: Public Taxation and Social Relations*. Baltimore, MD.
Gagarin, M. 1997. *Antiphon: The Speeches*. Cambridge.
Gagarin, M. 2002. *Antiphon the Athenian: Oratory, Law and Justice in the Age of the Sophists*. Austin, TX.
Gagarin, M. 2012. 'Law, Politics, and the Question of Relevance in the Case On the Crown', *Classical Antiquity* 31: 293–314.
Gager, J. G. 1992. *Curse Tablets and Binding Spells from the Ancient World*. Oxford.
Gagné, R. 2009. 'Mystery Inquisitors: Performance, Authority and Sacrilege at Eleusis', *Classical Antiquity* 28: 211–47.
Gallant, T. W. 1991. *Risk and Survival in Ancient Greece: Reconstructing the Rural Domestic Economy*. Stanford, CA.
Galt, A. H. 1982. 'The Evil Eye as Synthetic Image and its Meanings on the Island of Pantelleria, Italy', *American Ethnologist* 9: 664–81.
Galt, A. H. 1991. *Far from the Church Bells: Settlement and Society in an Apulian Town*. Cambridge.
Gardner, A., ed. 2004a. *Agency Uncovered: Archaeological Perspectives on Social Agency, Power and Being Human*. London.
Gardner, A. 2004b. 'Introduction: Social Agency, Power and Being Human', in Gardner 2004a: 1–15.

Gardner, A. 2004c. 'Agency and Community in 4th Century Britain: Developing the Structurationist Project', in Gardner 2004a: 33–49.
Garland, R. 1990. *The Greek Way of Life: From Conception to Old Age*. Ithaca, NY.
Garland, R. 1992. *Introducing New Gods: The Politics of Athenian Religion*. Ithaca, NY.
Garnsey, P. 1984. 'Religious Toleration in Classical Antiquity', in W. Shiels, ed. *Persecution and Toleration: Papers read at the 22nd Summer Meeting and the 23rd Winter Meeting of the Ecclesiastical History Society*. Studies in Church History 21, 1–28. London.
Garnsey, P. 1988. *Famine and Food Supply in the Graeco-Roman World: Responses to Risk and Crisis*. Cambridge.
Garnsey, P. 1998. *Cities, Peasants and Food in Classical Antiquity: Essays in Social and Economic History*, ed. with addenda by Walter Scheidel. Cambridge.
Gawlinski, L. 2012. *The Sacred Law of Andania: A New Text with Commentary*. Berlin.
Geertz, A. W. 2004. 'Cognitive Approaches to the Study of Religion', in P. Antes, A. W. Geertz, and R. R. Warne, eds. *New Approaches to the Study of Religion*, ii: *Textual, Comparative, Sociological and Cognitive Approaches*, 347–440. Berlin and New York.
Geertz, C. 1960. *The Religion of Java*. Chicago.
Gendron, M., and Barrett, L. F. 2009. 'Reconstructing the Past: A Century of Ideas about Emotion in Psychology', *Emotions Review* 1: 316–39.
Gendron, M., Lindquist, K. A., Barsalou, L., and Barrett, L. F. 2012. 'Emotion Words Shape Emotion Percepts', *Emotion* 12: 314–25.
Gerber, D. E., ed. and tr. 1999. *Greek Iambic Poetry from the Seventh to the Fifth Centuries BC: Archilochus, Semonides, Hipponax*. Loeb Classical Library. Cambridge, MA.
Gernet, L. 1968. *Anthropologie de la Grèce antique*. Paris.
Geschiere, P. 2013. *Witchcraft, Intimacy and Trust: Africa in Comparison*. Chicago.
Giammellaro, P. 2013. 'Ἀγύρται. Pratiche magiche, itineranza e marginalità religiosa nella Grecia antica', in M. Piranomonte and F. M. Simón, eds. *Contextos mágicos, Atti del Convegno Internazionale*, 279–82. Rome.
Gildersleeve, B. L. 1885. *Pindar: The Olympian and Pythian Odes*. New York.
Gill, C. 1996. *Personality in Greek Epic, Tragedy, and Philosophy: The Self in Dialogue*. New York.
Gilmore, D. 1978. 'Varieties of Gossip in a Spanish Rural Community', *Ethnology* 17: 89–99.
Gluckman, M. 1963. 'Papers in Honor of Melville J. Herskovits: Gossip and Scandal', *Current Anthropology* 4: 307–16.
Gluckman, M. 1968. 'Psychological, Sociological and Anthropological Explanations of Witchcraft and Gossip: a Clarification', *Man* NS 3: 20–34.

Godelier, M. 1999. *The Enigma of the Gift*. Chicago.
Godley, A. D., tr. 1920. *Herodotus: The Histories*. Loeb Classical Library. Cambridge, MA.
Goff, B. 2004. *Citizen Bacchae: Women's Ritual Practice in Ancient Greece*. Berkeley and Los Angeles.
Goffman, E. 1961. *Encounters: Two Studies in the Sociology of Interaction*. Indianapolis, IN.
Golden, M. 1981. 'Demography and the Exposure of Girls at Athens', *Phoenix* 35: 316–31.
Golden, M. 1990. *Children and Childhood in Classical Athens*. Baltimore, MD and London.
Golden, M. 2003. Childhood in Early Greece', in J. Neils, J. H. Oakley, K. Hart, and L. A. Beaumont, eds. *Coming of Age in Ancient Greece: Images of Childhood from the Classical Past*, 13–30. Hanover, NH.
Golden, M. 2009. 'Oedipal Complexities', in Hübner and Ratzan 2009a: 41–60.
Goldhill, S. 1991. *The Poet's Voice: Essays on Poetics and Greek Literature*. Cambridge.
Goode, E., and Ben-Yehuda, N. 2009. *Moral Panics: The Social Construction of Deviance*. 2nd edn. Chichester.
Goodman, B. F., and Ben-Ze'ev, A., eds. 1994. *Good Gossip*. Lawrence, KS.
Goodwin, M. H. 1982. '"Instigating": Storytelling as Social Process', *American Ethnologist* 9: 799–816.
Goodwin, M. H. 1990. *He-Said-She-Said: Talk As Social Organization Among Black Children*. Bloomington, IN.
Gordon, R. 1999. 'Imagining Greek and Roman Magic', in Ankarloo and Clark 1999: 159–276.
Gordon, R. 2004. 'Raising a Sceptre: Confession-Narratives from Lydia and Phrygia', *Journal of Roman Archaeology* 17: 177–96.
Gosden, C., 2004. 'Aesthetics, Intelligence and Emotions. Implications for Archaeology', in E. Demarrais, C. Gosden, and C. Renfrew, eds. *Rethinking Materiality: The Engagement of Mind with the Material World*, 33–40. Cambridge.
Gould, J. 2001a. 'Give and Take in Herodotus', in J. Gould, *Myth, Ritual, Memory and Exchange: Essays in Greek Literature and Culture*, 283–303. Oxford.
Gould, J. 2001b. 'The Idea of Society in the Iliad', in J. Gould, *Myth, Ritual, Memory and Exchange: Essays in Greek Literature and Culture*, 335–58. Oxford.
Graf, F. 1985. *Nordionische Kulte: Religionsgeschichtliche und epigraphische Untersuchungen zu den Kulten von Chios, Erythrai, Klazomenai und Phokaia*. Rome.
Graf, F. 1997. *Magic in the Ancient World*. Cambridge, MA.
Graf, F. 2000. 'Der Mysterienprozess', in L. Burckhardt and J. von Ungern-Sternberg, eds. *Große Prozesse im antiken Athen*, 114–27. Munich.

Graf, F. 2007. 'Untimely Death, Witchcraft, and Divine Vengeance: A Reasoned Epigraphical Catalog', *Zeitschrift für Papyrologie und Epigraphik* 162: 139–50.

Graf, F. 2010. 'Victimology: or, How to Deal with Untimely Death', in *Women and Gender in Ancient Religions: Interdisciplinary Approaches*, 228–40. Tübingen.

Graham, A. J. 1992. 'Abdera and Teos', *Journal of Hellenic Studies* 112: 44–73.

Greco, M., and Stenner, P. 2008. *Emotions: A Social Science Reader*. Oxford.

Griffiths, P. E. 1997. *What Emotions Really Are: The Problem of Psychological Categories*. Chicago.

Griffiths, P. E. 2004. 'Is Emotion a Natural Kind?', in Solomon 2004: 233–49.

Guarducci, M. 1978. *Epigrafia greca*, iv. Rome.

Guettel Cole, S. 2001. 'Achieving Political Maturity: *Stephanosis, Philotimia*, and *Phallephoria*', in D. Papenfuß and V. M. Strocka, eds. *Gab es das Griechische Wunder?*, 203–14. Mainz.

Hacking, I. 1999. *The Social Construction of What?* Cambridge, MA.

Halm-Tisserant, M. 1998. *Realités et imaginaire des supplices en Grèce ancienne*. Paris.

Halperin, D. 1990a. *One Hundred Years of Homosexuality and Other Essays on Greek Love*. New York and London.

Halperin, D. 1990b. 'Why is Diotima a Woman?', in D. Halperin, J. Winkler, and F. Zeitlin, eds. *Before Sexuality: The Construction of Erotic Experience in the Ancient Greek World*, 257–308. Princeton, NJ.

Hamel, D. 2003. *Trying Neaira: The True Story of a Courtesan's Scandalous Life in Ancient Greece*. New Haven, CT.

Hampe, B. 2005. 'Introduction: Image Schemas in Cognitive Linguistics', in B. Hampe and J. Grady, eds. *From Perception to Meaning: Image Schemas in Cognitive Linguistics*, 1–12. Berlin.

Handelman, D. 1973. 'Gossip in Encounters: The Transmission of Information in a Bounded Social Setting', *Man* NS 8: 210–27.

Hannerz, U. 1967. 'Gossip Networks and Culture in a Black American Ghetto', *Ethnos* 32: 35–59.

Hansen, M. H. 1975. *Eisangelia: The Sovereignty of the People's Court in Athens in the Fourth Century BC and the Impeachment of Generals and Politicians*. Odense.

Hansen, M. H. 1976. 'How Many Athenians Attended the Ecclesia?', *Greek, Roman, and Byzantine Studies* 17: 115–34.

Hansen, M. H. 1979. 'Misthos for Magistrates in Classical Athens', *Symbolae Osloensis* 54: 5–22.

Hansen, M. H. 1980. 'Perquisites for Magistrates in Fourth-Century Athens', *Classica et Mediaevalia* 32: 105–25.

Hansen, M. H. 1985. *Demography and Democracy: The Number of Athenian Citizens in the Fourth Century B.C.* Herning.

Hansen, M. H. 1988a. 'Athenian Population Losses, 431–403 BCE, and the Number of Athenian Citizens in 431', in M. H. Hansen, *Three Studies in Athenian Demography*, 14–28. Copenhagen.

Hansen, M. H. 1988b. 'Demography and Democracy Once Again', *Zeitschrift für Papyrologie und Epigraphik* 75: 189–93.

Hansen, M. H. 1991. *The Athenian Democracy in the Age of Demosthenes: Structure, Principles and Ideology*, tr. J. A. Cook. Cambridge, MA.

Hansen, M. H. 1994. 'The Number of Athenian Citizens *Secundum* Sekunda', *Échos du monde classique* 13: 299–310.

Hansen, M. H. 1995. *The Trial of Socrates—from the Athenian Point of View*. Historisk-filosofiske Meddelelser 71. Copenhagen.

Hansen, M. H. 2006a. *Studies in the Population of Aigina, Athens and Eretria*. Historisk-filosofiske Meddelelser 94. Copenhagen.

Hansen, M. H. 2006b. *The Shotgun Method: The Demography of the Ancient Greek City-State Culture*. Columbia, MO.

Hanson, V. D. 1983. *Warfare and Agriculture in Classical Greece*. Pisa.

Harding, P. 1974. 'The Purpose of Isokrates' *Archidamos* and *On the Peace*', *California Studies in Classical Antiquity* 6: 137–49.

Harding, P. 1987. 'Metics, Foreigners, or Slaves? The Recipients of Honours in *IG* II^{2}10', *Zeitschrift für Papyrologie und Epigraphik* 67: 176–82.

Harré, R., ed. 1986a. *The Social Construction of Emotion*. New York.

Harré, R. 1986b. 'An Outline of the Social Constructionist Viewpoint', in Harré 1986a: 2–14.

Harré, R., and Finlay-Jones, R. 1986. 'Emotion Talk Across Times', in R. Harré, ed. *The Social Construction of Emotion*, 221–33. New York.

Harris, E. M. 1988. 'When Was Aeschines Born?', *Classical Philology* 83: 211–14.

Harris, E. M. 1992. Review of D. M. MacDowell *Demosthenes: Against Meidias*. Oxford., *Classical Philology* 87: 71–80.

Harris, E. M. 2001a. 'How to Kill in Attic Greek', in E. Cantarella and G. Thür, eds. *Symposion 1997: Vorträge zur griechischen und hellenistischen Rechtsgeschichte*, 75–87. Cologne, Weimar, and Vienna.

Harris, E. M. 2001b. 'Lycurgus', in *Dinarchus, Hyperides, and Lycurgus*, tr. I. Worthington, C. R. Cooper, and E. M. Harris, 153–218. Austin, TX.

Harris, E. M. 2004. 'Notes on a Lead Letter from the Athenian Agora', *Harvard Studies in Classical Philology* 102: 157–70.

Harris, E. M. 2013. *The Rule of Law in Action*. Oxford.

Harris, O. J. T., and Sørensen, T. F. 2010a. 'Rethinking Emotion and Material Culture', *Archaeological Dialogues* 17: 145–63.

Harris, O. J. T., and Sørensen, T. F. 2010b. 'Talk about the Passion', *Archaeological Dialogues* 17: 186–98.

Harris, W. V. 2001. *Restraining Rage: The Ideology of Anger Control in Classical Antiquity*. Cambridge, MA.

Harrison, A. R. W. 1968. *The Law of Athens*, i: *The Family and Property*. Oxford.

Harrison, A. R. W. 1971. *The Law of Athens*, ii: *Procedure*. Oxford.
Harrison, S. 1993. Review of *Just Talk: Gossip, Meetings, and Power in a Papua New Guinea Village* by Karen J. Brison, *Man* NS 28: 618–19.
Haviland, J. B. 1977. 'Gossip as Competition in Zinacatan', *Journal of Communication* 27: 186–92.
Hawthorne, S. 1994. 'Diotima Speaks Through the Body', in Bat-Ami Bar On, ed. *Engendering Origins: Critical Feminist Readings in Plato and Aristotle*, 83–96. Albany, NY.
Heelas, P. 1986. 'Emotion Talk Across Cultures,' in Harré 1986a: 234–66.
Hendershot, C. 1999. *Paranoia, the Bomb and 1950s Science Fiction Films*. Bowling Green, OH.
Henderson, J. 1987. 'Older Women in Attic Old Comedy', *Transactions and Proceedings of the American Philological Association* 117: 105–29.
Henderson, J., ed. and tr. 2002. *Aristophanes*, iv: *Frogs, Assemblywomen, Wealth*. Loeb Classical Library. Cambridge, MA.
Henrichs, A. 2008. 'Introduction: What is a Greek Priest?', in B. Dignas and K. Trampedach, eds. *Practitioners of the Divine: Greek Priests and Religious Officials from Homer to Heliodorus*, 1–16. Cambridge, MA.
Heppenstall, M. A. 1971. 'Reputation, Criticism, and Information in an Austrian Village', in F. G. Bailey, ed. *Gifts and Poison: The Politics of Reputation*, 139–67. New York.
Herman, G., ed. 2011. *Stability and Crisis in the Athenian Democracy*. Historia Einzelschriften 220. Stuttgart.
Herriman, N. 2007. '"Sorcerer" Killings in Banyuwangi: A Re-Examination of State Responsibility for Violence', *Asian Studies Review* 31: 61–78.
Herriman, N. 2009. *The State in Indonesian Villages: Authority, Autonomy and Apparatus*. Monash.
Hesk, J. 2000. *Deception and Democracy in Classical Athens*. Cambridge.
Heskel, J. 1997. *The North Aegean Wars, 371–360 B.C.* Historia Einzelschriften 102. Stuttgart.
Hess, H. 1998. *Mafia and Mafiosi: Origin, Power and Myth*. New York.
Hicks, R. D., tr. 1925. *Diogenes Laertius: Lives of Eminent Philosophers*, i (*Books 1–5*). Loeb Classical Library. Cambridge, MA.
Hignett, C. 1952. *A History of the Athenian Constitution to the End of the Fifth Century B.C.* Oxford.
Hintzen-Bohlen, B. 1997. *Die Kulturpolitik des Eubulos und des Lykurg: Die Denkmäler- und Bauprojekte in Athen zwischen 355 und 322 v. Chr.* Berlin.
Holden, H. A. 1893. *Ploutarchou Dēmosthenēs*. Cambridge.
Holland, D. 1992. 'How Cultural Systems become Desire: A Case Study of American Romance', in D'Andrade and Strauss 1992: 61–89.
Homolle, T. 1901. 'Inscriptions d'Amorgos', *Bulletin de correspondance hellénique* 25: 412–30.

Hopfner, Th. 1928. 'Mageia', in A. F. Pauly, G. Wissowa, and W. Kroll, eds. *Realencyclopädie der classischen Altertumswissenschaft*, xiv.1, cols 301–93. Stuttgart.

Hopper, R. J. 1968. 'The Laurion Mines: A Reconsideration', *Annual of the British School at Athens* 63: 247–54.

Hornblower, S. 2006. *Thucydides and Pindar: Historical Narrative and the World of Epinikian Poetry*. Oxford.

Hornblower, S. 2011. *The Greek World 479–323 BC*. London.

Hornblower, S., and Morgan, C., eds. 2007. *Pindar's Poetry, Patrons, and Festivals: From Archaic Greece to the Roman Empire*. Oxford.

Hubbard, T. K. 1990. 'Envy and the Invisible Roar: Pindar, Pythian 11.30', *Greek, Roman, and Byzantine Studies* 31: 343–51.

Hübner, S., and Ratzan, D., eds. 2009a. *Growing up Fatherless in Antiquity*. Cambridge.

Hübner, S., and Ratzan, D. 2009b. 'Fatherless Antiquity? Perspectives on "Fatherlessness" in the Ancient Mediterranean', in Hübner and Ratzan 2009a: 3–28.

Hunt, P. 2010. *War, Peace and Alliance in Demosthenes' Athens*. Cambridge.

Hunter, V. 1989. 'The Athenian Widow and her Kin', *Journal of Family History* 14: 291–311.

Hunter, V. 1994. *Policing Athens: Social Control in the Attic Lawsuits, 420–320 B.C.* Princeton, NJ.

Hunter, V., and Edmondson, J., eds. 2000. *Law and Social Status in Classical Athens*. Oxford.

Iles Johnston, S. 1999. *Restless Dead: Encounters between the Living and the Dead in Ancient Greece*. Berkeley, CA.

Izard, C. 1971. *The Face of Emotion*. New York.

Jakov, D., and Voutiras, E. 2005. 'Gebet, Gebärden und Handlungen des Gebetes', in *Thesaurus Cultus et Rituum Antiquorum*, iii: 104–41. Los Angeles.

James, W. 1884a. 'The Physical Basis of Emotion', *Psychological Review* 1: 516–29; repr. 1994 in *Psychological Review* 101: 205–10.

James, W. 1884b. 'What is an Emotion?', *Mind* 9: 188–205.

James, W. 1890. (Repr. 1950.) 'The Emotions,' in *The Principles of Psychology*, ii: 442–85. New York.

Jameson, M. 1980. 'Apollo Lykeios in Athens', *Archaiognosia* 1: 213–36.

Jameson, M. 1997. 'Women and Democracy in Fourth-Century Athens', in P. Brulé and J. Oulhen, eds. *Esclavage, guerre, économie en Grèce ancienne: Hommages à Yvon Garlan*, 95–107. Rennes.

Janko, R. 2001. 'The Derveni Papyrus (Diagoras of Melos, *Apopyrgizontes logoi?*): A New Translation', *Classical Philology* 96: 1–32.

Jebb, R. 1907. *Sophocles: The Plays and Fragments, Part ii: The Oedipus Coloneus*. Cambridge.

Jenkins, J. H. 1991. 'Anthropology, Expressed Emotions, and Schizophrenia', *Ethos* 19: 387–431.
Jensen, C. 1917. *Hyperidis Orationes sex.* Leipzig.
Johnson, M. 1987. *The Body in the Mind: The Bodily Basis of Meaning, Imagination, and Reason.* Chicago.
Johnson, P. C. 2002. *Secrets, Gossip, and Gods: The Transformation of Brazilian Candomblé.* Oxford.
Johnstone, S. 2011. *A History of Trust in Ancient Greece.* Chicago.
Jones, H. L., tr. 1928. *Strabo: Geography*, v (*Books 10–12*). Loeb Classical Library. Cambridge, MA.
Jones, N. 1999. *The Associations of Classical Athens: The Response to Democracy.* Oxford.
Jordan, D. R. 1979. 'An Appeal to the Sun for Vengeance (Inscriptions de Délos, 2533)', *Bulletin de correspondance hellénique* 103: 522–5.
Jordan, D. R. 1985. 'Defixiones from a Well near the Southwest Corner of the Athenian Agora', *Hesperia* 54: 205–59.
Jordan, D. R. 1999. 'Three Curse Tablets', in D. R. Jordan, H. Montgomery, and E. Thomassen, eds. *The World of Ancient Magic: Papers from the First International Samson Eitrem Seminar at the Norwegian Institute at Athens, 4–8 May 1996*, 115–17. Bergen.
Just, R. 1989. *Women in Athenian Law and Life.* London.
Kagarow, E. 1929. *Griechische Fluchtafeln.* Lviv.
Kamen, D. 2013. *Status in Classical Athens.* Princeton, NJ.
Kamerbeek, J., ed. 1984. *The Plays of Sophocles: Commentaries*, vii: *The Oedipus Coloneus.* Leiden.
Kantzia, C. 1997. 'Εὐχή κατὰ Ἑρμία Πυθιάδος. ἕνας εικονογραφημένος κατάδεσμος ἀπὸ τὴν Κω', in A.-Ph. Christides and D. R. Jordan, eds. *Γλώσσα και μαγεία: Κείμενα από την αρχαιότητα*, 170–92. Athens.
Kapferer, B., ed. 2003. *Beyond Rationalism: Rethinking Magic, Witchcraft and Sorcery.* Oxford.
Kapparis, K. 1999. *Apollodoros: Against Neaira [D. 59].* Berlin.
Kapparis, K. 2005. 'Immigration and Citizenship Procedures in Athenian Law', *Revue internationale des droits de l' antiquité* 52: 71–113.
Kapparis, K. 2012. Review of Richard V. Cudjoe, *The Social and Legal Position of Widows and Orphans in Classical Athens.* Symboles, 3. Athens, *Bryn Mawr Classical Review* (2012.02.22). doi: bmcr.brynmawr.edu/2012/2012-02-22.html.
Kaster, R. A. 2005. *Emotion, Restraint, and Community in Ancient Rome.* Oxford.
Katz, M. 1992. 'Ideology and "The Status of Women" in Ancient Greece', *History and Theory* 31: 70–97.
Keller, O. 1862. *Untersuchungen über die Geschichte der griechischen Fabel.* Leipzig.
Kemper, T. D. 1978. *A Social Interactional Theory of Emotions.* New York.

Kennedy, R. 2014. *Immigrant Women in Athens: Gender, Ethnicity, and Citizenship in the Classical City*. New York and Abingdon.

Keramopoullos, A., 1923. *Ho apotympanismos: sumbolē archaiologikē eis tēn istorian tou poinikou dikaiou kai tēn laographian*. Athens.

Kirk, A. 2007. 'Karl Polanyi, Marshall Sahlins, and the Study of Ancient Social Relations', *Journal of Biblical Literature* 126: 182–91.

Kirkwood, G. M. 1984. 'Blame and Envy in the Pindaric Epinician', in D. E. Gerber, ed. *Greek Poetry and Philosophy: Studies in Honour of Leonard Woodbury*, 169–84. Chico, CA.

Kirsch, S. 2006. *Reverse Anthropology: Indigenous Analysis of Social and Environmental Relations in New Guinea*. Stanford, CA.

Konstan, D. 1987. 'Between Courtesan and Wife: Menander's "Perikeiromene"' *Phoenix* 41: 122–39.

Konstan, D. 2003. 'Before Jealousy', in Konstan and Rutter 2003: 7–28.

Konstan, D. 2007. *The Emotions of the Ancient Greeks: Studies in Aristotle and Classical Literature*. Toronto.

Konstan, D., and Rutter, N., eds. 2003. *Envy, Spite and Jealousy: The Rivalrous Emotions in Ancient Greece*. Edinburgh.

Kourouniotis, K. 1911. 'Ἐξ Ἀττικῆς', *Arkhaiologike Ephemeris*: 246–56.

Kovacs, D., ed. and trt. 1994. *Euripides*, i: *Cyclops, Alcestis, Medea*. Loeb Classical Library. Cambridge, MA.

Kövecses, Z. 2010. *Metaphor*. Oxford.

Kowalski, G. 1947. 'De Phrynes Pectore Nudato', *Eos* 42: 50–62.

Krauter, S. 2004. *Bürgerrecht und Kultteilnahme: Politische und kultische Rechte und Pflichten in griechischen Poleis, Rom und antikem Judentum*. Beihefte zur Zeitschrift für die neutestamentliche Wissenschaft und die Kunde der älteren Kirche 127. Berlin.

Kremmydas, C. 2012. *Commentary on Demosthenes Against Leptines, with Introduction, Text, and Translation*. Oxford.

Kroeber, A. L., and Parsons, T. 1958. 'The Concepts of Culture and Social System', *American Sociological Review* 23: 582–3.

Kron, G. 2011. The Distribution of Wealth at Athens in Comparative Perspective', *Zeitschrift für Papyrologie und Epigraphik* 179: 129–38.

Kucharski, J. 2012. 'Vindictive Prosecution in Classical Athens', *Greek, Roman, and Byzantine Studies* 52: 167–97.

Kurke, L. 1997. 'Inventing the Hetaira: Sex, Politics, and Discursive Conflict in Archaic Greece', *Classical Antiquity* 116: 117–32.

Kurke, L. 1999. *Coins, Bodies, Games, and Gold: The Politics of Meaning in Archaic Greece*. Princeton, NJ.

Kurke, L. 2011. *Aesopic Conversations: Popular Tradition, Cultural Dialogue, and the Invention of Greek Prose*. Princeton, NJ.

Kurke, L. 2013. *The Traffic in Praise: Pindar and the Poetics of Social Economy*. Ithaca, NY. Available online at https://escholarship.org/uc/item/29r3j0gm. Accessed 18 August 2015.

Kurland, N. B., and Pelled, L. H. 2000. 'Passing the Word: Toward a Model of Gossip and Power in the Workplace', *The Academy of Management Review* 25: 428–38.
Kyle, D. 1993. *Athletics in Ancient Athens*. Mnemosyne Suppl. 95. Leiden.
Laidlaw, J. 2002. 'A Free Gift Makes No Friends', in M. Osteen, ed. *The Question of the Gift*, 45–66. London. Originally published 2000 in *Journal of the Royal Anthropological Institute* 6: 617–34.
Lakoff, G. 1987. *Women, Fire and Dangerous Things: What Categories Reveal about the Mind*. Chicago.
Lakoff, G., and Johnson, M. 1980. *Metaphors We Live By*. Chicago.
Lakoff, G., and Kövecses, Z. 1987. 'The Cognitive Model of Anger Inherent in American English', in D. Holland and N. Quinn, eds. *Cultural Models in Language and Thought*, 195–221. Cambridge.
Lamb, W. R. M., tr. 1930. *Lysias*. Loeb Classical Library. Cambridge, MA.
Lambert, S. 1993. *The Phratries of Attica*. Ann Arbor, MI.
Langacker, R. W. 1987. *Foundations of Cognitive Grammar*, i: *Theoretical Prerequisites*. Stanford, CA.
Lanni, A. 2006. *Law and Justice in the Courts of Classical Athens*. Cambridge.
Lanzillotta, L. R. 2010. 'The So-Called Envy Of The Gods: Revisiting a Dogma of Ancient Greek Religion', in J. Dijkstra, J. Kroesen, and Y. Kuiper, eds. *Myths, Martyrs, and Modernity: Studies in the History of Religions in Honour of Jan N. Bremmer*, 75–93. Leiden.
Larsen, J. T., Berntson, G. G., Poehlmann, K. M., Ito, T. A., and Cacioppo, J. T. 2008. 'The Psychophysiology of Emotion', in Lewis, Haviland-Jones, and Feldman Barrett 2008: 180–95.
Latte, K. 1920. *Heiliges Recht: Untersuchungen zur Geschichte der sakralen Rechtsformen in Griechenland*. Tübingen.
Latte, K., Hansen, P. A., and Cunningham, I. C. 1953–2009. *Hesychii Alexandrini Lexicon*, 4 vols. Sammlung griechischer und lateinischer Grammatiker. Copenhagen and Berlin.
Leaper, C., and Holliday, H. 1995. 'Gossip in Same-Gender and Cross-Gender Friends' Conversations', *Personal Relationships* 2: 237–46.
Lefkowitz, M. 1980. 'Autobiographical Fiction in Pindar', *Harvard Studies in Classical Philology* 84: 29–49.
Lévi-Strauss, C. 1965. 'The Principle of Reciprocity', in L. A. Coser and B. Rosenberg, eds. *Sociological Theory*, 74–84. New York.
Lévi-Strauss, C. 1987. *Introduction to the Work of Marcel Mauss*, tr. F. Baker. London.
Levy, H. L. 1963. 'Inheritance and Dowry in Classical Athens', in J. Pitt-Rivers, ed. *Mediterranean Countrymen: Essays in the Social Anthropology of the Mediterranean*, 137–43. Paris.
Lewis, M., Haviland-Jones, J. M., and Barrett, L. F., eds. 2008. *Handbook of Emotions*, 3rd edn. New York.
Lewis, S. 1996. *News and Society in the Greek Polis*. Durham, NC.

Limberis, V. 1991. 'The Eyes Infected by Evil: Basil of Caesarea's Homily, "On Envy"', *Harvard Theological Review* 84: 163–84.

Lindquist, K. A., and Barrett, L. F. 2008. 'Emotional Complexity', in Lewis, Haviland-Jones, and Barrett 2008: 513–30.

Lipsius, J. 1984. *Das attische Recht und Rechtsverfahren*. Hildesheim. Originally published in 3 vols, 1905–15. Leipzig.

Lloyd-Jones, H., and Wilson, N. 1990. *Sophoclea: Studies on the Text of Sophocles*. Oxford.

Loman, P. 2004. 'No Woman No War: Women's Participation in Ancient Greek Warfare', *Greece and Rome* 51: 34–54.

Long, N. J., and Moore, H. L. 2013. 'Introduction', in N. J. Long and H. L. Moore, eds. *Sociality: New Directions*, 1–24. Oxford and New York.

Loomis, W. T. 1998. *Wages, Welfare Costs and Inflation in Classical Athens*. Ann Arbor, MI.

Loraux, N. 1986. *The Invention of Athens*. New York. Originally published 1981 as *L'Invention d'Athènes: Histoire de l'oraison funèbre dans le 'cité classique'*. Paris.

Luciani-Zidane, L. 2009. *L'Acédie: Le Vice de forme du Christianisme, de saint Paul à Lacan*. Paris.

Lutz, C. A. 1986. 'The Domain of Emotion Words on Ifaluk', in Harré 1986a: 267–88. Oxford.

Lutz, C. A., and White, G. M. 1986. 'The Anthropology of Emotions', *Annual Review of Anthropology* 15: 405–36.

Lynch, J. P. 1972. *Aristotle's School: A Study of a Greek Educational Institution*. Berkeley, CA.

Lyons, W. 1999. 'The Philosophy of Cognition and Emotion', in T. Dalgliesh and M. J. Power, eds. *Handbook of Cognition and Emotions*, 21–44. Chichester.

Macan, R. W. 1908. *Herodotus: The Seventh, Eighth and Ninth Books*. Cambridge.

McClure, L. 1999. *Spoken Like a Woman: Speech and Gender in Athenian Drama*. Princeton, NJ.

MacDowell, D. M. 1963. *Athenian Homicide Law in the Age of the Orators*. Manchester.

MacDowell, D. M. 1978. *The Law in Classical Athens*. Oxford.

MacDowell, D. M. 1990. *Demosthenes: Against Meidias*. Oxford.

MacDowell, D. M. 2000. *Demosthenes: On the False Embassy (Oration 19)*. Oxford.

MacDowell, D. M. 2004. 'Epikerdes of Kyrene and the Athenian Privilege of Ateleia', *Zeitschrift für Papyrologie und Epigraphik* 150: 127–33.

MacDowell, D. M. 2009. *Demosthenes the Orator*. Oxford and New York.

MacFarlane, A. 1976. *The Family Life of Ralph Josselin, a Seventeenth-Century Clergyman: An Essay in Historical Anthropology.* Cambridge.
McGinn, T. 2008. *Widows and Patriarchy: Ancient and Modern.* London.
McKechnie, P. 1989. *Outsiders in the Greek Cities in the Fourth Century BC.* London and New York.
Mackie, H. 2003. *Graceful Errors: Pindar and the Performance of Praise.* Ann Arbor, MI.
Maidment, K. J., tr. 1941. *Minor Attic Orators,* i: *Antiphon, Andocides.* Loeb Classical Library. Cambridge, MA.
Marchant, E. C., and Todd, O. J., tr., and rev. Henderson, J. 2013. *Xenophon: Memorabilia, Oeconomicus, Symposium, Apology.* Loeb Classical Library. Cambridge, MA.
Marzi, M. 1977. 'Iperide,' in M. Marzi, P. Leone, and E. Malcovati, eds. *Oratori Attici minori,* i: 9–328. Turin.
Massumi, B. 2002. *Parables for the Virtual: Movement, Affect and Sensation.* Durham, NC.
Mate, M. E. 1998. *Daughters, Wives and Widows after the Black Death: Women in Sussex, 1350–1535.* Woodbridge.
Mathews, H. F. 1992. 'The Directive Force of Morality Tales in a Mexican Community', in D'Andrade and Strauss 1992: 127–62.
Matsumoto, D., Keltner, D., Shiota, M. N., O'Sullivan, M., and Frank, M. 2008. 'Facial Expressions of Emotion', in Lewis, Haviland-Jones, and Barrett 2008: 211–34.
Mauss, M. 1990. *The Gift,* tr. W. D. Halls. London. Originally published 1950 as 'Essai sur le Don', in M. Mauss. *Sociologie et Anthropologie,* pp. ix–lii. Paris.
Meineck, P., and Konstan, D. 2014. *Combat Trauma and the Ancient Greeks.* New York.
Mendonsa, E. L. 1982. *The Politics of Divination: A Processual View of Reactions to Illness and Deviance among the Sisala of Northern Ghana.* Berkeley, CA.
Meritt, B. D. 1940. 'Greek Inscriptions', *Hesperia* 9: 53–96.
Merry, S. E. 1997. 'Rethinking Gossip and Scandal', in D. B. Klein, *Reputation: Studies in the Voluntary Elicitation of Good Conduct,* 47–74. Ann Arbor, MI. Originally published 1984, in D. Black, ed. *Toward a General Theory of Social Control,* i: *Fundamentals,* 271–302. Orlando, FL.
Merton, R. K. 1938 [1996]. 'Social Structure and Anomie', in P. Sztompka, ed. *Robert K. Merton on Social Structure and Science,* 132–51. Chicago.
Meskell, L. 1998. 'Intimate Archaeologies: The Case of Kha and Merit', *World Archaeology* 29: 363–79.
Michelson, G., van Iterson, A., and Waddington, K. 2010. 'Gossip in Organizations: Contexts, Consequences, and Controversies', *Group Organization Management* 35: 371–90.

Miller, W., tr. 1914. *Xenophon. Cyropaedia, Volume II. Books 5–8*. Loeb Classical Library. Cambridge, MA.

Mills, C. W. 1940. 'Situated Actions and Vocabularies of Motive', *American Sociological Review* 5: 904–13.

Mintel. 2008. *Gift Registries—US (May)*. http://academic.mintel.com/.

Mirhady, D. C., and Too, Y. L. 2000. *Isocrates*, i. Austin, TX.

Möbius, H. 1967. 'Diotima', in H. Möbius, *Studia varia: Aufsätze zur Kunst und Kultur der Antike mit Nachträgen*, ed. W. Schiering, 33–46. Wiesbaden.

Moore, H. L. 2013. 'Avatars and Robots: The Imaginary Present and the Socialities of the Inorganic', in N. J. Long and H. L. Moore, eds. *Sociality: New Directions*. Oxford and New York.

Moors, A. 2010. 'Theories of Emotion Causation: A Review', in J. de Houwer and D. Hermans, eds. *Cognition and Emotion: Reviews of Current Research and Theories*. New York.

Moraw, S. 1998. *Die Mänade in den attischen Vasenmalerei des 6. und 5. Jahrhunderts v. Chr.* Mainz.

Moreno, A. 2007. *Feeding the Democracy: The Athenian Grain Supply in the Fifth and Fourth Centuries BC*. Oxford.

Morris, I. 2000. *Archaeology as Cultural History*. Oxford.

Most, G. 1985. *The Measures of Praise: Structure and Function in Pindar's Second Pythian and Seventh Nemean Odes*. Göttingen.

Most, G. 1987. 'Two Leaden Metaphors in Pindar P. 2', *American Journal of Philology* 108: 569–84.

Most, G. 2003. 'Epinician Envies', in Konstan and Rutter 2003: 123–42.

Moysey, R. A. 1982. 'Isokrates' *On the Peace*: Rhetorical Exercise or Political Advice?', *American Journal of Ancient History* 7: 118–27.

Munn, N. D. 1986. *The Fame of Gawa: A Symbolic Study of Value Transformation in a Massim (Papua New Guinea) Society*. Cambridge. Rev. edn 1992. Durham. NC.

Munteanu, D. 2011. 'Comic Emotions: Shamelessness and Envy (Schadenfreude); Moderate Emotion', in D. Munteanu, ed. *Emotion, Genre and Gender in Classical Antiquity*, 89–112. London.

Murray, A. T., tr. 1936. *Demosthenes: Orations*, iv (27–40). Loeb Classical Library. Cambridge, MA.

Murray, A. T., tr. 1939a. *Demosthenes: Orations*, v (41–49). Loeb Classical Library. Cambridge, MA.

Murray, A. T., tr. 1939b. *Demosthenes: Orations*, vi (50–59). Loeb Classical Library. Cambridge, MA.

Murray, O. 1990. 'The Affair of the Mysteries: Democracy and the Drinking Group', in O. Murray, ed. *Sympotica: A Symposium on the Symposium*, 149–61. Oxford.

Mylonas, G. E. 1961. *Eleusis and the Eleusinian Mysteries*. Princeton, NJ.

Nagle, B. 2006. *The Household as the Foundation of Aristotle's Polis*. Cambridge.
Nagy, G. 1979. *The Best of the Achaeans*. Baltimore, MD.
Naiden, F. S. 2006. *Ancient Supplication*. Oxford.
Needham, R. 1978. 'Synthetic Images', in *Primordial Characters*, 23–50. Charlottesville, VA.
Newton, C. T., assisted by R. P. Pullan. 1862–3. *History of Discoveries at Halicarnassus, Cnidus and Branchidae*. 2 vols. London.
Nilsson, M. P. 1967. *Geschichte der griechischen Religion*, i: *Die Religion Griechenlands bis auf die griechische Weltherrschaft*. Handbuch der Altertumswissenschaft, Abt. 5.2. 3rd edn. Munich.
Noon, M., and Delbridge, R. 1993. 'News from Behind My Hand: Gossip in Organisations', *Organisation Studies* 14: 23–36.
Norlin, G., tr. 1929. *Isocrates*, ii: *On the Peace, Areopagiticus, Against the Sophists, Antidosis, Panathenaicus*. Loeb Classical Library. Cambridge, MA.
Norman, A. F., ed. and tr. 1992. *Libanius: Autobiography and Selected Letters*, i. Loeb Classical Library. Cambridge, MA.
Norman, A. F. 2000. *Antioch as a Centre of Hellenic Culture as Observed by Libanius*. Liverpool.
Noy, D., Panayotov, A., and Bloedhorn, H. 2004. *Inscriptiones Iudaicae Orientis*, i: *Eastern Europe*. Tübingen.
Nussbaum, M. 2003. 'Emotions as Judgments of Value and Importance', in Solomon 2003b: 271–83.
Ober, J. 1989. *Mass and Elite in Democratic Athens: Rhetoric, Ideology, and the Power of the People*. Princeton, NJ.
O'Connell, P. 2013. 'Hyperides and *Epopteia*: A New Fragment of the Defense of Phryne', *Greek, Roman, and Byzantine Studies* 53: 90–116.
Ogden, D. 1996. *Greek Bastardy in the Classical and Hellenistic Periods*. Oxford.
Ogden, D. 1999. 'Binding Spells: Curse Tablets and Voodoo Dolls in the Greek and Roman Worlds', in Ankarloo and Clark 1999: 1–90.
Ogden, D. 2002a. *Magic, Witchcraft, and Ghosts in the Greek and Roman Worlds: A Sourcebook*. Oxford.
Ogden, D. 2002b. 'Controlling Women's Dress: *Gynaikonomoi*', in L. Llewellyn-Jones, ed. *Women's Dress in the Ancient Greek World*, 203–25. London.
Olson, D., ed. and tr. 2010. *Athenaeus: The Learned Banqueters*, vi *(Books 12–13.594b)*. Loeb Classical Library. Cambridge, MA.
Omitowoju, R. 2002. *Rape and the Politics of Consent in Classical Athens*. Cambridge.
Ortony, A., Clore, G. L., and Collins, A. 1988. *The Cognitive Structure of Emotions*. Cambridge.
Osborne, M. J. 1981–2. *Naturalization in Athens*. 2 vols. Brussels.

Osborne, M. J. 2004–9. 'Five Hellenistic Decrees of the Salaminian Thiasotai of Bendis', *Horos* 17–21: 657–72.

Osborne, R. 1985. 'Law in Action in Classical Athens', *Journal of Hellenic Studies* 105: 40–58. Repr. in R. Osborne, ed. 2010. *Athens and Athenian Democracy*, 171–204. Cambridge.

Osborne, R. 1988. 'Social and Economic Implications of the Leasing of Land and Property in Classical and Hellenistic Greece', *Chiron* 18: 279–323.

Osborne, R. 1990. 'Vexatious Litigation in Classical Athens: Sykophancy and the Sykophant', in P. Cartledge, P. Millett, and S. Todd, eds. *Nomos: Essays in Athenian Law, Politics and Society*, 83–102. Cambridge.

Osborne, R. 1991. 'Pride and Prejudice, Sense and Subsistence: Exchange and Society in the Greek City', in J. Rich and A. Wallace-Hadrill, eds. *City and Country in the Ancient World*, 120–48. London.

Osborne, R. 1992. 'Is it a Farm?', in B. Wells, ed. *Agriculture in Ancient Greece: Proceedings of the Seventh International Symposium at the Swedish Institute at Athens, 16–17th May 1990*, 21–7. Stockholm.

Osborne, R. 1997. 'Law, the Democratic Citizen and the Representation of Women in Classical Athens,' *Past & Present* no. 155: 3–33.

Osborne, R. 2000. 'Religion, Imperial Politics and the Offering of Freedom to Slaves', in Hunter and Edmondson 2000: 75–92.

Osborne, R. 2003. 'Changing the Discourse', in K. Morgan, ed. *Popular Tyranny: Sovereignty and its Discontents in Ancient Greece*. Austin, TX.

Osborne, R., ed. 2007. *Debating the Athenian Cultural Revolution: Art, Literature, Philosophy and Politics 430–380 BC*. Cambridge.

Osborne, R. 2011. *The History Written on the Classical Greek Body*. Cambridge.

Osteen, M. 2002. 'Introduction: Questions of the Gift', in M. Osteen, ed. *The Question of the Gift: Essays Across Disciplines*, 1–42. London.

Ostling, M. 2011. *Between the Devil and the Host: Imagining Witchcraft in Early Modern Poland*. Oxford.

Ostwald, M. 1986. *From Popular Sovereignty to the Sovereignty of Law: Law, Society, and Politics in Fifth-Century Athens*. Berkeley and Los Angeles.

O'Sullivan, L. 1997. 'Athenian Impiety Trials in the Late Fourth Century B.C.' *Classical Quarterly* NS 47: 136–52.

O'Sullivan, L. 2009. *The Regime of Demetrius of Phalerum in Athens, 317–307 BCE: A Philosopher in Politics*. Leiden.

Paine, R. 1967. 'What is Gossip About? An Alternative Hypothesis', *Man* NS 2: 278–85.

Papadopoulos, J., Bejko, L., and Morris, S. P. 2007. 'Excavations at the Prehistoric Burial Tumulus of Lofkënd in Albania; A Preliminary Report of the 2004–2005 Seasons', *American Journal of Archaeology* 111: 105–47.

Parker, R. 1983. *Miasma: Pollution and Purification in Early Greek Religion*. Oxford.

Parker, R. 1996. *Athenian Religion: A History*. Oxford.

Parker, R. 2005a. *Polytheism and Society at Athens.* Oxford.
Parker, R. 2005b. 'Law and Religion', in M. Gagarin and D. Cohen, eds. *Cambridge Companion to Ancient Greek Law*, 61–81. Cambridge.
Parker, R. 2011. *On Greek Religion.* Ithaca, NY.
Parkinson, B. 1996. 'Emotions are Social', *British Journal of Psychology* 87: 663–83.
Parkinson, B. 2007. 'Getting from Situations to Emotions: Appraisal and Other Routes', *Emotion* 7: 21–5.
Parkinson, B. 2012. 'Piecing Together Emotion: Sites and Time-Scales for Social Construction', *Emotion Review* 4: 291–8.
Parrott, W. G., and Smith, R. H. 1993. 'Distinguishing the Experiences of Envy and Jealousy', *Journal of Personality and Social Psychology* 64: 906–20.
Parry, C. P. 1986. 'The *Gift*, the Indian Gift and the "Indian Gift"', *Man* NS 21: 453–73.
Patterson, C. 1991. 'Response to Claude Mossé', in M. Gagarin, ed. *Symposium 1990: Papers on Greek and Hellenistic Legal History*, 281–7. Cologne.
Pecírka, J. 1966. *The Formula for the Grant of Enktesis in Attic Inscriptions.* Acta Universitatis Carolinae, Philosophica et Historica Monographia 15. Prague.
Pelekidis, E. 1916. 'Ἀνασκαφὴ Φαλήρου', *Arkhaiologikon Deltion* 2: 13–64.
Pelling, C. 2006. 'Educating Croesus: Talking and Learning in Herodotus' Lydian *Logos*', *Classical Antiquity* 25: 141–77.
Pemberton, E. 1989. 'The Dexiosis on Attic Gravestones', *Mediterranean Archaeology* 2: 45–50.
Perry, B. E. 1936. *Studies in the Text History of the Life and Fables of Aesop.* Philological Monographs of the American Philological Association 7. Haverford, PA.
Perry, B. E. 1952. *Aesopica: A Series of Texts Relating to Aesop or Ascribed to Him or Closely Connected with the Literary Tradition that Bears his Name.* Urbana, IL.
Perry, B. E. 1959. 'Fable', *Studium Generale* 12: 17–37.
Perry, B. E. 1962. 'Demetrius of Phalerum and the Aesopic Fables', *Transactions and Proceedings of the American Philological Association* 93: 287–346.
Petit, P. 1979. *Libanios: Autobiographie (Discours I).* Paris.
Pettegree, A. 2005. *Reformation and the Culture of Persuasion.* Cambridge.
Petzl, G. 1988. 'Sünde, Strafe, Wiedergutmachung (Zur Inschrift [EA 12, 1988] p. 151f., Nr. 5)', *Epigraphica Anatolica* 12: 155–66.
Petzl, G. 1994. *Die Beichtinschriften Westkleinasiens* (= *Epigraphica Anatolica* 22). Bonn.
Pfeffer, J., and Salancik, G. R. 1978. *The External Control of Organizations: A Resource Dependence Perspective.* New York.
Pfohl, G. 1966. *Griechische Inschriften als Zeugnisse des privaten und öffentlichen Lebens.* Munich.

Phillips, III, C. R. 1991. 'Nullum Crimen sine Lege: Socioreligious Sanctions on Magic', in Faraone and Obbink, eds. *Magika Hiera: Ancient Greek Magic and Religion*, 1991: 260-76.
Pippidi, D. M. 1976/7. 'Tibi Commendo. À propos d'une inscription fragmentaire publiée par Pârvan,' *Rivista storica dell'antichità* 6/7: 37-44.
Poland, F. 1909. *Geschichte des griechischen Vereinswesens*. Leipzig.
Pomeroy, S. B. 1982. 'Charities for Greek Women', *Mnemosyne* 35: 115-35.
Pomeroy, S. B. 1983. 'Infanticide in Hellenistic Greece', in A. Cameron and A. Kuhrt, eds. *Images of Women in Antiquity*, 207-22. London.
Pouilloux, J. 1954. *Recherches sur l'histoire et les cultes de Thasos*, i. Paris.
Prauscello, L. 2014. *Performing Citizenship in Plato's Laws*. Cambridge.
Pritchard, D. M. 2010. 'The Symbiosis between Democracy and War: The Case of Ancient Athens', in D. M. Pritchard, ed. *War, Democracy and Culture in Classical Athens*, 1-62. Cambridge.
Pritchard, D. M. 2012. 'Costing Festivals and War: Spending Priorities of the Athenian Democracy', *Historia* 61: 18-65.
Pritchard, D. M. 2014. 'The Public Payment of Magistrates in Fourth-Century Athens', *Greek, Roman, and Byzantine Studies* 54: 1-16.
Pritchard, D. M. 2015. *Public Spending and Democracy in Classical Athens*. Austin, TX. http://espace.library.uq.edu.au/view/UQ:328969
Purkiss, D. 1996. *The Witch in History: Early Modern and Twentieth-Century Representations*. London and New York.
Purvis, A. 2003. *Singular Dedications: Founders and Innovators of Private Cults in Classical Greece*. Abingdon.
Putnam, R. D., Leonardi, R., and Nanetti, R. Y. 1994. *Making Democracy Work*. Princeton, NJ.
Raaflaub, K. A. 1998. 'The Transformation of Athens in the Fifth Century', in D. Boedeker and K. A. Raaflaub, eds. *Democracy, Empire and the Arts in Fifth-Century Athens*, 15-42. Cambridge, MA.
Raaflaub, K. A. 2003. 'Stick and Glue: The Function of Tyranny in Fifth-Century Athenian Democracy', in K. Morgan, ed. *Popular Tyranny*, 59-93. Austin, TX.
Race, W. H., ed. and tr. 1997a. *Pindar*, i: *Olympian Odes, Pythian Odes*. Loeb Classical Library. Cambridge, MA.
Race, W. H., ed. and tr. 1997b. *Pindar*, ii: *Nemean Odes, Isthmian Odes, Fragments*. Loeb Classical Library. Cambridge, MA.
Rackham, H. 1932. *Aristotle: Politics*. Loeb Classical Library. Cambridge, MA.
Ramsay, R. 1888. 'Antiquities of Southern Phrygia and the Border Lands (III)', *American Journal of Archaeology* 4: 263-83.
Rankin, D. 1987. 'Sokrates, an Oligarch?', *L'Antiquité classique* 56: 68-87.
Raubitschek, A. 1941. 'Phryne' in A. F. Pauly, G. Wissowa, and W. Kroll, eds. *Realencyclopädie der classischen Altertumswissenschaft*, xx.1, cols 893-907. Stuttgart.

Redfield, J. 2003. *The Locrian Maidens: Love and Death in Greek Italy.* Princeton, NJ.
Reed, C. M. 2003. *Maritime Traders in the Ancient Greek World.* Cambridge.
Reverdin, O. 1945. *La Religion de la cité platonicienne.* Paris.
Rhodes, P. J. 1979–80. 'Athenian Democracy after 403 BC', *Classical Journal* 75: 305–23.
Rhodes, P. J. 1981. *A Commentary on the Aristotelian* Athenaion Politeia. Oxford.
Rhodes, P. J. 1992. 'The Athenian Revolution', in D. M. Lewis, ed. *The Cambridge Ancient History*, v: *The Fifth Century B.C.*, 67–77. 2nd edn. Cambridge.
Rhodes, P. J. 1994. 'The Polis and the Alternatives', in *The Cambridge Ancient History*, vi: *The Fourth Century B.C.*, 565–591. 2nd edn. Cambridge.
Rhodes, P. J. 2004. 'Keeping to the Point', in E. M. Harris and L. Rubinstein, eds. The *Law and the Courts in Ancient Greece*, 137–58. London.
Rhodes P. J. 2010. *A History of the Classical Greek World, 478–323.* 2nd edn. Oxford.
Richards, R. J. 1989. *Darwin and the Emergence of Evolutionary Theories of Mind and Behavior.* Chicago.
Ricl, M. 1995. 'The Appeal to Divine Justice in the Lydian Confession Inscriptions', in E. Schwertheim, ed. *Forschungen in Lydien.* Asia Minor Studien 17. Bonn.
Riess, W. 2012. *Performing Interpersonal Violence: Court, Curse and Comedy in Fourth-Century Athens.* Berlin.
Robben, A. C. G. M. 2005. *Political Violence and Trauma in Argentina.* Philadelphia.
Robben, A. C. G. M., and Suárez-Orozco, M. M. 2000. 'Interdisciplinary Perspectives on Violence and Trauma', in A. C. G. M. Robben, and M. M. Suárez-Orozco, eds. *Cultures under Siege: Collective Violence and Trauma*, 1–41. Cambridge.
Robert, L. 1936. *Collection Froehner*, i: *Inscriptions grecques.* Paris.
Roberts, J. M. 1964. 'The Self-management of Cultures', in W. H. Goodenough, ed. *Explorations of Cultural Anthropology: Essays in Honor of George Peter Murdock*, 433–54. New York.
Roesch, E. B., Korsten, N., Fragopanagos, N. F., Taylor, J. G., Grandjean, D., and Sander, D. 2011. 'Biological and Computational Constraints to Psychological Modeling of Emotion', in P. Petta, R. Cowie, and C. Pelachaud, eds. *Emotion-Oriented Systems: The Humaine Handbook*, 47–64. Berlin and Heidelberg.
Roisman, J. 2006. *The Rhetoric of Conspiracy in Ancient Athens.* Berkeley and Los Angeles.
Roper, L. 1994. *Oedipus and the Devil.* London and New York.

Roper, L. 1996. 'Witchcraft and Fantasy in Early Modern Germany', in J. Barry, M. Hester, and G. Roberts, eds. *Witchcraft in Early Modern Europe*, 207–36. Cambridge.

Roper, L. 2012. *The Witch in the Western Imagination*. Charlottesville, NC and London.

Rosaldo, M. 1984. 'Toward an Anthropology of Self and Feeling', in R. A. Shweder and R. A. LeVine, eds. *Culture Theory: Essays on Mind, Self, and Emotion*, 137–57. Cambridge.

Roseman, I. J. 1991. 'Appraisal Determinants of Discrete Emotions', *Cognition and Emotion* 5: 161–200.

Rosenberg, E. L. 2005. 'Introduction: The Study of Spontaneous Facial Expressions in Psychology', in P. Ekman and E. L. Rosenberg, eds. *What the Face Reveals: Basic and Applied Studies of Spontaneous Expression Using the Facial Action Coding System (FACS)*, 3–18. 2nd edn. Oxford.

Rosenwein, B. 2002. 'Worrying about *Emotions* in History', *American Historical Review* 107: 821–45.

Rosenwein, B. 2006. *Emotional Communities in the Early Middle Ages*. Ithaca, NY.

Rosivach, V. J. 1987. 'Execution by Stoning in Athens,' *Classical Antiquity* 6: 232–49.

Rosnow, R. L. 2001. 'Rumor and Gossip in Interpersonal Interaction and Beyond: A Social Exchange Perspective', in R. M. Kowalski, *Behaving Badly: Aversive Behaviors in Interpersonal Relationships*, 203–33. Washington, DC.

Rosnow, R. L., and Georgoudi, M. 1985. '"Killed by Idle Gossip": The Psychology of Small Talk', in B. Rubin, ed. *When Information Counts: Grading the Media*, 59–73. Lexington, MA.

Rowlands, A. 2003. *Witchcraft Narratives in Germany: Rothenburg 1561–1652*. Manchester.

Roy, D. F. 1959. 'Banana Time: Job Satisfaction and Informal Interaction', *Human Organisation* 18: 158–68.

Rubel, A. 2000. *Stadt in Angst: Religion und Politik in Athen während des Peloponnesischen Krieges*. Darmstadt. (Tr. M. Vickers and A. Piftor. 2014. *Fear and Loathing in Ancient Athens: Religion and Politics during the Peloponnesian War*. Abingdon.)

Rubinstein, L. 1993. *Adoption in Fourth-Century Athens*. Copenhagen.

Rubinstein, L. 1999. 'Adoption in Classical Athens', in M. Cornier, ed. *Adoption et fosterage*, 45–62. Paris.

Rubinstein, L. 2000. *Litigation and Co-operation: The Use of Supporting Speakers in the Courts of Classical Athens*. Historia Einzelschriften 147. Stuttgart.

Rudhardt, J. 1960. 'La Définition du délit d'impiété d'après la législation attique', *Museum Helveticum* 17: 87–105.

Ruschenbusch, E. 1979. *Athenische Innenpolitik im 5. Jahrhundert v. Chr: Ideologie oder Pragmatismus?* Bamberg.
Russell, J. A. 2003. 'Core Affect and the Psychological Construction of Emotion', *Psychological Review* 110: 145–172.
Russell, J. A., Bachorowski, J.-A., and Fernández-Dols, J.-M. 2003. 'Facial and Vocal Expressions of Emotion', *Annual Review of Psychology* 54: 329–49.
Russell, J. A., and Fehr, B. 1994. 'Fuzzy Concepts in a Fuzzy Hierarchy: Varieties of Anger', *Journal of Personality and Social Psychology* 67: 186–205.
Rutherford, I. 2001. *Pindar's Paeans: A Reading of the Fragments with a Survey of the Genre*. Oxford.
Sabini, J., and Silver, M. 1986. 'Envy', in Harré 1986a: 167–83.
Sahlins, M. 1972. *Stone Age Economics*. London.
Sallares, R. 1991. *The Ecology of the Ancient Greek World*. Ithaca, NY.
Saller, R. P. 2007. 'Household and Gender', in W. Scheidel, I. Morris, and R. P. Saller, eds. *The Cambridge Economic History of the Greco-Roman World*, 87–112. Cambridge.
Salomon, N. 1997. *Le cleruchie di Atene: Caratteri e funzioni*. Studi e testi di storia antica 6. Pisa.
Salvo, I. 2012. 'Sweet Revenge: Emotional Factors in "Prayers for Justice"', in A. Chaniotis, ed. *Unveiling Emotions: Sources and Methods for the Study of Emotions in the Greek World*, 235–66. Stuttgart.
Sanders, E. 2008. 'Pathos Phaulon: Aristotle and the Rhetoric of Phthonos', in I. Sluiter and R. M. Rosen, eds. *Kakos: Badness and Anti-Value in Classical Antiquity*, 255–82. Leiden.
Sanders, E. 2014. *Envy and Jealousy in Classical Athens: A Socio-Psychological Approach*. Oxford.
Sandwell, B. 2005. 'Outlawing "Magic" or Outlawing "Religion"? Libanius and the Theodosian Code as Evidence for Legislation against "Pagan" Practices', in W. V. Harris, ed. *The Spread of Christianity in the First Four Centuries: Essays in Explanation*, 87–124. Leiden.
Sarbin, T. R. 1986a. 'Emotion and Act: Roles and Rhetoric', in Harré 1986a, 83–97.
Sarbin, T. R., ed. 1986b. *Narrative Psychology: The Storied Nature of Human Conduct*. Westport, CT.
Sarbin, T. R. 1995. 'Emotional Life, Rhetoric, and Roles', *Journal of Narrative and Life History* 5(3): 213–20.
Saunders, T. 1996. 'Plato on the Treatment of Heretics', in L. Foxhall and A. D. E. Lewis, eds. *Greek Law in its Political Setting: Justifications Not Justice*, 91–100. Oxford.
Scarborough, J. 1991. 'The Pharmacology of Sacred Plants, Herbs, and Roots', in Faraone and Obbink 1991: 138–74.

Scarborough, J. 2006. 'Drugs and Drug Lore in the Time of Theophrastus: Folklore, Magic, Botany, Philosophy, and the Rootcutters', *Acta Classica* 49: 1–29.

Schaps, D. M. 1977. 'The Woman Least Mentioned: Etiquette and Women's Names', *Classical Quarterly* NS 71: 323–30.

Schaps, D. M. 1979. *Economic Rights of Women in Ancient Greece*. Edinburgh.

Schaps, D. M. 1982. 'The Women of Greece in Wartime', *Classical Philology* 77: 193–213.

Scheer, M. 2012. 'Are Emotions a Kind of Practice (and is That What Makes Them Have a History)? A Bourdieuian Approach to Understanding Emotion', *History and Theory* 51: 193–220.

Scheidel, W. 1995. 'The Most Silent Women of Greece and Rome: Rural Labour and Women's Life in the Ancient World (1)', *Greece and Rome* 42: 202–17.

Scheidel, W. 2002. 'A Model of Demographic and Economic Change in Roman Egypt after the Antonine Plague', *Journal of Roman Archaeology* 15: 97–114.

Scheidel, W. 2007. 'Demography', in W. Scheidel, I. Morris, and R. P. Saller, eds. *The Cambridge Economic History of the Greco-Roman World*, 38–56. Cambridge.

Scheidel, W. 2009. 'The Demographic Background', in Hübner and Ratzan 2009a: 31–40.

Scheidel, W. 2010. 'Roman Wellbeing and the Economic Consequences of the "Antonine Plague"', with a contribution by John Sutherland, *Princeton/Stanford Working Papers in Classics*, 1–29. doi: http://www.princeton.edu/~pswpc/pdfs/scheidel/011001.pdf, accessed 7 Jan. 2014.

Scherer, K. R. 1984. 'On the Nature and Function of Emotion: A Component Process Approach', in K. R. Scherer and P. Ekman, eds. *Approaches to Emotion*, 293–318. Hillsdale, NJ.

Scherer, K. R. 2001. 'Appraisal Considered as a Process of Multilevel Sequential Checking', in K. R. Scherer, A. Schorr, and T. Johnstone, eds. *Appraisal Processes in Emotion: Theory, Methods, Research*, 92–120. New York.

Scherke, K. 2012. 'Comment on Brian Parkinson's "Piecing Together Emotion: Sites and Time-Scales for Social Construction"', *Emotion Review* 4: 303–4.

Scholz, P. 2000. 'Der Prozeß gegen Sokrates. Ein 'Sündenfall' der athenischen Demokratie?', in L. Burckhardt and J. von Unger-Sternberg, eds. *Große Prozesse im antiken Athen*, 157–73. Munich.

Schurgin O'Keeffe, G., and Clarke-Pearson, K. 2011. 'Clinical Report—The Impact of Social Media on Children, Adolescents, and Families', *Pediatrics* 127: 800–4.

Schwartz, B. 1967. 'The Social Psychology of the Gift', *American Journal of Sociology* 73: 1–11.

Sealey, R. 1984. 'On Lawful Concubinage in Athens', *Classical Antiquity* 3: 111–33.

Seeberg, A. 1967. 'A Boston Fragment with a Prisoner', *Bulletin of the Institute of Classical Studies* 14: 25–35.
Seibert, J. 1979. *Die politischen Flüchtlinge und Verbannten in der griechischen Geschichte*. Darmstadt.
Semenov, A. 1935. 'Hypereides und Phryne', *Klio* 28: 271–9.
Shapiro, H. A. 1991. 'The Iconography of Mourning in Athenian Art', *American Journal of Archaeology* 95: 629–56.
Shay, J. 2003. *Achilles in Vietnam: Combat Trauma and the Undoing of Character*. New York.
Shipton, K. M. W. 1997. 'The Private Banks in Fourth-Century B.C. Athens: A Reappraisal', *Classical Quarterly* NS 47: 396–422.
Shrimpton, G. S. 1991. *Theopompus the Historian*. Montreal and Kingston, ON.
Siegel, J. 2006. *Naming the Witch*. Stanford, CA.
Silk, M. 2000. *Aristophanes and the Definition of Comedy*. Oxford.
Silk, M. 2007. 'Pindar's Poetry as Poetry: A Literary Commentary on Olympian 12', in Hornblower and Morgan 2007: 177–98.
Sillar, B. 2004. 'Acts of God and Active Material Culture: Agency and Commitment in the Andes', in Gardner 2004a: 153–89.
Simmel, G. 1906. 'The Sociology of Secrecy', *American Journal of Sociology* 11: 4441–98.
Slater, N. W. 1993. 'Theozotides on Adopted Sons (Lysias fr. 6)', *Scholia* 2: 81–5.
Smith, A. T. 2010. 'Those Obscure Objects of Desire', *Archaeological Dialogues* 17: 172–6.
Smith, R. R. R. 2007. 'Pindar, Athletes, and the Early Greek Statue Habit', in Hornblower and Morgan 2007: 83–140.
Smolders, R. 2013. *Gemellus Horion. ArchID 90. Version 2*. Leuven Homepage of Papyrus Collections. http://www.trismegistos.org/arch/archives/pdf/90.pdf, accessed 22 July 2014.
Sobel, J. 2001. 'Another View of Trust and Gossip', in J. E. von Rauch and A. Casella, eds. *Networks and Markets*, 75–85. New York.
Soeter, J., and van Iterson, A. 2002. 'Blame and Praise Gossip in Organizations: Established, Outsiders and the Civilizing Process', in A. van Iterson, W. Mastenbroek, T. Newton, and D. Smith, eds. *The Civilized Organization: Norbert Elias and the Future of Organization Studies*, 25–40. Philadelphia.
Solomon, A. 2001. *The Noonday Demon*. London.
Solomon, R. C. 1976 [1973]. *The Passions*. Indianapolis, IN.
Solomon, R. C. 2003a. *Not Passion's Slave: Emotions and Choice*. Oxford.
Solomon, R. C., ed. 2003b. *What is an Emotion? Classic and Contemporary Readings*. Chichester.
Solomon, R. C., ed. 2004. *Thinking about Feeling: Contemporary Philosophers on Emotions*. Oxford.

Solomon, R. C. 2008. 'The Philosophy of Emotions', in Lewis, Haviland-Jones, and Barrett 2008: 3–16.
Sommerstein, A. H. 1984. 'Aristophanes and the Demon Poverty', *Classical Quarterly* NS 34: 314–33.
Sommerstein, A. H., ed. and tr. 1990. *Aristophanes: Lysistrata*. Comedies of Aristophanes 7. Oxford.
Sommerstein, A. H., ed. and tr. 1994. *Thesmophoriazusae. The Comedies of Aristophanes*, viii. Warminster.
Sommerstein, A. H., ed. and tr. 2008. *Aeschylus*, iii: *Fragments*. Loeb Classical Library. Cambridge, MA.
Sørensen, J. 2007. *A Cognitive Theory of Magic*. Plymouth.
Sourvinou-Inwood, C. 'Further Aspects of Polis Religion?', *AION* 10: 259–74. Repr. 2000 in R. Buxton, ed. *Oxford Readings in Greek Religion*, 38–55. Oxford.
Spacks, P. M. 1982. 'In Praise of Gossip', *Hudson Review* 35: 19–38.
Spengel, L., ed. 1856. *Rhetores Graeci*. 3 vols. Leipzig. Repr. 1966. Frankfurt am Main.
Spiro, M. E. 1984. 'Some Reflections on Cultural Determinism and Relativism with Special Reference to Emotion and Reason', in R. A. Shweder and R. A. LeVine, eds. *Culture Theory: Essays on Mind, Self, and Emotion*, 323–346. Cambridge.
Stamatopoulou, M. 2007. 'Thessalian Aristocracy and Society in the Age of the Epinikian', in Hornblower and Morgan 2007: 309–41.
Stearns, P. N., and Stearns, C. Z. 1985. 'Emotionology: Clarifying the History of Emotions and Emotional Standards', *American Historical Review* 90: 813–36.
Stears, K. 1995. 'Dead Women's Society: Constructing Female Gender in Classical Athenian Funeral Sculpture', in N. Spencer, ed. *Time, Tradition and Society in Greek Archaeology*, 109–31. New York.
Steiner, D. 2002. 'Indecorous Dining, Indecorous Speech: Pindar's First Olympian and the Poetics of Consumption', *Arethusa* 35: 297–314.
Stewart, C. 1991. *Demons and the Devil: Moral Imagination in Modern Greek Culture*. Princeton, NJ.
Stewart, C. 2014. 'The Modern Greek Devil: Cosmology or Rhetoric?' https://www.ucl.ac.uk/anthropology/people/academic_staff/c_stewart/downloadable-publications/The_Devil_in_Modern_Greece1.pdf, accessed Dec. 2014. Originally published 2008 as 'Le Diable chez les Grecs à l'époque contemporaine: cosmologie ou rhétorique', *Terrain*, 50: 100–13.
Stewart, K. 2007. *Ordinary Affects*. Chapel Hill, NC.
Stewart, P. J., and Strathern, A. 2004. *Witchcraft, Sorcery, Rumors and Gossip*. Cambridge.
Stirling, R. B. 1956. 'Some Psychological Mechanisms Operative in Gossip', *Social Forces* 34: 262–7.

Stocker, M. 2003. 'The Irreducibility of Affectivity', in Solomon 2003b: 258–64.
Stoddart, R. 1990. *Pindar and Greek Family Law*. New York.
Storey, I., ed. and tr. 2011a. *Fragments of Old Comedy*, i: *Alcaeus to Diocles*. Loeb Classical Library. Cambridge, MA.
Storey, I., ed. and tr. 2011b. *Fragments of Old Comedy*, ii: *Diopeithes to Pherecrates*. Loeb Classical Library. Cambridge, MA.
Stratton, K. 2007. *Naming the Witch: Magic, Ideology, and Stereotype in the Ancient World*. New York.
Strauss, B. 1986. *Athens After the Peloponnesian War: Class, Faction and Policy 403–386 B.C.* New York.
Strauss, C. 1992a. 'Models and Motives', in D'Andrade and Strauss 1992: 1–20.
Strauss, C., 1992b. 'What Makes Tony Run? Schemas as Motives Reconsidered', in D'Andrade and Strauss 1992: 191–224.
Strauss, C. 2005. 'Analyzing Discourse for Cultural Complexity', in N. Quinn, ed. *Finding Culture in Talk: A Collection of Methods*, 203–42. New York.
Strauss, C., and Quinn, N. 1997. *A Cognitive Theory of Cultural Meaning*. Cambridge.
Strothmann, M. 'Lais', in *Brill's New Pauly*. Antiquity volumes, ed. H. Cancik and H. Schneider. Brill Online, 2015. http://referenceworks.brillonline.com/entries/brill-s-new-pauly/lais-e629040, accessed 24 Apr. 2015.
Stroud, R. S. 1971. 'Greek Inscriptions, Theozotides and the Athenian Orphans', *Hesperia* 40: 280–301.
Stroud, R. S. 1974. 'An Athenian Law on Silver Coinage', *Hesperia* 43: 157–88.
Sugg, R. 2007. *Murder after Death: Literature and Anatomy in Early Modern England*. New York.
Suls, J. 1977. 'Gossip as Social Comparison', *Journal of Communication* 27: 164–8.
Sykes, K. 2005. *Arguing with Anthropology: An Introduction to Critical Theories of the Gift*. London and New York.
Sztompka, P. 2000. 'Cultural Trauma: The Other Face of Social Change', *European Journal of Social Theory* 3: 449–66.
Szwed, J. F. 1966. 'Gossip, Drinking and Social Control in a Newfoundland Parish', *Ethnology* 5: 434–41.
Talmy, L. 2000. *Towards a Cognitive Semantics*, i: *Concept Structuring Systems*. Cambridge, MA.
Tambiah, S. J. 1985. *Culture Thought and Social Action: An Anthropological Perspective*. Cambridge.
Tannen, D. 1990. *You Just Don't Understand: Women and Men in Conversation*. New York.
Tarlow, S. 2000. 'Emotion in Archaeology', *Current Anthropology* 41: 713–46.

Tarlow, S. 2010. 'Pale Reflections', *Archaeological Dialogues* 17: 183–6.
Taussig, M. 1984. 'Culture of Terror—Space of Death. Roger Casement's Putumayo Report and the Explanation of Torture', *Comparative Studies in Society and History* 26: 467–97.
Taussig, M. 1991. *Shamanism, Colonialism and the White Man: A Study in Terror and Healing*. Chicago.
Taussig, M. 1992. *The Nervous System*. London and New York.
Taylor, A. E. 1932. *Socrates*. New York.
Taylor, C. 2007. 'A New Political World', in Osborne 2007: 72–90.
Taylor, C. 2011. 'Migration and the Demes of Attica', in C. Holleran and A. Pudsey, eds. *Demography and the Graeco-Roman World: New Insights and Approaches*, 117–34. Cambridge.
Taylor, G. 1994. 'Gossip as Moral Talk', in Goodman and Ben-Ze'ev 1994: 34–46.
Taylor, J. 2010. *Careless Talk Costs Lives: Fougasse and the Art of Public Information*. London.
Tchernetska, N., Handley, E. W., Austin, C. F. L., and Horváth, L. 2007. 'New Readings in the Fragment of Hyperides' *Against Timandros* from the Archimedes Palimpsest', *Zeitschrift für Papyrologie und Epigraphik* 162: 1–4.
Thackeray, H. St. J., tr. 1926. *Josephus*, i: *The Life. Against Apion*. Loeb Classical Library. Cambridge, MA.
Thalheim, Th. 1896. 'Ἀσεβείας γραφή', in A. F. Pauly, G. Wissowa, and W. Kroll, eds. *Realencyclopädie der classischen Altertumswissenschaft*, ii.2, cols 1529–39. Stuttgart.
Theodoridis, C., ed. 1998. *Photii Patriarchae Lexicon*, ii. Berlin and New York.
Theodoridis, C., ed. 2013. *Photii Patriarchae Lexicon N–Φ*. Berlin.
Thomas, R. 2007. 'Fame, Memorial and Choral Poetry: The Origins of Epinikian Poetry—an Historical Study', in Hornblower and Morgan 2007: 141–66.
Thonemann, P. 2007. 'Magnesia and the Greeks of Asia (I.Magnesia 16.16)', *Greek, Roman, and Byzantine Studies* 47: 151–60.
Threatte, L. 1980. *The Grammar of Attic Inscriptions*, i: *Phonology*. Berlin.
Todd, S. 1993. *The Shape of Athenian Law*. Oxford.
Todd, S. 1996. 'Lysias against Nikomachos: The Fate of the Expert in Athenian Law', in L. Foxhall and A. D. E. Lewis, eds. *Greek Law in its Political Setting: Justifications Not Justice*, 101–32. Oxford.
Todd, S. 1997. 'Status and Gender in Athenian Public Records', in G. Thür and J. Vélissaropoulos-Karakostas, eds. *Symposion 1995: Akten der Gesellschaft für griechische und hellenistische Rechtsgeschichte*, 113–24. Cologne.
Todd, S., tr. 2000a. *Lysias*. The Oratory of Classical Greece 2. Austin, TX.

Todd, S. 2000b. 'How to Execute Someone in Fourth-Century Athens', in Hunter and Edmondson 2000: 31–51.

Tomkins, S. S. 1962. *Affect, Imagery, Consciousness*, i. New York.

Tomkins, S. S., and McCarter, R. 1964. 'What and Where are the Primary Affects? Some Evidence for Theory', *Perceptual and Motor Skills* 18: 119–58.

Tonkin, E. *Narrating Our Pasts: The Social Construction of Oral History*. Cambridge.

Too, Y. L. 1995. *The Rhetoric of Identity in Isocrates: Text, Power, Pedagogy*. Cambridge.

Too, Y. L. 2000. 'Part 2', in D. C. Mirhady, and Y. L. Too, eds. *Isocrates*, i, 135–264. Austin, TX.

Toobey, J., and Cosmides, L. 1990. 'The Past Explains the Present: Emotional Adaptations and the Structure of Ancestral Environments', *Ethology and Sociobiology* 11: 375–424.

Toohey, P. 2014. *Jealousy*. New Haven, CT.

Trampedach, K. 2001. 'Gefährliche Frauen. Zu athenischen Asebie-Prozessen im 4. Jh. v. Chr', in R. von den Hoff and S. Schmidt, eds. *Konstruktionen von Wirklichkeit: Bilder im Griechenland des 5. und 4. Jahrhunderts v. Chr.*, 137–55. Stuttgart.

Travlos, J. 1980. *Pictorial Dictionary of Ancient Athens*. New York.

Tredennick, H., and Armstrong, G. C., trs. 1935. *Aristotle. Metaphysics, ii (Books 10–14)*. Loeb Classical Library. Cambridge, MA.

Tsagalis, C. 2008. *Inscribing Sorrow: Fourth-Century Attic Funerary Epigrams*. Berlin.

Tuplin, C. 1977. 'The Athenian Embassy to Sparta 371/2', *Liverpool Classical Monthly* 2: 51–6.

Tuplin, C. 1993. *The Failings of Empire: A Reading of Xenophon Hellenica 2.3.11–7.5.27*. Stuttgart.

Turner, M., and Fauconnier, G. 1995. 'Conceptual Integration and Formal Expression', *Metaphor and Symbolic Activity* 10: 183–203.

Turner, M., and Fauconnier, G. 2003. 'Metaphor, Metonymy, and Binding', in A. Barcelona, ed. *Metaphor and Metonymy at the Crossroads: A Cognitive Perspective*, 133–48. Berlin.

Turner, V. 1980. 'Social Dramas and Stories about Them,' *Critical Inquiry* 7 (On Narrative): 141–68.

Ulf, C. 2006. 'The World of Homer and Hesiod', in K. A. Raaflaub and H. van Wees, eds. *A Companion to the Archaic Greek World*, 81–99. Oxford.

Usher, S., tr. 1974. *Dionysius of Halicarnassus: Critical Essays*, i. Loeb Classical Library. Cambridge, MA.

van Bremen, R. 1996. *The Limits of Participation: Women and Civic Life in the Greek East in the Hellenistic and Roman Periods*. Amsterdam.

van der Horst, P. W., and Newman, J. H. 2008. *Early Jewish Prayers in Greek: A Commentary.* Berlin and New York.
van de Ven, J. 2002. 'The Demand for Social Approval and Status as Motivation to Give', *Journal of Institutional and Theoretical Economics* 158: 464–82.
van de Ven, N. 2014. 'Malicious Envy and Schadenfreude', in W. W. van Dijk and J. W. Ouwerkerk, eds. *Schadenfreude: Understanding Pleasure at the Misfortune of Others,* 110–17. Cambridge.
van Dijk, W. W., and Ouwerkerk, J. W. 2014. 'Introduction', in W. W. van Dijk and J. W. Ouwerkerk, eds. *Schadenfreude: Understanding Pleasure at the Misfortune of Others,* 1–16. Cambridge.
van Dijk, W. W., Ouwerkerk, J. W., Goslinga, S., Nieweg, M., and Gallucci, M. 2006. 'When People Fall from Grace: Reconsidering the Role of Envy in Schadenfreude', *Emotion* 6, 156–60.
Van Hook, L., tr. 1945. *Isocrates,* iii. Loeb Classical Library. Cambridge, MA.
van Wees, H. 1998. 'The Law of Gratitude. Reciprocity in Anthropological Theory', in C. Gill, N. Postlethwaite, and R. Seaford, eds. *Reciprocity in Ancient Greece,* 13–49. Oxford.
van Wees, H. 2001. 'The Myth of the Middle-class Army: Military and Social Status in Ancient Athens', in T. Bekker-Nielsen and L. Hannestad, eds. *War as a Cultural and Social Force,* 45–71. Copenhagen.
van Wees, H. 2002. 'Greed, Generosity and Gift-Exchange in Early Greece and the Western Pacific', in W. Jongman and M. Kleijwegt, eds. *After the Past: Essays in Ancient History in Honour of H. W. Pleket,* 341–78. Leiden.
Versnel, H. S. 1990. *Inconsistencies in Greek and Roman Religion: Ter Unus-Isis, Dionysos, Hermes. Three Studies in Henotheism.* 2 vols. Studies in Greek and Roman Religion 6. Leiden.
Versnel, H. S. 1991. 'Beyond Cursing: The Appeal to Justice in Judicial Prayers', in Faraone and Obbink 1991: 60–106.
Versnel, H. S. 1994. '$Πεπρημένος$: The Cnidian Curse Tablets and Ordeal by Fire', in R. Hägg, ed. *Ancient Greek Cult Practice from the Epigraphical Evidence: Proceedings of the Second International Seminar on Ancient Greek Cult, Organized by the Swedish Institute at Athens, 22–24 November 1991,* 145–54. Stockholm.
Versnel, H. S. 1998. '$καὶ εἴ τι λ[οιπὸν] τῶν μερ[ῶ]ν [ἔσ]ται τοῦ σώματος ὅλ[ο]υ[..$ (... and any other part of the entire body there may be...): An Essay on Anatomical Curses', in F. Graf and W. Burkert, eds. *Ansichten griechischer Rituale: Geburtstags-Symposium für Walter Burkert,* 217–67. Stuttgart and Leipzig.
Versnel, H. S. 1999. '"Punish Those Who Rejoice in Our Misery." On Curse Tablets and Schadenfreude', in D. R. Jordan, H. Montgomery, and E. Thomassen, eds. *The World of Ancient Magic: Papers from the First International Samson Eitrem Seminar at the Norwegian Institute at Athens, 4–8 May 1996,* 125–62. Bergen.

Versnel, H. S. 2002a. 'Writing Mortals and Reading Gods: Appeal to the Gods as a Dual Strategy in Social Control', in D. Cohen and E. Müller-Luckner, eds. *Demokratie, Recht und soziale Kontrolle im klassischen Athen*, 37–77. Munich.
Versnel, H. S. 2002b. 'The Poetics of the Magical Charm: An Essay on the Power of Words', in P. Mirecki and M. Meyer, eds. *Magic and Ritual in the Ancient World*, 105–58. Leiden.
Versnel, H. S. 2010. 'Prayers for Justice, East and West: New Finds and Publications since 1990', in R. Gordon and M. Simón, eds. *Magical Practice in the Latin West: Papers from the International Conference held at the University of Zaragoza, 30th Sept.–1st Oct. 2005, Religions in the Graeco-Roman World*, 275–356. Leiden.
Versnel, H. S. 2013. *Coping With the Gods: Wayward Readings in Greek Theology*. Leiden.
Vince, C. A., tr. 1935. *Demosthenes: Orations*, iii (21–26). Loeb Classical Library. Cambridge, MA.
Vince, C. A., and Vince, J. H., trs. 1926. *Demosthenes: Orations*, ii (18–19). Loeb Classical Library. Cambridge, MA.
Vince, J. H., tr. 1930. *Demosthenes: Orations*, i. Loeb Classical Library. Cambridge, MA.
von Reden, S. 2003. *Exchange in Ancient Greece*. London.
Voutsaki, S. 2010. 'Agency and Personhood at the Onset of the Mycenaean Period', *Archaeological Dialogues* 17: 65–92.
Waithe, M. E. 1987. 'Diotima of Mantinea', in M. E. Waithe, ed. *A History of Women Philosophers*, i: *Ancient Women Philosophers, 600 BC–500 AD*, 83–116. Dordrecht.
Walcot, P. 1978. *Envy and the Greeks*. Warminster.
Wallace, R. W. 1989. *The Areopagus Council to 307 B.C.* Baltimore, MD and London.
Wallace, R. W. 1994. 'Private Lives and Public Enemies: Freedom of Thought in Classical Athens', in A. Scafuro and A. Boegehold, eds. *Athenian Identity and Civic Ideology*, 127–55. Baltimore, MD.
Wallace, R. W. 2010. 'Tecmessa's Legacy: Valuing Others in Athens' Democracy', in R. Rosen and I. Sluiter, eds. *Valuing Others in Classical Antiquity*, 136–54. Leiden.
Ward, M. K., and Broniarczyk, S. M. 2011. 'It's Not Me, It's You: How Gift Giving Creates Giver Identity Threat as a Function of Social Closeness', *Journal of Consumer Research* 38: 164–81.
Waterfield, R. 2009. *Why Socrates Died: Dispelling the Myths*. New York.
Watson, P. A. 1995. *Ancient Stepmothers: Myth, Misogyny and Reality*. Leiden.
Wehrli, F. R. 1969. *Die Schule des Aristoteles*, Part x: *Hieronymos von Rhodos, Kritolaos und seine Schüler*. 2nd edn. Basle and Stuttgart.
Wehrli, F. R. 1974. *Die Schule des Aristoteles*, Supplement i: *Hermippos der Kallimacheer*. Basle and Stuttgart.

Weinstein, F. 1990. 'Some Comments on the History of Emotion', *Psychohistory Review* 18: 293–302.
Weinstein, F. 1995. 'Psychohistory and the Crisis of the Social Sciences', *History and Theory* 34: 299–319.
Wenzel, S. 1967. *The Sin of Sloth: Accedie in Medieval Thought and Literature*. Chapel Hill, NC.
White, L. 1994. 'Between Gluckman and Foucault: Historicizing Rumour and Gossip', *Social Dynamics: A Journal of African Studies* 20: 75–92.
Whitehead, D. 1983. 'Competitive Outlay and Community Profit: Philotimia in Democratic Athens', *Classica et Mediaevalia* 34: 55–74.
Whitehead, D. 1984. 'A Thousand New Athenians', *Liverpool Classical Monthly* 9: 8–10.
Whitehead, D. 1990. *Aineias the Tactician: How to Survive Under Siege*. Oxford.
Whitehead, D. 1991. 'Who Equipped Mercenary Troops in Classical Greece?', *Historia* 40: 105–13.
Whitehead, D. 2009. 'Spiteful Heaven: Residual Belief in Divine Phthonos in Post-Fifth-Century Greece', *Acta Antiqua Academiae Scientiarum Hungaricae* 49: 327–33.
Widlok, T. 1997. 'Orientation in the Wild: The Shared Cognition of Hai||om Bushpeople', *Journal of the Royal Anthropological Institute* 3: 317–32.
Wilhelm, A. 1901. 'Zwei Fluchinschriften', *Jahreshefte des österreichischen archäologischen Institutes* in Wien 4, Beiblatt, cols 9–18.
Willi, A. 2003. *The Languages of Aristophanes: Aspects of Linguistic Variation in Classical Attic Greek*. Oxford.
Williams, R. 2009 [1977]. *Marxism and Literature*. Oxford.
Wilson, A. 1990. 'The Ceremony of Childbirth and its Interpretation', in V. Fildes, ed. *Women as Mothers in Pre-Industrial England*, 68–107. London.
Wilson-Mendenhall, C., Barrett, L. F., and Barsalou, L. W. 2013. 'Neural Evidence that Human Emotions Share Core Affective Properties', *Psychological Science* 24: 947–56.
Wilson-Mendenhall, C., Barrett, L. F., and Barsalou, L. W. 2015. 'Variety in Emotional Life: Within-Category Typicality of Emotional Experiences is Associated with Neural Activity in Large-Scale Brain Networks', *Social Cognitive and Affective Neuroscience* 10: 62–71.
Wolf, M. 1972. *Women and the Family in Rural Taiwan*. Stanford, CA.
Wood, J. L. 2007. 'Comedy, Malice and Philosophy in Plato's Philebus', *Ancient Philosophy* 27: 77–94.
Woodbury, L. E. 1973. 'Socrates and Aristides' Daughter', *Phoenix* 27: 24–5.
Worthington, I. 1992. *A Historical Commentary on Dinarchus: Rhetoric and Conspiracy in Fourth-Century Athens*. Ann Arbor, MI.
Worthington, I. 2001. 'Dinarchus', in I. Worthington, R. Craig, and E. Harris, *Oratory of Classical Greece*, v: *Dinarchus, Hyperides, and Lycurgus*, 1–58. Austin, TX.

Worthington, I. 2012. *Demosthenes of Athens and the Fall of Classical Greece*. New York.

Wycherley, R. E. 1970. 'Minor Shrines in Ancient Athens', *Phoenix* 24: 283–95.

Wyse, W. 1904. *The Speeches of Isaeus with Critical and Explanatory Notes*. Cambridge.

Young, D. C. 1968. *Three Odes of Pindar: A Literary Study of Pythian 11, Pythian 3, and Olympian 7*. Leiden.

Younger, J. G. 2002. 'Women in Relief: "Double Consciousness" in Classical Attic Tombstones', in N. Rabinowitz and L. Auanger, eds. *Among Women: From the Homosocial to the Homoerotic in the Ancient World*, 167–210. Austin, TX.

Youtie, H. C. 1974. 'P. Mich. Inv. 2920 = Sammelbuch IV 7361', *Zeitschrift für Papyrologie und Epigraphik* 15: 149–52.

Youtie, H. C., and Pearl, O. M. 1944. *Papyri and Ostraca from Karanis*. Michigan Papyri, 6. Ann Arbor, MI.

Yunis, H. 1988. *A New Creed: Fundamental Religious Beliefs in the Athenian Polis and Euripidean Drama*. Göttingen.

Zafiropoulos, C. A. 2001. *Ethics in Aesop's Fables: The Augustana Collection*. Leiden.

Zelnick-Abramowitz, R. 2004. 'Settlers and Dispossessed in the Athenian Empire', *Mnemosyne* 4th ser. 57: 325–45.

Ziehen, L. 1934. 'Theoris', in A. F. Pauly, G. Wissowa, and W. Kroll, eds. *Realencyclopädie der classischen Altertumswissenschaft*, v.2, cols 2237–9. Stuttgart.

Zingerle, 1926. 'Heiliges Recht', *Jahreshefte des Österreichischen Archäologischen Instituts* 23: 67–72.

Ziolkowski, J. M. 2003. '*Amaritudo Mentis*: The Archpoet's Interiorization and Exteriorization of Bitterness in its Twelfth-Century Contexts', in C. S. Jaeger and I. Kasten, eds. *Codierungen von Emotionen im Mittelalter*, 98–111. Berlin and New York.

General Index

abaskanta (untouched by evil eye) 163, see also *baskanos*
Abdera, Abderites 39, 109
Abrahams, Roger 178
accidie 91–2
accusations 8–9, 26, 38–67, 125, 161, 212, 256, 261, 331
acedia 91–2
Achaemenes 103, 147
actors 287
Adonis 53–4
adoption 196, 301, 321
Adrastus 183
Aegina, Aeginetans 117, 121, 288, 290
  athletes from 108, 114, 120–1
Aelian 72
Aemilius Saturninus, Quintus 156
Aeneas Tacticus 286–7
Aeschines (orator) 17, 19–20, 29, 45, 52–4, 57, 129–31, 134–5, 154, 170, 182, 184–5, 197, 199–200, 203–4, 209, 258–60, 262, 283, 294, *see also* Glaucothea
Aeschines (Socratic) 27
Aeschylus 52, 74, 187, 241, 309
Aesop's fables 5, 31, 33, 45, 55, 60
Agamemnon 111
Agathocles 217
Agathokleia (*thiasotes*) 28
Agathon 144
Agathursi 77, 147
age (as evidence of legal incapacity) 317, 323
Agesilaus 276
Aglaeon son of Leontius 226
agon timetos 48, 50
Agora (at Athens) 181, 186, 229, 258, 260, 281, 320
Agoratus 199
agurtai (beggar-priests) 13, 30, 46, 308–9
Aitherion (thiasotes) 29
Ajax 111, 120, 122

akosmousai (women without decorum) 334
Akragas 114, 124, *see also* Thero
Akrigg, Ben 270, 284–5
Alcathous 308
Alce 313–15
Alcestis 184, 188
Alcibiades 52, 56, 59, 106, 148, 205, 285, 322
Alexander, Jeffrey 330
Alexander of Aphrodisias 74
Alexander the Great 23
  exiles decree of 259, 286
Allen, Danielle 181, 238, 240
Allport, Gordon 172
Almirol, Edwin 178
Alston, Richard 157
Alvar Nuño, Anton 158
amae ('dependency' in Japanese) 89
amaritudo (bitterness) 92
Amasis 153
Amnesty of 403/2 BCE 59
Amorgos 63, 226, *see also* Semonides
Amphipolis 147, 274, 277
amulets 74, 168–9
  as metaphor 168
Amyntas 194
anakrisis (preliminary hearing) 49
analogical language, in spells 237
Anaxagoras 22, 57, 66
Anaximenes of Lampsacus (rhetorician) 23, 26
Andania 334
Andean analogy 79
Andersen, Øivind 295
Andocides 49, 51–2, 184, 187, 198, 200, 271, 273
Andrewes, Antony 18
Androcles 313
Andros, Andrians 271
anger 93, 98–9, 113, 209
  'basic' emotion 83–4
  of the gods 31–2, 83
anosios (profane) 41
Anthology, Greek 72

General Index

anthropology, anthropological
    findings 6, 83, 96, 140, 155–6,
    173–4, see also Candomblé, dan,
    Douglas, Fiji, gift, Gluckman, hau,
    Ilongots, Indonesia, Inkas, Lévi-
    Strauss, Maori, Mauss, potlatch,
    Soweto, Thailand, Trobrianders
Antidorus 313–14
Antigone (cursing woman) 215–16
Antimachus 206
Antinoopolis 157
Antioch 158
Antiochus (doctor) 214
Antiphanes (comic poet) 307
Antiphon 34–7, 39
anxiety 4, 206, 208, 223, 311–12, 329,
    see also fear
apagoge (privately directed judicial
    process) 242–3, 249
Apelles 25
    painted *Phthonos* 92, 121
Aphrodite 25, 53, 308
    Ourania 53
Apollo 149
    Lyceus 27
    Pythius 308
Apollodorus (orator, prosecutor of
    Neaera) 204–6, 276, 302, 307,
    317–18, 322
Apollodorus, estate of (subject of
    Isaeus 7) 196
apotumpanismos (crucifixion) 238,
    240–2, 249
appraisal processes 97
apprenticeship 299
Apsephion 133
Arcesilaus, name of kings of Cyrene
    III 152
    IV 113
archaeology 54, 79, see also iconography
Archestratus 206
Archias 38, 51, 319–20
Archilochus 118–20
Archippe 293
Archippus 51
archon, eponymous 198
archon basileus ('King Archon',
    Athenian magistrate) 49, 318
Areopagus 35–6, 42, 267–8
Aretaphila 37, 66–7
Arezzo 232
Arge (Hyperborean virgin) 309

Argenti, Nicholas 330, 332
Arginusae, battle of 270
Aristagora (*hetaira*) 323
Aristarchus (associate of Meidias) 258
Aristarchus (character in Xenophon's
    Memorabilia) 296
Aristippus 287, 307
Aristoclidas of Aegina 108
Aristocrates 125
Aristodemus 146
Aristogiton (prosecuted by
    Demosthenes) 11–12, 14, 16, 39,
    135, 187, 189, 302, 308
Aristogiton (tyrannicide) 132
Aristola (*thiasotes*) 28
Aristomenes of Aegina 120, 150
Ariston (opponent of Hyperides) 192
Ariston (plaintiff in Demosthenes
    54) 199
Aristophanes 28, 52, 153, 187, 241, 272,
    295, 303
    change of viewpoint in 272
    on female occupations 306
Aristotle 35, 36, 50, 130, 144, 189, 210,
    275, 287, 292, 298, 302, 312, 334
    charged with pro-Macedonian
        sympathies 49
    on gossip 188
    on *phthonos* 75, 77, 130, 210
'arms race', magical 223
army, armies 288, 305
    fund (*stratiotikon*) 277
Arnaoutoglou, Ilias 18, 63
Arnold, Magda 84, 87
Artabanus 152
Artabazus 276
Asclapiadas 215–16
Asclepius 169
Ascough, Richard 29
asebeia (impiety) 16, 23, 26–7, 32–3,
    40–1, 44, 48–52, 60–2, 66, 167, 192,
    323, 329
Ashforth, Adam 8, 136, 155–6
Aspasia 66, 192, 322–3
Aspendus 275
Assembly, Athenian 27, 40, 53, 148, 192,
    199, 205, 268
    pay for 271, 273
Astycratea 308
Astypalaia 105
Astyphilus, estate of (subject of
    Isaeus 9) 201

General Index

ataphos (unburied) 158
ateleia (exemption from taxes and liturgies) 132–3
Athenaeus 24–5, 28, 257, 323, 334
Athens, Athenians *passim*
   citizenship and citizen status 12, 189, 196, 208, 288, 301, 303–4, 307–8, 316–18, 321–2, 333
   economic situation after 400 BCE 5, 8–9, 207–311
   food supply of 208, 280–1
   foreigners, attitudes to 282–4, *see also* metics
   navy, difficulties of financing in fourth century 275–7
   oligarchs, oligarchy 49, 265, 269, 292, *see also* Four Hundred, Thirty
   population of 180, 266, 269–70, 280–1, 285, 293
   religious policies of 44, *see also* new gods and religions
atheos (godless) 41
athletes 105, 109, 113, 123
atimia (loss of civic rights) 50
Atrometus (father of Aeschines the orator) 17
Attica (territory of Athens) 47, 59, 62, 265, 269, 280, 285, 306, 322–3, *see also* Athens
Austin, Colin 40
Austin, Michel 274, 280, 281, 288
autochthony 269
Averill, James 90, 93, 94, 96
Ayim, Marianne 197

Babylon 183
Bacchis (*hetaira*) 26
Bacchylides 104, 124
Bailey, Frederick 175, 179
Bakewell, Geoff 283
bakers, women as 305
Bamberger, John 92
Banaras 142
barbaroi 282
Barrett, Lisa Feldman 82–8
Bartolini, Gianfranco 30
Basil of Caesarea 161
baskainein, baskanos, baskania (words implying abuse and malevolence) 74, 135–6, 154, 163, 169–70, *see also* evil eye
bastards 301, 322, *see also nothoi*

Bathippus 132–3
Bauman, Richard 49
Baumeister, Roy 173, 176, 178
Bean, George 214
beggar-priests *see agurtai*
begging 272, 308–9
Bell, Charles 80–1
belly-talkers 310
Bemarchius 160–1
Bendis, cult of 52–3, 59
benefaction(s) 106, 124, 138, 140, 145, 154, 158
Benoit, William 156
Benson, Larry 92
Ben-Yehuda, Nachman 10
Ben Ze'Ev, Aaron 76, 226, 231
Bergadaà, Michelle 143
Bergmann, J. (epigraphist) 213
Bergmann, Jörg 173, 176, 177
Berking, Helmuth 141
Berve, Helmut 23
Besnier, Niko 3, 172, 173, 175, 195, 196, 201
biaiothanatos (dead by violence) 158
Biezunska-Malowist, Iza 157
binding as metaphor 234–7
binding spells 7, 38, 65–6, 101, 162, 168–9, 224–55, 259, 261
   analogical language in 237
   apotumpanismos and 240–3
   blending and 246–50
   body parts listed in 233, 238–40
   emotions and 250–3
   gossip and 180
   Libanius and 160, 233
   metaphorical 234–7
   prayers for justice and 215
   purpose of 157, 240
   Schadenfreude and 225, 231, 250–3
   thieves frequently targeted in 242
Biton 152
bitterness 92
Björck, Gudmund 213, 214, 218
Black, John 82
Black Death 284, 305
Black Sea 232, 275, 308
blame 110–13, 137, 145, 175, 254, 295, *see also momos*
   'blame games' 125
   'blame poetry' 118
blending, conceptual 243–4, 246–7, 249
blood, avoided in Athenian executions 240

General Index

Blümel, Wolfgang 215, 218
boastfulness, boasting 32, 117, 119, 124, 132, 154
bocage (Northern France) 155
Bodman, Ida 265
body parts 98, *see also* binding spells
Boeotus 18–20, 189
Boiotia 64, 183, 234, 239
Bollansée, Jan 26
Bonner, Campbell 159
Bordia, Prashant 257
boredom 92
Borphor syllables 230
Borsch, Stuart 284
bottomry loans 299
Boulay, Juliet du 180
boule see Council
Bowie, Angus 146, 269
Bowie, Katherine 143
Brasidas 147
Braund, Susanna 6
breasts, Phryne's 24
Brenner, Robert 284
brephos see fetus
Breuer, Christine 306, 324
Brigantium 232
Brison, Karen 177
Brixhe, Claude 239
Brock, Roger 306
Broniarczyk, Susan 143
Brosch, Tobias 87
Brown, Christopher 119
Brown, Peter 159
Bryen, Ari 74, 156–8
Bulman, Patricia 77, 105
Burford, Alison 286
burial 14, 48, 282, 325
 legislation about 334
Burian, Peter 34
Burke, Kenneth 136–7
Burkert, Walter 53, 57, 169, 310, 329
Burkhardt, Frederick 81
Burnett, Ann 122
Burt, Ronald 256

Caillé, Alain 141–2
Cairns, Douglas 6, 77, 93, 126–8
Calhoun, Cheshire 90
Callaeschrus 126
Callias 184, 200
Callistratus (Athenian politician) 287

Callistratus (speaker of Demosthenes 48) 201
Cambyses 146
Camp, John 282
Campbell, John 155, 177, 225
Candomblé (Brazil) 255
cannibalism 99, 120
Cantarelli, Luigi 25
Canterbury Tales 92
Capelle, Wilhelm 158
'Careless talk . . . ' 162
Carey, Chris 103, 104, 113, 116, 123–4, 192–4, 259, 282, 307
Cargill, Jack 12
Carrier, James 142–3
Cartesianism 82
Cassandra 309
casualties 269
causal tautology 244–5
Cawkwell, George 276
Cebes 136
Cephisius 198
Cerasuolo, Salvatore 251
Chabrias 133
Chaerecrates 167
Chaerestratus 313
Chaeronea, battle of 281
Chambry, Émile 31–2
chameleon, Libanius and the 159–60
Chaniotis, Angelos 5–6, 217
Chares 276
charges 38–67, *see also* accusation
Chariades 271, 316
charis 104, 109, 149, 206, 295
Chaucer, Geoffrey 92
Chersonese 274, 281
children 270, 273, 282, 288–9, 292, 295–304, 307, 313, 324
 girls 288, 302, 326
 interactions of 256
Chios 63, 286, 313
 battle of (357/6 BCE) 133
choregos 257
Chremilus 272
Christ, Matthew 277–80
Christes, Johannes 325
Christianity, analogies with 14
Chrysilla 200
chthonic powers 249
Cimon 285
Cinesias 198
Ciron 198–9

citizen status, citizenship (Athenian) 12, 189, 196, 208, 288, 303–4, 306–8, 316–18, 321–2, 333
   Athenian law of 451 BCE 283, 301, 304
   Demophilus, decree of 305–6
   Milesian 288
Cleobis 152
Cleobule (mother of Demosthenes) 297
Cleomedes of Astypalaea 105
Cleomenes, king of Sparta 146, 183, 238
cleruchies 272, 281
clientship, Roman 141
Clore, Gerald 84, 87, 89
'clothing and jewellery' (*himatia kai chrusia*) 293
Clytemnestra 109, 111
Coan, James 89
cognitive:
   analysis of narrative 179
   approaches to emotions 83, 87, 90, 100
   blending 243–4, 246–7, 249
   'maps of social identities' 178
Cohen, David 16, 50, 57, 58, 60, 61, 62, 129, 180, 185, 190, 205
Cohen, Edward 279, 307
coinage, silver 276
Coleman, James 242, 256
Collins, Derek 17, 39, 42, 236
colour 88
combat trauma 328
conceptual blending *see* blending
confession inscriptions 180, 218–21
Congo 99–100
Connelly, Joan 15
Connor, W. Robert 49, 54, 49, 65
Conon (Athenian general) 133, 138
Conon (defendant in speech by Demosthenes) 199, 202
Constantinople 156, 158
constructionist theories of emotion
   psychological 87, 89
   social 89–90, 95
cooks, cookery 287
Cooper, Craig 25, 26, 28, 30
Corcyra 203, 280, 287
Corinth 188, 202, 293, 307
   Corinthian War 271, 274
corn supply and trade, Athenian 280, 282
Coronea 202
corrupting the youth 28, 52, 59
Cosmides, Lida 88

Council 40, 53, 258, 277, 315
courtroom space 247–9
courtroom spells 7, 247
cowl, used metonymically for death 245
Cox, Bruce 175
Crete, Cretans 124, 288, 308
Cribiore, Raffaella 158, 161
Critias 59, 126, 162, 265
Critobulus 167, 209
Croesus 151–2, 154, 183
Crook, Zeba 142
Crotty, Kevin 105, 107, 111–13, 151
Ctesiphon 128
Cudjoe, Richard 292–7, 299, 304, 306
cult(s) *see* Adonis, Drimacus, Pheme, Sabazius, *thiasos*
   ecstatic 54
   foreign 44, 64
   of dead athletes 105
Cummings, Frederick 80
Cumont, Franz 213, 214
Cunningham, William 89
Currie, Bruno 105
curses, curse tablets and -texts, cursing 7, 38–9, 65–7, 168–9, 180, 213, 215–24, 226, 229, 231, 232–3, 235–7, 239, 249–50, 254, 255, 261, 301, 326, *see also* Teos
   anatomical curses 235, *see also* body parts
   'border-area' curses 233
   motivation for 241
   public 39–40, 43
   see also binding spells
Cybele 29, 55
cyberbullying 265
Cyprus 53, 269, 280, 306
Cyrene, Cyrenaica 37, 66, 113, 152, 249
Cyrus (the Younger) of Persia 288
Cyrus, St. 233

daimon, plural *daimones* 29, 50, 260, *see also* demons
daimonion, plural *daimonia* (divine power) 52, 58, 154
'Dale Carnegie paradox' 141
Damophilus of Cyrene 113
dan (Indian charitable gifts) 142
Danae (woman in Polybius) 217
dancing, ecstatic 54
D'Andrade, Roy 96–8
'dangerous women' 312–21, 323, 333

General Index

Darwin, Charles 80–2, 84
David, Ephraim 272
Davidson, James 269
Davies, John 285
Dawson, Graham 4
dead, *phthonos* not felt towards the 102
death 212–14, see also *apotumpanismos*, execution, homicide, murder, poison, punishment
  as 'Grim Reaper' 244–6
  as penalty 22, 42, 193
  attitudes to 146, 152, 238
  binding spells and 250
  curse tablets and 234
  epitaphs describe manner of 214
  personification of 244
  result of gossip 265
  wish for 232
deceit, Demosthenes on 133
Decelea, Spartan occupation of 271
defixio, plural *defixiones* 217, 225, 236
Deianeira 34
Deissmann, Adolf 213
Delbridge, Rick 179
Delos, Delians 51, 58, 213, 218, 221–2, 309
Demades 49
Demaenetus affair 274
Demaratus 146–7
demes (villages of Attica) 285, 305
Demeter 16, 215–18, 220, 227–8
Demetriou, Denise 282
Demetrius of Phaleron 22, 31, 49, 73, 120, 287, 323, 334
Demetrius Poliorcetes 300
democracy 269, 312, 330
  cost of running 275
  phthonos and 128
  women and 189, 312
Democritus 74
demography 269, 293, 299, see also population
demons 14, 91–2, see also *daimons/daimones*
  'noonday' 91
Demophilus, decree of 305–6
Demosthenes 11–23, 40, 45, 50, 52, 128–30, 133–6, 163, 182, 205, 257–60, 276–8, 297, 303–5, 320, 322, 328
Den Boer, Willem 295, 299–300
depression 85, 92

Derrida, Jacques 13
Derenne, Eudore 22, 44, 51, 52, 57, 58
Descartes see Cartesianism
devils 9, 10, 14
Dewald, Carolyn 140
dexiosis (hand-clasping) 324
diabole (slander) 66, 121, 137, 192–4, 201, 209–10, 261, see also slander
Diagoras of Melos 22, 52
Diagoras of Rhodes 115, 118
Dicaeogenes 197
Dickie, Matthew 18, 19, 20, 21, 33, 37, 43, 45, 55, 61, 63, 117, 120–1, 151, 154, 158, 309
Difonzo, Nicholas 257
dikai emporikai (commercial courts) 282
dikastai 35, 315, see also jurors
dike pseudomarturion (case for false witness) 313
Dillon, Matthew 29, 309
Dinarchus 12, 21, 259–60
Dinka of Sudan 93
Diocles 189, 203, 296
Diodorus (character in Xenophon's *Memorabilia*) 228
Diodorus (litigant in Demosthenic speech) 40–1, 50
Diodorus of Sicily (historian) 300
Diodotus (in Lysias 32) 296–7
Diodotus (in Thucydides) 148
Diogenes Laertius 73
Diogenes of Sinope, the Cynic 286, 308
Diogiton (in Lysias 32) 297–8
Dionysus, 29, 55, 310
  festival (Dionysia) 257
  processions 134
  theatre of, at Athens 309
Diopeithes, decree of 57–8, 62
Dioscuri 149
Diotima of Mantinea 310–11
discourse 136–8
disgust 83–4
display rules 85
divination 311, see also dreams, *mantis*, seers
  as criminal offence 159
Dodds, Eric 44, 57, 184, 329
dokimasia 207–8
dolls 234, see also figurines
Douglas, Mary 143
Dover, Kenneth 22, 52, 57, 58, 154, 231

General Index

dowries 203, 294, 302-3, 307, 317, 321-2, 324
Draco 241
dramatism 136
dreams 48, 152, 159, 179, 183
Drimacus 63
Driscoll, Jeremey 92
drugs 12-13, 40-3, 168, 314, see also *pharmaka*, *philtra*
Dunbabin, Katherine 120, 158
Dunbar, Robin 172, 179
Duncan-Jones, Richard 284

Easterling, Patricia 34
eating as metaphor for *phthonos* 119-20
Edmonds III, Radcliffe 9, 213, 214, 222, 333
Edwards, Derek 97
Edwards, Michael 313, 315-17
Egypt(ians) 91, 156, 249, 269, 276, 284
Ehrenberg, Victor 270
Eidinow, Esther 7, 16, 38, 49, 51, 62, 96, 137, 145, 149, 154, 208, 216, 231, 237, 240, 247, 254, 260, 299, 301, 309, 333
eisangelia (type of prosecution process) 58, 61
eisphora (property tax) 277-8
ekklesia see Assembly
Ekman, Paul 81, 84-6
Eleusis 56, 59, 319, see also mysteries
Ellsworth, Phoebe 87
Emerson, Ralph 144
emigration 270
Emler, Nicholas 177, 180
emotional communities 95
'emotionology' 93
emotions 76-101, 160, 232, 252, see also anger, binding spells, envy, fear, hatred, jealousy, love, *nemesis*, *phthonos*
  'basic emotions' 83-5, 93
  behind curse texts 213
  cognitive approaches to 83, 87, 90, 100
  evolutionary theory of origins 93
  language of 89
  modern theories of 5-7, 76-101
  network theories of 97
  physiognomy and 80, 88
  psychological constructionist theories of 87, 89
  relational theory of 79, 90
  social constructionists theories of 89-90, 95
  talk 97-102
Empedocles 92
emporoi (traders) 282
Endius 315
engastrimuthoi (belly-talkers) 310
Engen, Darel 281-2
engue (betrothal) 322
enklema 41-2
Enquist, Magnus 172
envy 5, 7-9, 75-6, 109, see also *phthonos*
  as 'sense-making technique' 8
  divine 7, 149-55
  gossip and 9
  jealousy and 76, 94
  Plutarch on 158
  Schadenfreude and 251
  witchcraft and 93
Epaenetus 318
Epaphroditus 226-8
Epharmostus of Opous 117
Epictetus 227
epidemics 284, see also Black Death, plague
epigrams 306, 310
epigraphic evidence, epigraphy 28, 63, 66, 283, 310, see also curses, epigrams, epitaphs, inscriptions
epilepsy 13
epinikia (victory odes) 107, see also Bacchylides, Pindar, praise
epitaphs 180, 213-14, 218, 221-3, 228, 254-5, 261, 310, 323
epoidai (incantations) 13, 42, 46, 167, 169, see also incantations
epopteia (highest grade of Eleusinian initiation) 30
Eratidai 114
Eretria 14
Ergamenes 313
Ergoteles of Himera 124
Eridanos 224
Erinyes (Furies) 241
Erotis (*thiasotes*) 29
ethos 79
Euandrus 237
Eubulides 197, 320-1
Eubulus 257, 277
Euctemon (enemy of Demosthenes) 257
Euctemon (estate of, in Isaeus 6) 313-14
Eunomus 11-14

Euripides 35, 55, 144, 184, 187, 239, 303
Euryale 120
Eurymedon, battle of 183
eusebeia (piety) 41
Eutherus 172
Euthias 23–7, 30, 56
Euthycles 105
euthyna (account of period of office) 208
Euthyphro 49–50
eutuches 154
Eutychian 229
Euxitheus of Halimous 305, 320–1
Evagoras of Salamis in Cyprus 183
Evagrius, St. 91–2
Evans, Vyvyan 244
Evans-Pritchard, Edward 8
evolutionary psychology 172, 175
evil eye 7, 9, 74, 135, 151, 158, 161, 236
  eye disease connected with? 158
execution 39, 55, 237, 240, 242, 250, *see also* punishment, capital
exegetai (expounders of religious law) 41
exile, exiles 14, 113, 122–3, 193, 257, 260, 286, 290
  as penalty 42, 48, 159, 193
  decree of Alexander about 259, 286
exorcisms 14

Fahr, Wilhelm 52
Fähse, Gottfried 72
famine 159, *see also* food
Faraone, Chris 233, 240, 241
Fauconnier, Gilles 244–5, 247, 256
Favret-Saada, Jeanne 8, 155
Fayyum 156
fear 10, 49, 160, 231, *see also* anxiety
  as 'basic' emotion 83–4
  of betrayal 332
  of conspiracy 209, 332
  of mockery 225
  of returning athletes 106
  of slaves 63
  of sophists 265
  of tyranny 115
  of wrath of gods 61, 154
festivals, religious 25, 27–8, 48, 115, 314, *see also* Dionysus
  women and 31, 334, *see also* Thesmophoria
fetus 156–8

figurines 121
  found with spells 234, 239, 241, 247
Fiji, gossip in 177
Filonik, Jakub 4, 49, 50
Finlay-Jones, Robert 92
Finley, Moses 59
Firth, Raymond 141
Fisher, Nick 202, 228, 257–8
Flower, Michael 15, 23, 309, 310–11
Fluchhände 212–13
Fontenrose, Joseph 105
food 272, 280, 300, 305, *see also* famine, grain
  shortages of 280, 282
force dynamics 244
foreigners, attitudes to at Athens 282–4
Forsdyke, Sara 110, 273, 349
Foster, Eric 177, 256
Foucart, Paul 25, 30
Four Hundred (oligarchs in 411 BCE) 193
fox, slanderer as 113
Foxhall, Lin 270, 285, 293–4, 324
Frankenberg, Ronald 173
Frankfurter, David 157
Frede, Dorothea 250
'free riders' 172
French, Alfred 273–4
Friedrich, Johannes 239
Friesen, Wallace 84
Frijda, Nico 87
Frith, Uta and Chris 172–3
Fuks, Alexander 289

Gabrielsen, Vincent 271, 273, 275–80, 287
Gagarin, Michael 33–5, 41, 42, 43, 192
Gager, Joseph 63, 213, 233
Gagné, Renaud 56
Galen 233
Gallant, Thomas 299
Galt, Anthony 9, 155
Gambreion 334
Gardner, Andrew 79
Garland, Robert 53, 55, 58, 59, 65, 306
Garnsey, Peter 270, 280
Gawlinski, Laura 334
Geertz, Armin 172, 179
Geertz, Clifford 331
Gemellus Horion 156–8, 163
gender 4, 99, 153
  as factor in prosecutions 42, 63
  roles 305

Gendron, Maria 82, 84, 87
generals, freelance 276, 287
Gennadius of Constantinople 74
Georgoudi, Marianthe 265
Germany 155
Gernet, Louis 238, 241–3, 249
Geschiere, Peter 156, 331
Geta 304
geuomai (taste) 112
Giammellaro, Pietro 309
Gill, Christopher 137
Gilmore, David 171
girls, unmarried 302–8
Glaucothea (mother of Aeschines) 17–18, 20, 29, 45, 56
Glaucus 145
Gluckman, Max 173–5, 179, 186
Glycera 322
Godelier, Maurice 141–2
gods, traditional 55–7, *see also* new gods
god-sibbs 170
goes (sorcerer), *goeteia* (sorcery) 33, 44, 55, 135, 169–70
Goff, Barbara 320
Goffman, Erving 178
Golden, Mark 293, 298–9, 303
Goldhill, Simon 113, 124
Goode, Erich 10
Goodwin, Marjorie 175, 178, 256
Gordon, Richard 9, 13, 33, 40, 42, 55, 57, 62, 63, 64, 218, 219, 220, 333
Gorgias 169
Gosden, Chris 78
gossip 7–9, 170–260 *passim*
 ancient Greek words for 181
 Aristotle on 188
 as Mediterranean phenomenon 180
 as 'sense-making technique' 8
 as 'social glue' 174
 as weapon 175
 between classes 186
 etymology of word 171
 Euripides on 187
 Fijian evidence for 177
 in epitaphs 180
 in law courts 185, 189, 191–211, 259
 networks of 256
 operation of 170
 origins of 172
 pheme and 182
 phthonos and 161, 209–11, 253
 Pindar on 109, 112, 120, 188
 positive/negative 175
 private 212–23
 reputation and 173
 slander and 180, 191–209
 slaves and 187
 three-stage process of 254
 truth and 196–206
 witchcraft and 8
Gould, John 140
Graf, Fritz 9, 56, 63, 159, 213–15, 217, 222, 225, 232–5, 329
Graham, A. John 39
grain supply and trade, Athenian 208, 280–1
graphe, plural *graphai* 3, 40, 42, 49–50, 207
 aprostasiou 283
 asebeias 3, 48–9, 51, 57–8, 62, 65, 319
 nomon me epitedeion theinai (charge of proposing unsuitable law) 132
 xenias (charge of being a non-citizen) 317
Greco, Monica 89
Green, Melanie 244
Gregory the Great 91
Griffiths, Paul 6, 83, 86, 89–90
'Grim Reaper' (conceptual blend) 244–6
Guettel Cole, Susan 77, 126, 134
gunaikonomoi (controllers of women) 333–4
gymnasium 27

Hacking, Ian 90
Hades 240
Hagesias of Syracuse 104, 108–9, 112
Hagesidamus 108
Hagnon 316
Hagnotheus 316
Halimous (deme of Attica) 305, 320
Halliwell, Stephen 250–2
Halm-Tisserant, Monique 237, 239, 242
Halperin, David 311
Hamel, Debra 318
Hampe, Beate 243–4
Handelman, Don 175, 178
Hannerz, Ulf 173, 175
Hansen, Mogens Herman 18, 50, 59, 270, 271, 273, 275
Hanson, Victor 270
Harding, Phillip 268, 283
Harmodius (tyrannicide) 132
Harpalus affair 12, 259

Harpocration 11, 16, 26–7, 29, 45
Harré, Rom 90–3, 99
Harris, Edward 6, 21, 39, 42, 50, 58, 78, 79, 92, 194, 299
Harris, Oliver 78–9
Harris, William 92
Harrison, A. Robin W. 42, 49, 303, 304, 313, 322
Harrison, Simon 177
harvest 155–6, 227
 used metonymically for death 244, 246
hate, hatred 85, 119, 127, 209
 and *phthonos* 209–10
hau (soul of a thing) 141
Haviland, John 177
Hawthorne, Susan 311
Heelas, Paul 91, 93, 97–100
Hegesistratus (seer) 238
Heliaia 25
Helios 214, 218
Hendershot, Cyndy 223
Henderson, Jeffrey 295
hendiadys 13
Henrichs, Albert 17
Heppenstall. M. A. 177
Hera 16, 309
Hercules 34, 115, 239
Hermes 67, 149
Hermippus 24, 26
Hermocrates 148
Hermotimus 153
herms, mutilation of 51–2
hero(es), hero cults, heroization 63, 105–6
Herodotus (historian) 269, 309
 pheme in 182–3
 phthonos in 77–8, 103, 146–7, 151–3
 reciprocity and 140
Herodotus of Thebes (athlete) 108, 114, 122
Herriman, Nicholas 331
Hesiod 103, 140, 241
Hesk, Jon 132, 134, 136, 169
Hesychia (name of *thiasotes*) 29
hetaira (courtesan), plural *hetairai* 23, 26, 30, 63–4, 185, 287, 307, 315–17, 319, 321–3
Hierax 156
hiereia see priestesses
Hiero II of Syracuse 104
hierophant (high priest) 319
hierosulia (temple-robbery, sacrilege) 48

Hignett, Charles 303
Himera 124
Hintzen-Bohlen, Brigitte 27
Hippocleas of Thessaly 123, 150
Hippocrates, Hippocratic treatises 13, 56, 92, 287, 310
Hipponicus 184, 187
Holland, Dorothy 97
Holliday, Heithre 175
Homer 46, 107, 140
 on *pharmakon* 12
 on *phthonos* 145
homicide 42–3, *see also* murder
homosexuality 161
Hopfner, Th. 13
Hopper, Robert 274
Hornblower, Simon v, 105, 123, 124, 132, 150, 271, 285
horoi (mortgage) 279
Hubbard, Thomas 109, 111
hubris (outrage) 115, 117, 129, 151
Hübner, Sabine 298
humiliation 225–6, 231, 239, 242, 250
humnos desmios (binding song) 241
Hunt, Peter 268
Hunter, Virginia 180, 184–6, 188–9, 192, 194, 196, 199–200, 206–8, 238, 297
Hyacinthus 224
Hykkara (Sicily) 307
Hyperboreans 309
Hyperides 23–30, 51, 56, 191–3, 283, 302, 334

iconography
 of cursing 212–13
 of *phthonos* 120–1, 158, 209
 of women 323–4
'identity-expressive products' 143
Idomeneus of Lampsacus 26, 257
Iles Johnston, Sarah 33, 44
Ilongots (Philippines) 96
Imbros 281
immobility of victim (as wish in curse tablets) 232, 237, 242
impiety *see asebeia*
Inachos 309
Inarus 269
incantations 11, 13, 31–3, 40, 42–3, 46, 55, 60, 159, 168, 241, 311, *see also epoidai*
Indonesia 331–3

General Index

infanticide 288
information management 175–7
initiation 19, 53, 320, *see also* Eleusis, mysteries, *telete*
 into mysteries of Dionysus 310
 into mysteries of Sabazius 29, 45
Inkas 79
innocence, protestations of 215, 218, 220
inscriptions 15, 28, 39, 212–13, 221, 288, *see also* confession inscriptions, curse tablets, epigrams, epigraphic evidence, epitaphs
intolerance 4, 22–3, 53, 56, 329
Iphicrates 287
Isaeus 127, 189, 195–6, 302, 307, 313, 315, 322
Isis 53
Isocrates 28, 169, 183, 267–9, 282, 284–5, 289–90
 on Athenian economic situation in fourth century BCE 267–9 and 282–90 *passim*
Isodaites 29–30, 45, 59, 62
Isotimides, decree of 51
Izard, Carol 84

Jain religion 142
Jakov, David 213
James, William 81–3
Jameson, Michael 27, 312
Janko, Richard 49
Japanese analogy 89
Java, East 331–2
jealousy (*zelos*) 75–6, 85, 331
 and envy 76, 94
Jebb, Richard 72
Jenkins, Janis 79
jewellery 293, 324
Jewish culture and evidence 22, 213
John, St. 233
Johnson, Mark 243–4
Johnson, Paul 255
Jones, Nicholas 28
Jordan, David 67, 213, 214, 224, 229–30
Josephus 21–3, 45, 52
Josselin, Ralph 171
judges 42, 210
Julius 156–7
jurors 24–5, 40, 43, 320

kakologia (abuse) 118, 147
kakourgoi (malefactors) 242

kalathoi (wool baskets) 324
Kamarina, Kamarineans 114–15, 148
Kamen, Deborah 322
Kammerbeek, Jan 72
Kapferer, Bruce 225
Kapparis, Konstantinos 283, 304, 317
Karanis 156–7
Kaster, Robert 6, 84, 98
katharmoi (purifications) 13
kathodos (return i.e. of the democrats from Phyle, 403 BCE) 283
Katz, Marilyn 3–4
Keller, Otto 31
Kemper, Theodore 87
Kennedy, Rebecca 284, 322
Kephallenia 158
Kerameikos 224, 314, 324–5
Keramopoullos, Antonios 240–1
Kerykes 200
King Archon *see archon basileus*
Kirk, Alan 141
Kirkwood, Gordon 110
kithara (lyre) 324
Klaros 308
kledon 183–4
kleos (good report) 107, 110, 117, 145
 'economy of' 107, 113
kloios (collar) 238
Knidos, curses from 215, 219–22, 224
Knossos 124
komos (revel, drunken procession) 27–8
Konstan, David 6, 76, 126, 127, 322, 329
Kore ('Maiden') 215–16, *see also* Persephone
koros (excess) 115, 117, 151
Kövecses, Zoltán 98, 243–4
Kowalski, Gorgius 25
Krauter, Stefan 22, 48–9, 50, 54, 55, 58–60, 62, 65, 319, 329
Kremmydas, Christos 132, 133
Kroeber, Alfred 96
Kron, Geoffrey 278
Kucharski, Janek 207
kuphon (pillory) 238
Kurke, Leslie 31
Kurland, Nancy 177
Kyle, David 27
kyria, kyrios (words for legal competence or control) 294, 307

Lacedaemonius, sister of 320–1
Laches 202

Laidlaw, James 142
Lais (*hetaira*) 307
Lakoff, George 98, 243–4
Lakonia 280, *see also* Sparta
laleo and cognate words for babbling, gossiping 181, 188
Lampsacus 277
Lanni, Adriaan 192
Lanzillotta, Lautaro 103, 136, 151
Larsen, Jeff 82
Latte, Kurt 39
Laurion, silver mines at 274
law courts *passim*, esp. 185, 189, 191–211, 259
lead (metal for curse tablets and associated figurines) 237, 247
Leaper, Campbell 175
leases 279, 284
Leimar, Olof 172
Lemnos 12, 14, 64, 281
  women of (mythical) 14, 41–2
Leocrates 194, 204–5
Leptines 132
lesche, plural *leschai* (informal meeting-place) 182
Lévi-Strauss, Claude 141
Lewis, Sian 182, 186
Libanius 157–61, 233
Limberis, Vasiliki 161
Limenius 161
Lindquist, Kristen 85, 88
Lipsius, Justus 61
liturgies (civic financial obligations) 76, 132, 157–8, 206, 276–8
Llorona, La 99
Lloyd-Jones, Hugh 72
loans 278, 299, *see also* mortgages
Lokri, Epizephyrian 105, 123
logismoi '(tempting) thoughts' 91
logopoios and cognate words 181
loidoria (abuse) 129, 134–5, 154, 191
Loman, Pasi 288, 305
Long, Nicholas 96
Loomis, William 273
Loraux, Nicole 301
love 85, 243, 311
  love potions *see philtra*
Lucian 92, 121
Luciani-Zidane, Lucrèce 92
Lutz, Catherine 83, 93
Lyceum (Athenian gymnasium) 27–8
Lycia 290

Lycurgus of Athens 12, 58, 194, 204
Lydia(ns) 218, 221, 282
Lynch, John 27
lynchings 331
Lyons, William 82
Lysias 125–6, 188, 193, 203, 283, 295
Lysistrata 28, 303

Macan, Reginald 152
McClure, Laura 186
MacDowell, Douglas 12, 15, 18, 20, 35, 36, 40–3, 49, 50, 132, 258, 303, 320
MacFarlen, Alan 171
McGinn, Thomas 295
McKechnie, Paul 284, 286–8, 290
Mackie, Hilary 117
Maeandrius 146
maenads 29
magic, magical activities or practices 3–4, 7, 9, 12–14, 42–4, 46–8, 56, 60, 64, 66, 100, 141, 157, 159–61, 162–3, 168, 225, 233, 335, *see also* binding spells, Borphor syllables, curses
  'magical arms-race' 223
  manipulative 246
  medicine and 169
  monetization of 310
  new cults and 44, 46
  performative function of of 235
  religion and 13, 46–7
  rhetoric/sophistry and 42, 169
  'sympathetic' 236
Magnesia (on Maeander, Asia Minor) 334
magos, plural *magoi* 13, 31–3, 46, 55, 170
Malinowski, Bronislaw 141–2
mania (insanity), as evidence of legal incapacity 317, 323
Mantias 20
mantic books 289
Mantinea 310
  battle of 274
mantis (seer), plural *manteis* 16–17, 30, 46, 287, 310, *see also* seers
Mantitheus 20
Manto (daughter of Polyidus) 308
Manto (daughter of Tiresias) 308
Maori 140–1
marriage 292, 297, 299, 302–8, 321
Marzi, Mario 24, 30

Mate, Mavis 305
Mathews, Holly 99
Matsumoto, David 81, 86
Mauss, Marcel 140-1, 143, 153
Medea 35, 188
medicine 169, 287, 306
medimnos of barley (as limit on women's transactions) 293, 306
Medusa 120
Megacles 104, 123
megaloprepeia (magnificence, lavish public expenditure) 106, 114, 148
Megara 308
Megas 122
Meidias 51, 135, 181, 189, 198, 257-8
Melampus 308
Melesias 110
Melos 290
Menander 121, 188, 304-5, 322, 324, 334
Mendonsa, Eugene 333
Menecles (adopter of the speaker in Isaeus 2) 317
Menecles (prosecutor of Ninon) 18-21
mercenaries 287-9
Meritt, Benjamin 287
Merry, Sally 170, 173, 175-9, 254, 256
Merton, Robert 330
Meskell, Lynn 79
Mesopotamia 237
Messenia 276
metaphor(s) 243-50, *see also* amulets, binding, envy, poison, spells, water
Methymna (Lesbos) 334
metics (resident foreigners) 14, 270, 277, 281-4, 290, 308, 320
tax on 14, 277, 308
metonymy 244-5
miara, miaros (polluted) 11, 14, 42, *see also* pollution
Michelson, Grant 173
midwives 171, 306
migration, circular 285, 296
Miletos, Milesians 288, 310
Mills, C. Wright 156
mines, silver 274
Mintel 143
Mirhady, David 268
misthos (pay) 274
Mnesilochus 239, 242
mobility, increase of in fourth century BCE 284, 286, 307
Möbius, Hans 310

momos (blame) 112
monkeys 80-1
Moore, Henrietta 96
Moors, Agnes 83, 97
Mopsus 308
Moraw, Susanne 29
Moreno, Alfonso 280-1
Morgan, Catherine 105
Morris, Ian 285
mortality 287, 292
mortgages 279
mosaics 158
Most, Glenn 6, 72, 112, 113, 117, 119, 121-4
Moysey, Robert 268
Munteanu, Dana 250
murder 14, 31, 34-43, 50, 66, 111, 208, 213-4, 232, 257-60, 308, *see also* homicide, parricide, poison
Murray, Oswyn 45
muscle actions 80-1
Mykale, battle of 183
Mylonas, George 56
mysteries (cults requiring initiation) 22, *see also* initiation
Eleusinian (the 'real' Mysteries) 18, 19, 30, 45, 51-2, 56, 315, 323
mockery of 45, 52
of Sabazius 45
slaves and 59
myth 14, 34, 63, 105, 111-12, 114, *see also* Alcestis, Cassandra, Lemnos, Manto, Medea, Oedipus, Pentheus, Prometheus, Tiresias
binding in 236
foundation myths 115
Mytilene debate 148

Nagle, Brendan 334
Nagy, Gregory 110, 120
narrative(s) 4, 7, 94, 100, 179
Neaera 293, 304, 307, 317-20, 322
Needham, Rodney 9
Nemea, Nemean festival 110, 114
nemesis (righteous indignation) 75, 77
'nervous system' 95, 100
network(s) 7, 143
analysis, social 256
of gossip 256
personal semantic networks 100
theory of emotions 97
new gods and religions 44-5, 57-60

Newman, Judith 213
Newton, Charles 215, 218
Nicias 148, 153, 305
Nicocrates of Cyrene 37, 66
Nicodemus (in Isaeus 3) 195–6, 316
Nicodemus of Aphidna 257–61
Nicomachus 193
Nicomedia 158, 160
Nicostratus, estate of (subject of Isaeus 4) 271, 289, 316–17
Nilsson, Martin 153
Ninon 17–23, 46–7, 49, 52, 55–9, 63, 64, 66, 162, 261–2, 265, 312, 327–8, 332
nomizein theous (acknowledge the gods) 52
Noon, Mike 179
Norman, A. F. 159–60
nothoi (bastards) 301, 322
Nukulaelae (Pacific island) 175
Nussbaum, Martha 90
nymphs 59, 309

oaths 199–201, 237, 235
Ober, Josiah 106, 185–6, 200
occult aggression, attacks, and insecurity 136, 137, 155–6, 162, 223, 250, 254
occupations
  changes in 286
  of women 306
O'Connell, Peter 24, 26, 30
Odysseus 111
Odyssey 112, 145
Oebatas of Dyme 105
Oedipus 46, 309
Oenanthe 217
'Office Pollyanna' (game) 143
Ogden, Daniel 12, 13, 43, 223, 225, 239, 301, 304, 321, 322, 334
oikos (household) 114–15, 184, 295, 315, 319, 323–5
olbios (fortunate, happy) 154
oligarchs, oligarchy (at Athens) 49, 265, 269, 292, *see also* Four Hundred, Thirty
  at Siphnos 290
olive trees, offences against 48, 205
Olympia and festival 108, 115, 138
Olympiodorus 201
Olson, Douglas 40
Omitowoju, Rosanna 304–5
Opis (Hyperborean virgin) 309

oratory 61, 74, 103, 130, 148, 192, 196, 284, 286, *see also* Aeschines, Demosthenes, Isaeus, rhetoric
orphanistai, orphanophylakes (orphan guardians) 299
orphans 282–3, 292, 294–5, 298–302
  adopted 301
Ortony, Andrew 84, 87, 89
Osborne, Robin v, 4, 28, 59, 61, 207, 269, 278–9, 283, 334
Osteen, Michael 141
Ostling, Michael 9
ostracism 104, 123
Ostwald, Martin 61
O'Sullivan, Lara-Louisa 49, 334
Otanes 77, 103
Ouwekerk, Jaap 231, 251

Paine, Robert 174–5, 186
Palladium 35, 42
pallake, plural *pallakai* (concubine) 304, 316, 321–2
Pan 53
panic, moral 10
Panionius 153
Papadopoulos, John 241
paraleipsis 201
parents, mistreatment of 50–1
Parker, Robert 18, 20, 22, 23, 29, 36, 37, 39, 41, 45, 47, 49, 51, 52, 53, 54, 55, 57, 59, 61, 62, 64, 65, 329
Parkinson, Brian 6, 87, 95
Paros 290
parricide 40–1
Parrot, W. Gerrod 76
Parry, Jonathan 142
Parsons, Talcott 96
Parthenion (*thiasotes*) 29
Pasion 293
Patterson, Cynthia 322
Pausanias (Spartan regent) 152
Pausanias (travel writer) 154, 308
pay *see* Assembly, *misthos*
  for magistrates at Athens 275
Pearl, Orsamus 156, 158
pederasty 161, 283
Pelled, Lisa 177
Pelling, Christopher 152
Pelopidas 319
Peloponnesian War, First (*c.* 461–446 BCE) 269

General Index

Peloponnesian War, Second or Main (431–404 BCE), effects of at Athens 266–311
Pelops 111, 120
pentakosiomedimnoi ('500-bushel men') 281
Pentheus 55
Periander (Corinthian tyrant) 146
Periander (fourth-century Athenian) 278
Pericles 27, 49, 57, 66, 148, 168, 210, 289, 295, 300, 322–3
   and Aspasia 66, 322–3
   citizenship law of law (451 BCE) 283, 301, 304
Perry, Ben 31
Persephone 15, *see also* Kore
Persia, Persians 42, 152, 276
   Greek wars and battles against 122, 152, 183, 269, 274, 298
   negotiations with as criminal offence 40
Pettegree, Andrew 259
Petzl, Georg 218–20
Pfeffer, Jeffrey 256
Phaleron 240
phallephoria 134
Phano, daughter of Neaera 304, 317–19
pharmakeia (knowledge of drugs/spells) 36, 37, 40, 169, 326, 328
pharmakis (woman with expertise in drugs or spells) 12, 162
pharmakon, plural *pharmaka* (drugs or spells) 12–14, 17–18, 31, 34–6, 39–40, 42–3, 65–7, 167–70, 219, 314–15, 317, 319, 323, *see also* poison
   incantations and 42, 167
   legality or illegality of 12–13
   Teos curses about 39, 43, 169
   trials for 35–6, 39
pharmattein (treat) 41
pheme (rumour) 182–4, 200
Pheretime 152–3
Phile 204, 315–16, 322
Philip II of Macedon 258
Phillips III, C. Robert 13
Philochorus 11, 16, 27, 33, 55, 281, 310, 334
Philocrates, Peace of (346 BCE) 283
Philoctemon and estate of (subject of Isaeus 6) 127, 313–14
Philoneus 34

philosophy 287
philotimia (love of honour) 282
philtra (love-potions) 18, 34, 45–6, 59, 162, 167–8, 333
Phocion 312
phonos see homicide
phthonos and 72
Phormio (co-prosecutor of Leptines) 133
Phormio (prosecutor of Apollodorus) 205–6
Phormisius 283
Phrastor 304, 318
phratries (kinship groupings) 18, 196, 200, 314, 318
Phrygia(ns) 214, 218, 282
   religion of 52, *see also* Cybele
Phryne 23–30, 47, 49, 56, 58–9, 62, 64, 66, 162, 261–2, 265, 312, 327–8, 332
phthonos (envy) 5, 71–9, 102–63, 278, *see also* envy, Schadenfreude
   Aristotle on 75, 77, 130, 144
   as emotion 77, 145, 253
   as pain at good fortune of others 75, 162
   dead people, not felt towards 102
   democracy and 128
   Demosthenes and 128–30, 133–6, 163
   divine 7, 149–55
   eating as metaphor for 119–20
   evil eye and 9
   gifts and 140–5, 148
   good and bad varieties of 127–8
   gossip and 161, 209–11, 253
   hatred and 209–10
   Herodotus on 77–8, 103, 146–7, 151–3
   Hippias of Elis on 127
   Homeric epics and 145
   iconography of 120–1, 158, 209
   Isaeus on 127
   law courts and 126–7
   magic-making/*pharmakeia* and 37, 66
   phonos and 72
   Pindar on 71, 103–24, 138, 150, 154, 163, 167
   Plato on 209–10
   Plutarch on 116, 158
   Sophocles on 71–3
   Suda on 72–4, 77, 167
   Thucydides on 147–8
   tyranny and 116

General Index

Phylacidas of Aegina 108
Phylarchus 158
Phyle 199, see also *kathodos*
physiognomy and emotions 80, 88
Pindar 124, 169
  on gossip 109, 120, 188
  on *pharmaka* 168
  on *phthonos* 103–24, 138, 150, 154, 167
Pippidi, Dionisie 213, 214
piracy 280
Piraeus 54, 274, 280, 296, 313
Pisander 126
Pisidia 214
plague 159
  Antonine 284
  at Athens 270, 292, 310
Plangon 20, 322
Plataea(ns) 289, 305
  battle of 122, 183 ('battle in Boiotia')
Plato, Platonic dialogues 13, 44, 49–50, 52, 54, 56, 58, 295, 299–300, 310–12, 333
  on itinerant *agurtai* and *manteis* 30, 46
  on *pharmakeia* and *pharmakon* 13, 36, 40, 43, 47, 60, 169
  on *phthonos* 209–10
'pledge', Germanic 140
plemmeleia (error, offence) 50
Plutarch 15–16, 24–5, 37, 56, 57, 66, 116, 154, 158, 181, 319
Pluto 29, 215
Pnyx (meeting place of Athenian Assembly) 27–8
podokakke (stocks) 238–9, 241
poietoi (adopted orphans) 301
poison (literal), poisoning 13, 16, 34–6, 40–1, 43, 167–8, 212, 215, 216, 219, 223, 224, 326, 328, see also *pharmakeia, pharmakon*
  as metaphor 163, 168, 170, 261, 315, 326
Poland, Franz 18
Polemaenetus 290
Polemon 322
pollution (religious) 11, 14, 41, 51
Pollux 334
Polybius 123, 154, 217
Polycrates 151, 153
Pomeroy, Sarah 288, 300, 302
population(s) 5, 286, 335
  Aeginetan 288
Athenian 180, 266, 269–70, 280–1, 285, 293
  Poros building 229
Posidippus (epigrammatist) 310
Posidippus (writer of comedies) 25, 28
Poseidon 111
Postman, Leo 172
post-traumatic stress disorder 328
Potidaia 281, 288
potions, love see *philtra*
potlatch 141
Pouilloux, Jean 334
praeteritio 201
praise 103–20, 124, 148, 150, 295, 323
  of self 124, 128
praise poetry 103, 112, 163
Prauscello, Lucia 252
prayer(s) 213, 233
  for justice 9, 63, 215, 232–3, 249
Praxagora 272
priestesses 15, 17–18, 55, 306, 309, see also Diotima
  Ninon as 18–19, 21–2, 55
  of Aphrodite 25
  of Artemis 16
  of Athena 15, 16, 183 (on Acropolis of Athens)
  of Demeter 16
  of Dionysus 310
  of Hera 16
  of Hestia 15
  of Persephone 15
priests 21, 30, 46, 51, 55, 217, 219–21, 245, 319, see also *agurtai*
  of Banaras 142
  of Cybele 55
Pritchard, David 274–6
Prodicus of Keos 28
proeisphora (money advanced to pay the property tax) 132
profit motive of prophets 46
Prometheus 238, 241–2
propelakismos (insulting treatment) 129
Propontis 274
prostitutes, prostitution 26, 64, 186, 307, 313, 317, 320
Protagoras 22, 28
Psaumis of Kamarina 114–15
psuchagogomenos (beguiled, perhaps supernaturally) 318

General Index

psychology 6, 95, 185, *see also* constructionist theories, evolutionary
public charges *see graphe*
punishment
   capital 219, 241, see also execution, stoning
   civic 235, 237-8, 240, 253, see also *apotumpanismos*
   corporal 237, 242
   divine 39, 117, 217, 220
purification 199, 308, see also *katharmoi*
Purkiss, Diane 9, 171
Purvis, Andrea 53, 54
Putnam, Robert 256
Pyrrhus, estate of (subject of Isaeus 3) 196, 204, 315-16, 322
Pythian festival 120

Quinn, Naomi 97
Quintilian 129

Ramsay, William 214
Rankin, David 59
rape 304
Ratzan, David 298
Raubitschek, Antony 23, 25, 26, 30
reciprocity 108, 110, 138, 140-52, 155, 167, *see also* gifts
   negative 142
Redfield, James 105
relevance, forensic, notions of 43, 192-3
religion(s)
   foreign 44
   magic and 13, 46-7
   new 44-6
religious offences *see asebeia*
resentment 143-5
return *see kathodos*
   of athletes 106-8
revenge 152-3, 193, 214, 231, 233
   worse when carried out by women 153
Reverdin, Olivier 44, 58
Rhacius 308
Rheneia(ns) 51, 213
rhetoric, rhetorical devices and texts 42, 64, 72, 94-5, 99, 102-3, 122, 125, 127, 129, 134, 138, 158, 169, 189, 192, 195, 204, 208, 236, 268, 289, *see also* oratory
Rhodes, Peter 270, 271, 274, 277, 287
Rhodes, Rhodians 115, 118, 123, 205, 300, 302

Richards, Robert 81, 82
Ricl, Marijana 219-20
Riess, Werner 7, 236-7
risk 5
   binding-spells and 224, 231, 247, 250
   gift-giving and 141-2, 150
   gossip and 177
   leases and 279
   management of 7
   phthonos and 128, 138, 151, 251
   social construction of 10
   women and 265-6, 315, 317, 323, 327
ritual 13, 23, 44, 246
   abuse 134
   magical 246
   new, foreign 45-6, 53
   space 247-9
   traditional 61
'ritualism' 331
Rivera, Joseph De 87
Robben, Antonius 329-30
Robert, Jeanne and Louis 213
Robert, Louis 214, 219-20
Roberts, John 175, 177
Roesch, Etienne 86
Roisman, Joseph 208, 284
Roman evidence and analogies 44, 141, 232, 292
Romilly, Jacqueline de 169
Roper, Lyndal 9, 155, 333
Rosaldo, Michelle 94, 98
Roseman, Ira 87
Rosenberg, Erika 84, 86
Rosenwein, Barbara 95
Rosivach, Vincent 110
Rosnow, Ralph 171-3, 176-7, 256, 261, 265
Rowlands, Alison 9
Roy, Donald 178
Rubel, Alexander 269
Rubinstein, Lene 50, 301, 321
Rudhardt, Jean 22, 60
Ruschenbusch, Eberhard 270
Russell, James 86, 88, 89
Rutherford, Ian 109

Sabazius 29, 45, 54, 59
Sabini, John 102
Sabinus 160
sacred, definition of 54, 246
'sacred disease' *see* epilepsy
sacrifice 32-3, 158, 167, 310, 319, 334
Sahlins, Marshall 141

Salamis, battle of 146
Salancik, Gerald 256
Sallares, Robert 292, 296
Saller, Richard 292, 299
Salomon, Nicoletta 12
salvific capital 62
Salvo, Irene 9, 213, 214, 218, 221, 222
Samos 146, 281, 286
Sanders, Ed 6, 9, 76, 94, 125, 127, 129, 130, 144, 186, 250, 252
Sandwell, Bella 161
Sarbin, Theodore 94
Sarpedon 145
satyrs 29
Saunders, Trevor 60, 61
scandal 172-3, 195
Scarborough, John 12, 13, 168
Schachter, Stanley 84
Schadenfreude 86, 225, 231, 250-3
Schaps, David 286, 293-4, 303, 306, 316
Scheer, Monique 94
Scheidel, Walter 270, 284, 292, 299, 306
schemas 6-7, 96-7, 99-101
Scherer, Klaus 87
Scherke, Katharina 95
Scholz, Peter 329
Schramm, Katharina 330, 332
Schwartz, Barry 143
scythe (used metonyically for death) 244-5
Scythia(ns) 203, 239
Scythopolis (Palestine) 161
Sealey, Raphael 321-2
Second Athenian League 275
Second Sophistic 72
secrecy, secrets 56, 180, 255, *see also* mysteries
Secundus 230
seers 16, 238, 290, 308, 310, see also *mantis*
Seibert, Jakob 286
Semenov, Anatol 25
Semonides of Amorgos 186-7
Seriphos 146
Sestos 281
Seven Deadly Sins 91
Shay, Jonathan 329
Shipton, Kirsty 279
Shrimpton, Gordon 102
Sicily 121, 124, 148, 232, 286, 307, *see also* Akragas, Hiero, Hykkara, Kamarina, Syracuse, Thero

disaster (Athenian) in 181, 269, 303, 305
sickness (as evidence of legal incapacity) 317, 323
Siegel, James 149, 329-33
Sigeum 277
Silk, Michael 72, 124
Sillar, Bill 79
silver 276, *see also* Laurion
Silver, Maury 102
Simmel, Georg 254-5
Singer, Jerome 84
Sinope (city on Black Sea) 308
Sinope (woman in Demosthenes 59) 319-20
sins *see* Seven Deadly Sins
Siphnos 290
Sirens 168
skeleton 244 (used metonymically for death) 244
Skyros 281
slander 112, 130, 137, 195, 198, see also *diabole*
  gossip and 180, 186-7, 191-2, 205
  phthonos and 11, 210
  Plutarch on 127
Slater, Niall 301
slaves 41, 59, 63, 188, 228, 270, 293, 296
  curse tablets and 226-7
  gossip and 187
  initiation and 59
  murder of 41
  numbers of (at Athens) 270-1
  punishment of 239
  sources of anxiety 312
  teaching of (as criminal charge) 15-16, 38, 52, 59, 63
Smith, R. R. R. (Bert) 117
Smith, Richard 76
Smolders, Ruben 157
Smyrna 120, 219
Sobel, Joel 256
social construction *see* constructionist
  network analysis 256
'sociality' 96
Social War (Athenian, 350s BCE) 132, 274, 276, 281, 355
Socrates (Athenian philosopher) 13, 28, 33, 46, 58, 76, 136, 167-9, 209-10, 226, 251-3, 272, 294, 295, 296, 303, 307, 310, 329

General Index

trial and execution of 21–2, 28, 46–50, 51–2, 57–60, 62, 65–6, 167, 209, 253, 262, 265
Socrates (son of Tatias) 220
Soeter, J. 175
Solomon, Robert 90, 92
Solon 28, 152, 154, 300, 315
Sommerstein, Alan 272, 303, 309
sophists, sophistry 28, 65, 158, 169, 262
Sophronius 233
Sopolis 290
sorcerer *see goes*
Sørensen, Jesper 246
Sørensen, Tim 78–9
Sostrata 304
Sotas 156
Soweto, South Africa 136, 155
space (generic, courtroom, ritual) 247–8
spells 12–14, 19, 23, 38, 42, 163, 224–5, *see also* binding spells, *pharmaka*
  as metaphor for oratory 168
Sparta(ns) 146–7, 181, 238, 269, 273–4, 276, 286
Spiro, Melford 98
Stamatopoulou, Maria 123
stasis, plural *staseis* (civil strife) 72, 123–4, 147, 286
Stearns, Carol and Peter 78, 93
Steiner, Deborah 119–20
stele, plural *stelai* (stone monument) 218, 310, 323–5
Stenner, Paul 89
Stephanus (of the deme Acharnae, prosecuted by Apollodorus for false witness) 198
Stephanus (of the deme Eroeadae, allegedly married to Neaera) 198, 317–18
Stewart, Charles v, 9, 14, 95, 134, 231, 261, 333
Stewart, Kathleen 95
Stewart, Pamela 8, 172, 261
Stilpo the Megarian 49
Stirling, Rebecca 261
Stocker, Michael 90
Stoddart, Robert 109
Stoics 90
stoning 110
Strabo 52
strategies, poetic 113
Strathern, Andrew 8, 72, 261
stratiotikon (army fund) 277

Stratton, Kimberly 333
Strauss, Barry 271
Strauss, Claudia 94, 97, 100
Strepsiades (in Aristophanes) 182
Strepsiades of Thebes (in Pindar) 110, 122
Stroud, Ronald 276, 300–1
Suárez-Orozco, Marcelo 329–30
Suda 72–4, 77, 167
Sugg, Richard 171
Suharto, President of Indonesia 331–2
Sukarno, President of Indonesia 331
Suls, Jerry 173
sycophancy (malicious prosecution), sycophants 14, 19–20, 26, 49, 130, 207
Sykes, Karen 141
Syloson 146
symmories (groups of taxpayers) 277
syntaxeis (contributions) 275
synthetic images 9
syntrierarchies 277–8
Syracuse, Syracusans 148, 188, *see also* Hagesias, Hiero
Syria 158, 214
  Syrian gods 218
Sztompka, Piotr 328–30
Szwed, John 211

talk 111–24, 256, *see also* gossip
  emotion talk 97–102
Talmy, Leonard 244
Tambiah, Stanley 235
Tannen, Deborah 173
Tantalus 111, 117
Tarlow, Sarah 5, 79, 98, 335
tasting 112
Tatias 219–21
Taussig, Michael 95, 100, 155
tautology, causal 244–5
Taylor, Alfred 59
Taylor, Claire 285, 296, 299
Taylor, Gabriele 175
Taylor, James 162
tax, taxation 14, 157, 205, 277, 308, *see also eisphora*
taxiarchs 20, 202
Tchernetska, Natalie 302
Tegea 286
telete (initiation ritual) plural *teletai* 29–30
Tellus 152
Ten Thousand, the 305

Teos, curses from 39, 43, 169
Teuta 217
Thailand, gifts in 143
Thais (*hetaira*) 322
Thalassius 160
Thalheim, Theodor 60
Thasos 214, 300, 302, 334
Theagenes (man cursed on Delos) 218, 221
Thebes, Thebans 114, 121–4, 274, 286, 308, 319, *see also* Herodotus, Pelopidas, Strepsiades, Thrasydaeus
medism of 123
Themistocles 133–4, 138, 146–7, 152, 168
Theodote 168, 294
Theogenes 304, 318
Theopompus (historian) 15, 102
Theodorus the atheist 49
Theophilus 233
theoric fund 277
Theoris of Lemnos 11–17, 39–40, 47, 55, 57–9, 61–4, 66, 162, 261–2, 265, 327–8, 332
Theosebes of Xypete 48
Theozotides and decree of 283, 301
Theramenes 125–6
Thero 106, 108, 121, 124
Thesmophoria (female festival) 217, 314–15
Thespiai 24
Thessaly, Thessalians 123, 150, 271, 307
thiasos, plural *thiasoi* (subgroups of phratries; cultic subgroups) 17–18, 27–9, 45, 59
at Eleusis (slaves) 59
of Bendis 59
thiasotai (members of *thiasoi*) 28
thieves targeted in binding spells 232
'Thirty', the (oligarchs at Athens) 59, 126, 262, 282, 288, 299, 301, 303
Thomas, Rosalind 117
Thonemann, Peter 288
Thorikos (Attic deme) 20
Thrasybulus (Athenian general and politician) 275, 282
Thrasybulus of Acragas 124
Thrasydaeus 109, 123
Thrasylochus 290
Thrasyllus (litigant in Isaeus 7) 196
Thrasyllus (seer in Isocrates 19) 290

Thucydides 106, 147–8, 153, 269–70, 288, 300
on *phthonos* 147–8
thusiai (sacrifices) 334, *see also* sacrifice
Timarchus 199, 204, 258–8, 262
Timasarchus of Aegina 114
Timocles 334
Timocrates 203–4
Timodemus of Aphidna 146–7
Timotheus 204, 276, 278, 287
Tiresias 46, 308–9
Todd, Stephen v, 16, 49, 50, 59, 65, 77, 168, 238, 240, 242
Tomkins, Sylvan 84
tongue
binding of 239–40
cutting out of 257, 259
Tonkin, Elizabeth 8
Too, Yun Lee 268
Toobey, John 88
Toohey, Peter 76
torture 34, 233, 235, 237–8
in Congo 99–100
tragedy 74, 154, 184, 188
Trampedach, Kai 14, 21, 22, 27, 63
trauma, social 9, 269, 328–35
Travlos, John 27
trials *passim*
of Aretaphila 37
of fictional women 31–7
of intellectuals at Athens 22
of Ninon 17–23
of Phryne 23–30
of Socrates *see* Socrates, trial and execution of
of Theoris 11–17
'Triballi' (young disorderly Athenians) 199
tribute 275
trierarchs, trierarchy (as liturgy) 132, 276–8
Trobrianders 140, 143
Troezen 290
truth 194, 196–206
Tsagalis, Christos 306, 323–5
tuche, personified as *Tuche* (chance, luck) 149, 154
tumpanon (cudgel?) 238
Tuplin, Christopher 282, 287
Turner, Mark 244–5, 247, 256
Turner, Victor 256
Typhon 230

tyranny and tyrants 37, 66, 106, 108, 117, 121, 123, 188
  fear of 115
  legislation about 40
  phthonos and 116
  tyrannicides 132

uncertainty
  in accusations 9, 214, 222
  of divine gifts 150, 155
  of experience of loss resulting from trauma 331
underworld gods 41, *see also* Hades
unmarried girls 302–8

Van Bremen, Riet 4
Van de Ven, Jeroen 142
Van de Ven, Niels 251
Van der Horst, Pieter 213
Van Dijk, Wilco 231, 251
Van Iterson, Ad 175
Van Wees, Hans 140, 271
Versnel, Henk 9, 20, 22, 23, 25, 28, 29, 33, 44–6, 51, 51–3, 55, 57–8, 63, 213, 215, 218–21, 225–6, 228–9, 231–3, 235, 250, 329
Vincent, St. (Caribbean island) 178
Von Reden, Sitta 145
Voutsaki, Sofia 78–9
Voutiras, Emmanuel 213

Waithe, Mary 311
Walcot, Peter 74–6, 127, 145
Wallace, Robert 35, 283
war *see* Corinthian War, Peloponnesian War, Persia, Social War
Ward, Morgan 143
war-dead, provision for families of 300–2
water, as metaphor in Pindar 113, 122
Waterfield, Robin 59
Watson, Patricia 298
weddings 334
'Weeping Woman' folktale 99
Weinstein, Fred 78, 93, 330
Welsh villages, gossip in 173
Wenzel, Siegfried 92
wet nurses 306, 320–1
White, Geoffrey 93
White, Luise 8, 195
Whitehead, David 106, 154, 282, 283, 287

Widlok, Thomas 179
widows 292–300, 303
wife, wives 64, 99, 171, 203, 214–15, 292–3, 294, 297, 314–17, 321–3, 325
Willi, Andreas 239
Williams, Raymond 95
Wilson, Adrian 171
Wilson, Nigel 72
Wilson-Mendenhall, Christine 88, 89
witchcraft 8–9, 13, 93, 149, 156, 171, 256, 261, 331–3
  gossip and 8
witches 9, 93, 136, 155–6, 332–3
witch-hunts 10, 331
Wolf, Margery 177
wolf, poet as 113
women *passim*, *see also* Aspasia, democracy, *hetaira*, Neaera, Ninon, Phryne, priestesses, Tatias, Theoris, widows
  armies and 288, 305
  'dangerous' 312–21, 323, 333
  festivals and 31, 314
  history of 3–4
  iconography of 323–4
  lack political role at Classical Athens 3, 265
  legal limitations on ownership of property by 293–4
  naming of, in court 316
  occupations of 306
Wood, James L. 250
Woodbury, Leonard 303
wool-working 324
Worthington, Ian 257, 259
wrestling 120, 229–30
Wycherley, Richard 54
Wypustek, Andrzej 74, 156–8
Wyse, William 314–15, 317

Xenocles of Kopros 315
Xenocrates of Acragas 124
xenoi (foreigners, temporary non-Athenian visitors) 282
Xenophon (Athenian author) 13, 58, 76, 123, 167, 169, 209, 228, 271, 272, 274, 282–3, 288, 296, 305
Xenophon of Corinth (athlete) 123, 150
Xerxes 103, 146–7, 151–2
xulon ('wood'; instrument of punishment) 238

Younger, John 323–4
Youtie, Herbert 156–8
Yunis, Harvey 52

Zaphiropoulos, Christos 32
Zelazo, Philip 89
Zelnick-Abramowitz, Rachel 12

zelos (jealousy) 75, 104 (*zalotos*)
Zenas 156
Zeus 106, 107, 115, 127, 150, 153
Zingerle, Josef 219
Ziolkowski, Jan 92
Zobia 14, 187, 308

Index Locorum

Aelian
Varia Historia
 2.7 300
 5.19 52
Fragments
 335 (Domingo-Forasté = 338 Hercher) 72

Aeschines
1. *Against Timarchus*
 44–5 200
 53 200, 281
 55–6 200
 69 200
 94–105 279
 99 199
 107–15 204
 116 200
 127 182
 128 182
 130 200
 158 200
 170 295
 171 258
 172 257, 259
 173 59
2. *The Speech on the Embassy*
 71 276
 145 182
 148 257
3. *Against Ctesiphon*
 117 154
 154 300, 301
 172 203
 174 209
 187 282
 195 282
 258 302

Aeschines the Socratic
 fr. 15 27

Aeschylus
Agamemnon
 468–70 74
 483–7 187
 832–7 103
 927 184
 938 182
 947 74
 1269–74 309
Choephoroe
 505 184
Eumenides
 306 241
 959–60 303
Persae
 744–5 238
Fragments
 220a–c (Sommerstein 2008 = fr. 168 Radt) 309
 220a 16–17 309

[Aeschylus]
Prometheus Vinctus 241

Aesop
Fables
 56 (Perry) 31
 91 (Chambry) 32

Alciphron
 4.3.1 26
 4.4.4 26
 4.4.5 26
 4.5.3 26

Alexander of Aphrodisias
In Topica 141.31–142.2 74

Alexis (K-A)
 fr. 25 28
 fr. 52 252

Amphis (K-A)
 fr. 22.12 308

Andocides
1. *On the Mysteries*
 10 52
 29–32 52
 45 238
 54 181
 58 52
 71 52

Andocides (*cont.*)
  124–9 200
  130 184
  139 198
  149 271

2. On His Return
  6 128

3. On the Peace with Sparta
  15 274
  35 181
  36 273

4. Against Alcibiades
  10 205

Anonymus Seguerianus
  215 (= Euthias fr. 2 Baiter–
    Sauppe) 27

Anthologia Palatina (Cougny)
Anthologiae Graecae, App. VII
  (*Problemata, aenigmata*)
  47, 42.6–7 (Basilii Megalomytis) 72

Antiphanes (K-A)
  fr. 120 28
  fr. 166.2 181
  fr. 210 307, 308, 323
  fr. 247 186

Antiphon
*1. Against the Stepmother for
    Poisoning* 34, 37, 44
  3 208
  5 208
  9 208
  21 208
  23 35
  25–7 208
  26 35
  27 35

*2. Anonymous Prosecution for Murder
(First Tetralogy)*
  1.6 48

5. On the Murder of Herodes
  9 242
  79 192

6. On the Choreutes 34, 44
  1 35
  7 192

Apollonius Rhodius
Argonautica
  4.1669 ff. 158

Aristophanes
Acharnenses
  731–5 302
Aves
  987–8 44
  1071 52
  1441 186
  1534 54
  1649–68 304
Ecclesiazousae
  120 187
  184–8 271
  210–13 294
  230 181
  293 271
  308 271
  380–90 271
  415–21 272
  591–3 271
  676–90 272
Equites
  103 138
  367 237, 238, 240
  580 76
  705 238, 240
  1048 237, 238
  1085 44
  1320 182
  1375–6 186
Lysistrata
  1–5 28
  3 54
  492–7 294
  591–7 303
  680 238
  1192 144
Nubes
  447 182
  592 238
  1003 186
Pax
  119–23 302
  353–7 27
  1052–119 44
  1061–86 44
Plutus
  87–92 153
  218 ff. 273
  338 186
  476 238

Index Locorum

503 ff. 273
535–47 273
606 238
627 ff. 273
750 ff. 273

Ranae
156
376 181
619 237
1344 310

Thesmophoriazousae
41
146 252
249 144
252 144
332–67 40
393 187
418–23 294
443–58 306
534 40
930–46 240
942 237
1001–2 240
1012 240
1019 237
1022 237
1031 237

Vespae
9 60
380 44
1489 130

Aristotle
De virtutibus et vitiis
1251a30 50

Ethica Nicomachea
1108a35 75
1111a10 52

Politica
1268a8–11 300
1277b 188
1293a1–10 275
1306b 237, 238
1313b11–15 188
1323a 300

Rhetorica
1372b 210
1382b 240
1385a 240
1387a1–3 252
1387b 75, 144
1387b28–31 144
1388a30–3 75

[Aristotle]
Athenaion Politeia
24.3 300
40.2 282
41.3 271
42.3 287
45.1 238, 240, 242
52.1 242
55.2–4 208
56.6–7 299, 302
57.2–3 49
57.3 35
62.2 271
67.1 192

De Mundo
400a16 213

Magna Moralia
1188b35–38 (= 1.16.2) 36

Oeconomica
1350a3 276

Rhetorica ad Alexandrum
1440a35–1440b4 128
1445a13–29 128

Athenaeus
Deipnosophistae
4.167 323
6.245a 334
6.265c–266e 64
8.344 182
13.555d–556b 303
13.577c 322
13.588c 307
13.588e 307
13.589a 307
13.589a–b 308
13.590d 26
13.590d–e 24
13.591e 26
13.591e–f 25
13.591f 25
13.592–3 257
14.661e 287

Basil of Caesarea
On Envy 161

Callimachus
Aetia
1.1.16 182

Epigrammata
2.3 182

Fragments
84–5 (Pfeiffer) 105

Cicero
Brutus
217 231

Epistulae ad Atticum
12.45.1 93

Pro Balbo
16 102

Cratinus (K-A)
Drapetides 311
183 300

Demosthenes
2. Second Olynthiac
22 198
28–9 277

4. First Philippic
22–3 276
28 276
36 278
37–8 274
48 181

6. Second Philippic
19 181

8. On Affairs in the Chersonese
19 134
22 134
61 240

9. Third Philippic
54 125, 135, 154, 252
61 240

10. Fourth Philippic
43–5 279
63 240

15. On the Freedom of the Rhodians
3 274
15 125, 274

16. For the Megalopolitans
19 134

18. On the Crown
3 134
3–4 130
12 129
30 40
102–8 278
108 134
119 134
121–2 130
127 182
129 197, 238
132 134
139 134
189 134
234 275
242 134
252 154
258 21
259 29
259–60 17, 54
276 134
279 130
307 134
317 134
321 134
315 102, 131

19. On the False Embassy
70 40
109 134
137 240
194 298
199 29
199–200 200
226 200
281 18
313 102
293 48

20. Against Leptines
24 134
56–7 133
74 128, 133, 138
115 302

21. Against Meidias
1 51
12 51
20 51
34 51
51 51
55 51
102–22 258
103–4 257
104 186
104–5 240, 258
105 240
116–19 258
139 203
148 189
149 200

149-50 198
156 279
160-7 279
195 198
196 127
198 181
209 134

22. Against Androtion
2 51
2-3 40
21 134
22 134
23 134
61 307

23. Against Aristocrates
66 35
97 40
188-9 208
213 204

24. Against Timocrates
11-14 276
15 186
94 208
105 238
127 204
202 203

25. Against Aristogiton 1 302
28 14
32 14
41 14
52 186
54 14
55 308
56 294
57 187, 308
58 14
62 14
65 308
67-71 189
79-80 11
80 13, 136
82 186

27. Against Aphobus 1 297
4-5 299
5 297
13-15 295
53-5 294

28. Against Aphobus 2
15-16 297
18 127
21 303

29. Against Aphobus for Phanus
3 284
26 295
32 169
43 297

30. Against Onetor 1
33 297

32. Against Zenothemis 208

34. Against Phormio
37 281

35. Against Lacritus
25 181
48 49
51 281

37. Against Pantaenetus
45 299
52 127, 189

38. Against Nausimachus and Xenopeithes
19-20 297

39. Against Boeotus 1
2 19
15-17 192
16 197
17 20
26 202, 322
34 125

40. Against Boeotus 2
3 20
6-7 297
8 322
9 19
18 20
20-2 297
22 189
27 322
56-7 297

41. Against Spoudias
8-11 294
11 294
17 294
21 294
25-6 296
27 294

42. Against Phaenippus
24 201

43. Against Macartatus
1-10 208

Demosthenes (*cont.*)
  51 304
  54 297, 302
  57 41
  75 294, 299
48. Against Olympiodorus
  12 279
  33 279
  35 279
  55 192, 201
51. On the Trierarchic Crown 132
  5 276
54. Against Conon
  33 207
  34 197, 200
  39 199, 200
  44 202
56. Against Dionysodorus 208
57. Against Eubulides 208, 283, 320
  3 304
  8 321
  17 134
  18–19 178, 306
  25 304
  30 192
  30–45 321
  35 306
  36 192
  42 306, 321
  45 305
  52 192
  59–60 197
  61 197

[Demosthenes] (following MacDowell 2009)
7. On Halonnesus 208
36. For Phormio
  14–16 294
  36–9 206
  44–5 206
44. Against Leochares 283
45. Against Stephanus 1 297
  27 204
  28 293
  63–5 197
  66 198, 279
46. Against Stephanus 2
  14 317, 323
  20 296

47. Against Euergus and Mnesibulus
  20 132
  23 276
  44 132
  68–73 41
49. Against Timotheus
  9–15 279
  12 277
  16 277
  22–7 279
  66 204
  66–7 204
50. Against Polycles
  6 280
  7 132
  12 280
  19 280
  48 188
53. Against Nicostratus
  1–3 207
  15 207
  29 298
58. Against Theocrines
  28 197
  49 207
  52 207
59. Against Neaera 299
  1 207
  7–8 297
  8 302
  14–15 207
  16 304, 307
  18 293
  21 320
  30 200
  35 294
  38 318
  46 294
  50 304
  50–1 318
  50–62 318
  55 318
  72 304, 318
  73–87 318
  74–7 319
  104 286
  111–14 307
  112 208, 302
  113 297
  116 38

116-17 317
119 320

Digest
  47.22.4 (= Solon fr. 76a Ruschenbusch) 28

Dinarchus
1. Against Demosthenes
  30 197, 198
  15 198
  32 181
  54 192
  66 169
  92 169
2. Against Aristogiton
  8 197, 200
  11 197
  16 40

Diodorus Siculus
  4.4.3 318
  13.6.7 52
  13.65.4 286
  13.114.1 286
  14.94 275
  14.99.4-5 275
  15.59.2 286
  16.21-2 276
  16.42.8 280
  16.88.1 58
  18.8.1-5 286
  18.18.4-5 270

Diogenes Laertius
  1.55 301
  2.26 303
  2.40 33, 52
  2.75 308
  2.85 287
  9.54 28
  5.80 31
  5.12-13 300
  5.22 287
  5.50 287
  5.76 73
  5.76-7 120
  5.81 287
  6.38 286
  6.49 286

Dionysius Halicarnassensis
De Dinarcho
  11 21
De imitatione
  5.6 24

DT
  1 (*IK* I 147) 216, 219
  4 (*IK* I 150) 216
  8 (*IK* I 154) 217, 224
  43 237
  49 234, 235, 240
  50 240
  51 240
  52 240
  68 234
  69 249
  85 233
  87 240
  92 232
  93a 232
  129 232

DTA
  45 237
  65 234, 240
  66 240
  68 240
  74-5 240
  79 240
  84 240
  86 240
  87 240
  88 240
  89 240
  94 240
  95 240
  97 240
  75 232
  77 239
  99 237
  100 237
  102 237
  103 237
  105 234

Euripides
Alcestis
  315-16 184, 188
Andromeda 241
Bacchae
  421-3 29
  680 18
Cyclops
  234 237
Hecuba
  416-18 303
  612 303

Euripides (cont.)
Hercules Furens 241
Hippolytus
　384 182, 187
　1056 182
Iphigenia Aulidensis
　461 303
　1059 18
Iphigenia Taurica
　369–71 303
Medea
　214–15 188
　219–21 189
　985 303
Orestes
　1109 303
Phoenissae
　796 18
Supplices 76
　241 77
Fragments (Collard and Cropp, also Kannicht, *TrGF*)
　88a (*Alcmene*) 231
　122 (*Andromeda*) 237
　128 (*Andromeda*) 237

Evagrius Ponticus
Praktikos 12 (Bamberger) 92

Gennadius of Constantinople
Commentary on Romans (Theodoridis) 74

Harpocration
Epopteukoton 30
Euthias 26
Isodaites 29
Hoti Chilias 334
Lykeion 27
Sitos 300
Theoris 16
Thiasos 18

Heliodorus
Aethiopica
　3.7–9 158

Hermippos (*FGrH* 1026)
　F 46 24
　F 67 26

Herodas
　5.10 237

　5.18 237

Herodotus
　1.31 182
　1.32.1 151
　1.32.8–9 151
　1.43.2–3 183
　1.164–8 287
　2.32.1 182
　2.135.5 182
　3.30.1 146
　3.40 151
　3.40.2 153
　3.52.5 146
　3.80.3 103
　3.80.3–5 77
　3.143.2 237
　3.146.1 146
　3.153.1–2 183
　4.104 77
　4.104.1 147
　4.205 152
　5.66 54
　5.72.2 183
　5.72.4 183, 237
　6.61.1 146
　6.75.2 237, 238
　7.16–18 152
　7.33.1 240
　7.46.1 152
　7.139.1 146, 152
　7.236.1 103
　7.237.2 147
　7.237.3 147
　8.41.1 299
　8.69.1 146
　8.105.6 153
　8.109.3 152
　8.124.1 146
　8.125.1 146
　9.37.2 238
　9.71.3 182
　9.71.4–72 146
　9.79.2 152
　9.100 182
　9.100.2 183
　9.120.4 240

Hesiod
Opera et Dies
　25–6 103
　493 182
　760 182

763 182

Theogonia
522 242
652 237
718 237

Fragments (Merkelbach and West)
25.18–25 34

Hesychius (Latte, Hansen, and Cunningham)
Agurtes (alpha 461) 310
Isodaites (iota 952) 29
Lykaion kai Thumbraion (lambda 1368) 27
platanos (pi 2475) 334
thiasos (theta 573)

Hippias of Elis (D-K 86)
B16 127

Hippocratic Treatises
De arte 287
De prisca medicina 287
De decente habitu 287
Epidemiae
5.63 310
7.28 310
De glandulis 92
De morbo sacro
1.9 56
2.3–4 13
4 40

Homer
Iliad
5.385–91 237
9.318–20 107
12.310–21 145
18.110 113
21.60–3 112
22.446 ff. 309

Odyssey
17.411–13 112
18.329 182
19.284 309
20.100 182
20.178 ff. 112
21.98 112
22.8–14 112
22.189–90 237

Horace
Carmina
3.24.31 102

Hyperides (Burtt)
1. In Defence of Lykophron
1 fr. IVb.3 295
1 fr. IVb.7 295
1 fr. IVb.9 191
1 fr. IVb.10–11 192
1 fr. IVb.12–13 303
1 fr. IVb.14 192

4. In Defence of Euxenippus
4.5 51
4.10 192
4.21 186
4.22 198

6. Funeral Speech
6.27 295
fr. 68a I
fr. 70

Against Timandrus
Tchernetska et al. 2007 302

Fragments (Jensen)
14 334
172 26
174 30
175 30
176 26
177 29
179 26
198 30

IDélos
98 [B, frg. a1] ll. 26–7 51
2532 I A–B 213
2532 II 213
2533 214

Inscriptiones Graecae
I^2 115 41
I^3 104 41
I^3 105 28
II^2 10 283
II^2 43 275
II^2 337 = *LSCG* 34 53
II^2 1177 54, 63
II^2 1283 53
II^2 1611 276
II^2 1613.284–310 276
II^2 1629.180–271 278
II^2 1635 51
II^2 2343–61 18
II^2 2346 28
II^2 2347 28
II^2 2934 59

Fragments (Jensen) (*cont.*)
II² 4650 59
XI 2532 I A 213
XII 8.450 214

Isaeus

1. On the Estate of Cleonymus
39 302

2. On the Estate of Menecles
9 294
19 317
43 189

3. On the Estate of Pyrrhus 283
11 316
17–18 307
10–14 204
13 204, 316
13–14 185
17 316
37 196, 198, 283
39 321
40 200

4. On the Estate of Nicostratus
7 284
10 317
21 272, 289
27 284

5. On the Estate of Dicaeogenes
9–11 298
39 197
43 279

6. On the Estate of Philoctemon 313
10–16 284
12 283
19 200, 314
21 314
29 314
38–40 314
47 304
48 314
48–50 314
49–50 315
50 315
51 295
52 283
61 127

7. On the Estate of Apollodorus 289, 297
31–3 279
39–41 279

8. On the Estate of Ciron
7–8 297
8–9 296
36–7 189
38 199
40–3 203
44 189

9. On the Estate of Astyphilus 289
16–18 201
27–9 295
37 317

10. Against Xenaenetus on the Estate of Aristarchus
10 293

11. On the Estate of Hagnias
6 299
39 297
44–50 279

12. On Behalf of Euphiletus 283
2 304

Isocrates

1. To Demonicus 287
26 76

4. Panegyricus
47 125
68 300
157 40
167–8 289

5. Philippus
11 135
134 182

6. Archidamus 268
73–4 298
82 300

7. Areopagiticus
54 267

8. On the Peace 132, 268
21 282
24 289
48 287
51 127
50 269
79 287
88 269

9. Evagoras
21 182, 183
39 128

12. Panathenaicus
18–20 28

Index Locorum

33 28
94 286
155 135

14. Plataicus
20 125
48 284
51-2 286

15. Antidosis
8 134
62 135
90 242
109 276
259 125

16. De Bigis
6 56
46 285

17. Trapeziticus
33-4 197

18. Special Plea against Callimachus
9 186

19. Aegineticus
9 290
11 290
19 290
20-2 290
24 290
25 290
40 290

20. Against Lochites
10-13 208

John Chrysostom (Migne *PG*)
In 1 Cor. Hom.
31.4 (*PG* 61.264) 72

In 2 Cor. Hom.
27.3 (*PG* 61.587) 121

Josephus
Contra Apionem
2.267 22

Libanius
Orationes
1.43 160
1.44 160
1.45-7 161
1.49 160
1.62 160
1.64-6 160
1.91 158
1.98 160
1.194 160
1.241-2 159
1.243-4 159
1.245 159
1.247 159
1.248 159
1.249 159
2.14 158
30.15 161
36 160
38.6 161
42.12 161
58.30-1 161

Epistulae
37 161

LIMC
8.1 120, 121, 158

[Longinus]
Περὶ ὕψους or *De sublimitate*
34.2-4 24

LSAM
32 334
48 310

LSCG
34 53
127 334

Lucan
Calumniae non temere credendum
5 121, 209

Lycurgus
1.11 192
1.11-13 192
1.19 205
1.27 281
1.123 194
1.149 192
fr. 14.1 [Berlin Papyrus 11748] 58

Lysias
1. On the Murder of Eratosthenes
15-16 188
48-50 208

2. Funeral Oration
34 298
48 125
66 282
67 125
75 295

3. Against Simon
3-4 194, 205

Lysias (cont.)
  6 296
  6–7 297
  9 252
  29 296, 297
  30 194, 205
  44–6 192, 202
5. *For Callias*
  3–5 61
6. *Against Andocides*
  11–12 51
  17 52
  21 237
  32 197
  54 56
7. *On the Olive Stump*
  14–18 205
  16 61
  20 207
  28 205
  39 205
9. *For the Soldier*
  1 192
  3 192
  18–19 192
10. *Against Theomnestus 1*
  10 242
  16 238
12. *Against Eratosthenes* 208, 283
  19 294
  21 303
  66 126
  97 288, 298
13. *Against Agoratus* 208
  1 207
  45 303
  45–6 299
  56 240
  65–9 193
  67 203, 240, 242
  68 240, 242
  77 199
14. *Against Alcibiades 1*
  7–8 285
  25 198
  28 203
  31 285
15. *Against Alcibiades 2*
  12 201

16. *For Mantitheus*
  4 298
18. *On the Confiscation of the Property of the Brother of Nicias*
  23 208
19. *On the Property of Aristophanes*
  5–6 192
  9 297
  11 297
  32–5 297
20. *For Polystratus*
  11 300
  13 271
  23 279
  32 208
21. *Defence against a Charge of Taking Bribes*
  1–5 106
  15 128
  20 198
22. *Against the Corn Dealers*
  5–6 281
  8 281
  12 281
23. *Against Pancleon* 286
  3 186
24. *On the Refusal of a Pension* 125
  2 207
  3 125
  20 186
25. *Defence against a Charge of Subverting the Democracy*
  12–13 106
26. *On the Scrutiny of Evandros* 208
27. *Against Epicrates and his Fellow Envoys*
  1 279
28. *Against Ergocles* 275
  1–4 276
  6 276
  10 276
29. *Against Philocrates*
  2 276
  5 276
  8–11 276
  14 276
30. *Against Nicomachus* 59, 208
  2 204

7-9 193
15 193
15-16 193
22 279

31. Against Philon 283
9 284
20 203
27-9 199

32. Against Diogiton
24-5 299

34. Against the Subversion of the Ancestral Constitution of Athens 283

Fragments (Carey)
1.34-47 282
128-50 282
299 307

Maximus of Tyre
19.3 55

Menander
Aspis 303
Dyskolos
260-3 48

Kitharistes
64-5 186

Samia
301-3 294
510 186
553-4 305

Sikyonioi
281-2 298

Fragments (K-A)
208 334
298 305
761 72, 121

Milet.
I.3 33-93 288
I.3 62 288

ML
23.6-8 298
30 39, 169
33 269

NGCT
24 67, 224, 250, 261
89 249

Nymphodorus of Syracuse (*FGrH* 572)
F 4 63

Papyri
P. Hib. I 54, 20-2 249
P. Hib. I 14 301
P. Mich. VI 370 157
P. Mich. VI 422 156
P. Mich. VI 423 156
P. Mich. VI 425 157
P. Mich. VI 426 158
P. Mich. VI 428 157
P. Mil. Vogl. VIII 309 310

Pausanias
1.9.3 27
3.14.2 182
6.3.8 105
6.9.6-8 105
7.3.1-2 308
7.17.6-7 105

Philemon (K-A)
fr. 92.2 76

Philochorus (*FGrH* 328)
F 37 27
F 41 277
F 60 16
F 65 334
F 78 310
F 154 281

Philostratus
Vita Apollonii
5.20 182

Photius (Theodoridis)
Phthonos (phi 154) 74

Pindar
Isthmian Odes
1 115
1.32-8 122
1.41-5 105
1.41-6 116
1.42-6 118
1.43-5 108
1.44 121
1.52-4 149
1.62-3 117
1.62-8 124
1.63 117
1.64-7 114
2 124
2.13-19 149
2.37-42 118
2.43 108, 109, 121
2.44-5 118
2.44-6 117

Pindar (*cont.*)
  3.1–3 116, 118
  3.6–7 106
  3.18b 149
  4.4–21 149
  4.7–12 118
  4.12 106
  4.31–5 149
  4.37–45 118
  5.11 149
  5.14–15 106
  5.21–5 116
  5.22–5 108
  5.24 104, 121
  5.51 117
  6.3–7 149
  6.16–18 149
  6.24–5 118
  6.69–72 118
  7.16–19 110
  7.20–3 118
  7.23–5 123
  7.39 121
  8.61–60 149

Nemean Odes
  1.24 113, 118
  1.17–21 119
  2.23–35 118
  3.9 104, 108, 121
  3.19–22 106
  3.29 107
  3.70–5 106
  4.11 114
  4.12–13 114
  4.39 121
  4.39–40 112, 116, 119
  5.1a 117
  5.2–6 118
  5.4–5 114
  5.7–8 114
  5.40 118
  6.1–7 149
  6.28–30 117
  6.57b 118
  7 113
  7.11–13 118
  7.20–23 118
  7.31–2 151
  7.61–2 113
  7.61–3 110
  7.64–9 122
  7.64–74 113

  7.86–9 112
  8.19–21 117
  8.20–2 114
  8.21 73, 112, 116, 118, 119, 121, 167
  8.23 120
  8.26 113
  8.33 111
  9.6–7 118
  9.53–5 118
  10 114
  10.20 117
  10.49–54 149
  11.13–16 118
  11.13–17 116
  11.17–21 118

Olympian Odes
  1.5–17b 117
  1.28–9 118
  1.47 113, 121
  1.47–51 112
  1.53 113
  1.99–100 106
  2.5–7 106
  2.21 149
  2.35 149
  2.53–6 106
  2.92–7 117
  2.94 104, 108, 117, 121
  2.95–8 114, 120
  2.96–100 121
  3.44–5 106
  4.8–12 114
  4.17 119
  5.15–16 109
  5.23–4 117, 118
  6.6 108
  6.6–7 105
  6.7 104, 121
  6.72–4 118
  6.73–7 109
  6.74 116, 121
  6.74–7 104, 110
  6.77–81
  6.101–2 151
  7 115
  7.6 123
  7.7 104
  7.11 118
  7.11–12 149
  7.80–5 115
  7.87–95 151
  7.89–90 107

7.89-91 149
7.89-92 118
7.93-4 118
8 110
8.10-11 151
8.12-14 149
8.54-61 110
8.55 121, 122
8.74-84 107
9.21-30 151
9.27-39 106
9.28-9 149
9.35-9 119
9.38-9 117
9.100-4 149
10.21 149
10.86-94 110
11.7 104, 107, 108, 123
11.5-6 118
11.8-9 108
11.8-11 118
11.10 151
12.10-12a 149
13 114
13.5 104
13.10 117
13.25 119, 123
13.43-50 119
13.52 119
13.105-6 149
14.5-6 149
19.97-9 114

Pythian Odes
1.41-2 149
1.42-5 114
1.81-3 108, 112
1.82-4 117
1.83-4 75, 104
1.85 121, 124
1.91-3 118
1.98-101 107
2 105
2.21-41 151
2.24-9 117
2.52-6 120
2.55 119
2.55-6 119
2.75-7 112
2.76-7 119
2.78-80 113
2.81-2 112, 113
2.82 118

2.89-90 117, 150
2.89-91 112
2.90 121
2.90-1 116
2.93-6 150
3.51-3 169
3.59-60 117
3.71 121
3.114-15 118
4.283-4 113
5 110
5.1-4 106
5. 23-31 149
5.30-1 149
5.54-5 149
5.108-15 108
6.7-9 151
7.18-19 104, 108, 116
7.19 116, 123
7.19-21 149
8.15 117
8.32 117
8.72 121
8.76-7 149
8.86-7 120
8.95 149
9.93-6 118
10.20 123
10.29-30 106
10.55-9 118
10.57-60 118
11.22-9 109
11.29 121
11.29-30 111
11.50-4 123
11.50-8 106
11.54 121
11.54-8 108, 115
12.4-6 114
12.21 120
12.30 149

Paeans
2.50-8 109

Partheneia
1.8 108
1.8-10 76

Fragments (Maehler)
38 149
94a 107, 108
121 107
181 110

418 — Index Locorum

Fragments (Maehler) (*cont.*)
  212 116
  232 149

Plato
Apologia
  18c 210
  18d 210
  23 38
  24b–c 52
  26a–c 58
  26b 59
  37d 210

Euthydemus
  271a 28

Euthyphro
  2a
  2b7–9 49
  3b–c
  3e–4b 41
  7a 50
  272d–273b 27

Laches
  183a–b 287
  184c1–4 252

Leges
  672b 182
  721b 292
  772d 292
  785b 292
  805e 294
  845e3 310
  855c 237, 238
  882b 237
  886d–e 329
  889b–890a 329
  907d4–909d2 47
  908d 46
  909b 46, 318
  909d–910a 54
  909e–910a 48
  910b1–6 61
  910d 47, 61
  925a–b 299
  932e–933e 333
  933a 169
  933a–b 223
  933b 46
  933b–e 43
  967a–d 329

Lysis
  221d 181

Meno
  80a 44
  80a–b 55
  80a3 40

Phaedo
  95b5–6 136
  111b 182
  116a 295

Phaedrus
  240a5–6 252

Philebus
  48a 251
  48b 251
  49d 251
  49d–e 252
  50a 251

Respublica
  329e6–330a 146
  336d 181
  362 240
  364b–c 46, 169
  364b2–365a3 310
  364c 17
  364e 46
  365a 39
  381d4–7 309
  560d8–561a8 106
  578e–579a 228

Symposium
  194a5 40
  201d 311
  203d 169
  222d 192
  223d 28

Theaetetus
  174c 135
  176b 181

Timaeus
  70e 237

[Plato]
Eryxias
  397c–d 28

Menexenus
  248d 295
  248e 295
  249a3–249b2 301

Index Locorum

Plutarch
Amatorius
  767f 308
An seni respublica gerenda sit
  787c 113
De amore prolis
  497e 300
De capienda ex inimicis utilitate
  10.91f 116
De cohibenda ira
  2.456c 182
De E
  389a 29
De invidia et odio
  537e 158
De mulierum virtutibus
  256b-c 37, 66
  257f1 16
  262d2 16
De recta ratione audiendi
  39e 120
De tranquillitate animi
  2.473a 182
Parallela minora
  314f5 16
Praecepta gerendae reipublicae
  804d 113
Quaestiones convivales
  5.7.680-3 74
Quaestiones Romanae
  292a6 16
Vitae decem oratorum
  835f-836a 282
  836d 279
  841b 58
  849e 26
  852b 58
Vitae:
Agesilaus
  31.1-2 280
  40 276
Alcibiades
  22 56
  36 182
  39 308
  65b 182
  74 113
Aristides
  27.1-3 302

Demosthenes
  14.4 15
  31.7 15
Pericles
  22 52
  28 240
  32 57, 323
  32.2 66
Lycurgus
  16.24 182
Nicias
  3.1-3 106
  13.6.3 15
  30.1 181
Pelopidas
  10.3-4 319
Phocion
  28.7 270
  34 312
Romulus
  3.3.4 15
Timoleon
  8.1.2 15
[Plutarch]
Life of Isaeus
  839f 313
Pollux
Onomasticon
  8.112 334
  8.118 41
  8.123-4 24, 30
Polybius
  4.31.6 123
Posidippus (1), comic poet
Ephesian Woman 25
Posidippus (2), epigrammatist
P. Mil. Vogl. VIII 309 AB 26 (IV 36-9) 310
Quintilian
Institutio oratoria
  3.1.21 102
  10.5.2 24
  11.1.22 129
RO
  18 275
  22 275
  28 51

SEG
  4.648 219
  7.1239 214
  12.100 48
  14.505 213
  19.227 27
  24.223 60
  27.19 287
  31.985 39
  35.626 310
  37.687 213
  46.966 213
  47.1291 218

Semonides (Gerber)
  fr. 7.7–20 187

Servius
Serv. *Aen.* 8.187 22

SGD
  9 234
  14 224
  24–38 229
  38 229
  46 240
  48 234
  57 239
  58 239
  60 63, 226
  75 240
  89 232
  95 240
  99 240
  100 240
  108 240
  150 249
  170 235

Solon (Ruschenbusch)
  fr. 76a 28

Sophocles
Ajax
  108 237
  157 73
  240 237
  512 299

Andromeda 241
Antigone
  654 303
  810–13 303

Electra
  188 303
  1109 182

Oedipus at Colonus
  167 182
  258 184
  1234–5 72

Oedipus Tyrannus
  43 182
  86 182
  386 46
  388–9 309
  475 182
  723 182
  386 182

Trachiniae 34
  1150 182

Strabo
  10.3.18 52

Suda (Adler)
Anaximenes (alpha 1989) 23
Euthias (epsilon 3497) 26
Leipandrein (lambda 377) 303
Orphaniston (omicron 652) 299
Phthonos (phi 508) 74
Phthonos (phi 509) 73
Phthonos (phi 510) 71, 74
Sitos (sigma 502) 300
Thiasos (theta 379 and 380) 18

Supplementum Magicum 2
  54 249

Syll.^{3}
  736.26 334
  736.32 334
  1219 334

TAM
  V.1 318 219

Theopompus (*FGrH* 115)
  F 136 27
  F 395 102

Thucydides
  1.11 182
  1.89.3 298
  2.6.4 298
  2.13 271
  2.14 ff. 285
  2.17 271
  2.24.2 278
  2.27.1 288
  2.35.2 148
  2.45 131
  2.45.1 148
  2.45.1–2 103
  2.45.2 295

Index Locorum

2.46.1 300
2.64.5 148
2.70.3-4 288
2.78.3 298, 305
3.55.3 286
3.63.2 286
3.82.8 147
4.108.7 147
4.123.4 298
6.12 106
6.15.2 192
6.16.3 76, 148
6.16.3-6 106
6.27 52
6.53 52
6.53.1 51
6.60 52
6.78.2 148
7.27.4-5 270
7.27-8 271
7.60.3 288
7.77.3 148
7.77.4 148
7.87.6 269
8.15 237
8.21 286

TM
8204 250
12174 157
12261 156
12262 156
12263 157
12264 157
12266 157
14456 157
61454 301

Xenophon
Anabasis
1.9.19 76
2.1.7 287
4.3.19 305
5.3.1 288
5.4.33 305
6.1.12 305
6.4.8 288

Apologia Socratis
10 52
14.3 209
32.2 209

Cyropaedia
7.5.77 76
3.1.39 144

8.7.3 182

De equitum magistro
3.1.6-7 27

De vectigalibus 132
2.3 282
2.7 299
6.1 279

Hellenica
1.1.33 27
1.2.4-5 276
1.4.13 52
1.4.14 52
1.4.20 52
1.6.24 271
1.7.22 48
3.3.11 237, 238
3.5.8-15 274
3.5.10 274
4.1.14 305
4.2.17 271
4.8.26-30 275
4.8.27 275
4.8.30 275
5.2.31 286
6.2.6 280
6.2.11-12 287
6.3.3 287
6.5.10 286

Hiero
4.3 228

Memorabilia
1.1-2 52
1.1.5 58
1.1.9-16
1.2.9 59
1.2.12-46 59
2.3.11 167
2.6.10 168
2.6.13 168
2.7.2 292, 296
2.8.1 272
2.10.1-2 228
3.9.8 76
3.10.6 318
3.11.4 294
3.11.16-18 168

Oeconomicus
3.12 294

Symposium
4.48 182

Printed and bound by CPI Group (UK) Ltd, Croydon, CR0 4YY